Rick Steves'®

GERMANY

2009

Hamburg
Bremerhaven
Emden
A29
A27
A1
A7
Groningen
Leeuwarden
Leer
A28
Bremen
Elbe
A7
Delmenhorst
A28
A31
A27
Bergen-Belsen
NETHERLANDS
A1
Celle
Wolfsburg
Hannover
Bad Bentheim
Hengelo
A2
A2
Braunschweig
A30
Rheine
Osnabrück
A1
Magdeburg
Hameln
Bielefeld
Halberstadt
Münster
Goslar
Arnhem
A2
Aschersleben
Nijmegen
Emmerich
A1
Paderborn
A3
HARZ MOUNTAINS
A57
Essen
Göttingen
A7
Duisburg
Dortmund
A73
A67
A44
Kassel
Venlo
Korbach
Düsseldorf
GERMANY
A1
Erfurt
Weimar
Bebra
Eisenach
A4
Maastricht
A4
Marburg
Köln
Aachen
A45
A48
E40
A1
Bonn
Suhl
Liege
A3
Remagen
Rhine
Wetzlar
Fulda
BELGIUM
A61
A3
Burg Eltz
Koblenz
Coburg
A5
Boppard
E25
Cochem
St. Goar
Frankfurt
Beilstein
Wiesbaden
A7
A70
A1
Zell
Bacharach
Bamberg
Bayreuth
Bingen
Frankfurt
Mosel
Mainz
A3
Main
LUXEMBOURG
Rudesheim
Würzburg
A73
Trier
A3
Steinach
Worms
Hahn
Luxembourg City
Mannheim
A81
Nürnberg
Heidelberg
FRANCONIA
Thionville
Kaiserslautern
Rothenburg
A6
Saarbrücken
Castle Road
Metz
Dinkelsbühl
A4
A9
Karlsruhe
A7
Romantic Road
LORRAINE
Nördlingen
Ingolstadt
Stuttgart
A4
Baden-Baden
A31
Schwäbisch Gmünd
Donauworth
Toul
Nancy
A35
LES VOSGES
BAVARIA
A5
Strasbourg
Kehl
A8
BLACK FOREST
Reutlingen
ALSACE
St Dié
A8
Augsburg
Ulm
Tübingen
A31
Ribeauvillé
Rhine
A81
Dachau
Hausach Open-Air Museum
Munich
Kaysersberg
A7
Colmar
Triberg
Danube
Herrsching
Furtwangen
Landsberg
Andechs Monastery
Eguisheim
Freiburg
A7
Bad Krozingen
Ravensburg
Ronchamp
Staufen
Meersburg
Lake Constance
Oberammergau
Mulhouse
Kempten
Rhinefalls
Konstanz
Neuschwanstein
Stein
Füssen
Belfort
Lindau
FRANCE
Reutte
Basel
A3
Bregenz
Zugspitze
A36
Ehrenberg
JURA MTNS.
Zürich
APPENZELL
Fallerschein
Feldkirch
Besançon
Appenzell
Ebenalp
Innsbruck
SWITZERLAND
LIECHTENSTEIN
Lech
Buchs
A3
Zug
Vaduz
TIROL
A1
Bludenz
Luzern
Neuchâtel
Murten
Bern
Lac de Neuchâtel
Avenches
Ballenberg Museum
Fluelen
Chur
Frasne
A12
Scuol
ITALY
Inter-laken
Fribourg
Susten Pass
A2
Spiez
Glacier Express
Lausanne
Gruyères
St. Moritz
Samedan
Bolzano

GERMANY
Freeway/Autobahn
Major Roads
Major Rail Line
Airport
St. Goar
Recommended Location*
Bebra
Just Passing Through**
Ruin, Museum, Other Point of Interest
Castle/Monument/Palace
* Black locations are places of interest to tourists, sized by importance.
** Gray locations are not places of interest to tourists and are sized by population.
0 km
50
100 km
0 miles
50 miles
POLAND
CZECH REPUBLIC
AUSTRIA
SLOVAKIA
HUNGARY
SLOVENIA
CROATIA
SAXONY
SILESIA
BOHEMIA
MORAVIA
WACHAU
SALZKAMMERGUT
Neustrelitz
Sachsenhausen
Tegel
Berlin
Frankfurt an der Oder
Schönefeld
Potsdam
Sanssouci Palace
Rzepin
Gorzow Wielkopolski
Zielona Góra
Wittenberg
Cottbus
Zary
Elbe
Lauchhammer
Bolesławiec
Leipzig
Moritzburg
Meissen
Bautzen
Görlitz
Zgorzelec
Dresden
Bad Schandau
Zittau
Chemnitz
Seiffen
Děčín
Swidnica
Opole
Nysa
Nachod
Ustí nad Labem
Litoměřice
Terezín
Hradec Kralove
Ruzyně
Lichkov
Karlovy Vary
Prague
Kutná Hora
Štramberk
Olomouc
Cheb
Marianské Lazne
Marktredwitz
Karlštejn Castle
Plzeň
Kromeriz
Zlin
Tabor
Český Kubice
Furth
Veseli nad Luznici
Telč
Brno
Slavonice
České Budejovice
Český Velenice
Gmund
Breclav
Kuty
Regensburg
Obertraubling
Český Krumlov
Passau
Summerau
Danube
Krems
Durnstein
Vienna
Grinzing
Bratislava
Linz
Mauthausen
Melk
Schönbrunn Palace
St. Valentin
Attnang Puchheim
Puchberg
Eisenstadt
Schneeberg
Salzach
Chiemsee
Salzburg
Bad Ischl
Sopron
Esterhazy Palace
Berchtesgaden
Hallstatt
Selzthal
Kufstein
Hallein
Leoben
Bruck an der Mur
Szombathely
Stainach Irdning
Worgl
Zell am See
Kitzbuhel
Piber
Graz
Badgastein
Grossglockner Pass
Spielfeld
Spittal
Klagenfurt
Nagykanizsa
Lienz
Maribor
Villach
Jesenice
Ptuj
ALPE DI SIUSI
Cortina
Tarvisio
Vršič Pass
Bled/Lesce
Dobbiaco
A11
A10
A12
A9
A13
A15
A4
A13
A72
A93
A3
A92
A8
A12
A10
A1
A2
A9
M1
E50
E65

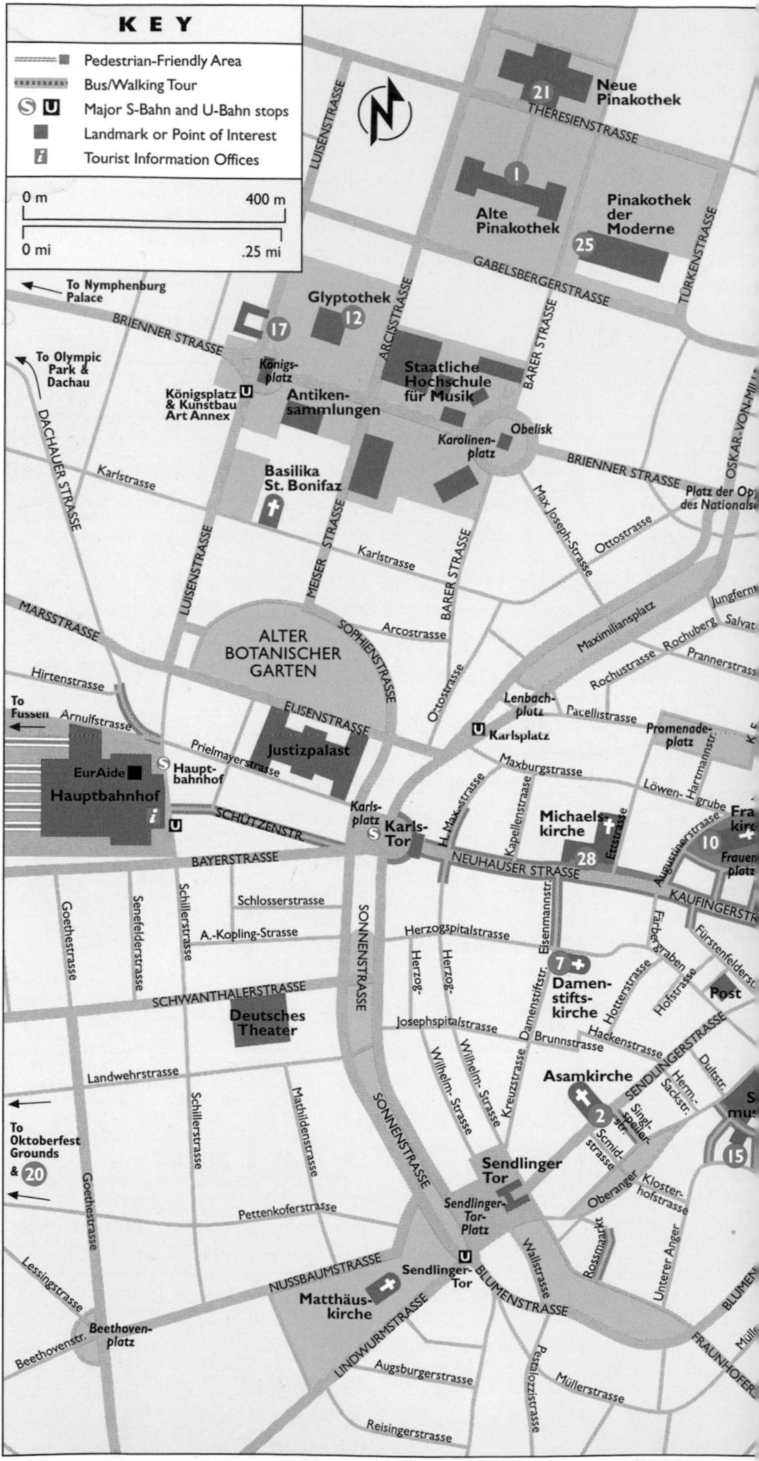
KEY
Pedestrian-Friendly Area
Bus/Walking Tour
Major S-Bahn and U-Bahn stops
Landmark or Point of Interest
Tourist Information Offices
0 m
400 m
0 mi
.25 mi
To Nymphenburg Palace
To Olympic Park & Dachau
To Fussen
To Oktoberfest Grounds & 20
Neue Pinakothek
21
Alte Pinakothek
1
Pinakothek der Moderne
25
Glyptothek
12
17
Königsplatz
Königsplatz & Kunstbau Art Annex
Antikensammlungen
Staatliche Hochschule für Musik
Obelisk
Karolinenplatz
Basilika St. Bonifaz
ALTER BOTANISCHER GARTEN
Justizpalast
EurAide
Hauptbahnhof
Karlsplatz
Karls-Tor
Lenbachplatz
Promenadeplatz
Michaelskirche
28
10
Frauenplatz
Damenstiftskirche
7
Post
Deutsches Theater
Asamkirche
2
15
Sendlinger Tor
Sendlinger-Tor-Platz
Sendlinger-Tor
Matthäuskirche
Beethovenplatz
THERESIENSTRASSE
GABELSBERGERSTRASSE
LUISENSTRASSE
TÜRKENSTRASSE
ARCISSTRASSE
BARER STRASSE
BRIENNER STRASSE
DACHAUER STRASSE
Karlstrasse
MEISER STRASSE
Max Joseph-Strasse
Ottostrasse
OSKAR-VON-MILLER
Platz der Opfer des Nationalsozialismus
MARSSTRASSE
SOPHIENSTRASSE
Arcostrasse
Maximiliansplatz
Jungfernturm
Salvatorstrasse
Rochuberg
Prannerstrasse
Rochusstrasse
Hirtenstrasse
Arnulfstrasse
ELISENSTRASSE
Ottostrasse
Pacellistrasse
Prielmayerstrasse
Maxburgstrasse
Hartmannstr.
Löwengrube
H.-Max-strasse
Kapellenstrasse
Ettstrasse
Augustinerstrasse
SCHÜTZENSTR.
BAYERSTRASSE
NEUHAUSER STRASSE
KAUFINGERSTR.
Schlosserstrasse
A.-Kopling-Strasse
Herzogspitalstrasse
Goethestrasse
Senefelderstrasse
Schillerstrasse
SONNENSTRASSE
Eisenmannstr.
Färbergraben
Fürstenfelderstr.
Herzog-Wilhelm-Strasse
Hotterstrasse
Hofstrasse
SCHWANTHALERSTRASSE
Josephspitalstrasse
Damenstiftstr.
Brunnstrasse
Hackenstrasse
SENDLINGERSTRASSE
Dultstr.
Landwehrstrasse
Kreuzstrasse
Hermann-Sack-Str.
Singlspielerstr.
Schmidstrasse
Mathildenstrasse
Oberanger
Klosterhofstrasse
Pettenkoferstrasse
Rossmarkt
Unterer Anger
Wallstrasse
NUSSBAUMSTRASSE
BLUMENSTRASSE
Lessingstrasse
Beethovenstr.
LINDWURMSTRASSE
Augsburgerstrasse
Pestalozzistrasse
Müllerstrasse
FRAUNHOFER
Reisingerstrasse

MUNICH

- Alte Pinakothek
- Asam Church
- Bavarian National Museum
- Beer and Oktoberfest Museum
- To Chinese Tower Beer Garden
- Cuvilliés Theater
- Damenstift Church
- 8 Deutsches Museum
- 9 English Garden
- 10 Frauenkirche
- 11 Fünf Höfe Shops
- 12 Glyptothek
- 13 Haus der Kunst
- 14 Hofbräuhaus
- 15 Jewish History Museum
- 16 Kunsthalle Art Center
- 17 Lenbachhaus
- 18 Marienplatz
- 19 Munich City Museum
- 20 To Museum of Transportation
- 21 Neue Pinakothek
- 22 New Town Hall & Glockenspiel
- 23 Odeonsplatz
- 24 Old Town Hall
- 25 Pinakothek der Moderne
- 26 Residenz Museum
- 27 Residenz Treasury
- 28 St. Michael's Church
- 29 St. Peter's Church
- 30 Viktualienmarkt

BERLIN

1. Alexanderplatz
2. Bauhaus Archive
3. Bebelplatz
4. Berlin Cathedral
5. Berlin Wall Documentation Center
6. Brandenburg Gate
7. Egyptian/Altes Museums
8. Erotic Art Museum
9. Europa Center
10. Gemäldegalerie
11. Gendarmenmarkt
12. German Cathedral
13. German History Museum
14. German Resistance Memorial
15. Hackesche Höfe Shops
16. Hauptbahnhof (Main Train Station) & EurAide
17. Jewish Museum Berlin
18. KaDeWe Department Store
19. Kaiser Wilhelm Memorial Church
20. Käthe Kollwitz Museum
21. (The) Kennedys Museum
22. Memorial to the Murdered Jews of Europe
23. Museum of Arts and Crafts
24. Museum of the Wall at Checkpoint Charlie
25. Musical Instruments Museum
26. Natural History Museum
27. Neue Wache Memorial
28. New National Gallery
29. New Synagogue
30. Old National Gallery
31. Pergamon Museum
32. Philharmonic Concert Hall
33. Potsdamer Platz & Sony Ce
34. Reichstag
35. Topography of Terror
36. TV Tower
37. Victory Column
38. Zoo

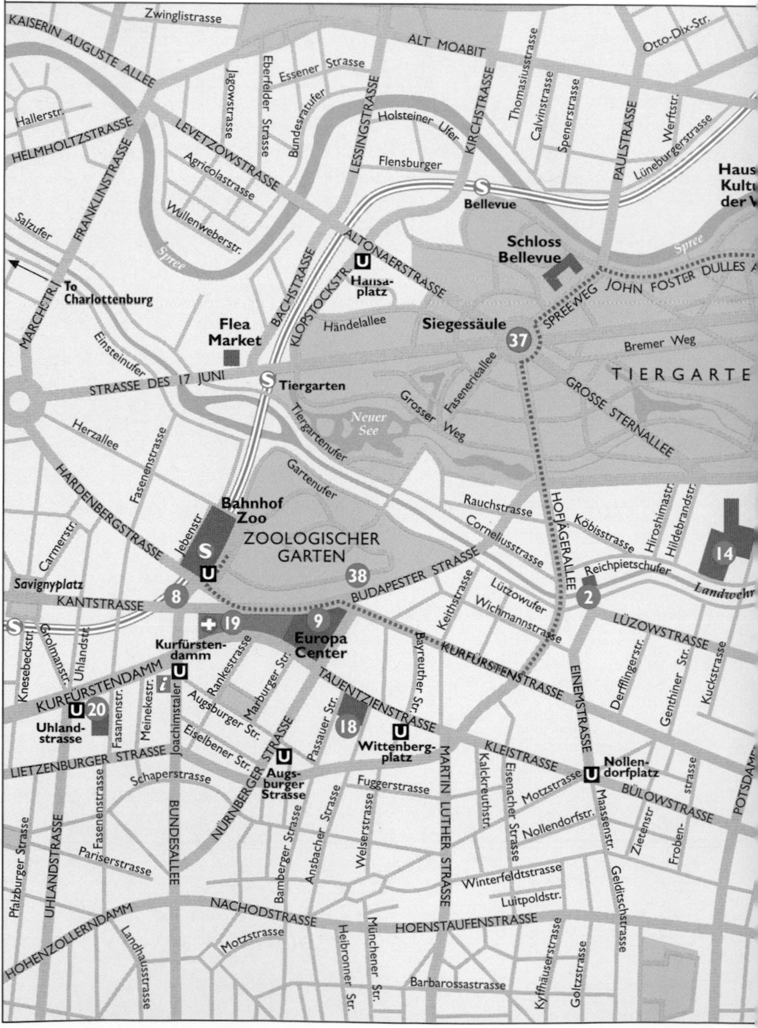

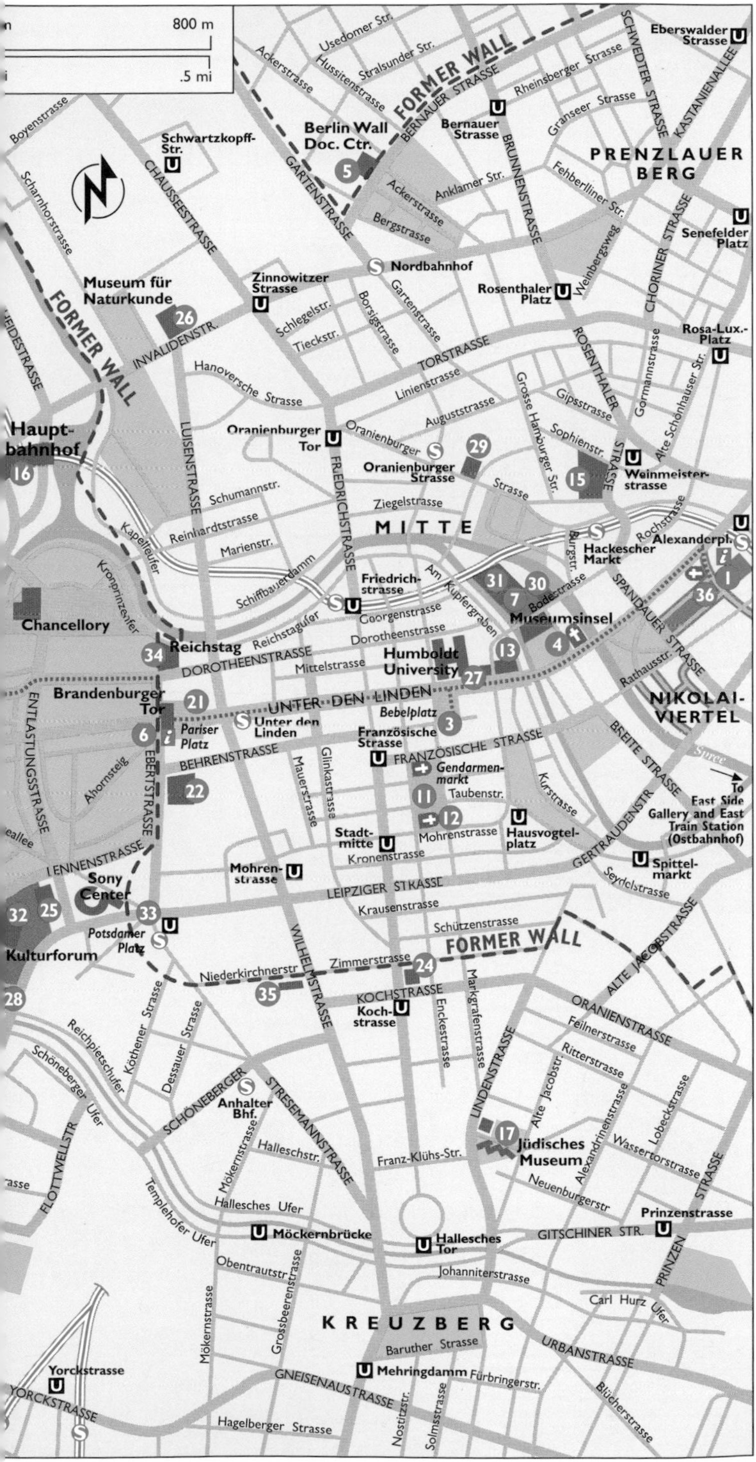

800 m
.5 mi
FORMER WALL
Usedomer Str.
Ackerstrasse
Hussitenstrasse
Stralsunder Str.
BERNAUER STRASSE
SCHWEDTER STRASSE
Eberswalder Strasse
Rheinsberger Strasse
Granseer Strasse
KASTANIENALLEE
Boyenstrasse
Schwartzkopff-Str.
Berlin Wall Doc. Ctr.
5
Bernauer Strasse
BRUNNENSTRASSE
PRENZLAUER BERG
Scharnhorststrasse
CHAUSSEESTRASSE
GARTENSTRASSE
Ackerstrasse
Anklamer Str.
Fehberlliner Str.
Bergstrasse
Senefelder Platz
Nordbahnhof
Weinbergsweg
CHORINER STRASSE
Museum für Naturkunde
26
Zinnowitzer Strasse
Rosenthaler Platz
Gartenstrasse
Schlegelstr.
Borsigstrasse
Tieckstr.
HEIDESTRASSE
INVALIDENSTR.
TORSTRASSE
ROSENTHALER STRASSE
Rosa-Lux.-Platz
Gormannstrasse
Alte Schönhauser Str.
Hanoversche Strasse
Linienstrasse
Grosse Hamburger Str.
Gipsstrasse
Auguststrasse
Hauptbahnhof
16
Oranienburger Tor
Oranienburger Strasse
29
Sophienstr.
Weinmeisterstrasse
15
LUISENSTRASSE
FRIEDRICHSTRASSE
Schumannstr.
Ziegelstrasse
Reinhardtstrasse
MITTE
Hackescher Markt
Rochstrasse
Alexanderpl.
Kapelleufer
Marienstr.
Burgstr.
Kronprinzenufer
Schiffbauerdamm
Friedrichstrasse
Am Kupfergraben
31
30
7
Bodestrasse
36
Chancellory
Georgenstrasse
Museumsinsel
Reichstagufer
Dorotheenstrasse
SPANDAUER STRASSE
34
Reichstag
13
4
DOROTHEENSTRASSE
Humboldt University
Mittelstrasse
27
Rathausstr.
Brandenburger Tor
21
UNTER DEN LINDEN
NIKOLAI-VIERTEL
ENTLASTUNGSSTRASSE
Bebelplatz
Unter den Linden
Pariser Platz
6
Französische Strasse
3
FRANZÖSISCHE STRASSE
BREITE STRASSE
Spree
BEHRENSTRASSE
EBERTSTRASSE
Gendarmenmarkt
Ahornsteig
Glinkastrasse
Mauerstrasse
22
11
Taubenstr.
Kurstrasse
To East Side Gallery and East Train Station (Ostbahnhof)
12
Hausvogtelplatz
Stadtmitte
Mohrenstrasse
Kronenstrasse
GERTRAUDENSTR.
LENNENSTRASSE
Mohrenstrasse
Spittelmarkt
Seydelstrasse
Sony Center
LEIPZIGER STRASSE
32
25
33
Krausenstrasse
Potsdamer Platz
Schützenstrasse
FORMER WALL
Kulturforum
Zimmerstrasse
24
ALTE JACOBSTRASSE
Niederkirchnerstr
28
35
KOCHSTRASSE
Kochstrasse
WILHELMSTRASSE
Enckestrasse
Markgrafenstrasse
ORANIENSTRASSE
Feilnerstrasse
LINDENSTRASSE
Reichpietschufer
Köthener Strasse
Dessauer Strasse
Ritterstrasse
Schöneberger Ufer
SCHÖNEBERGER
STRESEMANNSTRASSE
Anhalter Bhf.
Alte Jacobstr.
Alexandrinenstrasse
Lobeckstrasse
17
Jüdisches Museum
Wassertorstrasse
Halleschstr.
Franz-Klühs-Str.
Möckernstrasse
Neuenburgerstr
FLOTTWELLSTR.
Templehofer Ufer
Hallesches Ufer
Prinzenstrasse
Möckernbrücke
Hallesches Tor
GITSCHINER STR.
Obentrautstrasse
Grossbeerenstrasse
Johanniterstrasse
PRINZENSTRASSE
Carl Hurz Ufer
Mökernstrasse
KREUZBERG
Baruther Strasse
URBANSTRASSE
Yorckstrasse
Mehringdamm
Fürbringerstr.
GNEISENAUSTRASSE
YORCKSTRASSE
Nostitzstr.
Solmsstrasse
Blücherstrasse
Hagelberger Strasse

To Rothenburg
To Würzburg
Donauworth
Ingolstadt
To Nürnberg
Manching
A93
To Regens
Danube
Romantic Road
Pfaffenhofen
Landsh
A92
A9
Moosburg
Freising
B A V A R I A
A8
To Stuttgart
Augsburg
Unterschleissheim
Munich Strauss
Dachau
GERMANY
Munich
To Lindau
Buchloe
A96
Herrsching
Ammersee
Starnberg
Landsberg
A8
Andechs Monastery
Starnbergersee
Rosenh
Kaufbeuren
A95
Weilheim
Schongau
Bad Tolz
Steingaden
Tegernsee
Isar
Murnau
Wieskirche
Kempten
Tegelberg
Oberammergau
To Lindau
A7
Forggensee
Walchensee
Neuschwanstein
Ettal
Achenpass
Füssen
Pfronten
Linderhof
Ettal Monastery
Pinswang
Garmisch-Partenkirchen
Wo
Reutte
Plansee
Eibsee
Mittenwald
A12
Zugspitze
Ehrenberg
Ehrwald
Hinterhornalm
Fernpass
Lech
Telfs
Hafelekar
Zille Valle
Nassereith
Hall
Inn
Fallerschein
Seefeld
Imst
A12
Innsbruck
Zell
Igls
Mayrhofen
Arlberg Pass Tunnel
Europabrücke
T I R O L
Landeck
St. Anton
To Zürich
Ötztal Valley
Stubai Glacier
Sölden
Brenner Pass
Obergurgl
Timmelsjoch Pass
SWITZ.
ITALY
Nauders
Vipiteno
A22
Reifenstein Castle
0
25 kilometers
0
25 miles
Fortezza
Bru
To Bolzano & Verona
Merano
Bressanone

BAVARIA & TIROL
A24 Freeway/Autobahn
Major Roads
Rail Line
Airport
Ruin, Museum, Other Point of Interest
Castle/Monument/Palace
Mountain
Mountain Lift
Mountain Pass
Romantic Road
A3
Dingolfing
Danube
Pocking
Eggenfelden
Simbach
Mühldorf
Braunau
Inn River
Salzach
OBERÖSTERREICH
Wasserburg
Attnang-Puchheim
To Melk & Vienna
A1
Gmunden
Chiemsee
Traunstein
Mondsee
Attersee
Traunsee
Freilassing
Ebensee
Herrenchiemsee
SALZKAMMERGUT
Prien
A8
Salzburg
Schafberg
St. Gilgen
St. Wolfgang
Bad Ischl
Bad Reichenhall
Hallein
Hallstatt Station
Berchtesgaden
Hallstatt
Salt Mine
Kehlstein
Obertraun
Lofer
Obersalzberg (Hitler's Eagle's Nest)
Ice Caves
Kufstein
Dachstein Mtns.
Königssee
St. Johann
Kitzbühel
Bischofshofen
SALZBURG
Zell am See
Zellersee
Schwarzach St. Veit
Uttendorf
A10
Krimml
AUSTRIA
Bad Gastein
Katschberg Tunnel
Grossglockner Pass
Tauern Tunnel
Felbertauern Tunnel
KÄRNTEN
Winklern
To Villach, Venice & Ljubljana
Spittal
Drau River
Lienz
Arnbach
Dobbiaco
Cortina
San Candido
Plöckenpass
To Venice

CONTENTS

Schloßkellerstr.

Germany

Deutschland

Germany is blessed with some of Europe's most high-powered sights. There's spectacular scenery—the jagged Alps, flower-filled meadows, rolling hills of forests and farms, and rivers such as the raging Rhine and moseying Mosel. Germany has hundreds of castles, some ruined and mysterious; others stout, crenellated, and imposing; and still others right out of a Disney fairy tale. In this land of the Protestant Reformation—and Catholic Counter-Reformation—churches and cathedrals are another forté. Austere Lutheran houses of worship tower silently next to exuberantly overripe Baroque churches, dripping with curlicues.

Deutschland is energetic, efficient, and organized. It's Europe's muscleman, both economically and wherever people line up (Germans have a reputation for pushing ahead). It's the European Union's most populous country and biggest economy, with a geographic diversity and cultural richness that draws millions of visitors every year.

Germany's dark side is recalled in eerie Nazi remnants (stern office buildings, thoughtfully presented "documentation centers," haunting concentration camps) and chilling reminders of the Cold War (embodied in a few quickly disappearing sites—such as scant fragments of the notorious Berlin Wall).

And of course there are the cultural clichés—kept alive more by tradition-loving Germans than by tourist demand. The country is dotted with idyllic half-timbered villages where you can enjoy strudel at the bakery or sip a stein of brew while men in lederhosen play oompah music. Peruse a wonderland of chocolates, stock up on Hummels and cuckoo clocks, and learn how to polka.

All of this stands at sharp contrast with the "real" Germany of today. Despite its respect for the past, this is a truly 21st-century country. At the forefront of human progress, Germany is a world of high-tech trains, gleaming cities, social efficiency, and world-class museums of history's greatest cultural achievements.

Modern Germany bustles. Its cities hold 75 percent of its people, and average earnings are among the highest in the world. Most workers get at least a month of paid vacation, and, during the other 11 months, they create a Gross Domestic Product (GDP) that's about one-quarter of the United States'. Germany has risen from the ashes of World War II to become the world's fifth-largest industrial power.

People all over the world enjoy the fruits of Germany's labor. Their cars are legendary—BMW, Mercedes-Benz, Volkswagen, Audi, and Porsche. We talk on German mobile phones (T-Mobile), ride German elevators and trains (ThyssenKrupp and Siemens AG), take German medicines (Bayer), use German cosmetics (Nivea), ...and eat German goodies (Haribo's Gummi bears).

Germany beats out all but two countries in production of

books, Nobel laureates, and professors. In the world of physics, there's Einstein's Relativity, Planck's constant, and the Heisenberg Uncertainty Principle. German inventions range from Gutenberg's printing press to Zeppelin's zeppelins to Roentgen's X-rays to Daimler's and Benz's cars to Geiger's counter. Musically, Germany dominated the scene for more than two centuries—Bach, Beethoven, Brahms, Handel, Pachelbel, Wagner, and more. Germans have a reputation as profound analytical thinkers, sprouting philosophers such as Kant, Hegel, Nietzsche, Marx, and Engels.

Germany is geographically big (compared to other European countries) but closely knit by transportation. Its autobahns—miles and miles of high-quality freeway—are famous (or notorious) for their no-speed-limit system (more fully explained on page 556). InterCityExpress (ICE) trains zip by at up to 200 miles per hour, linking major cities quickly and efficiently.

As a nation, Germany is less than 140 years old ("born" in 1871), quite young compared to most of its European neighbors. In medieval times, there were 300 countries in what is now Germany, each with its own weights, measures, coinage, king, and lottery. By 1850, the number had dropped to a still formidable 35 countries. Today's Germany is a federation of states, each with its own cultural identity and customs.

Traditionally—and in some ways even today—German culture divides at a sort of North-South Mason-Dixon Line. Northern Germany was barbarian, is predominantly Protestant, and tackles life aggressively, while southern Germany (Bavaria) was Roman, is largely Catholic, and enjoys a more relaxed tempo. The romantic American image of Germany is beer-and-pretzel Bavaria (probably because that was "our" sector after the war). This historic North-South division is growing less pronounced as Germany becomes a more mobile society.

Germany's roots run deep. Thoughtful travelers can easily trace Germany's history in their sightseeing. Find Germany's Roman roots at the impressive Porta Nigra Gate and Basilica of scenic Trier. When Rome fell, German lands fragmented into hundreds of small feudal kingdoms, each with its own castle—many of which still dot the German countryside today. Magnificent Gothic cathedrals like the one in Köln attest to the faith of medieval people. As Germany's economy recovered, it became Europe's trade and transportation hub. Prosperous cities sprung up along the Romantic Road—today's prime tourist trail.

It was from Germany that a humble monk named Martin Luther rocked Europe with religious reform, and you'll see monuments, cities, and churches associated with him. Meanwhile, German Catholics decorated their churches (including the glorious Wieskirche) and palaces (in Munich and Würzburg) in the ornate Baroque/Rococo style, giving a glimpse of the heaven that awaited the faithful. Germany became a Europe-wide battleground for Protestants and Catholics in the Thirty Years' War that was duked out in towns such as Rothenburg (which today is besieged by tourists).

In the 1800s, Germany unified politically, and it became a cultural powerhouse. European nobles flocked to Baden-Baden's casino and thermal baths, while composer Richard Wagner spun operatic tales about German folk legends at the castle of Neuschwanstein with his friend "Mad" King Ludwig II.

Germany's prosperity ended in the humiliating defeat of World War I. You can see the rising specter of Hitler and Nazism at the Nürnberg Rally Grounds (where huge propaganda events were staged, now home to an excellent museum documenting the Nazis' rise to power), at Berlin's Reichstag (whose destruction helped the Nazis take control), and the sobering concentration camp museum at Dachau (one of many places where the Nazis snuffed out their opposition). Germany's utter destruction in World War II is evident in the skylines of today's cities. Some, like Munich and Dresden, were rebuilt in a faux-Baroque style, while Frankfurt sprouted skyscrapers.

At war's end, Germany was divided East-West between the victorious Allies, and the Cold War set in (1945–1990). In Berlin, you can see a few surviving stretches of the Wall that divided the country, and the famous Checkpoint Charlie that controlled the East-West flow. Even today, Eastern cities such as Dresden and Görlitz bear the scars and stunted growth of Soviet occupation. Some friction still exists between the residents of the former East Germany ("Ossies" in impolite slang) and those from West Germany ("Wessies"). Two decades after reunification, and despite billions of dollars of economic aid, the East lags behind the West, with a higher unemployment rate (about double the West's), lower income, potholed infrastructure, and a few old-timers who miss the good, Red, old days.

Many visitors can't help but associate Germany with its dark Nazi past. But while a small neo-Nazi skinhead element still survives in the back alleys of German society, for the most part the nation has evolved into a surprisingly progressive, almost touchy-feely place. A genuine sense of responsibility for World War II and the Holocaust pervades much of German society. If you visit a concentration camp memorial, you'll likely see several field-trip groups of German teens visiting there to learn the lessons of the past.

Germany was a founding member of the European Union, and continues to lead the way in creating a healthy Europe for the future—with peace, unity, tolerance (e.g., legalized gay marriage), and human rights as its central motivations. It's the world's second-biggest foreign-aid donor, after the US. Even to a skeptical visitor, it's clear that most Germans are trying to make up for the ugliness their ancestors subjected Europe to not so long ago.

How does a country achieve such robust economic and social success, despite losing two world wars? This is a country of "Type A" personalities. Bold, brassy Germans typically aren't shy to speak their minds. Their directness (some might say "bluntness") is refreshing to some, and startling to others. At least you'll know where you stand. People who enjoy trains that run on time are perfectly suited for travel in everything-has-its-place Germany. Those who like to play it fast and loose might find that improvisation has its limits here.

Paradoxically, the ultra-efficient Germans also have a weak spot for Hummel-esque quaintness and a sentimentality for their own history. They love nature. They love to go a-wandering along a mountain path with their hiking sticks,

Germany Almanac

Official Name: Bundesrepublik Deutschland, or simply Deutschland.

Population: Germany's 82 million people (four times the population of Texas) are largely of Teutonic DNA (88 percent), plus a small but significant minority (2.4 percent) of Turkish-descended citizens. A third of Germans are Catholic, and a third are Protestant. About 4 percent are Muslim; the remainder are unaffiliated.

Latitude and Longitude: 51°N and 9°E. The latitude is similar to Alberta, Canada.

Area: At 138,000 square miles, Germany is slightly smaller than Montana and about half the size of Texas. It's bordered by nine countries.

Geography: The terrain gradually rises—from flat land in the north to the rugged Alps in the south, culminating in the 9,700-foot Zugspitze mountain. The climate is temperate.

Biggest Cities: The capital city of Berlin has 3.4 million people, followed by Hamburg's 1.7 million and Munich's 1.5 million.

Economy: With a GDP of $2.75 trillion—similar to America's Midwest states combined—Germany is Europe's largest economy. Still, the GDP per capita is $33,450, or about 25 percent less than America's. It's one of the world's most advanced economies, producing steel, cars, chemicals, pharmaceuticals, consumer electronics, and more. Germany also has 1,280 breweries, but much of the production is consumed domestically. Germany trades almost equally with a half-dozen neighboring countries, and the United States.

Since the 1990 reunification, Germany's economy has been burdened by the cost (about $80 billion a year) of integrating the former East Germany into the modern West. Germany's expensive social security system gets even costlier as the population ages. Thanks to powerful trade unions, workers get good benefits. Unemployment hovers around 8 percent.

Government: Germany's September 2005 elections were extremely close, with no single party, left or right, sweeping to victory. Conservative Chancellor Angela Merkel now heads a coalition government that leans slightly to the right. A small but powerful minority party, the Greens, presses the pro-environment agenda. Germany's chancellor, similar to the prime minister in other countries, is not elected directly by the people but is the head of the lead party in parliament. The less-powerful president (Horst Köhler) is also elected by parliament. The legislative branch includes the *Bundestag* (613 seats, elected by both direct and proportional representation) and the *Bundesrat* (69 votes by local officials of Germany's 16 states).

Flag: Deutschland's flag is composed of three horizontal bands of (starting from the top) black, red, and gold.

The Average *Deutscher:* The average German is 43 years old—six years older than the average American—has 1.4 kids, and will live to be 79. He or she lives in a household with two other people, watches 2.5 hours of TV a day, and spends 20 minutes reading the daily newspaper. The average German drinks a pint of beer every 32 hours, which is slightly less than the average Irish or Czech.

rucksacks, and state-of-the-art gear. Dramatic cable cars whisk visitors to sweeping cut-glass panoramas. Learn the word *schön*—beautiful—because you'll hear it often, from little old ladies and grown men alike as they survey beautiful vistas of their homeland. They're also prone to get misty-eyed when, after a glass or two of white wine, they and their mates start singing a traditional song from their youth. Cutesy traditions are respected and celebrated. Germans wear dirndls and lederhosen on holidays, erect maypoles in spring, decorate Christmas trees and host exuberant Christmas markets in winter, and frequent Oktoberfest-type beer halls year-round.

Germans love to travel, through their own country and beyond. They're cosmopolitan and outward-looking. Two-thirds speak at least one other language (mostly English), and they enjoy watching TV and movies beamed in from other countries. Watch out—they may know American politics and history better than you do. They're products of high-quality schools that put kids on either fast- or slow-tracks, depending on ability and desire. To move on to college, they must pass a major SAT-like test. Once there, the university system is top-quality...with tuition of only a few hundred dollars a semester.

Germans aren't all work and no play. All Europeans love watching sports, but Germans actually play them. More than six million are registered

to play *Fussball* (soccer) every year in the official league. There's a big following for pro soccer Bundesliga, and Germany is always a strong contender for the World Cup and Euro Cup championship tournaments (runners-up in the 2008 Euro Cup).

Motorsports are big time, especially Formula One—the European answer to NASCAR—where racing legend Michael Schumacher is one of the world's highest-paid athletes. In the Olympics (winter and summer), Germany is consistently one of the world's top medal-finishers. Just try to keep up with them on one of their summer luge courses *(Sommerrodelbahn)* that allow amateur thrill-seekers to scream down a mountain at top speed.

As Germany speeds into the future, it's faced with a number of challenges—none bigger than immigration. After World War II, Germany needed cheap blue-collar laborers to help rebuild, and they welcomed in many Turkish people as *Gastarbeiters* (guest workers). While many earned money and went home, many others married, had kids, and stayed. Today, more than 10 million immigrants (12 percent of Germany's population) live within its borders—more than every country but the US and Russia. Of these, 2.3 million are Turks, most of whom are Muslims—not always the easiest fit within a traditionally Christian nation.

Germany today is trying to stay competitive in the global marketplace while maintaining generous social services. Neo-Nazism is a festering sore, and there's a declining birthrate (one of the world's lowest). And its enormous appetite for energy is increasingly at odds with its love for the environment (the government is working to phase out nuclear power and invest in sustainable energy).

Best Destinations in Germany

Since the end of World War II, when the US evolved from an occupying force to a close ally, Germany and the US have had a strong relationship. Today more than 100,000 Americans live in Germany (many of them at US military bases, such as Ramstein near the Rhine). Americans generally find Germany to be one of Europe's most accessible nations. It's efficient, the people are almost aggressively welcoming, the language barrier is minimal...and the German roots that pervade America's melting pot don't hurt matters, either. (More than 15 percent of Americans have some German ancestry—more than any other background.)

Germany today is reunited, a nation of cutting-edge industry, medieval castles, speedy autobahns, old-time beer halls, modern skyscrapers, and the best wurst. This young country with a long past continues to make history.

INTRODUCTION

This book breaks Germany into its top big-city, small-town, and rural destinations. It then gives you all the information and opinions necessary to wring the maximum value out of your limited time and money. If you plan a month or less in Germany and have a normal appetite for information, this book is all you need. If you're a travel-info fiend, this book sorts through all the superlatives and provides a handy rack upon which to hang your supplemental information.

Experiencing Europe's culture, people, and natural wonders economically and hassle-free has been my goal for three decades of traveling, tour guiding, and travel writing. With this new edition, I pass on to you the lessons I've learned, updated for your trip in 2009.

The German destinations covered in this book are balanced to include a comfortable mix of cities and villages, mountaintop hikes and forgotten Roman ruins, sleepy river cruises and sky-high gondola rides. I've also included a taste of neighboring Austria, with side-trips into Tirol and Salzburg. While you'll find the predictable biggies (such as Rhine castles and chunks of the Berlin Wall), I've also mixed in a healthy dose of Back Door intimacy (a soak in a Black Forest mineral spa, a beer with Bavarian monks, a thrilling mountain luge, and a ramble through traffic-free alpine towns). I've been selective, including only the most exciting sights. For example, of the many castles in the Mosel Valley, I guide you to the best: Burg Eltz.

The best is, of course, only my opinion. But after spending half of my adult life exploring and researching Europe, I've developed a sixth sense for what travelers enjoy. The places featured in this book will make anyone want to yodel.

About This Book

Rick Steves' Germany 2009 is your friendly Franconian, your German in a jam, a tour guide in your pocket.

This book is organized by destination—each a mini-vacation on its own, filled with exciting sights, homey and affordable places to stay, and memorable places to eat. In the following chapters, you'll find these sections:

Planning Your Time suggests a schedule with thoughts on how best to use your limited time.

Orientation includes tourist information, specifics on public transportation, local tour options, helpful hints, and easy-to-read maps designed to make the text clear and your arrival smooth.

Sights, described in detail, are rated:

▲▲▲—Don't miss.
▲▲—Try hard to see.
▲—Worthwhile if you can make it.
No rating—Worth knowing about.

Self-Guided Walks take you through interesting neighborhoods, with a personal tour guide in hand.

Sleeping describes my favorite hotels, from budget deals to cushy splurges.

Eating serves up a range of options, from inexpensive pubs to fancier restaurants.

Transportation Connections outlines your options for traveling to destinations by train and bus. In car-friendly regions, I've included route tips for drivers.

German History introduces you to some of the key people and events in this nation's complicated past, making your sightseeing that much more meaningful.

The **appendix** is a traveler's tool kit, with a handy packing checklist, recommended books and films, instructions on how to use the telephone, and useful phone numbers. You'll also find detailed information on driving and public transportation, as well as a climate chart, festival list, hotel reservation form, and German survival phrases.

Browse through this book and select your favorite sights. Then have a *wunderbar* trip! Traveling like a temporary local and taking advantage of the information here, you'll get the absolute most out of every mile, minute, and euro. As you visit places I know and love, I'm happy you'll be meeting some of my favorite German people.

PLANNING

Trip Costs

Five components make up your trip cost: airfare, surface transportation, room and board, sightseeing and entertainment, and shopping and miscellany.

Airfare: A basic round-trip flight from the US to Frankfurt costs $800–1,600, depending on what city you fly from and when (cheaper in winter). Always consider saving time and money in Europe by flying "open jaw"— into one city and out of another—for example, into Frankfurt and out of Berlin.

Surface Transportation: For a three-week whirlwind trip of all my recommended destinations, allow $650 per person for public transportation (trains and buses) or $800 per person (based on two people sharing) for a three-week car rental, parking, gas, and insurance. Leasing is worth considering for trips of two and a half weeks or more. Car rental and leases are cheapest when reserved from the US. Train passes are normally sold only outside of Europe. You may save money by simply buying tickets as you go (see "Transportation," page 547, for more details on renting cars and taking trains).

Room and Board: You can thrive in Germany on an average of $120 a day per person for room and board (less in small towns, more in big cities such as Berlin). A $120-a-day budget allows $15 for lunch, $20 for dinner, $5 for beer and *Eis* (ice cream), and $80 for lodging (based on two people splitting the cost of a $160 double room that includes breakfast). That's doable. Students and tightwads eat and sleep on $50 a day ($25 per hostel bed, $25 for meals and snacks).

Sightseeing and Entertainment: In big cities, figure $13–20 per major sight (Munich's Deutsches Museum-$13, Berlin's Museum of the Wall-$18), $5–7 for minor ones, and $25–50 for bus tours and splurge experiences (such as concert tickets, alpine lifts, and conducting the beer-hall band). An overall average of $30 a day works for most. Don't skimp here. After all, this category is the driving force behind your trip—you came to sightsee, enjoy, and experience Germany.

Shopping and Miscellany: Figure $3 per postcard, coffee, beer, and ice-cream cone. Shopping can vary in cost from nearly nothing to a small fortune. Good budget travelers find that this category has little to do with assembling a trip full of lifelong and wonderful memories.

Germany's Best Three-Week Trip by Car

Day	Plan	Sleep in
1	Fly into Frankfurt, pick up car, to Rhine	Bacharach
2	Rhine Valley	Bacharach
3	To Mosel Valley	Beilstein or Trier
4	Mosel Valley and/or Trier	Beilstein or Trier
5	To Baden-Baden	Baden-Baden
6	Relax and soak in Baden-Baden	Baden-Baden
7	Drive through the Black Forest	Staufen or Freiburg
8	To Bavaria and Tirol	Füssen or Reutte
9	Bavaria/Tirol and castles	Füssen or Reutte
10	More Bavaria/Tirol, then to Munich	Munich
11	Munich	Munich
12	More Munich, or side-trip to Salzburg	Munich
13	To Dachau, then follow Romantic Road to Rothenburg	Rothenburg
14	Rothenburg	Rothenburg
15	To Würzburg, drop car*, then train to Nürnberg	Nürnberg or Würzburg
16	Nürnberg	Nürnberg
17	Train to Dresden	Dresden
18	Train to Berlin	Berlin
19	Berlin	Berlin
20	Berlin	Berlin
21	Fly home	

*After Day 15, you're visiting well-connected cities, making a car unnecessary. Drop the car in Würzburg to save several days of car-rental costs and parking fees.

Smaller Towns vs. Bigger Towns: This itinerary (especially the first half) is heavy on half-timbered villages—a German specialty. But for some, a little cuteness goes a long way. Plan your overnights to either maximize or reduce quaintness. For example, for Days 3–4, 7, and 15, you can opt for smaller towns (Beilstein, Staufen, and the mid-size town of Würzburg) or bigger, more bustling cities (Trier, Freiburg, and Nürnberg).

With Less Time: This trip can be pared down to two weeks by making the following changes: Skip the Mosel (a sleepier version of the Rhine), and go directly from the Rhine to Baden-Baden. From Baden-Baden, head straight for Füssen/Reutte instead of overnighting in Staufen/Freiburg. Skip the Salzburg

side-trip; choose between Würzburg and Nürnberg, and stay just one night there; and reduce the stay in Berlin to two nights.

With More Time: Berlin and Salzburg are each easily worth another day. Depending on your interests, you could stay a day in Frankfurt (upon arrival); add another day for the Rhine to visit Köln from Bacharach; and see the town of Görlitz as a side-trip from Dresden (or as a detour en route to Berlin).

By Train: This itinerary is designed to be done by car, but could be done by train with some modifications: Skip the southern Black Forest and take the train from Baden-Baden to Munich, which works well as a home base for visiting Bavaria and Salzburg. Then take the train or bus to Rothenburg; from there, Würzburg, Nürnberg, and Dresden are all on the way to Berlin. Or, for the best of both worlds, consider using trains to connect major cities, and then renting a car strategically to explore worthwhile countryside regions (such as Bavaria/Tirol).

When to Go

The "tourist season" runs roughly from May through September. Book ahead for the holidays that occur throughout the year (see "Major Holidays and Weekends," next page).

Summer has its advantages: the best weather, snow-free alpine trails, very long days (light until after 21:00), and the busiest schedule of tourist fun.

Travel during "shoulder season" (May, June, Sept, and early Oct) is easier and a bit less expensive. Shoulder-season travelers get minimal crowds, decent weather, the full range of sights and tourist fun spots, and the ability to grab a room almost whenever and wherever they like—often at a flexible price. Also, in fall, fun harvest and wine festivals enliven many towns and villages, while forests and vineyards display beautiful fiery colors.

Winter travelers find concert seasons in full swing, with absolutely no tourist crowds, but some accommodations and sights are either closed or run on a limited schedule. Confirm your sightseeing plans locally, especially when traveling off-season. The weather can be cold and dreary, and nightfall draws the shades on sightseeing well before dinnertime. But dustings of snow turn German towns and landscapes into a wonderland, and December offers the chance to wander through Germany's famous Christmas markets.

You may find the climate chart in the appendix helpful.

Sightseeing Priorities

Depending on the length of your trip, and taking geographic proximity into account, the following are my recommended priorities.

3 days:	Munich, Bavarian castles
5 days, add:	Rhine Valley, Rothenburg
7 days, add:	More of Bavaria and Tirol, side-trip to Salzburg
10 days, add:	Berlin
14 days, add:	Baden-Baden, Black Forest, Dresden
17 days, add:	Nürnberg, Mosel Valley, Trier
21 days, add:	Würzburg, and slow down
More time:	Choose among Frankfurt, Köln, and Görlitz

(The itinerary and map on pages 4 and 5 include everything on this list.)

Travel Smart

Your trip to Germany is like a complex play—easier to follow and to really appreciate on a second viewing. While no one does the same trip twice to gain that advantage, reading this book in its entirety before your trip accomplishes much the same thing.

Design an itinerary that enables you to visit the various sights at the best possible times. Note the days when sights are closed. Saturday mornings are like weekday mornings, but by lunchtime,

Major Holidays and Weekends

Popular places are even busier on weekends, and holidays can bring many businesses to a grinding halt. Plan ahead and reserve your accommodations and transportation well in advance. Mark these dates in red on your travel calendar: New Year's Day, Easter (April 12 in 2009), Oktoberfest in Munich (Sept 19–Oct 4), Christmas, December 26, and New Year's Day. Also check the list of festivals and holidays on page 558 of the appendix.

many shops close down through Sunday. Sundays have the same pros and cons as they do for travelers in the US: Special events pop up, sights may have limited hours, shops and banks are closed, public transportation options are fewer, and there's no rush hour. Popular destinations are even more popular on weekends.

Be sure to mix intense and relaxed periods in your itinerary. To maximize rootedness, minimize one-night stands. Every trip (and every traveler) needs at least a few slack days. Pace yourself. Assume you will return. It's worth a long drive after dinner to be settled into a town for two nights. B&Bs are also more likely to give a good price to someone staying more than one night.

Reread this book as you travel, and visit local tourist information offices (abbreviated as TI in this book). Upon arrival in a new town, lay the groundwork for a smooth departure; write down the schedule for the train or bus you'll take when you depart.

Plan ahead for laundry and picnics. Get online at Internet cafés or your hotel to research transportation connections, confirm events, check the weather, and get directions to your next hotel. Buy a phone card and use it for reservations, reconfirmations, and double-checking hours.

Connect with the culture. Set up your own quest for the best beer-and-bratwurst, castle, cathedral, or whatever. Enjoy the hospitality of the Germanic people. Slow down and be open to unexpected experiences. Ask questions—most locals are eager to point you in their idea of the right direction. Keep a notepad in your pocket for organizing your thoughts. Wear your money belt, and learn the local currency and how to estimate prices in dollars. Those who expect to travel smart, do.

PRACTICALITIES

Red Tape: You need a passport—but no visa or shots—to travel in Germany. Your passport must be valid for at least six months beyond the time you leave Germany. Pack a photocopy of your

Know Before You Go

Your trip is more likely to go smoothly if you plan ahead. Check this list of things to arrange while you're still at home.

Be sure that your **passport** is valid at least six months after your ticketed date of return to the US. If you need to get or renew a passport, it can take up to two months (for more on passports, see www.travel.state.gov).

Book your rooms well in advance if you'll be traveling during any major **holidays,** such as Oktoberfest (see "Major Holidays and Weekends," on previous page). It's also smart to reserve rooms for your first night and during high season. Check if you'll be visiting **Frankfurt** and **Köln** during convention season (see page 277 and 372), and consider changing your dates in those cities to avoid peak prices.

Call your **debit and credit card companies** to let them know the countries you'll be visiting, so that they'll accept (and not deny) your international charges. Confirm your daily withdrawal limit; consider asking to have it raised so you can take out more cash at each ATM stop. Ask about international transaction fees.

If you're planning on **renting a car** in Germany, you'll need your US driver's license. It's recommended—but not required—that you also carry an International Driving Permit, available at your local AAA office ($15 plus the cost of two passport-type photos, www.aaa.com).

To get tickets to **Neuschwanstein Castle** in peak season, you can email, go online, or phone ahead (a minimum of 24 hours before your visit) to avoid long lines (see page 106 for tips).

Sign up in advance if you'd like a free **Munich BMW factory tour** (see page 67).

To see **Dresden's Historic Green Vault,** book your tickets ahead (ideally six months before)—or take your chances with same-day tickets (see page 418).

Tickets for the music-packed **Salzburg Festival** (late July through August) can go fast. Consider buying tickets ahead if there's a specific event you want to see (for details, see page 160).

Because **airline carry-on restrictions** are always changing, visit the Transportation Security Administration's website (www.tsa.gov/travelers) for an up-to-date list of what you can bring on the plane with you...and what you have to check. Remember to arrive with plenty of time to get through security.

passport in your luggage in case the original is lost or stolen.

Time: In Germany—and in this book—you'll use the 24-hour clock. It's the same through 12:00 noon, then keep going: 13:00, 14:00, and so on. For anything over 12, subtract 12 and add p.m. (14:00 is 2:00 p.m.).

Germany, like most of continental Europe, is generally six/nine hours ahead of the East/West Coasts of the US. The exceptions are the beginning and end of Daylight Saving Time: Europe "springs forward" the last Sunday in March (two weeks after most of North America), and "falls back" the last Sunday in October (one week before North America). For a handy online time converter, try www.timeanddate.com/worldclock.

Business Hours: Most shops throughout Germany are open from about 9:00 until 18:00–20:00 on weekdays, but close early on Saturday (generally between 12:00 and 17:00, depending on whether you're in a town or a big city), and are almost always closed on Sunday. By law, stores must close by 22:00, but very few stay open that late, and some shutter their doors as early as 18:30. The law makes an exception for shops in train stations, which often have grocery stores that are open daily until late. Banks are generally open Monday–Friday 8:00–12:00 and 14:00–16:00.

Catholic regions, including Bavaria, shut down during religious holidays. Turkish-owned shops are often open later than other stores. Many museums and sights are closed on Monday.

Shopping: For customs regulations and VAT refunds (the tax refunded on large purchases made by non-EU residents), see page 13.

Medical Help: If you get sick, do as the locals do and go to a pharmacist. They can help you with most any ailment. If a pharmacy is closed, a sign near the door indicates the nearest pharmacy that's open.

Watt's Up? Europe's electrical system is different from North America's in two different ways: the shape of the plug (two round prongs) and the voltage of the current (220 volts instead of 110 volts). For your North American plug to work in Europe, you'll need an adapter, sold inexpensively at travel stores in the US. As for the voltage, most newer electronics or travel appliances (such as hair dryers, laptops, and battery chargers) automatically convert the voltage—if you see a range of voltages printed on the item or its plug (such as "110–220"), it'll work in Europe. Otherwise, you can buy a converter separately in the US (about $20).

News: Americans keep in touch via the *International Herald Tribune* (published almost daily throughout Europe). Every Tuesday, the European editions of *Time* and *Newsweek* hit the stands with articles of particular interest to travelers. Sports

Just the FAQs, Please

Whom do I call in case of emergency?
Dial 112 for police or medical emergencies.

What if my credit card is stolen?
Act immediately. See "Damage Control for Lost Cards," page 12, for instructions.

How do I make a phone call to, within, and from Germany?
For detailed dialing instructions, refer to page 540.

How can I get tourist information about my destination?
Germany has a network of local tourist information offices (listed in each chapter of this book), as well as a national tourist information office in the US (see page 535). Note that tourist information office is abbreviated as **TI** in this book.

What's the best way to pack?
Light. For a recommended packing list, see page 562.

Does Rick have other resources that could help me?
For info on Rick's guidebooks, public television series, free audiotours, public radio show, website, guided tours, travel bags, accessories, and railpasses, see page 536.

Are there any updates to this guidebook?
Check www.ricksteves.com/update for changes to the most recent edition of this book.

Can you recommend any good books or movies for my trip?
For suggestions, see page 538.

addicts can get their daily fix online or from *USA Today*. Good websites include www.iht.com, http://news.bbc.co.uk, and www.europeantimes.com.

MONEY

Cash from ATMs

Throughout Europe, cash machines (ATMs) are the standard way for travelers to get local currency. Bring plastic—credit and/or debit cards. It's smart to bring two cards, in case one gets demagnetized or eaten by a temperamental machine.

Avoid using currency exchange booths (lousy rates and/or outrageous fees); if you have foreign currency to exchange, take it to a bank. Traveler's checks are a waste of time (long waits at slow banks) and a waste of money (in fees).

To use an ATM to withdraw money from your account, you'll need a debit card (ideally with a Visa or MasterCard logo for maximum usability), plus a PIN code. Know your PIN code in numbers; there are only numbers—no letters—on European keypads.

Do I need to speak some German?
Though most young or well-educated Germans—especially those in the tourist trade, and in big cities—speak at least some English, you'll get more smiles if you learn and use the German pleasantries. For background information on the language barrier, see page 541. For a list of survival phrases, see page 565.

Do you have information on driving, train travel, and flights?
See "Transportation" on page 547.

How much do I tip?
Relatively little. For tips on tipping, see page 13.

Will I get a student or senior discount?
While discounts are not listed in this book, seniors (age 60 and over), students with International Student Identification Cards, teachers with proper identification, and youths under 18 often get discounts—but you have to ask. To get a teacher or student ID card, visit www.statravel.com or www.isic.org.

How can I get a VAT refund on major purchases?
See the details on page 13.

How do I calculate metric amounts?
Germany uses the metric system. A liter is about a quart, four to a gallon. A kilometer is six-tenths of a mile. I figure kilometers to miles by cutting them in half and adding back 10 percent of the original (120 km: 60 + 12 = 72 miles, 300 km: 150 + 30 = 180 miles). For more metric conversions, see page 560.

Before you go, verify with your bank that your card will work overseas, and alert them that you'll be making withdrawals in Europe; otherwise, the bank may not approve transactions if it perceives unusual spending patterns. Also ask about international transaction fees; see "Credit and Debit Cards," next page.

The German word for "cash machine" is *Geldautomat* (*Bankomat* in Austria). Many ATMs don't issue receipts with your transaction.

Try to take out large sums of money to reduce your per-transaction bank fees. If the machine refuses your request, try again and select a smaller amount; some cash machines won't let you take out more than about €150 (don't take it personally). If that doesn't work, try a different machine.

To keep your cash safe, use a money belt—a pouch with a strap that you buckle around your waist like a belt, and wear under your clothes. Thieves target tourists. A money belt provides peace of mind, allowing you to carry lots of cash safely. Don't waste time every few days tracking down a cash machine—withdraw a week's worth of money, stuff it in your money belt, and travel!

Exchange Rate

1 euro (€) = about $1.50

To convert prices in euros to dollars, add about 50 percent: €20 = about $30, €50 = about $65. (To get the latest rate and print a cheat sheet, see www.oanda.com.) Just like the dollar, the euro is broken down into 100 cents. You'll find coins ranging from 1 cent to 2 euros, and bills from 5 euros to 500 euros.

So that €65 German cuckoo clock is about $100. Uh-oh.

Credit and Debit Cards

For purchases, Visa and MasterCard are more commonly accepted than American Express. Just like at home, credit and debit cards work easily at larger hotels, restaurants, and shops, but smaller businesses prefer payment in local currency (in small bills—break large bills at a bank or larger store). Note that receipts show your credit-card number; don't toss these thoughtlessly.

Fees: Some credit- and debit-cards transactions—whether purchases or ATM withdrawals—often come with tacked-on "international transaction" fees of up to 3 percent plus $5 per transaction. To avoid unpleasant surprises, call your bank or credit-card company before your trip to ask about these fees. If the fees are too high, consider getting a card just for your trip: Capital One (www.capitalone.com) and most credit unions have low-to-no international transaction fees.

Damage Control for Lost Cards

If you lose your credit, debit, or ATM card, you can stop people from using it by reporting the loss immediately to the respective global customer-assistance centers. Call these 24-hour US numbers collect: Visa (410/581-9994), MasterCard (636/722-7111), and American Express (623/492-8427).

At a minimum, you'll need to know the name of the financial institution that issued you the card, along with the type of card (classic, platinum, or whatever). Providing the following information will allow for a quicker cancellation of your missing card: full card number, whether you are the primary or secondary cardholder, the cardholder's name exactly as printed on the card, billing address, home phone number, circumstances of the loss or theft, and identification verification (your birth date, your mother's maiden name, or your Social Security number—memorize this, don't carry a copy). If you are the secondary cardholder, you'll also need to provide the primary cardholder's identification-verification details. You can generally receive a temporary card within two or three business days in Europe.

If you promptly report your card lost or stolen, you typically won't be responsible for any unauthorized transactions on your account, although many banks charge a liability fee of $50.

Tipping

Tipping in Germany isn't as automatic and generous as it is in the US, but for special service, tips are appreciated, if not expected. As in the US, the proper amount depends on your resources, tipping philosophy, and the circumstance, but some general guidelines apply.

Restaurants: Tipping is an issue only at restaurants that have table service. If you order your food at a counter, don't tip.

At German restaurants that have a wait staff, a service charge is generally included in the bill, although it's common to round up after a good meal (usually 5–10 percent; so, for an €18.50 meal, pay €20). Give the tip directly to your server. Rather than leaving coins, Germans usually pay with paper, saying how much they'd like the bill to be (for example, for an €8.10 meal, give a €20 bill and say *"Neun Euro"*—"Nine euros"—to get €11 change).

Taxis: To tip the cabbie, round up. For a typical ride, round up about 5–10 percent (to pay a €4.50 fare, give €5; or for a €28 fare, give €30). If the cabbie hauls your bags and zips you to the airport to help you catch your flight, you might want to toss in a little more. But if you feel like you're being driven in circles or otherwise ripped off, skip the tip.

Special Services: It's thoughtful to tip a couple of euros to someone who shows you a special sight and who is paid in no other way. Tour guides at public sites often hold out their hands for tips (€1–2) after they give their spiel; if I've already paid for the tour, I don't tip extra, though some tourists do give a euro, particularly for a job well done. I don't tip at hotels, but if you do, give the porter about a euro for carrying bags and leave a couple of euros in your room at the end of your stay for the maid if the room was kept clean. In general, if someone in the service industry does a super job for you, a tip of a euro or two is appropriate... but not required.

When in doubt, ask. If you're not sure whether (or how much) to tip for a service, ask your hotelier or the tourist information office; they'll fill you in on how it's done on their turf.

Getting a VAT Refund

Wrapped into the purchase price of your German souvenirs is a Value-Added Tax (VAT) of 19 percent. If you make a purchase of more than a certain amount (€25 in Germany) at a store that participates in the VAT-refund scheme, you're entitled to get most of that tax back. Getting your refund is usually straightforward and, if you buy a substantial amount of souvenirs, well worth the hassle. If you're lucky, the merchant will subtract the tax when you make your purchase. (This is more likely to occur if the store ships the goods to your home.) Otherwise, you'll need to:

Get the paperwork. Have the merchant completely fill out the necessary refund document, called a "Tax-Free Shopping Cheque." You'll have to present your passport at the store.

Get your stamp at the border or airport. Process your cheque(s) at your last stop in the EU (e.g., at the airport) with the customs agent who deals with VAT refunds. It's best to keep your purchases in your carry-on for viewing, but if they're too large or dangerous (such as knives) to carry on, track down the proper customs agent to inspect them before you check your bag. You're not supposed to use your purchased goods before you leave. If you show up at customs wearing your new lederhosen, officials might look the other way—or deny you a refund.

Collect your refund. You'll need to return your stamped document to the retailer or its representative. Many merchants work with a service, such as Global Refund (www.globalrefund.com) or Premier Tax Free (www.premiertaxfree.com), which have offices at major airports, ports, or border crossings. These services, which extract a 4 percent fee, can refund your money immediately in your currency of choice or credit your card (within two billing cycles). If the retailer handles VAT refunds directly, it's up to you to contact the merchant for your refund. You can mail the documents from home, or quicker, from your point of departure (using a stamped, addressed envelope you've prepared or one that's been provided by the merchant)—and then wait. It could take months.

Customs for American Shoppers

You are allowed to take home $800 worth of items per person duty-free, once every 30 days. The next $1,000 is taxed at a flat 3 percent. After that, you pay the individual item's duty rate. You can also bring in duty-free a liter of alcohol (slightly more than a standard-size bottle of wine; you must be at least 21), 200 cigarettes, and up to 100 non-Cuban cigars. Food in cans or sealed jars is permissible, as long as no meat is included. Some, but not all, types of cheese are allowed. Fresh fruits and vegetables are prohibited. Note that you'll need to carefully pack any bottles of wine and other liquid-containing items in your checked luggage, due to the three-ounce limit on liquids in carry-on baggage. To check customs rules and duty rates before you go, visit www.cbp.gov, and click on "Travel," then "Know Before You Go."

SIGHTSEEING

Sightseeing can be hard work. Use these tips to make your visits to Germany's finest sights meaningful, fun, fast, and painless.

Plan Ahead

Set up an itinerary that allows you to fit in all your must-see sights. For a one-stop look at opening hours in the bigger cities, see the "At a Glance" sidebars. Most sights keep stable hours, but you can easily confirm the latest by checking with the local TI.

Don't put off visiting a must-see sight—you never know when a place will close unexpectedly for a holiday, strike, or restoration. If you'll be visiting during a holiday, find out if a particular sight will be open by phoning ahead or visiting its website.

When possible, visit major sights first thing (when your energy is best) and save other activities for the afternoon. Hit the highlights first, then go back to other things if you have the stamina and time.

Going at the right time can also help you avoid crowds. This book offers tips on specific sights, such as Neuschwanstein Castle. Make reservations when possible, or try visiting very early, at lunch, or very late. Evening visits are usually peaceful with fewer crowds.

At the Sight

All sights have rules, and if you know about these in advance, they're no big deal.

Some important sights have metal detectors or conduct bag searches that will slow your entry.

At churches—which often offer interesting art (usually free) and a cool, welcome seat—a modest dress code (no bare shoulders or shorts) is encouraged.

Major museums and sights require you to check daypacks and coats. They'll be kept safely. If you have something you can't bear to part with, stash it in a pocket or purse. If you don't want to check a small backpack, carry it under your arm like a purse as you enter. From a guard's point of view, a backpack is generally a problem, while a purse is not.

Photography is sometimes banned at major sights. Look for signs or ask. If cameras are allowed, flashes or tripods are usually not. Flashes damage oil paintings and distract others in the room. Even without a flash, a handheld camera will take a decent picture (or buy postcards or posters at the museum bookstore). Video cameras are generally allowed.

Some museums have special exhibits in addition to their permanent collection. Some exhibits are included in the entry price; others come at an extra cost (which you may have to pay even if you don't want to see the exhibit).

Many sights rent audioguides, which generally offer excellent recorded descriptions in English (about $7.50). If you bring along your own pair of headphones and a Y-jack, two people can sometimes share one audioguide and save. Guided tours in English are most likely to occur during peak season (some are free, while others can cost up to $12 and range widely in quality).

Expect changes—paintings can be on tour, on loan, out sick, or shifted at the whim of the curator. To adapt, pick up any available free floor plans as you enter, and ask museum staff if you can't find a particular painting.

Most important sights have an on-site café or cafeteria (usually a good place to rest and have a snack or light meal). The WCs are free and generally clean.

Key sights and museums have bookstores selling postcards and souvenirs. Before you leave, scan the postcards and thumb through the biggest guidebook (or skim its index) to be sure you haven't overlooked something that you'd like to see.

Most sights stop admitting people 30–60 minutes before closing time, and some rooms close early (generally about 45 minutes before the actual closing time). Guards usher people out, so don't save the best for last.

Every sight or museum offers more than what is covered in this book. Use the information in this book as an introduction—not the final word.

SLEEPING

I favor accommodations (and restaurants) handy to your sightseeing activities. Rather than list hotels scattered throughout a city, I choose two or three favorite neighborhoods and recommend the best accommodations values in each, from $20 bunk beds to fancy-for-my-book $250 doubles.

While accommodations in Germany are fairly expensive, they are normally very comfortable and come with breakfast. Plan on spending $100–150 per hotel double in big cities, and $50–80 in towns and in private homes.

A triple is much cheaper than a double and a single. Single travelers save money at B&Bs (called *Pensions* in Germany), where the single price is often little more half the double-room price. Hotels, in contrast, charge almost as much for a single room as for a double. Hostels and dorms always charge per person. Especially in private homes, where the boss changes the sheets, people staying several nights are most desirable. One-night stays are sometimes charged extra.

I look for places that are friendly; clean; a good value; located in a central, safe, quiet neighborhood; English-speaking; and not

Sleep Code

(€1 = about $1.50, country code: 49)

To help you sort easily through these listings, I've divided the rooms into three categories based on the price for a standard double room with bath:

$$$ Higher Priced
$$ Moderately Priced
$ Lower Priced

To give maximum information in a minimum of space, I use the following code to describe the accommodations. Prices listed are per room, not per person.

When a price range is given for a type of room (such as double rooms listing for €100–150), it means the price fluctuates with the season, size of room, or length of stay.

- **S** = Single room (or price for one person in a double).
- **D** = Double or twin. Double beds are usually big enough for nonromantic couples.
- **T** = Triple (generally a double bed with a single).
- **Q** = Quad (usually two double beds).
- **b** = Private bathroom with toilet and shower or tub.
- **s** = Private shower or tub only (the toilet is down the hall).

According to this code, a couple staying at a "Db-€140" hotel would pay a total of €140 (about $210) for a double room with a private bathroom. Unless otherwise noted, breakfast is included, hotel staff speak basic English, and credit cards are accepted.

mentioned in other guidebooks. I'm more impressed by a handy location and a fun-loving philosophy than hair dryers and shoeshine machines.

I also like local character and simple facilities that don't cater to American "needs." Obviously, a place meeting every criterion is rare, and all of my recommendations fall short of perfection—sometimes miserably. But I've listed the best values for each price category, given the above criteria. The very best values are family-run places with showers down the hall and no elevator.

You should find most prices listed in this book to be good through 2009 (except for major holidays and festivals—see page 558). Prices can soften off-season, for stays of two nights or longer, or for payment in cash (rather than by credit card). Always mention that you found the place through this book—many of the hotels listed offer special deals to our readers.

Unless I note otherwise, the cost of a room includes breakfast (sometimes continental, but often buffet). The price is usually posted in the room. Before accepting, confirm your understanding of the complete price.

Germans depend heavily on expensive imported fuel and are very aware of their energy use. You'll endear yourself to *pension* and B&B owners by turning off lights when you leave and avoiding excessively long showers.

B&Bs

Compared to hotels, bed-and-breakfast places *(Pensions)* give you double the cultural intimacy for half the price. Throughout Germany, people rent out rooms *(Zimmer)* in their homes to travelers. Look for *Zimmer Frei* or *Privat Zimmer* signs. These are very common in areas popular with travelers (such as Germany's Rhine, Romantic Road, and southern Bavaria, and Austria's Tirol and Salzburg). In Germany, signs will clearly indicate whether they have available rooms (green) or not (orange). Booking direct saves both you and your host the cut the TI takes.

You'll get your own key to a private room that's clean, comfortable, and simple, though usually homey. Some B&Bs are like mini-hotels, with a separate entrance and several rooms, each with a private bath. Other B&Bs are family homes with spare bedrooms (the rooms sometimes lack sinks, but you have free access to the bathroom and shower in the home). Most B&Bs include a hearty continental breakfast.

*Pension*s and *Gasthof*s are similarly priced small, family-run hotels. Don't confuse B&Bs with the German *Ferienwohnung*, which is a self-catering apartment rented out by the week or fortnight.

Hostels

Hostelers can take advantage of the wonderful network of hostels. Follow signs marked *Jugendherberge* (with triangles) or with the logo showing a tree next to a house. Generally, travelers without a membership card ($28 per year, sold at hostels in most US cities or online at www.hiusa.org, US tel. 202/783-6161) are admitted for an extra $5.

Hostels are open to members of all ages. For decades, Bavaria's official hostels were the only ones in Europe that enforced a maximum age limit of 26. But now, even this has been relaxed, and everyone is welcome (though some slow-to-change Bavarian hostels still place some restrictions or charge slightly higher rates for older travelers). Hostel bunks usually cost $10–20 per night (cheaper for those under 27, plus $4 sheet rental if you don't have your own). Many hostels serve good, cheap meals and/or provide kitchen facilities. If you plan to stay in hostels, bring your own sheet. While many hostels have a few doubles or family rooms available upon request for a little extra money, plan on gender-segregated dorms with 4 to 20 beds per room. Hostels can be idyllic and peaceful, but school groups can raise the rafters. School groups are most common on summer weekends and on school-year weekdays. I like small hostels best. While many hostels may say over the telephone that they're full, most hold a few beds for people who drop in, or they can direct you to budget accommodations nearby.

Making Reservations

Given the quality of the places I've found for this book, I'd recommend that you reserve your rooms in advance, particularly during peak season. Book several weeks ahead, or as soon as you've pinned down your travel dates. Note that some holidays merit your making reservations far in advance (see "Major Holidays and Weekends," page 7). Just like at home, Monday holidays are preceded by busy weekends, so book the entire weekend in advance.

To make a reservation, contact hotels and B&Bs directly by email, phone, or fax. Email is the clearest and most economical way to make a reservation. In addition, many hotel websites now have online reservation forms. If phoning from the US, be mindful of time zones (see page 9). Most hoteliers listed are accustomed to English-only speakers. To ensure you have all the information you need for your reservation, use the form in this book's appendix (also at www.ricksteves.com/reservation).

When you request a room for a certain time period, use the European style for writing dates: day/month/year. Hoteliers need to know your arrival and departure dates. For example, for a two-night stay in July, I would request "2 nights, arrive 16/07/09, depart 18/07/09." Consider carefully how long you'll stay; don't just assume you can extend your reservation for extra days once you arrive.

If you don't get a response within a few days, call to follow up. If the response from the hotel gives its room availability and rates, it's not a confirmation. You must tell them that you want that room at the given rate.

For more spontaneity, you can make reservations as you travel, calling hotels or B&Bs a few days to a week before your visit. If you prefer the flexibility of traveling without any reservations at all, you'll have greater success snaring rooms if you arrive at your destination early in the day. When you anticipate crowds (weekends are worst), call hotels at about 9:00 on the day you plan to arrive, when the hotel clerk knows who'll be checking out and just which rooms will be available.

Whether you're reserving from home or on the road, the hotelier will sometimes request your credit-card number for a one-night deposit. While you can email your credit-card information (I do), some people prefer to share that personal info via phone call, fax, or secure online reservation form (if the hotel has one on its website).

If you must cancel your reservation, it's courteous to do so with as much advance notice as possible (at least three days; simply make a quick phone call or send an email). Family-run hotels and B&Bs lose money if they turn away customers while holding a room for someone who doesn't show up. Understandably, some hoteliers bill no-shows for one night. Hotels in larger cities such as Berlin sometimes have strict cancellation policies: For example, you might lose a deposit if you cancel within two weeks of your reserved stay, or you might be billed for the entire visit if you leave early. Ask about cancellation policies before you book.

Always reconfirm your room reservation a few days in advance from the road. If you'll be arriving after 17:00, let them know. Don't have the tourist office reconfirm rooms for you; they'll take a commission.

On the small chance that a hotel loses track of your reservation, bring along a hard copy of their emailed or faxed confirmation.

EATING

Germanic cuisine is heavy, hearty, and—by European standards—inexpensive. Though it's tasty, it can get monotonous if you fall into the schnitzel or wurst-and-potatoes rut. Be adventurous. Each region has its specialties, which, though not cheap, are often good values.

For breakfast, expect fresh-baked bread and jam, plus cereal, cold cuts, and cheese. Germans eat lunch and dinner about when we do, though they tend to eat a bigger lunch and smaller dinner.

Germans are health-conscious, but ironically many starchy, high-fat, high-calorie traditional foods remain staples of their diet. The classic dish is sausage—hundreds of varieties of *Brat-*, *Weiss-*, and other *wursts*—served with sauerkraut. Potatoes are the standard vegetable, along with cabbage and carrots. *Spargel* (giant white asparagus) is a must in early summer. Pork, fish, and venison are good here. When I need a break from pork, I order the *Salatteller* (big, varied dinner-size salad). Order house specials whenever possible. A good dish to try is *Maultaschen* ("mouth pockets"), a Swabian ravioli with meat smuggled inside a big piece of pasta—a custom that some say started as a culinary trick used by Catholics to eat meat when it wasn't allowed.

Ethnic restaurants provide a welcome break from Germanic fare. Foreign cuisine is either the legacy of a crumbled empire (Hungarian and Bohemian, from which German cuisine gets its goulash and dumplings) or a new arrival to feed the many hungry-but-poor guest workers. Italian, Turkish, and Greek food are good values. Middle Eastern places abound, serving *Döner Kebabs* (sliced meat and vegetables served in pita bread) and falafel (chickpea croquettes, also often served in pita bread).

There are many kinds of restaurants. Hotels often serve fine food. A *Gaststätte* is a simple, less-expensive restaurant. For smaller portions, order from the *kleine Hunger* (small hunger) section of the menu.

Most restaurants tack a menu onto their door for browsers and have an English menu inside. Only a rude waiter will rush you. Good service is relaxed (slow to an American). In Germany, you might be charged for bread or pretzels you've eaten from the basket on the table; have the waiter take it away if you don't want it. To wish others "Happy eating!" offer a cheery *"Guten Appetit!"* When you want the bill, say, *"Zahlen* (TSAH-lenn), *bitte."* For tips on tipping, see page 13.

For most visitors, the rich pastries, wine, and beer provide the fondest memories of Germanic cuisine. Wines range from the sweet, white "Rhine wines" to some good reds. The wine (85 percent white) from the Mosel, Rhine, and Danube river valleys is particularly good. Order wine by the *Viertel* (quarter-liter, or 8 oz.) or *Achtel* (eighth-liter, or 4 oz.). You can say, "*Ein Viertel Weisswein* (white wine), *bitte* (please)." Order it *süss* (sweet), *halb trocken* (medium), or *trocken* (dry). *Rotwein* is red wine and *Sekt* is German champagne. Menus list drink size by the tenth of a liter, or deciliter (dl). Ask for a *Weinschorle* and you'll get a spritzer—white wine pepped up with a little sparkling water.

The Germans enjoy a tremendous variety of great beer. The average German, who drinks 40 gallons of beer a year, knows that *dunkles* is dark, *helles* or *Lager* is light, *Flaschenbier* is bottled, and *vom Fass* is on tap. *Pils* is barley-based, *Weizen* or *Hefeweizen* is yeasty and wheat-based, *Bock* is a hoppy seasonal ale, and *Malzbier* is the malted soft drink that children learn with. *Radler* is half-beer and half-lemon-lime soda. When you order beer, ask for *eine Halbe* for a half-liter (not always available) or *eine Mass* for a whole liter (about a quart).

Tap water—which many waiters aren't eager to bring you—is *Leitungswasser.* They would rather you buy *Mineralwasser* (*mit/ohne Gas,* with/without carbonation). Popular soft drinks include *Apfelschorle* (half apple juice, half sparkling water) and *Spezi* (Coke and orange soda).

How Was Your Trip?

Were your travels fun, smooth, and meaningful? If you'd like to share your tips, concerns, and discoveries, please fill out the survey at www.ricksteves.com/feedback. I value your feedback. Thanks in advance—it helps a lot.

Cheap Meals: Try department-store cafeterias, *Schnell-Imbiss* (fast-food) stands, university cafeterias *(Mensas),* hostels, and—especially in big cities—*Döner Kebab* kiosks. For a quick, cheap bite, have a deli make you a *Wurstsemmel* (a meat sandwich). Enjoy the great snacks: Gummi bears are local gumdrops with a cult following (look for the Haribo brand), and Nutella is an Italian chocolate-hazelnut spread that may change your life.

TRAVELING AS A TEMPORARY LOCAL

We travel all the way to Europe to enjoy differences—to become temporary locals. You'll experience frustrations. Certain truths that we find "God-given" or "self-evident," such as cold beer, ice in drinks, bottomless cups of coffee, hot showers, and bigger being better, are suddenly not so true. One of the benefits of travel is the eye-opening realization that there are logical, civil, and even better alternatives.

Americans tend to be noisy in public places, such as restaurants and trains. My German friends place a high value on speaking quietly in these same places. Listen while on the bus or in a restaurant—the place can be packed, but the decibel level is low. Try to remember this nuance, and soften your speaking voice as a way of respecting their culture.

If there is a negative aspect to the image Germans have of Americans, it's that we are big, loud, aggressive, impolite, rich, superficially friendly, and a bit naive.

While Germans look bemusedly at some of our Yankee excesses—and worriedly at others—they nearly always afford us individual travelers all the warmth we deserve. Judging from all the happy feedback I receive from travelers who have used this book, it's safe to assume you'll enjoy a great, affordable vacation—with the finesse of an independent, experienced traveler.

Thanks, and *gute Reise!*

BACK DOOR TRAVEL PHILOSOPHY

From *Rick Steves' Europe Through the Back Door*

Travel is intensified living—maximum thrills per minute and one of the last great sources of legal adventure. Travel is freedom. It's recess, and we need it.

Experiencing the real Europe requires catching it by surprise, going casual..."Through the Back Door."

Affording travel is a matter of priorities. (Make do with the old car.) You can travel—simply, safely, and comfortably—nearly anywhere in Europe for $120 a day plus transportation costs (allow more for bigger cities). In many ways, spending more money only builds a thicker wall between you and what you came to see. Europe is a cultural carnival, and, time after time, you'll find that its best acts are free and the best seats are the cheap ones.

A tight budget forces you to travel close to the ground, meeting and communicating with the people, not relying on service with a purchased smile. Never sacrifice sleep, nutrition, safety, or cleanliness in the name of budget. Simply enjoy the local-style alternatives to expensive hotels and restaurants.

Extroverts have more fun. If your trip is low on magic moments, kick yourself and make things happen. If you don't enjoy a place, maybe you don't know enough about it. Seek the truth. Recognize tourist traps. Give a culture the benefit of your open mind. See things as different but not better or worse. Any culture has much to share.

Of course, travel, like the world, is a series of hills and valleys. Be fanatically positive and militantly optimistic. If something's not to your liking, change your liking. Travel is addictive. It can make you a happier American as well as a citizen of the world. Our Earth is home to six and a half billion equally important people. It's humbling to travel and find that people don't envy Americans. Europeans like us, but, with all due respect, they wouldn't trade passports.

Globe-trotting destroys ethnocentricity. It helps you understand and appreciate different cultures. Regrettably, there are forces in our society that want you dumbed down for their convenience. Don't let it happen. Thoughtful travel engages you with the world—more important than ever these days. Travel changes people. It broadens perspectives and teaches new ways to measure quality of life. Rather than fear the diversity on this planet, travelers celebrate it. Many travelers toss aside their hometown blinders. Their prized souvenirs are the strands of different cultures they decide to knit into their own character. The world is a cultural yarn shop, and Back Door travelers are weaving the ultimate tapestry. Join in!

MUNICH

München

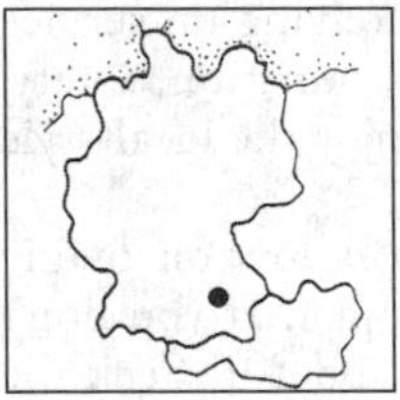

Munich, Germany's most livable and "yuppie" city, is also one of its most historic, artistic, and entertaining. It's big and growing, with a population of 1.5 million. Until 1871, it was the capital of an independent Bavaria. Its imperial palaces, jewels, and grand boulevards constantly remind visitors that this was once a political and cultural powerhouse. And its straightforward, somewhat sterile street plan reminds us that 80 years ago it provided a springboard for Nazism, and 65 years ago it lost a war. Today, Munich is a city of the 21st century, but still respects its past—in 2008, the city celebrated its 850th birthday.

Orient yourself in Munich's old center with its colorful pedestrian mall. Immerse yourself in the city's art and history—crown jewels, Baroque theater, Wittelsbach palaces, great paintings, and beautiful parks. Munich evenings are best spent in frothy beer halls, with their oompah, bunny-hopping, and belching Bavarian atmosphere. Pry big pretzels from buxom, no-nonsense beer maids.

Planning Your Time

Munich is worth two days, including a half-day side-trip to Dachau. If necessary, its essence can be captured in a day (walk the center, tour a palace and a museum, and enjoy a beer-filled evening). Those in a hurry and without a car can see "Mad" King Ludwig's castles (covered in the Bavaria and Tirol chapter) as a day trip from Munich by tour. Even Austria's Salzburg (1.5–2 hours one-way by train) is within day-tripping distance.

ORIENTATION

(area code: 089)

The tourist's Munich is circled by a ring road (site of the old town wall) marked by four old gates: Karlstor, also known as Stachus (near the main train station—the Hauptbahnhof); Sendlinger Tor; Isartor (near the river); and Odeonsplatz (no surviving gate, near the palace). Marienplatz marks the city's center. A great pedestrian-only zone (Kaufingerstrasse and Neuhauser Strasse) cuts this circle in half, running neatly from Karlstor and the train station through Marienplatz to Isartor. Orient yourself along this east–west axis. Ninety percent of the sights and hotels I recommend are within a 20-minute walk of Marienplatz and each other.

Despite its large population, Munich feels small. This big-city elegance is possible because of a law that no building can be taller than the church spires. Despite ongoing debate about changing this policy, there are still no skyscrapers in downtown Munich.

Tourist Information

Munich has two outlets for tourist information: the official TIs, and the handy travel agency called EurAide.

Official TIs

Munich has two helpful TIs (www.muenchen-tourist.de). One is in front of the **main train station** (with your back to the tracks, walk through the central hall, step outside, and turn right; April–Oct Mon–Sat 9:00–20:00, Sun 10:00–18:00; Nov–March Mon–Sat 9:00–18:30, Sun 10:00–18:00; tel. 089/233-0300). The other TI is on Munich's main square, **Marienplatz,** below the glockenspiel (Mon–Fri 10:00–20:00, Sat 10:00–16:00, Sun 14:00–16:00).

At either TI, pick up brochures and a city map (€0.30, often free in hotel lobbies) and confirm your sightseeing plans. Consider the *Monatsprogramm* (€1.65, German-language list of sights and events calendar) and the free, twice-monthly magazine *In München* (in German, lists all movies and entertainment in town). The TI can book you a room (you'll pay about 10 percent here, then pay the rest at the hotel), but you'll get a better value by contacting my recommended hotels directly. If you're interested in a Gray Line tour of the city or to nearby castles (described on page 36), don't buy your ticket at the TI; instead, you can get discounted tickets for these same tours at EurAide (see next page).

The **City Tour Card,** which covers public transportation and includes stingy sightseeing discounts on minor sights, is a bad deal (€10/1 day, €19/3 days, available at TIs or EurAide, validate before using). Two or more people traveling on a Munich "partner" all-day transit pass blow this deal out of the water (see "Getting Around Munich," page 29).

If the line at the TI is bad, go to EurAide.

EurAide

The industrious, eager-to-help EurAide office in the main train station is a godsend for Eurailers and budget travelers (May–Sept daily 7:45–12:45 & 14:00–18:00; Oct–April Mon–Fri 8:00–12:00 & 13:00–16:00, closed Sat–Sun; with your back to track 19, head toward the main entrance, turn left before the pretzel stand down the hallway, and find the EurAide office on the left—see map on page 76; tel. 089/593-889, www.euraide.com, see www.euraide.com/ricksteves for Rhine River cruise schedules and other useful information). EurAide sells a €0.50 city map and offers a free, information-packed newsletter, *The Inside Track* (described on page 28, always available in a rack at their door).

EurAide helps 600 visitors per day in the summer; do your homework, have a list of questions ready, and keep in mind that they're busiest in the morning. Chances are that your questions are already answered in their *Inside Track* newsletter—scan it first. Alan Wissenberg and his EurAide staff can answer your train-travel and accommodations questions in clear American English. Paid by the German rail company to help you design your train travels, EurAide makes reservations and sells tickets, *couchettes,* and sleepers for the train at the same price you'd pay at the station ticket windows.

EurAide also sells tickets for Gray Line city tours (see page 33), as well as for tours to Neuschwanstein and Linderhof castles (see page 36). EurAide offers a discount on these tickets with this book in 2009. For information on their Romantic Road bus tour tickets, see page 87.

Arrival in Munich

By Train: Munich's main train station (München Hauptbahnhof) is a sight in itself—one of those places that can turn a homebody into a fancy-free vagabond.

For a quick rest stop, Burger King's toilets (upstairs, €0.30) are as pleasant and accessible as its hamburgers. More toilets are downstairs near track 26 (clean, but €1.10). Check out the bright and modern complex of **restaurants and shops** opposite track 14.

For a quick train picnic, I shop at **Yorma's,** by track 26 and outside the station, next to the TI. The **k presse + buch** shop (across from track 23) is great for English-language books, newspapers, and magazines, including *Munich Found* (informative English-speaking residents' monthly, €3). You'll find two **tourist information** offices (the city TI and EurAide—see "Tourist Information," page 25) and **lockers** (€2, at tracks 18, 26, and 31). **Car-rental agencies** are up the steps opposite track 21 (Mon–Fri 7:00–21:00, Sat–Sun 8:00–17:00). A **pharmacy** is out the front door to the left, at the corner of Luisenstrasse and Elisenstrasse (Mon–Fri 8:00–19:00, Sat 9:00–14:00, closed Sun, tel. 089/595-444). A quiet, non-smoking **waiting room** *(Warteraum)* is open to anybody (across from track 23 and up the escalator), but the nearby, plush **DB Lounge** is only for those with a first-class ticket issued by Deutsche Bahn (railpasses don't get you in). **Radius Tours** (at track 32) rents bikes, organizes tours, and provides confused visitors with information.

Subway lines, trams, and buses connect the station to the rest of the city (though many of my recommended hotels are within walking distance of the station). If you get lost in the underground maze of subway corridors while you're simply trying to get to the train station, follow the signs for *DB* (Deutsche Bahn) to surface successfully. Watch out for the hallways with blue ticket stamping machines in the middle—these lead to the subway, where you could be fined if nabbed without a validated ticket.

By Plane: There are two good ways to connect Munich Airport and downtown Munich: subway and airport bus. You can take an easy 40-minute ride on the S-1 or S-8 **subway,** which runs every 20 minutes between the airport and Marienplatz (€9, or free with a validated and dated railpass). Or hop on the Lufthansa **airport bus,** which links the airport with the main train station (€11, 3/hr, 45 min, buses depart train station 5:10–19:50, buy tickets on bus; buses line up near taxi stands facing Arnulfstrasse—from inside the station, exit near track 26). A **taxi** from the airport makes no budgetary sense—it's cheaper to ride public transit into the center, and catch a taxi from there. Airport info: tel. 089/97500, www.munich-airport.de.

Helpful Hints

Museum Hours: The Alte Pinakothek, Munich City Museum, Jewish Museum, Pinakothek der Moderne, Lenbachhaus, Glyptothek, Bavarian National Museum, Beer and Oktoberfest Museum, and Dachau Concentration Camp are closed on Monday. The Neue Pinakothek closes Tuesday. The art galleries are generally open late one night a week. On Sunday, the Pinakotheks and Bavarian National Museum cost just €1 apiece, but you'll pay extra for the usually free audioguides.

Useful Phone Numbers: Pharmacy—tel. 089/595-444 (Mon–Fri 8:00–19:00, Sat 9:00–14:00, closed Sun, near train station on the corner of Luisenstrasse and Elisenstrasse); EurAide train info—tel. 089/593-889; Taxi—tel. 089/21610.

Bikes and Pedestrians: Signs painted on the sidewalk or blue-and-white street signs show which part of the sidewalk is designated for pedestrians and which is for cyclists. The strip of pathway closest to the street is usually reserved for bikes. Pedestrians wandering into the bike path may hear the cheery ding-ding of a cyclist's bell just before being knocked unconscious by a local biker.

Internet Access: There's plenty of online access in Munich. Hole-in-the-wall call centers near the station and all over town have Internet terminals. Most hotels also have a computer for guests. **Munich Walk**'s offices offer Internet access (15 extra minutes free with this book, near Isartor at Thomas-Wimmer-Ring 1—look for *Tourist info* sign, tel. 089/2423-1767).

Laundry: A handy self-service **Waschcenter** is a 10-minute walk from the train station (€6.50/15 lbs, €11/25 lbs, drop-off service for €8–16 depending on load size, daily 7:00–23:00, English instructions, Paul-Heyse-Strasse 21, near intersection with Landwehrstrasse—see map on page 76, tel. 089/531-311).

Private Driver: Johann Fayoumi is reliable and speaks English (€50/hr, mobile 0174-183-8473, johannfayoumi@gmail.com).

Car Rental: Several car-rental agencies are located upstairs at the train station, opposite track 21 (Mon–Fri 7:00–21:00, Sat–Sun 9:00–17:00).

***The Inside Track* Train Travelers' Newsletter:** Anyone traveling by train should pick up this wonk-ish yet brilliant quarterly newsletter published by Alan Wissenberg at EurAide (free, always available in a rack by the EurAide door—see listing on page 26). You'll find all the tedious but important details on getting to Neuschwanstein, Dachau, Nymphenburg, and Prague; the ins and outs of supplements and reservations necessary for railpass-holders; a daily schedule of various tours in Munich; and (of course) plenty of tips on how to take advantage of EurAide's services.

Need a Toilet? Munich had outdoor urinals until the 1972 Olympics and then decided to beautify the city by doing away with them. What about the people's needs? There's a new law: Any place serving beer must admit the public (whether or not they're customers) to use the toilets.

What's with Monaco? People walking around with guidebooks to Monaco aren't lost. "Monaco di Baviera" means "Munich" in *Italiano.*

Getting Around Munich

Much of Munich is walkable. To reach sights away from the city center, use the efficient tram, bus, and subway systems. Taxis are honest and professional, but expensive and generally unnecessary (except perhaps to avoid the time-consuming trip by tram and foot to Nymphenburg Palace).

By Public Transit

Subways are called U-Bahns and S-Bahns (actually an underground-while-in-the-city commuter railway). The U-Bahn mainly runs north–south, while the S-Bahn is generally east–west. Subway lines are numbered (for example, S-3 or U-5). Eurailpasses are good on the S-Bahn (but not the U-Bahn), but if you use a flexipass, it'll cost you a travel day.

The entire system (subway/bus/tram) works on the same tickets, sold at TIs and in the subway at booths and easy-to-use ticket machines (which take coins and €5 and €10 bills). There's a wide array of ticket types. A **regular ticket** *(Einzelfahrkarte)* costs €2.20 and is good for two hours in one direction, including changes. For the shortest rides (1 or 2 stops, no transfer), buy the €1.10 ***Kurzstrecke*** ("short stretch") ticket. The €5 **all-day pass** *(Single Tageskarte)* is a great deal for a single traveler. For small groups, the €9 **partner all-day pass** *(Partner Tageskarte)* is an even better deal—it covers all public transportation for up to five adults and a dog (two kids count as one adult, so two adults, six kids, and a dog can travel with this ticket). The **XXL** version of this all-day ticket includes the extended transportation network, which covers the trip to Dachau Concentration Camp (€6.70/person, €11.80/partner ticket). For longer stays, consider a **three-day ticket** (€12.30/person, €21/partner ticket for the gang, does not include transportation to Dachau). All-day and multi-day passes are valid until 6:00 the following morning.

Partner tickets—while seemingly impossibly cheap—are for real. Read it again and do the arithmetic. Even two people traveling together save money. And for groups, it's a real steal. The only catch is you've got to stay together.

You must stamp your ticket with the date and time prior to using it (for all-day or multi-day passes, you only have to stamp it the first time you use it). For the subway, punch your ticket in the blue machine *before* going down to the platform. For buses and trams, stamp your ticket once on board. Plainclothes ticket-checkers enforce this honor system, rewarding freeloaders with stiff €40 fines. There's a transit customer service center at Marienplatz (Mon–Fri 9:00–20:00, Sat 9:00–16:00, closed Sun, underground—directly beneath Beck's department store, tel. 089/4142-4344, www.mvv-muenchen.de). Note that bus #100 seems designed for tourists, as it connects the major museums (6/hr).

Important: All S-Bahn lines connect the Hauptbahnhof (main station) with Marienplatz (main square). If you want to use the S-Bahn and you're either at the station or at Marienplatz, follow signs to the S-Bahn (U is not for you), and concern yourself only with the direction (Hauptbahnhof/Pasing or Marienplatz). "Direction" in German is *Richtung.*

By Bike

Level, compact, and with plenty of bike paths, Munich feels made for those on two wheels. When biking in Munich, follow these simple rules: You must walk your bike through pedestrian zones; you can take your bike on the subway, but not during rush hour and only if you have an extra ticket; and cyclists are expected to follow the rules of the road, just like drivers.

You can rent bikes quickly and easily from two great places: Radius Tours (in the train station) and Munich Walk (at Isartor). Both have an extensive selection of bikes, and both provide helmets, maps, and advice on routes. You can get a 10 percent discount with this book in 2009 from either operation. **Radius Tours** is in front of track 32 in the train station (city bikes-€3/hr, €14.50/day, €17/24 hrs, €25/48 hrs, mountain bikes 25 percent more, €50 cash or credit-card deposit, ask about self-guided bike-tour info, April–Oct daily 9:30–18:00, closed in bad weather Nov–March, tel. 089/596-113, www.radiusmunich.com). **Munich Walk** is located at the other end of the tourist zone, near the river and Isartor (€3/hr, €15/24 hrs, 2-hour minimum, open daily 9:00–23:00, Thomas-Wimmer-Ring 1, storefront says *Tourist info,* tel. 089/2423-1767, www.munichwalktours.de).

For a great city ride, consider this day on a bike: English Garden to Olympic Park, then along the canal to Nymphenburg Palace, around the palace grounds, and back to the center (in 30 min) via Arnulfstrasse, which has a bike path the entire way. Or consider the Isar River bike ride described on page 68.

TOURS

Munich has three major tour companies. **Gray Line** specializes in bus tours of the city and to the Bavarian castles of "Mad" King Ludwig (Neuschwanstein and Linderhof; tel. 089/5490-7560, www.sightseeing-munich.com; you'll get a discount on these tours if you buy tickets at EurAide—see "Tourist Information" earlier in this chapter). The two other major companies compete directly with each other, offering walking tours, bike tours, and day trips

Munich

to Dachau Concentration Camp and Neuschwanstein Castle. In my experience, they're comparable: **Radius Tours** (office in the main train station, in front of track 32—see map on page 76, tel. 089/5502-9374, www.radiustours.com) and **Munich Walk** (near Isartor at Thomas-Wimmer-Ring 1—see map above, tel. 089/2423-1767, www.munichwalktours.de). Both Radius Tours and Munich Walk offer at least €1 off any of their walking tours with this book in 2009. If you do anything with either company, don't forget to show this book and request your discount.

In Munich

Walking Tours—Radius Tours runs two city walking tours, both with reliably good guides (daily April–Oct, fewer tours off-season): "Munich Highlights" (€10, €1 Rick Steves discount, at 10:00, 2 hours) and "Hitler and the Third Reich" (€13, €3 Rick Steves discount, at 15:00, 2.5 hours). They also offer an educational "Bavarian Beer and Food" tour that includes a visit to the Beer and Oktoberfest Museum (see page 44), samples of five varieties of the sudsy stuff, and regional food (€25, €3 Rick Steves discount; Tue, Thu, and Sat at 18:00; also Fri at 18:00 mid-April–mid-Oct; 3 hours). All tours depart from the Radius office (in front of track 32 at the train station, no need to register—just show up).

Munich Walk offers similar tours (€1 Rick Steves discount on each tour): a "City Walk" (€10, May–mid-Oct daily at 10:45 and 14:45) and "Hitler's Munich" (€10, April–Oct daily at 10:00, 10:30 in winter, 2.5 hours, extended 5-hour version Mon and Sat only). Their "Beer and Brewery" tour (like the Radius Tour version, described above) is more mature than your typical hard-partying pub crawl. You visit Munich's oldest brewery to learn, eat, and drink in the city that made beer famous. The price includes three stops and three different beers, and ends at the Hofbräuhaus (€18, May–mid-Sept daily at 18:15, fewer tours off-season, 3.5 hours). All Munich Walk tours depart from under the glockenspiel on Marienplatz. No reservations are necessary—just show up.

New Munich advertises free walking tours. This youthful outfit (which started with the same guerilla business plan in Berlin) has an irreverent, boisterous approach to walking tours—it's basically an hour of entertainment and stories sprinkled with some historical "facts." History and art information is kept very light (for example, guides might refer to the city's beloved Frauenkirche as "the church with the Pamela Anderson domes"). The first basic tour is free (although you'll be hit up for tips, as that's how their guides are paid). They sell the other standard Munich tours. Their nightly pub crawl offers a fun way to make drunken friends from around the world. For details, see their free magazine (all over town) or go to www.newmunich.com.

Local Guides—I've had great days with two good guides, each charging the same prices (€110/2 hrs, €130/3 hrs): **Georg Reichlmayr,** tel. 08131/86800, mobile 0170-341-6384, program explained at his website, www.muenchen-stadtfuehrung.de, info@muenchen-stadtfuehrung.de) and **Monika Hank** (tel. 089/311-4819, mobile 0175-923-2339, monika.hank@web.de). They helped me with much of the historical information in this chapter, and Georg was my sidekick on the Munich episode of my public television series.

Bike Tours—Munich lends itself to bike touring, and three outfits fit the bill: the original Mike's Bikes (€24); his spin-off competitor, Discover Munich (free but tip as you like); and Munich Walk (private hire only, for small groups).

Mike's Bike Tours, popular with the college crowd, are four-hour frat parties on wheels. The tours are high-energy, if a bit clunky with pacing, and the guides are better comedians than historians. Still, you get a great ride through the English Garden (€24, tips encouraged, bikes provided, 1-hour break in Chinese Tower beer garden, daily mid-April–Aug at 11:30 and 16:00, March–mid-April and Sept–mid-Nov at 12:30, no need to reserve, meet under tower of Old Town Hall on Marienplatz; for schedule, call or visit website, or pick up brochure at TI; tel. 089/2554-3987, mobile 0172-852-0660, www.mikesbiketours.com).

Discover Munich Free Bike Tours depart daily (same times as Mike's) from the Fish Fountain on Marienplatz. These tours (and use of the bike) really are free. You just tip as you are able and inclined after the 3.5-hour trip, which includes lots of information, silly jokes, and an hour to eat and drink at the Chinese Tower in the English Garden (25 people maximum, daily mid-April–Aug at 11:30 and 16:00, March–mid-April and Sept at 12:30, www.discovermunichnow.com). At this price, why not?

Munich Walk offers private guided bike tours to small groups at any time (€22/person for groups of at least four). Team up with a small gang, then call 089/2423-1767 and set a date.

Quickie Orientation City Bus Tour—Gray Line Tours has many itineraries, including one-hour orientation bus tours (3/hr, departs from Karstadt department store, Bahnhofplatz, directly in front of train station). This tour is actually well worthwhile—sitting upstairs on the topless double-decker bus, you'll see lots of things missed by the typical visitor wandering around the center. It complements the information in this book, though the live guide narrates (in German and English) as stiffly as a tape-recording. Just show up and pay the driver (cash only), or get a €1–2 discount by picking up your ticket in advance at EurAide. Choose from a basic, one-hour "Express Circle" that heads past the Pinakotheks, Marienplatz, and Karlsplatz; or the more extensive "Grand Circle" that lasts 2.5 hours and also includes the Nymphenburg Palace, Olympia Park, and the Schwabing neighborhood (€13 Express tour, €18 Grand tour, hop on and off privileges, daily in season, on the hour from 10:00–17:00, tel. 089/5502-8995, www.sightseeing-munich.com).

Outside Munich

"Mad" King Ludwig's Castles—Two spectacular Bavarian castles, Neuschwanstein and Linderhof, make a logical day trip from Munich. For more on these destinations, see the Bavaria and

Munich at a Glance

In the Center

▲▲**Marienplatz** Munich's main square, at the heart of a lively pedestrian zone, watched over by New Town Hall (and its glockenspiel show). **Hours:** Always open; glockenspiel jousts daily at 11:00 and 12:00, plus 17:00 May–Oct; New Town Hall tower elevator—daily 10:00–19:00. See page 36.

▲▲**Viktualienmarkt** Munich's "small-town" open-air market, perfect for a quick snack or meal. **Hours:** Mon–Sat, *Biergarten* open until late, closed Sun. See page 41.

▲▲**Hofbräuhaus** World-famous beer hall, worth a visit even if you're not chugging. **Hours:** Daily 9:00–24:00. See page 44.

▲▲**Munich City Museum** The city's history in five floors. **Hours:** Tue–Sun 10:00–18:00, closed Mon. See page 45.

▲▲**The Residenz** The elegant family palace of the Wittelsbachs, awash with Bavarian opulence. Complex includes the Residenz Museum (private apartments), Residenz Treasury (housing Wittelsbach family crowns and royal knickknacks), and the impressive, just-restored Cuvilliés Theater. **Hours:** Museum and treasury—daily April–mid-Oct 9:00–18:00, mid-Oct–March 10:00–16:00; theater—daily 10:00–17:00. See page 46.

▲▲**Alte Pinakothek** Bavaria's best painting gallery, with a wonderful collection of European masters from the 14th through the 19th centuries. **Hours:** Wed–Sun 10:00–18:00, Tue 10:00–20:00, closed Mon. See page 54.

▲▲**Deutsches Museum** Germany's version of our Smithsonian Institution, with 10 miles of science and technology exhibits. **Hours:** Daily 9:00–17:00. See page 60.

▲**Neue Pinakothek** The Alte's twin sister, with paintings from 1800 to 1920. **Hours:** Thu–Mon 10:00–18:00, Wed 10:00–20:00, closed Tue. See page 57.

▲**Pinakothek der Moderne** Hip contemporary-art museum near the Alte and Neue Pinakotheks—housed in a building that's as interesting as the art. **Hours:** Tue–Sun 10:00–18:00, Thu until 20:00, closed Mon. See page 57.

▲**Lenbachhaus** Collection of Blaue Reiter (Blue Rider) Expressionism. **Hours:** Tue–Sun 10:00–18:00, closed Mon. See page 57.

▲**English Garden** The largest city park on the Continent, packed with locals, tourists, surfers, and nude sunbathers. (I'd rate this ▲▲ on a bike.) **Hours:** Always open. See page 58.

St. Michael's Church Renaissance church housing Baroque decor and a crypt of 40 Wittelsbachs. **Hours:** Church—daily 9:00-19:00, Thu until 21:00, Sun until 22:00; crypt—Mon-Fri 9:30-16:30, Sat 9:30-14:30, closed Sun, less off-season. See page 39.

Frauenkirche Huge, distinctive twin-domed church looming over the city center. **Hours:** Church—daily 7:00-19:00; tower climb—April-Oct Mon-Sat 10:00-17:00, closed Sun and Nov-March. See page 39.

St. Peter's Church Munich's oldest church, packed with relics. **Hours:** Church—long hours daily; spire climb—Mon-Fri 9:00-18:30, Sat-Sun 10:00-18:30, off-season until 17:30. See page 40.

Away from the Center

▲▲**Nymphenburg Palace** The Wittelsbachs' impressive summer palace featuring a hunting lodge, coach museum, fine royal porcelain collection, and vast park. **Hours:** Daily April-mid-Oct 9:00-18:00, mid-Oct-March 10:00-16:00. See page 63.

▲▲**Dachau Concentration Camp** Notorious Nazi camp on the outskirts of Munich, now a powerful museum. **Hours:** Tue-Sun 9:00-17:00, closed Mon. See page 69.

▲**Museum of Transportation** Deutsches Museum's cross-town annex devoted to travel. **Hours:** Daily 9:00-17:00. See page 61.

▲**Olympic Park** Munich's 1972 Olympic stadium, now a lush park with a view tower and swimming pool. **Hours:** Grounds always open; tower daily 9:00-24:00, pool daily 7:00-23:00. See page 67.

▲**Andechs Monastery** Baroque church, hearty food, and Bavaria's best brew, in the countryside near Munich. **Hours:** *Biergarten* open daily 10:00-20:00, church open until 18:00. See page 68.

BMW Museum The carmaker's futuristic museum, including glimpses of rare models. **Hours:** Tue-Fri 9:00-18:00, Sat-Sun 10:00-20:00, closed Mon. See page 67.

Tirol chapter. If you're planning on visiting these sights as a day trip from Munich, you have three basic options: on your own by train, with an escorted train tour, or by guided bus tour.

Gray Line Tours offers rushed all-day bus tours of the two castles that also include 30 minutes in Oberammergau (€49, €7 Rick Steves discount if you buy your ticket at EurAide—cash only, two castle admissions-€15 extra, daily April–Oct, no tours Mon or Nov–March). In summer, it's wise to purchase tickets a day ahead. Tours meet at 8:10 and depart at 8:30 from the Karstadt department store (across from the station). While **Munich Walk** advertises a similar tour, they're simply selling tickets for this Gray Line trip.

Radius Tours runs all-day tours to Neuschwanstein Castle by train. Your guide will escort you onto public transportation, give you some general information, and help you into the castle for the standard tour that's included with any admission ticket (€32 with this book, €25 with railpass, castle admission-€9 extra; departs daily mid-April–Sept at 9:30 from in front of track 32 at train station, home by 19:00, book ahead; Oct–mid-April tours run Mon, Wed, and Sat at 10:30; tel. 089/5502-9374, www.radiustours.com).

Dachau Concentration Camp—**Radius Tours** offers English-language-only tours of the camp year-round (€21 includes the €6.70 cost of public transportation, €3 Rick Steves discount; April–mid-Oct Tue–Sun at 9:15 and 12:30; mid-Oct–March Tue–Sun at 11:00; no tours Mon, when camp is closed; depart from Radius office in Munich station—in front of track 32, smart to confirm times, but you can just show up). **Munich Walk** does a similar tour (€21 includes €6.70 transport costs, €3 Rick Steves discount, May–Oct Tue–Sun at 10:20 and 13:15, Nov–March Tue–Sun at 10:30, April Tue–Sun at 13:15, no tours Mon). While several other companies do Dachau tours, both Radius and Munich Walk are allowed to actually guide inside the camp. Considering how good and passionate their guides are, and that you're only paying about €10 for them, these tours are a great value. Allow about five hours total (including 20-min S-Bahn trip and 10-min bus trip each way, and about 3 hours at the site, with English film).

SIGHTS AND ACTIVITIES

Central Munich

▲▲City Views—Downtown Munich's three best city viewpoints (all described in this section) are from the tops of St. Peter's Church (stairs only), Frauenkirche (stairs plus elevator), and New Town Hall (elevator).

▲▲Marienplatz and the Pedestrian Zone—Riding the escalator out of the subway into sunlit Marienplatz ("Mary's Square") gives you a fine first look at the glory of Munich: great buildings

bombed flat and rebuilt, outdoor cafés, and people bustling and lingering like the birds and breeze with which they share this square. Take in the ornate facades of the gray, pointy Old Town Hall and the Neo-Gothic New Town Hall, with its beloved glockenspiel.

The **New Town Hall** (Neues Rathaus), built from 1867 until 1908, dominates the square. Munich was a very royal city. Notice the politics of the statuary. The 40 statues—though sculpted only in 1900—decorate New Town Hall not with civic leaders, but with royals and blue-blooded nobility. Because this building survived the bombs and had a central location, it served as the US military headquarters in 1945.

The New Town Hall is famous for its **glockenspiel**—only 100 years old—which "jousts" daily at 11:00 and 12:00 all year (also at 17:00 May–Oct). The *Spiel* recreates a royal wedding from the 16th century: The duke and his bride watch the action as the Bavarians (in white and blue) forever beat their enemies. Below, the barrel-makers—famous for being the first to dance in the streets after a deadly plague lifted—do their popular jig. The glockenspiel's 32 life-size figures were restored in 2008, as Munich celebrated the clock's 100th year of entertaining the city.

The New Town Hall tower offers **views** of the city (€2, elevator from under glockenspiel, daily 10:00–19:00).

Marienplatz is marked by a statue of the **Virgin Mary,** moved here in 1638 from its original location in the Frauenkirche out of thanks that the Swedes didn't sack the town during their occupation. It was also a rallying point for the struggle against the Protestants. The cherubs are fighting against the four great biblical enemies of civilization: the dragon of war, the lion of hunger, the snake of plague and disease, and the rooster-headed monster of heresy (Protestantism). The serpent that's being stepped upon represents the "wrong faith," a.k.a. Martin Luther.

The **Old Town Hall** (Altes Rathaus; at the right side of square as you face New Town Hall) was completely destroyed by WWII bombs and later rebuilt. Ludwig IV, an early Wittelsbach who was Holy Roman Emperor back in the 14th century, stands

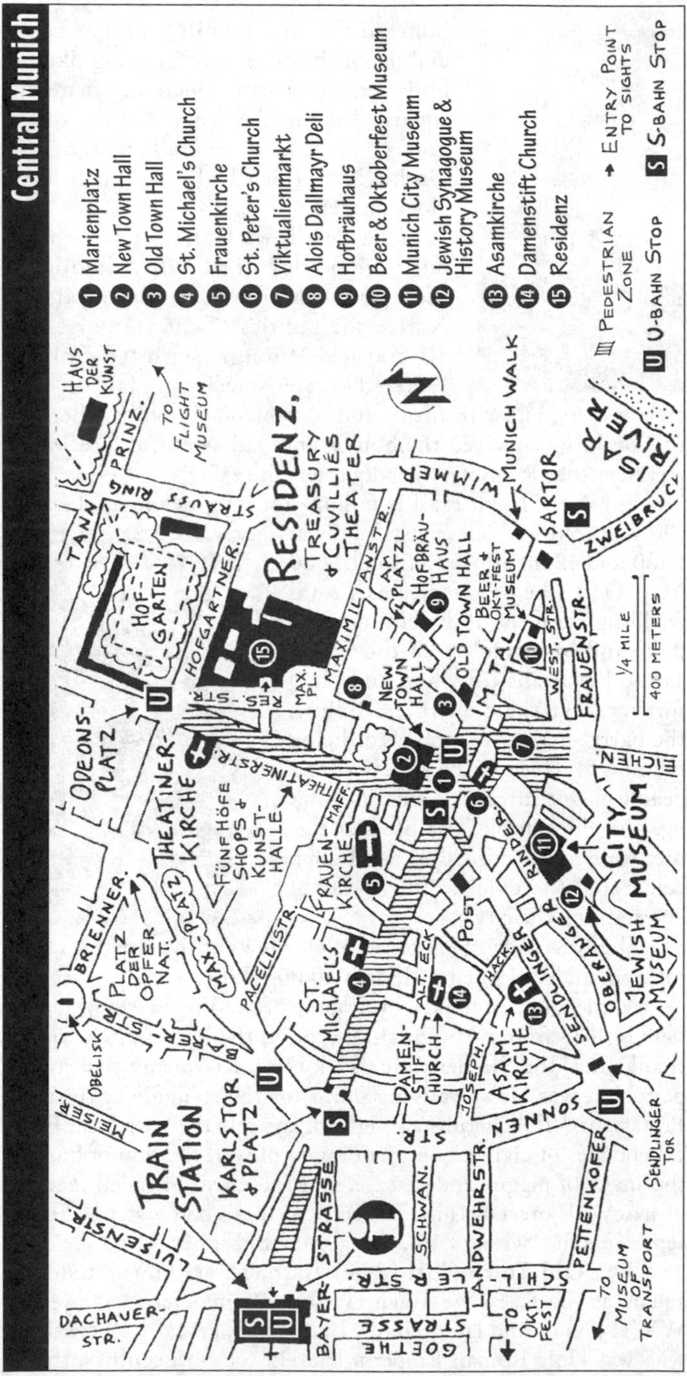
Central Munich
1 Marienplatz
2 New Town Hall
3 Old Town Hall
4 St. Michael's Church
5 Frauenkirche
6 St. Peter's Church
7 Viktualienmarkt
8 Alois Dallmayr Deli
9 Hofbräuhaus
10 Beer & Oktoberfest Museum
11 Munich City Museum
12 Jewish Synagogue & History Museum
13 Asamkirche
14 Damenstift Church
15 Residenz
PEDESTRIAN ZONE
ENTRY POINT TO SIGHTS
U-BAHN STOP
S-BAHN STOP
1/4 MILE
400 METERS
TRAIN STATION
KARLSTOR & PLATZ
DACHAUER-STR.
LUISENSTR.
MEISER-STR.
OBELISK
BRIENNER STR.
PLATZ DER OPFER NAT.
MAX-PLATZ
ODEONS-PLATZ
THEATINER-KIRCHE
FÜNF HÖFE SHOPS & KUNST-HALLE
TANN
HAUS DER KUNST
PRINZ.
RING
TO FLIGHT MUSEUM
HOF-GARTEN
HOFGARTNER.
STRAUSS
RESIDENZ, TREASURY & CUVILLIÉS THEATER
RES.-STR.
MAX. PL.
MAXIMILIANSTR.
AM PLATZL
HOFBRÄU-HAUS
WIMMER
MUNICH WALK
ISARTOR
ISAR RIVER
ZWEIBRUCK
BEER & OKT-FEST MUSEUM
WEST. STR.
FRAUENSTR.
OLD TOWN HALL
IM TAL
NEW TOWN HALL
THEATINERSTR.
MAFF.
FRAUEN-KIRCHE
PACELLISTR.
ST. MICHAEL'S
ALT. ECK
POST
RINDER
CITY MUSEUM
EICHEN
DAMEN-STIFT CHURCH
ASAM-KIRCHE
HACK.
SENDLINGER
OBERANGER
JEWISH MUSEUM
JOSEPH.
SONNEN
SENDLINGER TOR
PETTENKOFER
SCHILLER STR.
LANDWEHRSTR.
SCHWAN.
BAYER-STRASSE
GOETHE STRASSE
TO OKT-FEST
TO MUSEUM OF TRANSPORT

in the center of the facade. He donated this great square to the people. On the bell tower, find the city seal with its monk and towers. Munich flourished because, in its early days, all salt trade had to stop here on Marienplatz.

Back at Marienplatz, the **pedestrian mall** (Kaufingerstrasse and Neuhauser Strasse) leads you through a great shopping area, past carnivals of street entertainers and good old-fashioned slicers and dicers, the towering twin-domed Frauenkirche (built in the late 1400s, rebuilt after World War II), and several fountains, to Karlstor and the train station. As one of Europe's first pedestrian zones, the mall enraged shopkeepers when it was built in 1972 for the Olympics. Today, it is Munich's living room. Nearly 9,000 shoppers pass through it each hour. The shopkeepers are happy... and merchants nearby are begging for their streets to become traffic-free. Imagine this street in hometown USA.

Three Churches near Marienplatz—In the pedestrian zone around Marienplatz are three noteworthy churches: St. Michael's, the Frauenkirche, and St. Peter's. Each was heavily bombed in World War II, and each displays photos of that destruction near its entrance. As you face New Town Hall, St. Michael's is a few blocks down the pedestrian street to your left; the Frauenkirche is the big twin-domed church at 10 o'clock; and St. Peter's is over your right shoulder.

St. Michael's Church: While one of the first great Renaissance buildings north of the Alps, this church has a brilliantly Baroque interior. Inspired by the Gesù (the Jesuit's main church in Rome), it was built in the late 1500s as a home to the Jesuits in Bavaria. The statue of Michael fighting a Protestant demon (on the front facade) is a reminder that this leader of heaven's army invited the Jesuits to literally counter the Reformation from here. The interior is striking for its barrel vault, the largest in its day. The crypt contains 40 stark royal tombs, including the resting place of King Ludwig II. Judging by all the flowers, romantics are still mad about their "mad" king (church entry free, daily 9:00–19:00, Thu until 21:00, Sun until 22:00; crypt-€2, Mon–Fri 9:30–16:30, Sat 9:30–14:30, closed Sun, less off-season; frequent concerts—check the schedule outside).

Frauenkirche: These twin onion domes are the symbol of the city. Some say Crusaders, inspired by the Dome of the Rock in Jerusalem, brought home the idea. Others say these

domes are the inspiration for the characteristic domed church spires marking villages throughout Bavaria.

Go inside (free, daily 7:00–19:00). While much of the church was destroyed during World War II (see photos just inside the entrance, on the right), the towers survived, and the rest has been gloriously restored.

Built in Gothic style in the late 1400s, the Frauenkirche (Church of Our Lady) has been the city's cathedral since 1821. Construction was funded with the sale of indulgences, but money problems meant the domes weren't added until Renaissance times. Late-Gothic buildings in Munich were generally built of brick—easy to make locally and cheaper and faster to use than stone. This church was constructed in a remarkable 20 years. It's located on the grave of Ludwig IV (who died in 1347). His big, black, ornate, tomb-like monument (now in the back) was originally in front at the high altar. Standing in the back of the nave, notice how your eyes go right to the altar...Christ...and (until recently) Ludwig. Those Wittelsbachs—always trying to be associated with God. In fact, this alliance was instilled in people through the prayers they were forced to recite: "Virgin Mary, mother of our duke, please protect us." A plaque over the last pew on the left recalls the life story of Pope Benedict XVI, who occupied the archbishop's seat here from 1977 until 1982, when he moved into Pope John Paul II's inner circle in the Vatican.

You can ascend the tower for the city's highest public viewpoint, at 280 feet (€3, 86 steps to elevator, April–Oct Mon–Sat 10:00–17:00, closed Sun and Nov–March). On many Wednesday evenings in summer, you can catch an organ concert here (€8, 19:00, tickets available at München Ticket office inside Marienplatz TI).

St. Peter's Church: The oldest church in town overlooks Marienplatz from its perch near the Viktualienmarkt. It's built on the hill where Munich's original monastic inhabitants probably settled. (Founded in 1158, the city celebrated its 850th birthday in 2008.) Outside, notice the old tombstones plastered onto the wall—a reminder that in the Napoleonic age, the cemeteries surrounding most city churches were (for hygienic and practical space reasons) dug up and moved.

St. Peter's was badly damaged in World War II. Inside, photos show the bomb damage (near the entrance). As part of the soul of the city (according to a popular song, "Munich is not Munich without St. Peter's"), the church was lovingly rebuilt—half with Augustiner beer money, the rest with private donations—and the altar and ceiling frescoes were marvelously restored (possible with the help of Nazi catalog photos—see "The History of Munich: Part 2," on page 46).

Apostles line the nave, leading up to St. Peter above the altar. On the ceiling, you'll see Peter crucified upside-down. The finely crafted gray iron chapel fences were donated after World War II by the local blacksmiths of the national railway. The precious and fragile sandstone Gothic chapel altar (front left) survived the war only because it was buried in sandbags.

Munich has more relics than any city outside of Rome. For more than a hundred years, it was the pope's bastion against the rising tide of Protestantism in northern Europe during the Reformation. Favors done in the defense of Catholicism earned the Wittelsbachs neat relic treats. For instance, check out the tomb of Munditia (second side chapel on left as you enter). She's a third-century martyr (note the ancient Roman tombstone with red lettering), whose remains were given to Munich by Rome as thanks and a vivid reminder that those who die for the cause of the Roman Church go directly to heaven without waiting for Judgment Day.

It's a long climb to the top of the spire (306 steps, no elevator)—much of it with two-way traffic on a one-lane staircase—but the view is dynamite (€1.50, Mon–Fri 9:00–18:30, Sat–Sun 10:00–18:30, off-season until 17:30, last exit 30 min after closing). Try to be two flights from the top when the bells ring at the top of the hour, and then, when your friends back home ask you about your trip, you'll say, "What?"

▲▲Viktualienmarkt—Early in the morning, you can still feel small-town Munich here, long a favorite with locals for fresh produce and good service (open Mon–Sat, food stalls open late, closed Sun). The most expensive real estate in town could never really support such a market, but the town charges only a percentage of the gross income, enabling these old-time shops to carry on (and keeping out fast-food chains).

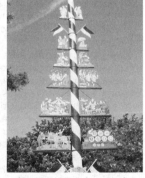

The huge **maypole** is a tradition. Fifteenth-century town market squares posted a maypole decorated with various symbols to explain which crafts and merchants were doing business in the market. Munich's maypole shows the city's six great brews, and the crafts and festivities associated with brewing. (You can't have a kegger without coopers—find the merry barrel-makers.)

Notice the beer counter. Munich's breweries take turns here.

The History of Munich: Part 1

Born from Salt (1100–1500)

Munich began in the 12th century, when Henry the Lion (Heinrich der Löwe) muscled in on the lucrative salt trade, burning a rival's bridge over the Isar River and building his own near a monastery of "monks"—München. (The town's coat of arms features the Münchner Kindl, a boy in monk's robes.) Henry built walls and towers, opened a market, and peasants flocked in from the countryside. Marienplatz—then as now—was the center of town, and the crossroads of the Salzstrasse (Salt Road) from Salzburg to Augsburg.

After Henry's death, the town was taken over by an ambitious merchant family, the Wittelsbachs (1240), and became the capital of the region (1255). Munich-born Louis (or Ludwig) IV (1282–1347) was elected king of Germany and Holy Roman Emperor, temporarily making Munich a major European capital.

By the 1400s, Munich's maypole-studded market bustled with trade. Besides salt, Munich gained a reputation for beer. More than 30 breweries pumped out the golden liquid that lubricated both trade and traders. The Bavarian Beer Purity Law assured quality control. Wealthy townspeople erected the twin-domed Frauenkirche and the Altes Rathaus on Marienplatz, and the Wittelsbachs built a stout castle that would eventually become the cushy Residenz. When the various regions of Bavaria united in 1506, Munich (pop. 14,000) was the natural capital.

Religious Wars, Plagues, Decline (1500–1800)

While Martin Luther and the Protestant Reformation raged in northern Germany, Munich became the ultra-Catholic heart of the Counter-Reformation. The devout citizens poured enormous funds into building the massive St. Michael's Church (1583) as a home for the Jesuits, and into the Residenz (early 1600s) as home of the Wittelsbachs. Both were showpieces of conservative power and the Baroque and Rococo styles.

During the Thirty Years' War, the Catholic city was surrounded by Protestants (1632). The Wittelsbachs surrendered quickly and paid a ransom, sparing the city from pillage, but it was soon hit by the bubonic plague. After that passed, the leaders erected the Virgin's column on Marienplatz to thank God for killing only 7,000 citizens. (Munich's many plagues are also remembered today when the glockenspiel's barrel-makers do their daily dance to ward off the plague.)

The double whammy of invasion and disease left Munich bankrupt and powerless, overshadowed by the more powerful Habsburgs of Austria. The Wittelsbachs took their cultural cues from France (Nymphenburg Palace is a mini-Versailles), England (the English Garden), and Italy (the Pitti Palace–inspired Residenz). While the rest of Europe modernized and headed toward democracy, Munich remained conservative and backward.

The Kings (1806–1918): Max I, Ludwig I, Max II, Ludwig II, Ludwig III

When Napoleon's army surrounded the city (1800), the Wittelsbachs again surrendered hospitably. Napoleon rewarded the Wittelsbach "duke" with more territory and a royal title: "king." Maximilian I (r. 1806–1825, see page 104), a.k.a. Max Joseph, now ruled the Kingdom of Bavaria, an independent nation bigger than Switzerland, with a constitution and parliament. When Max's popular son Ludwig got married (Sept 1810), it touched off a two-week celebration that became an annual event: Oktoberfest.

As king, Ludwig I (r. 1825–1848) set about rebuilding the capital in the Neoclassical style we see today. Medieval walls and ramshackle houses were replaced with grand buildings of columns and arches (including the Residenz and Alte Pinakothek). Connecting these were broad boulevards and plazas for horse carriages and promenading citizens (Ludwigstrasse and Königsplatz). Ludwig established the university and built the first railway line, turning Munich (pop. 90,000) into a major transportation hub, budding industrial city, and fitting capital for the new country.

In 1846, the skirt-chasing King Ludwig (see Nymphenburg's Gallery of Beauties, page 65) was beguiled by a notorious Irish dancer named Lola Montez. She became his mistress and he fawned over her in public, scandalizing Munich. The Münchners resented her spending their tax money and dominating their king (supposedly inspiring the phrase "Whatever Lola wants, Lola gets"). In 1848, as Europe was swept by a tide of revolution, the citizens rose up and forced Ludwig to abdicate. His son Maximilian II (r. 1848–1864) continued Ludwig's enlightened program of modernizing, while studiously avoiding dancers from Ireland.

In 1864, 18-year-old Ludwig II (r. 1864–1886) became king. He immediately invited the composer Richard Wagner to Munich, planning a lavish new opera house to stage Wagner's operas. Munich didn't like the idea, and Ludwig didn't like Munich. For most of his reign, Ludwig avoided the Residenz and Nymphenburg, instead building castles in the Bavarian countryside at the expense of Munich taxpayers. (For more on the king, see page 104.)

In 1871, Bavaria became part of the newly united Germany, and overnight, Berlin overtook Munich as Germany's power center. But turn-of-the-century Munich was culturally rich, birthing the abstract art of Wassily Kandinsky, Paul Klee, and the Blue Rider group. This artistic flourishing didn't last long.

World War I devastated Munich. Poor, hungry, disillusioned, unemployed Münchners roamed the streets. Extremists from the left and right battled for power. In 1918, a huge mob marched to the gates of the Residenz and drove the forgettable King Ludwig III (r. 1913–1918)—the last Bavarian king—out of the city, ending nearly 700 years of continuous Wittelsbach rule.

For "The History of Munich: Part 2," see page 46.

Changing every day or two, a sign *(Heute im Ausschank)* announces which of the six brews is being served. Here, under the standard beer-garden chestnut trees, you can order just half a liter—unlike at other *Biergarten* (handy for shoppers who want to have a quick sip and then keep on going).

The Viktualienmarkt is ideal for a light meal (see page 81). Or, for a more expensive selection, try the...

Alois Dallmayr Delicatessen—When the king called out for dinner, he called Alois Dallmayr. As you enter, read the black plaque with the royal seal by the door: Königlich Bayerischer Hof-Lieferant ("Deliverer for the King of Bavaria and his Court"). This place became famous for its exotic and luxurious food items: tropical fruits, seafood, chocolates, fine wines, and coffee. Catering to royal and aristocratic tastes (and budgets), it's still the choice of Munich's old rich. Today, it's most famous for its sweets, chocolates, and coffee—dispensed from fine hand-painted Nymphenburg porcelain jugs (Mon–Sat 9:30–19:00, closed Sun, Dienerstrasse 14, behind New Town Hall).

▲▲Hofbräuhaus—Whether or not you slide your lederhosen on its polished benches, it's a great experience just to see the world's most famous beer hall in all its rowdy glory. As you wander, look for the various *Stammtisch* signs (meaning "reserved"), hanging above tables where different clubs meet regularly; don't sit here unless you're specifically invited. Racks of locked steins, made of pottery and metal, are for regulars. You'll see locals stuffed into lederhosen and dirndls; giant gingerbread cookies that sport romantic messages; and postcards of the new German (and apparently beer-drinking) pope.

After being bombed in World War II, this venerable palace of beer was quickly rebuilt and back in business within a few years. Notice the quirky 1950s-style painted ceiling, with Bavarian colors, grapes, chestnuts, and fun "eat, drink, and be merry" themes. A slogan on the ceiling above the band reads, *Durst ist schlimmer als Heimweh* ("Being thirsty is worse than feeling homesick").

The men's room has two-dozen urinals around a vomitorium. The bouncer at the door nabs 20–50 people (mostly Italians, he says) each day trying to steal mugs as souvenirs. The staircase to the left of the entrance displays historic old Hofbräuhaus photos and prints (daily 9:00–24:00, live oompah music during lunch and dinner; €6 for upstairs dinner show, €20 includes all-you-can-stomach buffet, nightly from 19:00–22:30; a 5-min walk northeast of Marienplatz at Platzl 6). For more details, see page 81.

Beer and Oktoberfest Museum (Bier- und Oktoberfestmuseum)—Get a low-tech and underwhelming take on history at this humble museum, where exhibits and artifacts outline the centuries-old quest for the perfect beer (apparently perfected in Munich) and the origins of the city's Oktoberfest celebration. The oldest house in the city center, the museum's home is noteworthy in itself (€4; open Tue–Sat 13:00–17:00, closed Sun–Mon; between Isartor and Viktualienmarkt at Sterneckerstrasse 2, tel. 089/2423-1607).

▲▲Munich City Museum (Münchner Stadtmuseum)—Five floors of exhibits in this newly renovated museum tell the story of life in Munich through the centuries, including the history of "monk culture," the development of National Socialism (i.e., Nazism), and World War II—illustrated with paintings, photos, and models (€4, free on Sun, open Tue–Sun 10:00–18:00, closed Mon, few English descriptions, no crowds, bored and playful guards, 3 blocks off Marienplatz at St.-Jakobs-Platz 1, tel. 089/2332-2370, www.stadtmuseum-online.de). The museum's Stadt Café is handy for a good meal (see page 86).

Jewish Synagogue and History Museum (Jüdisches Museum München)—Thanks to Germany's acceptance of religious refugees from former USSR states, Munich's Jewish population has now reached its pre-Nazi size—10,000 people. The city's new synagogue and Jewish History Museum anchor a revitalized Jewish quarter, which includes a kindergarten and day school, children's playground, kosher restaurant, and bookstore.

While the **synagogue** is shut tight to the non-Jewish public, its architecture is striking from the outside. Lower stones of travertine evoke the Wailing Wall in Jerusalem, while an upper section represents the tent that held important religious wares during the 40 years of wandering through the desert until the Temple of Solomon was built, ending the Exodus. The synagogue's door features the first 10 letters of the Hebrew alphabet, symbolizing the Ten Commandments.

The cube-shaped **museum** is stark, windowless, and as inviting as a bomb shelter. Its small permanent exhibit in the basement is disappointing. The two floors of temporary exhibits, always Munich-specific, might justify the entry fee (€6, Tue–Sun 10:00–18:00, closed Mon, across the street from the Munich City Museum at St.-Jakobs-Platz 16, tel. 089/96096, www.muenchen.de/juedisches-museum).

Rococo Churches—Near the Munich City Museum, the private church of the Asam brothers **(Asamkirche)** is a gooey, drippy, Baroque-concentrate masterpiece by Bavaria's top two Rococonuts. A few blocks away, the small **Damenstift Church** has an incredibly realistic sculptural rendition of the Last Supper (at intersection of Altheimer Ecke and Damenstiftstrasse, a block south of the pedestrian street).

The History of Munich: Part 2

This picks up where "Part 1" leaves off (see page 42).

Nazis, World War II, and Munich Bombed (1918–1945)

Germany after World War I was in chaos. In quick succession, the prime minister was gunned down, Communists took power, and the army restored the old government. In the hubbub, one fringe group emerged—the Nazi party, centered around the charismatic war veteran Adolf Hitler.

Hitler—an Austrian who'd settled in Munich—made stirring speeches in Munich's beer halls (including the Hofbräuhaus) and galvanized the city's disaffected. On November 8–9, 1923, the Nazis launched a coup d'état known as the Beer Hall Putsch. They kidnapped the mayor, and Hitler led a mob to overthrow the German government in Berlin. The march got as far as Odeonsplatz before Hitler was arrested and sent to prison in nearby Landsberg. Though the Nazis eventually gained power in Berlin, they remembered their roots, dubbing Munich "Capital of the Movement." The Nazi headquarters stood near today's obelisk on Brienner Strasse, Dachau was chosen as the regime's first concentration camp, and Odeonsplatz was designated as a place where all who passed by were required to perform the Nazi salute.

As World War II drew to a close, it was clear that Munich would be destroyed. Hitler did not allow the evacuation of much of the town's portable art treasures and heritage—a mass emptying of churches and civil buildings would have caused hysteria and been a statement of no confidence in his leadership. While museums were closed (and could be systematically emptied over the war years), public buildings were not. Rather than save the treasures, the Nazis photographed everything.

Munich was indeed pummeled mercilessly by air raids, leveling nearly half the city. What the bombs didn't get was destroyed by 10 years of rain and freezing winters.

The Residenz

For a long hike through corridors of gilded imperial Bavarian grandeur, tour the Wittelsbachs' family palace (largely rebuilt after World War II). The Wittelsbachs, who ruled Bavaria for nearly 700 years, modeled the front of their enormous palace on the Medici family's Pitti Palace in Florence. The sprawling place evolved from the 14th through the 19th centuries—as you'll see on the charts near the entrance. Whatever happened to the Wittelsbachs, the longest continuously ruling family in European history? They're

Munich Rebuilds (1945–Present)

After the war, with generous American aid, the Münchners set to reconstructing their city. During this time, many German cities established commissions to debate their rebuilding strategy: They could restore the old towns, or bulldoze and go modern. While Frankfurt decided to start from scratch (hence its Manhattan-like feel today), Munich voted—by a close margin—to rebuild its old town.

Münchners took care to preserve the original street plan and recreate the medieval steeples, Neo-Gothic facades, and Neoclassical buildings. They blocked off the city center to cars, built the people-friendly U-Bahn system, and opened up Europe's first pedestrian-only zone (Kaufingerstrasse and Neuhauser Strasse). Only now, nearly 65 years after the last bombs fell, are the restorations—based on those Nazi photographs—finally being wrapped up. And those postwar decisions still shape the city: Buildings cannot exceed the height of the church spires.

The 1972 Olympic Games, featuring a futuristic stadium and a squeaky-clean city, were to be Munich's postwar statement that it had arrived. However, the Games turned tragic when a Palestinian terrorist group stormed a dormitory and kidnapped (and eventually killed) 11 Israeli athletes. In 1989, when Germany reunited, Berlin once again became the focal point of the country, relegating Munich to the role of sleepy Second City.

These days, Munich seems to be comfortable just being itself rather than trying to keep up with Berlin. In fact, the city seems to be on a natural high, especially since the ascension of Joseph Ratzinger (the local archbishop) to the papacy in 2005, his wildly successful homecoming visit in 2006, and Munich hosting the World Cup soccer tournament that same year.

Today's Munich is rich—home to BMW and Siemens AG, and a producer of software, books, movies, and the latest fashions. It's consistently voted one of Germany's most-livable cities—safe, clean, cultured, a university town, built on a people scale, and close to the beauties of nature. Though it's the capital of Bavaria and a major metropolis, Munich's low-key atmosphere has led Germans to dub it *Millionendorf*—the "village of a million people."

still around—but since they're no longer royalty, most of them have real jobs now. If you're torn between Munich's top two palaces, I'd say the Residenz interior is best, while Nymphenburg (see page 63) has the finest garden.

Cost, Hours, Location: €6 each to visit the Residenz Museum (palace apartments) and the Treasury, including audioguides; €9 combo-ticket covers both. The Halls of the Nibelungen are free (but closed until 2010). All parts of the palace are open daily April–mid-Oct 9:00–18:00, mid-Oct–March 10:00–16:00, last entry one hour before closing. The complex is located three blocks north of Marienplatz.

Information: Your ticket includes a free English audioguide. For more in-depth information, consider the €10 English guidebook, but don't bother with the dry €3 version. Tel. 089/290-671, www.schloesser.bayern.de.

Orientation: While impressive, the Residenz can be confusing for visitors. Enter the complex from the main entrance on Max-Joseph-Platz (at the corner of the palace nearest Marienplatz) or from the entrance on Residenzstrasse. Just inside the main entrance are the Halls of the Nibelungen (free), as well as the ticket booth for both the Residenz Museum and the Treasury (located in separate wings).

Halls of the Nibelungen (Nibelungensäle)—The mythological scenes in these fascinating halls (closed until 2010) were the basis of Wagner's *Der Ring des Nibelungen.* Wagner and "Mad" King Ludwig were friends and spent time hanging out here (c. 1864). These very images could well have inspired Wagner to write his *Ring* and Ludwig to build his "fairy-tale castle," Neuschwanstein. Note that even if you're not touring the rest of the Residenz, these rooms (when open) are free to enter.

▲▲Residenz Museum (Residenzmuzeum)—This museum includes the most spectacular halls and private apartments in the Wittelsbachs' palace complex. It's the best place to get a glimpse of the opulent lifestyle of Bavaria's late, great royal family.

➲ Self-Guided Tour: Since it's so big, different sections of the Residenz Museum are open in the mornings and in the afternoons (after 13:30 in summer, 12:30 in winter). Leave the ticket office to your right (without going back outside), and follow the *Rundgang* signs. This self-guided tour is designed to coincide with the afternoon route (a little more interesting than the morning). Due to ongoing renovations, either tour route can change without notice. To help you find the highlights, I have numbered the rooms as they appear on the official map (free at entry), though be warned the rooms themselves aren't all numbered.

Shell Grotto (Room 6, actually outside, ground floor): This artificial grotto was an exercise in man controlling nature—a celebration of humanism. Renaissance humanism was a big deal when this was built in the 1550s. Imagine the ambience here during that time, with Mercury—the pre-Christian god of trade and business—overseeing the action, and red wine spurting from the mermaid's breasts and dripping from Medusa's head in the courtyard. The strange structure is made from Bavarian freshwater shells. This palace was demolished by WWII bombs. After the war, people had no money to contribute to the reconstruction—but they could gather shells. All the shells you see here were donated by small-town Bavarians as the grotto was rebuilt according to Nazi photos (see "The History of Munich: Part 2" sidebar, page 46). To the right of the shells, the door marked *OO* leads to public toilets.

Antiquarium (Room 7, ground floor): In the mid-16th century, Europe's royal families (such as the Wittelsbachs) collected and displayed busts of emperors—implying a connection between themselves and the ancient Roman rulers. Given the huge demand for these Classical statues in the courts of Europe, many of the "ancient busts" are fakes cranked out by crooked Romans. Still, a third of the statuary you see here is original. This was, and still is, a festival banquet hall. Two hundred dignitaries can dine here, surrounded by allegories of the goodness of just rule on the ceiling. Check out the small paintings around the room—these survived the bombs because they were painted in arches. Of great historic interest, these paintings show 120 Bavarian villages as they looked in 1550. Even today, when a Bavarian historian wants a record of how his village once looked, he comes here. Notice the town of Dachau in 1550 (above the door on the left as you enter).

Reliquary (Room 95, upper floor, often closed in the morning): Meet St. John the Baptist and his mother, Elizabeth (#47 and #48—skulls on jeweled pillows).

Private Chapel of Maximilian I (Room 98, upper floor, often closed in the morning): Duke Maximilian I, the dominant Bavarian figure in the Thirty Years' War, built one of the most precious rooms in the palace. The miniature pipe organ (from about 1600) still works. The room is sumptuous, from the gold leaf and the fancy hinges to the stucco marble. (Stucco marble is fake marble—a special mix of stucco, applied and polished. Designers liked it because it was less expensive than real marble and the color could be controlled.) Note the post-Renaissance perspective tricks decorating the walls; they were popular in the 17th century. The case (on the right as you enter) supposedly contains skeletons of three babies from the slaughter of the innocents in Bethlehem (where Herod, in an attempt to murder the baby Jesus, ordered all sons of a certain age killed).

Chapel (Room 89, ground floor, also viewable from Room 96 on the upper floor, often closed in the morning): Dedicated to Mary, this late-Renaissance/early-Baroque gem was the site of "Mad" King Ludwig's funeral after his mysterious murder—or suicide—in 1886. (He's buried in St. Michael's Church; see page 39.) Though Ludwig was not popular in the political world, he was beloved by his people, and his funeral drew huge crowds. "Mad" King Ludwig's grandfather (Ludwig I) was married here in 1810. After the wedding ceremony, carriages rolled his guests to a rollicking reception, which turned out to be such a hit that it became an annual tradition—Oktoberfest.

Red Room (Room 62, upper floor): The ultimate room is at the end of the corridor—the coral red room from 1740. (Coral red was *the* most royal of colors in Germany.) Imagine visiting the duke and having him take you here to ogle miniature copies of the most famous paintings of the day, composed with one-haired brushes. Notice the fun effect of the mirrors around you—the corner mirrors make things go forever and ever.

Precious Rooms (Rooms 55–62, upper floor): The Wittelsbachs were always trying to keep up with the Habsburgs, and this long string of ceremonial rooms was all for show. The decor and furniture are Rococo. The family art collection, now in the Alte Pinakothek, once decorated these walls. The bedroom (Room 60) was the official sleeping place, where the duke would publicly go to bed and awaken, à la Louis XIV.

Nymphenburg Porcelain (Room 5, at the end of the family gallery—described below, ground floor): In the 18th century, a royal family's status was bolstered by an in-house porcelain works (like Meissen for the Wettins in Dresden). The Wittelsbach family had their own Nymphenburg porcelain made for the palace. See how the mirrors and porcelain vases give the effect of infinite pedestals. If this inspires you to own some pieces of your own, head to the Nymphenburg Porcelain Store at Odeonsplatz (see "Shopping," page 73).

Gallery of the Wittelsbach Family (Room 4, ground floor): This room is from the 1740s (about 200 years younger than the Antiquarium). All official guests had to pass through here to meet the duke. The family tree in the center is labeled "genealogy of an imperial family." The big Wittelsbach/Habsburg rivalry was worked out through 500 years of marriages and battles—when they failed to sort out a problem through strategic weddings, they had a war. Opposite the tree are portraits of Charlemagne and Ludwig IV, each a Holy Roman Emperor and each wearing the same crown (now in Vienna). Ludwig IV was the first Wittelsbach HRE—an honor used for hundreds of years to substantiate the family's claim to power. You are surrounded by a scrapbook covering centuries of Wittelsbach family history.

Allied bombs took their toll on this hall. Above, the central ceiling painting has been restored, but since there were no photos of the other two ceiling paintings, those spots remain empty. Looking at the walls, you can see how each painting was hastily cut out of its frame. Museums were closed in 1939, then gradually evacuated in anticipation of bombings. But public buildings like this palace, which remained open to instill confidence in local people, could not prepare for the worst. It wasn't until 1944, when bombs were imminent, that the last-minute order was given to slice all portraits out of their frames and hide them away.

▲▲Residenz Treasury (Schatzkammer)—The Treasury, next door to the Residenz, shows off a thousand years of Wittelsbach crowns and knickknacks. Vienna's jewels are better, but this is Bavaria's best, with fine 13th- and 14th-century crowns and delicately carved ivory and glass (for cost and hours, see page 47).

➲ **Self-Guided Tour:** A long clockwise circle through the eight rooms takes you chronologically through a thousand years of royal treasure. (It's a one-way system—getting lost is not an option.) Your ticket includes an English audioguide, but I've explained the highlights below.

The oldest jewels in the first room are 200 years older than Munich itself. Many of these came from various prince-bishop collections when they were secularized (and their realms came under the rule of the Bavarian king from Munich) in the Napoleonic Era (c. 1800). The tiny mobile altar allowed a Carolingian king (from Charlemagne's family of kings) to pack light in 890—and still have a little Mass while on the road.

In Room 3, study the reliquary with St. George killing the dragon—sparkling with more than 2,000 precious stones (#58). Get up close (it's OK to walk around the rope posts)...you can almost hear the dragon hissing. It was made to contain the relics of St. George, who never existed (Pope John Paul II declared him nothing more than a legend). If you could lift the miniscule visor, you'd see that the carved ivory face of St. George is actually the Wittelsbach duke (the dragon represents the "evil" forces of Protestantism).

In the next room (#4), notice the vividly carved ivory crucifixes from 1630 (#157 and #158, on the right). These incredibly realistic sculptures were done by local artist Georg Petel, a friend of Peter Paul Rubens (whose painting of Christ on the cross—which you'll see across town in the Alte Pinakothek—is Petel's obvious inspiration). Look at the flesh of Jesus' wrist pulling around the nails.

Continue into Room 5. The freestanding glass case (#245) holds the never-used royal crowns of Bavaria. Napoleon ended the Holy Roman Empire and let the Wittelsbach family rule as kings of Bavaria. As a sign of friendship, this royal coronation gear was made in Paris by the same shop that crafted Napoleon's crown. But before the actual coronation, Bavaria joined in an all-Europe anti-Napoleon alliance, and suddenly these were too French to be used.

Cuvilliés Theater—Attached to the Residenz is the exquisite Cuvilliés Theater. Designed by the same brilliant dwarf architect who also did the Amalienburg Palace (see page 65), this newly restored theater is dazzling enough to send you back to the days of divine monarchs (€3, daily 10:00–17:00).

Max-Joseph-Platz—The centerpiece of this square, which faces the Residenz and National Theater, is a grand statue of King Maximilian I, a.k.a. Max Joseph, who was installed as Bavaria's first king in 1806 by Napoleon. Because Napoleon was desperate to establish his family as royal, crowning Max Joseph came with one condition: that his daughter marry Napoleon's stepson.

With the Holy Roman Empire gone and Napoleon history, modern 19th-century kings had little choice but to embrace constitutions that limited their power. Max Joseph liberalized his realm with a constitution, emancipated Protestants and Jews, and established the Viktualienmarkt (with his statue in the center). He was a particularly popular king, and both his reign and his son's reign were full of grand building projects designed to show that Bavaria was an enlightened state, Munich was a worthy capital, and the king was an equal with Europe's other royalty. The National Theater, which opened in 1818, celebrated Bavaria's strong culture, roots, and legitimacy.

Though Max Joseph was busy and had plenty of vision, his son and successor, Ludwig I, was the builder king who made Munich a grand capital. His Ludwigstrasse remains an impressive boulevard, with 60-foot-tall buildings stretching a mile from the Hall of Generals to the Arch of Victory, capped with a figure of Bavaria riding a lion-drawn chariot. And it was Ludwig I's wedding festival in 1810 that became an annual bash, giving Munich perhaps its greatest claim to fame: Oktoberfest.

Near the Residenz

Hofgarten—The elegant people's state garden (Hofgarten) is a delight on a sunny afternoon. The "Renaissance" temple centerpiece has great acoustics (and usually a musician performing for tips from lazy listeners). The lane leads to a building that houses the government of Bavaria and the Bavarian war

memorial, which honors the fallen *heroes* of World War I, but only the *fallen* of World War II. The venerable old **Café Tambosi,** with a Viennese elegance inside and a relaxing garden setting outside, is a good antidote to all the beer halls (daily 8:00–24:00, Odeonsplatz 18, tel. 089/298-322). Just beyond is a lazy gravel *boules* court.

Odeonsplatz and Nearby—This square near the Hofgarten is a part of the grand, imperial Munich vision. The church on Odeonsplatz (Theatinerkirche) contains about half of the Wittelsbach tombs. The loggia in the Hofgarten (honoring Bavarian generals) is modeled in the Florentine Renaissance style (in fact, after the famous loggia in Florence). A Roman-type triumphal arch hovers in the distance to the north (at the end of Ludwigstrasse). And to the west, a grand axis (Brienner Strasse) heads toward the Greek-inspired museum quarter.

Brienner Strasse: From Odeonsplatz, look (or wander) down Brienner Strasse to get a taste of the Wittelsbachs' ambitious city planning. At Karolinenplatz, the black obelisk commemorates the 30,000 Bavarians who marched with Napoleon to Moscow and never returned. Beyond that is the grand Königsplatz, or "King's Square," with its stern Neoclassicism, evocative of ancient Greece (and home to Munich's cluster of art museums, described below).

On the way to this imperial splendor, Brienner Strasse goes through a square called **Platz der Opfer des Nationalsozialismus** ("Square of the Victims of Nazism"). Nearby, you'll find two former Nazi administration buildings; one is now the music academy, though it's still very much fascist in its architecture. A plaque on the street explains the buildings' history.

Munich's Cluster of Art Museums

This cluster of blockbuster museums (Alte, Neue, and Moderne Pinakotheks; Lenbachhaus; and Glyptothek) displays art spanning from the 14th century to modern times. The Glyptothek and Lenbachhaus are on Königsplatz, while the three Pinakothek museums sit around a grassy square just to the northeast. The Pinakotheks are a 10-minute walk from the nearest U-Bahn stops, but handy tram #27 whisks you right to them from Karlsplatz (near the train station).

▲▲Alte Pinakothek

Bavaria's best painting gallery (the "Old Art Gallery," pronounced ALL-tuh pee-nah-koh-TAYK) shows off a world-class collection of European masterpieces from the 14th to 19th centuries, starring the two tumultuous centuries (1450–1650) when Europe went from medieval to modern. See paintings from the Italian Renaissance (Raphael, Leonardo, Botticelli, Titian) and the German Renaissance it inspired (Albrecht Dürer). The Reformation of Martin Luther eventually split Europe into two subcultures—Protestants and Catholics—with their two distinct art styles (exemplified by Rembrandt and Rubens, respectively).

Cost, Hours, Location: €5.50, €1 on Sun, open Wed–Sun 10:00–18:00, Tue 10:00–20:00, closed Mon, last entry 30 min before closing, free and excellent audioguide (€4 on Sun), obligatory lockers with refundable €2 deposit, no flash photos, U-2 or U-8: Königsplatz, Barer Strasse 27, tel. 089/2380-5216, www.pinakothek.de/alte-pinakothek.

➲ **Self-Guided Tour:** From the ticket counter, head toward the back wall and walk up the stairway to the left. All the paintings we'll see are on the upper floor, which is laid out like a barbell. Start at one fat end and work your way through the "handle" to the other end. Along the way you'll find the following paintings, roughly in this order.

German Renaissance—Room II: Albrecht Altdorfer's *The Battle of Issus (Schlacht bei Issus)* shows a world at war. Masses of soldiers are swept along in the currents and tides of a battle completely beyond their control, their confused motion reflected in the swirling sky. We see the battle from a great height, giving us a godlike perspective. Though the painting depicts Alexander the Great's victory over the Persians (find the Persian king Darius turning and fleeing), it could as easily have been Germany in the 1520s. Christians were fighting Muslims, peasants battled masters, and Catholics and Protestants were squaring off for a century of conflict. The armies melt into a huge landscape, leaving the impression that the battle goes on forever.

Albrecht Dürer's larger-than-life *Four Apostles* (*Johannes und Petrus* and *Paulus und Marcus*) are saints of a radical new religion: Martin Luther's Protestantism. Just as Luther challenged Church authority, Dürer—a friend of Luther's—strips these saints of any rich clothes, halos, or trappings of power and gives them down-to-earth, human features: receding hairlines, wrinkles, and suspicious eyes. The inscription warns German rulers to follow the Bible rather than Catholic Church leaders. The figure of Mark—a Bible in one hand and a sword in the other—is a fitting symbol of the dangerous times.

Alte Pinakothek

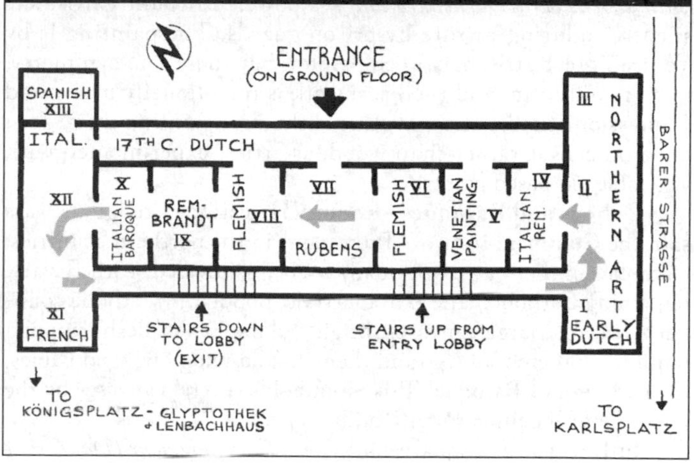

Dürer's *Self-Portrait in Fur Coat (Selbstbildnis im Pelzrock)* looks like Jesus Christ but is actually 28-year-old Dürer himself, gazing out, with his right hand solemnly giving a blessing. This is the ultimate image of humanism: the artist as an instrument of God's continued creation. Get close and enjoy the intricately braided hair, the skin texture, and the fur collar. To the left of the head is Dürer's famous monogram—"A.D." in the form of a pyramid.

Italian Renaissance—Room IV: With the Italian Renaissance—the "rebirth" of interest in the art and learning of ancient Greece and Rome—artists captured the realism, three-dimensionality, and symmetry found in classical statues. Leonardo da Vinci's *Virgin and Child (Maria mit dem Kind)* need no halos—they radiate purity. Mary is a solid pyramid of maternal love, flanked by Renaissance-arch windows that look out on the hazy distance. Baby Jesus reaches out to play innocently with a carnation, the blood-colored symbol of his eventual death.

Raphael's *Holy Family at the Canigiani House (Die hl. Familie aus dem Hause Canigiani)* takes Leonardo's pyramid form and runs with it. Father Joseph forms the peak, with his staff as the strong central axis. Mary and Jesus (on the right) form a pyramid-within-the-pyramid, as do Elizabeth and baby John the Baptist on the left. They all exchange meaningful contact, safe within the bounds of the stable family structure.

In Botticelli's *Lamentation over Christ (Die Beweinung Christi),* the Renaissance "pyramid" implodes, as the weight of the dead Christ drags everyone down, and the tomb grins darkly behind them.

Venetian Painting—Room V: In Titian's *Christ Crowned with Thorns (Die Dornenkronung),* a powerfully built Christ sits silently enduring torture by prison guards. The painting is by Venice's greatest Renaissance painter, but there's no symmetry, no pyramid form, and the brushwork is intentionally messy and Impressionistic. By the way, this is the first painting we've seen done on canvas rather than wood, as artists experimented with vegetable oil–based paints.

Rubens and Baroque—Room VII: Europe's religious wars split the Continent in two—Protestants in the northern countries, Catholics in the south. (Germany itself was divided, with Bavaria remaining Catholic.) The Baroque style, popular in Catholic countries, featured large canvases, bright colors, lots of flesh, rippling motion, wild emotions, grand themes...and pudgy winged babies, the sure sign of Baroque. This room holds several canvases by the great Flemish painter Peter Paul Rubens.

In Rubens' 300-square-foot *Great Last Judgment (Das Grosse Jüngste Gericht),* Christ raises the righteous up to heaven (left side) and damns the sinners to hell (on the right). This swirling cycle of nudes was considered risqué and kept under wraps by the very monks who'd commissioned it.

Rubens and Isabella Brant shows the artist with his first wife, both of them the very picture of health, wealth, and success. They lean together unconsciously, as people in love will do, with their hands clasped in mutual affection. When his first wife died, 53-year-old Rubens found a replacement—16-year-old Hélène Fourment, shown here in her wedding dress. You may recognize Hélène's face in other Rubens paintings.

The Rape of the Daughters of Leucippus (Der Raub der Tochter des Leukippos) has many of Rubens' most typical elements—fleshy, emotional, rippling motion; bright colors; and a classical subject. The legendary twins Castor and Pollux crash a wedding and steal the brides as their own. The chaos of flailing limbs and rearing horses is all held together in a subtle X-shaped composition. Like the weaving counterpoint in a Baroque fugue, Rubens balances opposites.

Notice that Rubens' canvases were—to a great extent—cranked out by his students and assistants from small "cartoons" the master himself made (displayed in the next room).

Rembrandt and Dutch—Room IX: From Holland, Rembrandt van Rijn's *Six Paintings from the Life of Christ* are a down-to-earth look at supernatural events. The *Adoration (Die Anbetung der Hirten)* of Baby Jesus takes place in a 17th-century Dutch barn with ordinary folk as models. The canvases are dark brown, lit by strong light. The *Adoration*'s light source is the Baby Jesus himself—literally the "light of the world." In the *Deposition (Kreuzabnahme),* the light bounces off Christ's pale body onto his mother Mary, showing how his death also hurts her. The drama is underplayed, with subdued emotions. Looking on is a man dressed in blue—a self-portrait of Rembrandt.

▲Neue Pinakothek

The Alte Pinakothek's sister is a twin building across the square, showing off paintings from 1800 to 1920: Romanticism, Realism, Impressionism, *Jugendstil,* Claude Monet, Pierre-Auguste Renoir, Vincent van Gogh, Francisco Goya, and Gustav Klimt (€5.50, €1 on Sun, open Thu–Mon 10:00–18:00, Wed 10:00–20:00, closed Tue, well-done audioguide is usually free but €4 on Sun, classy Café Greco in basement spills into park and offers fine salads, U-2 or U-8: Theresienstrasse, Barer Strasse 29 but enter on Theresienstrasse, tel. 089/2380-5195, www.pinakothek.de/neue-pinakothek).

MUNICH

▲Pinakothek der Moderne

This museum picks up where the other two leave off, covering the 20th century. Four permanent displays (graphics, design, architecture, and paintings) are layered within the striking minimalist architecture. You'll find works by Pablo Picasso, Salvador Dalí, Joan Miró, René Magritte, Max Beckmann, Max Ernst, and abstract artists. The big, white, high-ceilinged building itself is worth a look. Even if you don't pay to visit the exhibits, step into the free entrance hall to see the sky-high atrium and the colorful blob-column descending the staircase (€9.50, €1 on Sun, open Tue–Sun 10:00–18:00, Thu until 20:00, closed Mon, U-2 or U-8: Königsplatz, Barer Strasse 40, tel. 089/2380-5360, www.pinakothek.de/pinakothek-der-moderne). This far-out collection offers little information in English—and there's no English audioguide. However, some temporary exhibits may have an English flyer; ask at the information desk.

▲Lenbachhaus

Housed in a beautiful, late 19th-century Tuscan-style villa (owned by painter Franz von Lenbach), this museum features the most complete collection of the early Modernist movement known as Blaue Reiter (Blue Rider), a branch of Expressionism that flourished from 1911 to 1914. When Wassily Kandinsky, Paul Klee, Franz Marc, Gabriele Münter, and some of their art-school cronies got fed up with being told how and what to paint, they formed the Blaue Reiter around a common ideology: to strive for new forms

that expressed spiritual truth. Already controversial in their own day, their work was later targeted by the Nazis as *entartete Kunst* ("degenerate art"). As you tour the museum, trace Kandinsky's progression from his earlier, more realistic works to the complete abstraction he's best known for. Münter, Kandinsky's lover and a great painter in her own right, donated her entire private collection (90 paintings and 330 other works) to Lenbachhaus in 1957, putting this little museum on the world art map (€5–10 depending on exhibits, Tue–Sun 10:00–18:00, closed Mon, worthwhile €3 audioguide, €8 guidebook is a nice souvenir but otherwise unnecessary, small café, U-2 or U-8: Königsplatz, Luisenstrasse 33, enter through small archway, tel. 089/2333-2000, www.lenbachhaus.de). Your Lenbachhaus admission includes the Kunstbau modern art gallery in the Königsplatz U-Bahn station.

Glyptothek

A collection of Greek and Roman sculpture started by King Ludwig I, the Glyptothek includes the famous *Barberini Faun,* statues from the Greek Classical period, funerary monuments of wealthy Athenian families, and pediments of the Temple of Aegina. For a Who's Who of ancient celebrities, visit the Room of Ancient Portraits, where you'll come face to face with Alexander the Great and other luminaries from ancient political and philosophical spheres (€3.50, €1 on Sun, not much in English so invest in the worthwhile €1 guidebook, Tue–Sun 10:00–17:00, Thu until 20:00, closed Mon, U-2 or U-8: Königsplatz, on Königsplatz, tel. 089/286-100).

In and near the English Garden

▲English Garden (Englischer Garten)—Munich's "Central Park," the largest one on the Continent, was laid out in 1789 by an American. More than 100,000 locals commune with nature here on sunny summer days. The park stretches three miles from the center, past the university to the trendy and bohemian Schwabing quarter. For the best quick visit, follow the river from the

Green Munich

Although the capital of a very conservative part of Germany, Munich has long been a liberal stronghold. For nearly two decades, the city council has been controlled by a Social Democrat/Green Party coalition. The city policies are pedestrian-friendly—you'll find much of the town center closed to normal traffic, with plenty of bike lanes and green spaces. Talking softly and hearing birds rather than motors, it's easy to forget you're in the center of a big city. On summer Mondays, the peace and quiet make way for "blade Monday"—when streets in the center are closed to cars and as many as 30,000 inline skaters swarm around town in a giant rolling party.

surfers (under the bridge just past Haus der Kunst) downstream into the garden. Just beyond the hilltop temple (walk up for a postcard view of the city), you'll find the big Chinese Tower beer garden and other places to enjoy a drink or a meal (see page 84). A rewarding respite from the city, the park is especially fun—and worth ▲▲—on a bike under the summer sun and on warm evenings (unfortunately, there are no bike-rental agencies in or near the park; to rent some wheels, see page 30). Caution: While local law requires sun-worshippers to wear clothes on the tram, the park is sprinkled with buck-naked sunbathers—quite a shock to prudish Americans (they're the ones riding their bikes into the river and trees).

Haus der Kunst—Built by Hitler as a temple of Nazi art, this bold and fascist building is now an impressive shell for various temporary art exhibits. Ironically, the art now displayed in Hitler's "house of art" is the kind that annoyed the Führer most—modern (€5–9 per exhibit, €12 combo-ticket if there are two exhibits, daily 10:00–20:00, Thu until 22:00, little information in English but some exhibits may have English handouts, at south end of English Garden, tram #17 or bus #100 to Nationalmuseum/Haus der Kunst, Prinzregentenstrasse 1, tel. 089/211-270, www.hausderkunst.de).

Just beyond the Haus der Kunst, where Prinzregentenstrasse crosses the Eisbach canal, you can watch adventure-seekers surfing in the rapids created as the small river tumbles underground.

Bavarian National Museum (Bayerisches Nationalmuseum)—This tired but interesting collection features Tilman Riemenschneider woodcarvings, manger scenes, traditional living rooms, and old Bavarian houses (€7, €1 on Sun, open Tue–Sun 10:00–17:00, Thu until 20:00, closed Mon, tram #17 or bus #100 to Nationalmuseum/Haus der Kunst, Prinzregentenstrasse 3, tel. 089/211-2401, www.bayerisches-nationalmuseum.de).

Deutsches Museum

Germany's answer to our Smithsonian Institution, the Deutsches Museum traces the evolution of science and technology. The main branch of the Deutsches Museum is centrally located. The two branches—the Museum of Transportation and the Flight Museum—are situated outside the city center, but are worth the effort for enthusiasts. You can pay separately for each museum, or buy one €15 combo-ticket, which covers all three. Since this ticket has no time limit, you can spread out your visits to the various branches over your entire stay.

▲▲Deutsches Museum (Main Branch)

Enjoy wandering through well-described rooms of historic airplanes (Hitler's "flying bomb"—Wernher von Braun's notorious V-2 rocket—from 1944), spaceships, mining, the harnessing of wind and water power, hydraulics, musical instruments, printing, chemistry, computers, clocks, and astronomy...it's the Louvre of technical know-how. The museum is designed to be hands-on; if you see a button, push it. But with 10 miles of exhibits, from astronomy to zymurgy, even those on roller skates will need to be selective. While the museum was a big deal a generation ago, today it feels to many a bit dated, dusty, and overrated.

Cost, Hours, Information: €8.50, €15 combo-ticket includes Museum of Transportation and Flight Museum, daily 9:00–17:00, worthwhile €4 English guidebook, self-service cafeteria, tel. 089/21791, www.deutsches-museum.de. Most sections of the museum are well-described in English. The much-vaunted high-voltage demonstrations (3/day, 15 min, all in German) show the noisy creation of a five-foot bolt of lightning.

Getting There: Take the S-Bahn to Isartor, then walk 300 yards over the river, following signs.

➲ **Self-Guided Tour:** First head to the **mines,** which trace the history of mining since prehistoric times (mines closed during daily German-language tours at 9:45 and 13:45). As you follow the spiral stairs down to them, notice the 19th-century miners' chapel on the left. (Also notice the handy WC on the right.) While descriptions are only in German, the reconstructions of coal, potash, and salt mines are still impressive. It's a fun, haunted house–type experience, with creepy life-like miners tucked away in dark corners. Enjoy the photo ops, like the chairlift that used to transport workers. (Hop in!) Apart from the fun and games, the museum has made great efforts to include realistic, accurate details to show what rigorous, dangerous work mining has always been. When you emerge from the mines, skip the mineral oil and natural gas section *(Erdöl und Erdgas)* and follow the signs for *Ausgang* (exit).

The fascinating, compact exhibit on **marine navigation** (on the ground floor) has models of sail, steam, and diesel vessels, from early canoes to grand sailing ships. Take the staircase down into the galley, below the main floor, to check out how life on passenger ships has changed—and don't miss the bisected U1 submarine. This first German submarine, dating from 1906, has been in the museum since 1921.

Flying high above the masts of the marine navigation exhibit is the section on **aeronautics** (first floor). Displays cover the most basic airborne flights (flying insects and seed pods), Otto Lilienthal's successful efforts in 1891 to imitate bird flight, and the development of hot-air balloons and gas-powered zeppelins. Many of the planes here are original, including the Wright brothers' Type A (1909), fighters and cargo ships from the two World Wars, and the first functioning helicopter, made in 1936. Climb into the planes whenever permitted, and try out the flight simulator.

The **astronautics** exhibit is located on the second floor. Back in the 1920s, Germany was working on rocket-propelled cars and sleds. Germany's research provided the US and Soviet space teams with much of their technical know-how. Here, you can peer at models of the V-2 (one of the first remote-controlled rockets/weapons, from World War II), an early Messerschmitt jet fighter, motors from the American Saturn rockets, and various space capsules, including Spacelab. The main focus is the walk on the moon, the Apollo missions, and the dogs-in-space program (monkeys, too)...but if you've ever been curious about space underwear, you'll find your answer here. Skip the nearby Altamira Caves exhibit, a replica of the 15,000-year-old drawings found in a cave in northern Spain; they're so dark that you can barely see anything.

The third floor traces the **history of measurement,** including time (from a 16th-century sundial and an 18th-century clock to a scary Black Forest wall clock complete with grim reaper), weights, geodesy (surveying and mapping), and computing (from 18th-century calculators to antiquated computers from the 1940s and 1950s).

On your way to the state-of-the-art **planetarium** (worth a visit if open, requires €2 extra ticket, lecture in German), poke your head out into the **sundial garden** located above the third floor. Even if you're not interested in sundials, this is a great place for a view of the surrounding landscape. On a clear day, you can see the Alps.

▲Museum of Transportation (Verkehrszentrum)

You don't need to be an engineer or race-car driver to get a kick out of this fun museum. The Deutsches Museum celebrated its

100th anniversary in 2003 by opening this annex across town that shows off all aspects of transport, from old big-wheeled bikes to Benz's first car (a three-wheeler from the 1880s) to sleek ICE super-trains. It's housed in a recently renovated, early 20th-century conference hall and three giant hangar-like exhibition halls near the Oktoberfest grounds, a.k.a. Theresienwiese.

Cost, Hours, Location: €5, €15 combo-ticket includes Deutsches Museum and Flight Museum, daily 9:00–17:00, Thu until 20:00, Theresienhöhe 14a, U-4 or U-5: Schwanthalerhöhe, tel. 089/2179-529, www.deutsches-museum.de.

Tours: The free tours Sat–Sun at 14:30 (kid-focused) and 15:30 (general) are primarily in German, but English-speaking guides are happy to share.

➲ **Self-Guided Tour:** True to the Deutsches Museum's interactive spirit, the Museum of Transportation is totally hands-on, and comes with plentiful English explanations. Without getting too academic, it traces the physiological and socioeconomic origins of motion and travel, from basic human and animal anatomy (try to identify those paw prints) to nomadic herders and camel caravans. What would our lives be like without transportation? Exhibits show how modes of transportation developed from sheer necessity into entertainment and competition, from Neolithic "bone" skates (predecessors to today's Rollerblades), to 19th-century Lapland skis, to today's snowboards and fast cars.

Hall 1 takes an inside-out look at Munich's public-transportation system—ride the tram and marvel at a cross-section of the intricate and multi-layered subway system.

Hall 2 gives you a look at the development of transportation for the sake of overland travel. Although it focuses primarily on trains, don't miss the chance to climb into the old carriage: The metal track simulates what it would have felt like to travel in the 18th century over different terrain (grass and cobblestones—pretty uncomfortable). Admire the Maffei S3/6, a.k.a. "The Pride of Bavaria" (in its heyday the fastest steam engine, at nearly 80 miles per hour); the clever old postal train (complete with a mail slot on the side); and the 1950s panorama bus that shuttled eager tourists to fashionable destinations such as Italy.

Hall 3 is all about fun: motorcycles, bicycles, skis, and race cars. Famous prewar models include the deluxe Mercedes-Benz 370 (1930s) and the Auto Union Type C "Grand Prix" race car. Other tiny racers—which resemble metal pickles to the uninitiated—include the 1950s Mercedes-Benz 300 SLR and the famous Messerschmitt 200. You'll also find early 18th-century bicycles based on Leonardo da Vinci's drawings. Before the invention of the pedal crank, bikes were just silly-looking scooters for adults.

Flight Museum (Flugwerft Schleissheim)

Fans of all things winged will enjoy the Deutsches Museum's Flight Museum, with more than 50 planes, helicopters, gliders, and an original Europa rocket housed in a historical aerodrome on a former military airfield. Inside the museum is the glass-walled workshop, where visitors can watch as antique planes are restored (€5, €15 combo-ticket includes Deutsches Museum and Museum of Transportation, daily 9:00–17:00, about 8 miles outside of town, take S-1 direction: Freising Flughafen and get off at Oberschleissheim, Effnerstrasse 18, tel. 089/315-7140, www.deutsches-museum.de).

Nymphenburg Palace Complex

Nymphenburg Palace and the surrounding one-square-mile park are good for a royal stroll or bike ride. Here you'll find a pair of palaces, the Royal Stables Museum, and playful extras such as a bathhouse, pagoda, and artificial ruins.

Cost and Hours: €10 for everything, less for each of the six individual parts. All sights are open daily April–mid-Oct 9:00–18:00, mid-Oct–March 10:00–16:00. The park is open daily 6:00 to dusk. Tel. 089/179-080, www.schloesser.bayern.de.

Getting There: The palace is three miles northwest of central Munich. Getting there from the center is easy, if a bit time-consuming: Take tram #17 from Karlstor (20 min to palace) or the train station (15 min to palace) to the Schloss Nymphenburg stop. From the bridge by the tram stop, you'll see the palace, but you'll have to walk another 10 minutes to get there. A pleasant bike path follows Arnulfstrasse from the train station all the way to Nymphenburg (a 30-min pedal).

▲▲Nymphenburg Palace

In 1662, after 10 years of trying, the Bavarian ruler Ferdinand Maria and his wife, Henriette Adelaide of Savoy, finally had a son, Max Emanuel. In gratitude for a male heir, Ferdinand gave this land to his Italian wife, who proceeded to build an Italian-style Baroque palace. Their son expanded the palace to today's size. For 200 years, this was the Wittelsbach family's summer escape from Munich. (They still refer to themselves as princes and live in one wing of the palace.) If "Wow!" is your first impression, that's intentional.

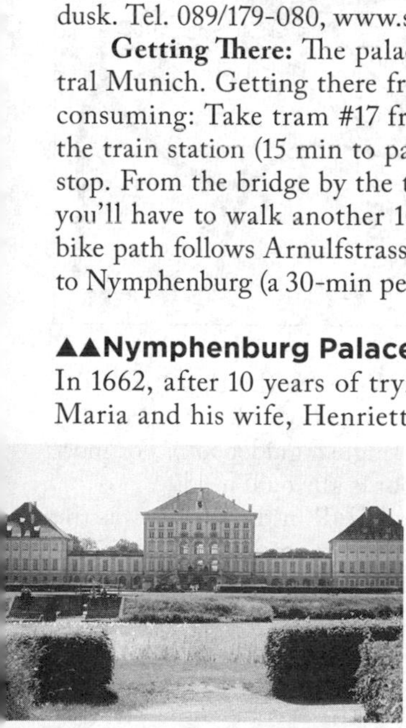

Your visit is limited to 16 main rooms on one floor: the Great

Greater Munich

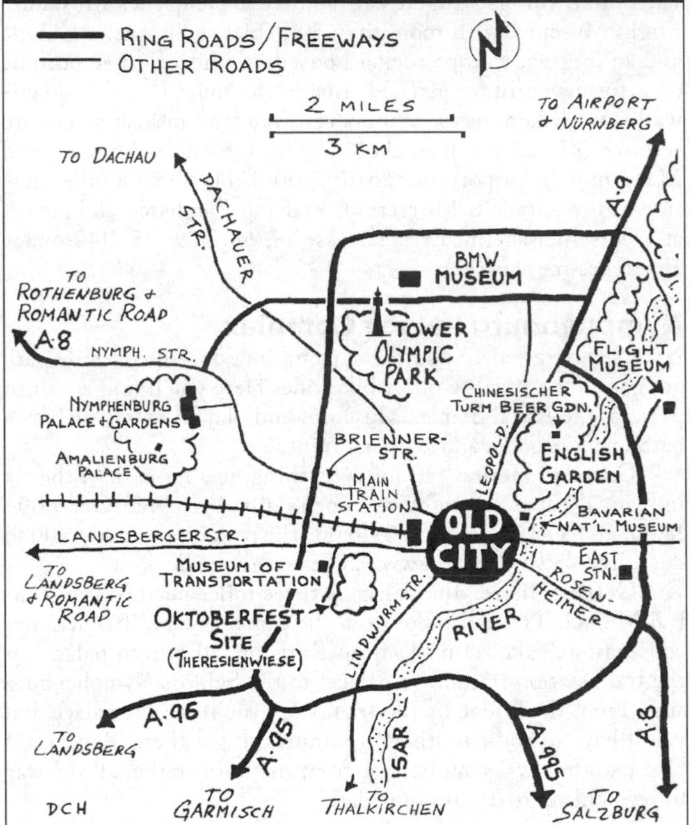

Hall (where you start), the King's Wing (to the right), and the Queen's Wing (on the left). The €2.50 audioguide is informative and easy to use (better than the €6 English guidebook). For most visitors, the following self-guided tour is all you'll need.

➲ **Self-Guided Tour:** The **Great Hall** in the middle was the dining hall. One of the grandest Rococo rooms in Bavaria, it was decorated by Johann Baptist Zimmermann (of Wieskirche fame) and François de Cuvilliés in about 1760. The painting on the ceiling shows Olympian gods keeping the peace (the ruler's duty).

The **King's Wing** (right of entrance) has walls filled with Wittelsbach portraits and stories. In the second room straight ahead, notice the painting showing the huge palace grounds, with Munich (and the twin onion domes of the Frauenkirche) three miles in the distance. Imagine the logistics when the royal family—with their entourage of 200—decided to move out to the summer palace. The Wittelsbachs were high rollers; from 1624 until 1806, one of the seven electors of the Holy Roman Emperor was a Wittelsbach. In 1806, Napoleon ended that institution and made the Wittelsbachs kings. (Note: For simplicity, I often refer to the Wittelsbachs as kings and queens, even though before 1806, these rulers were technically dukes, duchesses, and electors—and some were even Holy Roman Emperors.)

In the **Queen's Wing** (left of entrance), enter the first room, then head to the right to find the very red room. You'll see the founding couple, Henriette Adelaide and Ferdinand Maria (after the Counter-Reformation, Bavarian men were named Maria—but his high heels and leggings were another story altogether). The inlaid table was a wedding present. The real pay-off, this palace, didn't come until Henriette (who was 14 when she married) got pregnant. The green room is the ceremonial bedroom. The painting to the right of the bed shows Max Emanuel as a kid in a double portrait with his older sister. Both are dressed in the latest French fashions.

King Ludwig I's Gallery of Beauties, near the end of the long hall in the Queen's Wing, is decorated with portraits of 36 beautiful women—all of them painted by Joseph Stieler from 1827 to 1850. King Ludwig I was a consummate girl-watcher who prided himself on the ability to appreciate beauty regardless of social rank. He would pick the prettiest women from the general public and invite them to the palace for a portrait. The women range in status from royal princesses to a humble cobbler's daughter...but Ludwig seemed to prefer brunettes. The portraits reflect the modest Biedermeier style, as opposed to the more flamboyant Romanticism of the same period. If only these creaking floors could talk. Something about the place feels highly sexed, in a Prince Charles kind of way.

The next rooms are decorated in the Neoclassical style of the Napoleonic Era. At the rope, see the room where Ludwig II was born (August 25, 1845). Royal births were carefully witnessed. The mirror allowed for a better view. While Ludwig's death was shrouded in mystery (see page 104), his birth was well-documented.

Amalienburg Palace

Three hundred yards from the Nymphenburg Palace, hiding in the park (ahead and to the left as you go through to the back of the palace), you'll find one of the finest Rococo buildings in all of Europe. In 1734, Elector Karl Albrecht had this hunting lodge built for his wife, Maria Amalia—another Rococo jewel designed by François de Cuvilliés and decorated by Johann Baptist Zimmermann. Above the pink-and-white grand entryway, notice

Diana, goddess of the chase, flanked by busts of satyrs. Look for the perch atop the roof where the queen would do her shooting. Behind a wall in the garden, dogs would scare non-flying pheasants. When they jumped up in the air above the wall, the sporting queen—as if shooting skeet—would pick the birds off.

Tourists enter this tiny getaway through the back door. The first room has doghouses under gun cupboards. Next, in the fine yellow-and-silver bedroom, see Vulcan forging arrows for amorous cupids at the foot of the bed. The bed is flanked by portraits of Karl Albrecht and Maria Amalia—decked out in hunting attire. She liked her dogs. The door under the portrait leads to stairs to the rooftop pheasant-shooting perch.

The mini–Hall of Mirrors is a blue-and-silver commotion of Rococo nymphs designed by Cuvilliés in the mid-1700s. Cuvilliés, short and hunchbacked, showed a unique talent for art and was sent to Paris to study. In the next room, paintings depict court festivities, formal hunting parties, and no-contest kills (where the animal is put at an impossible disadvantage—like shooting fish in a barrel). Finally, the kitchen is decorated with Chinese picnics on blue Dutch tiles.

Royal Stables Museum (Marstallmuseum)

This huge garage is lined with gilded Cinderella coaches. The highlight is just inside the entrance: the 1742 Karl Albrecht coronation coach. When the Elector Karl Albrecht was chosen as Emperor, he rode in this coach, drawn by eight horses. Kings got only six.

Wandering through the collection, you can trace the evolution of 300 years of coaches—getting lighter and with better suspension as they were harnessed to faster horses. The carousel for the royal kids made development of dexterity fun—lop off noses and heads and toss balls through the snake. The glass case is filled with accessories.

In the room after the carousel, find the painting on the right of "Mad" King Ludwig on his sleigh at night. In his later years, Ludwig was a Howard Hughes–type recluse who stayed away from the public eye and only went out at night. (At his nearby Linderhof Palace, he actually had a hydraulic-powered dining table that would rise from the kitchen below, completely set for the meal—so he wouldn't be seen by his servants.) In the next room, you'll find Ludwig's actual sleighs. Next to them is the coach designed for his wedding, but it was never used. Ludwig's over-the-top coaches were Baroque. But this was 1870. The coaches, like the king, were in the wrong century. Notice the photos (c. 1865, in the glass case) of Ludwig with the Romantic composer Richard Wagner. Ludwig cried on the day Wagner was married. Hmmm.

Across the passage from the museum entrance, the second hall is filled with coaches for everyday use. Upstairs is a collection of **Nymphenburg porcelain** (described by an English loaner booklet at the entrance). Historically, royal families such as the Wittelsbachs liked to have their own porcelain plants to make fit-for-a-king plates, vases, and so on. The Nymphenburg Palace porcelain works is still in operation. Ludwig ordered the masterpieces of his royal collection (now at the Alte Pinakothek) to be copied in porcelain for safekeeping into the distant future. Take a close look—these are exquisite.

Olympic Park and Nearby

▲Olympic Park (Olympiapark München)—Munich's great 1972 Olympic stadium and sports complex is now a lush park. You can get a good look at the center's striking "cobweb" style of architecture while enjoying the park's picnic potential. In addition, there are several activities on offer at the park, including a tower with a commanding but so-high-it's-boring view from 820 feet (Olympiaturm, €4, daily 9:00–24:00, last trip 23:30, tel. 089/3066-8585) and an excellent swimming pool (Olympia-Schwimmhalle, €3.50, daily 7:00–23:00, last entry 22:00, tel. 0180-179-6223, www.olympiapark-muenchen.de).

With the construction of Munich's new Allianz soccer stadium for the 2006 World Cup, Olympic Park has been left in the past. It will now melt into the neighborhood as simply a fine park and swimming pool. To reach the park, take U-3 to Olympia-Zentrum direct from Marienplatz.

BMW Museum—The museum at BMW headquarters is now open after a complete remodel. The bowl-shaped building encloses a floating urban streetscape, with exhibits highlighting BMW design and technology through the years. The museum also includes a good look at rare cult models, though the Deutsches Museum's Museum of Transportation has a much better old-car exhibit—see page 61 (€12, Tue–Fri 9:00–18:00, Sat–Sun 10:00–20:00, closed Mon, last entry 45 min before closing, U-3: Olympia-Zentrum, tel. 0180-211-8822, www.bmw-museum.de). Visitors can also stop by the futuristic glass-and-steel BMW World building (where lucky customers go to pick up their new Beamers) to check out the latest cars and down-the-road technologies (free, daily 9:00–20:00). Factory tours are available for true BMW fans—register online or call several weeks in advance (€6, 2.5 hrs, by appointment, books up fast July–Aug, tel. 0180-211-8822, www.bmw-werk-muenchen.de).

Near Munich

For day trips to many Bavarian destinations, including the first four listed here, consider traveling by train with the **Bayern-Ticket.** It covers up to five people from Munich to anywhere in Bavaria (plus Salzburg) and back for only €27 (valid until 3:00 in the morning on the day after purchase, not valid before 9:00 Mon–Fri, www.bayern-takt.de). The ticket is explained in *The Inside Track* newsletter and sold at EurAide (see page 28). Note that on weekdays, the Bayern-Ticket is only valid after 9:00—so if you're visiting "Mad" King Ludwig's Castles, you'll need to plan your entrance time accordingly.

▲▲▲"Mad" King Ludwig's Castles—The spectacular Neuschwanstein and Linderhof castles make a great day trip. Your easiest option is to take a tour (see page 30). Without a tour, only Neuschwanstein is easy (2 hrs by train to Füssen, then 10-min bus ride to Neuschwanstein). Or spend the night there. For all the details, see the next chapter.

▲▲Nürnberg—A handy express train gets you to Nürnberg in about an hour (departures several times an hour), making this very historic city a viable day trip from Munich. For information, see the Nürnberg chapter, page 378.

▲▲Salzburg—This Austrian city is an easy day trip, and offers some exciting sightseeing (hourly trains from Munich get you there in less than 2 hrs). For details, see "Salzburg," page 135.

▲Berchtesgaden—This resort, near Hitler's Eagle's Nest getaway, is easier as a side-trip from Salzburg (just 12 miles from there). For more, see page 178.

▲Isar River Bike Ride—Munich's river, lined by a gorgeous park, leads bikers into the pristine countryside in just a few minutes. From downtown (easy access from the English Garden or Deutsches Museum), follow the riverside bike path south (upstream) along the east (left) bank. You can't get lost. Just stay on the lovely bike path. It crosses the river after a while, passing tempting little *Biergartens* and lots of Bavarians having their brand of fun—including gangs enjoying Munich's famous river party rafts. Go as far as you like, then retrace your route to get home. The closest bike rental is at Munich Walk, near Isartor (see page 30).

▲Andechs Monastery—This monastery crouches quietly with a big smile between two lakes just south of Munich. For a fine

Near Munich

Baroque church in a rural Bavarian setting at a monastery that serves hearty cafeteria-quality food and perhaps the best beer in Germany, consider a short side-trip here. The cafeteria terrace offers first-class views and second-class prices (*Biergarten* open daily 10:00–20:00, church open until 18:00, tel. 08152/3760). Reaching Andechs from Munich without a car is frustrating (take the S-5 train to Herrsching, then catch a shuttle bus or taxi, or hike 3 miles). Don't miss the stroll up to the church, where you can sit peacefully and ponder the striking contrasts a trip through Germany offers.

▲▲Dachau Concentration Camp Memorial (KZ-Gedenkstätte Dachau)—Dachau was the first Nazi concentration camp (1933). Today, it's the most accessible camp for travelers and an effective voice from our recent but grisly past, pleading "Never again." A visit here is a valuable experience and, when approached thoughtfully, well worth the trouble. After this most powerful sightseeing experience, many people gain more respect for history and the dangers of mixing fear, blind patriotism, and an evil government. You'll likely see lots of students here, as all

German schoolchildren are required to visit a concentration camp. It's interesting to think that a couple of generations ago, people greeted each other with a robust, "Sieg Heil!" Today, almost no Germans know the lyrics of their national anthem, and German flags are a rarity outside of major soccer matches.

Cost and Hours: Free, Tue–Sun 9:00–17:00, closed Mon except holidays, last entry 30 min before closing. Though the museum shuts down at 17:00, the grounds are open until 18:00.

Information and Tours: For maximum understanding, rent the €3 audioguide and consider the English guided walk (€3; May–Sept daily at 13:30, also at 12:00 on weekends; Oct–April Sat–Sun and Thu at 13:30; 2.5 hours, call 08131/669-970 or ask at door to confirm; extensive website at www.memorial-site-dachau.org). You can also take a tour from Munich (see page 36).

Getting There: Dachau is a 45-minute trip from downtown Munich. Take S-2 (direction: Petershausen) to Dachau. Then, from the Dachau station, catch bus #726 to KZ-Gedenkstätte, near the camp entrance and the new-for-2009 Dachau visitors center (on Sun, when #726 doesn't run, take bus #724 to Robert-Bosch-Strasse, a 5-min walk from the camp entrance). The XXL ticket covers the entire trip, both ways (€6.70/person, €11.80/partner ticket). Drivers follow Dachauer Strasse from downtown Munich to Dachau-Ost, then follow *KZ-Gedenkstätte* signs.

The Town: The town of Dachau is more pleasant than its unfortunate association with the camp (TI tel. 08131/75286). With 40,000 residents, located midway between Munich and its airport, it's now a high-priced and in-demand place to live.

Orientation: A visit to the Dachau memorial consists of the museum, the bunker behind the museum, the restored barracks, and a pensive walk across the huge but now-empty camp to the shrines and crematorium at the far end. A new visitors center should open in 2009 near the entrance. Upon arrival, pick up the €0.50 mini-guide, consider the excellent €2 booklet, and note when the next documentary film in English will be shown (20 min, normally shown at 11:30, 14:00, and 15:30, verify times on board as you enter museum).

Background: In the 1930s, the camp was outside the town, surrounded by a mile-wide restricted area. A huge training center stood next to the camp. While a relatively few 32,000 inmates died in Dachau between 1933 and 1945 (in comparison, more than a million were killed at Auschwitz in Poland), the camp is notorious because the people who ran the entire concentration-camp system

Dachau

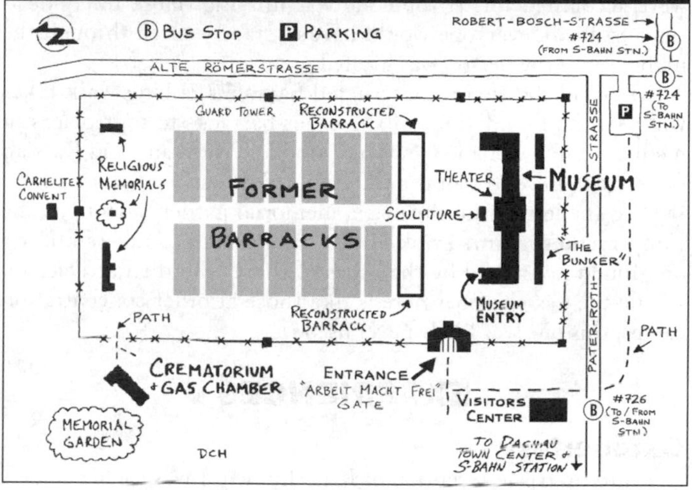

were trained here. Given the strict top-down Nazi management style, it's safe to assume that most of the demonic innovations for Hitler's mass killing originated at Dachau. This was a work camp, where inmates were used for slave labor. It was also a departure point for people shipped to gas chambers in the east, mostly in Nazi-occupied Poland—where most of the mass murder took place (conveniently distant, far out of view of the German public).

Few realize that Dachau actually housed people longer *after* the war than during the war. After liberation, the fences were taken down, but numerous survivors who had nowhere else to go stayed. It later served as a prison for camp officials convicted in the Dachau trials. Still later, it housed refugees from Eastern Europe. Until the 1960s, it was like a small town, with a cinema, shops, and so on.

➲ **Self-Guided Tour:** You enter, like the inmates did, through the infamous **iron gate** with the taunting slogan *Arbeit macht frei* ("Work makes you free"). The **museum**—which tries valiantly to personalize the plight of the inmates—is thoughtfully described in English. Computer touch-screens let you watch early newsreels. The **theater** shows a powerful documentary movie (see previous page for times).

The **bunker** behind the theater was for "special prisoners," such as failed Hitler assassins and politicians who challenged Nazism. It contains an exhibit on the notorious SS (you have direct access to the bunker after the movie lets out, otherwise walk around museum past the *Arbeit macht frei* sign).

The big **square** between the museum and the reconstructed barracks was used for roll call. Twice a day, the entire camp population assembled here. They'd stand at attention until all were accounted for. If someone was missing (more likely dead than escaped), everyone would have to stand—often through the night—until the person was located.

Beyond the two reconstructed **barracks,** a long walk takes you past the foundations of the other barracks to four places of meditation and worship (Jewish, Catholic, Protestant, and Russian Orthodox). Beyond that is a Carmelite Convent.

To the left of the shrines, a memorial garden surrounds the camp **crematorium.** Look at the smokestack. You're standing on ground nourished by the ashes of those who died at Dachau. While the gas chamber here is like those at other concentration camps, this one was likely never used.

EXPERIENCES

Oktoberfest

The 1810 marriage reception of King Ludwig I was such a success that it turned into an annual bash. These days, the Oktoberfest lasts

just over two weeks (Sept 19–Oct 4 in 2009), starting on the third Saturday in September and usually ending on the first Sunday in October (but never before Oct 3—the day Germany celebrates its recent reunification).

Oktoberfest kicks things off with an opening parade of more than 6,000 participants. Every night, it fills eight huge beer tents with about 6,000 people each. A million gallons of beer later, they roast the last ox.

It's best to reserve a room early, but if you arrive in the morning (except Fri or Sat) and haven't called ahead, the TI can usually help. The Theresienwiese fairground (south of the main train station), known as the "Wies'n," erupts in a frenzy of rides, dancing, and strangers strolling arm-in-arm down rows of picnic tables while the beer god stirs tons of brew, pretzels, and wursts in a bubbling cauldron of fun. The triple-loop roller coaster must be the wildest on earth (best before the beer-drinking). During the fair, the city functions even better than normal. It's a good time to sightsee, even if beer-hall rowdiness isn't your cup of tea. For details, see www.oktoberfest.de.

If you're not visiting while the party's on, don't worry: You can still dance to oompah bands, dunk huge pretzels, and show off your stein-hoisting skills any time of year at Munich's classic beer halls, including the venerable **Hofbräuhaus** (see page 44). Also in the city center, the **Beer and Oktoberfest Museum** gives a historical take on the festival (see page 44).

SHOPPING

You'll find beer steins to take home at shops on the pedestrian zone by St. Michael's Church and at the gift shops that surround the Hofbräuhaus. Münchners take their shoes very seriously; the pedestrian zone abounds with shoe stores featuring everything from expensive Italian models to Birkenstocks.

Here are a few areas and stores to consider:

Department Stores: You'll see lots of modern department stores. Locals rate them this way: **C&A** (which sells only clothing) is considered cheap yet respected; **Kaufhof** (which sells everything) is mid-range; and **Karlstadt/Herti** is upmarket.

On Marienplatz: Beck's has been a local institution since 1861, when it began meeting the needs of the royal family, including "Mad" King Ludwig. This shop has long been to fabrics what Alois Dallmayr is to fine food (see page 44). Today, it's an upscale department store, with stationery, cosmetics, and its own clothing label and designer duds (Mon–Sat 10:00–20:00, closed Sun). If you're facing the glockenspiel on New Town Hall, look to your right—you can't miss it on the corner. Also on Marienplatz is the **Hugendubel** bookstore, with an extensive selection of English-language books (Mon–Sat 9:30–20:00, closed Sun, coffee shop on top floor).

Weinstrasse/Theatinerstrasse: Shoppers will want to stroll from Marienplatz down the pedestrianized Weinstrasse, which becomes Theatinerstrasse. As you walk down Weinstrasse (it runs alongside the left of New Town Hall, as you face it), look for **Fünf Höfe** on your left, a delightful mall filled with Germany's top shops (open until 20:00, www.fuenfhoefe.de). Named for its five courtyards, this is where tradition meets modern. Note how its Swiss architects (who also designed Munich's grand new Allianz soccer stadium for the 2006 World Cup) play with light and color. Even if you're not a shopper, wander through the **Kunsthalle** to appreciate the architecture, the elegant window displays, and the sight of Bavarians living very well. There's an all-English branch of the Hugendubel bookstore behind Fünf Höfe (down Salvatorplatz).

For fine-quality (and very expensive) traditional clothing, visit **Loden-Frey Verkaufshaus** (two blocks west of Wienstrasse). The third floor of this fine department store is dedicated to classic Bavarian wear for men and women (Mon–Sat 10:00–20:00, closed Sun, Maffeistrasse 7, tel. 089/210-390, www.loden-frey.com).

Theatinerstrasse spills out onto Odeonsplatz, where you'll

find the **Nymphenburg Porcelain Store** (Mon–Fri 10:00–18:30, Sat 10:00–16:00, closed Sun, Odeonsplatz 1, tel. 089/282-428).

Maximilianstrasse: For the most exclusive shops, stroll this street. Ludwig I made the grand but very impersonal Ludwigstrasse. As a reaction to this unpopular street by this unpopular king, his son Maximilian built a street designed for the people and for shopping. It leads from the National Theater, over the Isar River to the Bavarian Parliament (which you can see from the theater end).

SLEEPING

Unless you hit Munich during a fair, convention, or big holiday, you can sleep reasonably here. Lots of student hotels around the station house anyone who's young at heart for €20, and it's easy to find a fine double with breakfast in a good basic hotel for €80. I've listed accommodations in two neighborhoods: within a few blocks of the central train station (Hauptbahnhof) and in the old center. Many of these places have complicated, slippery pricing schemes. I've listed the normal non-convention, non-festival prices. There are major conventions about 30 nights a year—prices increase from 20 percent to as much as 300 percent during Oktoberfest (Sept 19–Oct 4 in 2009; reserve well in advance). On the other hand, during slow times, you may be able to do better than the rates listed here—always ask. Sunday is very slow and usually comes with a huge discount if you ask. EurAide's website (www.euraide.com/ricksteves) has a schedule of conventions, festivals, and high-price days for hotels.

Near the Train Station

Budget hotels cluster in the area immediately south of the station. It feels seedy after dark (erotic cinemas and men with moustaches loitering in the shadows), but it's dangerous only for those in search of trouble. Still, hotels in the old center (see page 78) might feel more comfortable to many readers.

$$ Hotel Europäischer Hof is a huge, impersonal business hotel with 150 decent rooms. They have four categories of rooms, ranging from fairly cheap to outrageous (official rates are sky-high, but actual rates are usually closer to S-€50, Sb-€85, smaller "tourist class" D with head-to-toe twin beds-€57, Db-€92; 10 percent discount on prevailing rate in 2009 with this book and advance reservation, *or* if you pay cash—no double discounts; no discounts during conventions, major events, and Oktoberfest weekends; non-smoking rooms, family rooms, free Internet access, Bayerstrasse 31, tel. 089/551-510, fax 089/5515-11444, www.heh.de, info@heh.de). They also run **$$ Hotel Mark** around the corner, with a large

Sleep Code

(€1 = about $1.50, country code: 49, area code: 089)
S = Single, **D** = Double/Twin, **T** = Triple, **Q** = Quad, **b** = bathroom, **s** = shower only. Unless otherwise noted, credit cards are accepted, a buffet breakfast is included, there is no air-conditioning, and English is spoken.

To help you sort easily through these listings, I've divided the rooms into three categories based on the price for a standard double room with bath:

$$$ Higher Priced—Most rooms €100 or more.
$$ Moderately Priced—Most rooms between €70–100.
$ Lower Priced—Most rooms €70 or less.

lobby, dim hallways, 95 fine rooms, and a similar institutional 1970s ambience (S-€50, Sb-€75, D-€60, basic Db-€82, ask for 10 percent discount described above, Internet access, Senefelderstrasse 12, tel. 089/559-820, fax 089/5598-22444, www.heh.de, info@heh.de).

$$ Hotel Monaco is a delightful and welcoming little hideaway, tucked inside the fifth floor of a giant, nondescript building two blocks from the station. Emerging from the elevator, you're warmly welcomed by Christine into her flowery, cherub-filled oasis. It's homey, with 24 clean and fresh rooms (Sb-€45–70, Db-€55–75, breakfast-€8, Wi-Fi, Schillerstrasse 9, entrance on Adolf-Kolping-Strasse, tel. 089/545-9940, fax 089/550-3709, www.hotel-monaco.de, info@hotel-monaco.de).

$$ Litty's Hotel advertises cheap and cozy, and that's exactly what it delivers. Opened in 2008, the hotel is all new, with 34 rooms and charming managers Litty and Bernd (S-€45, Sb-€66, D-€66, Ds-€74, Db-€82, T-€93, Wi-Fi, near Schillerstrasse at Landwehrstrasse 32, tel. 089/5434-4211, fax 089/5434-4212, www.littyshotel.de, littyshotel@web.de).

$$ Hotel Deutsches Theater, managed by the Hotel Reinbold's Johannes, is a brass-and-marble-filled place with 28 tight, modern, three-star rooms. The back rooms face the courtyard of a neighboring theater—when there's a show, there can be some street noise (Sb-€65, Db-€79, Tb-€95, these rates promised in 2009 with cash and this book, prices higher during events, pricier suites, non-smoking floor, Landwehrstrasse 18, tel. 089/545-8525, fax 089/5458-5261, www.hoteldeutschestheater.de, info@hoteldeutschestheater.de).

$$ Hotel Reinbold has 65 sunny rooms close to the station. Manager Johannes promises these special cash-only rates with this book in 2009 when you reserve online and request the

MUNICH

Hotels near the Train Station

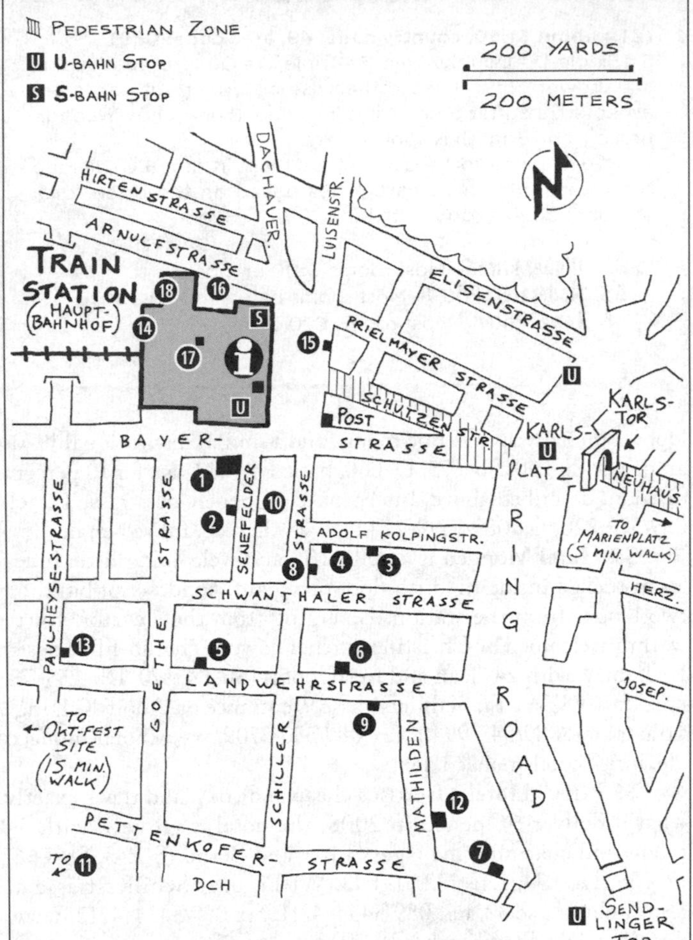

1. Hotel Europäischer Hof
2. Hotel Mark
3. Hotel Reinbold
4. Hotel Monaco
5. Litty's Hotel
6. Hotel Deutsches Theater
7. Hotel Bristol
8. Hotel Royal
9. CVJM (YMCA)
10. Wombat's Hostel, Euro Youth Hotel & Jaeger's Hostel
11. To Hotel Uhland
12. La Vecchia Masseria Rest.
13. Launderette
14. Radius Tours
15. City Tour Bus Stop
16. Airport & Romantic Road Bus Stops
17. EurAide Office
18. Trains to Füssen

Rick Steves discount (Sb-€61, Db-€79, Tb-€91, elevator, Adolf-Kolping-Strasse 11, tel. 089/5999-3902, fax 089/5999-3994, www.eckelmann-hotels.de, info@hotel-reinbold.de).

$$ Hotel Bristol has 57 comfortable business-class rooms. While a longer walk from the station, it's bright, efficient, and pleasantly located just across the street from the Sendlinger Tor U-Bahn stop (Sb-€89, Db-€99, hearty buffet breakfast, non-smoking rooms, elevator, free Internet access and Wi-Fi, one U-Bahn stop from station, U-1 or U-2: Sendlinger Tor, Pettenkoferstrasse 2, tel. 089/5434-8880, fax 089/5434-888111, www.bristol-munich.de, info@bristol-munich.de).

$$ Hotel Royal is perhaps the best value in its price range (if you don't mind the strip joints flanking the entry). While a bit institutional, it's clean, entirely non-smoking, and plenty comfortable. Most importantly, it's energetically run by Pasha and Changiz. Each of its 40 rooms is fresh and bright (Sb-€59, Db-€79–84, Tb-€99–109, book direct for a 10 percent discount off the prevailing price with this book in 2009, ask for a room on the quiet side—especially in summer when you'll want the window open, Internet access and Wi-Fi, Schillerstrasse 11a, tel. 089/591-021, fax 089/550-3657, www.hotel-royal.de, info@hotel-royal.de).

$ The **CVJM (YMCA),** open to all ages, rents 85 beds in modern rooms (S-€35, D-€60, T-€82.50, €27.50/bed in a shared triple, those over 26 pay about 10 percent more, cheaper for 3 nights or more and in winter, only €5/night per person more during Oktoberfest; includes showers, sheets, breakfast, and Internet access, but no lockers; Landwehrstrasse 13, tel. 089/552-1410, fax 089/550-4282, www.cvjm-muenchen.org, hotel@cvjm-muenchen.org).

"Hostel Row" on Senefelderstrasse, a Block from the Station

All three of the following hostels are casual and well-run, with friendly and creative management, and all cater expertly to the needs of young beer-drinking backpackers enjoying Munich on a shoestring. There's no curfew at any of these places, and each one has a lively bar that rages until the wee hours, along with staff who speak English as the primary language. Sleep cheap in big dorms, or spend a little more for a two-, three-, or four-bed room.

$ Wombat's Hostel rents cheap doubles and six- to eight-bed dorms with lockers. All bedrooms are fresh and modern, with good bathrooms, and there's a relaxing and peaceful winter garden (374 beds, dorm bed-€25, Db-€68, breakfast-€4, cheaper off-season, open 24 hours, Senefelderstrasse 1, tel. 089/5998-9180, www.wombats-hostels.com, office@wombats-munich.de).

$ Euro Youth Hotel fills a rare pre-WWII building and is probably the most comfortable hostel for older travelers (200 beds,

20-bed dorm-€18/bed, 4-bed dorm-€21/bed, D-€45, great breakfast, earplugs free at reception, Senefelderstrasse 5, tel. 089/5990-8811, www.euro-youth-hotel.de, info@euro-youth-hotel.de, run by Alfio).

$ Jaeger's Hostel rounds out this trio of station-neighborhood hostels, with 240 cheap beds and all the fun and efficiency you'd hope for in a hostel (40-bed dorm-€19/bed, 8-bed dorm-€22/bed, 3- to 6-bed rooms-€25/bed, includes breakfast, reception open 24/7/365, Senefelderstrasse 3, tel. 089/555-282, www.jaegershostel.de, info@jaegershostel.de).

In the Old Center

$$$ Mercure München Altstadt Hotel is a huge, impersonal, basic business-class hotel with all the modern comforts on a boring street very close to the Marienplatz action. If you want an American-style hotel room buried deep in Munich for a decent price, this place has 70 of them (Sb-€100, Db-€120 for most days, breakfast-€13, non-smoking floors, air-con, a block south of the pedestrian zone at Hotterstrasse 4, tel. 089/232-590, fax 089/2325-9127, www.mercure.com, h3709@accor.com).

$$$ Hotel Blauer Bock, formerly a dormitory for Benedictine monks, has been on the same corner across from the Munich City Museum since 1841. It's a little pricey and feels spartan, but offers clean, decent rooms and a straightforward pricing system (the same rates every day, except during fairs). Breakfast is served in its very mod and sleek restaurant next door, though most of the decor feels like the monks still run the place. Doubles with twin beds are normally smaller and cheaper (S-€45–53, Sb-€64–72, twin D-€72, D-€72, twin Db-€96, Db-€100–118, Tb-€130–135, Qb-€155, Sebastianplatz 9, tel. 089/231-780, fax 089/2317-8200, www.hotelblauerbock.de, info@hotelblauerbock.de).

$$ Pension Lindner is clean, quiet, and modern, with 10 pastel-bouquet rooms, mediocre plumbing, and reserved service (S-€39, D-€60, Ds-€70, Db-€80, these special prices promised with this book through 2009, cash preferred, elevator, Dultstrasse 1, tel. 089/263-413, fax 089/268-760, www.pension-lindner.com, info@pension-lindner.com, Marion Sinzinger).

$$ Hotel Atlanta is conveniently located 50 yards from the Sendlinger Tor U-Bahn stop and a 10-minute walk from Marienplatz. Its 20 rooms are split between two buildings connected by a peaceful patio. To minimize street noise, ask for a room in the older back building (S-€40, Ss-€55, Sb-€70, Ds-€70, Db-€80–90, family rooms, Sendlinger Strasse 58, tel. 089/263-605, fax 089/260-9027, www.hotel-atlanta.de, info@hotel-atlanta.de).

$$ Hotel Münchner Kindl is jolly, with 22 decent rooms above a friendly neighborhood bar (S-€45, D-€72, Db-€92,

Central Munich Hotels and Restaurants

1. Mercure München Altstadt Hotel
2. Hotel Blauer Bock
3. Pension Lindner
4. Hotel Atlanta
5. Hotel Münchner Kindl
6. Hofbräuhaus
7. Münchner Suppenküche (2)
8. To Augustiner Beer Garden
9. Jodlerwirt Pub
10. Nürnberger Bratwurst Glöckl am Dom & Andechser am Dom
11. Altes Hackerhaus
12. Der Pschorr Beer Hall & Schrannenhalle
13. Spatenhaus
14. Heilig-Geist-Stüberl Pub
15. To Chinesischer Turm Biergarten & Seehaus
16. Glockenspiel Café & Hugendubel Bookstore
17. Alois Dallmayr Deli
18. Buxs Self-Service Vegetarian Restaurant
19. Stadt Café (in City Museum)
20. Prinz Myshkin Veggie Rest.
21. Riva Bar Pizzeria
22. Café Tambosi
23. Nymphenburg Porcelain Store
24. Beer & Oktoberfest Museum
25. Munich Walk Office

Tb-€115, Qb-€130, these prices through 2009 with this book except during Oktoberfest and special events, lower rates possible in summer—ask, non-smoking rooms, no elevator, night noises travel up central courtyard, no air circulation in courtyard-facing rooms so they can get hot in summer—request a fan, Internet access, Damenstiftstrasse 16, tel. 089/264-349, fax 089/264-526, www.hotel-muenchner-kindl.de, reservierung@hotel-muenchner-kindl.de, Gunter and Renate).

Away from the Center

$$ Hotel Uhland is a stately mansion that rents 31 delightful rooms in a safe-feeling residential neighborhood near the Theresienwiese Oktoberfest grounds. It's been in the same wonderful Hauzenberger family for 50 years (Sb-€70–85, small Db-€85, big Db-€95, Tb-€120, save about €10 a night by booking through their website, great family rooms and deals, non-smoking floor, Wi-Fi, free parking; from station, take bus #58 to Georg-Hirth-Platz, or walk 15 minutes: go up Goethestrasse and turn right on Pettenkoferstrasse, cross Georg-Hirth-Platz to Uhlandstrasse and find #1; tel. 089/543-350, fax 089/5433-5250, www.hotel-uhland.de, info@hotel-uhland.de).

$ Munich's venerable **International Youth Camp Kapuzinerhölzl** (a.k.a. "The Tent") offers 400 spots on the wooden floor of a huge circus tent and never fills up. You'll get a mattress (€7.50) or bed (€10.50), or pitch your own tent (€5.50/tent plus €5.50/person). Blankets, hot showers, lockers, self-service laundry, and Wi-Fi are all included; breakfast is a few euros extra. It can be a fun but noisy experience—kind of a cross between a slumber party and Woodstock. There's a cool table-tennis-and-Frisbee atmosphere throughout the day, nightly campfires, and no curfew (open early-June–mid-Oct only, prices a little higher during Oktoberfest, Internet access, bikes-€8/day, catch tram #17 from train station for 17 minutes to Botanischer Garten, direction Amalienburgstrasse, and follow the crowd down Franz-Schrank-Strasse, tel. 089/141-4300, www.the-tent.com, info@the-tent.com).

EATING

Munich cuisine is best seasoned with beer. You have two basic types of places to choose from: beer halls such as the Hofbräuhaus, where you'll find music and tourists; or the mellower beer gardens, where you'll find the Germans. I'm here for the beer-garden fun. But when the *Wurst und Kraut* get to be too much for you, Munich has more Michelin-star restaurants than any other German city, plus a galaxy of good, more affordable alternatives. All restaurants are now smoke-free. The only ashtrays you'll see throughout Bavaria are outside.

In beer halls, beer gardens, or at the Viktualienmarkt, try the most typical meal in town: *Weisswurst* (white-colored veal sausage—peel off the skin before eating) with *süsser Senf* (sweet mustard), a salty *Brezel* (pretzel), and *Weissbier* ("white" wheat beer). Another traditional favorite is *Obatzda* (a.k.a. *Obatzter*), a mix of soft cheeses and butter with paprika and raw onions that's spread on bread. *Brotzeit,* meaning "time for bread," gets you a wooden platter of cold cuts, cheese, and pickles and is a good option for a light dinner. Also unique and memorable is a *Steckerlfisch*—fish on a stick (great with a pretzel and a big beer).

Beer Halls and Beer Gardens

These are my favorite places to sip or chug some Munich brew. For tips on enjoying this quintessential Munich experience, see "Munich's Beer Scene," next page.

The **Hofbräuhaus** (HOFE-broy-howze) is the world's most famous beer hall. Although it's grotesquely touristy, it's a Munich must. Even if you don't eat here, check it out; it's fun to see 200 Japanese people drinking beer in a German beer hall...across from a Hard Rock Café. Germans go for the entertainment—to sing "Country Roads," see how Texas girls party, and watch tourists try to chug beer (daily 9:00–24:00, music during lunch and dinner, 5-min walk from Marienplatz at Platzl 6, tel. 089/290-1360, www.hofbraeuhaus.de). You can drop by anytime for a large or light meal (my favorite: €6.60 for *ein paar Schweinswurst mit Kraut*—two pork sausages with sauerkraut), or just order a drink. They only sell beer by the one-liter mug, or *Mass* (€6.20). And they sell 10,000 of these liters every day. The Hofbräuhaus is the only beer hall in town offering regular live oompah music. This music-every-night atmosphere is thick, and the fat, shiny-leather bands even get church mice to stand up and conduct three-quarter time with breadsticks. They also host a gimmicky folk evening in the upstairs *Festsaal* (second floor) nightly from 19:00 to 22:30 (buffet with show-€20, show only-€6). Walk up the stairs to the left of the entrance just to see the historic old Hofbräuhaus photos and prints. For more on this Munich institution, see page 44.

The **Viktualienmarkt Beer Garden** taps you into about the best budget eating in town (closed Sun, see page 41). Countless stalls surround the beer garden and sell wurst, sandwiches, produce, and so on. This B.Y.O.F. tradition goes back to the days

Munich's Beer Scene

In Munich's beer halls *(Bräuhäuser)* and beer gardens *(Biergartens),* meals are inexpensive, white radishes are salted and cut in delicate spirals, and surly beer maids pull mustard packets from their cleavage. Unlike with wine, spending more money on beer doesn't get you a better drink. Beer is truly a people's drink, and you'll get the very best here in Munich. The big question among connoisseurs (local and foreign) is, "Which brew today?"

Beer gardens go back to the days when monks brewed their beer and were allowed to sell it directly to the thirsty public. They stored their beer in cellars under courtyards kept cool by the shade of bushy chestnut trees. Eventually, tables were set up, and these convivial eateries evolved. The tradition (complete with chestnut trees) survives, and any real beer garden will keep a few tables (identified by not having a tablecloth) available for customers who buy only beer and bring in their own food.

Huge liter beers (called *ein Mass* in German, or "*ein* pitcher" in English) cost about €6. You can order your beer *helles* (light but not "lite"—which is what you'll get if you say "*ein* beer"), *dunkles* (dark), or *Radler* (half lemon-lime soda, half beer). Beer gardens have a deposit system for their big glass steins: You pay €1 extra, and when you're finished, you can take the mug to the return man for your refund, or leave it on the table and lose your money. (Men's rooms come with vomitoriums.)

Many beer halls have a cafeteria system. Eating outside is made more pleasant by the *Föhn* (warm winds that come over the Alps from Italy), which gives this part of Germany 30 more days of sunshine than the North—and sometimes even an Italian ambience. (Many natives attribute the city's huge increase in outdoor dining to global warming.)

Beer halls take care of their regular customers. You'll notice many *Stammtische* (tables reserved for regulars and small groups, such as the "Happy Saturday Club"). They have a long tradition of being launch pads for grassroots action. The Hofbräuhaus was the first place Hitler talked to a big crowd.

when monks served beer but not food. To picnic, choose a table without a tablecloth. This is a good spot to grab a typical Munich *Weisswurst* and some beer. **Die Münchner Suppenküche,** a self-service soup kitchen at the Viktualienmarkt, is fine for a small, cozy, sit-down lunch (€4–6 soup meals, Mon–Fri 10:00–19:00, Sat 9:00–17:00, closed Sun; the statue of the woman in the fountain faces it about 30 yards away). There's another branch behind the New Town Hall (described on page 85).

Augustiner Beer Garden is a sprawling haven for well-established local beer-lovers on a balmy evening. For a true under-the-leaves beer garden packed with Münchners, this is a delight. In fact, most Münchners consider Augustiner the best beer garden in town. There's no music, it's away from the tourist hordes, and it serves up great beer, good traditional food, huge portions, reasonable prices, and the perfect conviviality. While there's plenty of indoor seating, the outdoor ambience is best—making this place ideal on a nice summer evening (daily 10:00–24:00, self-service food until 22:00, across from train tracks, 3 loooong blocks from station, away from the center at Arnulfstrasse 52, tram #17, taxis always waiting at the gate).

Jodlerwirt is tiny and cramped—a smart-alecky, yodeling kind of pub. The food is great, and the ambience is as Bavarian as you'll find. Avoid the basic ground-floor bar and climb the stairs into the action. Good food and lots of belly laughs...completely incomprehensible to the average tourist (Tue–Sat 18:00–3:00 in the morning, food until 23:00, closed Mon except Sept–April, always closed Sun, accordion act nightly from 20:30, between Hofbräuhaus and Marienplatz at Altenhofstrasse 4, tel. 089/221-249).

Nürnberger Bratwurst Glöckl am Dom, popular with tourists, offers a classier, fiercely Bavarian evening. Dine outside under the trees or in the dark, medieval, cozy interior—patrolled by wenches and spiked with antlers. I come here to enjoy the explosively tasty little *Nürnberger* sausages with kraut (€8–15 dinners, daily 10:00–24:00, at the rear of the twin-domed Frauenkirche, Frauenplatz 9, tel. 089/291-9450).

The trendier **Andechser am Dom,** on the same breezy square, serves Andechs beer and great food to appreciative regulars. Münchners favor the dark beer (ask for *dunkles*), but I love the light *(helles)*. The €10.50 *Gourmetteller* is a great sampler of their specialties, and the *Rostbratwurst* with kraut (€6.50) gives you the virtual *Nürnberger* bratwurst experience with the better Andechs beer (€5–15 main dishes, daily 10:00–24:00, Weinstrasse 7, reserve during peak times, tel. 089/298-481).

Altes Hackerhaus is popular with locals—especially the workers from the newspaper—for its traditional *Bayerischer* (Bavarian) fare served with a fancier white-tablecloth feel in one of the oldest buildings in town. It offers a small courtyard and a fun forest of characteristic nooks festooned with old-time paintings and posters (€10–20 meals, €5–10 wurst dishes, daily 10:00–24:00, Sendlinger Strasse 14, tel. 089/260-5026).

Der Pschorr, a new beer hall occupying a former slaughterhouse with a terrace overlooking the Viktualienmarkt, serves a special premium version of what many consider Munich's finest beer. With organic "slow food" and chilled glasses, this place mixes modern concepts—no candles, industrial-strength conviviality—with traditional, quality, classic dishes (Viktualienmarkt 15, tel. 089/5181-8500).

Spatenhaus is the opera-goers' beer hall, serving more elegant food in a woodsy, traditional setting since 1896. You can also eat outside, on the square facing the opera and palace. It's pricey, but you won't find better-quality *Biergarten* cuisine (€20 meals, daily 9:30–24:00, on Max-Joseph-Platz opposite opera, Residenzstrasse 12, tel. 089/290-7060).

Heilig-Geist-Stüberl ("Holy Ghost Pub") is a funky, retro little hole–in-the-wall where you are sure to meet locals (the German cousins of those who go to Reno because it's cheaper than Vegas, and who consider karaoke high culture). The interior, a 1980s time warp, makes you feel like you're stepping into an alcoholic cuckoo clock (just off the Viktualienmarkt at Heiliggeiststrasse 1, tel. 089/297-233).

In the English Garden

For outdoor ambience and a cheap meal, spend an evening at the English Garden's **Chinesischer Turm** (Chinese Tower) *Biergarten***.** You're welcome to B.Y.O. food and grab a table, or buy from the picnic stall *(Brotzeit)* right there. Don't bother to phone ahead—they have 6,000 seats. This is a fine opportunity to try a *Steckerlfisch,* sold for €9 at a separate kiosk (daily, long hours in good weather, usually live music, tel. 089/3838-7327, www.chinaturm.de; take tram #17 from main train station or Sendlinger Tor to Tivolistrasse, or U-3 or U-6 to Universität). **Seehaus im Englischen Garten** is famous among Münchners for its idyllic lakeside setting and excellent Mediterranean and traditional cooking. It's dressy and a bit snobbish, and understandably filled with locals who fit the same description. Choose from classy indoor or lakeside seating (€20–25 meals, daily 10:00–24:00, a pleasant 15-min hike into the English Garden—located on all the city maps—or take tram #44 or a taxi to the doorstep, Kleinhesselohe 3, tel. 089/3816-130). **Seehaus Beer Garden,** adjacent to the fancy Seehaus restaurant, is a less expensive, more casual beer garden with all the normal wurst, kraut, pretzels, and fine beer at typical prices. What makes this spot special: You're buried in the English

Garden, enjoying the fine lakeside setting (daily, long hours from 11:00 when the weather's fine).

Non-Beer Hall Restaurants

Man does not live by beer alone. Well, maybe some do. But for the rest of us, I recommend the following alternatives to the beer-hall scene.

On or near Marienplatz

With a Bird's-Eye Marienplatz View: **Glockenspiel Café** is good for a coffee or a meal with a view down on the Marienplatz action. There are several dining zones. Locals like the sunroof, but regardless of the weather, I grab a seat overlooking Marienplatz (Mon–Sat 10:00–24:00, Sun 10:00–19:00, ride elevator from Rosenstrasse entrance, opposite glockenspiel at Marienplatz 28, tel. 089/264-256). For a quicker and less crowded option, go to the Starbucks-style café on the top floor of **Hugendubel** bookstore (described under "Shopping" on page 73).

An Elegant Picnic or Café: The crown in **Alois Dallmayr**'s emblem indicates that the royal family assembled its picnics at this historic and expensive delicatessen. Explore this dieter's purgatory and put together a royal picnic to munch in the nearby Hofgarten. A classy but pricey café serves light meals on the ground floor (Mon–Sat 9:30–19:00, closed Sun, behind New Town Hall, Dienerstrasse 14). For more information, see page 44.

Soup-Kitchen Chain: **Die Münchner Suppenküche,** famous for its location in Viktualienmarkt (see page 83), has taken its cheap-and-cheery, locals-pleasing formula into town with six locations. A handy one is just off the Weinstrasse shopping street on Schafflerstrasse am Dom (behind the New Town Hall, look for the two coopers greeting shoppers; €4–6 for a great selection of today's soups, open for lunch daily except Sun).

A Budget Picnic: To save money, browse at Dallmayr's but buy in the basement **supermarkets** of the **Kaufhof** stores across Marienplatz or at Karlsplatz (Mon–Sat 9:30–20:00, closed Sun), or the **Minimal** at Fünf Höfe (Mon–Sat 7:00–20:00, closed Sun).

Trendy Eateries South of Marienplatz

The area south of Marienplatz is becoming a kind of SoHo, with lots of fun shops, wine bars, and bistros handy for a healthy and quick lunch. Most of these recommended restaurants are located on the map on page 79.

Buxs Self-Service Vegetarian Restaurant is a cafeteria where you'll find exactly what you want—as long as it's vegetarian. Fill a plate with your choice of organic soups, salads, and hot dishes, then pay by weight and eat inside or pleasantly outdoors (about

€10 for a meal, Mon–Fri 11:00–18:45, Sat 11:00–15:00, closed Sun, non-smoking, at bottom end of Viktualienmarkt at Frauenstrasse 9, tel. 089/291-9550).

Schrannenhalle, an old grain hall that burned in the 1930s, was reconstructed with original pieces and reopened in 2005 as a fun little mall/food circus. In the evenings, it feels like a community center, with people grabbing a bite from whatever eatery appeals and sitting down for a free movie, sporting event, or concert on the central big screen. The basement hosts a dance club for "over-30s." Pop in, if for no other reason than to see the fine reconstruction job on the amazingly preserved old beams (Pralat-Zistl-Strasse, 1 block from Viktualienmarkt).

Stadt Café is a lively diner/café serving healthy fare, with great daily specials (€5–8) and an inventive menu of Italian, German, salads, and vegetarian dishes. This high-energy, no-frills restaurant is packed with enthusiastic local eaters, newspaper-readers, and coffee-sippers. Dine in the quiet cobbled courtyard, inside, or outside facing the new synagogue (2-course lunch specials-€6, see the blackboard for today's specials, daily 10:00–24:00, in Munich City Museum, St.-Jakobs-Platz 1, tel. 089/266-949).

Prinz Myshkin is everybody's favorite upscale vegetarian eatery in the old center. You'll find a clever, appetizing selection of €8–15 plates. The decor is modern, the arched ceilings are cool, the outside seating is on a quiet street, and the clientele is entirely local. Don't miss the enticing appetizer selection on display as you enter (they do a fine mixed appetizer plate). They also have vegetarian sushi and their own baker, so they're proud of their sweets (€6 lunch specials, daily 11:30–23:00, Hackenstrasse 2, tel. 089/265-596).

Riva Bar Pizzeria is a long, skinny bar with an open oven popping out great pizzas to a crowd of young Münchners. It's very popular for its fresh, homemade-quality pizzas, "salad pizzas," pastas, and salads. There's a crowded dining area in back and a few pleasant tables outside on the busy sidewalk (€9–11 pizzas, Mon–Sat 8:00–24:00, Sun 12:00–24:00, 50 yards toward Marienplatz from Isartor at Im Tal 44, tel. 089/220-240).

La Vecchia Masseria serves simple Italian food inside amid a cozy Tuscan farmhouse decor, or outside in a beautiful flowery courtyard. Try the €24 tasting *menu* (€6 pizza or pasta, €14 main courses, daily 11:30–23:00, reservations smart, cash or AmEx only, near train station, Mathildenstrasse 3—see map on page 76, tel. 089/550-9090).

TRANSPORTATION CONNECTIONS

Munich is a super transportation hub (one reason it was the target of so many WWII bombs). For quick help at the main train station, stop by the service counter in front of track 18. For better English and more patience, drop by EurAide in a small hallway off the main entryway (with your back to track 19, head toward the main entrance; before the pretzel stand, turn left—the EurAide office is on the left; see page 26). Train info: tel. 11861 (€0.60/min). For flight information, see page 27.

From Munich by Train to: Füssen (hourly, 2 hrs; for a Neuschwanstein Castle day trip, depart at 6:50 and arrive at 9:00 with transfer in Buchloe; or go direct at 8:52 and arrive at 11:00—confirm times at station), **Reutte,** Austria (every 2 hrs, 2.5 hrs, best transfer in Garmisch), **Oberammergau** (nearly hourly, 1.75 hrs, change in Murnau or Oberau), **Salzburg,** Austria (2/hr, 1.5–2 hrs), **Berchtesgaden** (roughly hourly, 2.5–3 hrs, most with change in Salzburg or Freilassing), **Nürnberg** (2–3/hr, 1–1.25 hrs), **Würzburg** (1–2/hr, 2 hrs), **Rothenburg** (hourly, 2.5–3 hrs, 1–2 transfers), **Frankfurt** (hourly, 3–4 hrs) and **Frankfurt Airport** (hourly, 3.5 hrs), **Dresden** (about hourly, 5.75–6.25 hrs, transfer in Leipzig or Nürnberg), **Berlin** (hourly, 5.75–6.25 hrs, a few with change in Nürnberg), **Vienna** (3/day direct, 4.25 hrs; otherwise about hourly, 5–5.75 hrs, transfer in Salzburg), **Venice** (1/day direct, 7 hrs, more with change in Verona), **Paris** (2/day direct, 6 hrs, 1 direct overnight, 10 hrs, reservation required), **Prague** (2/day direct, 6 hrs, more with changes), **Zürich** (4/day direct, 4.25 hrs, more with changes), **Bern** (hourly, 5.5–6.5 hrs, 1–2 changes). Night trains run daily to Berlin, Vienna, Venice, Florence, Rome, Paris, Amsterdam, Budapest, Copenhagen (at least 6 hrs to each city). To use a railpass for a night train to Italy, your pass must include all countries on the train route (i.e., Austria or Switzerland), or you'll have to buy the segment that's not included.

Romantic Road Bus: For information on the Romantic Road bus tour, which connects "Mad" King Ludwig's castles, Munich, Dinkelsbühl, Rothenburg, and Frankfurt, see page 244. If going from Munich to Rothenburg, you can hitch a ride on the Romantic Road bus tour for €30 one-way by purchasing tickets at EurAide. This is a more scenic alternative to the train, allowing you to view some of the Romantic Road towns such as Augsburg, Nördlingen, and Dinkelsbühl (no advance reservations needed, daily early May–mid-Oct, departs Munich at 11:10, arrives Rothenburg at 16:00).

BAVARIA and TIROL

Füssen • King's Castles • Wieskirche • Oberammergau • Linderhof Castle • Ettal Monastery • Zugspitze • Reutte, Austria

Two hours south of Munich, between Germany's Bavaria and Austria's Tirol, is a timeless land of fairy-tale castles, painted buildings shared by cows and farmers, and locals who still yodel when they're happy.

In Germany's Bavaria, tour "Mad" King Ludwig II's ornate Neuschwanstein Castle, Europe's most spectacular. Stop by the Wieskirche, a textbook example of Bavarian Rococo bursting with curly curlicues, and browse through Oberammergau, Germany's woodcarving capital and home of the famous Passion Play. Then, just over the border in Austria's Tirol, explore the ruined Ehrenberg Castle and scream down the mountain on an oversized skateboard.

In this chapter, I'll cover Bavaria first, then Tirol. Austria's Tirol is easier and cheaper than touristy Bavaria. My favorite home base for exploring Bavaria's castles is actually in Austria, in the town of Reutte (see page 121). Füssen, in Germany, is a handier home base for train travelers.

Planning Your Time

While Germans and Austrians vacation here for a week or two at a time, the typical speedy American traveler will find two days' worth of sightseeing. With a car and more time, you could enjoy three or four days, but the basic visit ranges anywhere from a long day trip from Munich to a three-night, two-day visit. If the weather's good and you're not going to Switzerland on your trip, be sure to ride a lift to an alpine peak.

Highlights of Bavaria and Tirol

By Car: Here's a good, one-day circular drive from Reutte (or from Füssen, starting half an hour later): 7:30—Breakfast; 8:00—Depart hotel; 8:30—Arrive at Neuschwanstein to pick up tickets for the two castles (Neuschwanstein and Hohenschwangau); 9:00—Tour Hohenschwangau; 11:00—Tour Neuschwanstein; 13:00—Drive to Oberammergau, and spend an hour there to browse the carving shops; 15:00—Drive to Ettal Monastery for a half-hour stop (if you're not otherwise seeing the Wieskirche), then on to Linderhof Castle; 16:00—Tour Linderhof; 18:00—Drive along scenic Plansee lake back into Austria (or return to Füssen); 19:00—Back at hotel; 20:00—Dinner at hotel. Off-season

(Oct–March), start your day an hour later, since Neuschwanstein and Hohenschwangau don't open until 10:00; and skip Linderhof, as it closes an hour early.

The next morning, you could stroll through Reutte, hike to the Ehrenberg ruins, and ride the luge on your way to Munich, Innsbruck, Switzerland, Venice, or wherever.

By Public Transportation: Train travelers can use Füssen as a base and bus or bike the three miles to Neuschwanstein. Reutte is connected by bus with Füssen (except Sat–Sun; taxi €30 one-way). If you're based in Reutte, you can bike to the Ehrenberg ruins (just outside Reutte) and to Neuschwanstein Castle/Tegelberg luge (90 min). A one-way taxi from Reutte to Neuschwanstein costs about €35. Or, if you stay at the recommended Gutshof zum Schluxen hotel (in Pinswang, Austria—see page 132), it's a one-hour hike through the woods to Neuschwanstein.

Getting Around Bavaria and Tirol

By Car: This region is ideal by car. All the sights are within an easy 60-mile loop from Reutte or Füssen. Even if you're doing the rest of your trip by train, consider renting a car in Füssen (see page 94) or in Reutte (see page 122).

By Public Transportation: Local bus service in the region is spotty for sightseeing. If you're rushed and without wheels, Reutte, the Wieskirche, Linderhof, Ettal Monastery, and the Biberwier luge ride are probably not worth the trouble (speed freaks should instead consider the Tegelberg luge near Neuschwanstein, which is within walking distance of the castle and served regularly by bus). I've listed connections below for each of the possible home-bases in the region: Füssen (best overall base for non-drivers, especially for Ludwig's castles, also decent for Oberammergau and Reutte); Oberammergau (good base for Linderhof, Ettal Monastery, and Garmisch/Zugspitze); and Reutte (most challenging home-base for non-drivers). Note that the bus connections listed below are for summer weekdays; on weekends and out of season, frequency plummets. Confirm all bus schedules locally: Check the big board at the bus stop across from the Füssen train station, buy the indispensable bus timetable (€0.30, *OVG Fahrpläne der Linienbusse*) at the TI or train station, check online at www.rva-bus.de, or call 08362/939-0505. For longer-distance bus trips (such as side-tripping from Füssen to Oberammergau), you'll likely save money if you buy a ***Tagesticket*** (day pass). If you'll be taking a lot of trains in Bavaria (for example, day-tripping from Munich to the castles), consider the **Bayern-Ticket** (covers up to five people from Munich to anywhere in Bavaria and back for only €27/day, not valid Mon–Fri before 9:00; for more information, see page 68 in the Munich chapter).

From Füssen: Füssen is connected by hourly train with **Munich** (2-hour trip, some with transfer in Buchloe). Füssen is three miles from Ludwig's castles (Neuschwanstein and Hohenschwangau), easily reachable by bus (or by bike—see page 92).

From Füssen, handy buses connect to **Ludwig's castles** and the **Tegelberg luge** (buses #73 and #78, 2/hr, 10 min). There's also a bus connection to **Oberammergau** (bus #73 to Echelsbacher Brücke, change there to bus #9622—often marked *Garmisch*, confirm with driver that bus will stop in Oberammergau; 4–6/day in summer, 1.5 hrs total); the same bus continues to **Garmisch,** where you can ascend the **Zugspitze.** (From Oberammergau, you can also connect to **Linderhof Castle** and **Ettal Monastery**—see "From Oberammergau," below—but sparse buses make these sights challenging to do in a day from Füssen; rent a car instead.) To reach **Reutte,** you can take the bus (#74, Mon–Fri 6/day—but only 4 return buses/day, no buses at all Sat–Sun, less off-season, 35 min, €3.40) or a taxi (€30). You can reach the **Wieskirche** relatively easily (various buses, 4–5/day, 40–50 min each way, more frequently with a transfer in Steingaden; or just hop on the Romantic Road bus, leaving Füssen early May–late Oct daily at 8:00); however, return connections from the Wieskirche to Füssen are infrequent, likely leaving you with more time at the church than you want.

From Oberammergau: Oberammergau is a fine home-base for seeing Linderhof Castle, Ettal Monastery, and the Zugspitze. Bus #9622 heads from Oberammergau to **Linderhof** (nearly hourly, 25–40 min); some also stop at **Ettal Monastery** en route. Buses also go to **Garmisch** (nearly hourly, 40 min; also possible by train with a transfer in Murnau, 1.5 hrs), where you can head up to the **Zugspitze.** Oberammergau is also reasonably well-connected to **Füssen** (4–6/day in summer, transfer at Echelsbacher Brücke, 1.5 hrs total). The trip between Oberammergau and **Munich** is better directly by train (nearly hourly, 1.75 hrs, change in Murnau or Oberau) than via Füssen by bus.

From Reutte: Reutte is the most challenging home base for non-drivers. It's a 35-minute bus ride from Füssen (Mon–Fri 6/day, none Sat–Sun, less off-season, €3.40; taxis from Reutte to Ludwig's castles are €35 one-way; to Füssen, €30). There are only four return buses (from Reutte back to Füssen), but Reutte is planning a more regular bus service to Füssen and the sights across the border—ask your hotel for the latest information. In Füssen, you can connect to **Ludwig's castles, Oberammergau,** and other sights (see "From Füssen," above). From Reutte, a train departs every two hours to **Ehrwald** (30 min) and then **Garmisch** (1 hr), each of which has connections up to the **Zugspitze;** in Garmisch, you can also connect to **Oberammergau.**

By Tour: If you're interested only in Bavarian castles, consider an all-day organized bus tour of the Bavarian biggies as a side-trip from Munich (see page 36 in the Munich chapter).

By Bike: This is great biking country. Shops in or near train stations rent bikes for €8–15 per day. The ride from Reutte to Neuschwanstein and the Tegelberg luge (90 min) is a natural.

By Thumb: Hitchhiking, always risky, is a slow-but-possible way to connect the public-transportation gaps. For example, even reluctant hitchhikers can catch a ride from Linderhof back to Oberammergau, as virtually everyone leaving there is a tourist like you and heading that way.

Füssen

Dramatically situated under a renovated castle on the lively Lech River, Füssen is a handy home base for exploring the region. Füssen has been a strategic stop since ancient times. Its main street sits on the Via Claudia Augusta, which crossed the Alps (over the Brenner Pass) in Roman times. The town was the southern terminus of a medieval trade route, now known among modern tourists as the "Romantic Road." Today, while Füssen is overrun by tourists in the summer, few venture to the back streets...where you'll find the real charm. Apart from my self-guided walk (described on page 94) and the City Museum, there's little to do here. It's just a pleasant small town with a big history and lots of hardworking people in the tourist business.

Halfway between Füssen and the border (as you drive, or a woodsy walk from the town) is the **Lechfall,** a thunderous waterfall (with a handy WC).

ORIENTATION

(area code: 08362)

Füssen's train station is a few blocks from the TI, the town center (a cobbled shopping mall), and all my hotel listings (see "Sleeping," page 98).

Tourist Information

The TI is in the center of town (June–mid-Sept Mon–Fri 9:00–18:00, until 17:00 off-season, Sat 10:00–14:00, Sun 10:00–12:00, one free Internet terminal, 3 blocks down Bahnhofstrasse from station, tel. 08362/93850, www.fuessen.de). If necessary, the TI can help you find a room. After hours, the little self-service info pavilion near the front of the TI features an automated room-finding service (7:00–24:30).

Füssen

1. Hotel/Rest. Kurcafe
2. Hotel Hirsch
3. Hotel Sonne
4. Altstadthotel zum Hechten & Restaurant Ritterstub'n
5. Suzanne's B&B
6. Hotel Bräustüberl
7. Gasthof Krone
8. House LA
9. Allgäuer Gästehaus
10. To Magdalena Höbel
11. Haus Peters
12. To Youth Hostel
13. Aquila das Restaurant
14. Markthalle Food Court
15. Bike Rental
16. Car Rental
17. To Car Rental
18. Internet Café

Arrival in Füssen

From the train station (lockers available, €2–3), exit to the left and walk a few straight blocks to the center of town and the TI. Buses leave from the station to Neuschwanstein (2/hr) and Reutte (6/day Mon–Fri in summer).

Helpful Hints

Internet Access: Beans & Bytes is the best place to get online, with fast terminals and good drink service (€1/30 min, Wi-Fi, Skype, disc-burning for your photos, daily 10:00–22:00, down the pedestrian alley off the main drag at Reichenstrasse 33, tel. 08362/926-8960).

Bike Rental: Bike Station, sitting right where the train tracks end, outfits sightseers with good bikes and tips on two-wheeled fun in the area (€8/24 hrs, April–Sept Mon–Fri 9:00–18:00, Sat 10:00–14:00, Sun 9:00–12:00 in good weather, closed Oct–March, mobile 0176-2205-3080). For a strenuous but enjoyable 20-mile loop trip, see page 109.

Car Rental: Peter Schlichtling, in the town center, rents cars for reasonable prices (€62/day, includes insurance, Mon–Fri 8:00–18:00, Sat 9:00–12:00, closed Sun, Kemptener Strasse 26, tel. 08362/922-122, www.schlichtling.de).

Auto Osterried/Europcar rents at similar prices, but is an €8 taxi ride away from the train station. Their cheapest car is a fun-to-try SmartCar going for about €40 per day (daily 8:00–19:00, across river from Füssen at Tiroler Strasse 65, tel. 08362/6381).

Local Guide: Silvia Beyer speaks English and knows the region very well (silliby@web.de, mobile 0160-901-13431).

SELF-GUIDED WALK

Welcome to Füssen

For most, Füssen is just a touristy home base for visiting Ludwig's famous castles. But the town has a rich history and hides some evocative corners, as you'll see when you follow this short orientation walk. Throughout the town, "City Tour" information plaques explain points of interest in English. Use them to supplement the information I've provided.

• *Begin at the square in front of the TI, three blocks from the train station.*

❶ **Kaiser-Maximilian-Platz:** The entertaining "Seven Stones" fountain on this square (in front of the TI) was built in 1995 to celebrate Füssen's 700th birthday. The stones symbolize community, groups of people gathering, conviviality...each is different, with "heads" nodding and talking. It's granite on granite.

Füssen Walk

1. Kaiser-Maximilian-Platz
2. Hotel Hirsch & Medieval Wall
3. Historic Cemetery of St. Sebastian
4. Town View from Franciscan Monastery
5. Lech Riverbank
6. Church of the Holy Ghost, Bread Market & Lute-Makers
7. Benedictine Monastery
8. City Museum
9. St. Magnus Basilica
10. High Castle

The moving heads are not connected, and nod only with water-power. While frozen in winter, it's a popular and splashy play zone for kids on hot summer days.

• *Just half a block down the busy street stands...*

❷ **Hotel Hirsch and Medieval Wall:** Hotel Hirsch, one of the first hotels in town, dates from the 19th century, when aristocratic tourists started coming to appreciate the castles and natural wonders of the Alps. Across the busy street stands one of two surviving towers from Füssen's medieval town wall (c. 1515). Farther down the street (50 yards, just before the second tower), a gate leads into the old town (see information plaque).

• *Step through the gate (onto today's Klosterstrasse), and immediately turn left into the old cemetery.*

❸ **Historic Cemetery of St. Sebastian (Alter Friedhof):** This peaceful oasis of Füssen history, established in the 16th century, fills a corner between the town wall and the Franciscan monastery. It's technically full, and only members of great and venerable Füssen families (who already own plots here) can join those who are buried (free, daily 7:30–19:00).

Just inside the gate (on right) is the tomb of Dominic Quaglio, who painted the Romantic scenes decorating the walls of Hohenschwangau Castle in 1835. Over on the old city wall is the World War I memorial, listing all the names of men from this small town killed in that devastating conflict (along with each one's rank and place of death). A bit to the right, also along the old wall, is a statue of the hand of God holding a fetus—a place to remember babies who died before being born. And in the corner, farther to the right, are the simple wooden crosses of Franciscans who lived just over the wall in the monastery. Note the fine tomb art from many ages collected here, and the loving care this community gives its cemetery.

• *Exit on the far side, just past the dead Franciscans, and continue toward the big church.*

❹ **Town View from Franciscan Monastery (Franziskanerkloster):** From the Franciscan Monastery (which still has big responsibilities, but only a handful of monks in residence), there's a fine view over the medieval town. The Church of St. Magnus and the High Castle (the summer residence of the Bishops of Augsburg) break the horizon. The chimney (c. 1886) on the left is a reminder that when Ludwig built Neuschwanstein, the textile industry (linen and flax) was very big here.

• *Go down the steps into the flood zone, and stay left, following the roar of the charging river, through the medieval "Bleachers' Gate," to the riverbank.*

❺ **Lech Riverbank:** This low end of town, the flood zone, was the home of those whose work depended on the river—bleachers, rafters, and fishermen. The Lech River was—in its day—an expressway to Augsburg (about 70 miles to the north). Around the year 1500, the rafters established the first professional guild in Füssen. As Füssen was on the Via Claudia, cargo from Italy passed here en route to big German cities farther north. Rafters would assemble rafts, and pile them high with goods—or with people needing a lift. If the water was high, they could float all the way to Augsburg in as little as one day. There they'd disassemble their raft and sell off the lumber along with the goods they'd carried, then make their way home to raft again. Today you'll see no water sports here, as there's a hydroelectric plant just downstream.

• *Walk upstream a bit, and head inland immediately after crossing under the bridge.*

❻ **Church of the Holy Ghost, Bread Market, and Lute-Makers:** Climbing uphill, you pass the colorful Church of the Holy Ghost (Heilig-Geist-Spitalkirche) on the left. As this was the church of the rafters, their patron, St. Christopher, is prominent on the facade. Today it's the church of Füssen's old folks' home (it's adjacent—notice the easy-access skyway).

Farther up the lane (opposite the entry to the big monastery) is Bread Market Square (Brotmarkt), with its fountain honoring the famous 16th-century lute-making family, the Tieffenbruckers. In its day, Füssen was a huge center of violin- and lute-making, with about 200 workshops. Today only two survive.

• *Backtrack and enter the courtyard in the huge monastery just across the street.*

❼ **Benedictine Monastery (Kloster St. Mang):** From 1717 until secularization in 1802, this was the powerful center of town. Today the courtyard is popular for concerts, and the building houses the City Hall and City Museum (and a public WC).

❽ **City Museum:** This is Füssen's one must-see sight (€2.50, €3 includes castle gallery; April–Oct Tue–Sun 11:00–17:00, closed Mon; Nov–March Fri–Sun 13:00–16:00, closed Mon–Thu; tel. 08362/903-146). Pick up the loaner English translations and follow the one-way route. In the St. Anna Chapel, you'll see the famous *Dance of Death.* This was painted shortly after a plague devastated the community in 1590. It shows 20 social classes, each dancing with the Grim Reaper—starting with the pope and the emperor. The words above say, essentially, "You can say yes or you can say no, but you must ultimately dance with death." Leaving the chapel, you walk over the metal lid of the crypt. Farther on, exhibits illustrate the rafting trade and violin- and lute-making (with a complete workshop). The museum also includes an exquisite *Festsaal* (main festival hall), an old library, a textile factory, and a Ludwig's "castle dream room."

• *Leaving the courtyard, hook left around the monastery and uphill. The square tower marks...*

❾ **St. Magnus Basilica (Basilika St. Mang):** St. Mang (or Magnus) is Füssen's favorite saint. In the eighth century, he worked miracles all over the area with his holy rod. For centuries, pilgrims came from far and wide to enjoy art depicting the great works of St. Magnus. Above the altar dangles a glass cross containing his relics (including that holy stick). Just inside the door is a chapel remembering a much more modern saint—Franz Seelos (1819–1867), the local boy who went to America (Pittsburg and New Orleans) and lived such a saintly life that in 2000 he was made a saint. If you're in need of a miracle, there are cards to fill out next to the candles.

• *From the church, a lane leads high above, into the castle courtyard.*

❿ **High Castle (Hohes Schloss):** This castle, long the summer residence of the Bishop of Augsburg, houses a painting gallery. Its courtyard is interesting for the striking perspective tricks painted onto its flat walls. From below the castle, the city's main drag (once the Roman Via Claudia and now Reichenstrasse) leads from a grand statue of St. Magnus past lots of shops, cafés, and strolling people to Kaiser-Maximilian-Platz and the TI...where you began.

SLEEPING

(country code: 49, area code: 08362)

Though I prefer sleeping in Reutte (see page 121), convenient Füssen is just three miles from Ludwig's castles and offers a cobbled, riverside retreat. It's very touristy, but it has plenty of rooms. All recommended accommodations are within a few blocks of the train station and the town center. Parking is easy at the station. Prices listed are for one-night stays. Most hotels give about 5 to 10 percent off for two-night stays—always request this discount. Competition is fierce, and off-season prices are soft. High season is mid-June through September. Rooms are generally about 12 percent less in shoulder season and much cheaper in off-season. To locate these hotels, see the map on page 93.

$$$ Hotel Kurcafe is deluxe, with 30 spacious rooms and all of the amenities. The standard rooms are comfortable, and the newer, bigger rooms have elegant touches and fun decor—such as canopy drapes and cherubic frescoes over the bed (Sb-€89, standard Db-€109–125, bigger Db-€135–149 depending on size, Tb-€135, Qb-€149, 4-person suite-€179–209, high prices are for July–Aug, €10 more for weekends and holidays, you'll likely save money by booking via their website, elevator, Internet access, parking-€5/day, a block from station at Bahnhofstrasse 4, tel. 08362/930-180, fax 08362/930-1850, www.kurcafe.com, info@kurcafe.com, Norbert and the Schöll family).

Sleep Code

(€1 = about $1.50, Germany country code: 49, Austria country code: 43)

S = Single, **D** = Double/Twin, **T** = Triple, **Q** = Quad, **b** = bathroom, **s** = shower only. Unless otherwise noted, credit cards are accepted, English is spoken, and breakfast is included. The €1.35 per person, per night "tourist tax" is not included in these rates.

To help you sort easily through these listings, I've divided the rooms into three categories, based on the price for a standard double room with bath:

$$$ Higher Priced—Most rooms €100 or more.
$$ Moderately Priced—Most rooms between €60-100.
$ Lower Priced—Most rooms €60 or less.

$$$ Hotel Hirsch is a big, romantic, old tour-class hotel with 53 rooms on the main street in the center of town. Their standard rooms are fine, and their theme rooms are a fun splurge (Sb-€65–85, standard Db-€110–140, theme Db-€140–170, price depends on room size and demand, cheaper Nov–March and during slow times, family rooms, elevator, free parking, Kaiser-Maximilian-Platz 7, tel. 08362/93980, fax 08362/939-877, www.hotelhirsch.de, info@hotelhirsch.de).

$$$ Hotel Sonne, in the heart of town, rents 51 stylish and spacious rooms (Sb-€93–109, Db-€93–159, Tb-€118–148, Qb-€164–200, higher prices are for huge rooms in the new wing, cheaper Oct–mid-May, elevator, Internet access, free sauna, parking-€4/day, kitty-corner from TI at Prinzregentenplatz 1, tel. 08362/9080, fax 08362/908-100, www.hotel-sonne.de, info@hotel-sonne.de).

$$ Altstadthotel zum Hechten, with 35 rooms, offers all the modern comforts in a friendly, traditional building right under Füssen Castle in the old-town pedestrian zone (Sb-€57, Db-€90, Tb-€117, Qb-€140, request Rick Steves discount, beds can be short, fun miniature bowling alley in basement, free parking with this book; from TI, walk down pedestrian street and take second right to Ritterstrasse 6; tel. 08362/91600, fax 08362/916-099, www.hotel-hechten.com, hotel.hechten@t-online.de, Pfeiffer and Tramp families).

$$ Suzanne's B&B is run by a plainspoken, no-nonsense American woman who strikes some travelers as a brusque drill sergeant. Suzanne runs a tight ship, offering travel advice, local cheese, a children's yard, garden, and bright, woody, spacious rooms (Db-€90, huge Db with waterbed and balcony-€110, Tb-€120, Qb-€156, suite sleeps up to 10, cash only, non-smoking, €8/day bike rental; exit station right and backtrack 2 btlocks along tracks, cross tracks at Venetianerwinkel to #3; tel. 08362/38485, fax 08362/921-396, www.suzannes.de, svorbrugg@t-online.de).

$$ Hotel Bräustüberl has 17 decent rooms at fair rates attached to a gruff, musty, old beer hall. Don't expect much service (Db-€84, cash only, Rupprechtstrasse 5, 1 block from station, tel. 08362/7843, fax 08362/923-951, www.brauereigasthof-braeustueberl.de, brauereigasthof-fuessen@t-online.de).

Füssen's Budget Beds

$ Gasthof Krone, a rare bit of pre-glitz Füssen in the pedestrian zone, has dumpy halls and stairs and 12 big, worn time-warp rooms (S-€31, D-€58, extra bed-€26, extra bed for kids under 12-€20, €3 more per person for 1-night stays, closed Nov–June; from TI, head down pedestrian street and take first left to Schrannengasse 17; tel. 08362/7824, fax 08362/37505, www.krone-fuessen.de, info@krone-fuessen.de).

$ House LA offers nine basic, clean rooms at rock-bottom prices near the town center (4-bed dorms-€18/bed, Db-€42, Wachsbleichstrasse 2, mobile 0170-624-8610, www.housela.de, info@housela.de). They also rent four very basic rooms and one apartment at Welfenstrasse 39 (D-€40, light breakfast served in room).

$ Allgäuer Gästehaus has four cheap and slightly run-down rooms on a busy street near the center of town (Db-€54, Luitpoldstrasse 10, tel. 08362/926-8425, hdnet@web.de).

$ Magdalena Höbel, your quintessential German grandmother, rents two double rooms in a quiet neighborhood about a 10-minute walk from the train station. Magdalena speaks some English (D-€36, Frauensteinweg 42c, tel. 08362/2950).

$ At Haus Peters, Frau Peters rents great rooms in a clean and homey setting with an inviting garden that's a five-minute stroll from the train station (Db-€52, Augustenstrasse 5-1/2, tel. 08362/7171). Frau Peters plans to retire after 2009.

$ Füssen Youth Hostel, a fine, German-run place, welcomes travelers, especially younger ones (bed in 2- to 6-bed dorm rooms-€20, D-€56, €3 more for non-members, includes breakfast and sheets, guests over age 26 pay €4 penalty for being so old, laundry-€3.20/load, cheap dinners, office open 7:00–12:00 & 17:00–23:00, until 22:00 off-season, from station backtrack 10 min along tracks, Mariahilfer Strasse 5, tel. 08362/7754, fax 08362/2770, www.fuessen.jugendherberge.de, jhfuessen@djh-bayern.de).

EATING

Aquila das Restaurant serves modern international dishes in a simple, traditional *Gasthaus* setting with great seating outside on the delightful little Brotmarkt square (€10 plates, serious salads, daily from 11:30 and from 17:00, Brotmarkt 9, tel. 08362/6253).

Restaurant Ritterstub'n offers delicious, reasonably priced fish, salads, veggie plates, and a fun kids' menu. They have three eating zones: dressy in front, casual in back, and courtyard. Demure Gabi serves while her husband cooks standard Bavarian fare (€5 lunch specials, €6–12 plates, Tue–Sun 11:30–14:30 & 17:30–23:00, Ritterstrasse 4, tel. 08362/7759).

Schenke & Wirtshaus (inside the Altstadthotel zum Hechten) dishes up hearty, traditional Bavarian fare. They specialize in pike *(Hecht)* pulled from the Lech River, served with a tasty, fresh herb sauce (€8–13 plates, salad bar, cafeteria ambience, daily 10:00–22:00, Ritterstrasse 6, tel. 0836/91600).

Hotel Kurcafe's fine restaurant, right on Füssen's main traffic circle, has good weekly specials. Choose between a traditional dining room and a pastel winter garden, and enjoy the live Bavarian zither music most Fridays and Saturdays during dinner (open daily 11:30–14:30 & 17:30–21:30, Bahnhofstrasse 4, tel. 08362/930-180).

Markthalle, just across the street from Gasthof Krone, is a fun food court offering a wide selection of reasonably priced, wurst-free food. Located in an old warehouse from 1483, it's now home to a fishmonger; Chinese, Turkish, and Italian delis; a fruit stand; a bakery; and a wine bar. Buy your food from one of the vendors, park yourself at any one of the tables, then look up and admire the Renaissance ceiling (Mon–Fri 7:30–18:30, Sat 7:30–14:00, closed Sun, corner of Schrannengasse and Brunnengasse).

Gelato: **Hohes Schloss Italian Ice Cream** is a good gelateria on the main drag, with cheap ice cream to go and an inviting perch for a coffee or dessert while people-watching (Reichenstrasse 14).

Picnic Supplies: Bakeries and *Metzger*s (butcher shops) abound and frequently have ready-made sandwiches. For groceries, try the **Plus** supermarket at the roundabout on your way into town from the train station (Mon–Sat 8:30–20:00, closed Sun).

TRANSPORTATION CONNECTIONS

From Füssen to: Neuschwanstein (bus #73 or #78, departs from train station, continues to Tegelberg lift station after castles, 2/hr, 10 min, €2 one-way, €3.50 round-trip; taxis cost €10 one-way); **Oberammergau** (bus #73 to Echelsbacher Brücke, change there to bus #9622—often marked *Garmisch,* confirm with driver that bus will stop in Oberammergau; 4–6/day in summer, 1.5 hrs total)—

from Oberammergau you can connect to **Linderhof Castle, Ettal Monastery,** or **Garmisch/Zugspitze; Reutte** (bus #74, Mon–Fri 6 buses/day, none Sat–Sun, 35 min, €3.40 one-way; taxis cost €30 one-way); **Wieskirche** (4–5/day, 40–50 min each way, more frequently with a transfer in Steingaden; or take Romantic Road bus—see below); **Munich** (hourly trains, 2 hrs, some change in Buchloe); **Innsbruck** (5 trains/day, 4.25 hrs, change in Munich). Train info: tel. 11861 (€0.60/min).

Romantic Road Buses: The northbound Romantic Road bus departs Füssen at 8:00; the southbound bus arrives in Füssen at 19:00 (bus stops at train station). A railpass gets you a 20 percent discount on the Romantic Road bus (without using up a day of a flexipass). Note that the northbound bus stops at the **Wieskirche** for 17 minutes, but the southbound bus stops there only by request. For more details on the bus, see page 244 in the Rothenburg chapter.

The Best of Bavaria

Within a short drive of Füssen and Reutte, you'll find some of the most enjoyable—and most tourist-filled—sights in Germany. The otherworldly "King's Castles" of Neuschwanstein and Hohenschwangau capture romantics' imaginations, the ornately decorated Wieskirche puts the faithful in a heavenly mood, and the little town of Oberammergau overwhelms visitors with cuteness. Yet another impressive castle (Linderhof), another fancy church (Ettal), and a sky-high viewpoint (the Zugspitze) round out Bavaria's top attractions.

The King's Castles

The most popular tourist destinations in Bavaria are the "King's Castles" *(Königsschlösser)*. The older Hohenschwangau, King Ludwig's boyhood home, is less touristy but more historic. The more dramatic Neuschwanstein, which inspired Walt Disney, is the one everyone visits. I'd recommend visiting both, and planning some time to hike above Neuschwanstein to Mary's Bridge—and if you enjoy romantic hikes, down through the gorge below. With fairy-tale turrets in a fairy-tale alpine setting built by a fairy-tale king, these castles are understandably a huge hit.

Getting There

If arriving by **car,** note that road signs in the region refer to the sight as *Königsschlösser,* not Neuschwanstein. There's plenty of parking (all lots-€4.50). The first lots require more walking. Drive right through Touristville and past the ticket center, and park in lot #4 by the lake for the same price.

From **Füssen,** those without cars can catch the twice-hourly **bus** #73 or #78 (€2 one-way, €3.50 round-trip, 10 min, catch bus at train station), take a **taxi** (€10 one-way), or ride a rental **bike** (two level miles).

From **Reutte,** take bus #74 to the Füssen train station (Mon–Fri 4/day, none Sat–Sun, €3.40, 35 min), then hop on bus #73 or #78 to the castle.

For a romantic twist, hike or mountain-bike from the trailhead at the recommended hotel **Gutshof zum Schluxen** in Pinswang, Austria (see page 132, they rent bikes). When the dirt road forks at the top of the hill, go right (downhill), cross the Austria-Germany border (marked by a sign and deserted hut), and follow the narrow paved road to the castles. It's a 60- to 90-minute hike or a great circular bike trip (allow 30 min; cyclists can return to Schluxen from the castles on a different 30-min bike route via Füssen).

SIGHTS

For all the logistics, see "Visiting the Castles" on page 105.

▲▲▲Hohenschwangau Castle

Standing quietly below Neuschwanstein, the big, yellow Hohenschwangau (hoh-en-SHVAHN-gow) Castle was Ludwig's boyhood home. Originally built in the 12th century, it was ruined by Napoleon. Ludwig's father, King Maximilian II, rebuilt it in 1830. Hohenschwangau ("High Land of the Swans") was used by the royal family as a summer hunting lodge until 1912. This was Ludwig's boyhood escape.

The interior decor is harmonious, cohesive, and original—all done in 1835, with paintings inspired by Romantic themes. The Wittelsbach family (which ruled Bavaria for nearly seven centuries) still owns the place (and lived in the annex—today's shop—until the 1970s). As you tour the castle, imagine how the paintings must have inspired young Ludwig. For 17 years, he followed the construction of his dream castle from his dad's place—you'll see the telescope still set up and directed at Neuschwanstein.

The excellent 30-minute tours give a better glimpse of Ludwig's life than the more-visited and famous Neuschwanstein Castle tour. Tours here are smaller (35 people rather than 60) and more relaxed.

▲▲▲Neuschwanstein Castle

Imagine "Mad" King Ludwig as a boy, climbing the hills above his dad's castle, Hohenschwangau, dreaming up the ultimate

"Mad" King Ludwig

A tragic figure, Ludwig II (a.k.a. "Mad" King Ludwig) ruled Bavaria for 22 years until his death in 1886 at the age of 40. Bavaria was weak. Politically, Ludwig's reality was to "rule" either as a pawn of Prussia or a pawn of Austria. Rather than deal with politics in Bavaria's capital, Munich, Ludwig frittered away most of his time at his family's hunting palace, Hohenschwangau. He spent much of his adult life constructing his fanciful Neuschwanstein Castle—like a kid builds a tree house—on a neighboring hill upon the scant ruins of a medieval castle. Although Ludwig spent 17 years building Neuschwanstein, he lived in it only 172 days.

Ludwig was a true romantic living in a Romantic age. His best friends were artists, poets, and composers such as Richard Wagner. His palaces are wallpapered with misty medieval themes—especially those from Wagnerian operas. Eventually he was declared mentally unfit to rule Bavaria and taken away from Neuschwanstein. Two days after this eviction, Ludwig was found dead in a lake. To this day, people debate whether the king was murdered or committed suicide.

fairy-tale castle. Inheriting the throne at the young age of 18, he had the power to make his dream concrete and stucco. Neuschwanstein (noy-SHVAHN-shtine) was designed by a theater set designer first...then by an architect. It looks medieval, but it's modern iron-and-brick construction with a sandstone veneer—only about as old as the Eiffel Tower. It feels like something you'd see at a home show for 19th-century royalty. Built from 1869 to 1886, it's the epitome of the Romanticism popular in 19th-century Europe. Construction stopped with Ludwig's death (only a third of the interior was finished), and within six weeks, tourists were paying to go through it.

Today, guides herd groups of 60 through the castle, giving an interesting—if rushed—30-minute tour. You'll go up and down more than 300 steps, through lavish rooms based on Wagnerian opera themes, the king's gilded-lily bedroom, and his extravagant throne room. You'll visit 15 rooms with their original furnishings and fanciful wall paintings. After the tour, before you descend to the king's kitchen, see the 20-minute video about the king's life and passions accompanied by Wagner's music (next

Neuschwanstein and Hohenschwangau Castles

to the café, alternates between English and German, schedule board at the entry says what's playing and what's on deck). After the kitchen (state of the art for this high-tech king in its day), you'll see a room lined with fascinating drawings (described in English) of the castle plans, construction, and drawings from 1883 of Falkenstein—a whimsical, over-the-top, never-built castle that makes Neuschwanstein look stubby. Falkenstein occupied Ludwig's fantasies the year he died.

Visiting the Castles

Cost: Each castle costs €9, a *Königsticket* for both castles costs €17, and children under 18 (accompanied by an adult) are admitted free.

Hours: Both castles are open April–Sept daily from 9:00 with last tour departing at 18:00, Oct–March daily from 10:00 with last tour at 16:00.

Getting Tickets for the Castles: Every tour bus in Bavaria converges on Neuschwanstein, and tourists flush in each morning from Munich. A handy reservation system (described below) sorts out the chaos for smart travelers. Tickets come with admission times. To tour both castles, you must do Hohenschwangau first (logical, since this gives a better introduction to Ludwig's short life). You'll get two tour times: Hohenschwangau and then, two hours later, Neuschwanstein. If you miss your appointed tour time, you can't get in.

A **ticket center** for both castles is located at street level between the two (daily April–Sept 8:00–17:00, Oct–March 9:00–15:00, last tickets sold for Neuschwanstein one hour before closing, for Hohenschwangau 30 min before closing). Arrive by 8:00 in summer, and you'll likely be touring by 9:00. During August, tickets for English tours can run out by 16:00.

Reservations: While chaotic crowd scenes are largely a thing of the past, it's smart to reserve in peak season (July–Sept, especially Aug). Reservations cost €2 per person per castle, and you should make them a minimum of 24 hours in advance by phone (tel. 08362/930-830), email (info@ticket-center-hohenschwangau.de), or online (www.ticket-center-hohenschwangau.de).

Tour Procedure: You must pick up tickets well before the appointed entry time (30 min before your Hohenschwangau tour, one hour before your Neuschwanstein tour). Why the long wait? Many of the businesses serving tourists are owned by the old royal family...so they require more waiting time than necessary in the hope that you'll spend more money. The same applies to the minimum allowable time between the two castle tours: two hours. After completing the Hohenschwangau tour, this leaves you with about 45 minutes to kill. Ask for the minimum between tours. If they give you a longer gap, request less downtime.

For each castle, tourists jumble at the entry, waiting for their ticket number to light up on the board. When it does, power through the mob (most waiting there are holding higher numbers) and go to the turnstile. Warning: You must use your ticket while your number is still on the board. If you space out while waiting for a polite welcome, you'll miss your entry window and never get in.

Getting to the Castles: From the ticket booth, Hohenschwangau is an easy 10-minute climb, and Neuschwanstein is a steep 30-minute hike. To minimize hiking to Neuschwanstein, you can take a shuttle bus (leaves every few minutes from in front of Hotel Lisl, just above ticket office and to the left) or a horse-drawn carriage (in front of Hotel Müller, just above ticket office and to the right), but neither gets you to the castle doorstep. The shuttle bus drops you off near Mary's Bridge, leaving you a steep, 10-minute downhill walk to the castle—be sure to see the view from Mary's Bridge before hiking down (€1.80 one-way, the €2.60 round-trip is not worth it since you have to hike uphill to the bus stop for your return trip). Carriages (€5 up, €2.50 down) are slower than walking and stop below Neuschwanstein, leaving you a five-minute uphill hike. Here's the most economic and least strenuous plan: Ride the bus to Mary's Bridge for the view, hike down to Neuschwanstein, and then catch the horse carriage from the castle back down to the parking lot.

Services: The helpful TI, bus stop, ATM, WC (€0.50), and telephones cluster around the main intersection (**TI** open daily May–Sept 11:00–19:00, Oct–April 11:00–17:00, tel. 08362/819-765, www.schwangau.de).

Eating: The "village" at the foot of Europe's Disney castle feeds off the droves of hungry, shop-happy tourists. The Bräustüberl cafeteria serves the cheapest grub (€4 gut-bomb meals, often with live folk music, from 11:30). The Alpsee lake is ideal for a picnic, but there are no grocery shops nearby. Your best bet is to get food to go from one of the many bratwurst stands (between the ticket center and TI) or a sandwich at the shop adjacent the ticket booth. Enjoy a lazy lunch at the lakeside park or in one of the old-fashioned rowboats (rented by the hour in summer).

Near the Castles

Mary's Bridge (Marienbrücke)—Before or after the Neuschwanstein tour, climb up to Mary's Bridge to marvel at Ludwig's castle, just as Ludwig did. This bridge was quite an engineering accomplishment 100 years ago. From the bridge, the frisky can hike even higher to the *Beware—Danger of Death* signs and an even more glorious castle view. (Access to the bridge is closed in bad winter weather, but many travelers walk around the barriers to get there—at their own risk, of course.) For the most interesting descent from Neuschwanstein (15 min longer but worth it, especially with new steel walkways and railings that make the slippery area safer), follow signs to the Pöllat Gorge *(Pöllatschlucht)*.

▲Tegelberg Gondola—Just north of Neuschwanstein is a fun play zone around the mighty Tegelberg Gondola. For €16 round-trip (€10 one-way), you can ride the lift to the 5,500-foot summit (daily 9:00–17:00, closed Nov, 4/hr, last ride at 16:30, in bad weather call first to confirm, tel. 08362/98360; remember, buses #73 and #78 from Füssen continue from the castles to Tegelberg). On a clear day, you get great views of the Alps and Bavaria and the vicarious thrill of watching hang gliders and paragliders leap into airborne ecstasy. Weather permitting, scores of adventurous Germans line up and leap from the launch ramp at the top of the lift. With someone leaving every two or three minutes, it's great for spectators. Thrill-seekers with exceptional social skills may talk themselves into a tandem ride with a paraglider. From the top of Tegelberg, it's a steep and demanding 2.5-hour hike down to Ludwig's castle. (Avoid the treacherous trail directly below the gondola.) At the base of the gondola, you'll find a playground, a cheery eatery, the stubby remains of an ancient Roman villa, and a luge ride (below).

▲Tegelberg Luge—Next to the Tegelberg Gondola is a luge course. A luge is like a bobsled on wheels (for more details, see "Luge Lesson" on page 128). This stainless-steel track is heated, so it's often dry and open, even when drizzly weather shuts down the concrete luges. It's not as scenic as Austria's Biberwier luge (see page 127), but it's handy and half the price (€2.50/ride, 6-ride sharable card-€10, July–Sept daily 10:00–18:00, otherwise same hours as gondola, in winter sometimes opens late due to wet track, in bad weather call first to confirm, no children under 6, tel. 08362/98360). A funky cable system pulls riders (in their sleds) to the top without a ski lift.

▲Royal Crystal Baths (Königliche Kristall-Therme)—This pool/sauna complex just outside Füssen is the perfect way to relax on a rainy day, or to cool off on a hot one. The downstairs contains two heated indoor pools and a café; outside you'll find a shallow kiddie pool, a lap pool, a heated "Kristallbad" with massage jets and a whirlpool, and a salty mineral bath. The extensive saunas upstairs are well worth the few extra euros, as long as you're OK with nudity. (Swimsuits are required in the downstairs pools, but *verboten* in the upstairs saunas.) You'll see pool and sauna rules in German all over, but don't worry—just follow the locals' lead. To enter the baths, first choose the length of your visit and your focus (big outdoor pool only, all ground-floor pools but not the saunas, or the whole enchilada—a flyer explains all the prices in English). You'll get a wristband and a credit-card-sized ticket with a bar code. Insert that ticket into the entry gate, and keep it—you'll need it to get out. Enter through the yellow changing stalls—where you'll change into your bathing suit—then choose a storage locker (€1 coin deposit). When it's time to leave, reinsert your ticket in the gate—if you've gone over the time limit, feed extra euros into the machine (€8.50/2 hrs, €12.20/4 hrs, €15.80/day, saunas-€4, towel rental-€2, bathing suit rental-€3, daily 9:00–22:00, Fri–Sat until 23:00, nude swimming everywhere Tue and Fri after 19:00; from Füssen, drive, bike, or walk across the river, turn left toward Schwangau, and then, about a mile later, turn left at signs for *Kristall-Therme,* Am Ehberg 16; tel. 08362/819-630).

Bike Ride Around Forggensee—On a beautiful day, nothing beats a bike ride around the bright turquoise Forggensee lake. This 20-mile ride is almost exclusively on bike paths, with just a few stretches on country roads. Locals swear that going clockwise is less work, but either way has a couple of strenuous uphill parts. Still, the amazing views of the surrounding Alps will distract you from your churning legs—so this is still a great way to spend the afternoon. Rent a bike (see page 94), pack a picnic lunch, and figure about a three-hour round-trip. From Füssen, follow *Festspielhaus* signs; once you reach the theater, follow *Forggensee Rundweg* signs. From the theater, you can also take a boat ride on the Forggensee (€7/50 min, 6/day; €9.50/2 hrs, 6/day; fewer departures Nov–May, confirm schedule at Füssen TI, tel. 08362/921-363).

SLEEPING

In Hohenschwangau, near Neuschwanstein Castle

(€1 = about $1.50, country code: 49, area code: 08362)

Inexpensive farmhouse *Zimmer* (B&Bs) abound in the Bavarian countryside around Neuschwanstein, offering drivers a decent value. Look for *Zimmer Frei* signs ("room free," or vacancy). The going rate is about €50–65 for a double, including breakfast.

$$ Alpenhotel Meier is a small, family-run hotel with 18 rooms in a bucolic setting within walking distance of the castles, just beyond the lower parking lot (Sb-€48–58, perfectly fine older Db-€80, newer Db-€88, Tb-€110, these are book-direct prices, 5 percent discount with cash and this book in 2009, all rooms have porches or balconies—some with castle views, family rooms, elevator, sauna, free parking, just before tennis courts at Schwangauer Strasse 37, tel. 08362/81152, fax 08362/987-028, www.alpenhotel-allgaeu.de, info@alpenhotel-allgaeu.de, Frau Meier).

$ Beim "Landhannes," a 200-year-old working dairy farm run by Connie Schon, rents six creaky but sunny rooms, and keeps flowers on the balconies, big bells and antlers in the halls, and cows in the yard (Sb-€30, Db-€60, 20 percent discount for 3 or more nights, apartment with kitchen, cash only, poorly signed in the village of Horn on the Füssen side of Schwangau, look for the farm down a tiny lane through the grass 100 yards in front of Hotel Kleiner König, Am Lechrain 22, tel. 08362/8349, www.landhannes.de, mayr@landhannes.de).

$ Sonnenhof is a big, woody, old house with four spacious traditionally decorated rooms (all with balconies) and a cheer garden. It's a 15-minute walk through the fields to the castl

(S-€35, D-€50, Db-€60, cash only; at Pension Schwansee on the Füssen-Neuschwanstein road, follow the small lane 100 yards to Sonnenweg 11; they'll pick you up from the train station if you request ahead, tel. 08362/8420, Frau Görlich).

Wieskirche

Germany's greatest Rococo-style church, this "Church in the Meadow" is newly restored and looking as brilliant as the day it floated down from heaven. It's worth ▲▲. Overripe with decoration but bright and bursting with beauty, this church is a divine droplet, a curly curlicue, the final flowering of the Baroque movement.

Cost and Hours: Donation requested, summer daily 8:00–19:00, winter daily 8:00–17:00, tel. 08862/932-930, www.wieskirche.de.

Getting There: The Wieskirche is a 30-minute drive north of Neuschwanstein. The Romantic Road bus tour stops here for 17 minutes—but only on the northbound route to Frankfurt. Southbound buses stop here to pick up and drop off only on request. For information on taking the bus from Füssen to the Wieskirche, see page 91 in "Getting Around Bavaria and Tirol," earlier in this chapter. By car, head north from Füssen, turn right at Steingaden, and follow the signs. Take a commune-with-nature-and-smell-the-farm detour back through the meadow to the parking lot (€1/hr).

➲ **Self-Guided Tour:** This pilgrimage church is built around the much-venerated statue of a scourged (or whipped) Christ, which supposedly wept in 1738. The carving—too graphic to be accepted by that generation's church—was the focus of worship in a peasant's barn. Miraculously, it shed tears—empathizing with all those who suffer. Pilgrims came from all around. A tiny and humble chapel was built to house the statue in 1739. (You can see it where the lane to the church leaves the parking lot.) Bigger and bigger crowds came. Two of Bavaria's top Rococo architects, the Zimmermann brothers (Johann Baptist and Dominikus), were commissioned to build the Wieskirche that stands here today.

Follow the theological sweep from the altar to the ceiling: Jesus whipped, chained, and then killed (notice the pelican above the altar—recalling a pre-Christian story of a bird that opened its breast to feed its young with its own blood); the painting of a baby Jesus posed as if on the cross; the sacrificial lamb; and finally, high on the ceiling, the resurrected Christ before the Last Judgment. This is the most positive depiction of the Last Judgment around. Jesus, rather than sitting on the throne to judge, rides high on a rainbow—a symbol of forgiveness—giving any sinner the feeling that there is still time to repent, with plenty of mercy on hand. In the back, above the pipe organ, notice the empty throne—waiting for Judgment Day—and the closed door to paradise.

Above the entrances to both side aisles are murky glass cases with 18th-century handkerchiefs. People wept, came here, were healed, and no longer needed their hankies. Walk up either aisle flanking the high altar to see votives—requests and thanks to God (for happy, healthy babies, and so on). Notice how the kneelers are positioned so that worshippers can meditate on scenes of biblical miracles painted high on the ceiling and visible through the ornate tunnel frames. A priest here once told me that faith, architecture, light, and music all combine to create the harmony of the Wieskirche.

Two paintings flank the door at the rear of the church. One shows the ceremonial parade in 1749 when the white-clad monks of Steingaden carried the carved statue of Christ from the tiny church to its new big one. The second painting, from 1757, is a votive from one of the Zimmermann brothers, the artists and architects who built this church. He is giving thanks for the successful construction of the new church.

If you can't visit the Wieskirche, visit one of the other churches that came out of the same heavenly spray can: Oberammergau's church (see next page), Munich's Asamkirche, Würzburg's Hofkirche Chapel (at the Residenz), the splendid Ettal Monastery (free and near Oberammergau, next page and described on page 117), and, on a lesser scale, Füssen's basilica.

Route Tips for Drivers: If you're driving from Wieskirche to Oberammergau, you'll cross the **Echelsbacher Bridge,** which arches 230 feet over the Pöllat Gorge. Thoughtful drivers let their passengers walk across (for the views) and meet them at the other side. Any kayakers? Notice the painting of the traditional village woodcarver (who used to walk from town to town with his art on his back) on the first big house on the Oberammergau side. It holds the Almdorf Ammertal shop, with a huge selection of overpriced carvings and commission-hungry tour guides.

Oberammergau

The Shirley Temple of Bavarian villages, and exploited to the hilt by the tourist trade, Oberammergau wears way too much makeup. If you're passing through anyway, it's a ▲ sight—worth a wander among the half-timbered *Lüftlmalerei* houses frescoed (in a style popular throughout the town in the 18th century) with biblical scenes and famous fairy-tale characters. It's also a relatively convenient home base for visiting Linderhof Castle, Ettal Monastery, and the Zugspitze (via Garmisch).

Tourist Information: The TI is at Eugen-Papst-Strasse 9A (Mon–Fri 9:00–18:00, Sat 10:00–13:00, Sun 10:00–12:00; Nov–May closed Sun; tel. 08822/922-740, www.oberammergau.de).

Getting There

From Füssen to Oberammergau, four to six **buses** run daily (fewer in winter, 1.5 hrs). All buses start at the train station and stop two minutes later near the TI closer to the center. **Trains** run from Munich to Oberammergau (nearly hourly, 1.75 hrs, change in Murnau or Oberau). **Drivers** entering the town from the north should cross the bridge, take the second right, and park in the free lot a block beyond the TI. Leaving town (to Linderhof or Reutte), head out past the church and turn toward Ettal on Road 23. You're 20 miles from Reutte via the scenic Plansee. If heading to Munich, Road 23 takes you to the autobahn, which gets you there in less than an hour.

SIGHTS

Oberammergau Church—Visit the town church, a poor cousin of the one at Wies. Being in a woodcarving center, it's only logical that all the statues are made of wood, and then stuccoed and gilded to look like marble or gold. Saints Peter and Paul flank the altar, where the central painting can be raised to reveal a small stage decorated to celebrate special times during the church calendar. In the central dome, a touching painting shows Peter and Paul bidding each other farewell (with the city of Rome as a backdrop) on the day of their execution—the same day in the year A.D. 67. On the left, Peter is crucified upside-down. On the right, Paul is beheaded with a sword. (A fine little €3 booklet explains it all.) Wander through the lovingly maintained graveyard. A stone WWI and WWII memorial at the gate reads, "We honor and remember the victims of the violence that our land gave the world."

Passion Play—Back in 1633, in the midst of the bloody Thirty Years' War and with horrifying plagues devastating entire cities, the people of Oberammergau promised God that if they were

Oberammergau

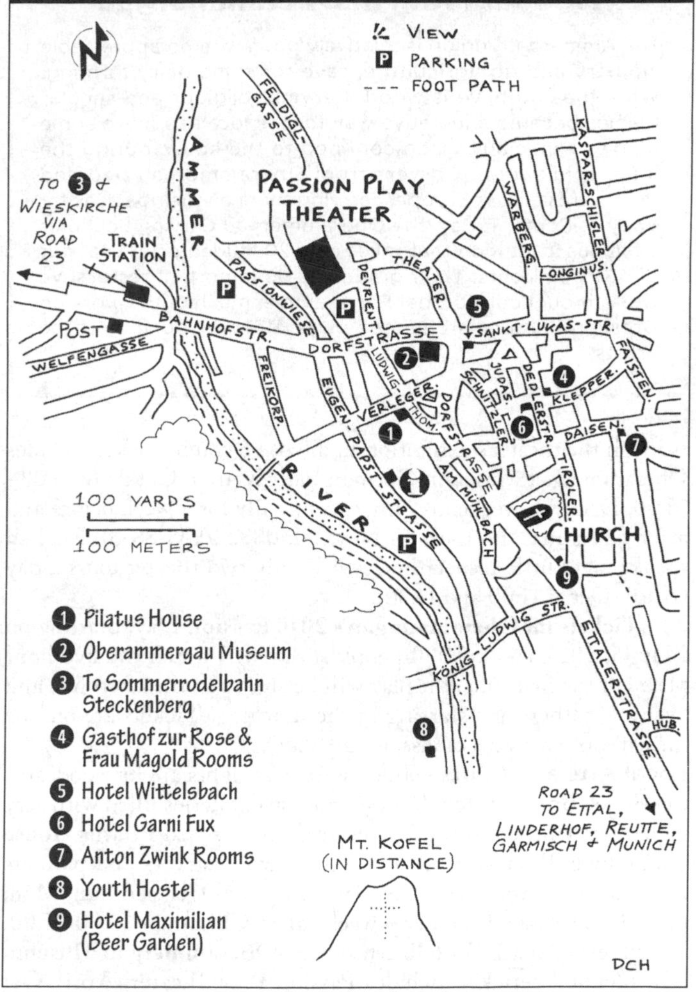

spared from extinction, they'd "perform a play depicting the suffering, death, and resurrection of our Lord Jesus Christ" every decade thereafter. The town survived and, heading into its 41st decade, the people of Oberammergau are still making good on the deal. For 100 days every 10 years (the last one was 2000, the next one is 2010), about half of the town's population (a cast of 2,000) is involved in the production of this extravagant, five-hour Passion Play—telling the story of Jesus' entry into Jerusalem, Crucifixion, and Resurrection. Until 2010, you'll have to settle for reading the book, seeing Nicodemus tool around town in his VW, or browsin

Woodcarving in Oberammergau

The Ammergau region is relatively poor, with no appreciable industry and no agriculture, save for some dairy farming. What they *do* have is wood. Carving religious and secular themes became a lucrative way for the locals to make some money, especially when confined to the house during the long, cold winter. Carvers from Oberammergau peddled their wares across Europe, carrying them on their back as far away as Rome. Today, the Oberammergau Carving School is a famous institution that takes only 20 students per year out of 450 applicants. Their graduates do important restorative work throughout Europe. For example, much of the work on Dresden's Frauenkirche (see page 415) was done by these artists.

through the theater's exhibition hall (€4, €6 combo-ticket includes Oberammergau Museum, German tours March–Oct daily 10:00–16:00, Dec–Feb weekends only except daily for a week before and after Christmas, no tours in Nov, tel. 08822/945-8833). English speakers get little respect here, with only two theater tours a day (April–Oct at 11:00 and 14:30).

Tickets for Oberammergau's 2010 Passion Play: Starting on May 15, 2010, about 5,000 people a day will watch the five-hour play. For the first time, the play will be shown in the afternoon and evening, rather than starting in the morning. Tickets are on sale for €50–165 (www.passionsspiele2010.de).

Local Arts and Crafts—The town's best sights are its woodcarving shops. Browse through these small art galleries filled with very expensive whittled works. The beautifully frescoed **Pilatus House** on Ludwig-Thomas-Strasse often has woodcarvers and painters at work (free; April–Oct Tue–Sat 13:00–18:00, closed Sun–Mon; open Dec weekends and two weeks after Christmas 13:00–17:00; closed rest of year). For folk art, see the **Oberammergau Museum** (€4, €6 combo-ticket includes Passion Play Theater, April–Oct and Dec–Jan Tue–Sun 10:00–17:00, closed Mon; closed Nov and Feb–March, Dorfstrasse 8, tel. 08822/94136, www.oberammergau museum.de).

Sommerrodelbahn Steckenberg—This stainless-steel luge track (near Oberammergau) is faster than the Tegelberg luge, but not quite a wicked as the one in Biberwier (€2.50/ride, €11/6 rides, May–Oct daily 10:00–18:00, closed when wet, Liftweg 1 in Unterammergau, clearly marked and easy 2.5-mile bike ride to Unterammergau along Bahnhofstrasse/Rottenbucherstrasse, take the first left when entering Unterammergau, tel. 08822/4027).

SLEEPING

(€1 = about $1.50, country code: 49, area code: 08822)

$$ Gasthof zur Rose is a big, central, family-run place with 21 rooms (Sb-€40, Db-€65, Tb-€75, Qb-€86, Internet access, Dedlerstrasse 9, tel. 08822/4706, fax 08822/6753, www.hotel-oberammergau.de, gasthof-rose@t-online.de, Frank family).

$$ Hotel Wittelsbach is a romantic, tourist-class hotel. Its creaky, 1970s-style public areas hide 40 deluxe, spacious rooms, many with geranium-clad balconies (Sb-€55–85, Db-€80–110, Tb-€100–140, Dorfstrasse 21, tel. 08822/92800, www.hotelwittelsbach.de, info@hotelwittelsbach.de).

$$ Hotel Garni Fux, quiet and romantic, rents six large rooms and eight apartments decorated in the Bavarian *Landhaus* style (Sb-€65, Db-€84, apartments €106–168, cheaper Nov–April, free Internet access and Wi-Fi, Mannagasse 2a, tel. 08822/93093, www.firmafux.de, info@firmafux.de).

$ Anton Zwink offers 10 small, quiet, no-frills rooms in a neighborhood adjacent to the town center (Sb-€30, Db-€50, behind Gasthof zur Rose at Daisenbergerstrasse 10, tel. 08822/6334, www.pension-zwink.de, info@pension-zwink.de).

$ Frau Magold's is a homey, grandmotherly place with three bright and spacious rooms—twice as nice as the cheap hotel rooms, and for much less money (Db-€48, cash only, also has two family apartments, immediately behind Gasthof zur Rose at Kleppergasse 1, tel. & fax 08822/4340, Christine).

$ The **youth hostel,** on the river, is a short walk from the center (€18 beds, includes breakfast and sheets, tel. 08822/4114, fax 08822/1695, jhoberammergau@djh-bayern.de).

EATING

Locals won't be caught dead inside the chic **Hotel Maximilian.** But they fill its serene beer garden to enjoy the hotel's homemade beer and summertime grill, which cooks up delicious chicken, sausage, and spareribs for under €10 (daily 9:00–22:00, right behind the church, Ettaler Strasse 5, tel. 08822/948-740).

TRANSPORTATION CONNECTIONS

From Oberammergau to: Füssen (4–6 buses/day in summer, transfer at Echelsbacher Brücke, 1.5 hrs total), **Linderhof Castle** (bus #9622, nearly hourly, 25–40 min; some of these also stop at **Ettal Monastery**), **Garmisch** (nearly hourly buses, 40 min; also possible by train with a transfer in Murnau, 1.5 hrs; from Garmisch you can ascend the **Zugspitze**), **Munich** (nearly hourly trains, 1.75 hrs, change in Murnau or Oberau).

Linderhof Castle

This homiest of "Mad" King Ludwig's castles is small and comfortably exquisite—good enough for a minor god, and worth ▲▲. Set in the woods 15 minutes from Oberammergau and surrounded by fountains and sculpted, Italian-style gardens, it's the only palace I've toured that actually had me feeling envious.

Ludwig was king for 22 of his 40 years. He lived much of his last eight years here—the only one of his castles that was finished in his lifetime. Frustrated by the limits of being a "constitutional monarch," he retreated to Linderhof, inhabiting a private fantasy world where extravagant castles glorified his otherwise weakened kingship. He lived here as a royal hermit; his dinner table—pre-set with dishes and food—rose from the kitchen below into his dining room, so he could eat alone.

Beyond the palace is Ludwig's **grotto.** Inspired by Wagner's *Tannhäuser* opera, this performance space is 300 feet long and 70 feet tall. Its rocky walls are actually made of cement poured over an iron frame. The grotto provided a private theater for the reclusive king to enjoy his beloved Wagnerian operas by himself. The first electricity in Bavaria was generated here, to change the colors of the stage lights and to power Ludwig's fountain and wave machine.

Cost and Hours: €7, daily April–Sept 9:00–18:00, Oct–March 10:00–16:00, last tour 30 min before closing, fountains often erupt on the half-hour, tel. 08822/92030.

Getting There: Without a car, getting to (and back from) Linderhof is a royal headache, unless you're staying in Oberammergau. From that village, there is a bus nearly hourly in summer (less frequently off-season; see "Transportation Connections" for Oberammergau, page 115). If you're driving, park near the ticket office (obligatory €2.50).

Visiting the Castle: The complex sits isolated in natural splendor. Plan for lots of walking and a two-hour stop to fully enjoy this royal park. Your ticket comes with an entry time to tour the palace, which is a five-minute hike from the ticket office. At the palace entrance, wait in line for your number to take the required, 30-minute English-language tour. Afterwards, hike 10 minutes uphill to the grotto (take the brief but interesting free tour in English, no reservations necessary). Then see the other royal buildings dotting the king's playground if you like.

Crowd-Beating Tips: July and August crowds can cause delays at the palace of up to two hours. During this period, you're wise to arrive after 15:00. Any other time of year, you should get your palace tour time shortly after you arrive.

Ettal Monastery and Pilgrimage Church

In 1328, the Holy Roman Emperor was returning from Rome with what was considered a miraculous statue of Mary and Jesus. He was in political and financial trouble, so to please God, he founded a monastery with this statue as its centerpiece. The monastery was located here because it was suitably off the beaten path, but today Ettal is on one of the most-traveled tourist routes in Bavaria. Stopping here (free and easy for drivers) offers a convenient peek at a splendid Baroque church.

Cost and Hours: Free, daily 8:00–19:45 in summer, until 18:00 off-season.

Getting There: The Ettal Monastery is a few minutes' **drive** (or a delightful **bike** ride) from Oberammergau. Just park for free and wander in. Some Oberammergau-to-Linderhof **buses** stop here (see "Transportation Connections" for Oberammergau, page 115).

➲ **Self-Guided Tour:** As you enter the more than 1,000-square-foot **courtyard,** imagine the 14th-century Benedictine abbey, an independent religious community. It produced everything it needed right here. In the late Middle Ages, abbeys like this had jurisdiction over the legal system, administration, and taxation of their district. Since then, the monastery has had its ups and downs. Secularized during the French Revolution and Napoleonic age, the Benedictines' property was confiscated by the state and sold. Religious life returned a century later. Today the abbey survives, with 50 or 60 monks. It remains a self-contained community, with living quarters for the monks, workshops, and guests' quarters. Along with their religious responsibilities, the brothers make their famous liqueur, brew beer, run a hotel, and educate 380 students in their private high school.

At the front of the church, you pass a **tympanum** over the door dating from 1350. It shows the founding couple, Emperor Louis the Bavarian and his wife Margaret, directing our attention to the crucified Lord and inviting us to enter the church contemplatively.

Stepping inside, the light draws our eyes to the **dome** (it's a double shell design 230 feet high) rather than to the high altar.

20 † C † M † B † 09

All over Germany (and much of Catholic Europe), you'll likely see written on doorways a mysterious message: "20 † C † M † B † 09." This is marked in chalk on Epiphany (Jan 6), the Christian holiday celebrating the arrival of the Magi to adore the newborn Baby Jesus. In addition to being the initials of the three wise men (Caspar, Melchior, and Balthazar), the letters also stand for the Latin phrase *Christus mansionem benedicat*—"May Christ bless the house." The little crosses separating the letters remind all who enter that the house has been blessed in this year (20†09). Epiphany is a bigger deal in Catholic Europe than in the US. The holiday includes gift-giving, feasting, and caroling door to door—often collecting for a charity organization. Those who donate get their doors chalked up as in thanks, and these marks are left on the door through the year.

Illusions—with the dome opening right to the sky—merge heaven and earth. The dome fresco shows hundreds of Benedictines worshipping the Holy Trinity...the glory of the Benedictine Order. This is classic "south German Baroque."

Statues of the **saints** on the altars are either engaged in a holy conversation with each other or singing the praises of God. Broken shell-style patterns seem to create constant movement, with cherubs adding to the energy. Side altars and confessionals seem to grow out of the architectural structure; its decorations and furnishings become part of an organic whole. Imagine how 18th-century farmers and woodcutters, who never traveled, would step in here on Sunday and be inspired to praise their God.

The origin of the monastery is shown over the **choir arch:** An angel wearing the robe of a Benedictine monk presents the emperor with a marble Madonna and commissions him to found this monastery. (In reality, the statue was made in Pisa, circa 1300, and given to the emperor in Italy.)

Dwarfed by all the magnificence and framed by a monumental tabernacle is that tiny, most precious statue of the abbey—the miraculous **statue of Mary and the baby Jesus**.

Zugspitze

The tallest point in Germany, worth ▲▲, is also a border crossing. Lifts from both Austria and Germany meet at the 9,700-foot summit of the Zugspitze. You can straddle the border between two great nations while enjoying an incredible view. Restaurants, shops, and telescopes await you at the summit.

German Approach: There are two ways to ascend the Zugspitze from Garmisch, Germany (which you can reach by bus from Füssen or Oberammergau—see "Getting Around Bavaria and Tirol," page 90): the whole way by cogwheel train (1.25 hrs one-way), or a faster cogwheel train-plus-cable car option (about 45 min one-way). Both cost the same (€47 round-trip). Although the train ride takes longer, many travelers enjoy the more involved cog-railway experience. The train departs from Garmisch, stops at Eibsee for the cable-car connection, and then continues up—and through—the mountain. The cable car simply zips you to the top in five minutes from the Eibsee station. Cable cars go up daily from 8:15–14:15. The last cable car down departs at about 16:30 (tel. 08821/7970, www.zugspitze.de). Allow plenty of time for afternoon descents: If bad weather hits in the late afternoon, cable cars can be delayed at the summit, causing tourists to miss their train connection from Eibsee back to Garmisch.

Drivers can park for €3 at the cable-car station at Eibsee. Hikers can enjoy the easy six-mile walk around the lovely Eibsee (start 5 min downhill from cable-car station).

Austrian Approach: The Tiroler Zugspitzbahn ascent is less crowded and cheaper. Departing from above the village of Ehrwald (a 30-min train trip from Reutte, every 2 hrs), the tram zips you to the top in 10 minutes (€33 round-trip, departures in each direction at :00, :20, and :40 past the hour, daily 8:40–16:40 except closed April–mid-May and most of mid-Oct–Nov, drivers follow signs for *Tiroler Zugspitzbahn,* free parking, Austrian tel. 05673/2309, www.zugspitze.com). While the German ascent from Garmisch is easier for those without a car, buses connect the Ehrwald train station and the Austrian lift nearly every hour (or pay €8 for the 5-minute taxi ride from Ehrwald train station).

➲ **Self-Guided Tour:** Whether you ascended from the Austrian or German side, you're high enough now to enjoy a little tour of the summit. The two terraces—Bavarian and Tirolean—are connected by a narrow walkway, which was the border station before Germany and Austria opened their borders. The Austrian (Tirolean) side was higher until the Germans blew its top off in World War II to make a flak tower, so let's start there.

Tirolean Terrace: Before you stretches the Zugspitzplatt glacier. Each summer, a 65,000-square-foot reflector is spread over

BAVARIA AND TIROL

the ice to try to slow the shrinking. Since metal ski lift towers collect heat, they, too, are wrapped to try to save the glacier. Many ski lifts fan out here, as if reaching for a ridge that defines the border between Germany and Austria. The circular metal building is the top of the cog-railway line that the Germans cut through the mountains in 1931. Just above that, find a small square building—the wedding chapel *(Hochzeitskapelle)* consecrated in 1981 by Cardinal Joseph Ratzinger (now Pope Benedict XVI).

Both Germany and Austria use this rocky pinnacle for communication purposes. The square box on the Tirolean Terrace provides the Innsbruck airport with air-traffic control, and a tower nearby is for the German *Kathastrophenfunk* (civil defense network).

This highest point in Germany (there are many higher points in Austria) was first climbed in 1820. The Austrians built a cable car that nearly reached the summit in 1926. (You can see it just over the ridge on the Austrian side—look for the ghostly abandoned concrete station.) In 1964, the final leg, a new lift, was built connecting that 1926 station to the actual summit, where you stand now. Before then, people needed to hike the last 650 feet to the top. Today's lift dates from 1980, but was renovated after a 2003 fire. The Austrian station, which is much nicer than the German station, has a fine little museum—free with Austrian ticket, €2 if you came up from Germany—that shows three interesting videos (6-min 3-D mountain show, 30-min making-of-the-lift documentary, and 45-min look at the nature, sport, and culture of the region).

Looking up the valley from the Tirolean Terrace, you can see the towns of Ehrwald and Lermoos in the distance, and the valley that leads to Reutte. Looking farther clockwise, you'll see the Eibsee lake below. Hell's Valley, stretching to the right of Eibsee, seems to merit its name.

Bavarian Terrace: The narrow passage connecting the two terraces used to be a big deal—you'd show your passport here at the little blue house, and shift from Austrian shillings to German marks. Notice the regional pride here: no German or Austrian banners, but regional ones instead—Freistaat Bayern and Land Tirol.

The German side features a golden cross marking the summit... the highest point in Germany. A priest and his friends hauled it up in 1851. The historic original was shot up by Americans soldiers using it for target practice in the late 1940s, so what you see today is a modern replacement. In the summer, it's easy to "summit" the Zugspitze, as there are steps and handholds all they way to the top. Or you can just stay behind and feed the birds. The yellow-beak ravens get chummy with those who share a little pretzel or bread.

The oldest building up here is the rustic, tin-and-wood weather tower, erected in 1900 by the *Deutscher Wetterdienst* (German weather service). The first mountaineers' hut was built in 1897, but didn't last. The existing one—entwined with mighty cables that cinch it down—dates from 1914. In 1985, observers clocked 200-mph winds up here—those cables were necessary. Step inside the restaurant to enjoy museum-like photos and paintings on the wall (including a look at the team who hiked up with the golden cross in 1851).

Reutte, Austria

Reutte (ROY-teh, with a rolled *r*), a relaxed Austrian town of 5,700, is located 20 minutes across the border from Füssen. While overlooked by the international tourist crowd, it's popular with Germans and Austrians for its climate. Doctors recommend its "grade 1" air. I like Reutte for the opportunity to simply be in a real community. As an example of how the town is committed to its character, real estate can be sold only to those using it as a primary residence. (Many formerly vibrant alpine towns made a pile of money but lost their sense of community by becoming resorts. They allowed wealthy foreigners—who just drop in for a week or two a year—to buy up all the land, and are now shuttered up and dead most of the time.)

Reutte's one claim to fame with Americans: As Nazi Germany was falling in 1945, Hitler's top rocket scientist, Werner von Braun, joined the Americans (rather than the Russians) in Reutte. You could say that the American space program began here.

Reutte isn't featured in any other American guidebook. While its generous sidewalks are filled with smart boutiques and lazy coffeehouses, its charms are subtle. It was never rich or important. Its castle is ruined, its buildings have painted-on "carvings," its churches are full, its men yodel for each other on birthdays, and its energy is spent soaking its Austrian and German guests in *Gemütlichkeit.* Most guests stay for a week, so the town's attractions are more time-consuming than thrilling.

ORIENTATION

(country code: 43, area code: 05672)
Remember, Reutte is in a different country. While Austrians use the same currency the Germans do, postage stamps and phone cards only work in the country where you buy them.

To **telephone** from Germany to Austria, dial 00-43- and then the number listed in this section (omitting the initial zero). To call from Austria to Germany, dial 00-49- and then the number (again, omitting the initial zero).

Tourist Information

Reutte's TI is a block in front of the train station (Mon–Fri 8:00–12:00 & 14:00–17:00, no midday break July–Aug, Sat 8:30–12:00, closed Sun, tel. 05672/62336, www.reutte.com). Go over your sightseeing plans, ask about a folk evening, pick up city and biking maps and the *Sommerprogramm* events schedule (in German only), and ask about discounts with the hotel guest cards. Their free informational booklet has a good self-guided town walk.

Arrival in Reutte

If you're coming by car from Germany, skip the north *(Nord)* exit and take the south *(Süd)* exit into town. For parking in town, blue lines denote pay-and-display spots. There is a free lot (P-1) near the train station on Muhlerstrasse.

While Austria requires a **toll sticker** *(Vignette)* for driving on its highways (€8/10 days, buy at the border, gas stations, car-rental agencies, or *Tabak* shops), those just dipping into Tirol from Bavaria do not need one.

Helpful Hints

Internet Access: There's a **call shop** at Untermarkt 22 in the town center (Tue–Sun 11:00–22:00, closed Mon), and **Café Alte Post** at Untermarkt 15 has Internet access. Otherwise, rely on your hotel.

Laundry: There isn't an actual launderette in town, but the recommended hotels Maximilian and Ernberg let even non-guests use their self-service machines (see page 130).

Bike Rental: Try **Intersport** (€15/day, Mon–Fri 9:00–18:00, Sat 9:00–17:00, closed Sun, Lindenstrasse 25, tel. 05672/62352), or check at Hotel Maximilian (see page 130).

Car Rental: Autoreisen Köck rents cars at Muhlerstrasse 12 (€80/24 hrs, tel. 05672/62233).

"Nightlife": Reutte is pretty quiet. For any action at all, there's a strip of bars, dance clubs, and Italian restaurants on Lindenstrasse.

SIGHTS AND ACTIVITIES

▲▲Ehrenberg Castle Ensemble (Festungsensemble Ehrenberg)

If Neuschwanstein was the medieval castle dream, Ehrenburg is the medieval castle reality. Just a mile outside of Reutte are the brooding ruins of four castles that once made up the largest fort in Tirol. This impressive "castle ensemble" was built to defend against the Bavarians and to bottle up the strategic Via Claudia trade route, which cut through the Alps as it connected Italy and Germany. Today, these castles have become a European "castle museum," showing off 500 years of military architecture in one swoop. The European Union is helping fund the project (paying a third of its €9 million cost) because it promotes the heritage of a multinational region—Tirol—rather than a country.

The complex has four parts: the fortified Klause toll both on the valley floor, the oldest castle on the first hill above (Ehrenberg), a mighty and more modern castle high above (Schlosskopf, built in the age when cannon positioned there made the original castle vulnerable), and a smaller fourth castle across the valley (Fort Claudia, an hour's hike away). All four were a fortified complex once connected by walls. Signs posted throughout the castle complex help visitors find their way and explain some background on the region's history, geology, geography, culture, flora, and fauna. (While the castles are free and open all the time, the museum and multimedia show at the fort's parking lot charge admission.)

Getting to the Castle Ensemble: The Klause, Ehrenberg, and Schlosskopf castles are on the road to Lermoos and Innsbruck. These are a pleasant walk or a short bike ride from Reutte; bikers can use the *Radwanderweg* along the Lech River (the TI has a good map).

▲Klause Valley Fort Museum—Historians estimate that about 10,000 tons of precious salt passed through this valley (along the route of Rome's Via Claudia) each year in medieval times, so it's no wonder the locals built this complex of fortresses and castles. Beginning in the 14th century, the fort controlled traffic and levied tolls on all who passed. Today, these scant remains hold a museum and a theater with a multimedia show (€8 for museum, €11 comboticket also includes multimedia show, €18 family pass for 2 adults and any number of kids, daily 10:00–17:00, closed Nov–mid-Dec, tel. 05672/62007, www.ehrenberg.at).

Reutte

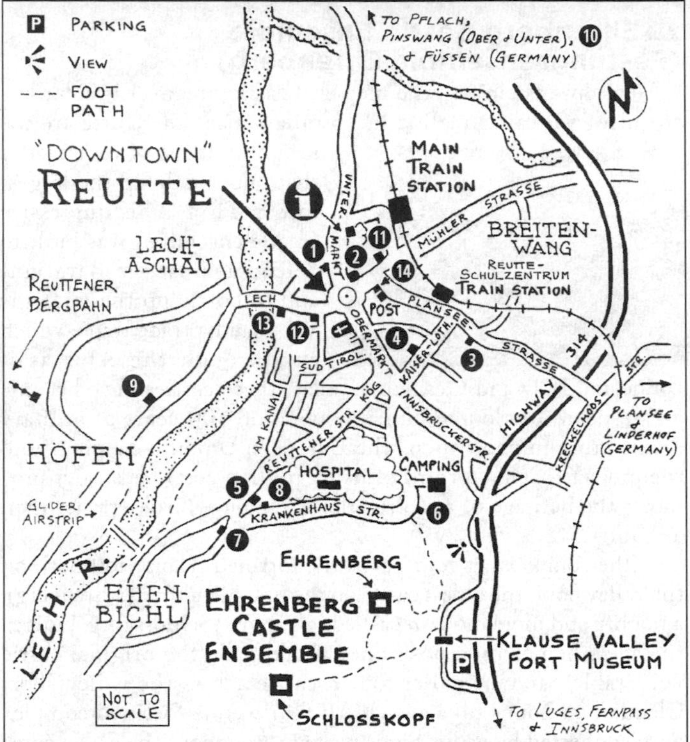

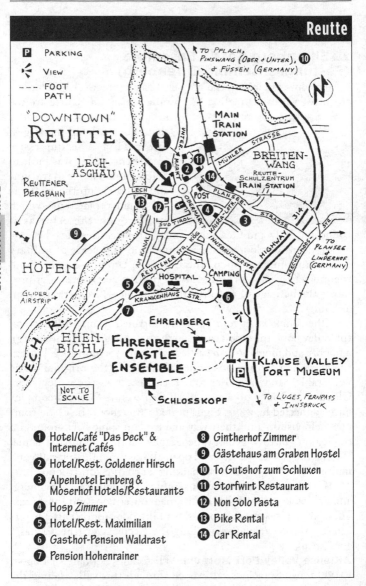

1. Hotel/Café "Das Beck" & Internet Cafés
2. Hotel/Rest. Goldener Hirsch
3. Alpenhotel Ernberg & Moserhof Hotels/Restaurants
4. Hosp *Zimmer*
5. Hotel/Rest. Maximilian
6. Gasthof-Pension Waldrast
7. Pension Hohenrainer
8. Gintherhof Zimmer
9. Gästehaus am Graben Hostel
10. To Gutshof zum Schluxen
11. Storfwirt Restaurant
12. Non Solo Pasta
13. Bike Rental
14. Car Rental

While there are no real artifacts here (other than the sword used in A.D. 2008 to make me the honorary First Knight of Ehrenberg), the clever, kid-friendly **museum** takes one 14th-century decade (1360–1370) and attempts to bring it to life. It's a hands-on experience, well-described in English. You can try on a set of armor (and then weigh yourself), see the limited vision knights had to put up with when wearing their helmet, empathize with victims of the plague, and join a Crusade.

The **multimedia show** takes you on a 30-minute spin through the 2,000-year history of this valley's fortresses, with images projected on the old stone walls and modern screens (generally in German, in English at 13:00 or sometimes by request).

▲▲**Ehrenberg Ruins**—Ehrenberg, a 13th-century rock pile, provides a super opportunity to let your imagination off its leash.

Hike up 30 minutes from the parking lot of the Klause Valley Fort Museum for a great view from your own private ruins. Ehrenberg (which means "Mountain of Honor") was the first castle here, built in 1296. Thirteenth-century castles were designed to stand boastfully tall. With the advent of gunpowder, castles dug in. (Notice the 18th-century **ramparts** around you.)

Approaching Ehrenberg Castle, look for the small **door** to the left. It's the night entrance (tight and awkward, and therefore safer against a surprise attack). Entering this castle, you go through two doors. Castles allowed step-by-step retreat, giving defenders time to regroup and fight back against invading forces.

Before climbing to the top of the castle, follow the path around to the right to a big, grassy courtyard with commanding views and a fat, newly restored **turret.** This stored gunpowder and held a big cannon that enjoyed a clear view of the valley below. In medieval times, all the trees approaching the castle were cleared to keep an unobstructed view.

Look out over the valley. The pointy spire marks **Breitenwang,** which was a stop on the ancient Via Claudia. In A.D. 46, there was a Roman camp there. In 1489, after the Reutte bridge crossed the Lech River, Reutte (marked by the onion-domed church) was made a market town and eclipsed Breitenwang in importance. Any gliders circling? They launch from just over the river in Höfen.

For centuries, this castle was the seat of government—ruling an area called the "judgment of Ehrenberg" (roughly the same as today's "district of Reutte"). When the emperor came by, he stayed here. In 1604, the ruler moved downtown into more comfortable quarters, and the castle was no longer a palace.

Now climb to the top of Ehrenberg Castle. Take the high ground. There was no water supply here—just kegs of wine, beer, and a cistern to collect rain.

Ehrenberg repelled 16,000 Swedish soldiers in the defense of Catholicism in 1632. Ehrenberg saw three or four other battles, but its end was not glorious. In the 1780s, a local businessman bought the castle in order to sell off its parts. Later, in the late 19th century, when vagabonds moved in, the roof was removed to make squatting miserable. With the roof gone, deterioration quickened, leaving only this evocative shell and a whiff of history.

▲**Schlosskopf**—From Ehrenberg, you can hike up another 30 minutes to the mighty Schlosskopf ("Castle Head"). When the Bavarians captured Ehrenberg in 1703, the Tiroleans climbed up to the bluff above it to rain cannonballs down on their former fortress. In 1740, a mighty new castle—designed to defend against modern artillery—was built on this sky-high strategic location. By the end of the 20th century, the castle was completely overgrown with trees—you literally couldn't see it from Reutte. But today the trees are shaved away, and the castle has been excavated. In 2008, the Castle Ensemble project, led by local architect Armin Walch, opened the site with English descriptions and view platforms. One spot gives spectacular views of the strategic valley. The other looks down on the older Ehrenberg Castle ruins, illustrating the strategic problems presented with the advent of cannon.

In Reutte

Reutte Museum (Museum Grünes Haus)—Reutte's city museum, offering a quick look at the local folk culture and the story of the castles, is more cute than impressive. Perhaps someday a little English will bring more meaning to the exhibits (€2, May–Oct Tue–Sun 10:00–16:00, closed Mon and Nov–April, in the bright-green building on Untermarkt, around corner from Hotel Goldener Hirsch, tel. 05672/72304, www.museum-reutte.at).

▲▲**Tirolean Folk Evening**—Ask the TI or your hotel if there's a Tirolean folk evening scheduled. During the summer (July–Aug), nearby towns (such as Höfen on Tuesdays) occasionally put on an evening of yodeling, slap dancing, and Tirolean frolic. These are generally free and worth the short drive. Off-season, you'll have to do your own yodeling. There are also weekly folk concerts featuring the local choir or brass band in Reutte's Zeiller Platz (free, July–Aug only, ask at TI). For listings of these and other local events, pick up a copy of the German-only *Sommerprogramm* schedule at the TI.

▲**Flying and Gliding**—For a major thrill on a sunny day, drop by the tiny airport in Höfen across the river and fly. A small, single-prop plane can buzz the Zugspitze and Ludwig's castles and give you a bird's-eye peek at Reutte's Ehrenberg ruins (2 people for 30 min-€110, 1 hr-€220, tel. 05672/63207, phone rarely answered and then not in English, so your best bet is to show up at the Höfen airport on good-weather afternoons). Or, for something more angelic, how about *Segelfliegen?* For €40, you get 30 minutes in a glider for two (you and the pilot, €60/1 hr) from Segelflugverein

Ausserfern. Just watching the towrope launch the graceful glider like a giant, slow-motion rubber-band gun is exhilarating (May–mid-Sept 12:00–19:00, sometimes in April and Oct if not too snowy, in good but breezy weather only, find someone in the know at the "Thermik Ranch," tel. 05672/71550, mobile 0676-557-1085, www.segelflugverein-ausserfern.at).

Reuttener Bergbahn—This mountain lift swoops you high above the tree line to a starting point for several hikes and an alpine flower park, with special paths leading you past countless varieties of local flora. Unique to this lift is a barefoot hiking trail *(Barfusswanderweg),* designed to be walked without shoes—no joke (€10 one-way, €14 round-trip, flowers best in late July, runs usually mid-June–Oct daily 9:00–12:00 & 13:00–17:00, weekends only in spring and fall, across the river in Höfen, tel. 05672/62420, www.reuttener-seilbahnen.at).

Near Reutte

Bird Lookout Tower—Between Reutte and Füssen is a pristine (if you get past the small local industrial park) nature preserve with an impressive wooden tower from which to appreciate the vibrant bird life in the wetlands along the Lech River. Look for *Vogel-Erlebnispfad* signs as you're driving through the village of Pflach (on the road between Reutte and Füssen). The EU gave half the money needed to enjoy the nature preserve—home to 110 different species of birds that nest here. The best action is early in the day. Be quiet, as eggs are being laid.

▲▲Biberwier Luge Course—Near Lermoos, on the road from Reutte toward Innsbruck, you'll find the Biberwier *Sommerrodelbahn*. At 4,250 feet, it's the longest in the Tirol (20 min from Reutte, stay on main road, Biberwier is the first exit after a long tunnel). The only drawbacks are its brief season, short hours, and a proclivity for shutting down sporadically—even at the slightest bit of rain (€6.60/ride, less for 3-, 5-, and 10-ride tickets, late May–mid-Oct daily 9:00–16:30, closed mid-Oct–late May, tel. 05673/2111, regional TI is more likely to have info in English—tel. 05673/20000). If you don't have a car, this is not worth the trouble; consider the luge near Neuschwanstein instead (see "Tegelberg Luge," page 108). Daredevils may want to rent the "monster roller" to literally skateboard down the mountain (€7 for the roller, €10/2 hrs lift usage). The ugly cube-shaped building marring the countryside near the luge course is a hotel for outdoor adventure enthusiasts. You can ride your mountain bike right into your room, or skip the elevator by using its indoor climbing wall.

▲Fallerschein—Easy for drivers and a special treat for those who may have been Kit Carson in a previous life, this extremely remote log-cabin village is a 4,000-foot-high, flower-speckled world of

Luge Lesson

Taking a wild ride on a luge (pronounced "loozh") is a quintessential alpine experience. It's also called a *Sommerrodelbahn,* or "summer toboggan run." To try one of Europe's great accessible thrills (€3-6), take the lift up to the top of a mountain, grab a wheeled, sled-like go-cart, and scream back down the mountainside on a banked course. Then take the lift back up and start all over again.

Luge courses are highly weather-dependent, and can close at the least hint of rain. If the weather's questionable, call ahead to confirm that your preferred luge is open. Stainless-steel courses are more likely to stay open in drizzly weather than concrete ones.

Operating the sled is simple: Push the stick forward to go faster, pull back to apply brakes. Even a novice can go very, very fast. Most are cautious on their first run, speed demons on their second...and many end up bruised and bloody on their third. A woman once showed me her travel journal illustrated with her husband's dried, five-inch-long luge scab. He had disobeyed the only essential rule of luging: Keep both hands on your stick. To avoid getting into a bumper-to-bumper traffic jam, let the person in front of you get way ahead before you start. You'll emerge from the course with a windblown hairdo and a smile-creased face.

serene slopes and cowbells. Thunderstorms roll down the valley like it's God's bowling alley, but the pint-size church on the high ground, blissfully simple in a land of Baroque, seems to promise that this huddle of houses will survive, and the river and breeze will just keep flowing. The couples sitting on benches are mostly Austrian vacationers who've rented cabins here. Some of them, appreciating the remoteness of Fallerschein, are having affairs.

Sleeping in Fallerschein: **$ Lottes Fallerscheiner Stube** is a family-friendly mountain-hut restaurant with a low-ceilinged attic space that has basic beds for up to 17 sleepy hikers. The accommodations aren't fancy, but if you're looking for remote, this is it (dorm bed-€9, sheets-€4, open May–Oct only, closed Tue, wildlife viewing deck, tel. 05632/2140, www.alpe-fallerschein.at, Gapp family).

Getting to Fallerschein: From Reutte, it's a 45-minute drive. Take road 198 to Stanzach (passing Weisenbach am Loch, then Forchach), then turn left toward Namlos. Follow the L-21 Berwang road for about five miles to a parking lot. From there, it's a two-mile walk down a drivable but technically closed one-lane road. Those driving in do so at their own risk.

SLEEPING

In and near Reutte

(€1 = about $1.50, country code: 43, area code: 05672)
Reutte is a mellow Füssen with fewer crowds and easygoing locals with a contagious love of life. Come here for a good dose of Austrian ambience and lower prices. While it's workable on public transit, staying here makes most sense for those with a car. Reutte is popular with Austrians and Germans, who come here year after year for one- or two-week vacations. The hotels are big, elegant, and full of comfy, carved furnishings and creative ways to spend lots of time in one spot. They take great pride in their restaurants, and the owners send their children away to hotel-management schools. All include a great breakfast, but few accept credit cards. Most hotels give about a 5 percent discount for stays of two nights or longer.

The Reutte TI has a list of 50 private homes that rent out generally good rooms *(Zimmer)* with facilities down the hall, pleasant communal living rooms, and breakfast. Most charge €20 per person per night, and the owners speak little or no English. As these are family-run places, it is especially important to cancel in advance if your plans change. I've listed a few favorites below, but the TI can always find you a room when you arrive.

Reutte is surrounded by several distinct "villages" that basically feel like suburbs—many of them, such as Breitenwang (described on next page), within easy walking distance of the Reutte town center. If you want to hike through the woods to Neuschwanstein Castle, stay at Gutshof zum Schluxen (listed on page 132). To locate the recommended accommodations, see the map on page 124. Remember, to call Reutte from Germany, dial 00-43- and then the number (minus the initial zero).

In Central Reutte

$$ Hotel "Das Beck" offers 16 clean, sunny rooms (many with balconies) filling a modern building in the heart of town. It's a great value, and guests are personally taken care of by Hans, Inge, Tamara, and Pipi. Enjoy their homemade marmalade at breakfast in the open kitchen/coffee bar or on the pleasant patio. Their small café offers tasty snacks and specializes in Austrian and Italian wines. Expect good conversation overseen by Hans (Sb-€45, Db-€68, Tb suite-€89, Qb suite-€106, Internet access free for Rick Steves readers, free parking, they'll pick you up from the train station, Untermarkt 11, tel. 05672/62522, fax 05672/625-2235, www.hotel-das-beck.at, info@hotel-das-beck.at).

$$ Hotel Goldener Hirsch, located in the center of Reutte just two blocks from the station, is a grand old hotel with 56 rooms and one lonely set of antlers (Sb-€58–62, Db-€85–90, Db suite-€90–98, Tb-€125–135, Qb-€140–145, 2-night discounts, elevator, tel. 05672/62508, fax 05672/625-087, www.goldener-hirsch.at, info@goldener-hirsch.at; Monika, Helmut, and daughters Vanessa and Nina).

In Breitenwang

Right next door to Reutte is the older and quieter village of Breitenwang (with good *Zimmer* and a fine bakery). It's a 20-minute walk from the Reutte train station: At the post office roundabout, follow Planseestrasse past the onion-dome church to the pointy straight-dome church near the two hotels. The Hosps—as well as other B&Bs—are along unmarked Kaiser-Lothar-Strasse, the first right past this church. If your train stops at the tiny Reutte-Schulzentrum station, hop out here—you're just a five-minute walk from here.

$$ Alpenhotel Ernberg is run with great care by friendly Hermann, who combines Old World elegance with modern touches. Nestle in for some serious coziness among the carved-wood eating nooks, tiled stoves, and family-friendly backyard (Sb-€45, Db-€84, less for longer stays, self-service laundry for €7—also available for non-guests, restaurant, Planseestrasse 50, tel. 05672/71912, fax 05672/191-240, www.ernberg.at, info@ernberg.at).

$$ Moserhof Hotel has 30 new-feeling rooms plus an elegant dining room (Sb-€52, Db-€88, these special rates promised in 2009 if you ask for the Rick Steves discount when you reserve, extra bed-€35, most rooms have balconies, elevator, restaurant, free parking, Planseestrasse 44, tel. 05672/62020, fax 05672/620-2040, www.hotel-moserhof.at, info@hotel-moserhof.at, Hosp family).

$ Walter and Emilie Hosp rent three rooms in a comfortable, quiet, and modern house two blocks from the Breitenwang church steeple. You'll feel like you're staying at Grandma's (D-€40, or €36 for 4 nights or more, T-€60, Q-€80, cash only, Kaiser-Lothar-Strasse 29, tel. 05672/65377).

In Ehenbichl, near the Ehrenberg Ruins

The next listings are a bit farther from central Reutte, a couple of miles upriver in the village of Ehenbichl (under the Ehrenberg ruins). From central Reutte, go south on Obermarkt and turn right on Kög, which becomes Reuttener Strasse, following signs to *Ehenbichl.*

$$ Hotel Maximilian is a great value. It includes free bicycles, table tennis, a children's playroom, a pool table, and the friendly service of Gabi, Monika, and the rest of the Koch family. They host many special events, and their hotel has lots of wonderful extras such as a sauna and a piano (Sb-€48–52, Db-€76–84, ask for these special Rick Steves prices when you reserve, family deals, elevator, free Internet access and Wi-Fi, laundry service for €12—or €16 for non-guests, good restaurant, tel. 05672/62585, fax 05672/625-8554, www.maxihotel.com, info@hotelmaximilian.at). They rent cars to guests only (one Renault, one VW van—€0.72/km, book in advance) and bikes to anyone (€6/half-day, €10/day).

$ Gasthof-Pension Waldrast, separating a forest and a meadow, is run by the farming Huter family. The place feels hauntingly quiet and has no restaurant, but it's inexpensive and offers 10 nice rooms with generous sitting areas and castle-view balconies (Sb-€37, Db-€60, Tb-€75, Qb-€95; discounts with this book in 2009: 5 percent for 2 nights, 10 percent for 3 nights or more; cash only, all rooms non-smoking, free parking; about a mile from Reutte, just off main drag toward Innsbruck, past campground and under castle ruins on Ehrenbergstrasse; tel. & fax 05672/62443, www.waldrasttirol.com, info@waldrasttirol.com, Gerd).

$ Pension Hohenrainer, a big, quiet, no-frills place, is a good value with 12 modern rooms and some castle-view balconies (Sb-€25–30, Db-€49–55, €3 per person extra for one-night stays, cheaper for longer stays and in April–June and Sept–Oct, cash only, family rooms, non-smoking rooms, free Internet access, restaurant across the street, follow signs up the road behind Hotel Maximilian into village of Ehenbichl, tel. 05672/62544 or 05672/63262, fax 05672/62052, www.hohenrainer.at, hohenrainer@aon.at).

$ Gintherhof is a working farm that provides its guests with fresh milk, butter, and bacon. Christl and Rudi Ginther offer geranium-covered balconies, six nice rooms with carved-wood ceilings, and a Madonna in every corner (Db-€46–50, Unterried 7, just up the road behind Hotel Maximilian, tel. 05672/67697, www.gintherhof.com, gintherhof@aon.at).

A Hostel Across the River

$ The homey **Gästehaus am Graben hostel** has 2–6 beds per room and includes breakfast and sheets. It's lovingly run by the Reyman family—Frau Reyman, Rudi, and Gabi keep the 50-bed place traditional, clean, and friendly, and they serve guests a great €7 dinner. This is a super value less than two miles from Reutte, and the castle views are fantastic. If you've never hosteled and are curious (and have a car or don't mind a bus ride), try it. If traveling with kids, this is a great choice. The double rooms are hotel-grade, and they accept non-members of any age (dorm bed-€22, bunk-bed D-€44, hotel-style Db-€56, cash only, non-smoking rooms, laundry service, no curfew, closed April and Nov–mid-Dec; from downtown Reutte, cross bridge and follow main road left along river, or take the bus—hourly until 19:30, ask for Graben stop, no buses Sun; Graben 1, tel. 05672/626-440, fax 05672/626-444, www.hoefen.at, info@hoefen.at).

In Pinswang

The village of Pinswang is closer to Füssen (and Ludwig's castles), but still in Austria.

$$ Gutshof zum Schluxen gets the "Remote Old Hotel in an Idyllic Setting" award. This family-friendly working farm offers rustic elegance draped in goose down and pastels, and a chance to pet a rabbit and feed the deer. Its picturesque meadow setting will turn you into a dandelion picker, and its proximity to Neuschwanstein will turn you into a hiker; the castle is just an hour's hike away—see page 103 (Sb-€45, Db-€78, extra person-€22, these prices with this book in 2009, 5 percent discount for stays of 3 or more nights, self-service laundry, mountain-bike rental, restaurant, fun bar, between Reutte and Füssen in village of Pinswang, free pick-up from Reutte or Füssen, call ahead if you'll arrive after 18:00, tel. 05677/8903, fax 05677/890-323, www.schluxen.com, welcome@schluxen.com).

EATING

In Reutte

The hotels here take great pride in serving local cuisine at reasonable prices to their guests and the public. Rather than go to a cheap restaurant, eat at a hotel. Most offer €8–14 dinners from 18:00 to 21:00 and are closed one night a week. Reutte itself has plenty of inviting eateries, including traditional, ethnic, fast food, grocery stores, and delis.

Since hospitality is such a big part of the local scene, **hotel restaurants** are generally your best bet for a good meal. Hotel Goldener Hirsch, Alpenhotel Ernberg, Moserhof Hotel, and Hotel Maximilian all offer fine restaurants (see each listing under "Sleeping," earlier in this section).

Storfwirt is *the* place for a quick and cheap lunch or light dinner. You can get the usual sausages here, as well as baked potatoes and salads (€5–8 daily meals, salad bar, always something for vegetarians, Mon–Fri 8:30–15:00, Sat 9:00–14:30, closed Sun, Schrettergasse 15, tel. 05672/62640).

Non Solo Pasta, just off the traffic circle, is a local favorite for Italian food (€7 pizzas, €7–10 entrées, Mon–Fri 11:30–14:00 & 18:00–23:00, Sat 18:00–23:00, closed Sun, Lindenstrasse 1, tel. 05672/72714).

Picnic Supplies: **Billa** supermarket has everything you'll need (across from TI, Mon–Fri 8:00–19:00, Sat 8:00–17:00, closed Sun).

TRANSPORTATION CONNECTIONS

From Reutte by Train to: Ehrwald (at base of Zugspitze lift, every 2 hrs, 30 min), **Garmisch** (every 2 hrs, 1 hr), **Innsbruck** (every 2 hrs, 2.5 hrs, change in Garmisch), **Munich** (every 2 hrs, 2.5 hrs, change in Garmisch).

By Bus to: Füssen (Mon–Fri 4/day, none Sat–Sun, 35 min, €3.40, buses depart from in front of the train station, pay driver). Taxis cost €30 one-way to Füssen, or €35 to the King's Castles.

SALZBURG (AUSTRIA) and BERCHTESGADEN

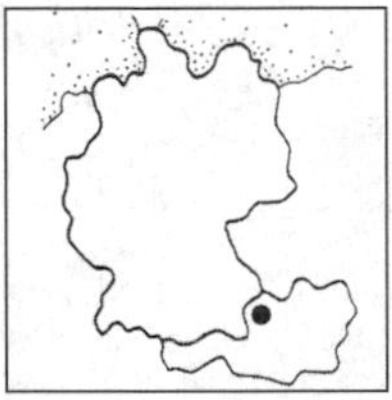

Salzburg, just over the Austrian border, makes a fun day trip from Munich (two hours by direct train). Salzburg is forever smiling to the tunes of Mozart and *The Sound of Music.* Thanks to its charmingly preserved old town, splendid gardens, Baroque churches, and Europe's largest intact medieval fortress, Salzburg feels made for tourism. It's a museum city with class. Vagabonds wish they had nicer clothes.

Nearly next door to Salzburg is Berchtesgaden, a German alpine town enjoyed by Hitler and nature-lovers.

Planning Your Time

While Salzburg's sights are mediocre, the town itself is a Baroque museum of cobbled streets and elegant buildings—simply a touristy stroller's delight. Even on a day trip from Munich, consider allowing half a day for the *Sound of Music* tour. The *S.O.M.* tour kills a nest of sightseeing birds with one ticket (city overview, *S.O.M.* sights, and a fine drive through the lakes).

You'd probably enjoy two nights for Salzburg—nights are important for swilling beer in atmospheric local gardens and attending concerts in Baroque halls and chapels. Seriously consider one of Salzburg's many evening musical events (a few are free, some are as cheap as €12, and most average €30–40).

To get away from it all, bike down the river or hike across the Mönchsberg. Or consider a day trip to Berchtesgaden, just 12 miles away in Germany. Berchtesgaden is much easier to reach from Salzburg (30-minute direct bus ride) than Munich (2.5- to 3-hour train ride with transfer).

Salzburg

Even without Mozart and the von Trapps, Salzburg is steeped in history. In about A.D. 700, Bavaria gave Salzburg to Bishop Rupert for his promise to Christianize the area. Salzburg remained an independent state until Napoleon came (about 1800). Thanks in part to its formidable fortress, Salzburg managed to avoid the ravages of war for 1,200 years...until World War II. Much of the city was destroyed by WWII bombs (mostly around the train station), but the historic old town survived.

Eight million tourists crawl its cobbles each year. That's a lot of Mozart balls—and all that popularity has led to a glut of businesses hoping to catch the tourist dollar. Still, Salzburg is both a must and a joy.

ORIENTATION

(country code: 43, area code: 0662)
Salzburg, a city of 150,000 (Austria's fourth-largest), is divided into old and new. The old town, sitting between the Salzach River and its mini-mountain (Mönchsberg), holds nearly all the charm and most of the tourists. The new town, across the river, has its own share of sights and museums, plus some good accommodations.

Tourist Information

Salzburg has three helpful TIs (main tel. 0662/889-870, www.salzburg.info): at the **train station** (daily June–Sept 8:15–20:00, often later July–Aug, Oct–May 8:45–19:00, tel. 0662/8898-7340), on **Mozartplatz** in the old center (daily 9:00–18:00, July–mid-Sept until 19:00, tel. 0662/8898-7330), and at the **Salzburg Süd park-and-ride** (generally open 10:00–18:00, often closed Mon–Tue, closed in winter, tel. 0662/8898-7360). At any TI, you can pick up a free city-center map (the €0.70 map has a broader coverage and more information on sights, but probably isn't necessary), the Salzburg Card brochure (listing sights with current hours and prices), and a bimonthly schedule of events. Book a concert upon arrival. The TIs also book rooms for a fee.

Salzburg Card: The TIs sell the Salzburg Card, which covers all your public transportation (including elevator and funicular) and admission to all the city sights (including Hellbrunn Castle and the river cruise). The card is pricey (€23/24 hrs, €31/48 hrs, €36/72 hrs), but if you'd like to pop into all the sights without concern for the cost, this can save money and enhance your experience. To analyze your potential savings, here are the major sights and what you'd pay without the card: Hohensalzburg Fortress and funicular-€10; Mozart's Birthplace and Residence-€10; Hellbrunn Castle-€8.50; Salzburg Panorama 1829-€2; Salzach River cruise-€13; 24-hour transit pass-€3.40. Busy sightseers can save plenty. Get this card, feel the financial pain once, and the city will be all yours.

Arrival in Salzburg

By Train: The Salzburg station is user-friendly. The TI is at track 2A. Downstairs at street level, you can store your luggage, buy tickets, and get train information. Bike rental is nearby (see "Getting Around Salzburg"). City buses depart from the lot facing the station (monitors clearly show each bus' destination—any bus heading for *Zentrum* stops near the main bridge in the old town, including buses #1, #5, #6, and #25; get off at the first stop after you cross the river for most sights and city-center hotels, or just before the bridge for Linzergasse hotels). Figure €7 for a taxi to the center. To walk downtown (15 minutes), leave the station ticket hall to the left, and walk straight down Rainerstrasse, which leads under the tracks past Mirabellplatz, turning into Dreitaltigkeitsgasse. From here, you can turn left onto Linzergasse for many of the recommended hotels, or cross the Staatsbrücke bridge for the old town (and more hotels). For a more dramatic approach, leave the station the same way but follow the tracks to the river, turn left, and walk the riverside path toward the fortress.

By Car: Follow *Zentrum* signs to the center, and park short-term on the street (3-hour limit, pay at meter) or longer in the various garages (best under Mönchsberg mountain, €14/day). Ask at your hotel for suggestions. (For more driving and parking tips, see "Transportation Connections," page 177.)

Helpful Hints

Recommendations Skewed by Kickbacks: Salzburg is addicted to the tourist dollar, and it can never get enough. Virtually all hotels are on the take when it comes to concert and tour recommendations, influenced more by their potential kickback than by what's best for you. Take their advice with a grain of salt.

Internet Access: The Internet kiosk a few doors down from the Mozartplatz TI is well-located, but too expensive (€2/10 min). Cheaper places around the old town aren't hard to find. Two Internet cafés at the bottom of the cliff, between Getreidegasse and the Mönchsberg lift, have good prices and hours (€2/hr, daily 10:00–22:00).

Across the river, there's a big, handy Internet café on Theatergasse (near Mozart's Residence, €2/hr, daily 9:00–23:00), and plenty more near the station (including **Bubblepoint,** a modern launderette—see "Laundry" below). Readers of this book can get online free at the Panorama Tours terminal on Mirabellplatz (daily 8:00–18:00).

Post Office: A full-service post office is located in the heart of town, in the new Residenz (Mon–Fri 7:00–18:30, Sat 8:00–10:00, closed Sun).

Laundry: The launderette at the corner of Paris-Lodron-Strasse and Wolf-Dietrich-Strasse, near my recommended Linzergasse hotels, is handy (€10 self-service, €15 same-day full-service, Mon–Fri 7:30–18:00, Sat 8:00–12:00, closed Sun, tel. 0662/876-381).

To do your laundry and email at the same time, head to **Bubblepoint** (wash and dry for €7, six Internet terminals, daily 7:00–23:00, in CityCenter Mall opposite train station, Karl-Wurmb-Strasse 2, tel. 0664/471-1484).

Lockers in the Old Town: The TI generously provides lockers right on Mozartplatz (€1/day, pick up key at the desk).

Getting Around Salzburg

By Bus: Single-ride tickets for central Salzburg *(Einzelkarte–Kernzone)* are sold on the bus for €1.80. At machines and *Tabak/Trafik* shops, you can buy €1.60 single-ride tickets or a €3.40 day pass (*Tageskarte,* good for 24 hours, €4.20 if you buy it on the bus). To signal the driver that you want to get off, press the buzzer on the pole. Bus info: tel. 0662/4480-1500.

By Bike: Salzburg is fun for cyclists. The following two bike-rental shops offer 20 percent off with a valid train ticket or Eurailpass—ask for it. **Top Bike** rents bikes from two outlets: at the river side of the train station (exit to the left and walk 50 yards), and on the river next to the Staatsbrücke (€6/2 hrs, €10/4 hrs, €15/24 hrs, usually daily April–June and Sept–Oct 10:00–17:00, July–Aug 9:00–19:00, closed Nov–March, tel. 06272/4656, mobile 0676-476-7259, www.topbike.at, Sabine).

Velo-Active rents bikes on Mozartplatz, in the old town (€4.50/1 hr, €7/2 hrs, €15/24 hrs; mountain bikes-€6/hr, €18/24 hrs; daily 9:00–18:00, until 19:00 July–Aug, but hours unreliable—you may have to call or let the Panorama Tours man nearby help you, shorter hours off-season and in bad weather, passport number for security deposit, tel. 0662/435-595, mobile 0676-435-5950).

By Funicular and Elevator: The old town is connected to the top of the Mönchsberg mountain (and great views) via funicular and elevator. The **funicular** *(Festungsbahn)* whisks you up to the imposing Hohensalzburg Fortress (included in castle admission, goes every few minutes—for details, see page 152). The **elevator** *(MönchsbergAufzug)* on the east side of the old town propels you to the recommended Gasthaus Stadtalm café and hostel, the Museum of Modern Art, wooded paths, and more great views (€2 one-way, €3 round-trip, Tue–Sun 8:00–1:00 in the morning, Mon 8:00–19:00, until 24:00 in Aug).

By Taxi: Meters start at about €3 (from train station to your hotel, allow about €7). As always, small groups can taxi for about the same price as riding the bus.

By Buggy: The horse buggies *(Fiaker)* that congregate at Residenzplatz charge €33 for a 25-minute trot around the old town (www.fiaker-salzburg.at).

TOURS

Walking Tours—On any day of the week, you can take a two-language, one-hour guided walk of the old town without a reservation—just show up at the TI on Mozartplatz and pay the guide. The tours are informative, but you'll be listening to a half-hour of German (€8, daily at 12:15 and 14:00, tel. 0662/8898-7330). To save money (and avoid all that German), you can easily do it on your own using my self-guided walk, page 142. There's also a *Sound of Music* walking tour (€8, 1 hour, English only, leaves from Mozartplatz TI at 11:00, tel. 0662/834-833).

Local Guides—Christiana Schneeweiss ("Snow White"), a hardworking young guide and art historian with a passion for fitting local history into the big picture, gives spirited private tours (€80/1 hr, €129/2 hrs, €150/3 hrs, tel. 0664/340-1757, www.kultur-tourismus.com, info@kultur-tourismus.com). Check her website for bike tours, private minibus tours, and more. **Bärbel Schalber,** one of Salzburg's senior guides, offers a two-hour walk packed with information and spicy opinions (€75 per family, €108 for a group of adults, tel. 0662/632-225, mobile 0664-412-3708, schalber.salzburg@aon.at). Salzburg has many other good guides (to book, call 0662/840-406).

▲▲*Sound of Music* Tour—I took this tour skeptically (as part of my research) and liked it. It includes a quick but good general city tour, hits the *S.O.M.* spots (including the stately home, flirtatious gazebo, and grand wedding church), and shows you a lovely stretch of Austria's Salzkammergut Lake District. This is worthwhile for *S.O.M.* fans and those who won't otherwise be going into the Salzkammergut. Warning: Many think rolling through the

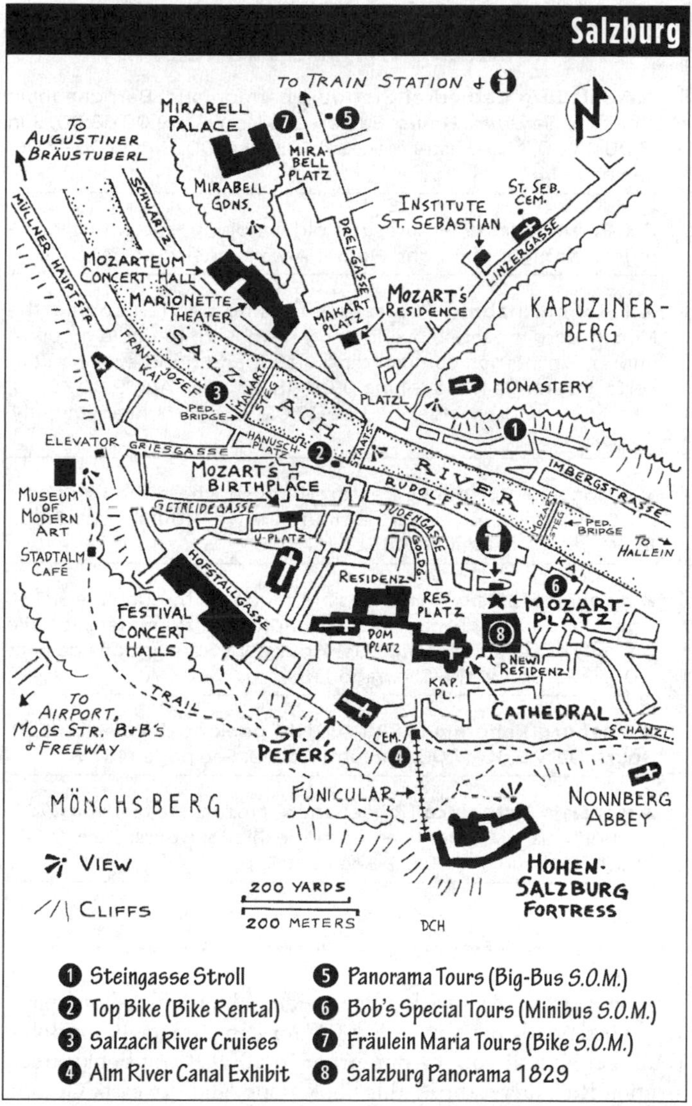

Austrian countryside with 30 Americans singing "Doe, a Deer" is pretty schmaltzy. Local Austrians don't understand all the commotion, and the audience is mostly native English speakers. For more on the *S.O.M.*, see the "*The Sound of Music* Debunked" sidebar on page 162.

Of the many companies doing the tour, consider Bob's Special Tours (usually uses a minibus) and Panorama Tours (more typical and professional, big 50-seat bus). Each one provides essentially the

Salzburg at a Glance

▲▲**Salzburg Cathedral** Glorious, harmonious, Baroque main church of Salzburg. **Hours:** Easter–Oct Mon–Sat 9:00–18:00, Sun 13:00–18:00; Nov–Easter Mon–Sat 10:00–17:00, Sun 13:00–17:00. See page 146.

▲▲**Getreidegasse** Picturesque old shopping lane with characteristic wrought-iron signs. **Hours:** Always open. See page 150.

▲▲**Hohensalzburg Fortress** Imposing castle capping the Mönchsberg mountain overlooking town, with tourable grounds, impressive interior, commanding views, and good evening concerts. **Hours:** Daily May–June 9:00–18:30, July–Aug 9:00–19:00, Sept 9:00–18:00, Oct–April 9:30–17:00. Concerts nearly nightly. See page 152.

▲▲**Mozart's Residence** Restored house where the composer lived, with the best Mozart exhibit in town. **Hours:** Daily 9:00–18:00, July–Aug until 19:00. See page 156.

▲▲***Sound of Music* Tour** Cheesy but fun tour through the *S.O.M.* sights of Salzburg and the surrounding Salzkammergut Lake District, by minibus or big bus. **Hours:** Various options daily at 9:00, 9:30, and 14:00. See page 138.

▲**Salzburg Panorama 1829** A vivid peek at the city in 1829. **Hours:** Daily 9:00–17:00, Thu until 20:00. See page 145.

▲**Mozart's Birthplace** House where Mozart was born in 1756, featuring his instruments and other exhibits. **Hours:** Daily 9:00–18:00, July–Aug until 19:00. See page 151.

same tour (in English with a live guide, 4 hours, free hotel pick-up) for essentially the same price: €37 for Panorama, €40 for Bob's. You'll get a €5 discount from either in 2009 if you book direct, mention Rick Steves, bring this book along, and pay cash. Getting a spot is simple—just call and make a reservation (calling Bob's a week or two in advance is smart). Note: Your hotel will be eager to call to reserve for you—to get their commission—but if you let them do it, you're unlikely to get the discount I've negotiated.

Minibus Option: Most of **Bob's Special Tours** use an eight-seat minibus and therefore have good access to old-town sights, promote a more casual feel, and spend less time waiting to load and unload. Calling well in advance increases your chances of getting a seat (€40 for adults, or €35 with this book if you pay cash and book

▲**Mönchsberg Walk** "The hills are alive" stroll you can enjoy right in downtown Salzburg. **Hours:** Doable anytime during daylight hours. See page 154.

▲**Mirabell Gardens and Palace** Beautiful palace complex with fine views, Salzburg's best concert venue, and *Sound of Music* memories. **Hours:** Gardens—always open; concerts—free in the park May–Aug Sun at 10:30 and Wed at 20:30, in the palace nearly nightly. See page 156.

▲**Steingasse** Historic cobbled lane with trendy pubs—a tranquil, tourist-free section of old Salzburg. **Hours:** Always open. See page 157.

▲**St. Sebastian Cemetery** Baroque cemetery with graves of Mozart's wife and father, and other Salzburg VIPs. **Hours:** Daily April–Oct 9:00–18:30, Nov–March 9:00–16:00. See page 158.

▲**Hellbrunn Castle** Palace on the outskirts of town featuring gardens with trick fountains. **Hours:** Daily May–Sept 9:00–17:30, July–Aug until 22:00, April and Oct 9:00–16:30, closed Nov–March. See page 158.

St. Peter's Cemetery Atmospheric old cemetery with mini-gardens overlooked by cliff face with monks' caves. **Hours:** Cemetery—daily April–Sept 6:30–19:00, Oct–March 6:30–18:00; caves—May–Sept Tue–Sun 10:30–17:00, closed Mon, shorter hours Oct–April. See page 148.

St. Peter's Church Romanesque church with Rococo decor. **Hours:** Open long hours daily. See page 148.

direct in 2009, €35 for kids and students with ID, €30 for kids in car seats, daily at 9:00 and 14:00 year-round, buses leave from Bob's office along the river just east of Mozartplatz at Rudolfskai 38—or they'll pick you up at your hotel for the morning tour, tel. 0662/849-511, mobile 0664-541-7492, www.bobstours.com). Nearly all of Bob's tours stop for the luge ride when the weather is dry (mountain bobsled-€4 extra, generally April–Oct, confirm beforehand). Some travelers looking for Bob's tours at Mozartplatz have been hijacked by other companies...have Bob's pick you up at your hotel (morning only) or meet the bus at their office (see map on page 139). If you're unable to book with Bob's, and still want a minibus tour, try **Kultur Tourismus** (€50, tel. 0664/340-1757, www.kultur-tourismus.com, info@kultur-tourismus.com).

SALZBURG

Big-Bus Option: Salzburg Panorama Tours depart from their smart kiosk at Mirabellplatz daily at 9:30 and 14:00 year-round (€37, or €32 with this book if you book direct and pay cash in 2009, book by calling 0662/874-029 or online at www.panoramatours.com, sightseeing@panoramatours.com). Many travelers appreciate their more businesslike feel, roomier buses, and slightly higher vantage point.

Bike Option: For some exercise with your tour, you can meet **Fräulein Maria** in the Mirabell Gardens (at Mirabellplatz 4, 50 yards to the left of palace entry) for a *S.O.M.* bike tour. The main attractions that you'll pass during the seven-mile pedal include the Mirabell Gardens, the horse pond, St. Peter's Cemetery, Nonnberg Abbey, Leopoldskron Palace and, of course, the gazebo (€24 includes bike, €2 discount with this book in 2009, kids 6–15 pay €15, kids under 6 pay €10, daily at 9:30, allow 3.5 hours, May–Sept only, family-friendly, tel. 0650/342-6297, www.mariasbicycletours.com).

Walking Option (City Only): Those with a little less time or enthusiasm for the movie can take a one-hour *S.O.M.*-themed walking tour within the city (€8, leaves from Mozartplatz TI at 11:00, tel. 0662/834-833).

More Tours—Both Bob's and Panorama Tours also offer an extensive array of other day trips from Salzburg (Berchtesgaden/Eagle's Nest, salt mines, and Salzkammergut lakes and mountains are the most popular, with the same discount in 2009—€5 off with this book, book direct, and pay cash). The tours are all explained in their brochures, which litter hotel lobbies all over town.

City Cruise Line runs a basic 40-minute round-trip cruise with recorded commentary (€13, 9/day July–Aug, 7/day in June, fewer in other months, no boats Nov–March). For a longer cruise, ride to Hellbrunn and return by bus (€16, 1–2/day April–Oct). Boats leave from the old-town side of the river just downstream of the Makartsteg bridge (tel. 0662/8257-6912). While views can be cramped, passengers are treated to a fun finale just before docking, when the captain twirls a fun "waltz."

SELF-GUIDED WALK

▲▲▲Salzburg's Old Town

I've linked the best sights in the old town into this handy self-guided orientation walk.

• *Begin in the heart of town, just up from the river, near the TI on...*

Mozartplatz

All the happy tourists around you probably wouldn't be here if not for the man honored by this statue (erected in 1842): Wolfgang Amadeus Mozart. Mozart spent much of his first 25 years

Salzburg's Old Town Walk

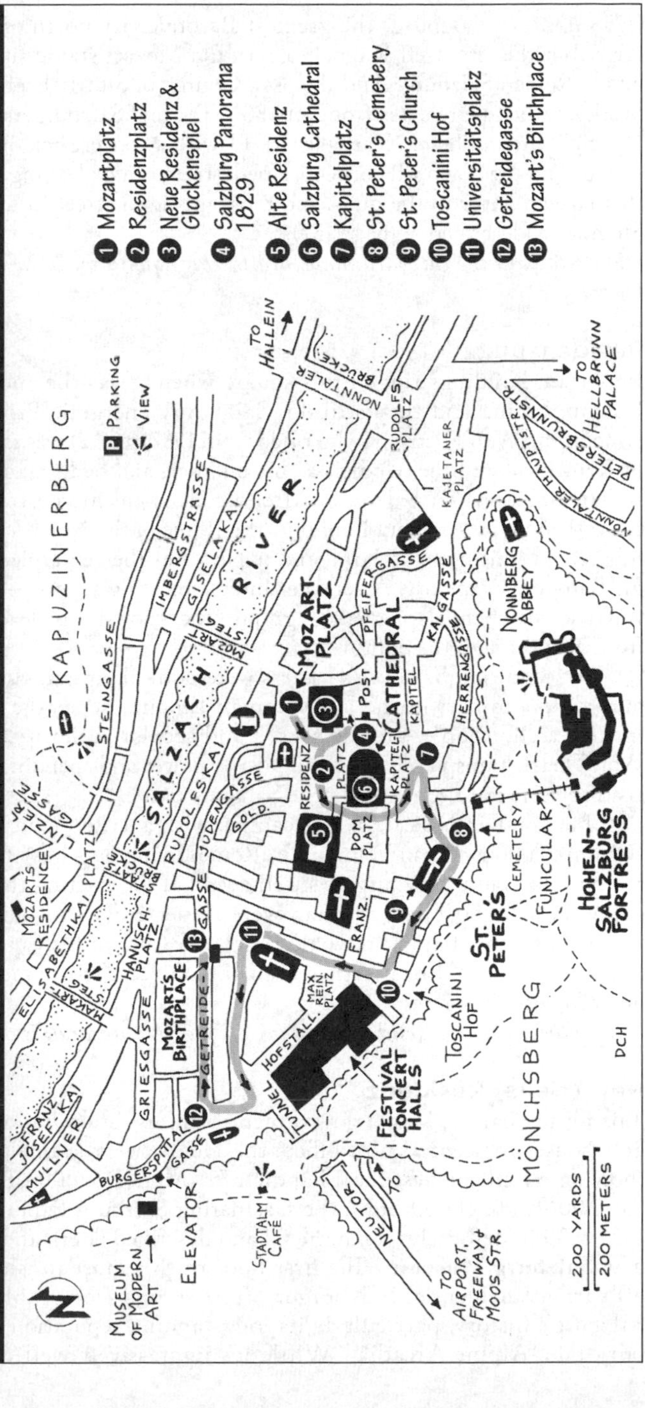

(1756–1777) in Salzburg, the greatest Baroque city north of the Alps. But the city itself is much older: The Mozart statue sits on bits of Roman Salzburg. And the pink Church of St. Michael that overlooks the square dates from A.D. 800. The first Salzburgers settled right around here. Nearby is the TI with a concert box office. Just around the downhill corner is a pedestrian bridge leading over the Salzach River to the quiet and most medieval street in town, Steingasse (described on page 157).

• *Walk toward the cathedral and into the big square with the huge fountain.*

Residenzplatz

Important buildings ringed this square when it was the ancient Roman forum...and they still do. Salzburg's energetic Prince-Archbishop Wolf Dietrich (who ruled from 1587 to 1612) was raised in Rome, counted the Medicis as his buddies, and had grandiose Italian ambitions for Salzburg. After a convenient fire destroyed the cathedral, he set about building "the Rome of the North." This square, with his new cathedral and palace, was the centerpiece of his Baroque dream city. A series of interconnecting squares—like you'll see nowhere else—make a grand processional way, leading from here through the old town.

For centuries, Salzburg's leaders were both important church officials *and* princes of the Holy Roman Empire, hence the title "prince-archbishop"—mixing sacred and secular authority. But Wolf Dietrich misplayed his hand, losing power and spending his last five years imprisoned up in the Salzburg castle.

The fountain is as Italian as can be, with a Triton matching Bernini's famous Triton Fountain in Rome. Lying on a busy trade route to the south, Salzburg was well aware of the exciting things going on in Italy. Things Italian were respected (as in colonial America, when a bumpkin would "stick a feather in his cap and call it macaroni"). Local artists even Italianized their names in order to raise their rates.

• *Along the left side of Residenzplatz (as you face the cathedral) is the...*

New (Neue) Residenz

This former palace, long a government administration building, now houses the central post office, the Heimatwerk (a fine shop showing off all the best local handicrafts, Mon–Fri 9:00–18:00, Sat 9:00–17:00, closed Sun), the fascinating Salzburg Panorama 1829 exhibit (definitely worth the €2 and described later), and the new **Salzburg Museum.** The first floor of this museum shows off various influential Salzburgers. The second floor explores Salzburg's history, particularly its longstanding reputation as a fairy-tale "Alpine Arcadia." While it's impressively well-done and described in English, the museum is only enjoyable to the extent that you're fascinated with the city—so most will find this merely a good rainy-day option (€7, €8 combo-ticket with Salzburg Panorama, both tickets €2 cheaper on Sun, includes audioguide, Tue–Sun 9:00–17:00, Thu until 20:00, closed Mon except July–Aug and Dec—when it's open Mon 9:00–17:00, tel. 0662/6208-080).

• *Atop the new Residenz rings the famous...*

Glockenspiel

This bell tower has a carillon of 35 17th-century bells (cast in Antwerp) that chimes throughout the day and plays tunes (appropriate to the month) at 7:00, 11:00, and 18:00. There was a time when Salzburg could afford to take tourists to the top of the tower to actually see the big barrel with adjustable tabs turn (like a giant music-box mechanism)...pulling the right bells in the right rhythm. Notice the ornamental top: an upside-down heart in flames surrounding the solar system (symbolizing that God loves all of creation).

Look back, past Mozart's statue, to the 4,220-foot-high Gaisberg—the forested hill with the television tower. A road leads to the top for a commanding view. Its summit is a favorite destination for local nature-lovers and kids learning to ski.

• *Before continuing our walk, round the corner toward the back of the cathedral and drop into the...*

▲Salzburg Panorama 1829

In the early 19th century, 360-degree "panorama" paintings of great cities or events were popular. These creations were even taken on extended road trips. Salzburg, at a stagnant stage in its development, had this circular view painted by Johann Michael Sattler: the city as seen from the top of its castle. When complete, it spent 10 years touring the great cities of Europe, showing off Salzburg's breathtaking setting. Today, the exquisitely restored painting offers a fascinating look at the city in 1829. The river was slower and had beaches. The old town looks essentially as it does today, and Moosstrasse still leads into idyllic farm country. Paintings from that era of other great cities around the world are hung around the outside wall with numbers but without labels, as a kind of quiz game. A flier gives the cities names on one side, and keys them to the numbers. See how many 19th-century cities you can identify (€2, €8 combo-ticket with Salzburg Museum, combo-ticket is €2 cheaper on Sun, open daily 9:00–17:00, Thu until 20:00, Residenzplatz 9).

• *Backtrack into Residenzplatz and head to the opposite end from the new Residenz. This building is the...*

Old (Alte) Residenz

Opposite the new Residenz is Wolf Dietrich's skippable palace, the old Residenz, which is connected to the cathedral by a skyway. A series of ornately decorated rooms and an art gallery are open to visitors with time to kill (€6, Tue–Sun 10:00–17:00, closed Mon, tel. 0662/840-4510).

• *Walk under the prince-archbishop's skyway and step into Cathedral Square (Domplatz), where you'll find the...*

▲▲Salzburg Cathedral

This was one of the first Baroque buildings north of the Alps. It was consecrated in 1628, during the Thirty Years' War. (Pitting Roman Catholics against Protestants, this war devastated much of Europe and brought most grand construction projects to a halt.) Experts differ on what motivated the builders: to emphasize Salzburg's commitment to the Roman Catholic cause and the power of the Church here, or to show that there could be a peaceful alternative to the religious strife that was racking Europe at the time. Salzburg's archbishop was technically the top papal official north of the Alps, but the city managed to steer clear of the war. With its rich salt production, it had enough money to stay out of the conflict and carefully maintain its independence from the warring sides.

The dates on the iron gates refer to milestones in the church's history: In 774, the previous church (long since destroyed) was founded by St. Virgil, to be replaced in 1628 by the church you see today. In 1959, the reconstruction was completed after a WWII bomb blew through the dome.

Cathedral Square is surrounded by the prince-archbishop's secular administration buildings. The **statue of Mary** (1771) is looking away from the church, welcoming visitors. If you stand in the rear of the square, immediately under the middle arch, you'll see that she's positioned to be crowned by the two angels on the church facade.

Step inside the cathedral (donation requested; Easter–Oct Mon–Sat 9:00–18:00, Sun 13:00–18:00; Nov–Easter Mon–Sat 10:00–17:00, Sun 13:00–17:00). Enter the cathedral as if part of a festival procession—drawn toward the resurrected Christ by the brightly lit area under the dome, and cheered on by ceiling paintings of the Passion. The stucco, by a Milanese artist, is exceptional. Sit under the dome—surrounded by the tombs of ten 17th-century archbishops—and imagine all four organs playing, each balcony filled with musicians...glorious surround-sound. Mozart, who was the organist here for two years, would advise you that the acoustics are best in pews immediately under the dome. Study the symbolism of the decor all around you—intellectual, complex, and cohesive. Think of the altar in Baroque terms, as the center of a stage, with sunrays as spotlights in this dramatic and sacred theater. In the left transept, stairs lead down into the crypt *(Krypta),* where you can see foundations of the earlier church, more tombs, and a tourist-free chapel (reserved for prayer) directly under the dome.

Built in just 14 years (1614–1628), the church boasts harmonious architecture. When Pope John Paul II visited in 1998, 5,000 people filled the cathedral (330 feet long and 230 feet tall). The baptismal font (dark bronze, left of the entry) is from the previous cathedral (basin from about 1320, although the lid is modern). Mozart was baptized here ("Amadeus" means "beloved by God"). Concert and Mass schedules are posted at the entrance; the Sunday Mass at 10:00 is famous for its music.

The **Cathedral Museum** (Dom Museum) has a rich collection of church art (entry at portico, €5, mid-May–Oct Mon–Sat 10:00–17:00, Sun 11:00–18:00, closed Nov–mid-May, tel. 0662/844-189).

• From the cathedral, exit left and walk toward the fortress into the next square...

Kapitelplatz

Head past the free underground public WCs and the giant chessboard to the pond. This was a **horse bath,** the 18th-century equivalent of a car wash. Notice the puzzle above it—the artist wove the date of the structure into a phrase. It says, "Leopold the Prince Built Me," using the letters LLDVICMXVXI, which total 1732 (add it up...it works)—the year it was built. A small road (back by the chessboard) leads uphill to the fortress (and fortress lift). With your back to the cathedral, leave the square through a gate in the right corner that reads *zum Peterskeller.* It leads to a waterfall and St. Peter's Cemetery.

The **waterwheel** is part of a canal system that has brought water into Salzburg from Berchtesgaden, 16 miles away, since the 13th century. Climb uphill a few steps to feel the medieval water power. The stream, divided from here into smaller canals, was channeled through town to provide fire protection, to flush out the streets (Saturday morning was flood-the-streets day), and to power factories (there were more than 100 watermill-powered firms as late as the 19th century). Drop into the fragrant and traditional **bakery** at the waterfall. It's hard to beat their rocklike *Roggenbrot* (various fresh rolls for less than €1, Thu–Tue 7:00–17:30, Sat until 12:00, closed Wed). There's a good view of the funicular climbing up to the castle from here. For more on the canal system, check out the free Alm River Canal exhibit nearby (described on page 154).

• *Now find the* Katakomben *sign and step into...*

St. Peter's Cemetery

This collection of lovingly tended mini-gardens abuts the Mönchberg's rock wall (free, silence is requested, daily April–Sept 6:30–19:00, Oct–March 6:30–18:00). Walk in about 50 yards to the intersection of lanes at the base of the cliff marked by a stone ball. (It's seemingly made-to-order for a little back-stretching break. Go ahead...I'll wait.) You're surrounded by three churches, each founded in the sixth century atop a pagan Celtic holy site. St. Peter's Church is closest to the stone ball. Notice the fine Romanesque stonework on the chapel nearest you, and the fancy rich guys' Renaissance-style tombs decorating its walls.

Wealthy as those guys were, they ran out of caring relatives. The graves surrounding you are tended by descendants of the deceased. In Austria, gravesites are rented, not owned. Rent bills are sent out every 10 years. If no one cares enough to make the payment, your remains are chucked. Iron crosses were much cheaper than tombstones. The cemetery where the von Trapp family hid out in *The Sound of Music* was a Hollywood set, but it was inspired by this one.

Look up the cliff. Legendary medieval hermit monks are said to have lived in the hillside—but "catacombs" they're not. For €1, you can climb lots of steps to see a few old caves, a chapel, and some fine views (May–Sept Tue–Sun 10:30–17:00, closed Mon; Oct–April Wed–Thu 10:30–15:30, Fri–Sun 10:30–16:00, closed Mon–Tue).

• *Continue downhill through the cemetery and out the opposite end. Just outside, hook right and drop into...*

St. Peter's Church

Just inside, enjoy a carved Romanesque welcome. Over the inner doorway, a fine tympanum shows Jesus on a rainbow flanked by Peter and Paul over a stylized Tree of Life and under a Latin inscription reading, "I am the door to life, and only through me can you find eternal life." Enter the nave and notice how the once purely Romanesque vaulting has since been iced with a sugary Rococo finish. Salzburg's only Rococo interior feels Bavarian (because it is—the fancy stucco work was done by Bavarian artists). Up the right side aisle is the tomb of St. Rupert, with a painting showing Salzburg in 1750 (one bridge, salt ships sailing the river, and angels hoisting barrels of salt to heaven as St. Rupert prays for his city). On pillars farther up the aisle are faded bits of 13th-century Romanesque frescos. Similar frescoes hide under Rococo whitewash throughout the church.

Leaving the church, notice the Stiftskeller St. Peter restaurant (on the left—described under "Eating," page 172, and for its Mozart Dinner Concert, page 162). Charlemagne ate here in A.D. 803—allowing locals to claim it's the oldest restaurant in Europe. Opposite where you entered the square (look through the arch), you'll see St. Rupert waving you into the next square (early 20th-century Bauhaus-style dorms for student monks), with a modern crucifix (1926) on the far wall. To the right of the crucifix (at #8), press the red button on the bronze door, enter, and see an unforgettable Expressionist-carved crucifix (also from the 1920s, free, open until 11:30 only).

• *Walk through the archway next to the crucifix into...*

Toscanini Hof

This square faces the 1925 Festival Hall. The hall's three theaters seat 5,000. This is where Captain von Trapp nervously waited before walking onstage (in the movie, he sang "Edelweiss"), just before he escaped with his family. On the left is the city's 1,500-space, inside-the-mountain parking lot; ahead, behind the *Felsenkeller* sign, is a tunnel (generally closed) leading to the actual concert hall; and to the right is the backstage of a smaller hall where carpenters are often building stage sets (door open on hot days). The stairway leads to the top of the cliff and eventually to the Stadtalm Café and hostel (more easily reached by elevator, see page 174).

• *Walk downhill through Max-Reinhardt-Platz, to the right of the church and past the public WC, into...*

Universitätsplatz

This square hosts an open-air produce market—Salzburg's liveliest (mornings Mon–Sat, best on Sat). Locals are happy to pay more here for the reliably fresh and top-quality produce. (These days, half of Austria's produce is grown organically.) The market really bustles on Saturday mornings, when the farmers are in town. Public marketplaces have fountains for washing fruit and vegetables. The fountain here—a part of the medieval water system—plummets down a hole and to the river. The sundial (over the water hole) is accurate (except for the daylight savings hour) and two-dimensional, showing both the time (obvious) and the date (less obvious). The fanciest facade overlooking the square (the yellow one) is the backside of Mozart's Birthplace (described on page 151).

• *Continue past the fountain to the end of the square, passing several characteristic and nicely arcaded medieval tunnels (on right) that connect the square to Getreidegasse. Cross the big road for a look at the giant horse troughs, adjacent to the prince's stables. Paintings show the various breeds and temperaments of horses in his stable—Salzburg had a passion for the equestrian arts.*

Take two right turns and you're at the start of...

▲▲Getreidegasse

This street was old Salzburg's busy, colorful main drag. It's lined with *Schmuck* (jewelry) shops. Famous for its old wrought-iron signs (best viewed from this end), the architecture on the street still looks much as it did in Mozart's day—though its former elegance is now mostly gone, replaced by chain outlets.

On the right at #39, **Sporer** serves up homemade spirits (€1.30 per shot). This has been a family-run show for a century—fun-loving, proud, and English-speaking. *Nuss* is nut, *Marille* is apricot (typical of this region), the *Kletzen* cocktail is like a super-thick Baileys with pear, and *Edle Brande* are the stronger schnapps. The many homemade firewaters are in jugs at the end of the bar.

Continue down Getreidegasse, noticing the old doorbells—one per floor. At #40, **Eisgrotte** serves good ice cream. Across from Eisgrotte, a tunnel leads to **Bosna Grill,** the local choice for the very best sausage in town (see page 175). Farther along, you'll pass McDonald's (while required to keep its arches Baroque and low-key, it just couldn't hang anything less than the biggest sign on the street).

The knot of excited tourists and salesmen hawking goofy gimmicks marks the home of Salzburg's most famous resident. **Mozart's Birthplace** (Geburtshaus)—the house where Mozart was born, and where he composed many of his early works—is worth a visit for his true fans (described next). But for most, his Residence, across the river, is more interesting (described on page 156).

• *Our walk is finished. From here, you can head up to the Hohensalzburg Fortress on Mönchsberg mountain over the old town (see page 152); or continue to some of the sights across the river. To reach the sights across the river, head for the river, jog left (past the fast-food fish restaurant and free WCs), climb to the top of the Makartsteg pedestrian bridge, and turn to page 155.*

SIGHTS AND ACTIVITIES

▲Mozart's Birthplace (Geburtshaus)

Mozart was born here in 1756. It was in this building—the most popular Mozart sight in town—that he composed most of his boy-genius works. For fans, it's almost a pilgrimage. American artist Robert Wilson was recently hired to spiff up the exhibit, to make it feel more conceptual and less like a museum. But I was unimpressed. If you're tackling just one Mozart sight, skip this one. Instead, walk 10 minutes from here to Mozart's Residence (described on page 156), which provides a more informative visit. But if you want to max out on Mozart, a visit here is worthwhile.

Cost, Hours, Location: €6.50, or €10 for combo-ticket that includes Mozart's Residence, daily 9:00–18:00, July–Aug until 19:00, last entry 30 min before closing, Getreidegasse 9, tel. 0662/844-313.

➲ **Self-Guided Tour:** Here's what you'll see as you shuffle through with the herd:

Room 1: Around a baby crib showing an infant both old and young (Mozart's music is timeless...get it?) are walls heavy with historic etchings, portraits, and documents. Most important: an engraving of the family (lower right) and a fine "portrait with a bird's nest" of Mozart, painted from life when he was nine years old (upper left).

Room 2: The living room shows off authentic family portraits: Wolfgang's mom, dad, sister, and wife. Wolfgang composed his first pieces as a child on a clavichord (like the one in this room). A predecessor of the piano, it hit the strings with simple teeter-totter keys that played very softly...ideal for composers living in tight apartment quarters.

Room 3: The nursery is decorated like Mozart's music: light and free as a bird (hence the flying birds). Embedded in the walls are Mozart's personal possessions—his ring, silk wallet, and violin. He was born in this room, and the entire family slept here until Wolfgang was 14.

Room 4: Exactly what Mozart looked like is a bit of a mystery. Various portraits in this room give us something to go on.

Corridor: The neon phrase shows his juvenile sense of humor. It's a rhyme: *Madame Mutter, ich esse gerne Butter.* ("Dear mother, I love to eat butter.") The next room is wallpapered with reproductions of actual circa-1840 photos of Mozart's wife and son (as an old man). More strange Wilson-designed rooms follow: Mozart loved to turn things upside-down—so the Salzburg cityscapes are that way, with stars on the floor. Downstairs, just before the shop, rooms dedicated to Mozart's operas play various video clips continuously.

Atop the Cliffs Above the Old Town

The main "sight" above town is the Hohensalzburg Fortress. But if you just want to enjoy the sweeping views over Salzburg, you have a couple of cheap options: Take the elevator up the cliffs of Mönchsberg (explained under "Getting Around Salzburg," page 138), head up to the castle grounds on foot, or visit the castle in the evening on a night when they're hosting a concert (about 300 nights a year). This is the only time you can buy a funicular ticket without paying for the castle entrance—since the castle museum is closed, but the funicular is still running to bring up concert-goers.

▲▲Hohensalzburg Fortress (Festung)—Built on a rock (called Festungsberg) 400 feet above the Salzach River, this fortress was never really used. That's the idea. It was a good investment—so foreboding, nobody attacked the town for a thousand years. The city was never taken by force, but when Napoleon stopped by, Salzburg wisely surrendered. After a stint as a military barracks, the fortress was opened to the public in the 1860s by Emperor Franz Josef. Today, it remains one of Europe's mightiest castles, dominating Salzburg's skyline and offering incredible views.

Cost: Your daytime ticket includes the price of the funicular up and down, as well as admission to the fortress grounds and all the museums inside—whether you want to see them or not (€10, €23.10 family ticket, €7 per person for museum entry if you hike to the castle without using the funicular). If you'd rather save money than see the museums, head up the hill in the evening (within one hour of the museum's closing time, it's €5.90 one-way/€7.20 round-trip for funicular and entry to castle grounds; after closing time, funicular is €3.40 round-trip).

Hours: The complex is open daily year-round (May–June 9:00–18:30, July–Aug 9:00–19:00, Sept 9:00–18:00, Oct–April 9:30–17:00, last entry 30 min before closing, tel. 0662/8424-3011). On nights when there's a concert, the castle grounds are free and open after the museum closes until 21:30.

Concerts: The fortress also serves as a venue for evening concerts (Festungskonzerte). For details, see page 161 in the "Entertainment" section.

Café: The café between the funicular station and the castle entry is a great place to nibble on apple strudel while taking in the jaw-dropping view.

Orientation: The fortress visit has three parts: a relatively dull courtyard with some fine views from its various ramparts; the fortress itself (with a required and escorted 45-minute audio tour); and the palace museum (by far the best exhibit of the lot). At the bottom of the funicular, you'll pass through an interesting little exhibit on the town's canal system (free, described on page 154).

➲ **Self-Guided Tour:** Climb from the top of the funicular to the inner courtyard. Immediately inside, circling to the left (clockwise), you'll encounter cannons (still poised to defend Salzburg against a Turkish invasion), the marionette exhibit, the palace museum, the Kuenburg bastion, scant ruins of a Romanesque church, the courtyard (with path down for those walking), toilets, shops, a restaurant, and the fortress tour.

• *Begin at the...*

Marionette Exhibit: Several fun rooms show off this local tradition, with three videos playing continuously: two with peeks at Salzburg's ever-enchanting Marionette Theater performances of Mozart classics (see listing, page 161), and one with a behind-the-scenes look at the action. Give the hands-on marionette a whirl.

• *Hiking through the former palace, you'll find the site's best exhibits at the...*

Palace Museum (Festungsmuseum Carolino Augusteum): The second floor has exhibits on castle life, from music to torture. The top floor shows off fancy royal apartments, a sneak preview of the room used for the nightly fortress concerts, and the Rainier military museum, dedicated to the Salzburg regiments that fought in both World Wars.

Castle Courtyard: The courtyard was the main square of the castle residents, a community of a thousand—which could be self-sufficient when necessary. The square was ringed by the shops of craftsmen, blacksmiths, bakers, and so on. The well dipped into a rain-fed cistern. The church is dedicated to St. George, the protector of horses (logical for an army church) and decorated by fine red marble reliefs (c. 1502). Behind the church is the top of the old lift that helped supply the fortress. (From near here, steps lead back into the city, or to the mountaintop "Mönchsberg Walk," described on next page.) The scant remains of a Romanesque chapel are well-described.

• *Near the chapel, turn left into the Kuenburg Bastion (once a garden) for fine city and castle views.*

Kuenburg Bastion: Notice how the castle has three parts: the original castle inside the courtyard, the vast whitewashed walls (built when the castle was a residence), and the lower, beefed-up fortifications (added for extra defense against the expected Turkish invasion). Survey Salzburg from here and think about fortifying an important city by using nature. Mönchsberg (the little mountain you're on) naturally cradles the old town, with just a small gate between the mountain

and the river needed to bottle up the place. The new town across the river needed a bit of a wall arcing from the river to its hill. Back then, only one bridge crossed the Salzach into town, and it had a fortified gate.

• *Back inside the castle courtyard, continue your circle. The Round Tower (1497) helps you visualize the inner original castle.*

Fortress Interior: Tourists are allowed in this part of the fortified palace only with an escort. (They say that's for security, though while touring it, you wonder what they're protecting.) A crowd assembles at the turnstile, and every quarter-hour 40 people are issued their audioguides and let in for the escorted walk. You'll go one room at a time, listening to a 45-minute commentary. While the interior furnishings are mostly gone—taken by Napoleon—the rooms survived as well as they did because no one wanted to live here after 1500, so the building was never modernized. Your tour includes a room dedicated to the art of "excruciating questioning" ("softening up" prisoners, in current American military jargon)—filled with tools of that gruesome trade. The highlight is the commanding city view from the top of a tower.

• *After seeing the fortress, consider hiking down to the old town, or along the top of Mönchsberg (see "Mönchsberg Walk," below). If you take the funicular down, keep an eye out for the...*

Alm River Canal Exhibit: At the base of the funicular, below the castle, is this fine little exhibit on how the river was broken into five smaller streams—powering the city until steam took up the energy-supply baton. Pretend it's the year 1200 and follow (by video) the flow of the water from the river through the canals, into the mills, and as it's finally dumped into the Salzach River (free, access from the bottom of the lift as you're leaving, or through Amber shop next door if you're not riding the funicular).

▲Mönchsberg Walk—For a great 30-minute hike, exit the fortress by taking the steep lane down from the castle courtyard. At the first intersection, right leads into the old town, and left leads across the Mönchsberg. The lane leads 20 minutes through the woods high above the city (stick to the high lanes, or you'll end up back in town), taking you to the Gasthaus Stadtalm café (light meals, cheap beds—see page 168 of "Sleeping," and page 174 of "Eating"). From the Stadtalm, pass under the medieval wall and walk left along the wall to a tableau showing how it once looked. Take the switchback to the right and follow the lane downhill to the Museum of Modern Art (described next), where the elevator zips you back into town (€2 one-way, €3 round-trip, Tue–Sun 8:00–1:00 in the morning, Mon 8:00–19:00, until 24:00 in Aug). If you stay on the lane past the elevator, you eventually pass the Augustine church that marks the rollicking Augustiner Bräustübl (see page 175).

In 1669, a huge Mönchsberg landslide killed more than 200 townspeople. Since then the cliffs have been carefully checked each spring and fall. Even today, you might see crews on the cliff, monitoring its stability.

Museum of Modern Art on Mönchsberg—The modern-art museum on top of Mönchsberg, built in 2004, houses Salzburg's Rupertinum Gallery, plus special exhibitions. While the collection is not worth climbing a mountain for, the M32 restaurant has some of the best views in town (€8, €9.70 including elevator ticket, Tue–Sun 10:00–18:00, Wed until 21:00, closed Mon; restaurant open Tue–Sat 9:00–24:00, Sun 9:00–18:00, closed Mon except during festival; both at top of Mönchsberg elevator, tel. 0662/842-220, www.museumdermoderne.at).

In the New Town, North of the River

The following sights are across the river from the old town. I've connected them with walking instructions.

• *Begin at the Makartsteg pedestrian bridge, where you can survey the...*

Salzach River—Salzburg's river is called "salt river" not because it's salty, but because of the precious cargo it once carried—the salt mines of Hallein are just nine miles upstream. Salt could be transported from here all the way to the Danube, and on to the Mediterranean via the Black Sea. The riverbanks and roads were built when the river was regulated in the 1850s. Before that, the Salzach was much wider and slower-moving. Houses opposite the old town fronted the river with docks and "garages" for boats. The grand buildings just past the bridge (with their elegant promenades and cafés) were built on reclaimed land in the late 19th century, in the historicist style of Vienna's Ringstrasse.

Scan the cityscape. Notice all the churches. Salzburg, nicknamed the "Rome of the North," has 38 Catholic churches (plus two Protestant churches and a synagogue). Find the five streams gushing into the river. These date from the 13th century, when the river was split into five canals running through the town to power its mills. Hotel Stein (upstream, just left of next bridge), described on page 158, has a popular roof-terrace café. Downstream, notice the Museum of Modern Art atop Mönchsberg, with a view restaurant and a faux castle (actually a water reservoir). The Romanesque bell tower with the copper dome in the distance is the Augustine church, site of the best beer hall in town (the Augustiner Bräustübl—see page 175).

• *Cross the bridge, pass the Café Bazar (a fine place for a drink—see page 176), walk two blocks inland, and take a left past the heroic statues into...*

▲Mirabell Gardens and Palace (Schloss)—The bubbly gardens laid out in 1730 for the prince-archbishop have been open to the public since 1850 (thanks to Emperor Franz Josef, who was rattled by the popular revolutions of 1848). The gardens are free and open until dusk. The palace is only open as a concert venue (explained later). The statues and the arbor (far left) were featured in *The Sound of Music*. Walk through the gardens to the palace. Look back, enjoy the garden/cathedral/castle view, and imagine how the prince-archbishop must have reveled in a vista that reminded him of all his secular and religious power. Then go around to the river side of the palace and find the horse.

The rearing **Pegasus statue** (rare and very well-balanced) is the site of a famous *Sound of Music* scene where the kids all danced before lining up on the stairs (with Maria 30 yards farther along). The steps lead to a small mound in the park (made of rubble from a former theatre, and today a rendezvous point for Salzburg's gay community).

Nearest the horse, stairs lead between two lions to a pair of tough dwarfs (early volleyball players with spiked mittens) welcoming you to Salzburg's **Dwarf Park.** Cross the elevated walk (noticing the city's fortified walls) to meet statues of a dozen dwarfs who served the prince-archbishop—modeled after real people with real fashions in about 1600. This was Mannerist art, from the hyper-realistic age that followed the Renaissance.

There's plenty of **music,** both in the park and in the palace. A brass band plays free park concerts (May–Aug Sun at 10:30 and Wed at 20:30, unless it's raining). To properly enjoy the lavish Mirabell Palace—once the prince-archbishop's summer palace, and now the seat of the mayor—get a ticket to a Schlosskonzerte (my favorite venue for a classical concert—see page 161).

• *To visit Salzburg's best Mozart sight, go a long block southeast to Makartplatz, where you'll find...*

▲▲Mozart's Residence (Wohnhaus)—This reconstruction of Mozart's second home (his family moved here when he was 17) is the most informative Mozart sight in town. The English-language audioguide (included with admission, 90 min) provides fascinating insight into Mozart's life and music, with the usual scores, old pianos, and an interesting 30-minute film (#17 on your audioguide for soundtrack) that runs continuously (€6.50, or €10 for combo-ticket that includes Mozart's Birthplace in the old town, daily 9:00–18:00, July–Aug until 19:00, last entry one hour before closing, allow at least one hour for visit, Makartplatz 8, tel. 0662/8742-2740).

In the main hall—used by the Mozarts to entertain Salzburg's high society—you can hear original instruments from Mozart's time. Mozart was proud to be the first in his family to compose a duet. Notice the family portrait (circa 1780) on the wall, showing Mozart with his sister Nannerl, their father, and their mother—who'd died two years earlier in Paris. Mozart also had silly crude bull's-eyes made for the pop-gun game popular at the time (licking an "arse," Wolfgang showed his disdain for the rigors of high society). Later rooms feature real artifacts that explore his loves, his intellectual pursuits, his travels, and more.

• *From here, you can walk a few blocks back to the main bridge (Staatsbrücke), where you'll find Platzl, a square once used as a hay market. Pause to enjoy the kid-pleasing little fountain. Near the fountain (with your back to the river), Steingasse leads darkly to the right.*

▲Steingasse—This street, a block in from the river, was the only street in the Middle Ages going south over the Alps to Venice (this was the first stop north of the Alps). Today, it's wonderfully tranquil and free of Salzburg's touristy crush.

At #9, a plaque (of questionable veracity) shows where Joseph Mohr, who wrote the words to "Silent Night," was born—poor and illegitimate—in 1792. There is no doubt, however, that the popular Christmas carol was composed and first sung in the village of Oberndorf, just outside of Salzburg, in 1818. Stairs lead from near here up to the monastery.

On the next corner, the wall is gouged out. This scar was left even after the building was restored, to remind locals of the American GI who tried to get a tank down this road during a visit to the town brothel—two blocks farther up Steingasse. Inviting cocktail bars along here come alive at night (described on page 177).

At #19, find the carvings on the old door. Some say these are notices from beggars to the begging community (more numerous after post-Reformation religious wars, which forced many people out of their homes and towns)—a kind of "hobo code" indicating whether the residents would give or not. Trace the wires of the old-fashioned doorbells to the highest floors.

Farther on, you'll find a commanding Salzburg view across the river. Notice the red dome marking the oldest nunnery in the German-speaking world (established in 712) under the fortress and to the left. The real Maria from *The Sound of Music* taught in this nunnery's school. In 1927, she and Captain von Trapp were married in the church you see here (not the church filmed in the movie). He was 47. She was 22. Hmmmm.

From here look back, above the arch you just passed through, at part of the town's medieval fortification. The coat of arms on the arch is of the prince-archbishop who paid Bavaria a huge ransom to stay out of the Thirty Years' War (smart move). He then built this fortification (in 1634) in anticipation of rampaging armies from both sides.

Today, this street is for making love, not war. The Maison de Plaisir (a few doors down, at #24) has for centuries been a Salzburg brothel. But the climax of this walk is more touristic.

• *For a grand view, head back to Platzl and the bridge, enter the Stein Hotel (left corner, overlooking the river), and ride the elevator to...*

Stein Terrasse—This café offers perhaps the best views in town (aside from the castle). Hidden from the tourist crush, it's a trendy, professional, local scene. You can discretely peek at the view, or enjoy a drink or light meal (indoor/outdoor seating, daily 9:00–24:00).

• *Back at Platzl and the bridge, you can head straight up Linzergasse (away from the river) into a neighborhood packed with recommended accommodations, as well as our final new-town sight...*

▲St. Sebastian Cemetery—Wander through this quiet place, so Baroque and so Italian (free, daily April–Oct 9:00–18:30, Nov–March 9:00–16:00, entry at Linzergasse 43 in summer, around the corner to the right in winter). Mozart is buried in Vienna, his mom's in Paris, and his sister is in Salzburg's old town (St. Peter's)—but Wolfgang's wife Constantia and his father Leopold are buried here (from the black iron gate entrance on Linzergasse, walk 17 paces and look left). When Prince-Archbishop Wolf Dietrich had the cemetery moved from around the cathedral and put here, across the river, people didn't like it. To help popularize it, he had his own mausoleum built as its centerpiece. Continue straight past the Mozart tomb to this circular building (English description at door).

Near Salzburg

For information on Berchtesgaden—also near Salzburg—see the end of this chapter.

▲Hellbrunn Castle—About the year 1610, Prince-Archbishop Sittikus (after meditating on stewardship and Christ-like values) decided he needed a lavish palace with a vast and ornate garden purely for pleasure. He built this and just loved inviting his VIP guests out for a fun with his trick fountains. Today, the visit is worthwhile for the garden full of clever fountains...and the sadistic joy the tour guide gets from soaking tourists. (Hint: When you see a wet place, cover your camera.) After buying your ticket, you wait for the English tour, laugh and scramble through the entertaining 40-minute trick-water toy tour, and are then free to tour the forgettable palace with an included audioguide (€8.50, daily May–Sept 9:00–17:30, July–Aug until 22:00, April and Oct 9:00–16:30, closed Nov–March, tel. 0662/820-3720, www.hellbrunn.at).

Hellbrunn is nearly four miles south of Salzburg (bus #25 from station or from Staatsbrücke bridge, 2/hr, 20 min). While it can be fun—especially on a hot day or with kids—for many, it's a

Greater Salzburg

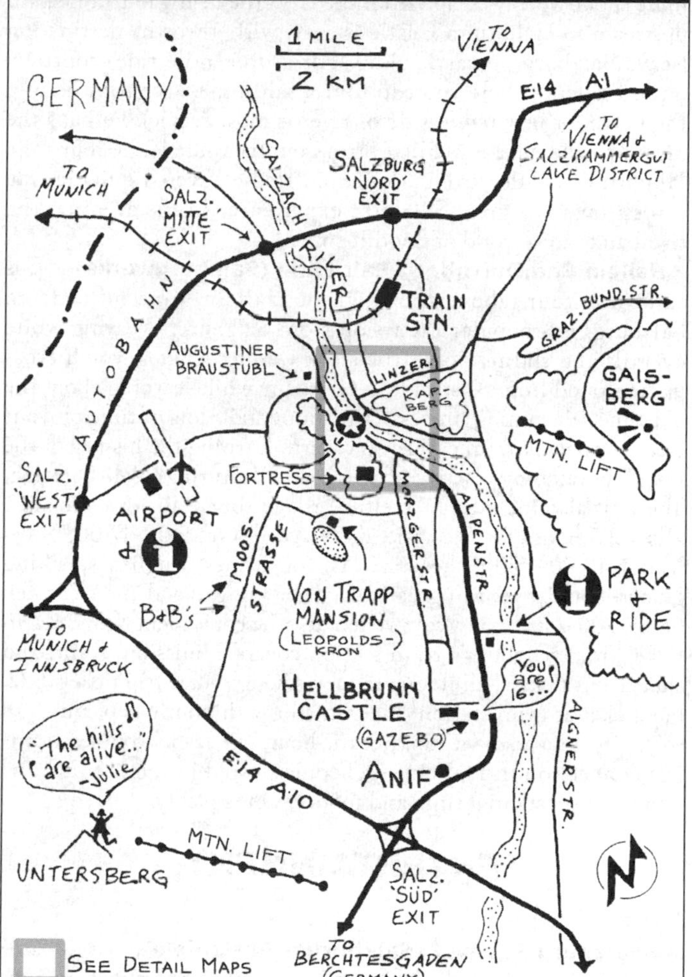

lot of trouble for a few water tricks. The Hellbrunn Baroque garden, one of the oldest in Europe, now features *S.O.M.*'s "Sixteen Going on Seventeen" gazebo.

Hellbrunn makes a good 30-minute bike excursion along the riverbank from Salzburg (described next).

▲▲Riverside or Meadow Bike Ride—The Salzach River has smooth, flat, and scenic bike lanes along each side (thanks to medieval tow paths—cargo boats would float downstream and be dragged back up by horse). On a sunny day, I can think of no more shout-worthy escape from the city. The nearly four-mile path upstream to Hellbrunn Castle is easy, with a worthy destination (leave Salzburg on castle side). For a nine-mile ride, continue on to Hallein (where you can tour a salt mine—see next listing; the north, or new town, side of river is most scenic). Perhaps the most pristine, meadow-filled farm-country route is the four-mile Hellbrunner Allee from Akademiestrasse. Even a quickie ride across town is a great Salzburg experience. In the evening, the riverbanks are a world of floodlit spires.

▲Hallein Bad Dürrnberg Salt Mine (Salzbergwerke)—This salt-mine tour (above the town of Hallein, nine miles from Salzburg) is a popular excursion from Salzburg. Wearing white overalls and sliding down the sleek wooden chutes, you'll cross underground from Austria into Germany while learning about the old-time salt-mining process. The tour entails lots of time on your feet as you walk from cavern to cavern, learning the history of the mine by watching a series of video skits featuring Wolf Dietrich. The visit also includes a "Celtic Village" open-air museum (€17, allow 2.5 hours for the visit, daily April–Oct 9:00–17:00, Nov–March 10:00–15:00, these are last tour times, English-speaking guides—but let your linguistic needs be known loud and clear, tel. 06132/200-2400, www.salzwelten.at). The convenient *Salz Erlebnis* ticket from Salzburg's train station covers admission, train, and shuttle bus tickets, all in one money-saving round-trip ticket (€22, buy ticket at train station; 40-min trip with hourly departures in each direction at about :15 after the hour, with synchronized train-bus connection in Hallein—schedule posted in flier). Salt mine tours cost substantial time and money. One's plenty.

SALZBURG

ENTERTAINMENT

Music Scene

▲▲Salzburg Festival (Salzburger Festspiele)—Each summer, from late July to the end of August, Salzburg hosts its famous Salzburg Festival, founded in 1920 to employ Vienna's musicians in the summer. This fun and festive time is crowded, but there are plenty of beds (except for a few August weekends). There are three big halls: the Opera and Orchestra venues in the Festival House, and the Landes Theater, where German-language plays are performed. Tickets for the big festival events are generally expensive (€50–200) and sell out well in advance (bookable from Jan). Most tourists think they're "going to the Salzburg Festival" by seeing smaller non-festival events that go on during the festival weeks. For these lesser events, same-day tickets are normally available (the ticket office on Mozartplatz, in the TI, prints a daily list of concerts and charges a 30 percent fee to book them). For specifics on this year's festival schedule and tickets, visit www.salzburgfestival.at, or contact the Austrian National Tourist Office in the United States (P.O. Box 1142, New York, NY 10108-1142, tel. 212/944-6880, fax 212/730-4568, www.austria.info, travel@austria.info). While I've never planned in advance, I've enjoyed great concerts with every visit.

▲▲Musical Events Year-Round—Salzburg is busy throughout the year, with 2,000 classical performances in its palaces and churches annually. Pick up the events calendar at the TI (free, bimonthly). Whenever you visit, you'll have a number of concerts (generally small chamber groups) to choose from. Here are some of the more accessible events:

Concerts at Hohensalzburg Fortress (Festungskonzerte): Nearly nightly concerts—Mozart's greatest hits for beginners—are held atop Festungsberg, in the "prince's chamber" of the fortress, featuring small chamber groups (open seating after the first six more expensive rows, €31 or €38 plus €3.40 for the funicular; at 19:30, 20:00, or 20:30; doors open 30 min early, tel. 0662/825-858 to reserve, pick up tickets at the door). The medieval-feeling chamber has windows overlooking the city, and the concert gives you a chance to enjoy the grand city view and a stroll through the castle courtyard. (The funicular ticket costs €3.40 within an hour of the show—ideal for people who just want to ascend for the view.) For €50, you can combine the concert with a four-course dinner (starts two hours before concert).

SALZBURG

Concerts at the Mirabell Palace (Schlosskonzerte): The nearly nightly chamber music concerts at the Mirabell Palace are performed in a lavish Baroque setting. They come with more sophisticated programs and better musicians than the fortress concerts. Baroque music flying around a Baroque hall is a happy bird in the right cage (open seating after the first five pricier rows, €29, usually at 20:00—but check flyer for times, doors open one hour ahead, tel. 0662/848-586, www.salzburger-schlosskonzerte.at).

"Five O'Clock Concerts" (5-Uhr-Konzerte): These concerts—next to St. Peter's in the old town—are cheaper, since they feature young artists (€12, July–Sept Thu–Tue at 17:00, no concerts Wed or Oct–June, 45 min, tel. 0662/8445-7619, www.5-uhr-konzerte.com). While the series is formally named after the brother of Joseph Haydn, it offers music from various masters.

Mozart Piano Sonatas: St. Peter's Abbey hosts these concerts each weekend (€18, €9 for children, €45 for a family of four, Fri and Sat at 19:00 year-round, tel. 0662/423-5645). This short and inexpensive concert is ideal for families.

Marionette Theater: Salzburg's much-loved marionette theater offers operas with spellbinding marionettes and recorded

The Sound of Music Debunked

Rather than visit the real-life sights from the life of Maria von Trapp and family, most tourists want to see the places where Hollywood chose to film this fanciful story. Local guides are happy not to burst any *S.O.M.* pilgrim's bubble, but keep these points in mind:

- "Edelweiss" is not a cherished Austrian folk tune or national anthem. Like all the "Austrian" music in the *S.O.M.*, it was composed for Broadway by Rodgers and Hammerstein. It was, however, the last composition that the famed team wrote together, as Hammerstein died in 1960—nine months after the musical opened.
- The *S.O.M.* implies that Maria was devoutly religious throughout her life, but Maria's foster parents raised her as a socialist and atheist. Maria discovered her religious calling while studying to be a teacher. After completing school, she joined the convent not as a nun, but as a novitiate (that is, she hadn't taken her vows yet).
- Maria's position was not as governess to all the children, as portrayed in the musical, but specifically as governess and teacher for the Captain's second-oldest daughter, Maria, who was bedridden with rheumatic fever.
- The Captain didn't run a tight domestic ship. In fact, his seven children were as unruly as most. But he did use a whistle to call them—each kid was trained to respond to a certain pitch.
- Though the von Trapp family did have seven children, the show changed all their names and even their genders. Rupert, the eldest child, responded to the often-asked tourist question, "Which one are you?" with a simple, "I'm Liesl!"
- The family didn't escape by hiking to Switzerland (which is a five-hour drive away). Rather, they pretended to go on one of their frequent mountain hikes. With only the

music. Music-lovers are mesmerized by the little people on stage (€18–35, nearly nightly at 19:30 June–Sept except Sun, also 3–4/week in May, some matinees, box office open Mon–Sat 9:00–13:00 and 2 hours before shows, near the Mirabell Gardens and Mozart's Residence at Schwarzstrasse 24, tel. 0662/872-406, www.marionetten.at). For a sneak preview, check out the videos playing at the marionette exhibit up in the fortress.

Mozart Dinner Concert: For those who'd like some classical music but would rather not sit through a concert, Stiftskeller St. Peter offers a traditional candlelit meal with Mozart's greatest hits performed by a string quartet and singers in historic costumes gavotting among the tables. In this elegant Baroque setting, tourists clap between movements and get three courses of food possessions in their backpacks, they "hiked" all the way to the train station (it was at the edge of their estate) and took a train to Italy. The movie scene showing them climbing into Switzerland was actually filmed near Berchtesgaden, Germany...home to Hitler's Eagle's Nest, and certainly not a smart place to flee to.

- The von Trapp family house exists...but it's not the one in the film. The mansion in the movie is actually two different buildings—one used for the front, the other for the back. The interiors were all filmed on Hollywood sets.
- For the film, Boris Levin designed a reproduction of the Nonnberg Abbey courtyard so faithful to the original (down to its cobblestones and stained-glass windows) that many still believe the cloister scenes were really shot at the abbey. And no matter what you hear in Salzburg, the graveyard scene (in which the von Trapps hide from the Nazis) was also filmed on the Fox lot.
- In 1956, a German film producer offered Maria $10,000 for the rights to her book. She asked for royalties, too, and a share of the profits. The agent explained that German law forbids film companies from paying royalties to foreigners (Maria had by then become a US citizen). She agreed to the contract and unknowingly signed away all film rights to her story. Only a few weeks later, he offered to pay immediately if she would accept $9,000 in cash. Because it was more money than the family had seen in all of their years of singing, she accepted the deal. Later, she discovered the agent had swindled them—no such law existed. (Rodgers, Hammerstein, and other producers did give the von Trapps a small percentage of the royalties, even though they weren't required to—but it was a small fraction of what they otherwise would have earned.)

(from Mozart-era recipes) mixed with three 20-minute courses of crowd-pleasing music (€48, Mozart-lovers with this guidebook pay €39 when booking direct in 2009, almost nightly at 20:00, dress is "smart casual," call to reserve at 0662/828-6950, www.mozartdinnerconcert.com). When they run out of space, they book a second quartet to perform in the adjacent Haydn Zimmer. I find the ambience much nicer in the main Baroque Hall—when making the booking, get a promise that that's where you'll be seated. For more details, see page 172.

Sound of Salzburg Dinner Show: The show at the Sternbräu Inn (see page 174) is Broadway in a dirndl with tired food. But it's a good show, and *Sound of Music* fans leave with hands red from clapping. A piano player and a hardworking quartet of singers wearing historical costumes perform an entertaining mix of *S.O.M.* hits and traditional folk songs (€46 for dinner, begins at 19:30). You can also come by at 20:30, pay €32, skip the dinner, and get the show. Those who book direct (not through a hotel) and pay cash get a 10 percent discount with this book in 2009 (nightly mid-May–mid-Oct, Griesgasse 23, tel. 0662/826-617, www.soundofsalzburgshow.com).

Music at Mass: Each Sunday morning, three great churches offer a Mass generally with glorious music. The Salzburg Cathedral is likely your best bet for fine music to worship by (10:00). The Franciscan church (9:00) and St. Peter's Church (10:30) are also enthusiastic about their musical Masses. See the Salzburg events guide for details.

Free Brass Band Concert: A traditional brass band plays in the Mirabell Gardens (May–Aug Sun at 10:30 and Wed at 20:30).

SLEEPING

Finding a room in Salzburg, even during its music festival (mid-July–Aug), is usually easy. Rates rise significantly (20–30 percent) during the music festival, and sometimes around Easter and Christmas; these higher prices do not appear in the ranges I've listed. You'll often be charged 10 percent extra for a one-night stay.

In the New Town, North of the River

These listings, clustering around Linzergasse, are in a pleasant neighborhood (with easy parking) a 15-minute walk from the train station (for directions, see "Arrival in Salzburg," earlier in this chapter) and a 10-minute walk to the old town. If you're coming from the old town, simply cross the main bridge (Staatsbrücke) to the mostly traffic-free Linzergasse. If driving, exit the highway at Salzburg-Nord, follow Vogelweiderstrasse straight to its end, and turn right.

$$$ Altstadthotel Wolf-Dietrich, around the corner from Linzergasse on pedestrians-only Wolf-Dietrich-Strasse, is well-located (with half its rooms overlooking St. Sebastian Cemetery). With 27 tastefully plush rooms, it's the best value I could find for a big, stylish hotel (Sb-€85–105, Db-€140–190, price depends on size, family deals, €20–40 more during festival time, complex pricing but readers of this book get a 10 percent discount on prevailing price in 2009—insist on this discount deducted from whatever price is offered that day, elevator, pool with loaner suits, sauna, free DVD library, Wolf-Dietrich-Strasse 7, tel. 0662/871-275, fax 0662/871-2759, www.salzburg-hotel.at, office@salzburg-hotel.at). Their annex across the street has 14 equally comfortable rooms (but no elevator, and therefore slightly cheaper prices).

Sleep Code

(€1 = about $1.50, country code: 43, area code: 0662)
S = Single, **D** = Double/Twin, **T** = Triple, **Q** = Quad, **b** = bathroom, **s** = shower only. Unless otherwise noted, credit cards are accepted and breakfast is included. All of these places speak English.

To help you sort easily through these listings, I've divided the rooms into three categories, based on the price for a standard double room with bath:

$$$ Higher Priced—Most rooms €90 or more.
$$ Moderately Priced—Most rooms between €60-90.
$ Lower Priced—Most rooms €60 or less.

$$$ Hotel Trumer Stube, three blocks from the river just off Linzergasse, has 20 clean, cozy rooms and a friendly, can-do owner (Sb-€65, Db-€105, Tb-€128, Qb-€147, about €30 more during music festival, top-floor rooms have lower ceilings and are €7 less expensive, 10 percent discount if you book direct with this book and pay cash in 2009—except during festival, entirely non-smoking, elevator, Internet access, Bergstrasse 6, tel. 0662/874-776, fax 0662/874-326, www.trumer-stube.at, info@trumer-stube.at, pleasant Silvia).

$$$ Hotel Goldene Krone, about five blocks from the river, is plain and basic, but a good value. Its 25 rooms are big, quiet, creaky, and well-kept—it'll feel like home right away (Sb-€69, Db-€119, Tb-€159, Qb-€189, claim your 10 percent discount off these prices with this book in 2009, elevator, parking €12/day, relaxing backyard garden, Linzergasse 48, tel. 0662/872-300, fax 0662/8723-0066, www.hotel-goldenekrone.com, office@hotel-goldenekrone.com, Claudia and Günther Hausknost). Ask about Günther's tours (€10/person, 2 hrs, 5 people minimum) and their "Rick Steves Two Nights in Salzburg" deal, which covers your room, a 24-hour Salzburg Card, a concert in Mirabell Palace, and a tour with Günther (Sb-€171, Db-€304, Tb-€429, Qb-€532).

$$ Institute St. Sebastian is in a somewhat sterile but very clean historic building next to St. Sebastian Cemetery. From October through June, the institute houses female students from various Salzburg colleges, and also rents 40 beds for travelers (men and women). From July through September, the students are gone and they rent all 100 beds (including 20 doubles) to travelers. The building has spacious public areas, a roof garden, a piano that guests are welcome to play, and some of the best rooms and dorm beds in town for the money. The immaculate doubles

Central Salzburg Hotels

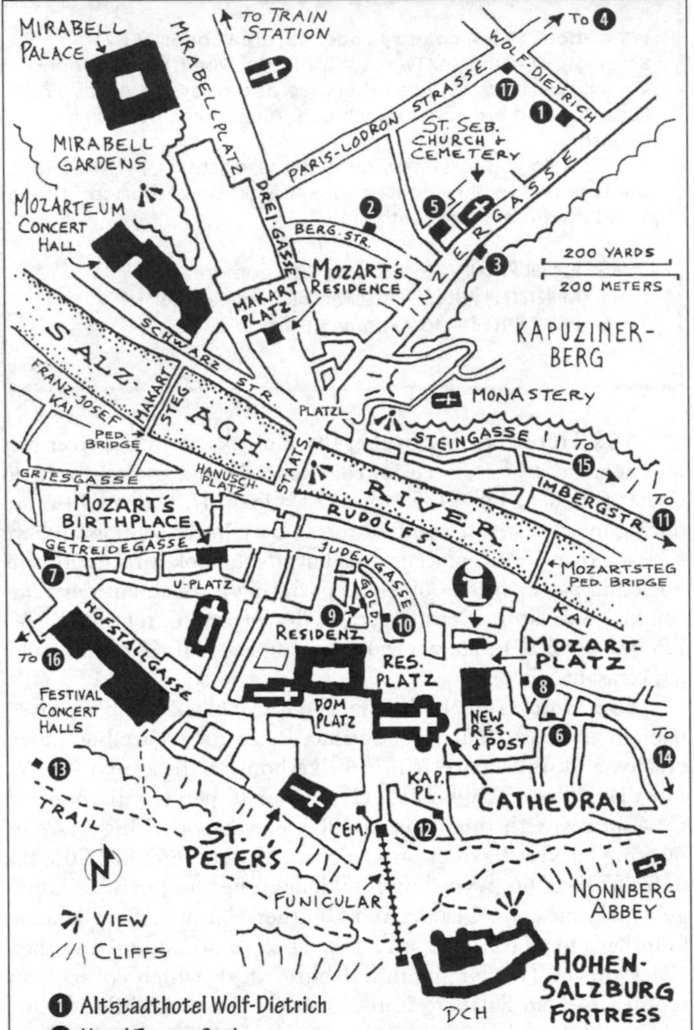

1. Altstadthotel Wolf-Dietrich
2. Hotel Trumer Stube
3. Hotel Goldene Krone
4. To Bergland Hotel & Hotel-Pension Jedermann
5. Institute St. Sebastian
6. Hotel-Pension Chiemsee
7. Blaue Gans Arthotel
8. Hotel Weisse Taube
9. Gasthaus zur Goldenen Ente
10. Hotel am Dom
11. To Hotel Rosenvilla
12. Christkönig Pension
13. Gasthaus Stadtalm
14. To Jugendgästehaus Salzburg
15. To Haus Arenberg
16. To Moosstrasse Zimmer
17. Launderette

come with modern baths and head-to-toe twin beds (S-€34, Sb-€42, D-€54, Db-€67, Tb-€81, Qb-€96, €2.50/person extra for 1-night stay, includes very basic breakfast, elevator, self-service laundry-€4/load; reception open daily July–Sept 7:30–12:00 & 13:00–21:30, Oct–June 8:00–12:00 & 16:00–21:00; Linzergasse 41, enter through arch at #37, tel. 0662/871-386, fax 0662/8713-8685, www.st-sebastian-salzburg.at, office@st-sebastian-salzburg.at). Students like the €21 bunks in 4- to 10-bed dorms (€2 less if you have sheets, no lockout time, free lockers, free showers). You'll find self-service kitchens on each floor (fridge space is free; request a key).

Pensions on Rupertgasse: These two hotels are about five blocks farther from the river on Rupertgasse, a breeze for drivers but with more street noise than the places on Linzergasse. They're both modern and well-run—good values if you don't mind being a bit away from the old town. **$$$ Bergland Hotel** is charming and classy, with comfortable, neo-rustic rooms. It's a modern building, and therefore spacious and solid (Sb-€65, Db-€95, Tb-€117, Qb-€140, elevator, Internet access, English library, bike rental-€6/day, Rupertgasse 15, tel. 0662/872-318, fax 0662/872-3188, www.berglandhotel.at, kuhn@berglandhotel.at, Kuhn family). The similar, boutique-like **$$$ Hotel-Pension Jedermann,** a few doors down, is tastefully done and comfortable, with an artsy painted-concrete ambience and a backyard garden (Sb-€65–85, Db-€90–130, Tb-€120–160, Qb-€160–200, much more during music festival, 5 percent discount with cash and 2-night stay, Internet access, Rupertgasse 25, tel. 0662/873-241, fax 0662/873-2419, www.hotel-jedermann.com, office@hotel-jedermann.com, Herr und Frau Gmachl).

In or Above the Old Town

Most of these hotels are near Residenzplatz. While this area is car-restricted, you're allowed to drive your car in to unload, pick up a map and parking instructions, and head for the €14-per-day garage in the mountain.

$$$ Blaue Gans Arthotel is ultra-modern, giving you a break from charming old Salzburg with artsy public spaces and 40 sleek but nothing-special rooms. It's beautifully located at the far end of Getreidegasse (Sb-€115–125, standard Db-€135–160, bigger superior Db-€185–195, fancier suites, elevator, free Internet access and Wi-Fi, Getreidegasse 41, tel. 0662/842-4910, fax 0662/842-4919, www.blauegans.at, office@blauegans.at).

$$$ Gasthaus zur Goldenen Ente is in a 600-year-old building with medieval stone arches and narrow stairs. Located above a good, smoke-free restaurant, it's as central as you can be on a pedestrian street in old Salzburg. The 17 rooms are modern and newly renovated (most of the year: Sb-€85, Db-€140; late July–Aug and Dec: Sb-€95, Db-€160; extra person-€29, non-smoking, elevator, free Internet access, Goldgasse 10, tel. 0662/845-622, fax 0662/845-6229, www.ente.at, hotel@ente.at). While this hotel's advertised rates are too high, travelers with this book get 10 percent off through 2009. Ulrika, Franziska, and Anita run a tight ship for the absentee owners.

$$$ Hotel Weisse Taube has 30 comfortable rooms in a quiet, dark-wood furnished 1365 building, well-located about a block off Mozartplatz (Sb-€67–85, Db with shower-€98–138, bigger Db with bath-€119–162, 10 percent discount with this book and cash in 2009 if you book direct, elevator, Internet access, tel. 0662/842-404, fax 0662/841-783, Kaigasse 9, www.weissetaube.at, hotel@weissetaube.at).

$$$ Hotel am Dom is perfectly located—on Goldgasse a few steps from the cathedral—but may close for renovation in 2009. Its 14 rooms are big, old, and basic, but well-maintained and filled with hand-painted furniture (Db-€88–106 depending on season, extra bed-€36, non-smoking, Goldgasse 17, tel. 0662/842-765, fax 0662/8427-6555, www.amdom.at, bach@salzburg.co.at).

$$$ Hotel-Pension Chiemsee is a stony dollhouse nestled in a quiet lane just behind the cathedral. Hardworking Frau Höllbacher rents 10 big, beautifully renovated rooms and two suites (Sb-€48–58, Db-€88–98, Tb-€110–120, suite-€110 for 2 people, €28 each additional person up to 5; during music festival and Dec: Sb-€68, Db-€98–116, Tb-€120–130; these special Rick Steves prices available through 2009 if you book direct and pay cash, Chiemseegasse 5, tel. 0662/844-208, fax 0662/8442-0870, www.hotel-ami.de/hotel/chiemsee, hotel-chiemsee@aon.at).

$$ Christkönig Pension makes you feel like a guest of the bishop because, in a sense...you are. With 20 rooms in a 14th-century church building just under the castle and behind the cathedral, this is where the bishop's visitors stay. It's a charming, quiet, and unique way to sleep well and affordably in the old center (S-€35, Ss-€41, Sb-€46, Ds-€68, Db-€80, suite for 2–4 people roughly €45/person, twin beds only, €3/person extra for 1-night stays, cash only, Kapitelplatz 2a, tel. 0662/842627, www.christkoenig-kolleg.at, christkoenig-pension@salzburg.co.at). Heavenly Frau Anna Huemer will take excellent care of you.

Hostels

For another hostel (on the other side of the river), see "International Youth Hotel," next page.

$ Gasthaus Stadtalm (a.k.a. the Naturfreundehaus) is a local version of a mountaineer's hut and a great budget alternative. Snuggled in a forest on the remains of a 15th-century castle wall atop the little mountain overlooking Salzburg, it has magnificent town and mountain views. While the 26 beds are designed-for-backpackers rustic, the price and view are the best in town—with the right attitude, it's a fine experience (€18.50/person in 2-, 4-, and 6-bed dorms, same price for room with double bed; includes breakfast, sheets, and shower; lockers, 2 minutes from top of €3 round-trip Mönchsberg elevator, Mönchsberg 19C, tel. & fax 0662/841-729, www.diestadtalm.com, ng.esterer@utanet.at, Peter and Roland). Once again, be warned: This is a rustic hostel on the mountaintop in a forest, an elevator ride above the city.

$ Jugendgästehaus Salzburg is just steps from the old town center, and yet removed from the bustle. While its dorm rooms are the standard crammed-with-beds variety, the doubles and family rooms are modern, roomy, and bright. The hallways will bring back high-school memories, but the recent renovation has made the public spaces quite pleasant (bed in 8-person dorm-€20–22, Db-€65–68, Qs-€98–104, higher prices are for May–Sept, €3 more for 1 or 2-night stays, non-members pay €1.50 extra, includes breakfast and sheets, free parking, just around the east side of the castle hill at Josef-Preis-Allee 18; from train station take bus #5 or #25 to the Justizgebäude stop, head left, cross the street after one block, and walk down Josefs-Preis-Alle for a few minutes—it's the big renovated building on the right; tel. 0662/842-670, fax 0662/841-101, www.jfgh.at/salzburg.php, salzburg@jfgh.at). The new hotel at the back of the hostel isn't as cheap, but does offer more standard hotel amenities (Db-€82–96 depending on season, includes breakfast).

SALZBURG

Near the Train Station

$$ Pension Adlerhof, a plain and decent old pension, is two blocks in front of the train station (left off Kaiserschutzenstrasse), but a 15-minute walk from the sightseeing action. It has a quirky staff, a boring location, and 30 stodgy-but-spacious rooms (Sb-€49–68, Db-€69–108, Tb-€93–123, Qb-€108–156, cash only, elevator, Elisabethstrasse 25, tel. 0662/875-236, fax 0662/873-663, www.gosalzburg.com, adlerhof@pension-adlerhof.at).

$ International Youth Hotel, a.k.a. the "Yo-Ho," is the most lively, handy, and American of Salzburg's hostels. This easygoing place speaks English first; has cheap meals, 160 beds, lockers, Internet access, laundry, tour discounts, and no curfew; plays *The Sound of Music* free daily at 10:30; runs a lively bar; and welcomes anyone of any age. The noisy atmosphere and lack of a curfew can make it hard to sleep (€18–19 in 6- to 8-bed dorms, €21–22 in dorms with bathrooms, D-€44, Ds-€56, Q-€76, Qs-€88, includes sheets, cheap breakfast, 6 blocks from station toward Linzergasse and 6 blocks from river at Paracelsusstrasse 9, tel. 0662/879-649, fax 0662/878-810, www.yoho.at, office@yoho.at).

Four-Star Hotels in Residential Neighborhoods away from the Center

Two plush, modern hotels in nondescript residential neighborhoods a 15-minute walk from the old town are a fine value for those wanting elegant, stylish furnishings, spacious public spaces, generous balconies, gardens, and free parking. While not ideal for train travelers, drivers in need of no-stress comfort for a home base should consider these.

$$$ Hotel Rosenvilla, closer to the river, offers 14 rooms with modern art, minimalist furnishings, and an organic closeness to nature (Sb-€79, Db-€128, bigger Db-€142, Db suite-€188, at least €30 more during music festival, Höfelgasse 4, tel. 0662/621-765, fax 0662/625-2308, www.rosenvilla.com, hotel@rosenvilla.com).

$$$ Haus Arenberg, higher up opposite the old town, rents 17 big, breezy rooms—most with generous balconies—in a quiet garden setting (Sb-€79–88, Db-€125–142, Tb-€148–158, Qb-€158–165, €25 more during music festival, Blumensteinstrasse 8, tel. 0662/640-097, fax 0662/640-0973, www.arenberg-salzburg.at, info@arenberg-salzburg.at, family Leobacher).

Zimmer (Private Rooms)

These are generally roomy and comfortable, and come with a good breakfast, easy parking, and tourist information. Off-season, competition softens prices. While they are a bus ride from town, with a €3.40 transit day pass *(Tageskarte)* and the frequent service, this shouldn't keep you away. In fact, most will happily pick you up at the train station if you simply telephone them and ask. Most will also do laundry for a small fee for those staying at least two nights. I've listed prices for two nights or more—if staying only one night, expect a 10 percent surcharge. Most push tours and concerts to make money on the side. As they are earning a commission, if you go through them, you'll probably lose the discount I've negotiated for my readers who go direct.

Beyond the Train Station

$ Brigitte Lenglachner rents eight basic, well-cared-for rooms in her home in a quiet, suburban-feeling neighborhood that's a 25-minute walk, 10-minute bike ride, or easy bus ride away from the center. Frau Lenglachner serves breakfast in the garden (in good weather) and happily provides plenty of local information and advice (S-€25, D-€40, Db-€48, T-€53, Qb-€96, 5b-€113; apartment with kitchen-€56 for Db; €90 for Tb, €110 for Qb; easy and free parking, Scheibenweg 8, tel. & fax 0662/438-044, bedandbreakfast4u@yahoo.de). It's a 10-minute walk from station: Head for the river, cross the pedestrian Pioneer Bridge (Pioniersteg), turn right, and walk along the river to the third street (Scheibenweg).

Turn left, and it's halfway down on the right.

On Moosstrasse

The busy street called Moosstrasse, which runs southwest of Mönchsberg (behind the mountain and away from the old town center), is lined with *Zimmer*. Handy bus #21 connects Moosstrasse to the center frequently (Mon–Fri 4/hr until 17:00, evenings and weekends 2/hr). To get to these from the train station, take bus #1, #5, #6, or #25 to Makartplatz, where you'll change to #21. If you're coming from the old town, catch bus #21 from Hanuschplatz, just downstream of the Staatsbrücke bridge near the *Tabak* kiosk. Buy a €1.60 *Einzelkarte–Kernzone* ticket (for 1 trip) or a €3.40 *Tageskarte* (day pass, good for 24 hours) from the streetside machine and punch it when you board the bus. The bus stop you use for each *Zimmer* is included in the following listings. If you're driving from the center, go through the tunnel, continue straight on Neutorstrasse, and take the fourth left onto Moosstrasse. Drivers exit the autobahn at *Süd* and then head in the direction of *Grodig*.

$$ Pension Bloberger Hof, while more a hotel than a pension, is comfortable and friendly, with a peaceful, rural location and 20 farmer-plush, good-value rooms. It's the farthest out, but reached by the same bus #21 from the center (Sb-€50–60, Db-€70, big new Db with balcony-€90, Db suite-€120, extra bed-€20, family apartment with kitchen, Inge und her daughter Sylvia offer those booking direct with this book and paying cash a 10 percent discount in 2009, non-smoking, free Internet access and Wi-Fi, restaurant for guests, free loaner bikes, free station pick-up if staying 3 nights, Hammerauer Strasse 4, bus stop: Hammerauer Strasse, tel. 0662/830-227, fax 0662/827-061, www.blobergerhof .at, office@blobergerhof.at).

$ Frau Ballwein offers four cozy, charming, and fresh rooms in two buildings, all with intoxicating view balconies (Sb-€35–37, D-€48, Db-€55–60 Tb-€78, Qb-€80–85, family deals, cash only, farm-fresh breakfasts, non-smoking, small pool, free parking, Moosstrasse 69-A, bus stop: Gsengerweg, tel. & fax 0662/824-029, www.haus-ballwein.at, haus.ballwein@gmx.net).

$ Helga Bankhammer rents four nondescript rooms in a farmhouse, with a real dairy farm out back (D-€46, Db-€52, no surcharge for 1-night stays, family deals, non-smoking, laundry-about €6 per load, Moosstrasse 77, bus stop: Marienbad, tel. & fax 0662/830-067, www.privatzimmer.at/helga.bankhammer, bank hammer@aon.at).

$ Haus Reichl, with three good rooms at the end of a long lane, feels the most remote (Db-€60, Tb-€75, Qb-€92–97, cash preferred, doubles and triples have balcony and view, non-smoking, between Ballwein and Bankhammer B&Bs, 200 yards down

Reiterweg to #52, bus stop: Gsengerweg, tel. & fax 0662/826-248, www.privatzimmer.at/haus-reichl, haus.reichl@telering.at). Franziska offers free loaner bikes for guests (20-min pedal to the center).

EATING

In the Old Town

Salzburg boasts many inexpensive, fun, and atmospheric eateries. I'm a sucker for big cellars with their smoky, Old World atmosphere, heavy medieval arches, time-darkened paintings, antlers, hearty meals, and plump patrons. Most of these restaurants are centrally located in the old town, famous with visitors, but also enjoyed by the locals.

Gasthaus zum Wilden Mann is *the* place if the weather's bad and you're in the mood for *Hofbräu* atmosphere and a hearty, cheap meal at a shared table in one small, smoky, well-antlered room. Notice the 1999 flood photo on the wall. For a quick lunch, get the *Bauernschmaus,* a mountain of dumplings, kraut, and peasant's meats (€9.50). Owner Robert—who runs the restaurant with Schwarzenegger-like energy—enjoys fostering a convivial ambience (you'll share tables with strangers) and serving fresh traditional cuisine at great prices. I simply love this place (€7–11 daily specials, Mon–Sat 11:00–21:00, closed Sun, 2 min from Mozart's Birthplace, enter from Getreidegasse 22, tel. 0662/841-787).

Stiftskeller St. Peter has been in business for more than 1,000 years—it was mentioned in the biography of Charlemagne. It's classy and central as can be, serving uninspired traditional Austrian cuisine (€10–25 meals, daily 11:30–22:30, indoor/outdoor seating, next to St. Peter's Church at foot of Mönchsberg, restaurant tel. 0662/841-268). They host the Mozart Dinner Concert described on page 162 (€48, nearly nightly at 20:00, call 0662/828-6950 to reserve, ask about a discount if you book direct with this guidebook). Through the centuries, they've learned to charge for each piece of bread and not serve free tap water.

St. Paul's Stub'n Beer Garden is tucked secretly away under the castle with an ignore-the-tourists-attitude (menu in German only). The food is better than a beer hall, and a young, Bohemian-chic clientele fills its two smoky, troll-like rooms and its idyllic, tree-shaded garden. *Kasnock'n* is a tasty mountaineers' pasta with cheese served in an iron pan with a side salad for €8 (€6–9 daily specials, €7–15 plates, Mon–Sat 17:00–23:00, open later for drinks only, closed Sun, Herrengasse 16, tel. 0662/843-220).

Fisch Krieg Restaurant, on the river where the fishermen used to sell their catch, is a great value. They serve fast, fresh, and inexpensive fish in a casual dining room—where trees grow

Central Salzburg Restaurants

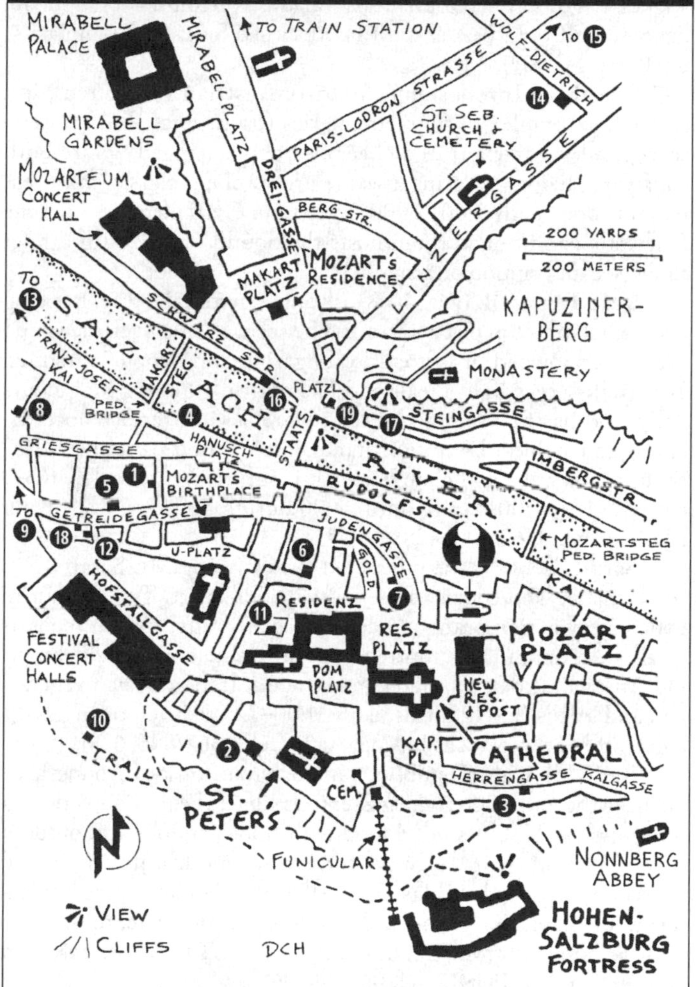

1. Gasthaus zum Wilden Mann
2. Stiftskeller St. Peter Rest.
3. St. Paul's Stub'n Beer Garden
4. Fisch Krieg Rest.
5. Sternbräu Inn
6. Café Tomaselli
7. Saran Essbar
8. Bar Club Café Republic
9. To Afro Coffee
10. Gasthaus Stadtalm
11. Toskana Cafeteria Mensa
12. Bosna Grill
13. To Augustiner Bräustübl
14. Spicy Spices
15. To Biergarten die Weisse
16. Café Bazar
17. Steingasse Pub Crawl
18. Sporer Schnapps Pub
19. Stein Terrasse

through the ceiling—as well as great riverside seating (€2 fishwiches to go, self-serve €7 meals, salad bar, Mon–Fri 8:30–18:30, Sat 8:30–13:00, July–Aug until 14:00, closed Sun, Hanuschplatz 4, tel. 0662/843-732).

Sternbräu Inn, a sloppy, touristy Austrian food circus, is a sprawling complex of popular eateries (traditional, Italian, self-serve, and vegetarian) in a cheery garden setting. Explore both courtyards before choosing a seat (Bürgerstube is classic, most restaurants open daily 9:00–24:00, enter from Getreidegasse 34). One fancy, air-conditioned room hosts the Sound of Salzburg dinner show (see description on page 163).

Café Tomaselli (with its Kiosk annex across the way) has long been Salzburg's top place to see and be seen. While overpriced and often overcrowded, it is good for lingering and people-watching. Tomaselli serves light meals and lots of drinks, keeps long hours daily, and has fine seating on the square, a view terrace upstairs, and indoor tables. Despite its fancy inlaid wood paneling, 19th-century portraits, and chandeliers, it is surprisingly low-key (€3–7 entrées, daily 7:00–21:00, until 24:00 during music festival, Alter Markt 9, tel. 0662/844-488).

Saran Essbar is the product of hardworking Mr. Saran (from the Punjab), who cooks and serves with his heart. This delightful little eatery is rich orange under medieval vaults. Its fun menu is small (Mr. Saran is committed to both freshness and value), mixing Austrian (great schnitzel and strudel), Italian, Asian vegetarian, and salads (€9–12 meals, daily 11:00–22:00, often open later, a block off Mozartplatz at Judengasse 10, tel. 0662/846-628).

Bar Club Café Republic, a hip hangout for local young people near the end of Getreidegasse, feels like a theater lobby during intermission. It serves good food with smoky indoor and outdoor seating. It's ideal if you want something mod, untouristy, and un-wursty (trendy breakfasts 8:00–18:00, Asian and international menu, €7–12 plates, lots of hard drinks, daily until late, music with a DJ Fri and Sat from 23:00, salsa music on Tue night, no cover, Anton Neumayr Platz 2, tel. 0662/841-613).

Afro Coffee, between Getreidegasse and the Mönchsberg lift, is understandably popular with its student clientele. They serve tea, coffee, cocktails, and tasty food with a dose of '70s funk and a healthy sense of humor. The menu includes pan-African specialties—try the spicy chicken couscous—as well as standard soups and salads (€9–13 main dishes, Mon–Sat 9:00–24:00, closed Sun, between Getreidegasse and cliff face at Bürgerspitalplatz 5, tel. 0662/844-888).

On the Mountaintop Above the Old Town: **Gasthaus Stadtalm,** Salzburg's mountaineers' hut, sits high above the old town on the edge of the cliff with cheap prices, good food, and great views. If hiking across Mönchsberg, make this your goal (traditional food, salads, cliffside garden seating or cozy-mountain-hut indoor seating, an indoor view table booked for a decade of New Year's celebrations, 2 min from top of €3 round-trip Mönchsberg elevator, also reachable by stairs from Toscanini Hof, Mönchsberg 19C, tel. & fax 0662/841-729, Peter and Roland). While they're open daily 10:00–24:00, they close in bad weather and in Jan–Feb.

Eating Cheaply in the Old Town

Toskana Cafeteria Mensa is the students' lunch canteen, fast and cheap—with indoor seating and a great courtyard for sitting outside with students and teachers instead of tourists. They serve a daily soup-and-main-course special for €4 (Mon–Fri 9:00–15:00, hot meals served 11:00–13:30 only, closed Sat–Sun, behind the Residenz, in the courtyard opposite Sigmund-Haffnergasse 16).

Sausage stands serve the town's favorite "fast food." The best stands (like those on Universitätsplatz) use the same boiling water all day, which gives the weenies more flavor. Key words: *Weisswurst*—boiled white sausage; *Bosna*—with onions and curry; *Käsekrainer*—with melted cheese inside; *Debreziner*—spicy Hungarian; *Frankfurter*—our weenie; *frische*—fresh ("eat before the noon bells"); and *Senf*—mustard (ask for *süss*—sweet; or *scharf*—sharp). Only a tourist puts the sausage in a bun like a hot dog. Munch alternately between the meat and the bread ("that's why you have two hands"), and you'll look like a native. Generally, the darker the weenie, the spicier it is. The Salzburgers' favorite spicy sausage is sold at the 55-year-old **Bosna Grill,** run by chatty Frau Ebner (€2.70; survey the four spicy options—described in English—and choose a number; take-away only, steady and sturdy local crowd, Mon–Fri 11:00–19:00, May–Dec also Sat 11:00–17:00, July–Dec also Sun 16:00–20:00, hours vary according to demand, hiding down the tunnel at Getreidegasse 33 across from Eisgrotte).

Picnickers will appreciate the bustling morning **produce market** (daily except Sun) on Universitätsplatz, behind Mozart's house (see page 149).

Away from the Center

Augustiner Bräustübl, a huge 1,000-seat beer garden within the monk-run Augustiner brewery, is rustic and crude. Don't be fooled by second-rate gardens serving the same beer nearby. The Augustiner is closed for lunch, but on busy nights, it's like a Munich beer hall with no music but the volume turned up. When it's cool, you'll enjoy a historic setting with beer-sloshed and smoke-stained halls. On balmy evenings, it's like a Monet painting—but with beer breath—under chestnut trees in the garden. Local students

mix with tourists eating hearty slabs of schnitzel with their fingers or cold meals from the self-serve picnic counter, while children frolic on the playground kegs. For your beer: Pick up a half-liter or full-liter mug (*schank* means self-serve price, *bedienung* is the price with waiter service), pay the lady, wash your mug, give Mr. Keg your receipt and empty mug, and you will be made happy. Waiters don't bring food—instead, go up the stairs, survey the hallway of deli counters, and assemble your own meal (or, as long as you buy a drink, you can bring in a picnic). Classic pretzels from the bakery and spiraled, salty radishes make great beer even better. For dessert—after a visit to the strudel kiosk—enjoy the incomparable floodlit view of old Salzburg from the nearby Müllnersteg pedestrian bridge and a riverside stroll home (open daily 15:00–23:00, Augustinergasse 4, tel. 0662/431-246). It's about a 15-min walk along the river (with the river on your right) from the Staatsbrücke bridge. Head up Müllner Hauptstrasse northwest along the river and ask for "Müllnerbräu" (MEWL-ner-broy), its nickname.

North of the River, near Recommended Linzergasse Hotels

Spicy Spices is a trippy vegetarian-Indian restaurant where Suresh Syad serves tasty take-out curry and rice, samosas, organic salads, vegan soups, and fresh juices (€6 specials, Mon–Sat 10:00–22:00, Sun 12:00–21:00, Wolf-Dietrich-Strasse 1, tel. 0662/870-712).

Biergarten die Weisse, close to the hotels on Rupertgasse and away from the tourists, is a longtime hit with the natives. If a beer hall can be happening, this one—modern yet with antlers—is it. Their famously good beer is made right there; favorites include their fizzy wheat beer *(Weisse)* and their seasonal beers (on request). Enjoy the beer with their good, cheap traditional food in the great garden seating, or in the wide variety of indoor rooms—sports bar, young and noisy, or older and more elegant (daily specials, Mon–Sat 10:00–24:00, Sun 9:00–18:00, Rupertgasse 10, east of Bayerhamerstrasse, tel. 0662/872-246).

Café Bazar, overlooking the river between Mirabell Gardens and the Staatsbrücke bridge, is as close as you'll get to a Vienna coffee house in Salzburg. It's *the* venerable spot for a classy drink with an old-town-and-castle view (daily €7 plate and light meals, Mon–Sat 7:30–23:00, Sun 9:00–18:00, Schwarzstrasse 3, tel. 0662/874-278).

Steingasse Pub Crawl

For a fun post-concert activity, crawl through medieval Steingasse's trendy pubs (all open until the wee hours). This is a local and hip scene, but accessible to older tourists: dark bars filled with well-dressed Salzburgers lazily smoking cigarettes and talking philosophy, with avant-garde Euro-pop throbbing on the soundtrack. Most of the pubs are in cellar-like caves...extremely atmospheric. (For more on Steingasse, see page 157.) These four pubs are all within about 100 yards of each other. Start at the Linzergasse end of Steingasse.

Pepe Cocktail Bar, with Mexican decor and Latin music, serves tostadas with fun toppings *con* cocktails (nightly 19:00–3:00 in the morning, live DJs Fri–Sat from 23:00, Steingasse 3, tel. 0662/873-662).

Shrimps, next door and less claustrophobic, is more a restaurant than a bar, serving creative international dishes (spicy shrimp sandwiches and salads, nightly 18:00–24:00, Steingasse 5, tel. 0662/874-484).

Saiten Sprung wins the "Best Atmosphere" award. The door is kept closed to keep out the crude and rowdy. Ring the bell and enter its hellish interior—lots of stone and red decor, with mountains of melted wax beneath age-old candlesticks and a classic soul music ambience. Stelios, who speaks English with Greek charm, serves cocktails, fine wine, and wine-friendly Italian antipasti (nightly 21:00–4:00 in the morning, Steingasse 11, tel. 0662/881-377).

Fridrich, a tiny place next door with lots of mirrors and a silver ceiling fan, specializes in wine. Bernd Fridrich is famous for his martinis, and passionate about Austrian wines and food (€5–12 small entrées, nightly from 18:00 in summer or 17:00 in winter, Steingasse 15, tel. 0662/876-218).

TRANSPORTATION CONNECTIONS

By train, Salzburg is the first stop over the German–Austrian border. This means that if Salzburg is your only stop in Austria, and you're using a Eurail Selectpass that does not include Austria, you do not have to pay extra or add Austria to your pass to get here.

From Salzburg by Train to: Berchtesgaden (hourly, 45–60 min; bus easier—hourly, 30 min, buses leave across from Salzburg train station), **Reutte** (hourly, 5 hrs, change either in Munich and Kempten, or in Innsbruck and Garmisch), **Munich** (2/hr, 1.5–2 hrs), **Nürnberg** (hourly with change in Munich, 3 hrs), **Innsbruck** (direct every 2 hrs, 2 hrs), **Vienna** (hourly, 3 hrs). Train info: tel. 051-717 (to get an operator, dial 2, then 2).

Route Tips for Drivers

From Munich (or the Autobahn) into Salzburg: After crossing the border, stay on the autobahn, taking the Salzburg Süd exit in the direction of Anif. First, you'll pass Schloss Hellbrunn (and zoo), then the Salzburg Süd TI and a park-and-ride service—a smart place to park for your time in Salzburg. Get sightseeing information and transit tickets from the TI (generally open 10:00–18:00, often closed Mon–Tue, closed in winter, tel. 0662/8898-7360). Park your car (€5) and catch the shuttle bus into town (€1.60 for a single ticket, or covered by €3.40 *Tageskarte* day pass, both sold at the TI, more expensive if you buy tickets on board, every 5 min, bus #3 or #8). Mozart never drove in the old town, and neither should you. If you don't believe in park-and-rides, the easiest, cheapest, most central parking lot is the 1,500-car Altstadt lot in the tunnel under the Mönchsberg (€14/day, note your slot number and which of the twin lots you're in, tel. 0662/846-434). Your hotel may provide discounted parking passes.

Berchtesgaden

This alpine ski town in the region of the same name (just across the border in Germany's southeastern tip, 12 miles south of Salzburg) is famous for its fjord-like lake and its mountaintop Nazi retreat. Long before its association with Hitler, it was one of the classic Romantic corners of Germany. In fact, Hitler's propagandists capitalized on the Führer's love of this region to establish the notion that the former Austrian was truly German at heart.

Getting There

From Salzburg, the bus is more scenic and direct than the train (bus runs hourly, 30 min, bus station across street from Salzburg's train station, bus also stops in Salzburg's old town—on Rudolfskai, near the Staatsbrücke). You can also visit Berchtesgaden from Munich (at least hourly, 2.5–3 hrs, train to Salzburg or Freilassing, then train or—more frequently—bus to Berchtesgaden). From the Berchtesgaden station, bus #840 goes to the salt mines (a 20-min walk otherwise), bus #838 goes to the Nazi Documentation Center (Obersalzberg stop, plus a 5-min walk—meet Eagle's Nest shuttle bus here), and bus #841 goes to the Königsee.

Planning Your Time

Berchtesgaden's attractions include the **town** (a touristy mess); **salt mines** (similar to tours across the border in Austria); the romantic, pristine lake called **Königsee** (extremely popular with less-adventurous Germans); and Obersalzberg with **Hitler's Eagle's Nest** (fascinating if you're into Nazi history, and stunningly scenic from the top).

ORIENTATION

Berchtesgaden can be inundated with Germans on vacation. During peak season, you may find yourself in a traffic jam of tourists desperately trying to turn their money into fun. Still, its sights are impressive, connections from Salzburg (and Munich) are excellent, and its various attractions are quite handy by local bus from the train station.

Tourist Information: The TI is across from the train station (tel. 08652/656-500, from Austria tel. 00-49-8652/656-500, www.berchtesgadener-land.com).

Eagle's Nest Historical Tours: For 20 years, David and Christine Harper—who rightly consider this visit more an educational opportunity than simple sightseeing—have organized thoughtful tours of the Hitler-related sites of Berchtesgaden. Their well-organized bus tours depart from the Visitors Center opposite the Berchtesgaden train station (€48, English only, daily at 13:30 mid-May–Oct, 4 hours, 25 people maximum, reservation required, tel. 08652/64971, www.eagles-nest-tours.com). While the price is €48, your actual cost for the guiding is only about €26, as the tour includes the (otherwise obligatory) bus connections and admissions. They also arrange private guides and *Sound of Music* excursions to Salzburg (see their website for details).

SIGHTS

▲Salt Mines—At the Berchtesgaden salt mines, you put on traditional miners' outfits, get on funny little trains, and zip deep into the mountain. For one hour, you'll cruise subterranean lakes; slide speedily down two long, slick, wooden banisters; and learn how they mined salt so long ago. Call for crowd-avoidance advice. When the weather gets bad, this place is mobbed. You can buy a ticket early and browse through the town until your appointed tour time. While tours are in German, English-speakers get audioguides (€14, daily May–Oct 9:00–17:00, Nov–April 11:30–15:00, German tel. 08652/600-220, from Austria tel. 00-49-8652/600-220).

▲Königsee—The idyllic Königsee stretches like a fjord through pristine mountain scenery from Berchtesgaden to the dramatically situated Church of St. Bartholomew, and beyond. Most visitors simply glide scenically for 35 minutes on the silent, electronically propelled boat ride to the church, enjoy that peaceful setting, then glide back. Boats, going at a sedate Bavarian speed and filled with

Germans chuckling at the captain's commentary, leave with demand—usually three per hour (€11 round-trip, bus #841 runs from train station to boat dock, parking-€3). At a rock cliff midway through the journey, your captain stops, and the first mate pulls out a trumpet to demonstrate the fine echo.

The remote red onion-domed **Church of St. Bartholomew** (once home of a monastery, then a hunting lodge of the Bavarian royal family) is surrounded by a fine beer garden, rustic fishermen's pub, and inviting lakeside trails. The family living next to St. Bartholomew's in the middle of this national park has a license to fish—so very fresh trout is the lunchtime favorite.

▲▲▲Obersalzberg and Hitler's Eagle's Nest (Kehlsteinhaus)—Early in his career as a wannabe tyrant, Adolf Hitler was inspired by this dramatic corner of Bavaria, so steeped in legend and close to the soul of the German people. This place, partly Austrian and partly Bavarian, held a special appeal to the Austrian-German Hitler. In the 1920s, just out of prison, he checked into an alpine hut here to finish up work on his memoir and Nazi primer, *Mein Kampf.* Because it was here that he claimed to be inspired and laid out his vision, some call Obersalzberg the "cradle of the Third Reich."

In the 1930s, as the German Führer, Hitler chose this place for his mountain retreat (and later, had it prepared for his last stand). His handlers crafted Hitler's image here—surrounded by nature, gently receiving alpine flowers from adoring little children, lounging around with farmers in lederhosen...no modern arms industry, no big-time industrialists, no ugly extermination camps. In reality, rather than an alpine chalet, it was a huge compound of 80 buildings—closed to the public after 1936—where the major decisions leading up to WWII were hatched. It was here that Hitler hosted world leaders, wowing them with the aesthetics and engineering of his mountain palace, the adoration of his people... and National Socialism.

Orientation: Visitors are often confused by the lay of the land. Your visit has three parts: the Obersalzberg complex and its small, modern **Nazi Documentation Center museum** (a short bus ride above Berchtesgaden, with free parking; also the terminus for the shuttle bus providing the only access to the Eagle's Nest high above); the vast and tourable remains of the **bunker system** (below the museum and included in that ticket); and the actual **Eagle's Nest** (a small yet mighty stone chalet capping the mountain high above).

Between 1945 and 1952, almost everything was destroyed by the victorious Allies (wanting to leave nothing as a magnet for future neo-Nazi pilgrims). If looking for actual pre-1945 artifacts, you'll only see this: the foundations of the Documentation Center (now mostly a modern building); the stripped-bare yet still evocative bunkers under it; the dramatic road to the Eagle's Nest; the stonework, elevator, and fireplace of the actual Eagle's Nest; and a very few papers and memorabilia in glass cases in the Documentation Center.

Nazi Documentation Center: This exhibit is built upon the remains of what was the second seat of Nazi administration. It's small—three floors of exhibits—with almost no actual artifacts, but evocative for the setting. This center, with only German descriptions (rent the €2 English audioguide), is designed primarily for Germans to learn and understand their recent history. Only since the late 1990s has interest in Nazi history been considered healthy rather than taboo. Non-Germans, too, can learn from a thoughtful visit (€3; April–Oct daily 9:00–17:00; Nov–March Tue–Sun 10:00–15:00, closed Mon; last entry one hour before closing, allow 90 min for visit, German tel. 08652/947-960, from Austria tel. 00-49-8652/947-960, www.obersalzberg.de). Buses depart from here to the Eagle's Nest.

Bunkers: From the Documentation Center, stairs lead into a complex and vast bunker system (same ticket and hours as Documentation Center). Construction began in 1943, after the Battle of Stalingrad ended the Nazi aura of invincibility. This is an incredibly engineered underground town with meeting rooms, offices, archives for the government, and lavish living quarters for Hitler—all connected by four miles of tunnels cut by slave labor through solid rock. It was stripped bare after the war. Today, you can wander among the concrete and marvel at megalomania gone mad.

Eagle's Nest: While many call the entire area "Hitler's Eagle's Nest," that name actually refers only to the mountaintop

chalet given to the Führer for his 50th birthday in 1939. While a fortune was spent to build this perch, Hitler made only 14 official visits. Today, the chalet is basically a restaurant with a scenic terrace 100 yards below the summit of a mountain. The views are magnificent. Wander into the fancy back dining room (the best-preserved from Hitler's time) where you can see the once-sleek marble fireplace chipped up by souvenir-seeking troops in 1945. From the bus stop, a finely crafted tunnel (which will have you humming the *Get Smart* TV theme song) leads to a polished brass elevator—one of the rare original elements of the complex. The site is open to visitors from mid-May through October. The round-trip bus ride up the private road and the lift to the top (a 2,000-foot altitude gain) together cost €19 from the Berchtesgaden train station, or €15 from the parking lot at the Nazi Documentation Center.

BADEN-BADEN and THE BLACK FOREST

Baden-Baden • Freiburg • Staufen • Best of the Black Forest

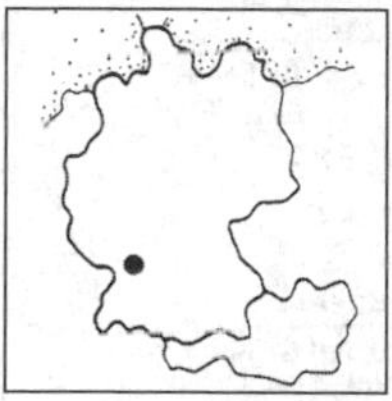

Combine Edenism and hedonism as you explore this most romantic of German regions and dip into its mineral spas. The Black Forest ("Schwarzwald" in German) is a range of hills stretching along the French border 100 miles from Switzerland north to Karlsruhe. Its highest peak is the 4,900-foot Feldberg. Because of its thick forests, people called it black.

Until the last century, the Schwarzwald was cut off from the German mainstream. The poor farmland drove medieval locals to become foresters, glassblowers, and clockmakers. Strong traditions continue to be woven through the thick dialects and thatched roofs. On any Sunday, you will find Germans in traditional costumes coloring the Black Forest on *Volksmärsche* (group hikes—open to anyone).

Popular with German holiday-goers and those looking for some serious R&R, the Black Forest offers clean air, cuckoo clocks, cherry cakes, cheery villages, and countless hiking possibilities.

The area's two biggest tourist traps are the tiny Titisee (a lake not quite as big as its tourist parking lot) and Triberg, a small town filled with cuckoo-clock shops. In spite of the crowds, the drives are scenic, the hiking is *wunderbar,* and the attractions listed in this chapter are well worth a visit.

The two major (and very different) towns are Baden-Baden in the north and Freiburg in the south. Their proximity to France lends both cities a sunny elegance. Freiburg is the Black Forest's capital and university town. Baden-Baden is Germany's grandest 19th-century spa resort. Stroll through its elegant streets and casino. Soak in its famous baths.

The Black Forest

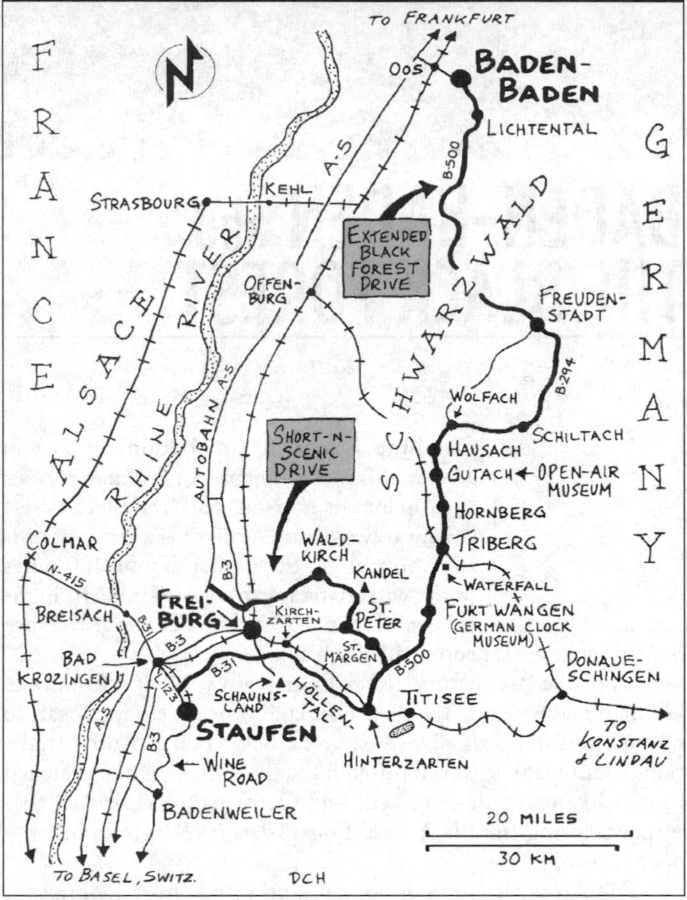

Planning Your Time

By **train,** Freiburg and Baden-Baden are easy, as is a short foray into the forest from either. Save a day and two nights for Baden-Baden. Tour Freiburg by day, and then sleep in charming and overlooked Staufen.

With more time and a **car,** do the whole cuckoo thing: two nights and a relaxing day in Baden-Baden, a busy day doing the small-town forest medley south (with stops at the Black Forest Open-Air Museum and Furtwangen's German Clock Museum), a quick visit to Freiburg, and a night in Staufen.

Baden-Baden

Of all the high-class resort towns I've seen, Baden-Baden is the easiest to enjoy in jeans with a picnic. The town makes a great first stop in Germany, especially for honeymooners (1.5 hours from Frankfurt's airport, direct trains every 2 hours).

Baden-Baden was the playground of Europe's high-rolling elite 150 years ago. Royalty and aristocracy would come from all corners to take the *Kur*—a soak in the curative (or at least they feel that way) mineral waters—and enjoy the world's top casino. Wrought-iron balconies on handsome 19th-century apartment buildings give Baden-Baden an elegant, Parisian feel.

The town remains popular today. How popular? Hoteliers in typical convention towns expect that 85 percent of their guests will need single rooms and 15 percent will need doubles. As spouses insist on coming to conventions held in Baden-Baden, hoteliers flip-flop those figures, anticipating that 85 percent of the demand will be for doubles.

Along with conventioneers, this lush resort town attracts a middle-class crowd consisting of tourists in search of a lower pulse, and Germans enjoying the fruits of their generous health-care system.

ORIENTATION

(area code: 07221)

Baden-Baden, with 50,000 residents, is made for strolling with a poodle. Except for the train station, youth hostel, and a recommended hotel on the opposite side of town, everything that matters is clustered within a 10-minute walk between the baths and the casino.

Although you'll barely notice if you just stick around the center, Baden-Baden is actually a long, skinny town, strung over several miles along the narrow valley of the Oosbach River (conveniently tied together by bus #201—see "Getting Around Baden-Baden," page 188). The train station is at the lower (northern) end of the valley, in a suburb called Baden-Oos, three miles from downtown; the Lichtentaler Abbey marks the upper end. The casino and town center are about halfway between, at the point where a small side valley joins the Oosbach. The church, castle, baths, and oldest sections of town are a few blocks uphill on the north slope of this side valley.

Tourist Information

Baden-Baden's main TI is in the ornate Trinkhalle building. Pick up the free monthly events program, *Baden-Baden Aktuell,* with an excellent fine-print, fold-out map. The TI has enough recommended walks and organized excursions to keep the most energetic vacationer happy. If you're headed into the countryside, consider the good €1 *Outline Map* and the €5 Black Forest guidebook (Mon–Sat 10:00–17:00, Sun 14:00–17:00, WC-€0.50, tel. 07221/275-200, www.baden-baden.com).

The main TI shares space with a café (see page 200) and an agency that sells tickets to performances in town (theater, opera, orchestra, and musicals; Tue–Sat 10:00–18:00, Sun 14:00–17:00, closed Mon). Another TI is at the B-500 autobahn exit (Mon–Sat 9:00–18:00, Sun 9:00–13:00, Schwarzwaldstrasse 52).

Arrival in Baden-Baden

Walk out of the train station (lockers at platform 1, €1.50–3) and catch bus #201 in front of the kiosks on your right (€2 single ticket; see "Getting Around Baden-Baden," page 188). Get off in about 15 minutes at the 11th stop, Leopoldsplatz, usually also announced as *Stadtmitte* ("center of town"). Allow about €16 for a taxi from the train station to the center.

Helpful Hints

Shopping: The big **Wagener Galerie** at Lange Strasse 44 has just about everything, including a modern supermarket on the top floor (Mon–Sat 9:00–19:00, closed Sun, winner of a "Germany's best" award) and a post office on the ground floor (Mon–Fri 9:00–19:00, Sat 9:00–14:00, closed Sun).

Horse Races: Book well in advance if you'll be visiting Baden-Baden during its horse races (May 16–24, Aug 29–Sept 6, and Oct 16–18 in 2009; www.baden-galopp.de).

Internet Access: There are two good 10-terminal places at either end of downtown: **Internet and Callshop** in the north (€2/hr, daily 10:00–22:00, Lange Strasse 54, tel. 07221/398-400) and **Medialounge** in the south (€2.40/hr, Mon–Fri 10:00–22:00, Sat 10:00–18:00, Sun 12:00–18:00, in passage at Kreuzstrasse 3, tel. 07221/22522).

Laundry: The unstaffed **SB-Waschcenter** is a steep hike up from downtown—only for the committed or those with a car—and you'll need to bring €9 per load in €1 coins (€5 wash, €4 dry; Mon–Sat 7:30–20:00, last load 18:00, closed Sun; walk up Sophienstrasse, go right up Stephanienstrasse, then left on steeply uphill Scheibenstrasse to #14, then down the alley; tel. 07221/24819).

Baden-Baden

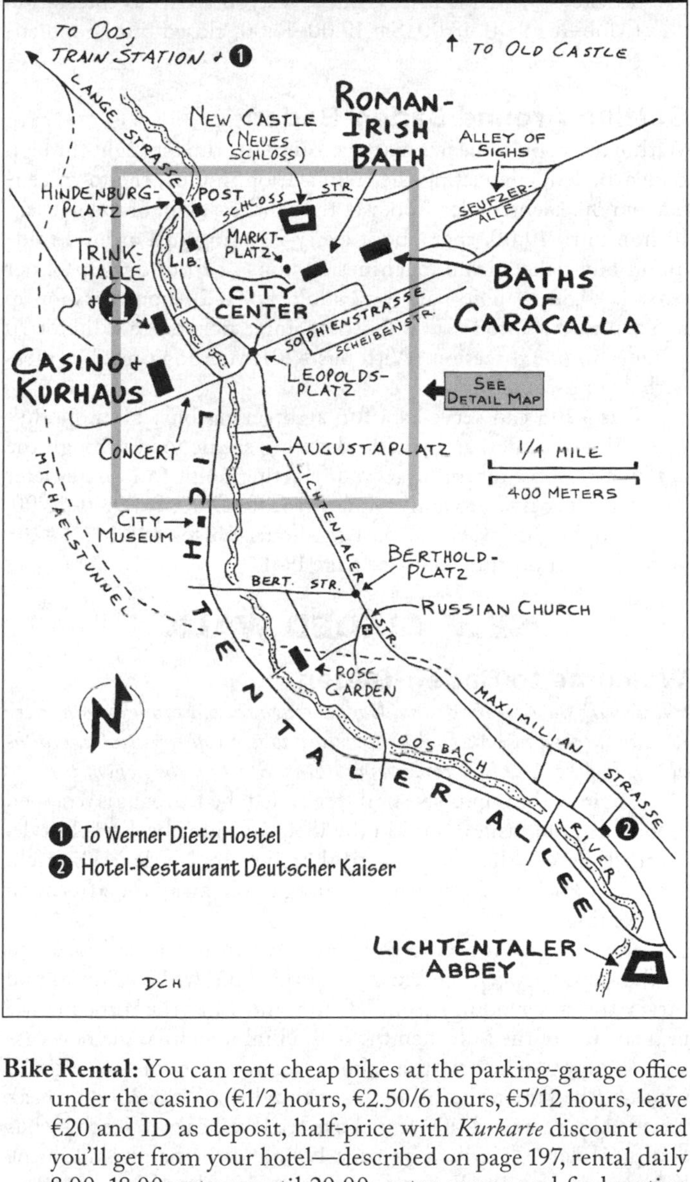

Bike Rental: You can rent cheap bikes at the parking-garage office under the casino (€1/2 hours, €2.50/6 hours, €5/12 hours, leave €20 and ID as deposit, half-price with *Kurkarte* discount card you'll get from your hotel—described on page 197, rental daily 8:00–18:00, return until 20:00; enter garage and find section A, space 52—easiest way down is from stairs off Kaiserallee marked *Kasse/Garage;* tel. 07221/277-203).

Train Info: The **Derpart** travel agency, between Leopoldsplatz and the casino, posts a train schedule outside. They'll charge you a €3.90 fee to answer your train questions and/or sell you a ticket—which is pricey, but saves you a trip to the station (Mon–Fri 9:00–18:00, Sat 10:00–14:00, closed Sun, Sophienstrasse 1B).

Getting Around Baden-Baden

Within town, only one bus matters: **Bus #201** runs straight through Baden-Baden, connecting the train station in Oos, the town center, and the Lichtentaler Abbey at the southeast end of town (every 10 min until 19:00, then about every 20 min until around midnight; buy tickets from machines at stops or from driver: €2 per person, €4.50 24-hour pass for 1 adult, €6.80 24-hour pass for up to 5 adults, bus info at www.kvv.de). Single tickets are valid for 90 minutes in one direction. With bus #201, you don't need to mess with downtown parking.

Bus #208 can serve as a fun sightseeing bus. Hop on anywhere in the center, and you'll take a big scenic loop through the outlying regions, returning to your starting point 55 minutes later (runs once per hour, roughly Mon–Fri 9:00–17:00, Sat 9:00–12:00, leaves Sophienstrasse at :07 past the hour). **Buses #204** and **#205** go to the Merkur funicular (see page 194).

SELF-GUIDED WALK

Welcome to Baden-Baden

• *This walk starts at the casino, loops through the old town to both of the famous baths, and ends back at the river where you can stroll up to the abbey. In other words, it covers everything. Start on the steps of the...*

Casino: The impressive building called the Kurhaus is wrapped around a grand casino. Built in the 1850s in wannabe-French style, it was declared "the most beautiful casino" by Marlene Dietrich. You can tour it in the morning, and gamble away the afternoon and evening.

To get a visual overview of the town from the casino, stand on the steps between the second and third big white columns and survey the surroundings from left to right: Find the ruined castle near the top of the hill, then the rock-climbing cliffs, the new castle (top of town) next to the salmon-colored spire of the Catholic Church (the famous baths are just behind that), the Merkur peak (marked by a tower, 2,000 feet above sea level, easy to reach by bus and funicular—described on page 194), and the bandstand in the Kurhaus garden. The Baden-Baden orchestra plays here most days (free, usually at 16:00).

Trinkhalle: Beyond the colonnade (about 100 yards to your left) is the old Trinkhalle—a long entrance hall decorated with nymphs and romantic legends (explained in the book *Trinkhalle*

Baden-Baden: Its Tales and Legends, sold inside for €9). It's now home to the TI, a recommended café, and a ticket agency. Wander its fancy portico, studying the romantic paintings that spa-goers a century ago could easily relate to.

• *From the Trinkhalle, walk down the steps, tip your hat to Kaiser Wilhelm (no moustache jokes), and go over the river. Walk one block inland, then go left on the pedestrian Lange Strasse. After a block, take a hard right, and climb up Hirschstrasse (under the "Bad" Hotel zum Hirsch skybridge) until you hit a big church.*

Catholic Church and Markt Platz: Baden-Baden's Catholic Church looks over the marketplace that has marked the center of town since Roman times. You're standing upon the "emperor's spa." Though it's not open to the public, city officials don oxygen masks and descend once a year (through the square metal hatch in the cobbles) to clean its sumptuous marble.

Enter the church (normally on the left side). Because it sits atop the spa, the Catholic Church is muggy and warm all year. There are no heaters inside. The floor stones are designed to transmit the natural spa heat in the winter. Since the air in the nave is at a steady 85 percent humidity level, the wooden pews have to be replaced every 50 years, all the art consists of copies (originals are stored safely in the regional museum), and it smells musty.

Back outside, you can see the edge of the "new castle" towering above the square. It's owned by a Kuwaiti woman who hopes to turn it into a fabulous five-star hotel at the cost of €500 million (if she can clear the hurdles that come with renovating a historic building).

From the Church to the Museum: Walk to the back of the church, then under a modern art installation holding jugs 20 yards high (reminders of the Roman spa that once stood here) and down a cobbled lane. Because the soil is spa-warmed, the vegetation is lush—Mediterranean pines and orange trees. At the end (top of stairs), enjoy the **viewpoint;** Baden-Baden's high-rent district—nicknamed "Paradise"—climbs the hills opposite.

Take the steps down to a water spigot called **Fettquelle** ("rich water source"). Taste the spa water. It's 105 degrees—as hot as a spa open to the public can legally be. Until recently, this was a practical source of hot water. Older locals remember being sent here to fetch hot water for their father's shave.

Find the **statue** on the lawn 50 yards farther. She's got her rear to the modern fun baths (Baths of Caracalla) and is eyeing the luxurious old-school Roman-Irish Bath (both described in "Experiences," on page 194).

• *Return halfway to the Fettquelle spigot and take the stairs down into the parking level (signposted* Römische Baderuinen*), to the small...*

Ancient Spa Museum: This spa, now in ruins, was built for Roman soldiers to use. While just one room—most of which you can see through the big windows—it's worth the €2.50 admission only if you want to use the included audioguide to learn the story of the ancient spa, including how it was engineered. As it was only for soldiers, this spa is just a simple terra-cotta structure with hollow walls and elevated floors to let the heat circulate (mid-March–mid-Nov daily 11:00–13:00 & 14:00–17:00, closed mid-Nov–mid-March).

• *Leaving the museum, jog left and head down...*

Gernsbacherstrasse: Walking down Gernsbacherstrasse, consider the 2,000-year heritage of guests who have been housed, fed, and watered here at the spa. Fyodor Dostoyevsky, Mark Twain, Johannes Brahms, and Russian princes all called this neighborhood home in its 19th-century heyday. Germany's oldest tennis and golf clubs were created here (for the English community) in the 19th century.

The late 20th-century German health-care system was very, very good for Baden-Baden. The government provided lavishly for spa treatment for its tired citizens. Now, doctors must make the case to insurance companies that their patients are more than tired... actually sick. And the insurance company then dictates where they'll go. The government will still pay for up to three weeks of recreation at a spa like this—but patients must go to the spa that is recommended and sleep in its clinic. If they want to sleep in a hotel, they lose their government funding—the gig is up.

• *After two blocks, you hit Sonnenplatz. Jog left, and at the corner (which has a little gifty shop selling all the local specialties), continue right down Sophienstrasse where a signpost directs you to Lichtentaler Allee.*

Sophienstrasse: This street enjoys the reliable shade of a long row of chestnut trees. In the 1870s, when it was lined exclusively by hotels, it was the town's aristocratic promenade. Back then there were 15,000 bedrooms for rent in Baden-Baden, triple what the city has today. (Note the bus stop just before Leopoldsplatz, where buses #204 and #205 go to the Merkur funicular—described on page 194.)

• *Sophienstrasse leads into...*

Leopoldsplatz: Until 1985, this square was a main traffic hub, with 30,000 cars muscling through it each day. Now a 1.5-mile long tunnel takes the east–west traffic under the city, and the peace and quiet you'd expect in a spa town has returned. Actually,

Baden-Baden had to get rid of the noise and pollution caused by the traffic in order to maintain its top rating as a spa resort—lose that, and Baden-Baden would lose half its business. The modern art decorating this square (and streets and squares throughout the city) rotates, as many artists want the exposure that an open-air exhibit in Baden-Baden brings.

• *From Leopoldsplatz, head left on Lichtentaler Strasse. You'll pass the venerable Café König (on right, described in "Eating"), antique shops (on left), and fine little malls. The big fountain in the distance marks Augustaplatz. Head toward it. At the fountain, go right, through the park, and over the petite bridge, where you'll come to a sweet riverside strolling path called Lichtentaler Allee (described on the next page). From here the casino is to your right. A stroll to the left—down Lichtentaler Allee—takes you to the rose garden, City Museum (a humble but well-displayed collection of artifacts and etchings showing the history of the spa town in an elegant old mansion), and out to Lichtentaler Abbey. You choose which way to go. My walk is done.*

SIGHTS

▲▲Casino and Kurhaus—Baden-Baden's grand casino occupies a classy building called the Kurhaus. Built in the 1850s, it was

inspired by the Palace of Versailles, and is filled with rooms honoring French royalty who never set foot in the place. But many other French people did. Gambling was illegal in 19th-century France... just over the border. The casino is licensed on the condition that it pays 92 percent of its earnings to the state. The amount of revenue it generates to help the state fund social services is a mystery, but insiders estimate that it's more than $30 million a year. The staff of 150 is paid by tips from happy gamblers.

You can visit the casino on a guided tour in the mornings, when it's closed to gamblers, but the casino is most interesting to see in action, after 14:00. You can gamble if you want, but a third of the visitors come only to people-watch under the chandeliers. The scene is more subdued than at an American casino; anyone showing emotion is a tourist. Lean against a gilded statue and listen to the graceful reshuffling of personal fortunes. Do some imaginary gambling or buy a few chips at the window near the entrance (an ATM is nearby).

The casino is open for gambling daily from 14:00 to 2:00 in the morning (Fri–Sat until 3:00; €3 entry, €1.50 entry with

Kurkarte discount card from your hotel—see page 197, €2 minimum bet, €10,000 maximum bet, no tennis shoes, tie and coat and collared shirt required for men and can be rented for €11 with an €11 deposit, nice jeans OK, passport required—driver's license isn't enough, under 21 not admitted, no photos, livelier after dinner and liveliest after 22:00, pick up English history and game rules as you enter, tel. 07221/30240, www.casino-baden-baden.de).

Lower rollers and budget travelers can try their luck downstairs at the casino's €1 slot machines, called *Automatenspiel* (€1 entry fee or included in €3 casino admission, same hours, passport required, no dress code).

Casino Tour: The casino gives 30-minute German tours every morning, departing from 9:30 to 11:30 (€4, 2/hr, Nov–March at 10:00; some guides speak English, or call ahead and pay €15 extra per group for an English tour—tel. 07221/30240, or just pick up the paltry English brochure). Even camera-toting peasants in T-shirts, shorts, and sandals are welcome on tours.

▲▲Strolling Lichtentaler Allee—Imagine yourself in top hat and tails as you promenade down the famous Lichtentaler Allee, a pleasant, picnic-perfect, 1.5-mile-long lane. You'll stroll through a park along the babbling, brick-lined Oosbach River, past old mansions and under hardy oaks and exotic trees (street-lit all night). By the elitist tennis courts, make sure to cross the footbridge into the free Art Nouveau rose garden (Gönneranlage, 100 labeled kinds of roses, great lounge chairs, best in early summer). If you wish, continue all the way to the historic Lichtentaler Abbey, a Cistercian convent founded in 1245. Either walk round-trip, or take city bus #201 one-way (runs along the main street, parallel to the promenade, on the other side of the river). Many bridges cross the river, making it easy to shortcut to bus #201 anytime. Biking is another option (see "Bike Rental," page 187), but you'll have to stay on the road in the bike lane, since the footpath is only for pedestrians.

Russian Baden-Baden—Many Russians, including Dostoyevsky and Tolstoy, flocked to Baden-Baden after the czars banned gambling in their motherland. Many lost their fortunes, borrowed a pistol, and did themselves in on the "Alley of Sighs" (Seufzerallee, near the Caracalla baths). You'll find a Russian **church** just south of the center (€1 donation requested, daily 10:00–18:00, services normally Sat 17:00–20:00 and Sun 9:40–11:30, near Gönneranlage rose garden across river from Lichtentaler Allee, or take bus #201 to Bertholdplatz stop). While the church dates from about 1900 and was quiet for generations, the current boom in the Russian population here has the church livelier than ever.

Many of Baden-Baden's top hotels are now Russian-owned. Ultra-wealthy Russians have sought out safe property investments all over Europe, and Baden-Baden is a favorite destination. While

Central Baden-Baden

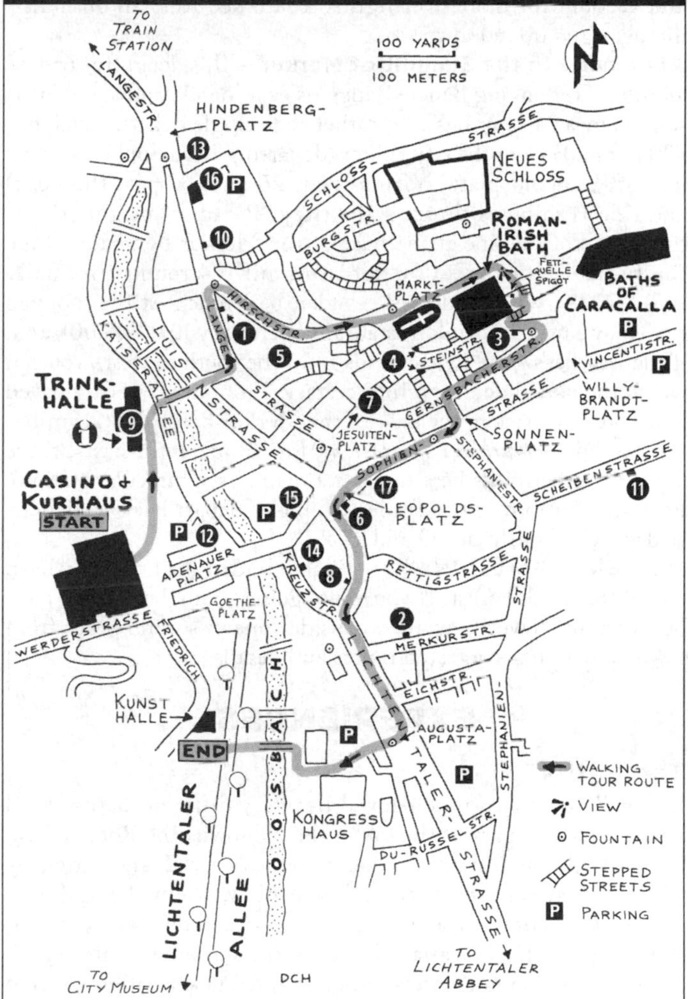

1. Hotel Colmar
2. Hotel Etol
3. Hotel Beeg
4. Hotel am Markt & Hotel/Rest. Rathausglöckel
5. Weinstube im Baldreit
6. Peter's am Leo Café
7. Jesuitenplatz Eateries
8. Café König
9. In der Trinkhalle Café
10. Böckeler Café
11. Launderette
12. Bike Rental
13. Internet & Callshop
14. Medialounge Internet Café
15. Derpart Travel Agency
16. Wagener Galerie (Grocery)
17. Bus to Merkur Bergbahn

more Americans visit Baden-Baden each year, Russians stay longer and account for more overnights. You'll see Russian on multilingual signs around town.

▲Funicular to the Summit of Merkur—This delightful trip, to a hilltop overlooking Baden-Baden, is easy, quick, and a good reason to buy a 24-hour bus card rather than single tickets. Catch bus #204 or #205 from the city center (departing from Sophienstrasse, just off Leopoldsplatz, normally at :26 and :52 past the hour) and ride 11 minutes through the ritzy "Paradise" neighborhood to the end of the line at the base of the Merkur Bergbahn. Take the funicular to the 2,000-foot summit (€4 round-trip, daily 10:00–22:00, www.stadtwerke-baden-baden.de). At the top, you can enjoy a meal or drink (restaurant open daily 10:00–18:00), and, if the weather's good (with winds from the south or west), you can watch the paragliders leap into ecstasy. From here, an easy paved lane takes you back to the base of the Merkur Bergbahn (2.5 miles, signposted *Merkurbahn Talstation*); for hiking enthusiasts, there are many other trails here (ask for a map at the funicular station). From the bottom of the funicular, buses depart back to Baden-Baden twice hourly (at :09 and :37).

Mini-Black Forest Walks—Baden-Baden is at the northern end of the Black Forest. If you're not going south, but want a taste of Germany's favorite woods, consider one of several hikes from town. The TI has suggested routes and details.

EXPERIENCES

The Baths

Baden-Baden's two much-loved but very different baths stand side-by-side in a park at the top of the old town. The Roman-Irish Bath is traditional, stately, indoors, not very social, and extremely relaxing...just you, the past, and your body. The perky, fun, and modern Baths of Caracalla are half the price, indoor and outdoor, and more social. Caracalla is better in the sunshine. Roman-Irish is fine anytime. Some hotels sell discounted tickets (10–15 percent off) to one or both of the baths—ask at your hotel.

At either bath, your admission ticket works like a subway token—you need it to get out. If you overstay your allotted time, you pay extra. You can relax while your valuables are stowed in very secure lockers. Both baths share a huge underground Bäder-Garage, which is free (for the first 2 hours, then €1/hr) if you validate your parking ticket before leaving either bath.

▲▲▲Roman-Irish Bath (Friedrichsbad)

The highlight of most visits to Baden-Baden is a sober two-hour ritual called the Roman-Irish Bath. Friedrichsbad pampered the rich and famous in its elegant surroundings when it opened 120 years ago. Today, this steamy world of marble, brass columns,

tropical tiles, herons, lily pads, and graceful nudity welcomes gawky tourists as well as locals.

Cost, Hours, Location: For €29, you get up to three hours and the works (€21 without the 10-minute massage). Daily 9:00–22:00, last entry 3 hours before closing if you're getting a massage, 2 hours before otherwise. Römerplatz 1, tel. 07221/275-920, www.carasana.de.

Dress Code: It is always nude. Men and women use parallel and nearly identical facilities. On "mixed" days (Tue–Wed and Fri–Sat), men and women share three pools in the center (yes, everyone's nude there, too). On Mondays and Thursdays, two of the shared pools are reserved for women only, but the biggest pool is available to both men and women. Shy bathers should avoid Sundays, when all of the rooms are mixed, including the steam and massage rooms. If you're concerned, there is no ogling going on. It's a very classy and respectful ritual—and a shame to miss just because you're intimidated by nudity.

Procedure: Read this carefully before stepping out naked: In your changing cabin, load all your possessions onto the fancy hanger. Then hang it in the locker across the way, slip your card into the lock, and strap the key around your wrist. (If you'll be having a massage, strap your plastic massage "coupon" to your wrist.) As you enter (in the "body crème" room), check your weight on the digital scale. Do this again as you leave to see how much you sweated off. You will lose a kilo...all in sweat. The complex routine is written (in English) on the walls with recommended time—simply follow the room numbers from 1 to 15. Instructions are repeated everywhere. For the first couple of stops only, you will use plastic slippers (marked with European sizes) and a towel (given to you by the attendant for the hot-room lounges) for hygienic reasons and because the slats are too hot to sit on without the towel.

Take a shower. Grab a towel and put on plastic slippers before hitting the warm-air bath for 15 minutes and the hot-air bath for five minutes. Shower again. If you paid extra, take the soap-brush massage—rough, slippery, and finished with a good Teutonic spank. Play Gumby in the shower; lounge under sunbeams in one of several thermal steam baths; and glide like a swan under a divine dome in a royal pool (one of three "mixed" pools—explained above). Don't skip the cold plunge. Dry in warmed towels and lie on a bed for 30 minutes, thinking prenatal thoughts, in the mellow, yellow, silent room. You don't appreciate how clean you are after this experience until you put your dirty socks back on. (Bring clean ones.)

All you need is money. You'll get a key, locker, and towel, and hair dryers are available. If you wear glasses, there are trays throughout for you to park them, but it's more relaxing if you can go without.

Afterward, before going downstairs, browse through the Roman artifacts upstairs in the Renaissance Hall (also accessible to non-bathers), sip just a little of the terrible but "magic" hot water *(Thermalwasser)* from the elegant fountain, and stroll down the broad royal stairway, feeling, as they say, five years younger—or, at least, 2.2 pounds lighter.

▲▲Baths of Caracalla (Caracalla Therme)

For a more modern experience, spend a few hours at the Baths of Caracalla, a huge palace of water, steam, and relaxed people.

More like a mini-water park, and with everyone clothed most of the time, this is a more fun and accessible experience for those intimidated by nudity.

Hours: Daily 8:00–22:00, last entry at 20:30, sometimes closed for 2 weeks in June or July for renovation, kids under 7 not allowed, those 7–14 must be with parents (it's not really a splashing and sliding kind of pool). Tel. 07221/275-940, www.carasana.de.

Cost and Procedure: Here you need to bring a towel (or pay €5 plus a €10 deposit to rent one) and a swimsuit (shorts are OK for men). Buy a card (€13/2 hours, €15/3 hours, €17/4 hours, 10 2-hour entries for repeat visits or to split among a group cost €113) and put it in the locker to get a key. Change clothes, strap the key around your wrist, and go play. Your key gets you into another poolside locker if you want to lock up glasses or money for a tan or a drink. Bring your towel to the pool (there are plenty of places to stow it). The baths are an indoor/outdoor wonderland of steamy pools, waterfalls, neck showers, Jacuzzis, hot springs, cold pools, lounge chairs, saunas, a cafeteria, and a bar. After taking a few laps around the fake river, you can join some kinky Germans for water spankings (you may have to wait a few minutes to grab a vacant waterfall). Then join the gang in the central cauldron. The steamy "inhalation" room seems like purgatory's waiting room, with a misty minimum of visibility, filled with strange, silently aging bodies.

Nudity is limited to one zone upstairs. The grand spiral

staircase leads to a naked world of saunas, tanning lights, cold plunges, and sunbathing outside on lounge chairs. At the top of the stairs everyone stows their suit in a cubbyhole and wanders around with their towel (some are modest and wrapped; others just run around buck naked). There are three eucalyptus-scented saunas of varying temperatures (80, 90, and 95 degrees) and two saunas in outdoor log cabins (with mesmerizing robotic steam-makers). Follow the instructions on the wall. Towels are required, not for modesty but to separate your body from the wood benches. The highlight is the arctic bucket in the shower room. Pull the chain. Only rarely will you feel so good. And you can do it over and over.

SLEEPING

(area code: 07221)

The TI can nearly always find you a room—but don't use the TI for places listed here, or you'll pay more. Go direct! The only tight times are during the horse races (May 16–24, Aug 29–Sept 6, and Oct 16–18 in 2009; www.baden-galopp.de). Hotel am Markt is a great value and worth reserving in advance.

All hotels and pensions are required to extract an additional €2.80 per person, per night "spa tax," so don't get upset when this is added to the bill. This comes with a "guest card" *(Kurkarte)*, offering small discounts on tourist admissions around town (including casino entry and bike rental). If you're coming into town by car or foot, look for the helpful green signs that direct you to each hotel by name.

In the Center, near the Casino

For locations, see the map on page 193.

$$$ Hotel Colmar, run with a personal touch by Hilde and Shaso Özcan and family, rents 26 pastel, elegant rooms, some

Sleep Code

(€1 = about $1.50, country code: 49)

S = Single, **D** = Double/Twin, **T** = Triple, **Q** = Quad, **b** = bathroom, **s** = shower only. Unless otherwise noted, credit cards are accepted, English is spoken, and breakfast is included.

To help you sort easily through these listings, I've divided the rooms into three categories based on the price for a standard double room with bath:

$$$ Higher Priced—Most rooms €100 or more.
$$ Moderately Priced—Most rooms between €80-100.
$ Lower Priced—Most rooms €80 or less.

with balconies (Sb-€78–85, Db-€100, 2-room apartment Db-€118, extra bed-€35, 10 percent discount off rack rates with cash and this book, non-smoking, elevator, parking-€11/day, Lange Strasse 34, between Hindenburgplatz and Leopoldsplatz stops on bus #201, tel. 07221/93890, fax 07221/938-950, www.hotel-colmar.de, info@hotel-colmar.de).

$$$ Hotel Etol is in the quiet courtyard of a renovated industrial complex, which celebrates its history as a tile and bathtub factory from around the year 1900. You'll climb the stairs to reach most of the 18 rooms, but natural light, tasteful design, friendly staff, and a central location make this a winning choice (Sb-€78–85, Db-€105–130, all rooms non-smoking, Wi-Fi in lobby, parking-€5/day, Merkurstrasse 7, 2-min walk from Augustaplatz stop of bus #201, tel. 07221/973-470, fax 07221/9734-7111, www.hotel-etol-badenbaden.de, info@hotel-etol-badenbaden.de).

In the Center, Uphill by the Baths

$$$ Hotel Beeg rents 15 attractive and comfortable rooms, run from a delectable pastry shop/café on the ground floor. It's wonderfully situated on a little square in a pedestrian zone and faces the baths, though the staff can be a bit formal (Sb-€85, Db-€109, balcony-€10 extra, apartment Db-€165, extra bed-€30, elevator, reception in café, on Römerplatz at Gernsbacher Strasse 44, tel. 07221/36760, fax 07221/367-610, www.hotel-beeg.de, info@hotel-beeg.de, Herr Beeg).

$$ Hotel am Markt is a warm, 25-room, family-run hotel with all the comforts a commoner could want in a peaceful, central, nearly traffic-free location, two cobbled blocks from the baths. For romantics, the church bells blast charmingly through each room every quarter-hour from 6:15 until 22:00; for others, they are a nuisance. Otherwise, quiet rules. The ambience and the clientele make it a joy to have breakfast or just kill time on the small terrace(S-€32, Sb-€44–47, D-€64–66, Db-€80–82, Tb-€100–115, extra bed-€20, free Internet access, pay Wi-Fi, Marktplatz 18, tel. 07221/27040, fax 07221/270-444, www.hotel-am-markt-baden.de, info@hotel-am-markt-baden.de, Herr und Frau Bogner-Schindler and Frau Jung).

$$ Hotel Rathausglöckel, around the corner and below the Hotel am Markt at Steinstrasse 7, is a 16th-century guest house with 10 cozy rooms and steep stairs (Sb-€60, Db-€80–90, third person-€20, 2-room apartment with kitchen-€80–150, depending on number of people and length of stay, Wi-Fi, church bells every 15 min 6:15–22:00, parking-€6/day, tel. 07221/90610, fax 07221/906-161, www.rathausgloeckel.de, info@rathausgloeckel.de, kind Michael Rothe).

Outside the Center

The following two listings are a few stops from the center by bus #201 (for locations, see map on page 187).

$ Hotel-Restaurant Deutscher Kaiser, a good choice for those on tighter budgets, is a traditional guest house with 22 simple, spacious, dated-but-clean rooms and a 1980s feeling, run by no-nonsense Frau Peter. Herr Peter cooks fine local-style meals in the hotel restaurant (€8–17 main dishes, restaurant closed Mon–Tue). It's right at the Eckerlestrasse stop of bus #201 (6/hr, 10 min from center, 20 min from train station) or a 25-minute stroll from the city center down polite Lichtentaler Allee—cross the river at the green *Restaurant Deutscher Kaiser* sign, then turn right (S-€35, Sb-€47–49, D-€46–49, Db-€61–69, family rooms, often impressive discounts on their website, non-smoking rooms, pay Internet access, free Wi-Fi, free and easy parking, Hauptstrasse 35, tel. 07221/72152, fax 07221/72154, www.hoteldk.de, info@hoteldk.de). Drivers: From the autobahn, skip the town center by following *Congress* signs into Michaelstunnel. Take the tunnel's first exit, then another right at the end of the exit (direction: Lichtental). Outside, the hotel is about a half-mile down on the left. From the Black Forest, follow *Zentrum* signs. Just 10 yards after the Aral gas station, turn left down the small road to Hauptstrasse.

$ Werner Dietz Hostel, between the station and the center, is big, modern, and has the cheapest beds in town (€18.70 per bed in 4- to 6-bed dorms, €3.30 less for 2 nights or more, €3 more if you're over 26, adult non-members pay €3.10 extra, S/D rooms €5 extra per person, includes sheets and breakfast, cash only, 23:30 curfew, outdoor swimming pool next door, Hardbergstrasse 34, tel. 07221/52223, www.jugendherberge-baden-baden.de, info@jugendherberge-baden-baden.de). To reach the hostel from the train station or downtown, take bus #201 to Grosse Dollenstrasse (also announced as *Jugendherberge*), six stops from the station or five from downtown; it's a steep, well-marked, 10-minute climb from there. Drivers should call the hostel for careful directions.

EATING

Dining with Elegance and Atmosphere

Hotel Rathausglöckel's restaurant, personal and homey, has long had a good reputation for great food. The setting is understated Old World elegance (all indoors, so eat elsewhere if the weather is really hot). Michael serves well-presented traditional dinners with good vegetarian options and is happy to explain the day's specials (€14–20 entrées, Wed–Sun 18:00–21:00, closed Mon–Tue, reservations smart, Steinstrasse 7, tel. 07221/90610).

Weinstube im Baldreit, with both a cozy cellar and a leafy back courtyard, is ideal on a hot evening. Dining here, I feel like a pampered salamander in a Monet terrarium. While her French husband Philippe cooks wonderful regional dishes, Nicole is happy to translate the daily specials chalked in German on the board. The priority here is near-gourmet food at great prices. Reservations are smart (€8–18 meals, Mon–Sat 12:00–14:00 & 17:00–22:00, closed Sun and closed for lunch Nov–March; several entrances: from Lange Strasse 10, walk up Küferstrasse, look for *Weinstube* signs and enter under archway, Küferstrasse 3; tel. 07221/23136).

Quick and Simple Meals near Leopoldsplatz

Peter's am Leo Café is a fun self-service place offering salads, pasta, omelets, pastries, and views over Baden-Baden's central square. (Try to snare one of the outdoor tables.) This is where commoners pile their plates high. The lively staff dons lederhosen for Oktoberfest, Hawaiian shirts in sunny weather, and striped shirts for the horse races (€5–7 entrées, Mon–Sat 6:30–19:00, Sun 8:00–19:00, on Leopoldsplatz at Sophienstrasse 10, tel. 07221/392-817).

Gasthaus Löwenbräu, on Jesuitenplatz at the bottom of Gernsbacherstrasse, is a sloppy, rude Bavarian *Biergarten* slinging good beer and basic schnitzel fare under a vine-covered trellis. Across the street, several decent restaurants offer curbside tables—great for people-watching. Just up Gernsbacherstrasse from here (at #17), the **Lotus Chinese Restaurant** serves big, cheap portions and has a few outdoor tables (daily 11:00–23:00).

Prime People-Watching Cafés

Café König is *the* place to bring your poodle and spend too much for an elegant cup of coffee and a slice of Black Forest cake. At the counter, you can buy pastry and candy to go (daily 8:30–18:30, counter opens Mon–Sat at 9:30 and Sun at 10:30, fine shady patio, look for sign with squiggly script, between Leopoldsplatz and Augustaplatz at Lichtentaler Strasse 12, tel. 07221/23573).

In der Trinkhalle, a café that shares the handsome Trinkhalle building with the TI, has comfy leather sofas, international newspapers and magazines, and a casino-view terrace (daily 10:00–24:00, Kaiserallee 3, tel. 07221/302-905).

Böckeler Café is reasonably priced and has good cakes, a praline counter, an ice-cream sundae menu, light meals, and outdoor tables along a lively pedestrian street (Mon–Fri 8:00–18:30, Sat–Sun 9:30–18:00, Lange Strasse 40–42, tel. 07221/949-594).

TRANSPORTATION CONNECTIONS

From Baden-Baden by Train to: Freiburg (direct trains every 1–2 hrs, 45 min), **Triberg** (hourly, 70 min), **Munich** (hourly, 4 hrs, some direct but most with 1–2 changes), **Frankfurt** (hourly, 1.5 hrs, direct or with a change in Mannheim or Karlsruhe), **Frankfurt Airport** (hourly, 1.5 hrs, mostly with a change in Mannheim or Karlsruhe), **Bacharach** (hourly, 3 hrs, 1–3 changes), **Strasbourg** (almost hourly, usually 60–90 min with a change in Appenweier), **Bern** or **Zürich** (every 1–2 hrs, 3 hrs, change in Basel). Train info: tel. 11861 (€0.60/min).

Freiburg

Freiburg im Breisgau is worth a quick look, if for nothing else than to appreciate its thriving center and very human scale. Bikers and hikers seem to outnumber cars, and trams run everywhere. This "sunniest town in Germany," with 30,000 students, lacks must-see attractions but offers the pleasures of a university town: small shops, cozy cafés, fine food, and fewer tourists than Baden-Baden.

Freiburg (FRY-burg), bombed nearly flat in 1944, skillfully put itself back together. This capital of the Schwarzwald, exuding an "I could live here" appeal, is surrounded by lush forests and filled with environmentally aware people so dedicated to solar power that they host an annual Intersolar trade fair.

Marvel at the number of pedestrian-only streets. Freiburg's trademark is its system of *Bächle,* tiny streams running down each street. These go back to the Middle Ages (serving as fire protection, cattle refreshment, and a constantly flushing disposal system). Local lore says that if you fall into a *Bächle,* you are destined to marry a Freiburger. A sunny day turns any kid-at-heart into a puddle-jumper. Enjoy the ice cream and street-singing ambience of the cathedral square, which has a great produce and craft market (Mon–Sat 7:30–13:00, biggest Wed and Sat, closed Sun). To get a glimpse of the historic Altstadt (old town), be sure to stroll down Gerberau Street to admire the 15th-century houses and medieval city gates (Martinstor and Schwabentor).

ORIENTATION

(area code: 0761)

Tourist Information

Freiburg's busy but helpful TI, on Rathausplatz, has free city maps and sells better maps for €1, as well as several city guidebooks that aren't necessary for a short stay (the €4 guide has tons of practical information, the €5 city guide with photos has the most info on sights, and the €7 book is geared toward students spending a semester in Freiburg, with lots of bar and nightlife suggestions). The TI also offers a room-booking service (€3 per booking plus a deposit for Freiburg and Black Forest area), weekly walking tours in English (€7, 1.5 hours, May–Oct Sat at 12:00, none off-season), and lots of information on the Black Forest region (including yet another €5 book; TI open June–Sept Mon–Fri 8:00–20:00, Sat 9:30–17:00, Sun 10:00–12:00; Oct–May Mon–Fri 8:00–18:00, Sat 9:30–14:30, Sun 10:00–12:00; tel. 0761/388-1880, www.freiburg.de).

Arrival in Freiburg

The bustling train station has lockers (€2–4 old-fashioned lockers by track 1B, or try the high-tech €4 ones—with English instructions—in the station hall), a WC (€0.80), and a helpful *Reisezentrum* that dispenses rail info and sells tickets (Mon–Sat 6:30–20:00, Sun 7:30–20:00). The bus station is next door.

Walk out of the train station, cross the street, and head straight up the tree-lined boulevard called Eisenbahnstrasse (passing the post office). Within three blocks, you'll take an underpass beneath a busy road. On the other side, it becomes Rathausgasse; follow it a little farther to Rathausplatz, where you'll find the Rathaus itself on your left, and the TI in the red building next door (attached by bridge to the Rathaus).

Helpful Hints

Internet Access: Call-Shop is in the building between the train and bus stations, across from McDonalds (€1.90/hr, Mon–Sat 9:00–22:00, Sun 10:00–22:00, Bismarckallee 5, tel. 0761/208-8191).

Laundry: Do your laundry while surfing the Net at **Wash Tours** (€6.50/load, Internet access-€2.50/hr, Mon–Sat 9:00–18:00, closed Sun, in the passage that runs from Salzstrasse 22 to Grünewaldstrasse 19, tel. 0761/288-866, www.washtours.com).

Bike Rental: Mobile, by the station, rents bikes and has free route maps (€7/4 hrs, €15/24 hrs, subsequent days-€5, €50–100 cash and ID for deposit, daily 8:00–20:00; from station, cross tram bridge over train tracks to round building on left and walk downstairs; Wentzingerstrasse 15, tel. 0761/292-7998).

Getting Around Freiburg and Surroundings

The city center (which includes all my recommended hotels) is completely walkable, though you might want to use a taxi or a tram to haul luggage from the station (from the train platforms, take the escalators up to the tram stop on the bridge above the tracks). Trams are also useful to reach outlying sights, such as Schauinsland (€2 per ride, €4.80 for 24-hour pass, buy tickets from machines at stops or inside cars). For local transport info in English, see www.vag-freiburg.de.

To visit **Staufen, St. Peter,** or **St. Märgen** by regional train and bus, you'll need a two-zone ticket (€3.40 each way) or a 24-hour regional pass (€10 for 1 adult, €16 for 2–5 adults, available from ticket machines). Also consider the SchwarzwaldCard (a.k.a. KONUS card), which includes three days of free public transport in Freiburg and surroundings, and admission to many sights (€31, available from participating hotels, more info at www.blackforest-tourism.com).

SIGHTS

▲Cathedral (Münster)—This impressive church, completed in 1513, took more than three centuries to build, and ranges in style from late Romanesque to lighter, brighter Gothic. It was one of the few buildings in town to survive WWII bombs (photos inside show the devastation). The lacy tower *(Münsterturm)* is as tall as the church is long...and not worth the 329-step ascent (tower-€1.50, Mon–Sat 9:30–17:00, Sun 13:00–17:00, enter from outside church). From this lofty perch, watchmen used to scan the town for fires.

While you could count the 123 representations of Mary throughout the church, most gawk at the "mooning" gargoyle outside (facing the entrance, walk around the right and look at the second butt-ress)...and wait for rain.

Take a clockwise spin around the cathedral exterior to appreciate the hodgepodge of architectural styles, ranging from 15th-century charming to 20th-century ugly (since much of the north side of the square was bombed flat in World War II). The fountain was moved here from another location in 1970. Noteworthy buildings include the Kornhaus (1489), which has served as a granary and theater. The ornate Historisches Kaufhaus (1532), across from the church, was the trading and customs center in the 16th century and briefly housed the state parliament after the war. The pale yellow Haus zum Ritter has morphed from a clubhouse for local knights to the residence of the archbishop, and today it remains property of the cathedral.

If you follow Buttergasse (near #28 on the square) to Schustergasse, jog right and immediately right, you'll end up at the...

Augustiner Museum—While this museum is undergoing extensive renovation (until early 2010, though some exhibits remain open), it feels more like a warehouse of crosses, goblets, broken statuary, and minor religious art. When completed, it is slated to be the Upper Rhine region's most significant collection of Black Forest art and culture. There are no descriptions in English as of yet, but most of the collection is self-explanatory. The highlights are a close-up look at some of the Münster's original medieval stained glass and statuary, as well as Wentzinger's *Immaculata,* a two-foot-tall terra-cotta statue from the 18th century (free while under renovation, Tue–Sun 10:00–17:00, closed Mon, 2 blocks south of cathedral in big yellow building on Augustinerplatz, tel. 0761/201-2531, www.freiburg.de/museen).

The area around Augustinerplatz is the heart of the **Gerberau district,** popular with locals. It's quieter and filled with little galleries and restaurants that are less expensive than on the Marktplatz. There's a great playground for kids and a beer garden just around the corner. From here, it's a five-minute walk to the base of Schlossberg.

Schlossberg (Castle Hill)—Schlossberg towers over the east end of Freiburg's old town. A 17th-century fort once stood here on "Castle Hill," built by the French to control the citizens of Freiburg during a period of French occupation. Schlossberg today is popular for its views over the city. Though the old fort is long gone, a new modern lookout tower (100 feet high) stands where the French Fort d'Aigle (eagle tower) once stood.

To get to the top of Schlossberg, you can either hike or take an elevator from Schwabentor, the half-timbered tower at the east end of the old town. From the tower, look for the footbridge on Oberlinden Street. Cross the bridge, bear left, and hike up 10 minutes. You can also continue straight (through the tunnel) to the free elevator *(Aufzug).* At the top of the elevator and trail, you'll come to the restaurant Greiffenegg Schlössle (see page 208). From there, walk another seven minutes up to the viewpoint. To continue 20 more minutes from the viewpoint to the Fort d'Aigle lookout tower, walk the level path to the left (with your back to the benches), then veer right uphill at the big white cross (look for small silver signs pointing through forest).

Schauinsland—Freiburg's own mountain, while little more than an oversized hill, is nine miles southeast of the center. The viewpoint at its 4,000-foot summit, which won't wow Americans from Colorado, offers the handiest panorama view of the Schwarzwald for those without wheels. The gondola system that takes you up—one of Germany's oldest—was designed for Freiburgers relying on public transportation (€11.50 round-trip, €26 family ticket includes 2 adults and up to 4 kids, daily July–Sept 9:00–18:00, Oct–June 9:00–17:00; catch tram #2—direction Günterstal—from town center to the end, then take bus #21 seven stops to Talstation stop for gondola; tel. 0761/292-930, www.bergwelt-schauinsland.de). At the top, you'll find a view restaurant, pleasant circular walks, and the Schniederli Hof, a 1592 farmhouse museum. A tower on a nearby peak offers an even more commanding Black Forest view.

Nightlife—Night owls flock around the Martinstor in the area affectionately called Freiburg's "Bermuda Triangle." Take the street to your right just before going through the gate and get sucked in. Look at the Burger King ahead of you; mischievous Puck does a little dance and plays the pan pipes. He's a fitting mascot for a district known for its fun, colorful bars.

SLEEPING

(€1 = about $1.50, country code: 49, area code: 0761)

Though I prefer nights in sleepy Staufen (see page 208), many will enjoy overnighting in lively Freiburg. Freiburg is also easier for non-drivers than Staufen. Of my listings, Schwarzwälder Hof is in the heart of the old town, and the others are just a block or two outside it. Schwarzwälder Hof and Hotel Alleehaus offer the most value for your money; Alleehaus has the most character. All hotels except Am Stadtgarten include breakfast in the room price.

$$ Schwarzwälder Hof is just steps from the cathedral, with odd bits of art in the hallways and 45 rooms over a reasonably priced restaurant. Ask for one of the new modern rooms (S-€45, Ss-€48, Sb-€70, D-€75, Ds-€78, Db-€95–105, Tb-€120, includes free local transport card, Wi-Fi, parking-€9/day, Herrenstrasse 43, walk 15 min from station or take tram #1 in direction Littenweiler three stops to Oberlinden, tel. 0761/38030, fax 0761/380-3135, www.shof.de, info@shof.de, Engler family).

$$ Hotel Alleehaus is tops. It has 19 comfy rooms with modern furniture and decorations at the south edge of the center, on a quiet, leafy street in a big house that feels like home. It's warmly run by Bernd, Claudia, and their team (S-€49, Sb-€68–75, small Db-€85, larger Db-€99, Tb-€135, Qb-€154, reception closed 19:30–6:00, call by 18:00 if arriving later than 19:30, Wi-Fi, parking-€6/day, Marienstrasse 7, tel. 0761/387-600, fax 0761/387-6099, www.hotel-alleehaus.de, wohlfuehlen@hotel-alleehaus.de). From the station, walk 20 minutes or take tram #3 (direction Vauban) or #5 (direction Rieselfeld) three stops to Holzmarkt; then walk along Holzmarkt, which becomes Wallstrasse, and turn right on Marienstrasse.

$$ Hotel am Stadtgarten, on the north side of town (a 20-min walk from the station), rents 73 comfortable rooms in two buildings across the street from each other. Ask for the older "Gästehaus" rooms in the building across the street from the reception, which are the best value (Sb-€64–86, Db-€74–99, more expensive rooms in new building, breakfast-€12.50, Wi-Fi, bike rental-€8/day, parking-€12/day in garage, coupons for local restaurants and discounts for walking tours, Karlstrasse 12 at intersection with Bernhardstrasse, near Siegesdenkmal stop on tram line #2—you'll have to change trams if coming from the station, tel. 0761/282-9002, fax 0761/282-9022, www.hotelamstadtgarten.de, kontakt@hotelamstadtgarten.de).

Near the Train Station

$$$ Hotel Barbara has 21 fine and bright rooms (Sb-€69–89, Db-€89–119, extra bed-€20, prices €10 higher during fairs, nearby parking garage-€9/day, Internet access and Wi-Fi, on quiet street 2 min from station, head toward TI but turn left at post office to Poststrasse 4, tel. 0761/296-250, fax 0761/26688, www.hotel-barbara.de, mail@hotel-barbara.de).

Hostels

$ Black Forest Hostel has 105 of the cheapest beds in town. Run by friendly Tania, with a young, bohemian attitude, it's bare-bones simple (€13–16 per person in 10- to 21-bed rooms, €17–21 per person in 3- to 8-bed rooms, S-€28, D-€46, sheets-€3, sleeping bags OK, cash only, no curfew, no smoking in rooms, lockers, Internet access-€2/hr, self-service kitchen, laundry-€5, Kartäuser Strasse 33—look for anchor sign and go down driveway; 20-min walk from station or take tram #1—direction: Littenweiler—to Oberlinden stop, then walk 5 more min; tel. 0761/881-7870, fax 0761/881-7895, www.blackforest-hostel.de, backpacker@blackforest-hostel.de). If full, they might direct you to the much larger, more distant **$ Freiburg Youth Hostel** at Kartäuser Strasse 151 (dorm bed-€22, includes sheets, €3 more for travelers over 26, tel. 0761/67656, www.jugendherberge-freiburg.de, info@jugendherberge-freiburg.de).

EATING

Freiburg has plenty of dining options. I've listed a few good places near Augustinerplatz (a few short blocks from the cathedral) and near the Rathaus, as well as a couple atop the scenic Schlossberg.

Near Augustinerplatz

Hausbrauerei Feierling is a microbrewery that also serves fine meals. On warm summer evenings, their *Biergarten* across the street offers cool, leafy shade and a bustling atmosphere (€5–13 entrées, daily 11:00–24:00, indoor section closed in afternoons when weather is hot, Gerberau 46, tel. 0761/243-480).

Sichlschmied is a good option rain or shine. Its timbered alcoves and cluttered interior give it a cozy living-room feel, and its creekside seating can't be beat. Be careful not to confuse it with a neighboring, lesser-value restaurant which shares the outdoor terrace. Come here for easygoing regional cuisine, good value, and a family-friendly ambience (€7–15 plates, daily 12:00–23:00, Insel 1, tel. 0761/35037).

Tacheles appeals to student-size appetites (big) and budgets (small). Who knew that schnitzel could be prepared in literally a dozen different ways? Here at the self-proclaimed *"Schnitzel Paradies,"* they serve up big schnitzels (€1 extra for *Pute*—turkey—instead of the traditional pork), a salad, and your choice of a side dish (french fries, *Spätzle*, and so on) for a mere €5.90 for lunch or €6.90 for dinner (after 18:00). Non-schnitzel lunch specials (Mon–Fri only) cost €6.30. The pub downstairs, a favorite hang-out, can be crowded and smoky; instead, opt for the quiet court-yard seating upstairs (daily 11:30–24:00, also vegetarian options, nightly drink specials, live *Fussball* broadcasts on some weekends, Grünwalderstrasse 17, tel. 0761/319-6669).

Chang Thai, next door to Tacheles, is where students satisfy their Asian-food cravings (€7–10 main dishes, Mon–Sat 12:00–23:00, Sun 13:00–22:30, Grünwalderstrasse 21).

Aran is an upscale sandwich shop and café (also serving soup, baked potatoes, and smoothies) with a "designy" interior and relaxing bamboo-screened outdoor seating (€4 sandwiches, daily May–Oct 9:00–23:00, Nov–April 9:00–19:00, on Augustinerplatz, tel. 0761/290-9664).

Near the Rathaus

Kleiner Meyerhof, between the train station and the Rathaus, offers typical German food in a comfortable indoor setting, with regional specialties and reasonable prices (€8–18 entrées, daily 10:00–24:00, kitchen closes at 22:00, Rathausgasse 27, tel. 0761/26941).

At **UC/Uni-Café,** join the cerebral grad-student crowd for cheap salads, sandwiches, and breakfasts—have a cappuccino outside on the square, or pop inside to drink beer and watch a *Fussball* match on the flat-screen TV (€4–8 salads and sandwiches, Mon–Sat 8:00–23:00, Sun 10:00–23:00, Niemensstrasse 7, at Universitätsstrasse, tel. 0761/383-355).

On Freiburg's Schlossberg

For directions on getting to these scenic eateries, see "Schlossberg (Castle Hill)," page 204.

Greiffenegg Schlössle offers rooftop views over Freiburg, but the meals are expensive and worth it only if you can get a table on the terrace in good weather (€17–25 entrées, daily 11:00–24:00, reservations smart, tel. 0761/32728). Consider instead their self-service, open-air **Biergarten Kastaniengarten,** just above the restaurant (€6–9 entrées, open April–Oct in good weather, same hours and phone).

Cheaper yet, consider a **picnic** at the Schlossberg viewpoint. Buy supplies before you ascend at the **Migros supermarket,** in the basement of the Karstadt department store on Kaiser-Joseph-Strasse, near the cathedral.

TRANSPORTATION CONNECTIONS

The full name of the town—and the station—is Freiburg im Breisgau, often abbreviated as "Freiburg (Brsg)" on schedules.

By Train to: Staufen (hourly until about 19:00, 30 min, most require transfer at Bad Krozingen; for more details, see "Transportation Connections" for Staufen, page 210), **Baden-Baden** (direct trains every 1–2 hrs, 45 min), **Munich** (hourly, 4.5 hrs, 1 change), **Basel,** Switzerland (hourly, 45 min), **Bern,** Switzerland (hourly, 2 hrs, most transfer in Basel), **Frankfurt** (hourly, 2–2.5 hrs, some direct, most require change in Mannheim or Frankfurt Airport), **Frankfurt Airport** (hourly, 2 hrs, direct or with a change in Mannheim). Train info: tel. 11861 (€0.60/min).

Staufen

The hotels in Staufen im Breisgau make a peaceful and delightful home base for your exploration of Freiburg and the southern trunk of the Black Forest. Hemmed in by vineyards, Staufen is small and off the beaten path, with a quiet pedestrian zone of colorful old buildings bounded by a happy creek that actually babbles. You can also make Staufen a half-day outing from Freiburg—better for lunch than for dinner, as the last public transport back from Staufen leaves around 19:00.

ORIENTATION

Tourist Information

The TI, on the main square in the Rathaus, has Internet access for €4 per hour (Mon–Fri 9:00–12:30 & 14:00–17:30, Sat 10:00–12:00, closed Sun, tel. 07633/80536, www.touristik-staufen.de).

Arrival in Staufen

The main square and Rathaus are a 10-minute walk from the station, and everything I list is along the way (or just off it). There are no lockers at the station, but try Bahnhof Hotel—see "Sleeping and Eating." To get to town, exit the station with your back to the pond and angle right up Bahnhofstrasse. Turn right at the post office onto Hauptstrasse, which leads through the town center to the Rathaus and TI.

SIGHTS

There's little to do in Staufen but enjoy the small lanes and shops, hike through the vineyards to the ruined castle overlooking the town (destroyed by Swedish troops in 1632), and savor a good meal with local wine. To learn more about the local vintners, visit Staufen's **bottling cooperative** *(Winzergenossenschaft)* at Haupstrasse 7, where you can both taste and buy (Mon–Fri 9:00–18:00, Sat 9:00–14:00, Sun 10:00–15:00, closed Sun in winter, tel. 07633/5510, www.winzergenossenschaft-staufen.de).

SLEEPING AND EATING

(€1 = about $1.50, country code: 49, area code: 07633)

$$ Gasthaus Krone, on the main pedestrian drag, has nine rooms that gild the lily but offer a good value in this price range (Sb-€65, Db-€85, Tb-€105, non-smoking, balconies, parking, Hauptstrasse 30, tel. 07633/5840, fax 07633/82903, www.die-krone.de, info@die-krone.de; Kurt Lahn, who looks a bit like Dan Rather, speaks a little English). Its **restaurant** appreciates vegetables and offers wonderful splurge meals (€19–25 main dishes, closed Fri lunch and all day Sat).

$$ Zum Hirschen, also with a storybook location on the main pedestrian street, is family-run, with 15 plush and thoughtfully appointed rooms, balconies, and a big roof deck (Sb-€62, Db-€82, Tb-€105, elevator, free and easy parking, on main pedestrian street at Hauptstrasse 19, cozy restaurant with €10-17 main dishes open Wed–Sun, tel. 07633/5297, fax 07633/5295, www.hirschen-staufen.de, for reservations on short notice it's best to fax, Dieter and Isabelle). Their top floor is a two-bedroom apartment (no kitchen) sleeping up to six people (€160 for 4 people).

$ Hotel Sonne, on a side street, offers eight simple rooms. Owner Antonio is particularly proud of his restaurant, serving tasty pizzas and Italian fare—a nice break from traditional *deutsche Küche* (Sb-€50, Db-€65, Tb-€85, Albert-Hugard-Strasse 1, tel. 07633/95300, fax 07633/953-014). With your back to the Rathaus, walk straight for 200 yards and turn left on Mühlegasse.

$ Bahnhof Hotel is the closest thing Staufen has to a hostel. Its seven cozy rooms (which share two bathrooms) are the cheapest in town. Packed full of old furniture, they make you feel like you're staying with an eccentric great-aunt. There's a dynamite castle view from the upstairs terrace, a self-service kitchen, and a tiny washing machine for guests. You can dine on its tree-shaded patio or in its antler-filled restaurant (€7.50 dinners). If you want to eat red meat under a tree at a table made out of a wine barrel, this is the place... it can get raucous (S-€21, D-€41, no breakfast, across from the train station, tel. 07633/6190, no English spoken).

TRANSPORTATION CONNECTIONS

By Train: Staufen is on a tiny branch line (called the Münstertalbahn) that connects to the main line at Bad Krozingen, a few stops south of Freiburg by slow milk-run train. Through connections from Freiburg leave roughly hourly; you need only a single two-zone local transport ticket, which costs €3.40 (available from ticket machines), and the whole trip takes about 30 minutes. First, take the train from Freiburg to Bad Krozingen. At Bad Krozingen station, find platform 12, from where the trains to Staufen leave. Sometimes, especially early and late, you have to take bus #113 instead of the Bad Krozingen-Staufen train (same ticket valid, bus stop is next to train station). A couple times a day, there is a through train from Freiburg to Staufen, with no need to change in Bad Krozingen. Plan ahead by checking schedules online, asking at the Freiburg train or bus station (pick up a printed schedule), calling the bus station at 0761/368-0388 during business hours, or calling the regional schedule helpline at 01805-779-966 (€0.14/min).

For those staying in Staufen, be aware of the last through connection from Freiburg (leaves Mon–Fri at 20:15, Sat–Sun at 19:15). For those visiting Staufen but sleeping elsewhere, the last through connection back to Freiburg leaves Staufen around 19:00 daily. If you really need to stay later in Staufen, a shared, subsidized taxi leaves from Staufen station for Bad Krozingen station at roughly 21:30 and 23:30, but only when riders reserve a seat at least 30 min in advance at tel. 07633/5386 (regular ticket required, taxi charges small "comfort supplement"). You can also call a regular taxi (same number).

The Best of the Black Forest

There are two great ways to see the most representative parts of the Black Forest: a short excursion from Freiburg and back (by public transport or car); or a longer route, if you have a day to connect Baden-Baden and Freiburg by car.

▲▲Short and Scenic Black Forest Joyride from Freiburg (by Car or Train and Bus)

This pleasant loop takes you through the most representative chunk of the area, avoiding the touristy, overcrowded Titisee.

By Car: Leave Freiburg on Schwarzwaldstrasse (signs to *Donaueschingen*), which becomes scenic road B-31 down the dark **Höllental** ("Hell's Valley") toward Titisee. Turn left at Hinterzarten onto road B-500, follow signs to St. Märgen and then to **St. Peter**—one of the healthy, go-take-a-walk-in-the-clean-air places that doctors actually prescribe for people from all over Germany. There's a fine four-mile walk between St. Märgen and St. Peter, with regular buses to bring you back.

For a longer drive, continue on from St. Peter, winding through idyllic Black Forest scenery up to **Mount Kandel.** At the summit is the Berghotel Kandel. You can park here and take a short walk to the 4,000-foot peak for a great view. Then the road winds steeply through a dense forest to **Waldkirch,** where a fast road takes you down to the Freiburg Nord autobahn entrance. From here you can return to Freiburg, or alternatively, drive on to Baden-Baden.

By Train and Bus: Trains run twice hourly from Freiburg to Kirchzarten Bahnhof, where you can take bus #7216 to St. Peter (40-min trip from Freiburg) and St. Märgen (55 min). Get off at St. Peter, hike four miles to St. Märgen, and bus/train back to Freiburg (through ticket €3.40 one-way, buy from machines). The Freiburg bus station has timetable booklets and more details on getting around the area (turn right out of Freiburg train station and walk 100 yards, tel. 0761/368-0388 during business hours; after hours, call 01805-779-966 for €0.12/min, or call Freiburg TI, tel. 0761/388-1880, www.rvf.de).

Town of St. Peter: The **TI,** just next to the Benedictine Abbey (private), can recommend a walk (TI open April–Oct Mon–Fri 9:00–12:00 & 15:00–17:00, Sat in July–Aug 10:00–12:00; Nov–March Mon–Fri 9:00–12:00; closed Sun year-round and Sat Sept–June; Klosterhof 11, tel. 07660/910-224). Sleep at the traditional old **$$ Gasthof Hirschen** on the main square (Sb-€39–44, Db-€66–82, Tb-€87–97, Qb-€103, parking-€4/day, St. Peter/Hochschwarzwald, Bertholdsplatz 1, tel. 07660/204, fax

07660/1557, www.gasthof-hirschen.de, info@gasthof-hirschen.de), or consider **$ Pension Kandelblick** (D-€50, cash only, Seelgutweg 5, tel. 07660/349).

▲▲Extended Black Forest Drive Between Baden-Baden and Freiburg

Of course, you could spend much more time in the land of cuckoo clocks and healthy hikes. For a more thorough visit, try this drive.

• *Assuming you're heading south from Baden-Baden, get on B-500, a.k.a. the Schwarzwald-Hochstrasse, which takes you along a ridge through 30 miles of pine forests (and becomes B-28—take it east, signs to* Freudenstadt*). Eventually you'll reach* ***Freudenstadt,*** *the capital of the northern Black Forest. From here, hop on B-294 southbound; in Turm (just before Hausach), turn south onto B-33/E-531 to* ***Gutach,*** *where you'll visit the...*

▲Black Forest Open-Air Museum (Schwarzwälder Freilichtmuseum Vogtsbauernhof)—This excellent museum offers the best look at this region's traditional folk life. (Note: It's different from the similarly named museum in Triberg, described below.) Built around one grand old farmhouse, the museum is a collection of several old farms filled with exhibits on the local dress and lifestyles. Make time for the grain mill (€6, daily April–Oct 9:00–18:00, until 19:00 July–Aug, last entry one hour before closing, closed Nov–March, English descriptions and €5 guidebook, in Gutach, tel. 07831/93560, www.vogtsbauernhof.org).

BLACK FOREST

Eating: The surrounding shops and restaurants are awfully touristy, but are a fair source for local specialties. Skip the indoor restaurant and instead try your *Frikadelle* (a spiced pork-and-beef patty) or *Schupfnudeln* (potato-based noodles, served fried up with sauerkraut) at the outdoor stands. Don't be shy to try a little of everything; the friendly ladies ladling the portions will fill up your plate with whatever you point to and charge about €6–7). Be sure to indulge in a creamy piece of Schwarzwald Kirschtorte.

• *After visiting the museum, continue south on B-33/E-531, turning off to see...*

Triberg—Deep in the Black Forest, Triberg is famous for its Gutach Waterfall (which falls 500 feet in several bounces, €2 to see it) and, more importantly, the **Black Forest Museum,** which gives a fine look at the costumes, carvings, and traditions of the local culture (€4.50, daily May–Sept 10:00–18:00, Oct–April

10:00–17:00, Wallfahrtstrasse 4, tel. 07722/4434, www.schwarzwaldmuseum.de). Touristy as Triberg is, it offers an easy way for travelers without cars to enjoy the Black Forest (TI located in Black Forest Museum, tel. 07722/866-490, www.triberg.de).

• *Now head south on B-500 to...*

Furtwangen—This town features the impressive **German Clock Museum** (Deutsches Uhrenmuseum). More than a chorus of cuckoo clocks, this museum traces (in English) the development of clocks from the Dark Ages to the Space Age. It has an upbeat combo of mechanical musical instruments as well (€4, daily April–Oct 9:00–18:00, Nov–March 10:00–17:00, tel. 07723/920-2800, www.deutsches-uhrenmuseum.de).

• *From Furtwangen, continue south on B-500. From this road, you have two options for joining up with different scenic areas (both described under "Short and Scenic Black Forest Joyride," page 211): Turn off for* ***St. Peter*** *(L-128 to St. Märgen, then L-127 to St. Peter), for a visit to that town and* ***Mount Kandel*** *and* ***Waldkirch;*** *or continue a bit farther south on B-500 to Hinterzarten, where you can turn right onto scenic B-31 and follow the claustrophobic* ***Höllental*** *("Hell's Valley"). Either option brings you to Freiburg's backyard.*

South-to-North Variation: To see these sights in reverse (from Freiburg to Baden-Baden), begin by following the "Short and Scenic" joyride, page 211, but continue north on B-500. Once on B-500, dip into Furtwangen's German Clock Museum, then Triberg. From Triberg, head north on B-33/E-531 to the open-air museum in Gutach, then continue north and pick up E-294 to Freduendstadt, and on to the Schwarzwald-Hochstrasse (B-28, then B-500), which dumps you right on Baden-Baden's back porch.

ROTHENBURG and the ROMANTIC ROAD

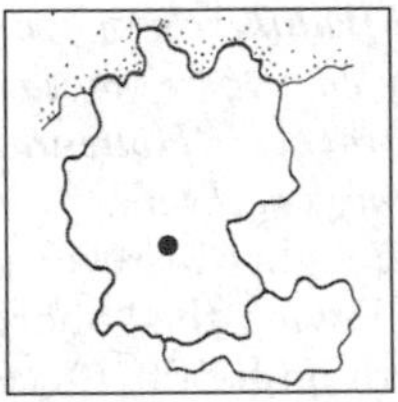

The Romantic Road takes you through Bavaria's medieval heartland, a route strewn with picturesque villages, farmhouses, onion-domed churches, Baroque palaces, and walled cities. The Romantic Road is the most scenic way to connect Frankfurt with Munich. Clearly marked for drivers, and well-described in a free brochure available at any TI, the route technically runs from Würzburg south to Füssen. Car travelers can follow the signposts, meandering from one medieval town to the next. No trains run along the entire Romantic Road, but rail travelers can linger for a night or two in Rothenburg (ROE-tehn-burg), the most interesting town along the route.

Countless travelers have searched for the elusive "untouristy Rothenburg." There are many contenders (such as Michelstadt, Miltenberg, Bamberg, Bad Windsheim, and Dinkelsbühl), but none holds a candle to the king of medieval German cuteness. Even with crowds, overpriced souvenirs, Japanese-speaking night watchmen, and, yes, even *Schneeballen*, Rothenburg is best. Save time and mileage and be satisfied with the winner.

Rothenburg ob der Tauber

In the Middle Ages, when Frankfurt and Munich were just wide spots on the road, Rothenburg ob der Tauber was a free imperial city. With a whopping population of 6,000, it was one of Germany's largest. Today, it's the country's best-preserved medieval walled town, enjoying tremendous tourist popularity without losing its charm.

During Rothenburg's heyday, from 1150 to 1400, it was a strategic stop on the trade routes between northern and southern Europe. Today, the great trade is tourism: Two-thirds of the townspeople are employed to serve you. While 2.5 million people visit each year, a mere 500,000 spend the night. Rothenburg is yours after dark, when the groups vacate and the town's floodlit cobbles wring some romance out of any travel partner.

Too often, Rothenburg brings out the shopper in visitors before they've had a chance to see the historic town. True, this is a fine place to do your German shopping, but appreciate Rothenburg's great history and sights, too.

Planning Your Time

If time is short, you can make just a two- to three-hour midday stop in Rothenburg, but the town is really best appreciated after the day-trippers have gone home. Spend at least one night in Rothenburg (hotels are cheap). With two nights and a day, you'll be able to see more than the essentials and actually relax a little.

Rothenburg in one day is easy, with four essential experiences: the Medieval Crime and Punishment Museum, Tilman Riemenschneider's wood carving in St. Jakob's Church, a walk along the city wall, and the entertaining Night Watchman's Tour (the first two sights are covered in my self-guided tour, later in this chapter). With more time, there are several mediocre but entertaining museums, scenic hikes and bike rides in the nearby countryside, and lots of cafés and shops.

Rothenburg is very busy through the summer and in the Christmas Market month of December. Spring and fall are a joy, but it's pretty bleak from January through March—when most locals are hibernating or on vacation. Many shops stay open on Sundays during the tourist season, but close on Sundays in November and from Christmas to Easter.

Rothenburg

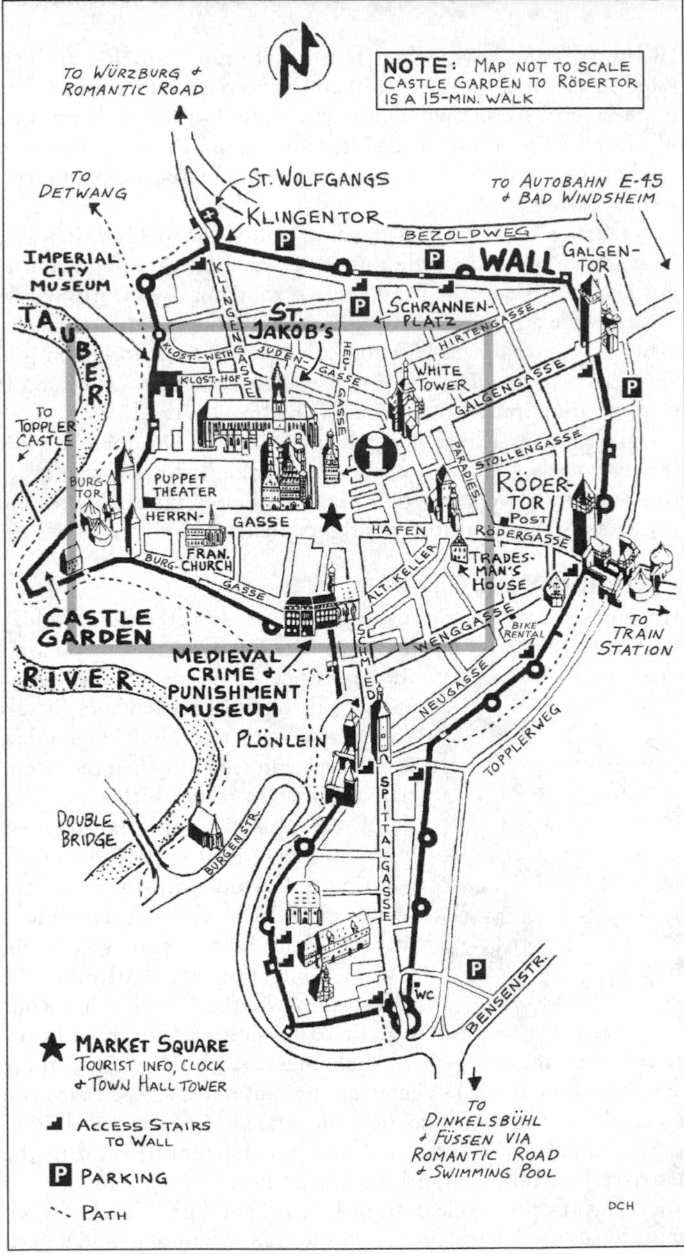
NOTE: MAP NOT TO SCALE
CASTLE GARDEN TO RÖDERTOR IS A 15-MIN. WALK
TO WÜRZBURG & ROMANTIC ROAD
TO DETWANG
ST. WOLFGANGS
KLINGENTOR
TO AUTOBAHN E-45 & BAD WINDSHEIM
BEZOLDWEG
WALL
GALGENTOR
IMPERIAL CITY MUSEUM
TAUBER
RIVER
SCHRANNENPLATZ
ST. JAKOB'S
KLINGENGASSE
JUDENGASSE
HEUGASSE
KLOST.-WETH
KLOST.-HOF
HIRTENGASSE
WHITE TOWER
GALGENGASSE
TO TOPPLER CASTLE
STOLLENGASSE
PARADIES
RÖDERTOR
POST
PUPPET THEATER
BURGTOR
HERRNGASSE
HAFEN
RÖDERGASSE
FRAN. CHURCH
BURGGASSE
TRADESMAN'S HOUSE
ALT. KELLER
CASTLE GARDEN
WENGGASSE
BIKE RENTAL
TO TRAIN STATION
MEDIEVAL CRIME & PUNISHMENT MUSEUM
SCHMIED
NEUGASSE
PLÖNLEIN
TOPPLERWEG
DOUBLE BRIDGE
BURGENSTR.
SPITTALGASSE
BENSENSTR.
WC
MARKET SQUARE
TOURIST INFO, CLOCK & TOWN HALL TOWER
ACCESS STAIRS TO WALL
PARKING
PATH
TO DINKELSBÜHL & FÜSSEN VIA ROMANTIC ROAD & SWIMMING POOL
DCH

There are several Rothenburgs in Germany, so make sure you are going to **Rothenburg ob der Tauber** (not "ob der" any other river); people really do sometimes drive or ride the train to other, nondescript Rothenburgs by accident.

ORIENTATION

(area code: 09861)
To orient yourself in Rothenburg, think of the town map as a human head. Its nose—the castle garden—sticks out to the left, and the skinny lower part forms a wide-open mouth, with the hostel and some of the best hotels in the chin. The town is a delight on foot. No sights or hotels are more than a 15-minute walk from the train station or each other.

Most of the buildings you'll see were in place by 1400. The city was born around its long-gone castle—built in 1142, destroyed in 1356—which was located where the castle garden is now. You can see the shadow of the first town wall, which defines the oldest part of Rothenburg, in its contemporary street plan. A few gates from this wall still survive. The richest and biggest houses were in this central part. The commoners built higgledy-piggledy (read: picturesque) houses farther from the center, but still inside the present walls.

Tourist Information

The TI is on Market Square (May–Oct and Dec Mon–Fri 9:00–18:00, Sat–Sun 10:00–15:00; Nov and Jan–April Mon–Fri 9:00–17:00, Sat 10:00–13:00, closed Sun; Marktplatz 2, tel. 09861/404800, www.rothenburg.de). If there's a long line, just raid the rack where they keep all the free pamphlets. The free *Map & Guide* comes with a walking guide to the town. The free *RoTour* monthly magazine lists all the events and entertainment (in German only; also look for current concert listing posters here and at your hotel). Ask about the daily English walking tour at 14:00 (€6, April–Oct and Dec; see "Tours," page 219). The TI has one free Internet terminal (15-min maximum). Visitors who arrive after closing can check the handy map highlighting which hotels have rooms available, with a free direct phone connection to them; it's just outside the door. A pictorial town map is available free with this book at the Friese shop, two doors west from the TI (toward St. Jakob's Church; see "Shopping," page 231).

Arrival in Rothenburg

By Train: It's a 10-minute walk from the station to Rothenburg's Market Square (following the brown *Altstadt* signs, exit left from station, turn right on Ansbacher Strasse, and head straight into the Middle Ages). Day-trippers can leave luggage in station lockers (€1–2, on platform) or at a local shop (try the Friese shop on Market Square, or Passage 12—see page 231). Arrange train and *couchette*/sleeper reservations at the combined ticket office and travel agency in the station (€0.50 charge for questions without ticket purchase, Mon–Fri 9:00–18:00, Sat 9:00–13:00, closed Sun, tel. 09861/7711). Free WCs are behind the snack bar next door to the station. Taxis wait at the station (€5 to any hotel).

By Car: For tips on getting here from Frankfurt, see "Route Tips for Drivers" on page 243. While much of the town is closed to traffic, anyone with a hotel reservation can drive in and through pedestrian zones to get to their hotel. But driving in town can be a nightmare, with many narrow, one-way streets. If you're packing light, just park outside the walls and walk five minutes to the center. Parking lots line the town walls: P1 costs €5 per day; P5 and the south half of P4 are free. Only those with a hotel reservation can park within the walls after hours (but not during festivals). The easiest way to enter and leave Rothenburg is generally via Spitalgasse and the Spitaltor (south end).

Helpful Hints

Festivals: *Biergartens* spill out into the street and Rothenburgers dress up in medieval costumes to celebrate Mayor Nusch's Meistertrunk victory (May 25–June 1 in 2009; see story of the draught that saved the town under "Meistertrunk Show" on page 220, more info at www.meistertrunk.de). The Reichsstadt festival every September celebrates Rothenburg's history (September 4–6 in 2009).

Christmas Market: Rothenburg is dead in November, January, and February, but December is its busiest month—the entire town cranks up the medieval cuteness with concerts and costumes, shops with schnapps, stalls filling squares, hot spiced wine, giddy nutcrackers, and mobs of earmuffed Germans. Christmas markets are big all over Germany, and Rothenburg's is considered one of the best. The festival takes place each year during Advent (Nov 27–Dec 23 in 2009). Virtually all sights listed in this chapter are open longer hours during these four weeks. Try to avoid Saturdays and Sundays, when big-city day-trippers really clog the grog.

Internet Access: When it comes to getting online, Rothenburg is still pretty medieval. Only some hotels have Internet access, and many have no phones in the rooms. **Inter@Play,** the only Internet café in town, has eight fast terminals (€3/hr, daily 8:00–24:00, 18 and older only, 2 blocks down Hafengasse from Market Square and around the corner to the left at Milchmarkt 3—see map on page 221, tel. 09861/935-599).

The **TI** has one free terminal for brief use (maximum 15 min). The **Passage 12** souvenir shop offers free use of the computer at their desk upstairs (see page 232).

Laundry: A handy launderette is near the station, off Ansbacher Strasse (€5.50/load, includes soap, English instructions, opens at 8:00, last load Mon–Fri at 18:00, Sat at 14:00, closed Sun, Johannitergasse 9, tel. 09861/2775).

Haircuts: At **Salon Wack** (pronounced vack, not wack), Horst and his team speak English and welcome both men and women (€17.50 for men, €27–32.50 for women, Tue–Fri 8:00–12:00 & 13:30–18:00, Sat 8:30–14:00, closed Sun–Mon, in the old center just off Wenggasse at Goldene Ringgasse 8, tel. 09861/7834).

Swimming: Rothenburg has a fine swimming complex, with a heated outdoor pool *(Freibad)* from mid-May to mid-September, and an indoor pool and sauna the rest of the year. It's about 15 minutes' walk south of Spitaltor along the main road toward Dinkelsbühl (adults-€3.50, kids-€2, swimsuit and towel rental-€2.50 each; outdoor pool open Fri–Tue 9:00–20:00, Wed 6:30–20:00, Thu 10:00–20:00; indoor pool open Mon 14:00–21:00, Tue–Thu 9:00–21:00, Fri–Sun 9:00–18:00; Nördlinger Strasse 20, tel. 09861/4565, www.stadtwerke-rothenburg.de).

Bike Rental: You can rent a bike and follow the suggested route on page 230. **Fahrradhaus Krauss** is a big bike shop that rents eight-gear bikes. It's cheap, reliable, and right in the old town (€5/6 hrs, €10/24 hrs, no helmets, Tue–Fri 9:00–18:00, Sat 9:00–13:00, closed Sun–Mon, Wenggasse 42, tel. 09861/3495).

TOURS

▲▲Night Watchman's Tour—This tour is flat-out the most entertaining hour of medieval wonder anywhere in Germany. The Night Watchman (a.k.a. Hans-Georg Baumgartner) jokes like a medieval Jerry Seinfeld as he lights his lamp and takes tourists on his rounds, telling slice-of-gritty-life tales of medieval Rothenburg (€6, free for kids, Easter–Dec nightly at 20:00, in English, meet at Market Square, www.nightwatchman.de). This is the best evening activity in town.

Old Town Historic Walk—The TI offers 90-minute guided walking tours in English (€6, April–Oct and Dec daily at 14:00, Jan–March Sat only at 11:00, no tours in Nov, departs from Market

Square). While the Night Watchman's Tour is fun, take this tour for the serious side of Rothenburg's history, and to make sense of the town's architecture. The tours are completely different, and it would be a shame not to take advantage of this informative tour just because you took the other.

Local Guides—A local historian can really bring the ramparts alive. Prices are standardized (€60/90 min, €78/2 hrs). **Gisela Vogl** (tel. 09861/4957, werner.vogl@t-online.de) and **Anita Weinzierl** (tel. 09868/7993, anitaweinzierl@aol.com) are both good. **Martin Kamphans,** a potter, also works as a guide (tel. 09861/7941, www.stadtfuehrungen-rothenburg.de, kamphans@t-online.de). Or you can reserve a guide by sending an email to the TI (info@rothenburg.de; also click "Guided Tours" at www.rothenburg.de).

Horse-and-Buggy Rides—These farm boys, who are generally about as charming as their horses, give a relaxing 30-minute clip-clop through the old town, starting from Market Square or Schrannenplatz. Good luck negotiating a fair price (private buggy for €30–50, or wait for one to fill up for €10 per person).

SELF-GUIDED WALK

Welcome to Rothenburg

This one-hour circular walk weaves Rothenburg's top sights together.

• *Start the walk on Market Square.*

Market Square Spin-Tour

Stand at the bottom of Market Square (10 feet below the wooden post on the corner) and spin 360 degrees clockwise, starting with the Town Hall tower. Now do it again, this time more slowly, following these notes:

Town Hall and Tower: Rothenburg's tallest spire is the **Town Hall tower** (Rathausturm). At 200 feet, it stands atop the old Town Hall, a white, Gothic, 13th-century building. Notice the tourists enjoying the best view in town from the black top of the tower (€2 and a rigorous but interesting climb, 214 steps, narrow and steep near the top—watch your head, April–Oct daily 9:30–12:30 & 13:00–17:00, closed Nov–March, enter on Market Square through middle arch of new Town Hall). After a fire burned down part of the original building, a new Town Hall was built alongside what survived of the old one (fronting the square). This half of the rebuilt complex is in the Renaissance style from 1570.

Meistertrunk Show: At the top of Market Square stands the proud Councillors' Tavern (clock tower from 1466). In its day, the city council—the rich guys who ran the town government—drank here. Today, it's the TI and the focus of most tourists' attention

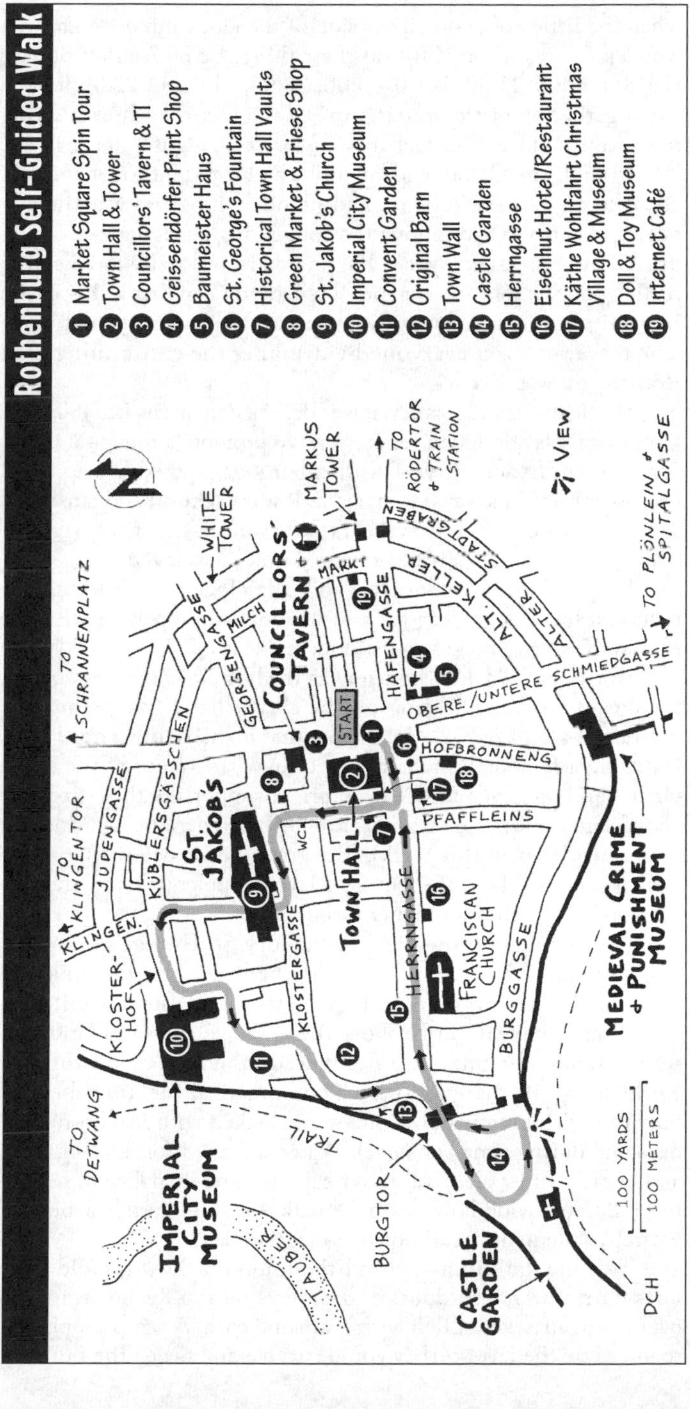
Rothenburg Self-Guided Walk
1 Market Square Spin Tour
2 Town Hall & Tower
3 Councillors' Tavern & TI
4 Geissendörfer Print Shop
5 Baumeister Haus
6 St. George's Fountain
7 Historical Town Hall Vaults
8 Green Market & Friese Shop
9 St. Jakob's Church
10 Imperial City Museum
11 Convent Garden
12 Original Barn
13 Town Wall
14 Castle Garden
15 Herrngasse
16 Eisenhut Hotel/Restaurant
17 Käthe Wohlfahrt Christmas Village & Museum
18 Doll & Toy Museum
19 Internet Café
TO SCHRANNENPLATZ
WHITE TOWER
MARKUS TOWER
TO RÖDERTOR + TRAIN STATION
VIEW
TO KLINGENTOR
JUDENGASSE
KÜBLERSGÄSSCHEN
GEORGENGASSE
MILCH
COUNCILLORS' TAVERN + i
MARKT
START
HAFENGASSE
STADTGRABEN
ALT. KELLER
ALTER
OBERE / UNTERE SCHMIEDGASSE
TO PLÖNLEIN + SPITALGASSE
HOFBRONNENG
PFAFFLEINS
ST. JAKOB'S
WC
TOWN HALL
KLINGEN.
KLOSTER-HOF
KLOSTERGASSE
HERRNGASSE
FRANCISCAN CHURCH
BURGGASSE
MEDIEVAL CRIME + PUNISHMENT MUSEUM
TO DETWANG
TRAIL
IMPERIAL CITY MUSEUM
BURGTOR
TAUBER
CASTLE GARDEN
100 YARDS
100 METERS
DCH

when the little doors on either side of the clock flip open and the wooden figures (from 1910) do their thing. Be on Market Square at 11:00, 12:00, 13:00, 14:00, 15:00, 20:00, 21:00, or 22:00 for the ritual gathering of the tourists to see the less-than-breathtaking reenactment of the Meistertrunk ("Master Draught") story:

In 1631, the Catholic army took the Protestant town and was about to do its rape, pillage, and plunder thing. As was the etiquette, the mayor had to give the conquering general a welcoming drink. The general enjoyed a huge tankard of local wine. Feeling really good, he told the mayor, "Hey, if you can drink this entire three-liter tankard of wine in one gulp, I'll spare your town." The mayor amazed everyone by drinking the entire thing, and Rothenburg was saved.

While this is a nice story, it was dreamed up in the late 1800s for a theatrical play designed (effectively) to promote a romantic image of the town. In actuality, if Rothenburg was spared, it happened because it bribed its way out of a jam. It was occupied and ransacked several times in the Thirty Years' War, and it never recovered—which is why it's such a well-preserved time capsule today.

For the best show, don't watch the clock; watch the open-mouthed tourists gasp as the old windows flip open. At the late shows, the square flickers with camera flashes.

Bottom of Market Square: On the bottom end of the square, the cream-colored building on the corner has a fine **print shop** (upstairs—see page 232). Adjoining that is the **Baumeister Haus,** featuring a famous Renaissance facade with statues of the seven virtues and the seven vices—the former supporting the latter. The statues are copies; the originals are in the Imperial City Museum (described later on this walk). The green house below that is the former home of the 15th-century Mayor Toppler (it's now the recommended Gasthof Goldener Greifen).

Keep circling to the big 17th-century **St. George's fountain.** The long metal gutters slid, routing the water into the villagers' buckets. Rothenburg had an ingenious water system. Built on a rock, it had one real source above the town, which was plumbed to serve a series of fountains; water flowed from high to low through Rothenburg. Its many fountains had practical functions beyond providing drinking water (some were stocked with fish on market days and during times of siege). Water was used for fighting fires, and because of its plentiful water supply—and its policy of requiring relatively wide lanes as fire breaks—the town never burned entirely, as so many neighboring villages did.

Two fine buildings behind the fountain show the old-time lofts with warehouse doors and pulleys on top for hoisting. All over town, lofts were filled with grain and corn. A year's supply was required by the city so they could survive any siege. The building behind the fountain is an art gallery showing off work by members of the local artists' association (free, Tue–Sun 14:00–18:00, closed Mon). To the right is Marien Apotheke, an old-time pharmacy mixing old and new in typical Rothenburg style.

The broad street running under the Town Hall tower is **Herrngasse.** The town originated with its castle (built in 1142 but now long gone; only the castle garden remains). Herrngasse connected the castle to Market Square. The last leg of this circular walking tour will take you from the castle garden up Herrngasse to where you now stand. For now, walk a few steps down Herrngasse and stand by the arch under the Town Hall tower (between the new and old town halls). On the left wall are the town's measuring rods—a reminder that medieval Germany was made of 300 independent little countries, each with its own weights and measures. Merchants and shoppers knew that these were the local standards: the rod (4.3 yards), the *Schuh* (or shoe, roughly a foot), and the *Ell* (from elbow to fingertip—four inches longer than mine...try it). Notice the protruding cornerstone. These are all over town—originally to protect buildings from reckless horse carts (and vice versa).

• *Under the arch, you'll find the...*

▲Historical Town Hall Vaults (Historiengewölbe)

This grade-schoolish little museum gives a waxy but interesting look at Rothenburg during the Catholics-vs.-Protestants Thirty Years' War. With helpful English descriptions, it offers a look at "the fateful year 1631," a replica of the mythical Meistertrunk tankard, and a dungeon complete with three dank cells and some torture lore (€2, April–Oct daily 9:30–17:30, closed Nov–March, tel. 09861/86751).

• *Leaving the museum, turn left (past a much-sketched and photographed venerable door), and walk through the courtyard to a square called...*

Green Market (Grüner Markt)

Once a produce market, this is now a parking lot that fills with Christmas shops during December. Notice the clay-tile roofs. These "beaver tail" tiles became standard after thatched roofs were outlawed to prevent fires. Today, all of the town's roofs are made of these. The little fences keep the snow from falling, and catch tiles that blow off during storms. The free public WC is on your left, the recommended **Friese shop** (see "Shopping," page 231) is on your right, and straight ahead is St. Jakob's Church.

Outside the church, you'll see 14th-century statues (mostly original) showing Jesus praying at Gethsemane, a common feature of Gothic churches. The artist is anonymous, because in the Gothic age (pre–Albrecht Dürer) artists were just nameless craftspeople working only for the glory of God. Five yards to the left (on the wall), notice the nub of a sandstone statue—a rare original, looking pretty bad after 500 years of weather and, more recently, pollution. Most original statues are now in the city museum. The better-preserved statues you see on the church are copies.

• *If it's your wedding day, take the first entrance. Otherwise, use the second (downhill) door to enter...*

▲▲St. Jakob's Church (St. Jakobskirche)

Built in the 14th century, this church has been Lutheran since 1544. The interior was "purified" by Romantics in the 19th century—cleaned of everything Baroque or not original, and refitted in the Neo-Gothic style. (For example, the baptismal font and the pulpit above the second pew *look* Gothic, but are actually Neo-Gothic.) The stained-glass windows behind the altar (most colorful in the morning light) are originals from the 1330s. Entrance costs €2 (April–Oct and Dec Mon–Sat 9:00–17:15, Sun 10:45–17:15; Nov and Christmas–March daily 10:00–12:00 & 14:00–16:00; free helpful English info sheet, concerts and tour schedule posted on the door). There are guided tours in English for no extra charge on Saturdays at 15:00.

At the back of the church, take the stairs that lead up behind the pipe organ. In the loft, you'll find the artistic highlight of Rothenburg and perhaps the most wonderful wood carving in all of Germany: the glorious 500-year-old, 35-foot-high ***Altar of the Holy Blood.*** Tilman Riemenschneider, the Michelangelo of German woodcarvers, carved this from 1499 to 1504 to hold a precious rock-crystal capsule, set in a cross that contains a scrap of tablecloth miraculously stained in the shape of a cross by a drop of communion wine. It's a realistic commotion, showing that Riemenschneider—while a High Gothic artist—was ahead of his time. Below, in the scene of the Last Supper, Jesus gives Judas a piece of bread, marking him as the traitor, while John lays his head on Christ's lap. Everything is portrayed exactly as described in the Bible. On the left: Jesus enters Jericho, with the shy tax collector Zacchaeus looking on from his tree. Notice the fun attention to detail—down to the nails on the horseshoe. On the right: Jesus prays in the Garden of Gethsemane. Notice how Judas, with his big bag of cash, could be removed from the scene—illustrated by photos on the wall nearby—as was the tradition for the four days leading up to Easter.

Head back down the stairs to the church's main hall. Go up front to take a close look at the main altar (from 1466, by Friedrich Herlin). Below Christ are statues of six saints. St. James (Jakob in German) is the one with the shell. He's the saint of pilgrims, and this church was a stop on the medieval pilgrimage route to Santiago ("St. James" in Spanish) de Compostela in Spain. Study the painted panels—ever see Peter with spectacles? Around the back of the altarpiece (upper left) is a painting of Rothenburg's Market Square in the 15th century—looking much like it does today, with the exception of the full-Gothic Town Hall (as it was before the big fire of 1501). Notice Christ's face on the veil of Veronica (center of back side). It follows you as you walk from side to side—it must have given the faithful the religious heebie-jeebies four centuries ago.

The small altar to the left is also worth a look. It's a century older than the main altar. Notice the unusual Trinity: the Father and Son are literally bridged by a dove, which represents the Holy Spirit. Stepping back, you can see that Jesus is standing on a skull—clearly "overcoming death."

Before leaving the front of the church, notice the old medallions above the carved choir stalls. They feature the coats of arms of Rothenburg's leading families and portraits of city and church leaders.

• *Leave the church and, from its outside steps, walk around the corner to the right and under the chapel (built over the road). Go two blocks down Klingengasse and stop at the corner of Klosterhof Street. Looking down Klingengasse, you see the...*

Klingentor

This cliff tower was Rothenburg's water reservoir. From 1595 until 1910, a copper tank high in the tower provided clean spring water (pumped up by river power) to the privileged. To the right of Klingentor is a good stretch of wall rampart to walk. To the left, the wall is low and simple, lacking a rampart because it guards only a cliff. Now find the shell decorating a building on the street corner next to you. That's the symbol of St. James (pilgrims commemorated their visit to Santiago de Compostela with a shell), indicating that this building is associated with the church.

• *Turn left down Klosterhof, passing the shell and, on your right, the colorful Altfränkische Weinstube am Klosterhof (see page 239), to reach the...*

▲▲Imperial City Museum (Reichsstadt-Museum)

You'll get a scholarly sweep through Rothenburg's history at this museum, housed in the former Dominican convent. Cloistered nuns used the lazy Susan embedded in the wall (to the right of museum door) to give food to the poor without being seen.

Highlights include *The Rothenburg Passion,* a 12-panel series of paintings from 1492 showing scenes leading up to Christ's crucifixion (in the *Konventsaal*); an exhibit of Jewish culture through the ages in Rothenburg *(Judaika);* a 14th-century convent kitchen *(Klosterküche)* with a working model of the lazy Susan and a massive chimney; romantic paintings of the town *(Gemäldegalerie);* the fine Baumann collection of weapons and armor; and sandstone statues from the church and Baumeister Haus (the seven vices and seven virtues). Follow the *Rundgang Tour* signs (€3.50, daily April–Oct 9:30–17:30, Nov–March 13:00–16:00, English info sheet and descriptions, Klosterhof 5, tel. 09861/939-043, www.reichsstadtmuseum.rothenburg.de).

• *Leaving the museum, go around to the right and into the Convent Garden (when locked at night, continue straight to the T-intersection and see the barn three doors to the right).*

Convent Garden

This spot is a peaceful place to work on your tan...or mix a poisoned potion (free, same hours as museum). Enjoy the herb garden. Monks and nuns, who were responsible for concocting herbal cures in the olden days, often tended herb gardens. Smell (but don't pick) the *Pfefferminze, Juniper* (gin), *Chamomilla* (disinfectant), and *Origanum.* Don't smell the plants in the poison corner (potency indicated by the number of crosses...like spiciness stars in a Chinese restaurant).

• *Exit opposite from where you entered, angling left through the nuns' garden (site of the now-gone Dominican church), eventually leaving via an arch at the far end. Looking to your left, you'll see the back end of an...*

Original Barn

This is the back side of a complex that fronts Herrngasse. Medieval Germans often lived in large structures like this that were like small villages in themselves, with a grouping of buildings and open spaces. The typical design included a house, a courtyard, a stable, a garden, and, finally, a barn. Notice how the bulging wall is corseted by a brace with iron washers. Crank on its nuts and the building will stand up straight.

• *Now go downhill to the...*

Town Wall

This part of the wall (view through bars, look to far right) takes advantage of the natural fortification provided by the cliff, and is therefore much smaller than the ramparts. Angle left along the wall to the big street (Herrngasse), then right under the Burgtor tower. Notice the tiny "eye of the needle" door cut into the big door. If trying to get into town after curfew, you could bribe the guard to let you through this door (which was small enough to keep out any fully armed attackers).

• *Step through the gate and outside the wall. Look around and imagine being locked out in the year 1400. This was a wooden drawbridge (see the chain slits above). Notice the "pitch nose" mask—designed to pour boiling Nutella on anyone attacking. High above is the town coat of arms: a red castle* (roten Burg).

Castle Garden (Burggarten)

The garden before you was once that red castle (destroyed in the 14th century). Today, it's a picnic-friendly park. The chapel (50 yards into the park on the left) is the only bit of the original castle to survive. It's now a memorial to local Jews killed in a 1298 slaughter. A few steps beyond that is a grapevine trellis that provides a fine picnic spot. If you walk all the way out to the garden's far end, you'll find a great viewpoint (well past the tourists, and considered the best place to kiss by romantic local teenagers). But the views of the lush Tauber River Valley below are just as good from the top end of the park. Facing the town, on the left, a path leads down to the village of Detwang (you can see the church spire below)—a town even older than Rothenburg (for a walk to Detwang, see "A Walk in the Countryside," page 230). To the right is a fine view of the fortified Rothenburg and the "Tauber Riviera" below.

• *Return to the tower, cross carefully under the pitch nose, and hike back up Herrngasse to your starting point.*

Herrngasse

Many towns have a Herrngasse, where the richest patricians and merchants (the *Herren*) lived. Predictably, it's your best chance to see the town's finest old mansions. Strolling back to Market Square, you'll pass the old-time puppet theater (German only, on left), the Franciscan church (from 1285, oldest in town, on right), and the hippie Sawasdee shop (where the Night Watchman spends his days dreaming of his next trip to Thailand while his girlfriend sells what they've imported, as well as "Night Watchman mementos," Herrngasse 23). The house at #18 is the biggest patrician house on the street. The family, which has lived here for three centuries, disconnected the four old-time doorbells. Their door—big enough to allow a carriage in (with a human-sized door cut into it)—is typical of the age. To see the traditional house-courtyard-stables-garden-barn layout, pop into either #14 (now an apartment block) or—if that's closed—the shop across the street, at #11. The Eisenhut Hotel, Rothenburg's fanciest, is worth a peek inside (see page 239). The Käthe Wohlfahrt Christmas shops (at Herrngasse 1 and 2, see "Shopping," page 231) are your last, and perhaps greatest, temptations before reaching your starting and ending point: Market Square.

SIGHTS AND ACTIVITIES

Museums Within a Block of Market Square

▲▲Medieval Crime and Punishment Museum (Mittelalterliches Kriminalmuseum)—This museum is the best of its kind, specializing in everything connected to medieval criminal justice. Learn about medieval police, medieval criminal law, and above all, instruments of punishment and torture—even a special cage complete with a metal gag for nags. The museum is more eclectic than its name, and includes exhibits on general history, superstition, biblical art, and temporary displays in a second building.

Follow the yellow arrows—the one-way traffic system makes it hard to double back. Exhibits are tenderly described in English (€3.80, daily April–Oct 9:30–18:00, Nov and Jan–Feb 14:00–16:00, Dec and March 10:00–16:00, last entry 45 min before closing, fun cards and posters, Burggasse 3–5, tel. 09861/5359, www.kriminalmuseum.rothenburg.de).

▲Doll and Toy Museum (Puppen- und Spielzeugmuseum)—These two floors of historic *Kinder* cuteness are a hit with many. Pick up the free English binder (just past the entry curtain) for an extensive description of the exhibits (€4, family ticket-€10, daily March–Dec 9:30–18:00, Jan–Feb 11:00–17:00, just off Market Square, downhill from the fountain at Hofbronnengasse 11–13, tel. 09861/7330, www.spielzeugmuseum.rothenburg.de).

▲German Christmas Museum (Deutsches Weihnachtsmuseum)—This excellent museum, upstairs in the giant Käthe Wohlfahrt Christmas Village shop, tells the history of Christmas decorations. There's a unique and thoughtfully described collection of Christmas-tree stands, mini-trees sent in boxes to WWI soldiers at the front, early Advent calendars, old-time Christmas cards, and a look at tree decorations through the ages—including the Nazi era and when you were a kid. The museum is not just a ploy to get shoppers to spend more money, but a serious collection managed by professional curator Felicitas Höptner (€4, April–Dec daily 10:00–17:30, Jan–March Sat–Sun 10:00–17:30 and irregularly on weekdays, Herrngasse 1, tel. 09861/409-365, www.germanchristmasmuseum.com). You can visit the museum at the €2.50 student rate with this book in 2009—if you promise to learn something.

More Sights and Activities in Rothenburg

▲▲Walk the Wall—Just longer than a mile and a half around, providing great views and a good orientation, this walk can be done by those under six feet tall and without a camera in less than an hour. The hike requires no special sense of balance. This walk is covered and is a great option in the rain. Photographers will stay very busy, especially before breakfast or at sunset, when the lighting is best and the crowds are fewest. You can enter or exit the ramparts at nearly every tower. The best fortifications are in the Spitaltor (south end). Climb the Rödertor en route (described next). The names you see along the way are people who donated money to rebuild the wall after World War II, and those who've recently donated €1,000 per meter for the maintenance of Rothenburg's heritage.

▲Rödertor—The wall tower nearest the train station is the only one you can climb. It's worth the 135 steps for the view and a short but fascinating rundown on the bombing of Rothenburg in the last weeks of World War II, when the east part of the city was destroyed (€1.50, pay at top, unreliable hours, usually open April–Oct daily 10:00–16:00, closed Nov–March, WWII photos have English translations). If you climb this, you can skip the more claustrophobic Town Hall tower climb.

▲▲The Allergic-to-Tourists Wall and Moat Walk—For a quiet and scenic break from the tourist crowds and a chance to appreciate the marvelous fortifications of Rothenburg, consider this hike: From the Castle Garden, go right and walk outside the wall to Klingentor. At Klingentor, climb up to the ramparts and walk on the wall past Galgentor to Rödertor. Then descend, leave the old town, and hike through the park (once the moat) down to Spitaltor. Explore the fortifications here before hiking a block up Spitalgasse, turning left to pass the youth hostel, popping back outside the wall, and heading along the upper scenic reaches of the "Tauber Riviera" and above the vineyards back to the Castle Garden.

▲Tradesman's House (Alt-Rothenburger Handwerkerhaus)—See the everyday life of a Rothenburger in the town's heyday in this restored 700-year-old home (€2.20; Easter–Oct Mon–Fri 11:00–17:00, Sat–Sun 10:00–17:00; Nov–Dec daily 14:00–16:00; closed Jan–Easter; Alter Stadtgraben 26, near Markus Tower, tel. 09861/94280).

St. Wolfgang's Church—This fortified Gothic church is built into the medieval wall at Klingentor. Its dungeon-like passages and shepherd's-dance exhibit are pretty lame (€1.50, April–Sept Wed–Mon 10:00–13:00 & 14:30–17:00, Oct Wed–Mon 10:00–16:00, closed Tue and Nov–March).

Near Rothenburg

▲A Walk in the Countryside—From the *Burggarten* (castle garden), head into the Tauber Valley. With your back to town, go down the hill, exiting the castle garden on your left. Once outside of the wall, walk around, keeping the castle and town on your right. The trail becomes really steep, taking you down to the wooden covered bridge on the valley floor. Across the bridge, the road goes left to Toppler Castle and right (downstream, with a pleasant parallel footpath) to Detwang.

Toppler Castle (Topplerschlösschen) is cute, skinny, sky-blue, and 600 years old. It was the castle/summer home of the medieval Mayor Toppler. The tower's top looks like a house—a sort of tree fort for grownups. It's in a farmer's garden, and it's open whenever he's around and willing to let you in (€1.50, normally Fri–Sun 13:00–16:00, closed Mon–Thu and Nov, 1 mile from town center at Taubertalweg 100, tel. 09861/7358). People say the mayor had this valley-floor escape to get people to relax about leaving the fortified town...or to hide a mistress.

To extend your stroll, walk back to the bridge and follow the river downstream to the peaceful village of **Detwang.** One of the oldest villages in Franconia, Detwang dates from 968. Like Rothenburg, it has a Riemenschneider altarpiece in its church.

Franconian Bike Ride—To get a fun, breezy look at the countryside around Rothenburg, rent a bike from Fahrradhaus Krauss (see "Helpful Hints," page 219). For a pleasant half-day pedal, escape the old town through Rödertor, bike along Topplerweg to Spitaltor, and follow the curvy road down into the Tauber Riviera. Turn right at the yellow *Leutzenbronn* sign to cross the double-arcaded bridge. From here a peaceful road follows the river downstream to **Detwang,** passing the cute Topplerschlösschen (described above). From Detwang, follow the main road to the old mill, and turn left to follow the *Liebliches Taubertal* bike path signs as far up the Tauber River (direction: Bettwar) as you like. After 2.5 miles, you'll arrive in the sleepy farming town of **Bettwar;** claim a spot among the chickens and the apple trees for a picnic or have a drink at one of the two restaurants in town.

Franconian Open-Air Museum (Fränkisches Freilandmuseum)—A 20-minute drive from Rothenburg—in the undiscovered "Rothenburgy" town of Bad Windsheim—is an open-air folk museum that, compared with others in Europe, is a bit humble. But it tries very hard and gives you the best look around at traditional rural Franconia (€5, daily mid-March–Sept 9:00–18:00, Oct–mid-Dec 10:00–16:00, closed mid-Dec–mid-March, last entry one hour before closing, tel. 09841/66800, www.freilandmuseum.de).

SHOPPING

Be warned...Rothenburg is one of Germany's best shopping towns. Do it here and be done with it. Lovely prints, carvings, wine glasses, Christmas-tree ornaments, and beer steins are popular. Rödergasse is the old town's everyday shopping street. There is also a modern shopping center across the street from the train station.

Christmas Souvenirs

Rothenburg is the headquarters of the **Käthe Wohlfahrt** Christmas trinkets empire, which is spreading across the half-timbered reaches of Europe. In Rothenburg, tourists flock to two Käthe Wohlfahrt stores (at Herrngasse 1 and 2, just off Market Square). Start with the **Christmas Village** (Weihnachtsdorf) at Herrngasse 1. This Christmas wonderland is filled with enough twinkling lights to require a special electrical hookup. You're greeted by instant Christmas mood music (best appreciated on a hot day in July) and American and Japanese tourists hungrily filling little woven shopping baskets with €5–8 goodies to hang on their trees. Let the spinning flocked tree whisk you in, but pause at the wall of Steiffs, jerking uncontrollably and mesmerizing little kids. (OK, I admit it, my Christmas tree sports a few KW ornaments.) The **Christmas Museum** upstairs is described under "Sights and Activities" (page 228). The smaller **Christmas Market** (Weihnachtsmarkt), across the street at Herrngasse 2, specializes in finely crafted wooden ornaments. A third, much smaller store is at Untere Schmiedgasse 19 (all stores open Mon–Sat 9:00–18:00, May–Dec also most Sun 10:00–18:00, Jan–April generally closed Sun, 10 percent discount on official KW products with this book in 2009, tel. 09861/4090, www.wohlfahrt.com or www.bestofchristmas.com). Käthe started the business in Stuttgart in 1964, and it's now run by her son Harald Wohlfahrt, who lives in Rothenburg.

Traditional German Souvenirs

The **Friese shop** has been welcoming readers of this book for more than 20 years (on the smaller square just off Market Square, west of TI, on corner across from free public WC). Cuckoo with friendliness, trinkets, and souvenirs, they give shoppers with this book tremendous service: a 10 percent discount, 19 percent sales tax deducted if you have purchases mailed, and a free pictorial map (normally €1.50). Anneliese Friese, who runs the place with her sons Frankie and Berni and grandson Rene, charges only her cost for shipping, and lets tired travelers leave their bags in her back room for free. If he's not busy, ask Rene to show you pictures of the local American football team he played on. For fewer crowds and more attentive service, visit after 14:00 (Mon–Sat 8:30–17:00, Sun 10:00–17:00, Grüner Markt 8, tel. 09861/7166, fax 09861/936-619, friese-kabalo@gmx.de).

Passage 12, a huge, more commercial souvenir shop with a vast selection of steins, knives, and noisy clocks, is locked in tooth-gnashing competition with the Friese shop. It's just a block below Market Square at Obere Schmiedgasse 12 (April–Dec Mon–Sat 9:00–19:00, Sun 10:00–19:00; Jan–March Mon–Sat 10:00–18:00, usually closed Sun; tel. 09861/8196). Martina, the manager, promises a 10 percent discount on prices with this book in 2009. Customers can check their email for free upstairs, use the WC, and stash their bags in lockers in the storage room.

Werkstattladen Lebenshilfe sells tasteful, original, unconventional souvenirs made in sheltered workshops by Germans with disabilities. It's a tiny shop down the side street behind Herrngasse 10 (daily 10:30–18:00, Jan–April closed Sun, Kirchgasse 1, tel. 09861/938-401).

Romantic Prints: The Ernst Geissendörfer print shop has sold fine prints, etchings, and paintings here since 1908. Enter through the teddy bear shop on the lower corner of Market Square, and go up the stairs in the back of the store. In 2009, show this book and Frau Geissendörfer will offer 10 percent off marked prices on all cash purchases (or minimum €50 credit-card purchases), plus a free shot of German brandy to sip while you browse (May–Dec Mon–Sat 11:00–18:00, Sun 11:00–17:00; Jan–April Mon–Sat 11:00–18:00, closed Sun; Obere Schmiedgasse 1 at corner of Hafengasse, go up one floor, tel. 09861/2005, www.geissendoerfer.de).

Wine Stuff: For characteristic wine glasses, winemaking gear, and the real thing from the town's oldest winemakers, drop by the **Weinladen am Plönlein** (daily 10:00–18:00, Untere Schmiedgasse 27—see "Wine-Drinking in the Old Center," page 242, for info on wine-tasting). Although Rothenburg is technically in Bavaria, the region around Rothenburg is called *Franken* (Franconia). You'll recognize Franconian wines by the shape of the bottle—short, stubby, and round.

Books: A good bookstore is **Rothenburger Büchermarkt**

at Rödergasse 3, on the corner of Alter Stadtgraben (Mon–Sat 9:00–18:30, Sun 11:00–18:00, Jan–April closed Sun).

Mailing Your Goodies Home: You can get handy yellow €2.50 boxes at the old town **post office** (Mon–Fri 9:00–13:00 & 14:00–17:30, Sat 9:00–12:00, closed Sun, inside photo shop at Rödergasse 11). The main post office is in the shopping center across from the train station.

Pastries: Those who prefer to eat their souvenirs browse the ***Bäckereien*** (bakeries). Their succulent pastries, pies, and cakes are pleasantly distracting...but skip the bad-tasting Rothenburger *Schneeballen*. Unworthy of the heavy promotion they receive, *Schneeballen* are bland pie crusts crumpled into a ball and dusted with powdered sugar or frosted with sticky-sweet glop. There's little reason to waste calories on a *Schneeball* when you can enjoy a curvy *Mandelhörnchen* (almond crescent), a triangular *Nussecke* (nut bar), a round *Florentiner* cookie, a couple of fresh *Krapfen* (like jelly doughnuts), or even just a soft, warm German pretzel.

SLEEPING

Rothenburg is crowded with visitors, but most are day-trippers. Except for the rare Saturday night and during festivals (see "Festivals," page 218), finding a room is easy throughout the year. If you want to splurge, you'll snare the best value by paying extra for the biggest and best rooms at the hotels I recommend.

Many hotels and guest houses will pick up tired heavy-packers at the station. If you're driving and unable to find where you're sleeping, stop and give them a call. They will likely come rescue you. Keep your key when out late. Rothenburg's hotels are small, and often lock the front entrance at about 22:00, asking you to let yourself in through a side door.

You may be greeted at the station by *Zimmer* skimmers who have rooms to rent. If you have reservations, resist them and honor your reservation. But if you haven't booked ahead, you could try talking one of these eager beavers into giving you a bed-and-breakfast room for a youth-hostel price. Be warned: These people are notorious for taking you to distant hotels and then charging you for the ride back if you decline a room. The automated hotel vacancy board at the TI (described on page 217) is another option for those without reservations.

Sleep Code

(€1 = about $1.50, country code: 49, area code: 09861)
S = Single, **D** = Double/Twin, **T** = Triple, **Q** = Quad, **b** = bathroom, **s** = shower only. Unless otherwise noted, credit cards are accepted, English is spoken, and breakfast is included.

To help you sort easily through these listings, I've divided the rooms into three categories, based on the price for a standard double room with bath:

$$$ Higher Priced—Most rooms €85 or more.
$$ Moderately Priced—Most rooms between €55–85.
$ Lower Priced—Most rooms €55 or less.

In the Old Town

$$$ Hotel Kloster-Stüble, deep in the old town near the castle garden, is my classiest listing. Rudolf does the cooking, while Erika—his fun and energetic first mate—welcomes guests. Twenty-one rooms fill two medieval buildings, connected by a modern atrium. The hotel is just off Herrngasse on a tiny side street (Sb-€55–75, traditional Db-€85, bigger and more modern Db-€115, Tb-€110–130, see website for suites and family rooms, kids under age 5 free, Internet access and Wi-Fi, Heringsbronnengasse 5, tel. 09861/938-890, fax 09861/6474, www.klosterstueble.de, hotel@klosterstueble.de).

$$$ Hotel Spitzweg is a rustic-yet-elegant 1536 mansion (never bombed or burned) with 10 big rooms, open beams, and endearing hand-painted antique furniture. It's run by gentle Herr Hocher, whom I suspect is the former Wizard of Oz—now retired and in a very good mood (Db-€85, family rooms, non-smoking, elegant breakfast room, free parking, Internet access at nearby hotel, Paradeisgasse 2, tel. 09861/94290, fax 09861/1412, www.hotel-spitzweg.de, info@hotel-spitzweg.de).

$$$ Hotel Gerberhaus is warmly run by Inge and Kurt and daughter Deborah, who mix modern comforts into 20 bright and airy rooms while maintaining a sense of half-timbered elegance. Enjoy the pleasant garden in back (Sb-€60–75, Db-€74–110, Tb-€129–139, Qb-€145, prices depend on room size; 2-room apartment with kitchen-€120/2 people, €155/4 people; 10 percent off the second and subsequent nights and a free *Schneeball* if you pay cash, non-smoking, 4 rooms have canopied 4-poster *Himmel* beds, Internet access, laundry-€7, Spitalgasse 25, tel. 09861/94900, fax 09861/86555, www.gerberhaus.rothenburg.de, gerberhaus@t-online.de). The downstairs café and *Biergarten* serve good soups, salads, and light lunches.

Rothenburg Accommodations

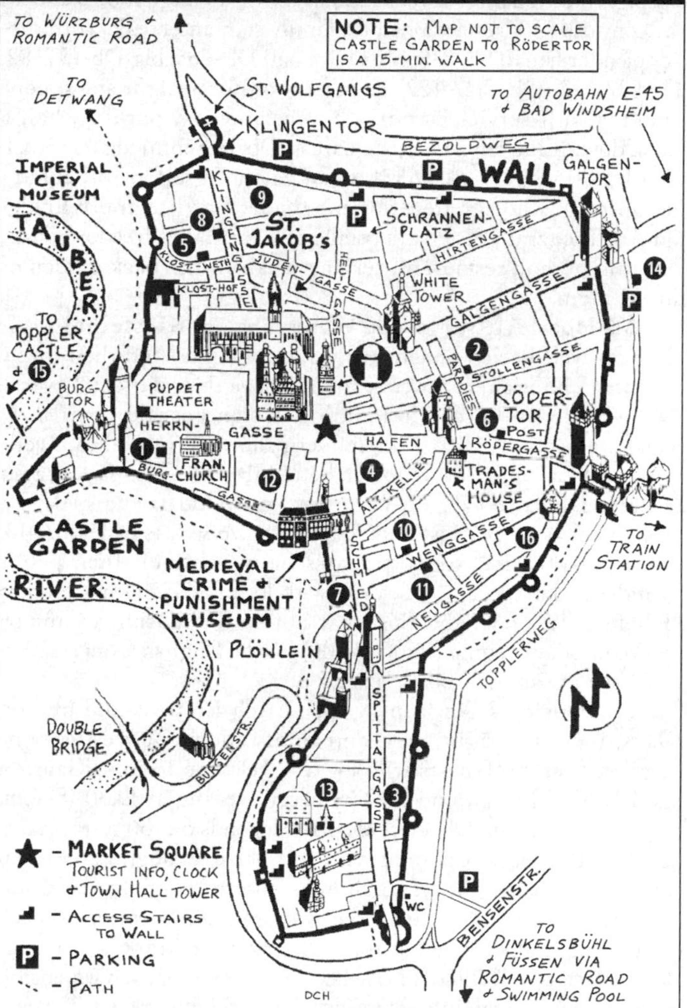

1. Hotel Kloster-Stüble
2. Hotel Spitzweg
3. Hotel Gerberhaus
4. Gasthof Goldener Greifen
5. Hotel Altfränkische Weinstube am Klosterhof
6. Pension Elke
7. Hotel Café Uhl
8. Gästehaus Flemming
9. Gästehaus Viktoria
10. Gästehaus Raidel
11. Pension Pöschel
12. Frau Liebler Rooms
13. Rossmühle Youth Hostel
14. Hotel Hornburg
15. To Pension Fuchsmühle
16. Bike Rental

$$ Gasthof Goldener Greifen, once Mayor Toppler's home, is a big, traditional, 600-year-old place with 15 large rooms and all the comforts. It's run by a helpful family staff and creaks with rustic splendor (small Sb-€38, Sb-€48, small Db-€65, big Db-€77–82, Tb-€97–102, Qb-€117–122, 10 percent off for 3-night stays, nonsmoking, full-service laundry-€8, free and easy parking, half a block downhill from Market Square at Obere Schmiedgasse 5, tel. 09861/2281, fax 09861/86374, www.gasthof-greifen-rothenburg.de, info@gasthof-greifen-rothenburg.de, Brigitte and Klingler family). The family also has a couple of loaner bikes free for guests, and runs a good restaurant, serving meals in the back garden or dining room.

$$ Hotel Altfränkische Weinstube am Klosterhof is *the* place for well-heeled bohemians. Mario, Hanne, and their lovely daughter Viktoria rent six cozy rooms above their dark and evocative pub in a 600-year-old building. It's an upscale, *Lord of the Rings* atmosphere, with TVs, modern showers, open-beam ceilings, and canopied four-poster beds (Sb-€48, Db-€59, bigger Db-€69, Db suite-€79, Tb-€79, prefer cash, kid-friendly, Wi-Fi, off Klingengasse at Klosterhof 7, tel. 09861/6404, fax 09861/6410, www.romanticroad.com/altfraenkische-weinstube). Their pub is a candlelit classic—and a favorite with locals, serving hot food to Hobbits until 22:30, and closing at 1:00 in the morning. Drop by on Wednesday evening (19:00–24:00) for the English Conversation Club (see "Meet the Locals," page 242).

$$ Pension Elke, run by spry Erich Endress and his son Klaus, rents 12 bright, airy, and comfy rooms above the family grocery store. Guests who jog are welcome to join Klaus on his half-hour run around the city every evening at 19:30 (S-€28, Sb-€38, D-€42–48, Db-€60–65, price depends on room size, extra bed-€15, 10 percent discount with this book through 2009 when you stay at least 2 nights, cash only, Internet access; reception in grocery store until 19:00, otherwise go around corner to back of building and ring bell at top of stairs; near Markus Tower at Rödergasse 6, tel. 09861/2331, fax 09861/935-355, www.pension-elke-rothenburg.de, info@pension-elke-rothenburg.de).

$$ Hotel Café Uhl offers 12 fine rooms over a bakery (Sb-€35–58, Db-€58–78, Tb-€78–92, Qb-€92–118, price depends on room size, 10 percent discount with this book and cash in 2009, reception in café, pay Internet access, parking-€6/day, closed Jan, Plönlein 8, tel. 09861/4895, fax 09861/92820, www.hotel-uhl.de, info@hotel-uhl.de, Paul and Robert the baker).

$$ Gästehaus Flemming has seven tastefully modern, fresh, and comfortable rooms and a peaceful garden behind St. Jakob's Church (Sb-€47, Db-€62, Tb-€84, cash only, nonsmoking, Klingengasse 21, tel. 09861/92380, fax 09861/976-384, www.gaestehaus-flemming.de, gaestehaus-flemming@t-online.de, Regina).

$$ Gästehaus Viktoria is a cheery little place right next to the town wall. Its three rooms overflow with furniture, ribbons, and silk flowers, and lovely gardens surround the house (Db-€59–69, larger Db suite-€79, ask about family specials, free Wi-Fi, a block from Klingentor at Klingenschutt 4, tel. 09861/87682, www.romanticroad.com/gaestehaus-viktoria, gaestehaus-viktoria@gmx.de).

$$ Gästehaus Raidel rents 12 rooms in a 500-year-old house filled with beds and furniture, all handmade by friendly Norry Raidel himself. The ramshackle ambience makes me want to sing the *Addams Family* theme song—but the place has a rare, time-passed family charm (S-€24, Sb-€39, D-€49, Db-€59, Tb-€70, cash only, Wenggasse 3, tel. 09861/3115, Norry asks you to use the reservations form at www.romanticroad.com/raidel). Norry, who plays in a Dixieland band, has invented a fascinating hybrid saxophone/trombone called the Norryphone...and loves to jam.

$ Pension Pöschel is simple and friendly, with six plain rooms in a concrete but pleasant building, and an inviting garden out back. Only one room has a private shower and toilet (S-€22, D-€40, Db-€45, T-€55, Tb-€60, small kids free, cash only, non-smoking, Wenggasse 22, tel. 09861/3430, www.pensionpoeschel.de, pension.poeschel@t-online.de, Bettina).

$ Frau Liebler rents two large, modern, ground-floor rooms with kitchenettes. They're great for those looking for real privacy—you'll have your own room fronting a quiet cobbled lane just below Market Square. She also rents a two-bedroom apartment (Db-€40, apartment-€50, extra bed-€10, 10 percent discount for 2 or more nights with this book in 2009, breakfast-€5, cash only, non-smoking, laundry-€5, behind Christmas shop at Pfäffleinsgässchen 10, tel. 09861/709-215, fax 09861/709-216).

$ Rossmühle Youth Hostel, run since 1981 by Eduard Schmitz, rents 186 beds in two buildings. While it's mostly four- to six-bed dorms, this charming hostel also has 15 doubles. Reception is in the droopy-eyed building—formerly a horse mill, it was used when the old town was under siege and the river-powered mill was inaccessible (dorm bed-€20, bunk-bed Db-€45, those over 26 pay €4 extra unless traveling with a family, includes breakfast and sheets, all-you-can-eat dinner-€6, pay Internet access, self-serve laundry including soap-€5, entrance on Rossmühlgasse, tel. 09861/94160, fax 09861/941-620, www.rothenburg.jugendherberge.de, jhrothenburg@djh-bayern.de).

Outside the Wall

$$$ Hotel Hornburg, a grand 1903 mansion, is close to the train station, a two-minute walk outside the wall. With groomed grounds, gracious sitting areas, and 10 spacious, tastefully decorated rooms, it's a super value (Sb-€58–79, Db-€78–108, Tb-€100–130, ground-floor rooms, non-smoking, family-friendly, avoid if you're allergic to dogs, free Internet access, expensive Wi-Fi, parking-€5/day; if walking, exit station and go straight on Ludwig-Siebert-Strasse, then turn left on Mannstrasse until you're 100 yards from town wall; if driving, the hotel is across from parking lot P4; Hornburgweg 28, at intersection with Mannstrasse, tel. 09861/8480, fax 09861/5570, www.hotel-hornburg.de, info@hotel-hornburg.de, friendly Gabriele and Martin).

$$ Pension Fuchsmühle is a guest house in a renovated old mill on the river below the castle end of Rothenburg, across from the Toppler Castle. It feels rural, but is a pleasant (though steep) 15-minute hike to Market Square, and a €10 taxi ride from the train station. Alex and Heidi Molitor, a young couple, run a book-lined café on summer weekends and offer a free look at the mill (in use until 1989). Eight bright, modern, light-wood rooms fill the building's three floors (Sb-€45, Db-€65, Tb-€90, Qb-€115, 6-bed apartment-€160, extra bed-€25, less for longer stays at some times of year, includes healthy farm-fresh breakfasts—or €9 less per person if you don't want breakfast, non-smoking, pay Wi-Fi, parking, flashlights provided for your walk back after dark, Taubertalweg 103, tel. 09861/92633, fax 09861/933895, www.fuchsmuehle.de, fuchsmuehle@t-online.de).

EATING

Many restaurants take a mid-afternoon break, and stop serving lunch at 14:00 and dinner as early as 20:00. My recommendations are all within a five-minute walk of Market Square. While all survive on tourism, many still feel like local hangouts. Your choices are typical German or ethnic. Any bakery will sell you a sandwich for a couple euros.

Traditional German Restaurants

Gasthof Goldener Greifen is in a historic building just off the main square. The Klingler family serves quality Franconian food at a good price...and with a smile. The wood is ancient and polished from generations of happy use, and the ambience is practical rather than posh—and that's just fine with me (€7–15 entrées, €12 three-course daily specials, super-cheap kids' meals, Mon–Sat 11:30–21:30, Sun 11:30–14:00, Obere Schmiedgasse 5, tel. 09861/2281).

Hotel Restaurant Klosterstüble, on a small street off Herrngasse near the castle garden, is a classy place for delicious and beautifully presented traditional cuisine. Chef Rudy's food is better than his English, so head waitress Erika makes sure communication goes smoothly. The shady terrace is nice on a warm summer evening. I prefer their traditional dining room to the stony, sleek, modern room (€7–17 main dishes, daily 11:00–14:00 & 18:00–21:00, Heringsbronnengasse 5, tel. 09861/938-890).

Bürgerkeller is a typical European cellar restaurant with a quiet, calming atmosphere, medieval murals, and pointy pikes. Without a burger in sight (*Bürger* means "townsman"), Harry Terian and his family pride themselves on quality local cuisine, offering a small but inviting menu and reasonable prices. Harry likes oldies, and you're welcome to look over his impressive playlist and request your favorite music (€6–13 entrées, cash only, Thu–Tue 11:30–14:00 & 18:00–21:00, closed Wed, a few sidewalk tables, near bottom of Herrngasse at #24, tel. 09861/2126).

Altfränkische Weinstube am Klosterhof seems designed for gnomes to celebrate their anniversaries. At this very dark pub, classically candlelit in a 600-year-old building, Mario whips up gourmet pub grub (€6–12 entrées, hot food served 18:00–22:30, closes at 1:00 in the morning, off Klingengasse at Klosterhof 7, tel. 09861/6404). If you'd like dinner company, drop by on Wednesday evening, when the English Conversation Club has a big table reserved from 19:00 on (see "Meet the Locals," page 242). You'll eat well and with new friends—both travelers and locals.

Altstadt-Café Alter Keller is just right for a light meal near the main square, but tucked away from the crowds. Eat indoors under walls festooned with old pots and jugs, or outdoors on a quiet little square. Herr Hufnagel, a baker and pastry chef, whips up a tempting array of cakes, pies, and giant meringue cookies, while gracious Christine makes sure you understand your options (€3 goulash soup with bread, €5–7 main dishes, Sat–Thu 11:00–20:00, Sun 11:00–18:00, closed Fri, Alter Keller 8, tel. 09861/2268).

Gasthof Rödertor, just outside the wall through the Rödertor gate, is a lively place where Rothenburgers go for a hearty meal at a good price. Their passion is potatoes—the menu is dedicated to spud cuisine. Try a €6.50 plate of *Schupfnudeln,* potato noodles with sauerkraut and bacon (€6–12 entrées, daily 11:30–14:00 & 17:30–22:30, Ansbacher Strasse 7, tel. 09861/2022). They also run a popular *Biergarten* (see below).

Eisenhut Restaurant, in Hotel Eisenhut, is a fine place for a dress-up splurge with surprisingly reasonable prices. You'll enjoy

Rothenburg Restaurants

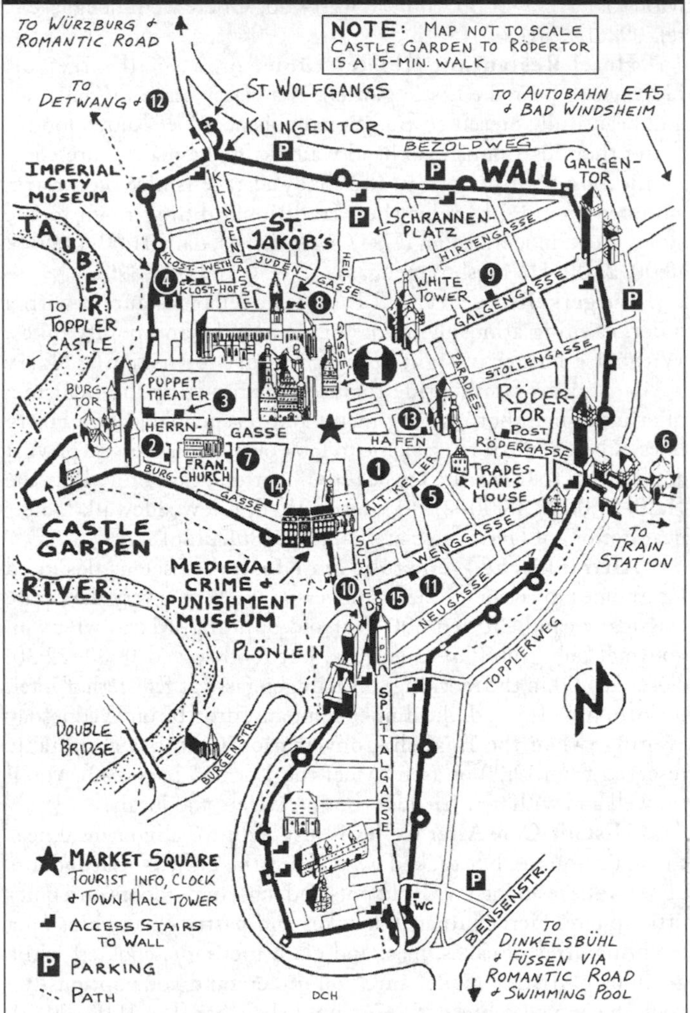

1. Gasthof Goldener Greifen
2. Hotel Restaurant Klosterstüble
3. Bürgerkeller
4. Altfränkische Weinstube am Klosterhof
5. Altstadt-Café Alter Keller
6. Gasthof Rödertor & Beer Garden
7. Eisenhut Restaurant
8. Reichs-Küchenmeister
9. Pizzeria Roma
10. China-Restaurant Peking
11. Döner Kebab Shop
12. To Unter den Linden Beer Garden
13. Eis Café D' Isep (Ice Cream)
14. Trinkstube zur Hölle
15. Restaurant Glocke

elegantly presented dishes, both traditional and international, with formal service. Sit in their royal dining room or on their garden sun terrace (€18–26 main dishes, fixed-price meals from €26, daily 11:00–23:00, Herrngasse 3, tel. 09861/7050).

Reichs-Küchenmeister is a forgettable, big-hotel restaurant, but on a balmy evening, its pleasant, tree-shaded terrace overlooking St. Jakob's Church is hard to beat. Their €12.50 *Vesperbrett* plate is a fine selection of cold cuts (€9–20 main dishes, daily 11:00–22:00, Kirchplatz 8, tel. 09861/9700).

Breaks from Pork and Potatoes

Pizzeria Roma is the locals' favorite for €6.50 pizza and pastas with good Italian wine. The Magrini family moved here from Tuscany in 1970 (many Italians immigrated to Germany in those years), and they've been cooking pasta for Rothenburg ever since (Thu–Tue 11:30–24:00, closed Wed and mid-Aug–mid-Sept, Galgengasse 19, tel. 09861/4540, Ricardo).

China-Restaurant Peking, at the Plönlein, has €5–7 two-course lunch specials (Mon–Sat only), and its noisy streetside tables have a fine tower view (daily 11:30–15:00 & 17:00–23:00, Plönlein 4, tel. 09861/938-738).

The ***Döner Kebab*** shop at Wenggasse 4, just off Untere Schmiedgasse, serves cheap and tasty food to go. This tiny place offers what must be the best €3 hot meal in Rothenburg (Mon–Sat 11:00–20:00, closed Sun).

Picnic Goodies: A small **grocery store** is in the center of town at Rödergasse 6 (Mon–Fri 7:30–19:00, Sat 7:30–18:00, April–Dec also Sun 10:00–18:00, closed Sun Jan–March). **Supermarkets** are outside the wall: Exit the town through Rödertor, turn left through the cobbled gate, and cross the parking lot to reach the Edeka supermarket (Mon–Fri 8:00–20:00, Sat 8:00–18:00, closed Sun); or head to the even bigger Kaufland in the shopping center across from the train station (Mon–Sat 7:00–20:00, closed Sun).

Beer Gardens (Biergartens)

Rothenburg's *Biergartens* can be great fun, but they're open only when the weather is balmy.

Unter den Linden, a bohemian yet family-friendly *Biergarten* in the valley along the river, is worth the 20-minute hike on a pleasant evening (daily in season with decent weather, 10:00–21:00 and sometimes later, self-service food and good beer, call first to confirm it's open, tel. 09861/5909). As it's in the valley on the river, it's cooler than Rothenburg; bring a sweater. Take a right outside the Burgtor, then a left on the footpath toward Detwang; it's at the bottom of the hill on the left.

Gasthof Rödertor, just outside the wall through the Rödertor gate, runs a backyard *Biergarten* that's great for a rowdy crowd, cheap food, and good beer (May–Sept daily 17:00–24:00, look for wooden gate, tel. 09861/2022). If the *Biergarten* is closed, their indoor restaurant (described earlier) is a good value.

Dessert

Eis Café D' Isep, with a pleasant "Venetian minimal" interior, is the town's ice-cream parlor, serving up cakes, drinks, fresh-fruit ice cream, and fancy sundaes. Their sidewalk tables are great for lazy people-watching (daily 9:30–22:00, closed mid-Oct–mid-Feb, 1 block off Market Square at Hafengasse 17, run by Paolo and Paola D'Isep).

Wine-Drinking in the Old Center

Trinkstube zur Hölle ("Hell") is dark and foreboding, offering a thick wine-drinking atmosphere, pub food, and a few main dishes. It's small and can get painfully touristy in summer (daily 17:00–24:00, closed Sun Jan–March, a block past Medieval Crime and Punishment Museum on Burggasse, with the devil hanging out front, tel. 09861/4229).

Mario's **Altfränkische Weinstube am Klosterhof** (listed under "Traditional German Restaurants," on page 239) is the liveliest place, and a clear favorite with locals for an atmospheric drink or late meal. When every other place is asleep, you're likely to find good food, drink, and energy here.

Eisenhut, behind the fancy hotel of the same name on Herrngasse, is a good bet for gentle and casual *Biergarten* ambience within the old center (also listed under "Traditional German Restaurants," page 239).

Restaurant Glocke, a *Weinstube* (wine bar) popular with locals, is run by Rothenburg's oldest winemakers, the Thürauf family. The menu, which has a very extensive wine list, is in German only because the friendly staff wants to explain your options in person. Their €4.40 deal, which lets you sample five Franconian wines, is popular (€8–17 entrées, Mon–Sat 11:00–23:00, Sun 11:00–14:00, Plönlein 1, tel. 09861/958-990).

Meet the Locals—English Conversation Club

For a rare chance to mix it up with locals who aren't selling anything, bring your favorite slang and tongue twisters to the English Conversation Club at Mario's Altfränkische Weinstube am Klosterhof (Wed 19:00–24:00; see restaurant listing under "Traditional German Restaurants," on page 238). This group of intrepid linguists has met more than 1,000 times. Hermann the German and his sidekick Wolfgang are regulars. Consider arriving early for dinner, or after 21:00, when the beer starts to sink in, the crowd grows, and everyone seems to speak that second language a bit more easily.

TRANSPORTATION CONNECTIONS

Reaching Rothenburg ob der Tauber by Train: A tiny branch train line connects Rothenburg to the outside world via **Steinach** in 14 minutes (generally 1/hr from Rothenburg at :06 and from Steinach at :35). If you plan to arrive in Rothenburg in the evening, note that the last train from Steinach to Rothenburg departs at about 20:30. All is not lost if you arrive in Steinach after the last train—there's a subsidized taxi service to Rothenburg (cheaper for the government than running an almost-empty train). To use this handy service, called AST *(Anrufsammeltaxi),* make an appointment with a participating taxi service (call 09861/2000 or 09861/7227) at least an hour in advance (2 hours ahead is better), and they'll drive you from Steinach to Rothenburg for the train fare (about €3.60/person) rather than the regular €25 taxi fare.

Train connections in Steinach are usually quick and efficient (trains to and from Rothenburg generally use track 5). The station at Steinach is not staffed, but has touch-screen terminals for fare and schedule information and ticket sales. Visit the ticket office in Rothenburg, or as a last resort call for train info at tel. 11861 (€0.60/min).

From Rothenburg by Train to: Würzburg (hourly, 1.25 hrs), **Nürnberg** (hourly, 1–1.5 hrs, change in Ansbach), **Munich** (hourly, 2.5–3 hrs, 1–2 changes), **Frankfurt** (hourly, 2.5–3 hrs, change in Würzburg), **Frankfurt Airport** (hourly, 3–3.5 hrs, change in Würzburg), **Berlin** (hourly, 5.5 hrs, 2 changes). Remember, all destinations also require a change in Steinach.

From Rothenburg by Bus: The Romantic Road bus stops at Schrannenplatz in Rothenburg once a day (early May–late Oct) on its way between Frankfurt and Füssen (and vice versa). See the schedule and tour description below.

ROTHENBURG

Route Tips for Drivers

From Frankfurt (and Other Points North) to Rothenburg: The three-hour autobahn drive from Frankfurt Airport to Rothenburg is something even a jet-lagged zombie can handle. It's a 75-mile straight shot to Würzburg on A-3; just follow the blue autobahn signs to *Würzburg.* While you can carry on to Rothenburg by autobahn, for a scenic back-road approach, leave the freeway at the Heidingsfeld–Würzburg exit. If going directly to **Rothenburg,** follow signs south to *Stuttgart/Ulm/Road 19,* then continue to Rothenburg via a scenic slice of the Romantic Road. If stopping at **Würzburg,** leave the freeway at the Heidingsfeld–Würzburg exit and follow *Stadtmitte,* then *Zentrum* and *Residenz* signs from the same freeway exit. From Würzburg, *Ulm/Road 19* signs lead to Bad Mergentheim and Rothenburg.

The Romantic Road

The Romantic Road (Romantische Strasse) winds you past the most beautiful towns and scenery in Germany's medieval heartland. Once Germany's north–south trade route, it connected the Rhine to the Roman road that crossed the Alps south of Munich. Now it's the most scenic way to connect the dots between Rothenburg and Munich, Frankfurt, Würzburg, or Füssen (www.romanticroad.com).

By car, you can wander through quaint hills and rolling villages, and stop wherever the cows look friendly or a town fountain beckons. My favorite sections are from Füssen to Landsberg and Rothenburg to Weikersheim. Drivers can follow the brown *Romantische Strasse* signs and use the free tourist brochure (available all over the place) that describes the journey. (Buy a good roadmap, as well.) To really enjoy the countryside, give yourself an extra day or two. If you're driving with limited time, just zero in on Rothenburg by autobahn.

The Romantic Road is the oldest and most famous of Germany's two dozen signposted scenic routes. Others celebrate toys, porcelain, architecture (Swabian Baroque or brick Gothic), clocks, and baths—and there are now two separate *Spargelstrassen* (asparagus roads). The "Castle Road" that runs between Rothenburg and Mannheim sounds intriguing, but it's nowhere near as interesting.

The Romantic Road Tour Bus

The Deutsche Touring company runs buses daily between Frankfurt and Munich in each direction (early May–late Oct, tel. 069/790-3261, www.romanticroadcoach.de). The bus leaves only once a day in each direction, stopping in most places only long enough to give you just a glimpse of what's there. Consider the bus only if you'd like to see most or all of the hard-to-reach villages en route, or if you prefer an 11-hour scenic bus ride to the four-hour fast train between Frankfurt and Munich. Most Romantic Roadsters, however, are happier visiting fewer places, and at their own pace. If that's more your style, the bus is useful only for its direct connections between two stops poorly served by public transportation (such as Dinkelsbühl and the Wieskirche; see "Public Transportation Along the Romantic Road," below).

If you do take the bus, confirm departures and arrivals when you buy your ticket—schedules aren't posted, and special events can temporarily change bus-stop locations and schedules.

The location of the bus stop in each town is listed on the bus brochure and website. The stops are not well-signed. The drivers usually hand out maps and brochures and play a recorded narration of the journey highlights in English. The bus takes short breaks (15–30 min) in Rothenburg, Dinkelsbühl, and a few other towns. This is too brief to really see each place, but long enough to slow down the overall journey. You can join or leave the trip where you like, but if you choose to stay at a particular stop, you'll have to wait until tomorrow for the next bus—or find another way to your next destination. If you prefer urban sights and speedy trains, this can seem like a glorified Greyhound ride with a beverage service (free coffee, €1 for cold drinks).

The entire ride (Frankfurt to Munich) costs €99 (pay cash on the bus). Shorter segments cost less (for example, Würzburg to Rothenburg is €14). Students and seniors—without a railpass—get a 10 percent discount. You can ride from Munich to Rothenburg for €30 if you purchase your ticket at the Munich EurAide office (see page 26).

You can get a 20 percent discount on your bus ticket if you have a German railpass, Eurailpass, or Eurail Selectpass (if Germany is one of your selected countries). You do not have to use a travel day of a flexipass to get this discount; if bus drivers say it takes a travel day, set them straight.

Bus reservations are almost never necessary. But they are free and easy, and, technically, without one you can lose your seat to someone who has one (reserve online at www.romanticroadcoach.de, or call 069/790-3261).

Public Transportation Along the Romantic Road

The Romantic Road has good, frequent train coverage for its major destinations (Rothenburg, Würzburg, and Füssen), and to towns such as Weikersheim, Nördlingen, and Augsburg. Some of its small, out-of-the-way sights, such as the Wieskirche, can only be reached by combining trains with local buses.

The Romantic Road

With limited time, focus on **Rothenburg** and **Würzburg** (in that order) as your best introduction to the Romantic Road. If you have lots of time, here are the three stops not served by trains most worth considering (listed in order of wow-value):

1. The **Wieskirche** (outside Füssen, see page 110). City buses run from Füssen to the Wieskirche (4–5/day, 40–50 min each way, more frequently with a transfer in Steingaden). But as I mention in the Bavaria chapter, you'll spend more time in transit than you will visiting the church.

2. The town of **Dinkelsbühl** (midway along the route). To get to Dinkelsbühl, take the train to Ansbach, then the easy one-hour

Romantic Road Bus Schedule

The Romantic Road bus runs daily from early May to late October. Every day, one bus goes north to south (Frankfurt to Munich), and another follows almost the same route south to north (Munich to Frankfurt). Along the way, both buses pass through towns and attractions such as Würzburg, Rothenburg, and Füssen (but only the northbound bus stops at the Wieskirche). You can begin or end your journey at any of these stops. The following times include only the main stops, based on the 2008 schedule. Check the full schedule at www.romanticroadcoach.de for any changes.

North to South

Depart Frankfurt	8:00
Arrive Würzburg	9:45
Depart Würzburg	9:45
Arrive Rothenburg	10:40
Depart Rothenburg	11:15
Arrive Dinkelsbühl	12:05
Depart Dinkelsbühl	12:40
Arrive Munich	16:25
Depart Munich	16:25
Arrive Füssen	19:00

South to North

Depart Füssen	8:00
Arrive Wieskirche	8:53
Depart Wieskirche	9:10
Arrive Munich	11:00
Depart Munich	11:10
Arrive Dinkelsbühl	14:40
Depart Dinkelsbühl	15:10
Arrive Rothenburg	16:00
Depart Rothenburg	16:35
Arrive Würzburg	17:30
Depart Würzburg	17:30
Arrive Frankfurt	19:15

bus that leaves hourly from Ansbach's train station (about €7).

3. The **Herrgottskirche,** in Creglingen, near Weikersheim. Creglingen is a half-hour from both Rothenburg and Weikersheim by local buses, which drop you off a mile's walk from the Herrgottskirche (to/from Rothenburg: 3/day Mon–Fri only, €3.30, change in Archshofen; to/from Weikersheim: 6/day Mon–Fri, 4/day Sat, no buses on Sun, €4.60).

SIGHTS

Along the Romantic Road

These sights are listed from north to south.

▲▲Würzburg—With its fancy palace and chapel, historic Würzburg is a good overnight stop (see next chapter).

Weikersheim—This untouristy town has a palace with fine Baroque gardens (luxurious picnic spot), a folk museum, and a picturesque town square.

▲Herrgottskirche—This peaceful church is graced with Tilman Riemenschneider's greatest carved altarpiece (€2, Easter–Oct daily 9:15–17:30, less off-season, tel. 07933/508, www.herrgottskirche.de). Across the street is the Fingerhut Museum, showing off thimbles—literally, "finger hats" (€1.50, April–Oct Tue–Sun 10:00–12:30 & 14:00–17:00, less off-season, tel. 07933/370, www.fingerhutmuseum.de). The southbound Romantic Road bus stops here for 10 minutes, long enough to see one or the other. The church and museum are a mile south of Creglingen (TI tel. 07933/631, www.creglingen.de).

▲▲▲Rothenburg—See page 215 for information on Germany's best medieval town.

▲Dinkelsbühl—Rothenburg's little sister is cute enough to merit a short stop. A moat, towers, gates, and beautifully preserved medieval wall surround this town. Dinkelsbühl's history museum is meager and without a word of English. The Kinderzeche children's festival celebrates the success of the local children who pleaded with the Swedish army during the Thirty Years' War, convincing them to spare the town. The festival turns Dinkelsbühl wonderfully on end for a week at the end of July (www.kinderzeche.de). The helpful **TI** on the main street sells maps with a short walking tour and can help find rooms (Mon–Fri 9:00–18:00, Sat 10:00–13:00 & 14:00–16:00, Sun 10:00–12:00, less off-season, tel. 09851/90240, www.dinkelsbuehl.de).

Sleeping in Dinkelsbühl: Consider **$$ Hotel Palmengarten,** run by the Danner-Bohl family (Sb-€35–48, Db-€68–78, Tb-€85–90, parking garage-€5/day, Untere Schmiedgasse 14, tel. 09851/57670, fax 09851/7548, www.sonne-palmengarten.de, info@sonne-palmengarten.de).

Nördlingen—Known for its 15-mile-wide valley, which is an impact crater blasted out by a meteor 15 million years ago, Nördlingen also gained fame as the "grain basket" because of its rich soil. Apollo astronauts did research and field training here; if you visit the museum dedicated to the study of the meteor (Riesenkrater Museum), so can you (Tue–Sun 10:00–12:00 & 13:30–16:30, closed Mon, Eugene-Shoemaker-Platz 1, tel. 09081/273-8220, www.rieskrater-museum.de).

Maypoles

Along the Romantic Road, and throughout Bavaria, you'll see colorfully ornamented maypoles decorating town squares (see an example on page 41). Many are painted in Bavaria's colors, white and blue. The decorations that line each side of the pole, which symbolize the craftspeople and businesses of that community, are festively replaced each May Day. Traditionally, rival communities try to steal each other's maypole. Locals guard their new pole night and day as May Day approaches. Stolen poles are ransomed only with lots of beer for the clever thieves.

Augsburg—Founded more than 2,000 years ago by Emperor Augustus, Augsburg enjoyed its heyday in the 15th and 16th centuries. Today, it's Bavaria's third largest city. The old town is pleasant, especially the small streets below the main square, where streams diverted from the River Lech run alongside pedestrians (www.augsburg.de).

Landsberg am Lech—Like many towns in this area, Landsberg (on the River Lech) has its roots in the salt trade. Every four years, the town returns to its medieval roots and hosts the Ruethenfest. The town, founded the same year as Munich (1158), was shaped by the architect Dominikus Zimmerman (of Wieskirche fame). Adolf Hitler wrote *Mein Kampf* while serving his prison sentence here after the Beer Hall Putsch of 1923 (when Hitler and his followers unsuccessfully attempted to take over the government of Bavaria).

Rottenbuch—This nondescript village has an impressive church in a lovely setting. The bus stops here only on request.

▲▲Wieskirche—This is Germany's most glorious Baroque-Rococo church, beautifully restored and set in a sweet meadow. Heavenly! Romantic Road buses stop here for 30 minutes—but only on the northbound Munich-to-Frankfurt run. Southbound buses will pick up and drop off here, but only on request. (See a description on page 110 of the Bavaria and Tirol chapter.)

Füssen—This town, three miles from the stunning Neuschwanstein Castle, is worth a stop on any sightseeing agenda. (See page 92 of the Bavaria and Tirol chapter for description and accommodations.)

WÜRZBURG

A historic city—though freshly rebuilt since World War II—Würzburg is worth a stop to see its impressive prince-bishop's Residenz, the bubbly Baroque chapel (Hofkirche) next door, and the palace's sculpted gardens. Surrounded by vineyards and filled with atmospheric *Weinstuben* (wine bars), this tourist-friendly town is easy to navigate by foot or streetcar. Today, 25,000 of its 130,000 residents are students—making the town feel young and very alive.

Planning Your Time

Würzburg has a few hours' worth of sightseeing. Begin at the Residenz (prince-bishop's palace), then take my self-guided walk through town to the Old Main Bridge. With more time, hike up to the hilltop Marienberg Fortress across the bridge.

ORIENTATION

(area code: 0931)

Tourist Information

Würzburg's helpful TI is in the Rococo-style Falken Haus on Market Square (May–Oct Mon–Fri 10:00–18:00, Sat–Sun 10:00–14:00; April and Nov–Dec same hours but closed Sun; Jan–March Mon–Fri 10:00–16:00, Sat 10:00–13:00, closed Sun; Marktplatz, tel. 0931/372-398, www.wuerzburg.de). Their free *Visitor's Guide* pamphlet and map covers the tourist's Würzburg well. The TI books rooms for free (in person only, not by

Würzburg's Beginnings

The city was born centuries before Christ at an easy-to-ford part of the Main River under an easy-to-defend hill. A Celtic fort stood where the fortress stands today. Later, three Irish missionary monks came here to Christianize the local barbarians. In A.D. 686, they were beheaded, and their relics put Würzburg on the pilgrimage map. About 500 years later, when the town was the seat of a bishop, Holy Roman Emperor Frederick Barbarossa came here to get the bishop's OK to divorce his wife. The bishop said "No problem," and the emperor thanked him by giving him secular rule of the entire region of Franconia. From then on, the bishop was also a prince, and the prince-bishop of Würzburg answered only to the Holy Roman Emperor.

phone), sells detailed maps for biking through the local wine country, and offers a one-hour walking tour in English (€5–6, mid-June–mid-Sept Sun–Fri at 18:30, Sat at 13:00). If you'll be continuing on the Romantic Road (see previous chapter), the TI has the *Romantische Strasse* brochure and a list of car-rental options. The TI also sells the Würzburg Welcome Card, offering minimal discounts on a few sights and restaurants (€3/7 days).

Arrival in Würzburg

By Train: Würzburg's train station is user-friendly and filled with handy services (coin-op lockers in main hall, WCs between main hall and tunnel to platforms). Walk out of the train station to the small square in front. A big **city map** board provides a quick orientation (on small building to the right). Farther right is the **post office** and the **Romantic Road bus stop** (track 13, curb closest and parallel to station building, look for *Touring* sign and schedule).

From the cul-de-sac in front of the station, **tram** #1, #2, #3, or #5 takes you one stop to the Juliuspromenade stop, near the recommended hotels (except Hotel-Pension Spehnkuch, which is near the station). Another stop (to Dom or Ulmer Hof) brings you close to Market Square and the TI. By **foot,** cross over the busy Röntgenring and head up the shop-lined Kaiserstrasse. To reach the **Residenz,** it's simplest to walk (15 min), or you can take tram #1, #3, or #5 to the Dom stop.

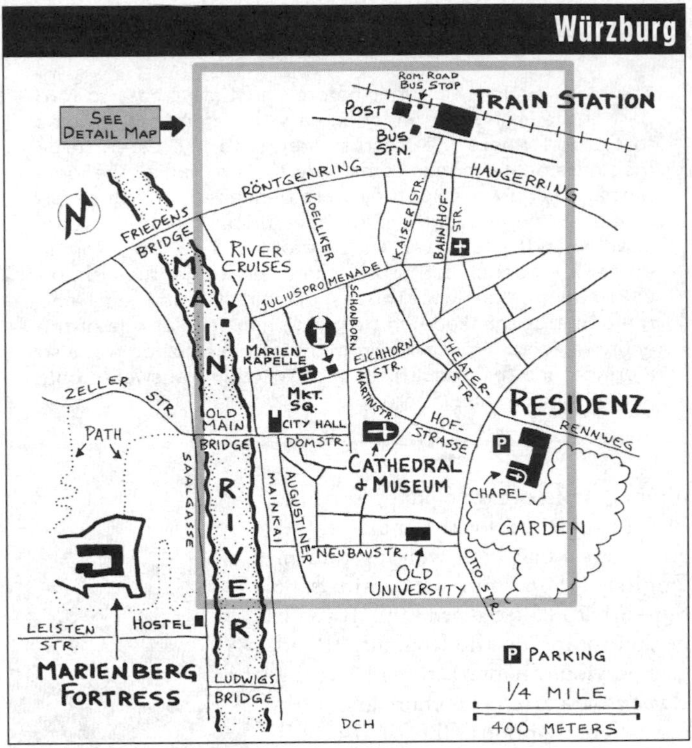

By Car: Drivers entering Würzburg can keep it simple by following signs to the *Residenz*, and parking in the vast cobbled square that faces the palace.

Helpful Hints

Festivals: Würzburg—always clever when it comes to trade—schedules its three annual festivals (wine, Mozart, and the Kiliani-Volksfest) in rapid succession, and keeps things busy from the beginning of June through late July.

Internet Access: Try the **Stadtbücherei** (city library), located in the same building as the TI, on Market Square (€2.40/hr plus €4 deposit, Mon–Fri 10:00–18:00, Thu until 19:00, Sat 10:00–15:00, closed Sun, check in with info desk on first floor, Falken Haus, Marktplatz).

Supermarket: Kupsch, at Domstrasse 10, is just a few doors from the Rathaus (Mon–Sat 8:00–20:00, closed Sun).

Bike Rental: Fahrrad Körner rents bikes right in the old town, a five-minute walk north of Market Square (€10/24 hrs, Bronnbachergasse 3, tel. 0931/52340).

Local Guide: Maureen Aldenhoff, who grew up in Liverpool but has been married to a German for 30 years, gives good private walking tours (€90/2 hrs, €115/3 hrs, €185/full day, tel. 0931/52135, maureen.aldenhoff@web.de).

Getting Around Würzburg

You can easily walk to everything but the hilltop Marienberg Fortress. For public transit, the same tickets work on all city bus and tram lines (including the bus up to the fortress). Your options include a single ticket (*Einzelfahrschein,* €2, good for 90 min in one direction with transfers) or a day pass (*Tageskarte Solo*—€4.10 for one person; or *Tageskarte Familie*—€8.30 for two adults and kids under age 15). You can buy either type of ticket from the bus driver or at a streetside machine (marked *Fahrausweise*). Single tickets are only valid if you stamp them, using the little box inside the tram or bus (day passes come pre-stamped). For transit info, call tel. 0931/362-320.

SIGHTS

Würzburg's Residenz

Würzburg's opulent palace and its associated sights—the Chapel (Hofkirche) and garden—are the town's main attraction.

Closures: The Residenz complex is undergoing a lengthy restoration. The palace's Imperial Hall is covered by scaffolding until mid-2009, and the Chapel is due to close in October of 2009.

▲▲Residenz Palace—This Franconian Versailles features grand rooms, 3-D art, and a massive (and recently restored) fresco by Giovanni Battista Tiepolo.

Cost, Hours, Location: €7, daily April–Oct 9:00–18:00, Nov–March 10:00–16:30, last entry 30 min before closing, no photos, tel. 0931/355-170 or 0931/355-1712. Don't confuse the Residenz (a 15-min walk southeast of the train station) with Marienberg Fortress (on the hilltop across the river). The Residenz is the far more important sight to visit. Easy parking is available in front of the Residenz (€1.50/hr for first 2 hrs, €1 each additional hr, pay at the machine marked *Kasse* before you drive out of the lot).

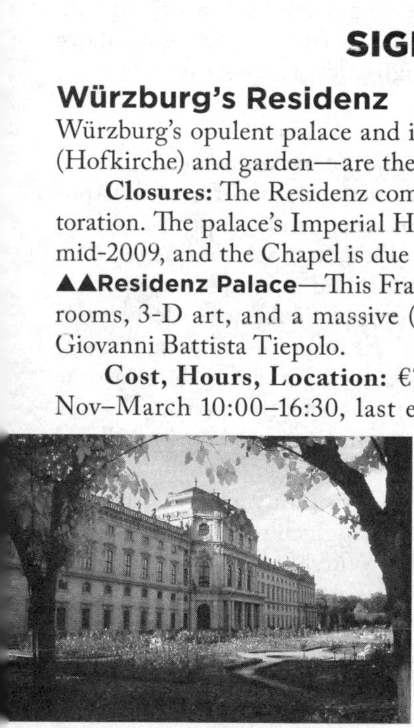

Tours, Information, Services: English tours, offered daily year-round at 11:00 and 15:00, include the normally closed South

Wing, which has the five best rooms (45 min, call ahead or tell the cashier you want to join the English tour, covered in entry price, but tips are welcome if the guide is good). The only other way to see the South Wing is to be trapped on a German tour (3/hr). The €5 English guidebook is dry and lengthy. Few English descriptions are provided in the Residenz; follow my self-guided tour for an overview. On the right as you exit the ticket office, you'll find free WCs and storage lockers (€1 deposit is returned).

Residenz Grounds: The elaborate Chapel (Hofkirche) is next door (as you exit the palace, go left). The entrance to the picnic-worthy garden is just beyond (for more on both, see next pages).

➲ **Self-Guided Tour:** The following self-guided tour gives you the basics to appreciate this fine palace.

• *Begin at the entrance.*

1. Vestibule: This area functioned as a grand circular driveway—just right for six-horse carriages to drop off their guests at the base of the stairs. The elegant stairway comes with low steps, enabling high-class ladies to glide up gracefully, heads tilted back to enjoy Europe's largest and grandest fresco opening up above them. Hold your lady's hand high and get into the ascending rhythm. Enjoy the climb.

• *Ascend the stairs and look up at the...*

2. Tiepolo Fresco: In 1752, the Venetian master Giovanni Battista Tiepolo was instructed to make a grand fresco illustrating the greatness of Europe, Würzburg, and the prince-bishop. And he did—in only 13 months. Find the four continents, each symbolized by a woman on an animal and pointing to the prince-bishop in the medallion above Europe. America—desperately uncivilized—sits naked with feathers in her hair on an alligator among severed heads. She's being served hot chocolate, a favorite import and nearly a drug for Europeans back then. Africa sits on a camel in a land of trade and fantasy animals (based on secondhand reports, and therefore inaccurate). Asia rides her elephant (with the backward ear) in the birthplace of Christianity and the alphabet. And Europe is shown as the center of high culture—Lady Culture points her brush not at Rome, but at Würzburg. The prince-bishop had a healthy ego. The ceiling features Apollo and a host of Greek gods, all paying homage to the PB.

3. The White Hall: This hall, actually gray, was kept plain to punctuate the colorful rooms on either side. It's a Rococo-stucco fantasy. (The word "Rococo" comes from the Portuguese word for the frilly rocaille shell.)

• *Straight ahead is the palace gift shop. Continue to your left, following signs for* Rundgang.

4. The Imperial Hall: This glorious hall will be emerging from under scaffolding in late spring 2009. (During the last months of the restoration period, you can learn about the process through an exhibit under the scaffolding.)

This hall is the ultimate example of Baroque: harmony, symmetry, illusion, and the bizarre; lots of light and mirrors facing windows; and all with a foundation of absolutism (a divine monarch, inspired by Louis XIV). If it happens to be open, take a moment to marvel at all the 3-D tricks in the ceiling. Here's another trick: As you enter the room, look left and check out the dog in the fresco. When you get to the window, have another look...notice that he has gotten older and fatter while you were crossing the hall.

The room features three scenes: On the ceiling, find Father Main (the local river) amusing himself with a nymph. The two walls tell more history. On one, the bishop presides over the marriage of a happy Barbarossa (whose bride was actually 12 years old, unlike the woman in the painting, who looks considerably older; for more on Barbarossa, see the sidebar on page 251). The bishop's power is demonstrated through his oversized fingers (giving the benediction) and through the details of his miter, which—unlike his face—is not shown in profile to allow you to see his coat of arms. Opposite that is the pay-off: Barbarossa, now the Holy Roman Emperor, gives the bishop Franconia and the secular title of prince. From this point onward, the prince-bishop rules. Also in the Imperial Hall, the balcony offers a great vantage point for surveying the Italian section of the garden (explained on the next page).

5. The North Wing: This wing is a string of lavish rooms—evolving from fancy Baroque to fancier Rococo—used for the prince-bishop's VIP guests. It's a straight shot, with short English descriptions in each room to the Green Room in the corner.

6. The Green Lacquer Room: This room is named for its silver-leaf walls, painted green. The Escher-esque inlaid floor was painstakingly restored after WWII bombings. Have fun multiplying in the mirrors before leaving. The nearby hall (look for the exit sign) shows photos of the city in rubble in 1945—and craftsmen bringing the palace back to its original splendor soon after. The little four-foot-tall doors were used by tiny servants who stoked the stoves, unseen from this hallway.

▲▲Chapel (Hofkirche)—This sumptuous chapel will close for 3–4 years of restoration in October of 2009. The chapel was for the exclusive use of the prince-bishop (private altar upstairs with direct entrance to his residence) and his court (ground floor). If it's open, take a look around: The decor and design are textbook Baroque. Architect Johann Balthasar Neumann was stuck with the existing walls. His challenge was to bring in light and create symmetry—essential to any Baroque work. He did it with mirrors and hidden windows. All the gold is real—if paper-thin—gold leaf. The columns are "manufactured marble," which

isn't marble at all but marbled plaster. This method was popular because it was uniform, economical, and the color could be controlled. Pigment was mixed into plaster, which was rolled onto the stone or timber core of the column. This half-inch veneer was then polished. You can tell if a "marble" column is real or fake by resting your hand on it. If it warms up, it's not marble. The faded painting high above the altar shows three guys in gold robes losing their heads (for more on these martyred Irish monks, see the sidebar on page 251). The two side paintings are by the great fresco artist Tiepolo. Since the plaster wouldn't dry in the winter, Tiepolo spent his downtime painting with oil (free, daily April–Oct 9:00–18:00, Nov–March 10:00–16:30, closed during Sun 10:00 Mass and on Catholic holidays; facing the palace, use separate entrance at far right just before garden entrance).

Residenz Garden—One of Germany's finest Baroque gardens is a delightful park (enter next to the chapel). By definition, Baroque gardens have three sections: English, French, and Italian. The French section is just inside the gate. It typically features statues of Greek gods (with lots of kidnapping action), carefully trimmed 18th-century yew trees, and an orangerie. The English section (to the right) is like a rough park. The Italian section, directly behind the palace around to the left, is grand—à la Versailles—but uses terraces to create the illusion of spaciousness (since it was originally hemmed in by the town wall). A modern feature has been added (WCs in the far-right corner).

SELF-GUIDED WALK

Welcome to Würzburg

This brief walk gets you from the Residenz, which you may want to tour first (described previously), to the Old Main Bridge (Alte Mainbrücke) via the key old-town sights.

• *Begin at the fountain in front of the Residenz palace.*

Fountain of Franconia: In 1814, the prince-bishop got the boot, and the region of Franconia was secularized and given to the Bavarian Wittelsbach dynasty. Technically, Franconia is a part of Bavaria, but that status is like Scotland being part of Great Britain. (Never call a Franconian a Bavarian.) This statue—a gift from the townspeople to their then-new royal family—turns its back to the palace and faces the town. It celebrates the artistic and intellectual genius of Franconia with statues of three great hometown boys (a medieval bard, the woodcarver Tilman Riemenschneider, and the Renaissance painter Matthias Grünewald).

• *If Franconia hopped down and ran 300 yards ahead down Hofstrasse, she'd hit the twin-spired cathedral. Meet her there.*

St. Kilian's Cathedral (Dom): This building's core is Romanesque (1040–1188), with Gothic spires and Baroque additions to the transepts. Enter through the back (the end nearest you, on the right-hand side).

Destroyed in World War II, the cathedral was rebuilt in the 1960s. Before 1945, the entire church was slathered in Baroque stucco decor, as the apse is today. The nave has a cohesive design, progressing from the menorah (representing the Old Testament) in the back, past tombstones of centuries of prince-bishops and a crucified Jesus (above the high altar), to the apse, where a resurrected Christ welcomes you into a hopeful future. The skulls of Würzburg's three favorite saints—those Irish monks martyred in the seventh century—lie in a box on the altar (for more on the monks, see the sidebar on page 251).

Halfway along the nave (on the left side, as you face the altar) is a fine memorial to the 15th-century Prince-Bishop Rudolf von Scherenberg, whose name means "scissors man" (see his coat of arms). Scherenberg ruled until he was 94 years old. Carved by Tilman Riemenschneider, this tombstone is an example of late-Gothic realism. Back then, it was outrageous to portray an old bishop as...an old bishop (looking at the tombstone, you can tell he needs dentures). The next prince-bishop, whose tomb is to the right of Scherenberg's, saw how realistic his predecessor's was, and insisted on having an idealized portrait (also by Riemenschneider) done to his satisfaction before he died. (He's looking unbelievably good.)

• *Leave the church through the side door, behind Mr. Scissors. Riemenschneider's tomb is on the church wall just outside the door. Stepping outside, look up at the three martyrs (before they were beheaded), turn left, and go into the museum.*

Central Würzburg

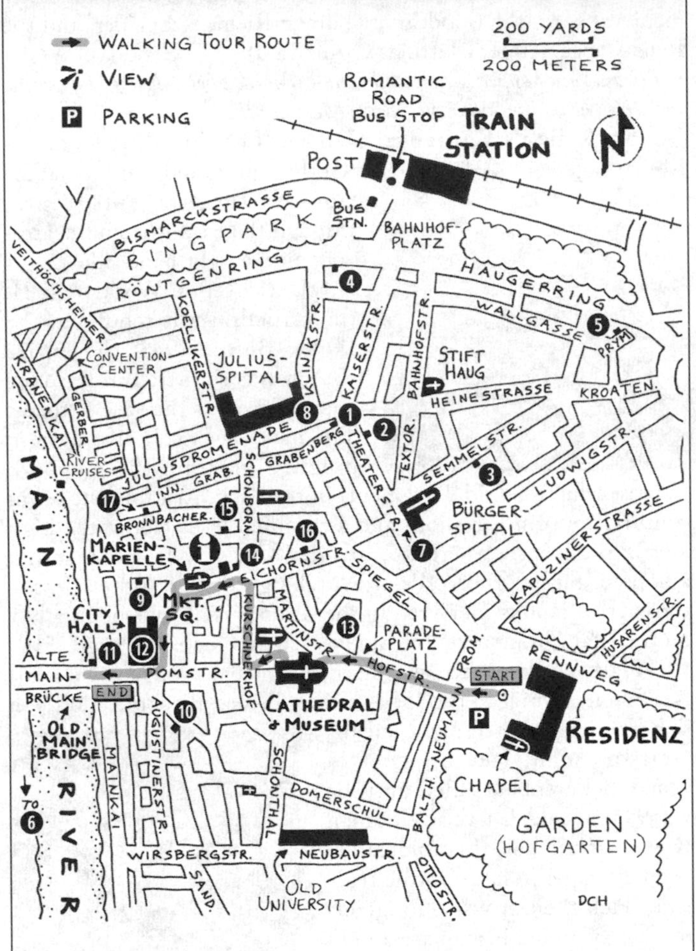

1. Hotel Barbarossa
2. City Hotel Schönleber
3. Sankt Josef Hotel
4. Hotel-Pension Spehnkuch
5. Babelfish Hostel
6. To Youth Hostel
7. Weinstube Bürgerspital & Hockerle Pub
8. Juliusspital
9. Zum Stachel Weinhaus
10. Backöfele
11. Alte Mainmühle
12. Würzburger Ratskeller
13. Martinz
14. Café Michel
15. Weinstube Maulaffenbäck
16. Pasta e Olio
17. Bike Rental

Cathedral Museum (Museum am Dom): This museum features a poignant combination of old and new religious art. It pairs 11th- to 18th-century works with modern interpretations, sprinkles it all with a Christian theme, and wraps it in a shiny new building (€3.50, €4.50 combo-ticket includes Cathedral Treasury, April–Oct Tue–Sun 10:00–18:00, Nov–March Tue–Sun 10:00–17:00, closed Mon year-round, tel. 0931/3866-5600, www.museum-am-dom.de).

• *Upon leaving, hook right through a tunnel, which emerges on a delightful urban scene. Domstrasse leads down to the spire of the City Hall and the Old Main Bridge (where this walk will end). On your left you'll see a sign for the* ***Cathedral Treasury*** *(Domschatz, €2, €4.50 combo-ticket includes Cathedral Museum, Tue–Sun 14:00–17:00, closed Mon, tel. 0931/3866-5600). But we're looping right. Go a block up Kurschner Hof. On your right, you'll pass the entrance to the...*

Neumünster Basilica: Like the cathedral, this church has a Romanesque body with a Baroque face. Go up the stairs to take a look inside, then continue up the street, noticing the vineyards in the distance. Appreciate this quiet pedestrian zone. Locals wouldn't have it any other way—electric trolleys, bikes, and pedestrians.

• *Enter the square on the left with the lacy, two-tone church.*

Market Square (Marktplatz): Imagine this square during the wine fest in June, with 75 vintners showing off their best wines, or during the Christmas market, when the square is full of quaint stalls selling holiday goodies. The fancy yellow-and-white Rococo-designed Falken Haus (House of the Falcon) once had three different facades. To fix it, the landlady gave a wandering band of stucco artists a chance to show their stuff...and ended up with this (inside are the TI and a prizewinning library with Internet access).

• *Set your eyes on the church.*

Marienkapelle: The two-tone, late-Gothic church was the merchants' answer to the prince-bishop's cathedral. Since Rome didn't bankroll the place, it's ringed with "swallow shops" (like swallows' nests cuddled up against a house)—enabling the church to run little businesses. The sandstone statues (replicas of Riemenschneider originals) depict the 12 apostles and Jesus. Walk downhill along the church to the lower marketplace, where the city's produce market bustles daily except Sunday (May–Oct 8:00–16:00). The famous Adam and Eve statues (flanking the side entrance to the church) show off Riemenschneider's mastery of the human body. Continue around the church to the west portal, where the carved Last Judgment (above the main doors) shows kings, ladies, and bishops—some going to heaven, others making up the chain gang bound for hell, via the monster's mouth. (This was commissioned by those feisty town merchants tired of snooty bluebloods.) Continue around to the next entry to see the Annunciation, with a cute angel Gabriel telling Mary (who is a virgin, symbolized by the lilies) the good news. Notice how God whispers through a speaking tube as baby Jesus slips down and into her ear.

• *Go back around to the lower market (Adam-and-Eve side) and leave—passing the obelisk—in the direction of the yellow building. Follow Schustergasse, a pedestrian lane lined with shops that leads back to Domstrasse. The cathedral is on your left, while the City Hall and bridge are to the right. Head right to the City Hall's tower.*

City Hall (Rathaus): Würzburg's City Hall is relatively humble because of the power of the prince-bishop. A side room (facing the building, around the left side, free, always open) holds the Gedenkraum 16, März 1945. This commemorates the 20-minute Allied bombing on March 16, 1945, that created a firestorm that destroyed (and demoralized) Würzburg six weeks before the end of World War II. Check out the sobering model, and ponder the names (lining the ceiling) of those killed. As you leave, notice the horizontal lines cut into the archway on your right. These mark the floodwaters *(Hochstand des Maines)* of the years 1342, 1682, and 1784.

• *Now, find the bridge.*

Old Main Bridge (Alte Mainbrücke): This isn't the town's "main" (as in primary) bridge; rather, it spans the Main (pronounced "mine") River, which also flows through Frankfurt.

The bridge, from 1133, is the second-oldest in Germany. The 12 statues lining the bridge are Würzburg saints and prince-bishops. Walk to the St. Kilian statue (with the golden sword)—one of the three monks who are shown being beheaded in the Residenz palace's Chapel (Hofkirche). Stand so that you can't see the white power-plant tower and enjoy the best view in town. Marienberg Fortress caps the hill. Squint up at Kilian pointing to God...with his head on.

The hillside is blanketed with grapevines destined to become the fine Stein Franconian wine. Johann Wolfgang von Goethe, the German Shakespeare, ordered 900 liters of this vintage annually. A friend once asked Goethe what he thought were the three most important things in life. He said, "Wine, women, and song." The friend then asked, "If you had to give one up, which would it be?" Without hesitating, Goethe answered "Song." Then, when asked what he would choose if he had to give up a second, Goethe paused and said, "It depends on the vintage."

• *Your walking tour is over. From here, consider paying a visit to the fortress on the hill above you (described next), or have lunch at the Alte Mainmühle restaurant, with a terrace overlooking the bridge* *(see page 264)*.

Marienberg Fortress (Festung Marienberg)

This 13th-century fortified retreat was the original residence of Würzburg's prince-bishops. After being stormed by the Swedish army during the 17th-century Thirty Years' War, the fortress was rebuilt in Baroque style. The **fortress grounds** (free) provide fine city views and a good place for a picnic. There's a restaurant inside (weekends only in the winter), and a summer *Biergarten* by the entrance (see "Eating"). The fortress houses two museums (both covered by a €5 combo-ticket): The **City History Museum and Prince's Mansion** (Stadtgeschichtliches Museum und Fürstenbaumuseum) is in the inner courtyard (€4, mid-March–Oct Tue–Sun 10:00–17:00, closed Mon and Nov–mid-March, tel. 0931/355-1750, www.schloesser.bayern.de). The **Mainfränkisches Museum,** which highlights the work of Riemenschneider, Germany's top woodcarver and onetime mayor of Würzburg, is in the red-and-white building at the back of the fortress, near the bus stop (€4, few English explanations, €3 audioguide, April–Oct Tue–Sun 10:00–17:00, Nov–March Tue–Sun 10:00–16:00, closed Mon year-round, good €2.60 guide, tel. 0931/205-940, www.mainfraenkisches-museum.de). Riemenschneider fans will also find his work throughout Würzburg's many churches.

Getting to Marienberg Fortress: Take bus #9 (€2 one-way, covered by *Tageskarte* passes, runs daily 10:00–18:00 every 45 min, departs from Residenzplatz and Juliuspromenade). To walk there, cross the Old Main Bridge and follow small *Festung Marienberg* signs to the right uphill for a heart-thumping 20 minutes (signs pointing left indicate a longer, more gradual 40-min path through vineyards).

SLEEPING

Würzburg's good-value hotels provide a stress-free first or last night when flying into or out of Frankfurt. Hourly trains connect Würzburg and Frankfurt's airport in 90 minutes.

The following listings (except the last one) are less than 10 minutes from the train station. To reach the two hotels on Theatergasse, head from the station up Kaiserstrasse to the circular awning at Barbarossaplatz and angle left, toward KFC, for Theaterstrasse. For the Sankt Josef Hotel, follow Theaterstrasse and take your first left onto Semmelstrasse. In these hotels, quieter rooms are in back, front rooms have street noise, and all rooms are entertained by church bells.

Sleep Code

(€1 = about $1.50, country code: 49, area code: 0931)
S = Single, **D** = Double/Twin, **T** = Triple, **Q** = Quad, **b** = bathroom, **s** = shower only. Credit cards are accepted, English is spoken, and breakfast is included.

To help you sort easily through these listings, I've divided the rooms into two categories, based on the price for a standard double room with bath:

$$ Higher Priced—Most rooms €80 or more.
$ Lower Priced—Most rooms less than €80.

$$ Hotel Barbarossa, tucked peacefully away on the fourth floor of an older building of doctors' and lawyers' offices, rents 18 simple, comfortable rooms (S-€30, Ss-€40, Sb-€50, Db-€80, Tb-€90, elevator, expensive Wi-Fi, across from KFC at Theaterstrasse 2, tel. 0931/321-370, fax 0931/321-3737, www.hotel-barbarossa-wuerzburg.de, marchiorello@t-online.de, Martina Marchiorello).

$$ City Hotel Schönleber has 33 good rooms (S-€42, Sb-€65, D-€62, Ds-€68, Db-€80–99 depending on size, Tb-€108, elevator, pay Wi-Fi in breakfast room, Theaterstrasse 5, tel. 0931/304-8900, fax 0931/3048-9030, www.cityhotel-schoenleber.de, reservierung@cityhotel-schoenleber.de, Ulrich Kölbel).

$$ Sankt Josef Hotel has 33 fine rooms and a pleasant breakfast room (Sb-€55–60, Db-€80–100 depending on size, non-smoking rooms, Wi-Fi, reserve ahead for parking-€8/day, Semmelstrasse 28–30, tel. 0931/308-680, fax 0931/308-6860, www.hotel-st-josef.de, hotel.st.josef@t-online.de, Herr and Frau Casagrande speak some English). The hotel also has a restaurant (€7–14 main dishes, Thu–Tue from 17:00, Sat–Sun also open for lunch 11:00–14:30, closed Wed).

$ Hotel-Pension Spehnkuch, the best budget option near the station, has seven rooms that share two sets of bathroom facilities. It overlooks a busy and uninviting street, but inside, it's quiet (behind double-paned windows), friendly, simple, clean, and comfortable, with a cheery breakfast room (S-€33, D-€58, T-€78–81, cash only, call 72 hours in advance to cancel, Wi-Fi; 3-min walk from station: exit station and take a right onto the first street, walk 500 feet to Röntgenring 7, ring bell, go up one floor; tel. 0931/54752, fax 0931/54760, www.pension-spehnkuch.de, info@pension-spehnkuch.de, Markus).

$ Babelfish Hostel, just a five-minute walk from the station, welcomes travelers of all ages. This laidback place is clean and feels safe. There's no breakfast, but you can store food and whip up your own treats in the community kitchen (dorm beds-€16–19, D-€48, sheets-€2.50, free Internet access and Wi-Fi, laundry-€4; free coffee, tea, parking, and lockers; wheelchair-accessible; bike rental-€5/day; exit the station, cross over main road, turn left and walk along Haugerring to Prymstrasse, hostel is on the corner at Prymstrasse 3; tel. 0931/304-0430, fax 0931/304-3632, www.babelfish-hostel.de, info@babelfish-hostel.de).

$ Würzburg's official **youth hostel,** across the river, has 246 beds (€21.50 per bed in 4- to 10-bed rooms, includes sheets and breakfast, non-members-€3 extra, over 26 years old-€4 extra, slightly cheaper Nov–March, family rooms, coin-op Internet access, no curfew—get night code; 20-min walk from station, cross Old Main Bridge and turn left on Saalgasse to Burkarderstrasse 44; tel. 0931/42590, www.wuerzburg.jugendherberge.de, jhwuerzburg@djh-bayern.de).

EATING

Restaurants and Wine Bars That Support the Needy

In medieval times, rich Würzburgers founded charitable foundations to support the city's elderly and poor. They began making and selling wine to fund their charity work, and this tradition continues today. Still occupying grand Baroque complexes, the foundations have restaurants, wine shops (selling wine in the area's distinctive, bulbous *Bocksbeutel* bottles), and extensive wine cellars (for serious buyers only).

The oldest and best-known of these foundations is the **Bürgerspital,** which now cares for about a hundred local seniors. Its characteristic restaurant, pub, and wine store are right downtown, near recommended hotels. The restaurant, **Weinstube Bürgerspital,** is candlelit but informal, with a cloistered feel and gorgeous courtyard seating (€5–12 main dishes, daily 10:00–24:00, Theaterstrasse 19, tel. 0931/352-880). The funky little **Hockerle** pub, adjacent to the wine store, is a time warp, filled with locals munching B.Y.O. sandwiches while sipping wine sold by the glass—as explained on its blackboard (both pub and store open Mon–Fri 9:00–18:00, Sat 9:00–15:00, closed Sun, corner of Theaterstrasse and Semmelstrasse at Theaterstrasse 19, tel. 0931/350-3403).

The **Juliusspital** has updated its traditional roots with a slightly modern, Mediterranean feel. Its courtyard is especially popular (€7–16 main dishes, daily 10:00–24:00, kitchen closes at 22:00, Juliuspromenade 19 at Barbarossaplatz, tel. 0931/54080).

More Restaurants in the Center

Zum Stachel, Würzburg's oldest *Weinhaus,* originated as the town's tithe barn—where people deposited 10 percent of their produce as tax. In 1413, it began preparing the produce and selling wine. Today, it's a worthy splurge, serving gourmet Franconian meals in an elegant stone-and-ivy courtyard and woody dining room. The ceiling depicts a medieval *Stachel* (mace) in deadly action (€19–24 entrées, €31 three-course fixed-price meals, Mon–Sat 11:00–24:00, closed Sun, reservations smart for this dressy place; from Marktplatz head toward river, turn right on Gressengasse to intersection with Marktgasse; Gressengasse 1, tel. 0931/52770).

Backöfele is a fun hole-in-the-wall (literally). Named "The Oven" for its entryway, this place is a hit with Germans, offering a rustic menu full of local specialties (€9–16 main dishes, daily 12:00–24:00, reservations smart; with your back to the City Hall, go straight on Augustinerstrasse, take the first left onto Wolfhartsgasse, then the first right to Ursulinergasse 2; tel. 0931/59059).

Alte Mainmühle, on the bridge in a converted mill, is a great place to end your walking tour. On a warm day, nothing beats a cold beer on their deck, which overlooks the river and the fortress—choose from their sunny top-floor terrace or the shade below. They have fresh fish specials (try their *Forelle* or *Zanderfilet*) and traditional fare with a Franconian twist. Their homemade sourdough bread *(Natursauerteigbrot)* is a delicious nod to their milling history (€7–8 wurst plates, €13–23 main dishes, Mon–Sat 10:00–24:00, kitchen open 11:00–22:30, closed Sun, Mainkai 1, tel. 0931/16777).

At **Würzburger Ratskeller,** enjoy traditional Franconian farmers' food, and choose from three seating options: an inviting courtyard (weather permitting), a stately restaurant (entrance on right side of building), and a cozy multi-room cellar accessed through the front entrance (€7–15 main dishes, daily 11:30–24:00, reservations smart, next to City Hall at Langgasse 1, tel. 0931/13021).

WÜRZBURG

Martinz, near the cathedral, serves a long list of sweet and savory Dutch pancakes *(Pfannkuchen)* for €6–9, as well as salads, steaks, and soups (€8–14 main dishes, daily 8:30–23:00, Martinsstrasse 21, tel. 0931/353-9290). In good weather, try their terrace.

Café Michel, right on Marktplatz and next to the TI, is a quiet, family-oriented bakery and tea house. It serves soups, small sandwiches, cakes, tea, coffee, and—until 16:00—inexpensive egg breakfasts. This place has been around since 1911 (€5–7 light meals, Mon–Sat 8:00–18:00, Sun 10:00–18:30, Marktplatz 11, tel. 0931/53776).

Weinstube Maulaffenbäck, tucked away in an alley near Marktplatz and the cathedral with a few outdoor tables, is a characteristic place for cheap Franconian meals and good wine. If you order wine, you're welcome to bring your own food—they'll provide the plate and fork. This is an old tradition unique to Würzburg. If you choose to follow this custom, consider stopping at the butcher shop next door (conveniently owned by the same family, Mon–Fri 7:30–18:00, Sat 8:00–14:00, closed Sun) to pick up great cold cuts before finding a table (€5–7 entrées, Mon–Thu 10:00–22:00, Fri–Sat 10:00–23:00, closed Sun, Maulhardgasse 9, tel. 0931/52351).

Pasta e Olio, a few blocks east of Marktplatz, features a fun and popular stand-up pasta lunch counter. Because Signora Aucone makes pasta fresh daily, the menu is limited, but usually includes a pasta dish, lasagna, a vegetarian option, and mixed antipasti. Place your order, then eat standing at one of the tables (€4.50–5 plates, Mon–Fri 11:00–17:00, Sat 11:00–15:00, closed Sun, Eichhornstrasse 6, tel. 0931/16699).

At Marienberg Fortress

A self-service ***Biergarten*** next to the Mainfränkisches Museum by the fortress entrance has typical sausage-and-pretzel fare and a great vineyard view (€4–7 light meals, daily April–Oct 10:00–19:00, weather permitting). The fancier **Burggaststätte,** in the inner courtyard next to the City History Museum, is a lesser value (€6–12 meals; May–Sept Tue–Sun 10:00–18:00, closed Mon; Oct–April Sat–Sun only 10:00–18:00; tel. 0931/47012).

TRANSPORTATION CONNECTIONS

From Würzburg by Train to: Rothenburg (hourly, 1.25 hrs, transfer in Steinach; 50 min to Steinach, then the tiny Steinach–Rothenburg train leaves usually from track 5 shortly after the Würzburg train arrives, then 14 min from Steinach to Rothenburg), **Frankfurt Airport** (1–2/hr, 1.5 hrs), **Frankfurt** (1–2/hr, 1.25 hrs), **Nürnberg** (2–3/hr, 1–1.25 hrs), **Munich** (1–2/hr, 2 hrs), **Köln** (almost hourly, 2.5 hrs, usually 1–2 changes), **Berlin** (hourly, 4 hrs, change in Göttingen). Train info: tel. 11861 (€0.60/min).

FRANKFURT

Frankfurt, while a bit low on Old World charm, offers a good look at today's no-nonsense, modern Germany. There's so much more to this country than castles and old cobbled squares. Cosmopolitan Frankfurt is a business hub of the united Europe, giving it a special sophistication and spice. Especially in the area around the train station, you'll notice the fascinating multi-ethnic flavor of the city. A third of its 650,000 residents carry foreign passports. For years, Frankfurt was a city to avoid... but today, it has a unique energy that makes it worth a look.

Planning Your Time

You might fly into or out of Frankfurt am Main, or at least pass through—this glossy city links the best wine-and-castles stretch of the Rhine to the north with the fairy-tale Romantic Road to the south. Even two or three hours in Frankfurt leaves you with some powerful impressions. The city's great sights are a 20-minute walk from its train station, which is a 12-minute train ride from its airport. At a minimum, wander the old town area (Römerberg) and head up to the top of the Main Tower for commanding city views. With more time or an overnight, Frankfurt has plenty of museums and other attractions to choose from.

ORIENTATION

(area code: 069)

Frankfurt, with its forest of skyscrapers perched on the banks of the Main (pronounced "mine") River, has been dubbed Germany's "Mainhattan." The city is Germany's trade and banking capital,

leading the country in skyscrapers (mostly bank headquarters)...and yet, a third of Frankfurt is green space.

The convention center (Messe), the red light district, and most of the skyscrapers are near the train station. Beyond that zone (to the east) is Frankfurt's old town, with the Römerberg, or central market square, as its focal point. Across the river, the south bank of the Main is lined with Frankfurt's top museums, and beyond that is Sachsenhausen, a residential neighborhood and prime restaurant zone.

Tourist Information

Frankfurt has several TIs. The handiest (though it's small) is inside the train station's main entrance, offering an abundance of brochures and a free hotel-booking service (Mon–Fri 8:00–21:00, Sat–Sun 9:00–18:00, tel. 069/2123-8800, www.infofrankfurt.de). You'll find other TIs on Römerberg's square (Mon–Fri 9:30–17:30, Sat–Sun 10:00–16:00), on the pedestrian shopping street Zeil, and at the airport. At any TI, buy the city/subway map (the basic €0.50 version is fine—skip the detailed €1 map) and consider the *Frankfurt Welcome* brochure (€0.50). The TI also offers bus tours of the city (see "Tours," page 269).

Discount Deals: Two discount passes compete for your attention, both sold at local TIs. The **Museum Ticket** gets you free entry into 26 museums (€12, valid 2 days). The **Frankfurt Card** gives you a transit pass (including connections to and from the airport), 50 percent off all major museums, and 25 percent off the city bus tour, which virtually pays for the pass (1 person: €8.70/1 day, €12.50/2 days; 2–5 people: €15/1 day, €24/2 days). If you're touring like mad for a day, the Frankfurt Card can be worthwhile.

Arrival in Frankfurt

By Train: The Frankfurt main train station (Hauptbahnhof) bustles with travelers. The TI is in the main hall just inside the front door. Baggage storage (€5/day, Mon–Fri 6:30–19:30, closed Sat–Sun) and lockers are in the main hall across from the TI. More lockers are at the end of the hall that starts by track 18, and along track 24. The post office is across from track 24 (Mon–Fri 7:00–19:30, Sat 8:00–16:00, closed Sun, automatic stamp machine outside—€1 for postcard to US or Canada). WCs (€0.70) are down the stairway by tracks 9 and 10. Inquire about train tickets in the *Reisezentrum* across from track 9 (Mon–Fri 6:00–22:00, Sat–Sun 7:00–22:00). Above the *Reisezentrum* is a peaceful lounge with a snack bar, clean WCs, telephones, and a children's play area (free entry with train ticket or railpass, free coffee and juice in first-class lounge). Pick up a snack at the good food court across from tracks 4 and 5. The station is a five-minute walk from the convention center (Messe), a three-minute subway ride or 20-minute walk from the center, and a 12-minute shuttle train from the airport.

By Plane: See "Frankfurt's Airport," page 282.

By Car: Follow signs for *Frankfurt,* then *Messe,* and finally *Hauptbahnhof* (train station). The Hauptbahnhof garage (€25/day) is under the station, near most recommended hotels.

Helpful Hints

Closed Day: Most museums are closed Monday, and most are open until 20:00 on Wednesday.

Internet Access: There are terminals underneath the train station—take the escalators down from track 19 to the shopping level, and look left (€2/hr, daily 5:30–24:00, must be over 18).

Laundry: An **SB-Waschsalon** is in Sachsenhausen, by the recommended Fichtekränzi restaurant (daily 6:00–23:00, Wallstrasse 8, instructions in German only).

Supermarket: Tengelmann, near the train station, is small but well-stocked (Mon–Fri 7:00–21:00, Sat 8:00–21:00, closed Sun; Karlstrasse 4, use Kaiserstrasse exit from underground passageway). On Sundays, the smaller **Supermarket im Bahnhof** in the underground passageway station is open until 22:00.

Getting Around Frankfurt

By Subway: Frankfurt's subway is easy to use, but a 10-minute wait for a train is common. From the train station, follow signs for *U-Bahn* (*U,* blue) or *S-Bahn* (*S,* green). Buy your tickets *(Fahrkarten)* from an RMV machine. Tickets are issued with a validating stamp already on them, and are valid only immediately after they're bought. Find your destination on the chart, key in the number, choose your ticket type, then pay. Choose *Einzelfahrt* for a regular single ticket (€2.10), *Kurzstrecke* for a short ride (€1.50—valid destinations listed on machines), *Tageskarte Frankfurt* for an all-day pass (€5.60 without the airport, €8.90 with), or *Gruppenkarte* for an all-day group ticket for up to 5 adults (€8.40 without the airport, €13.70 with). An individual one-way ticket to the airport costs €3.60 (no group rate for airport-only trips). For more information in English, see www.rmv.de.

By Taxi: A taxi stand is just outside the main entrance of the train station to your left. A typical ride to the Römerberg square should cost you €7 (or up to €10 in slow traffic). To get to the airport from any of my recommended hotels, count on at least €25.

TOURS

City Bus Tour—The basic city bus tour gives a 2.5-hour orientation to Frankfurt, including Römerberg and a visit to either the Goethe House or (summer only) the observation deck of the Main Tower (€25, 25 percent discount with Frankfurt Card, recorded narration; April–Oct daily at 10:00 and 14:00; Nov–March daily at 14:00, Sat–Sun also at 10:00). The bus picks up at the scheduled times at the Römerberg TI, then stops 15 minutes later at the Frankfurt train station TI.

Walking Tour—Insider Tours' three-hour walks hit the major sights, with native-English-speaking guides who give historical commentary (€12; €10 for youths, students, and seniors; daily from Römer/Paulskirche tram stop, just show up, Berlin tel. 030/692-3149, www.insidertour.com).

Local Guide—Elisabeth Lücke loves her city and shares it very well (€55/hr, reserve in advance, tel. 06196/45787, mobile 0173-913-3157, www.elisabeth-luecke.de, elisabeth.luecke@t-online.de).

SELF-GUIDED WALK

Welcome to Frankfurt's Römerberg

This sightseeing walk focuses on Römerberg, Frankfurt's lively market square, and begins at the train station (because that's where you'll likely arrive in Frankfurt). Allow 30–60 minutes, depending on whether you walk to the square from the station.

• *You'll probably start at the...*

Train Station: This is Germany's busiest train station: 350,000 travelers make their way to 25 platforms to catch 1,800 trains every day. While it was big news when it opened in the 1890s, it's a dead-end station, which, with today's high-speed trains, makes it outdated. In fact, the speedy ICE trains are threatening to bypass Frankfurt altogether unless it digs a tunnel to allow for a faster pass-through stop (a costly project now in the discussion stage).

• *To get to Römerberg, it's a 20-minute walk (up Kaiserstrasse), a €7–10 taxi ride, or a three-minute subway ride. To take the subway, buy a ticket (see "Getting Around Frankfurt," previous page) and follow signs to* U-4 *(direction: Seckbacher Landstrasse) or* U-5 *(direction: Preungesheim). Choose the track with the closest* Nächste Abfahrt *(next departure) time and go two stops to Römerberg. Exit the station following* Römerberg *signs (not* Domplatz*). As you surface, you'll see the tall, red tower of St. Bartholomew's Cathedral behind you, where we'll end this walk. For now, walk around the building in front of you and downhill to...*

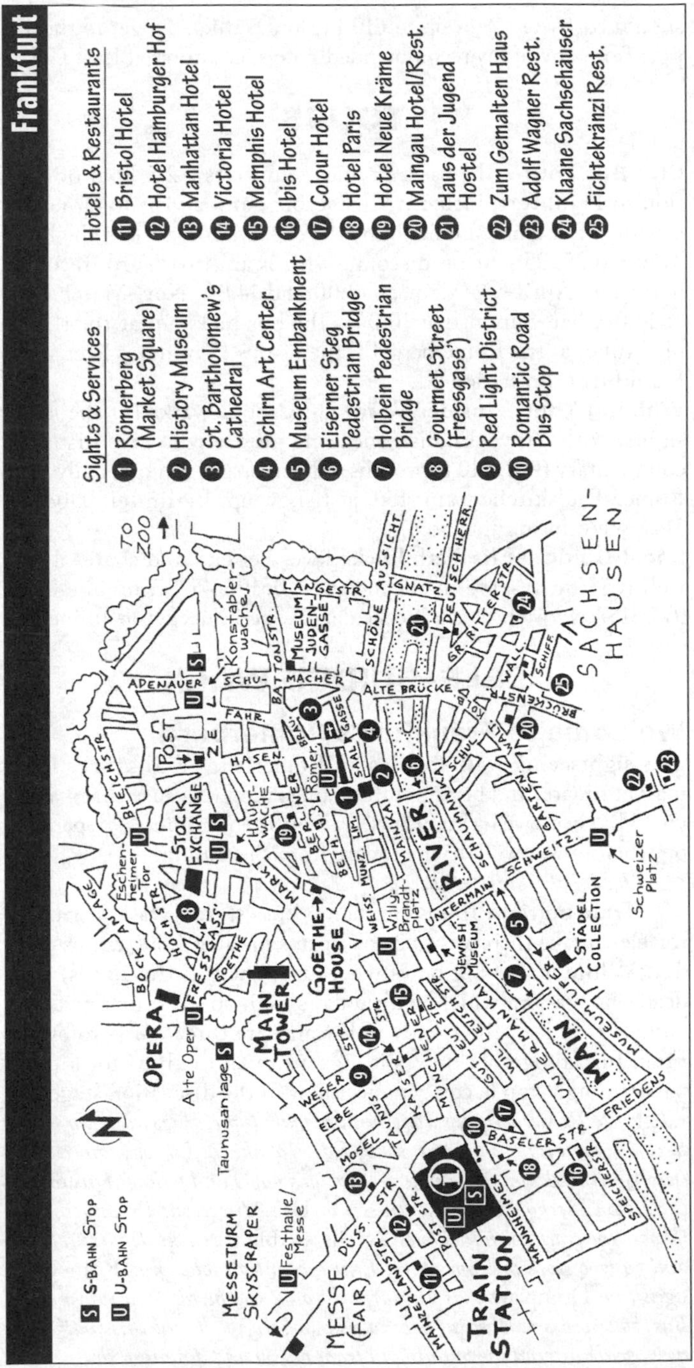
Frankfurt
Sights & Services
1 Römerberg (Market Square)
2 History Museum
3 St. Bartholomew's Cathedral
4 Schirn Art Center
5 Museum Embankment
6 Eiserner Steg Pedestrian Bridge
7 Holbein Pedestrian Bridge
8 Gourmet Street (Fressgass')
9 Red Light District
10 Romantic Road Bus Stop
Hotels & Restaurants
11 Bristol Hotel
12 Hotel Hamburger Hof
13 Manhattan Hotel
14 Victoria Hotel
15 Memphis Hotel
16 Ibis Hotel
17 Colour Hotel
18 Hotel Paris
19 Hotel Neue Kräme
20 Maingau Hotel/Rest.
21 Haus der Jugend Hostel
22 Zum Gemalten Haus
23 Adolf Wagner Rest.
24 Klaane Sachsehäuser
25 Fichtekränzi Rest.
S S-Bahn Stop
U U-Bahn Stop
MESSETURM SKYSCRAPER
MESSE (FAIR)
Festhalle/Messe
TRAIN STATION
OPERA
Alte Oper
Taunusanlage
MAIN TOWER
GOETHE HOUSE
STOCK EXCHANGE
Eschenheimer Tor
Hauptwache
Konstablerwache
Römer
MUSEUM JUDENGASSE
JEWISH MUSEUM
STADEL COLLECTION
Willy-Brandt-platz
Schweizer Platz
MAIN RIVER
ALTE BRÜCKE
SACHSENHAUSEN
TO ZOO

Römerberg: Frankfurt's market square, worth ▲, was the birthplace of the city. The Town Hall *(Römer)* houses the

Kaisersaal, or Imperial Hall, where Holy Roman Emperors celebrated their coronations. Today, the *Römer* houses the city council and mayor's office. The cute row of half-timbered houses (rebuilt in 1983) opposite the *Römer* is typical of Frankfurt's quaint old center before World War II.

• *Walk past the red-and-white church downhill toward the river to Frankfurt's...*

History Museum (Historisches Museum): Most won't want to hike through the museum upstairs, which has two floors

of artifacts, paintings, and displays—with very little English explanation (possibly closed for renovation in 2009, otherwise €4, Tue–Sun 10:00–18:00, Wed until 21:00, closed Mon, Saalgasse 19, tel. 069/2123-5599, www.historisches-museum.frankfurt.de). However, the models in the ground-floor annex are fascinating (€1, follow signs to *Altstadtmodelle*, English film and explanations). The big model in the middle of the room shows the town in the 1930s. Study the maps of medieval Frankfurt. The wall surrounding the city was torn down in the early 1800s to make the ring of parks and lakes you see on your modern map. The long, densely packed row of houses on the eastern end of town was Frankfurt's Jewish ghetto from 1462 to 1796. The five original houses that survive comprise one of the city's two Jewish Museums (described on page 275)—Frankfurt was the birthplace of Anne Frank and the Rothschild banking family.

Go up the steps and see the horror that befell the town in 1940, 1943, and on the "fatal night" of March 23, 1944. This last Allied bombing accomplished its goal of demoralizing the city. Find the facade of the destroyed Town Hall—where you just were. The film behind this model is a good 15-minute tour of Frankfurt through the ages (ask them to change the language for you—"*Auf Englisch, bitte?*").

• *Leaving the museum, turn right to...*

Saalgasse: Literally "Hall Street," this lane of postmodern buildings echoes the higgledy-piggledy houses that stood here until World War II. In the 1990s, famous architects from around the world were each given a ruined house of the same width and told to design a new structure to reflect the one that stood there before the war. As you continue down the street, guess which one is an upside-down half-timbered house with the stars down below. (Hint: Animals are on the "ground floor.")

Saalgasse leads to some ancient Roman ruins in front of St. Bartholomew's Cathedral (turn left when you first see the cathedral). The grid of stubs was the subfloor of a Roman bath (allowing the floor to be heated). The small monument in the middle of the ruins commemorates the 794 meeting of Charlemagne (king of the Franks and the first Holy Roman Emperor) with the local bishop—the first official mention of a town called Frankfurt. When Charlemagne and the Franks fled from the Saxons, a white deer led them to the easiest place to cross the Main—where the *Franks* could *ford* the river—hence, Frankfurt. The skyscraper with the yellow emblem in the distance is the tallest office block in Western Europe (985 feet). The shorter, glassy building next to it, also with a red-and-white antenna, is the Main Tower (open to the public—recommended and described on page 274).

• *Behind the Roman ruins is...*

St. Bartholomew's Cathedral (Kaiserdom): Ten Holy Roman Emperors were elected and crowned in this cathedral between 1562 and 1792. The church was destroyed in World War II, rebuilt, and reopened in 1955. Walk around the front of the church and enter on the side opposite the river. Twenty-seven scenes from the life of St. Bartholomew (Bartholomäus in German) flank the high altar and ring the choir. Everything of value was moved to safety before the bombs came. But the delightful red-sandstone chapel of Sleeping Mary (to the left of the high altar), carved and painted in the 15th century, was too big to move—so it was fortified with sandbags. The altarpiece and fine stained glass next to it survived the bombing (free, Sat–Thu 9:00–18:00, Fri 15:00–18:00). An in-depth English booklet about the cathedral is available for €2.50 in the adjoining Dom Museum (€3, Tue–Fri 10:00–17:00, Sat–Sun 11:00–17:00, closed Mon, not particularly interesting).

• *From the cathedral, it's a short walk to the Zeil, Frankfurt's lively department store–lined pedestrian boulevard (leading to the Opera and Main Tower, described later). Or circle back through the Römerberg to visit more old-town sights.*

SIGHTS

Near Römerberg

Paulskirche—Dominating a big square just across the street from Römerberg, this church is known as the "cradle of German democracy." It was here, during the political upheaval of 1848, that the first freely elected National Assembly met and the first German Constitution was drafted, paving the way for a united Germany in 1871. Following its destruction by Allied bombs on March 18, 1944, the church became the first historic building in the city to be rebuilt. Around the outside of the building, you'll see reliefs honoring people who contributed to the German nation, including Theodor Heuss, the first president, and John F. Kennedy, who spoke here on June 25, 1963.

Schirn Art Center (Schirn Kunsthalle)—Opened in 1986, this facility has quickly become one of Europe's most respected homes to modern and contemporary art. Rotating exhibits pay homage to everything and everyone from Kandinsky and Kahlo to contemporary artists, movements, and topics (€6–9 depending on exhibits, Tue–Sun 10:00–19:00, Wed–Thu until 22:00, closed Mon, Römerberg, tel. 069/299-8820, www.schirn.de).

▲Goethe House (Goethehaus)—Johann Wolfgang von Goethe (1749–1832), a scientist, minister, poet, lawyer, politician, and playwright, was a towering figure in the early Romantic Age. His birthplace, now a fine museum, is a five-minute walk northwest of Römerberg. It's furnished as it was in the mid-18th century, when the boy destined to become the "German Shakespeare" grew up here (€5, €2 high-tech but easy-to-use and informative audioguide, €1.50 English booklet has same info as free laminated cards—worthwhile only as a souvenir, Mon–Sat 10:00–18:00, Sun 10:00–17:30; 15-min walk from Hauptbahnhof up Kaiserstrasse, turn right on Am Salzhaus to Grosser Hirschgraben 23; tel. 069/138-800, www.goethehaus-frankfurt.de).

Borrow a laminated card at the bottom of the stairs for a refreshingly brief commentary on each of the 16 rooms. Since nothing's roped off and there are no posted signs, it's easy to picture real people living here. Goethe's father dedicated his life and wealth to cultural pursuits, and his mother told young Johann Wolfgang fairy tales every night, stopping just before the ending so that the boy could exercise his own creativity. Goethe's family gave him all the money he needed to travel and learn. His collection of 2,000 books was sold off in 1795. Recently, 800 of these have been located and repurchased by the museum (you'll see them in the library). This building honors the man who inspired the Goethe-Institut, dedicated to keeping the German language strong.

In the Skyscraper Zone, Northwest of Römerberg

Many of Frankfurt's skyscrapers—including the Main Tower, with its observation deck—cluster between the Römerberg and the train station. In this area, you'll also find some of Frankfurt's best shopping and fine dining.

▲**Main Tower**—Finished in 2000, this tower houses the Helaba Bank and offers the best public viewpoint from a Frankfurt skyscraper. A 45-second, ear-popping elevator ride—and then 50 stairs—takes you to the 55th floor, 650 feet above the city.

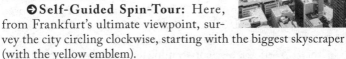

Cost, Hours, Location: €4.60; April–Sept Sun–Thu 10:00–21:00, Fri–Sat 10:00–23:00; Oct–March Sun–Thu 10:00–19:00, Fri–Sat 10:00–21:00; last entry 30 min before closing, enter at Neue Mainzer Strasse 52, near corner of Neue Schlesingerstrasse, tel. 069/3650-4777, www.maintower.de.

➲ **Self-Guided Spin-Tour:** Here, from Frankfurt's ultimate viewpoint, survey the city circling clockwise, starting with the biggest skyscraper (with the yellow emblem).

1. Commerzbank Building: Designed by Norman Foster (of Berlin Reichstag and London City Hall fame), the Commerzbank building was finished in 1997. It's 985 feet high, with nine winter gardens spiraling up its core. Just to the left is Römerberg—the old town center. Look to the right (clockwise).

2. European Central Bank: The blue-and-gold euro symbol (€) decorates the front yard of the Euro Tower, home of the European Central Bank (a.k.a. "City of the Euro"). Its 1,000 employees administer the all-Europe currency from here. Typical of skyscrapers from the 1970s, it's slim—to allow maximum natural light into all workplaces inside. The euro symbol in the park was unveiled on January 1, 2002, the day the euro went into circulation in the first 12 Eurozone countries.

The **Museum Embankment** (see page 276) lines Schaumainkai on the far side of the Main River, just beyond the Euro Tower.

3. Airport: The Rhine–Main airport, in the distance, is the largest employment complex in Germany (62,000 workers). Frankfurt's massive train station dominates the foreground. From the station, the grand Kaiserstrasse cuts through the city to Römerberg.

4. Messe: The Frankfurt fair (Messe), marked by the skyscraper with the pointy top, is a huge convention center—the size of 40 soccer fields. It sprawls behind the skyscraper that looks like a classical column sporting a visor-like capital. (The protruding lip of the capital is heated so that icicles don't form, break off, and impale people on the street below.) Frankfurt's fair originated in 1240, when the emperor promised all participating merchants safe passage. The black twin towers of the Deutsche Bank in the foreground are typical of mid-1980s mirrored architecture.

5. West End and Good Living: The West End—with vast green spaces and the telecommunications tower—is Frankfurt's trendiest residential quarter. The city's most enjoyable zone cuts from the West End to the right. Stretching from the classic-looking **Opera House** are broad and people-filled boulevards made to order for eating and shopping. Your skyscraper spin-tour is over. Why don't you go join them?

Opera House, Gourmet Street, and Zeil—From the Opera House to pedestrian boulevards, this is Frankfurt's good-living spine. The Opera House was finished in 1880 to celebrate German high culture and the newly created nation. Mozart and Goethe flank the entrance, reminders that this is a house of both music and theater. The original opera house was destroyed in World War II. Over the objections of a mayor nicknamed "Dynamite Rudy," the city rebuilt it in the original style (U-Bahn: Alte Oper). Facing the opera, turn right and walk down a restaurant-lined boulevard (Grosse Bockenheimer) nicknamed "Gourmet Street" (Fressgass'). (Frankfurt's version of Fifth Avenue, lined with top fashion shops, is the parallel Goethe Strasse.) Gourmet Street leads to Zeil, a lively, tree-lined festival-of-life pedestrian boulevard and department-store strip.

Near the Train Station

Jewish Museum (Jüdisches Museum)—Housed in the former Rothschild Palace (of the famous banking family), this worthwhile museum traces the history of Frankfurt's Jews since the 12th century. Rather than simply presenting artifacts, it tries to engage visitors in a dialogue about culture and society as a whole. The €7.80 English guidebook is unnecessary, since detailed English handouts are available on each floor (€4, €5 combo-ticket with Museum Judengasse—see next page, Tue–Sun 10:00–17:00, Wed until 20:00, closed Mon, Untermainkai 14/15, tel. 069/2123-5000, www.juedischesmuseum.de). The museum is just across the road from the lovely riverside promenade, a perfect place to rest your feet and watch people and planes go by.

The museum also runs the smaller and less interesting

Museum Judengasse, centering on the ruins of an ancient Jewish settlement. The exhibit consists of the medieval foundations of five houses, two ritual baths, and two wells (€2, €5 combo-ticket with Jewish Museum, same hours as Jewish Museum, just east of St. Bartholomew's Cathedral at Kurt-Schumacher-Strasse 10, tel. 069/297-7419).

▲Frankfurt's Red Light District—A browse through Frankfurt's sleazy red light district offers a fascinating way to kill time between trains. From the station, Taunusstrasse leads two blocks to the corner of Elbestrasse, where you'll find a zone of 20 "eros towers"—each a five-story brothel filled with prostitutes. Climbing a few of these towers may be one of the more memorable experiences of your European trip (€25, daily). While hiking through the towers feels safe, the aggressive women at the neighboring strip shows can be pretty unsettling. Ever since the Middle Ages, Frankfurt's thriving prostitution industry has gone hand-in-hand with its trade fairs. Today, it thrives with the Messe. Prostitutes note that business varies with the theme of the trade show—while the auto show is boom time, they complain that Frankfurt's massive book fair is a bust. Frankfurt's prostitutes are legal and taxed. Since they pay taxes, they are organizing to get the same benefits that other taxed workers receive.

This area can be dangerous if you're careless. If you take a wrong turn, you'll find creepy streets littered with drug addicts. In 1992, Frankfurt began offering "pump rooms" to its hard-drug users. These centers provide clean needles and a safe and caring place for addicts to go to maintain their habit and get counseling. More than a decade and a half later, while locals consider the program a success, wasted people congregate in neighborhoods like this one.

Across the River

The Schaumainkai riverside promenade (across the river, over the Eiserner Steg pedestrian bridge from Römerberg) is great for an evening stroll or people-watching on any sunny day. Keep your eyes peeled for nude sunbathers. On Saturdays, the museum strip street is closed off for a sprawling flea market. This is also near the inviting Sachsenhausen district, the best place in town for a meal (see "Eating," page 280).

Frankfurt's Museum Embankment (Museumsufer)—The Museum Embankment features nine museums lining the Main River along Schaumainkai (mostly west of the Eiserner Steg pedestrian bridge). In the 1980s, Frankfurt decided that it wanted to buck its "Bankfurt" and "Krankfurt" (*krank* means "sick") image. It went on a culture kick and devoted 11 percent of the city budget to the arts and culture. The result: Frankfurt has become a city of art. Today, locals and tourists alike enjoy an impressive strip of museums housed in striking buildings. These nine museums (including architecture, film, world cultures, and great European masters—the Städel Collection) and a dozen others are all well described in the TI's *Museumsufer* brochure (all museums here are covered by the 2-day, €12 Museum Ticket sold at TIs and participating museums—see page 267; most museums open Tue–Sun 10:00–17:00, Wed until 20:00, closed Mon; www.kultur.frankfurt.de).

SLEEPING

Planning to sleep in Frankfurt is a gamble, since the city's numerous trade fairs *(Messe)* send hotel prices skyrocketing—a €70 double can suddenly shoot up to €300. In 2009, the busiest months for trade fairs look to be January, March, May, and September, and based on previous years, they average about eight days a month. Visit www.messefrankfurt.com (and select "Trade fairs and events") for an exact schedule.

Keep overnights in Frankfurt to a minimum—pleasant Rhine and Romantic Road towns are just a quick drive or train ride away. During trade fairs, skip Frankfurt altogether and stay in Würzburg, Bacharach, or St. Goar.

Even when trade fairs aren't in town, room prices in most Frankfurt hotels fluctuate €20 or more with demand and the day of the week. The lower prices listed are usually for weekends, with the higher prices for weekdays. The ranges listed here are only approximate, and may skew higher or lower. If you'll be overnighting in Frankfurt during a non-convention summer weekend, you can land a great place relatively cheaply—call around to several places or comparison-shop online to get the best deal.

Near the Train Station

The following places are within a few blocks of the train station (and its fast and handy train to the airport; to sleep even nearer to the airport, see "Frankfurt's Airport," page 282). This isn't the safest part of town; don't wander into seedy-feeling streets, and be careful after dark. The first three hotels are on the north (and most sedate) side of the station. The Victoria and the Memphis are in a more middlebrow, mostly Turkish-immigrant neighborhood to the east of the station. The last three hotels are south of the station, where there are many Eastern European shops and services.

For a rough idea of directions to hotels, stand with your back to the main entrance of the station: Manhattan Hotel is across the street at 10 o'clock, Victoria Hotel at 1 o'clock, Memphis Hotel at 2 o'clock, Colour Hotel at 4 o'clock, Hotel Paris at 5 o'clock,

Sleep Code

(€1 = about $1.50, country code: 49, area code: 069)
S = Single, **D** = Double/Twin, **T** = Triple, **Q** = Quad, **b** = bathroom, **s** = shower only. Unless otherwise noted, credit cards are accepted, English is spoken, and breakfast is included. All listed hotels have non-smoking rooms.

To help you sort easily through these listings, I've divided the rooms into three categories, based on the price for a standard double room with bath:

$$$ Higher Priced—Most rooms €100 or more.
$$ Moderately Priced—Most rooms between €75-100.
$ Lower Priced—Most rooms €75 or less.

and Bristol Hotel and Hotel Hamburger Hof at 7 o'clock. The Ibis Hotel is on a nicer street two blocks beyond Hotel Paris.

$$$ Bristol Hotel is a swanky 145-room place, part of a new generation of train-station hotels. It serves up style and flair, from its nod to Pacific Rim architecture to its teak-furnished breakfast room and patio café. Although it's just two blocks from the station, it enjoys quiet and respectable surroundings. If you're looking to splurge on your first or last night in Europe, this is the place (Sb-€60–95, larger Sb-€80–120, Db-€95–160, larger Db-€115–180, huge breakfast buffet, elevator, Wi-Fi, Ludwigstrasse 15, tel. 069/242-390, fax 069/251-539, www.bristol-hotel.de, info@bristol-hotel.de). Exit the station by track 24, cross the street, turn left, then right on Ottostrasse, then left on Niddastrasse to Ludwigstrasse.

$$ Hotel Hamburger Hof, right next to the train station but in a quiet and safe-feeling location, has a shiny lobby and 66 elegantly simple, spacious rooms. The side facing the station is cheerfully sunny, while rooms on the other side are quieter (Sb-€55–70, Db-€75–95, Tb-€90–105, non-smoking floors, elevator, free Internet access, expensive Wi-Fi, Poststrasse 10–12, tel. 069/2713-9690, fax 069/235-802, www.hamburgerhof.com, hamburgerhof@t-online.de). Exit the station by track 24, cross the street, turn left, and walk to the end of the block.

$$ Manhattan Hotel, with 60 late-1980s-chic rooms, fronts a high-traffic street very close to the station (Sb-€55–85, Db-€69–105, mention this book when reserving to get a 10 percent discount during non-convention times in 2009, further discount when really slow—including weekends, kids under 12 free, elevator, Wi-Fi, Düsseldorfer Strasse 10, tel. 069/269-5970, fax 069/2695-97777, www.manhattan-hotel.com, manhattan-hotel@t-online.de).

Exit the station by track 24, cross the street, and go right until you see the hotel; to cross Düsseldorfer Strasse safely, walk up to the tram stop.

$$ Victoria Hotel, midway between the station and Römerberg on the grand Kaiserstrasse, is friendly, has 75 rooms, and feels a world apart from the red light district a block away (Sb-€65–85, Db-€75–95, Db suite-€105–120, free Internet access, expensive Wi-Fi, Kaiserstrasse 59, entrance on Elbestrasse, tel. 069/273-060, fax 069/2730-6100, www.victoriahotel.de, victoria-hotel@t-online.de). To reach the hotel, go down the escalators to the underground passageway below the station and follow the *Kaiserstrasse* signs.

$$ Memphis Hotel, three long blocks from the station on a colorful street in the Turkish district, has 42 rooms and is another stylish business hotel that's affordable when there's no convention in town (Sb-€55–85, Db-€70–90, prices soft—call for exact rates, ask for a room on the quiet side—*ruhige Seite,* Internet access, pay Wi-Fi, Münchener Strasse 15, tel. 069/242-6090, fax 069/2426-0999, www.memphis-hotel.de, memphis-hotel@t-online.de). To get here, use the same directions as for the Hotel Victoria, then cut one street right to the parallel Münchener Strasse.

$ Ibis Hotel Frankfurt Friedensbrücke, a reliable chain hotel, is a good value, with 233 rooms on a quiet riverside street away from the station (Sb/Db-€59–76, Tb-€109, breakfast-€9.50/person, elevator, Internet access, expensive Wi-Fi, parking-€10/day; exit station by track 1 and follow busy Baseler Strasse 3 blocks, before river turn right on Speicherstrasse to #4; tel. 069/273-030, fax 069/237-024, www.ibishotel.com, h1445@accor.com).

$ Colour Hotel is a funky, minimalist, primary-colors type of place on a busy street around the corner from the station. It has a bustling bar in the lobby and kind management, and it feels safe (S-€32, Sb-€42, D-€44, Db-€54, Tb-€69, Qb-€79, prices soft—check website for specials, breakfast-€8, Internet access, pay Wi-Fi, Baseler Strasse 52, tel. 069/3650-7580, fax 069/252-845, www.colourhotel.de, info@colourhotel.de). Exit the station by track 1, then go around the corner and cross Baseler Strasse.

$ Hotel Paris, on a street with Eastern European restaurants, has 20 small but fine rooms and a nice staff, making this a great value (Sb-€50, Db-€70, Tb-€85, Wi-Fi, Karlsruher Strasse 8, tel. 069/273-9963, fax 069/2739-9651, www.hotelparis.de, reservation@hotelparis.de). Exit the station by track 1, cross the street, turn right and go one block, and then turn left on Karlsruher Strasse.

Away from the Station

If you're in Frankfurt for one night, stay near the station—but if you're in town for a few days and want to feel like you belong, choose one of the following listings. Hotel Neue Kräme is near Römerberg, and the Maingau Hotel and the hostel are in the Sachsenhausen district (see below).

$$ Hotel Neue Kräme is a quiet little 21-room oasis tucked away above the center of Frankfurt's downtown action, just steps from Römerberg and the restaurant-filled Fressgass'. Friendly Hermann, who lived in the US and loves to revive his English, welcomes guests in this bright and cheerful little blue-and-white place (Sb-€70–85, Db-€85–105, prices much higher during conventions, elevator, expensive Wi-Fi, parking-€27/day, Neue Kräme 23, tel. 069/284-046, fax 069/296-288, www.hotel-neuekraeme.de, info@hotel-neuekraeme.de).

$$ Maingau Hotel, located across the river in the museum- and pub-friendly Sachsenhausen district, is in a quiet, residential neighborhood facing a park. The hotel hallways are dark, but the 90 rooms are bright. If you're looking for a little tranquility in an authentic residential neighborhood, stay here (Sb-€60–75, Db-€75–95, prices soft, pay Wi-Fi; fancy dinners at adjacent Maingau Stuben restaurant—see "Eating"; Schifferstrasse 38–40, tel. 069/609-140, fax 069/620-790, www.maingau.de, hotel@maingau.de).

$ ***Hostel:*** The **Haus der Jugend** hostel, with 434 beds, is open to guests of any age (€17 per bed in 8- and 10-bed dorms, €20 in 3- to 4-bed dorms, Sb-€35.50, Db-€61, €3.50 more for guests age 27 or older, families excepted; €3.10 more per day for non-members; includes sheets and breakfast; €5 for lunch or dinner, pay Internet access, laundry, 2:00 curfew; Deutschherrnufer 12; tel. 069/610-0150, fax 069/6100-1599, www.jugendherberge-frankfurt.de, jugendherberge_frankfurt@t-online.de). To reach the hostel, take bus #46 (3/hr, direction: Mühlberg) from the station to Frankensteiner Platz.

EATING

In the Sachsenhausen District

Instead of beer-garden ambience, Frankfurt entices visitors and locals to its apple-wine pub district. The cobbled and cozy Sachsenhausen district is both a well-heeled residential area and a traditional eating-and-drinking zone. There are more than a hundred characteristic apple-wine pubs here (and plenty of other options). *Apfelwein,* drunk around here since Charlemagne's time 1,200 years ago, became more popular in the 16th century, when local grapes were diseased. It enjoyed another boost two centuries later, when a climate change made grape-growing harder. Apple wine is about the strength of beer (5.5 percent alcohol), and is served spiced and warm in winter, cold in summer. To complement your traditional drink with a traditional meal, order Frankfurt sausage or pork chops and kraut.

All the places I've listed have both indoor and outdoor seating in a woodsy, rustic setting (except Maingau Stuben). Not just for tourists, these characteristic places are truly popular with Frankfurters, too. If you are craving *Leiterchen* ("mini-ladders," or spare ribs—surprisingly meaty and salty), these are your best bet. Two more widely available local specialties for the adventurous to try are boiled eggs (or beef) and potatoes topped with a green sauce of seven herbs, called *Grüne Sosse;* and an aged, cylindrical, ricotta-like cheese served with onions and vinegar, called *Handkäse mit Musik* ("hand cheese with music").

To get to Sachsenhausen, cross the river from Römerberg, either on the Alte Brücke or the pedestrian-only Eisener Steg. From the train station, take tram #16 to Schweizer Platz (at the west end of the apple-wine area, closer to the first two listings) or bus #46 to Frankensteiner Platz (at the east end, by the youth hostel, closer to the other listings).

Zum Gemalten Haus, named for the wall murals that adorn its facade, serves German cuisine and is deceptively mellow—it's rumored to get a little wild on the weekends (€5–12 entrées, Tue–Sun 10:00–24:00, closed Mon, Schweizer Strasse 67, tel. 069/614-559).

Adolf Wagner, two buildings away, is a traditional joint that serves a local constituency (€7–13 entrées, daily 11:00–24:00, Schweizer Strasse 71, tel. 069/612-565).

Klaane Sachsehäuser, owned by the same family for five generations, is popular with German tour groups and locals alike, and prides itself on its *Leiterchen* (€8–15 entrées, Mon–Sat 12:00–24:00, closed Sun, Neuer Wall 11, tel. 069/615-983).

Fichtekränzi offers the typical specialties (and some lighter fare), both in its cozy, bench-filled beer hall and outside under the trees. The staff is friendly and the atmosphere relaxed—expect to share a table and make some new friends (€8–13 entrées, daily from 17:00, Wall Strasse 5, tel. 069/612-778).

International Splurge: **Maingau Stuben** is often hailed as one of the best restaurants in Frankfurt. It boasts an extensive wine list, fancy "tasting *menus,*" recommended wine pairings, and an international lineup, including filet of venison and vegetarian options such as thyme-infused risotto. For less of an investment, come for lunch. Don't be fooled by its modest exterior—this place is elegant inside. Reservations are a must (most main dishes around €25; fixed-price meals are €16–33 for lunch, €56–78 for dinner, more with wine pairings, vegetarian dinner-€39; Tue–Fri 11:30–15:00 & 17:00–22:30, Sat 18:00–22:30, Sun 11:30–15:00, closed Mon, tel. 069/610-752, Schifferstrasse 38, www.maingau.de).

Pub Crawl: Irish pubs and salsa bars clutter the pedestrian zone around Rittergasse and Klappergasse, close to Frankensteiner Platz. The cobblestone streets and medieval buildings feel like Epcot Center, rather than historic Frankfurt. But if you're looking for a place to do a pub crawl, this is it.

TRANSPORTATION CONNECTIONS

Frankfurt am Main

From Frankfurt by Train to German Destinations: Rothenburg (hourly, 2.5–3 hrs, changes in Würzburg and Steinach; the tiny Steinach–Rothenburg train often leaves from track 5, shortly after the Würzburg train arrives), **Würzburg** (1–2/hr, 1.25 hrs), **Nürnberg** (1–2/hr, 2 hrs), **Munich** (hourly, 3–4 hrs, occasionally with 1 change), **Baden-Baden** (hourly, 1.5 hrs, direct or transfer in Mannheim or Karlsruhe), **Bacharach** (hourly, 1.5–2 hrs, change in Mainz or Bingen), **Freiburg** (hourly, 2–2.5 hrs, most with 1 change), **Bonn** (2/hr, 2 hrs, most with change in Mainz or Köln), **Cochem** (1–2/hr, 2.25–3 hrs, simplest routing with 1 change in Koblenz), **Köln** (direct trains hourly, 70 min; slower, cheaper trains show you more of the Rhine), **Berlin** (hourly, 4 hrs). Train info: tel. 11861 (€0.60/min).

By Train to International Destinations: Amsterdam (every 2 hrs, 4 hrs direct), **Bern** (every 1–2 hrs, 4 hrs, many with changes in Basel), **Zürich** (1–2/hr, 4–4.5 hrs), **Brussels** (every 2 hrs, 3.5 hrs direct or 4.5 with change in Köln), **Copenhagen** (4/day, 9–11 hrs, most change in Hamburg), **Paris** (every 1–2 hrs, 4–6 hrs, most with 1 change), **Vienna** (7/day direct, 7 hrs), **Prague** (almost hourly, 7–8.25 hrs).

Romantic Road Bus: The bus departs promptly at 8:00 (early May–late Oct) from the Deutsche Touring bus stop on the south side of the Frankfurt train station. Exit the station by track 1; the bus stop is to the right under the white canopy marked with a turquoise *Touring* sign (the Deutsche Touring/Eurolines office is across the street). You can either pay cash when you board, or buy your ticket at the Deutsche Touring office (Mon–Fri 7:00–19:00, Sat 7:00–14:00, Sun 7:00–13:00; entrance at Mannheimer Strasse 15—tel. 069/4609-7280 or 069/790-3261, www.romanticroadcoach.de). Book a seat for free by calling ahead. The Frankfurt–Munich bus trip costs €99. For more information, see the Romantic Road section on page 244.

Frankfurt's Airport

The airport *(Flughafen)* is just a few stops by S-Bahn from the city center, and has its own long-distance train station, which makes it a snap to connect from a flight to other German cities. There are two separate terminals (know your terminal—check your ticket or the airport website, www.airportcity-frankfurt.com). **Terminal 1,** a multi-level maze of check-in counters and shops, is linked to the train station. **Terminal 2** is small and quiet, with few services. A Skytrain and buses connect the two terminals. Pick up the free brochure *Your Airport Guide* for a map and detailed information (available at the airport and at most Frankfurt hotels). For flight information in English, visit www.airportcity-frankfurt.com, call 01805-372-4636, or contact your airline.

Services: The airport has three **baggage-storage** desks (*Gepäckausbewahrung*, €3.60/day per bag; the branch in Terminal 1A, Level 1 is open 24 hours). There is a **post office** (in Terminal 1B, Level 2, daily 7:00–22:00), a **pharmacy** (in Terminal 1B, Level 2, and also in Terminal 2, daily 7:00–22:00), a 24-hour **medical clinic** (Terminal 1C, Level 1), a good-sized **supermarket** (Terminal 1C, Level 0, daily 6:30–21:30), and expensive **Wi-Fi.** Take advantage of the **luggage carts,** ingeniously designed to ride on the airport's escalators (and even all the way up to, but not into, the Skytrain). But heed the instructions on the carts and at the escalator entrances. If you're meeting someone, each terminal has a hard-to-miss **"meeting point"** near where those arriving pop out. The public **showers** were closed for renovation on my last visit, but may reopen again. The **customs desk** in Terminal 2 keeps limited hours, so those claiming VAT refunds may need to go to the desk in Terminal 1. There's even McBeer at three McDonald's, one allegedly Europe's largest. McWelcome to Germany.

Frankfurt Airport Train Station

The airport's train station has two parts, both reachable from Terminal 1. Regional S-Bahn trains to downtown Frankfurt and nearby towns and suburbs depart from platforms 1–3. Long-distance trains to other German cities leave from the slightly more distant *Fernbahnhof*, platforms 4–7.

Getting Between the Airport and Downtown Frankfurt: The airport is a 12-minute train ride on the **S-Bahn** from Frankfurt's main train station, or Hauptbahnhof (€3.60, 4/hr, ride included in €8.70 Frankfurt Card and €8.90 version of all-day *Tageskarte Frankfurt* transit pass, but not in €5.60 version of *Tageskarte Frankfurt*). Figure about €25 for a **taxi** from any of my recommended hotels.

From Frankfurt Airport by Long-Distance Train: Train travelers can validate railpasses or buy tickets at the counters on the level above the long-distance train platforms. Destinations include **Rothenburg** (hourly, 3–3.5 hrs, with transfers in Würzburg and Steinach), **Würzburg** (1–2/hr, 1.5 hrs), **Nürnberg** (1–2/hr,

2.5 hrs), **Munich** (hourly, 3.5 hrs), **Baden-Baden** (roughly hourly, 1.5 hrs, change in Karlsruhe and/or Mannheim), **Köln** (1–2/hr, 1 hr), **Koblenz** (1–2/hr, 1.25–1.5 hrs, some transfer in Mainz), **Bacharach** (hourly, 1.25–1.5 hrs, most change in Mainz, some depart from regional platforms), **Berlin** (1–2/hr, 4.5–5 hrs, most with 1 change). There are also many **international connections** from here (such as Paris, London, Brussels, Amsterdam, Zürich, Bern, and Prague).

Sleeping at or near Frankfurt Airport

Because train connections to Frankfurt Airport are so good, if your flight doesn't leave too early, you can sleep in another city and still make it to the airport for your flight. If you wake up in Köln, Baden-Baden, Würzburg, or Bacharach, you can still make a late-morning or midday flight; you can often make it from Nürnberg, Rothenburg, Freiburg, the Mosel, and even Munich for an early-afternoon flight. But plan ahead and leave room for delays; don't take the last possible connection that allows making your plane.

Because of these easy connections—and since downtown Frankfurt is just 12 minutes away by frequent train—there's virtually no need to sleep at the airport. But if you're desperate, **$$$ Sheraton Frankfurt** is conveniently connected to Terminal 1 and has 1,008 international business-class rooms (Db-about €200–250, check website or the hotel desk in the airport for lower rates, tel. 069/69770, www.sheraton.com/frankfurt, reservations frankfurt@sheraton.com). In a pinch, you can also try the nearby, cheaper **$$ Airport Hotel Tanne** (Db-€82–90, Tannenstrasse 2 in Kelsterbach, tel. 06107/9340, www.airporthoteltanne.de, Laun family) or **$$ Ibis Frankfurt Hotel** (Sb/Db-€70–80, Langer Kornweg 9a–11 in Kelsterbach, tel. 06107/9870, www.ibishotel.com).

"Frankfurt" Hahn Airport

This smaller airport, misleadingly dubbed "Frankfurt" for marketing purposes, is actually almost two hours' drive away in the Mosel region. Regular buses connect Frankfurt Hahn Airport to Zell, Bullay, Trier, Mainz, and Frankfurt (more info at www.hahn-airport.de). Hahn Airport is popular with low-cost carriers (such as Ryanair). To avoid any confusion, double-check the three-letter airport code on your ticket (FRA for Frankfurt Airport, HHN for Frankfurt Hahn).

RHINE VALLEY

Best of the Rhine • Bacharach • St. Goar

The Rhine Valley is storybook Germany, a fairy-tale world of legends and robber-baron castles. Cruise the most castle-studded stretch of the romantic Rhine as you listen for the song of the treacherous Loreley. For hands-on thrills, climb through the Rhineland's greatest castle, Rheinfels, above the town of St. Goar. Castle connoisseurs will also enjoy the fine interior of Marksburg Castle. Spend your nights in a castle-crowned village, either Bacharach or St. Goar.

Planning Your Time

The Rhineland does not take much time to see. Both Bacharach and St. Goar are an easy 90-minute train ride or drive from Frankfurt Airport, and make a good first or last stop for air travelers.

The blitziest tour of the area is an hour at Köln's cathedral (see Köln chapter, page 360) and an hour looking at the castles from your train window. But for a better look, cruise in, tour a castle or two, sleep in a medieval town, and take the train out. If you have limited time, cruise less and explore Rheinfels Castle.

Ideally, if you have only two nights to spend here, sleep in Bacharach, cruise the best hour of the river (from Bacharach to St. Goar), and tour the Rheinfels Castle. Those with more time can ride the riverside bike path. With another day, mosey through the neighboring Mosel Valley or day-trip to Köln (both covered in different chapters).

If you have all the time in the world, you could visit countless castles without leaving this region. But with limited time and energy, you need to be selective in your castle-going. Aside from Rheinfels Castle, my favorites are Burg Eltz (see page 333 in next chapter; medieval interior, well-preserved, lost in a romantic forest in the next valley over), Marksburg Castle (page 297; rebuilt medieval interior, commanding Rhine setting), and Rheinstein Castle (page 301; 19th-century duke's hunting palace overlooking the Rhine). Of these, Rheinfels and Marksburg are the easiest to reach by train. Though only in German, www.burgen-am-rhein.de is a handy website with photos and opening times of the main Rhine castles.

The Best of the Rhine

Ever since Roman times, when this was the empire's northern boundary, the Rhine has been one of the world's busiest shipping rivers. You'll see a steady flow of barges with 1,000- to 2,000-ton loads. Tourist-packed buses, hot train tracks, and highways line both banks.

Many of the castles were "robber-baron" castles, put there by petty rulers (there were 300 independent little countries in medieval Germany, a region about the size of Montana) to levy tolls on passing river traffic. A robber baron would put his castle on, or even in, the river. Then, often with the help of chains and a tower on the opposite bank, he'd stop each ship and get his toll. There were 10 customs stops in the 60-mile stretch between Mainz and Koblenz alone (no wonder merchants were early proponents of the creation of larger nation-states).

Some castles were built to control and protect settlements, and others were the residences of kings. As times changed, so did the lifestyles of the rich and feudal. Many castles were abandoned for more comfortable mansions in the towns.

Most Rhine castles date from the 11th, 12th, and 13th centuries. When the pope successfully asserted his power over the German emperor in 1076, local princes ran wild over the rule of their emperor. The castles saw military action in the 1300s and 1400s, as emperors began reasserting their control over Germany's many silly kingdoms.

The castles were also involved in the Reformation wars, in which Europe's Catholic and Protestant dynasties fought it out using a fragmented Germany as their battleground. The Thirty Years' War (1618–1648) devastated Germany. The outcome: Each ruler got the freedom to decide if his people would be Catholic or Protestant, and one-third of Germany was dead. (Production of Gummi bears ceased entirely.)

The French—who feared a strong Germany and felt the Rhine was the logical border between them and Germany—destroyed most of the castles prophylactically (Louis XIV in the 1680s, the Revolutionary army in the 1790s, and Napoleon in 1806). Many were rebuilt in Neo-Gothic style in the Romantic Age—the late 1800s—and today are enjoyed as restaurants, hotels, hostels, and museums.

Getting Around the Rhine

The Rhine flows north from Switzerland to Holland, but the scenic stretch from Mainz to Koblenz hoards all the touristic charm. Studded with the crenellated cream of Germany's castles, it bustles with boats, trains, and highway traffic. Have fun exploring with a mix of big steamers, tiny ferries *(Fähre),* trains, and bikes.

By Boat: While some travelers do the whole Mainz–Koblenz trip by boat (5.5 hours downstream, 8.5 hours up), I'd just focus on the most scenic hour—from St. Goar to Bacharach. Sit on the top deck with your handy Rhine map-guide (or the kilometer-keyed tour in this chapter) and enjoy the parade of castles, towns, boats, and vineyards.

Two boat companies take travelers along this stretch of the Rhine. Most travelers sail on the bigger, more expensive, and romantic Köln–Düsseldorfer (K-D) Line (free with a German railpass or any Eurailpass that covers Germany, but uses up a day of any flexipass; otherwise about €9 for the first hour, then progressively cheaper per hour; recommended Bacharach–St. Goar trip: €9.90 one-way, €12.10 round-trip, bikes-€2.50; discounts: Mon and Fri—half-price for seniors over 60, Tue—bicyclists travel 2 for the price of 1; tel. 06741/1634 in St. Goar, tel. 06743/1322 in Bacharach, www.k-d.com).

Boats run daily in both directions April through October, with no boats off-season (see the abridged schedule above). Complete, up-to-date schedules are posted in any Rhineland station, hotel, or TI; at www.k-d.com; and at www.euraide.de/ricksteves. Purchase tickets at the dock up to five minutes before departure. (Confirm times at your hotel the night before.) The boat is never full. Romantics will enjoy the old-time paddle-wheel *Goethe,* which sails each direction once a day (noted on schedule above; €1.60 extra, confirm time locally).

The smaller Bingen–Rüdesheimer Line is slightly cheaper than K-D (railpasses not valid, buy tickets on boat, tel. 06721/14140, www.bingen-ruedesheimer.com), with three two-hour round-trip St. Goar–Bacharach trips daily April–October (€9 one-way, €11 round-trip; departing St. Goar at 11:00, 14:10, and 16:10; departing Bacharach at 10:10, 12:00, and 15:00).

By Car: Drivers have these options: 1) skip the boat; 2) take a round-trip cruise from St. Goar or Bacharach; 3) draw pretzels and let the loser drive, prepare the picnic, and meet the boat; 4) rent a bike, bring it on the boat for free, and bike back; or 5) take the boat

Rhine Overview

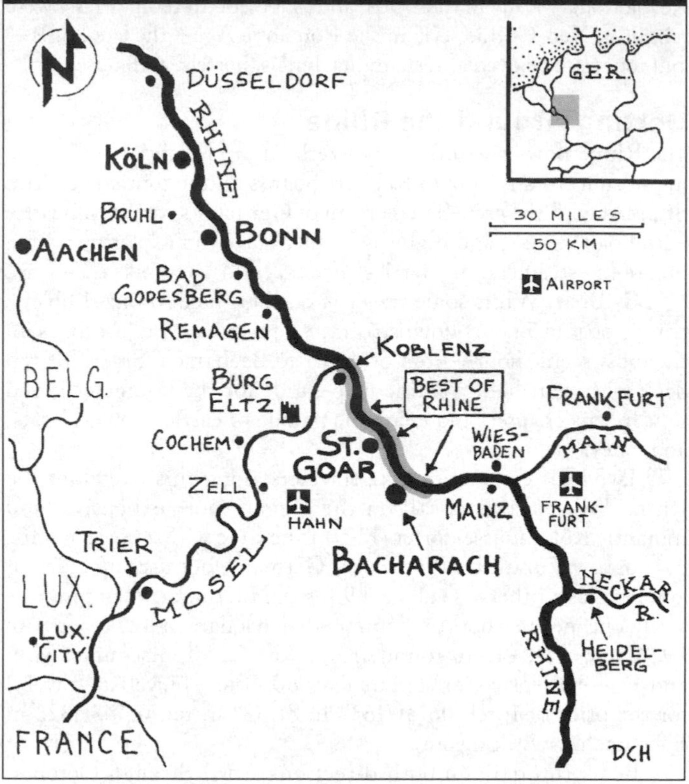

one-way and return by train. When exploring by car, don't hesitate to pop onto one of the many little ferries that shuttle across the bridgeless-around-here river (see below).

By Ferry: While there are no bridges between Koblenz and Mainz, you'll see car-and-passenger ferries (usually family-run for generations) about every three miles. Bingen–Rüdesheim, Lorch–Niederheimbach, Engelsburg–Kaub, and St. Goar–St. Goarshausen are some of the most useful routes (times vary; St. Goar–St. Goarshausen ferry departs each side every 15–20 min, Mon–Sat 6:00–21:00, Sun 8:00–21:00, May–Sept until 23:00; one-way fares: adult-€1.30, car and driver-€3.30, pay on the boat; www.faehre-loreley.de). For a fun little jaunt, take a quick round-trip with some time to explore the other side.

By Bike: You can bike on either side of the Rhine, but for a designated bike path, stay on the west side, where a 35-mile path runs between Koblenz and Bingen. The six-mile stretch between St. Goar and Bacharach is smooth and scenic, but mostly along the

K-D Line Rhine Cruise Schedule

Boats run May through September and on a reduced schedule for parts of April and October; no boats run November through March. These times are based on the 2008 schedule. Check www.k-d.com or www.euraide.de/ricksteves for changes.

Koblenz	*Boppard*	*St. Goar*	*Bacharach*
→			
—	9:00	10:20	11:30
*9:00	*11:00	*12:20	*13:30
11:00	13:00	14:20	15:30
—	14:00	15:20	16:30
14:00	16:00	17:20	18:30
←			
13:10	11:50	10:55	10:15
14:10	12:50	11:55	11:15
—	13:50	12:55	12:15
18:10	16:50	15:55	15:15
*20:10	*18:50	*17:55	*17:15

**These sailings are on the 1913 steamer* Goethe, *with working paddle wheel and viewable engine room.*

highway. The bit from Bacharach to Bingen hugs the riverside and is road-free. Either way, biking is a great way to explore the valley. Many hotels provide free or cheap bikes to guests; in Bacharach, anyone can rent bikes at Hotel Hillen (see page 303, €12/day for non-guests).

Consider biking one-way and taking the bike on the riverboat back, or designing a circular trip using the fun and frequent shuttle ferries. A good target might be Kaub (where a tiny boat shuttles sightseers to the better-from-a-distance castle on the island) or Rheinstein Castle.

By Train: Hourly milk-run trains down the Rhine hit every town (St. Goar–Bacharach, 12 min; Bacharach–Mainz, 60 min; Mainz–Koblenz, 90 min). Some train schedules list St. Goar but not Bacharach as a stop, but any schedule listing St. Goar also stops at Bacharach. Tiny stations are not staffed—buy tickets at the platform machines (user-friendly, takes paper money). Prices are cheap (for example, €3 between St. Goar and Bacharach); consider the Rhineland-Pfalz-Ticket, which covers travel on milk-run trains to anywhere in this chapter—and the Mosel and Trier chapters—for up to five people (€26, not good before 9:00 on weekdays). Express trains speed past the small towns, taking only 50 minutes between Koblenz and Mainz.

SELF-GUIDED TOUR

▲▲▲Rhine Blitz Tour by Train or Boat

One of Europe's great train thrills is zipping along the Rhine enjoying this blitz tour. Or, even better, do it relaxing on the deck of a Rhine steamer, surrounded by the wonders of this romantic and historic gorge. This quick and easy tour (you can cut in anywhere) skips most of the syrupy myths filling normal Rhine guides. You can follow along on a train, bike, car, or boat. By train or boat, sit on the left (river) side going south from Koblenz. While nearly all the castles listed are viewed from this side, train travelers need to clear a path to the right window for the times I yell, "Cross over!"

You'll notice large black-and-white kilometer markers along the riverbank. I erected these years ago to make this tour easier to follow. They tell the distance from the Rhinefalls, where the Rhine leaves Switzerland and becomes navigable. Now the river-barge pilots have accepted these as navigational aids as well. We're tackling just 36 miles (58 km) of the 820-mile-long (1,320-km) Rhine. Your Rhine Blitz Tour starts at Koblenz and heads upstream to Bingen. If you're going the other direction, it still works. Just hold the book upside-down.

Km 590—Koblenz: This Rhine blitz starts with Romantic Rhine thrills—at Koblenz. Koblenz is not a nice city (it was hit hard in World War II), but its place as the historic *Deutsche Eck* (German corner)—the tip of land where the Mosel joins the Rhine—gives it a certain historic charm. Koblenz, from the Latin for "confluence," has Roman origins. If you stop here, take a walk through the park, noticing the reconstructed memorial to the *Kaiser.* Across the river, the yellow Ehrenbreitstein Castle now houses a hostel. It's a 30-minute hike from the station to the Koblenz boat dock.

Km 585—Lahneck Castle (Burg Lahneck): Above the modern autobahn bridge over the Lahn River, this castle *(Burg)* was built in 1240 to defend local silver mines; the castle was ruined by the French in 1688 and rebuilt in the 1850s in Neo-Gothic style. Burg Lahneck faces another Romantic rebuild, the yellow Schloss Stolzenfels (out of view above the train, a 10-min climb from tiny parking lot, open for touring, closed Mon). Note that a *Burg* is a defensive fortress, while a *Schloss* is mainly a showy palace.

Km 580—Marksburg Castle: This castle (black and white, with the three modern chimneys behind it, just before the town of

The Best of the Rhine

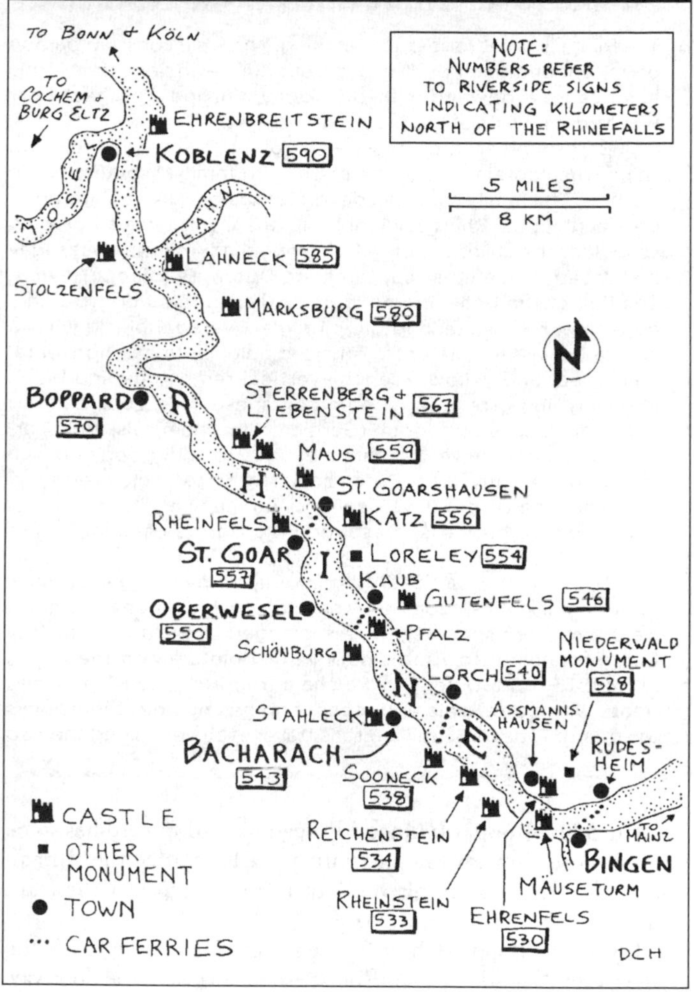

Spay) is the best-looking of all the Rhine castles and the only surviving medieval castle on the Rhine. Because of its commanding position, it was never attacked in the Middle Ages (though it was captured by the US Army in March of 1945). It's now open as a museum with a medieval interior second only to the Mosel's Burg Eltz (see page 297; for all the details on Burg Eltz, see page 333). The three modern smokestacks vent Europe's biggest car-battery recycling plant just up the valley.

If you haven't read the sidebar on river traffic on the next page, now's a good time.

Rhine River Trade and Barge-Watching

The Rhine is great for barge-watching. There's a constant parade of action, and each boat is different. Since ancient times, this has been a highway for trade. Today, Europe's biggest port (Rotterdam) waits at the mouth of the river.

Barge workers are almost a subculture. Many own their own ships. The captain lives in the stern, with family. Workers live in the bow. The family car often decorates the bow like a shiny hood ornament. In the Rhine town of Kaub, there was once a boarding school for the children of the Rhine merchant marine—but today it's closed, since most captains are Dutch, Belgian, or Swiss. The flag of the boat's home country flies in the stern (Dutch—horizontal red, white, and blue; Belgian: vertical black, yellow, and red; Swiss—white cross on a red field; German—horizontal black, red, and yellow; French—vertical red, white, and blue). Logically, imports go upstream (Japanese cars, coal, and oil) and exports go downstream (German cars, chemicals, and pharmaceuticals). A clever captain manages to ship goods in each direction. Recently, giant Dutch container ships (which transport five times the cargo) have been driving many of the traditional barges out of business, presenting the German economy with another challenge.

Tugs can push a floating train of up to five barges at once. Upstream it gets steeper and they can push only one at a time. Before modern shipping, horses dragged boats upstream (the faint remains of towpaths survive at points along the river). From 1873 to 1900, they laid a chain from Bonn to Bingen, and boats with cogwheels and steam engines hoisted themselves upstream. Today, 265 million tons travel each year along the 530

Km 570—Boppard: Once a Roman town, Boppard has some impressive remains of fourth-century walls. Notice the Roman towers and the substantial chunk of Roman wall near the train station, just above the main square.

If you visit Boppard, head to the fascinating church below the main square. Find the carved Romanesque crazies at the doorway. Inside, to the right of the entrance, you'll see Christian symbols from Roman times. Also notice the painted arches and vaults. Originally most Romanesque churches were painted this way. Down by the river, look for the high-water *(Hochwasser)* marks on the arches from various flood years. (You'll find these flood marks throughout the Rhine and Mosel valleys.)

Km 567—Sterrenberg Castle and Liebenstein Castle: These are the "Hostile Brothers" castles across from Bad Salzig. Take the wall between the castles (actually designed to improve the defenses of both castles), add two greedy and jealous brothers and a fair maiden, and create your own legend. Burg Liebenstein is now a miles from Basel on the German-Swiss border to the Dutch city of Rotterdam on the Atlantic.

Riverside navigational aids are of vital interest to captains who don't wish to meet the Loreley (see page 294). Boats pass on the right unless they clearly signal otherwise with a large blue sign. Since downstream ships can't stop or maneuver as freely, upstream boats are expected to do the tricky do-si-do work. Cameras monitor traffic all along and relay warnings of oncoming ships by posting large triangular signals before narrow and troublesome bends in the river. There may be two or three triangles per signpost, depending upon how many "sectors," or segments, of the river are covered. The lowest triangle indicates the nearest stretch of river. Each triangle tells whether there's a ship in that sector. When the bottom side of a triangle is lit, that sector is empty. When the left side is lit, an oncoming ship is in that sector.

The **Signal and Riverpilots Museum** (Wahrschauer- und Lotsenmuseum), located at the signal triangles at the upstream edge of St. Goar, explains how barges are safer, cleaner, and more fuel-efficient than trains or trucks (May-Sept Wed and Sat 14:00-17:00, outdoor exhibits always open).

fun, friendly, and affordable family-run hotel (9 rooms, Db-€115, suite-€140, giant king-and-the-family room-€215, easy parking, tel. 06773/308 or 06773/251, www.castle-liebenstein.com, hotel-burg-liebenstein@rhinecastles.com, Nickenig family).

Km 560: While you can see nothing from here, a 19th-century lead mine functioned on both sides of the river, with a shaft actually tunneling completely under the Rhine.

Km 559—Maus Castle (Burg Maus): The Maus (mouse) got its name because the next castle was owned by the Katzenelnbogen family. (*Katz* means "cat.") In the 1300s, it was considered a state-of-the-art fortification...until Napoleon had it blown up in 1806 with state-of-the-art explosives. It was rebuilt true to its original plans in about 1900. Today, the castle hosts a falconry show (€8, Tue–Sun at 11:00 and 14:30, also at 16:30 on Sun, closed Mon, 20-min walk up, tel. 06771/7669, www.burg-maus.de).

Km 557—St. Goar and Rheinfels Castle: Cross to the other side of the train. The pleasant town of St. Goar was named for a sixth-century hometown monk. It originated in Celtic times (really old) as a place where sailors would stop, catch their breath, send home a postcard, and give thanks after surviving the seductive and treacherous Loreley crossing. St. Goar is worth a stop to explore its mighty Rheinfels Castle. (For information, a self-guided castle tour, and accommodations, see page 313.)

Km 556—Katz Castle (Burg Katz): Burg Katz (Katzenelnbogen) faces St. Goar from across the river. Together, Burg Katz (built in 1371) and Rheinfels Castle had a clear view up and down the river, effectively controlling traffic. There was absolutely no duty-free shopping on the medieval Rhine. Katz got Napoleoned in 1806 and rebuilt in about 1900.

Today, the castle is shrouded by intrigue and controversy. In 1995, a wealthy and eccentric Japanese man bought it for about $4 million. His vision: to make the castle—so close to the Loreley that Japanese tourists are wild about—an exotic escape for his countrymen. But the town wouldn't allow his planned renovation of the historic (and therefore protected) building. Stymied, the frustrated investor just abandoned his plans. Today, Burg Katz sits empty...the Japanese ghost castle.

Below the castle, notice the derelict grape terraces—worked since the eighth century, but abandoned only in the last generation. The Rhine wine is particularly good because the local slate absorbs the heat of the sun and stays warm all night, resulting in sweeter grapes. Wine from the flat fields above the Rhine gorge is cheaper and good only as table wine. The wine from the steep side of the Rhine gorge—harder to grow and harvest—is tastier and more expensive.

About Km 555: A statue of the Loreley, the beautiful-but-deadly nymph (see next listing for legend), combs her hair at the end of a long spit—built to give barges protection from vicious ice floes that until recent years would rage down the river in the winter. The actual Loreley, a cliff (marked by the flags), is just ahead.

Km 554—The Loreley: Steep a big slate rock in centuries of legend and it becomes a tourist attraction—the ultimate Rhinestone. The Loreley (flags and visitors center on top, name painted near shoreline), rising 450 feet over the narrowest and deepest point of the Rhine, has long been important. It was a holy site in pre-Roman days. The fine echoes here—thought to be ghostly voices—fertilized legend-tellers' imaginations.

Because of the reefs just upstream (at kilometer 552), many ships never made it to St. Goar. Sailors (after days on the river) blamed their misfortune on a *wunderbares Fräulein* whose long blond hair almost covered her body. Heinrich Heine's *Song of Loreley* (the CliffsNotes version is on local postcards) tells the story of a count who sent his men to kill or capture this siren after she distracted his horny son, causing him to drown. When the soldiers cornered the nymph in her cave, she called her father (Father Rhine) for help. Huge waves, the likes of which you'll never see today, rose from the river and carried Loreley to safety. And she has never been seen since.

But alas, when the moon shines brightly and the tour buses are parked, a soft, playful Rhine whine can still be heard from the Loreley. As you pass, listen carefully ("Sailors...sailors...over my bounding mane").

Km 552—The Seven Maidens: Killer reefs, marked by red-and-green buoys, are called the "Seven Maidens." Okay, one more goofy legend: The prince of Schönburg Castle (*über* Oberwesel—described below) had seven spoiled daughters who always dumped men because of their shortcomings. Fed up, he invited seven of his knights to the castle and demanded that his daughters each choose one to marry. But they complained that each man had too big a nose, was too fat, too stupid, and so on. The rude and teasing girls escaped into a riverboat. Just downstream, God turned them into the seven rocks that form this reef. While this story probably isn't entirely true, there's a lesson in it for medieval children: Don't be hard-hearted.

Km 550—Oberwesel: Cross to the other side of the train. Oberwesel was a Celtic town in 400 B.C., then a Roman military station. It now boasts some of the best Roman-wall and medieval-tower remains on the Rhine, and the commanding Schönburg Castle. Notice how many of the train tunnels have entrances designed like medieval turrets—they were actually built in the Romantic 19th century. Okay, back to the river side.

Km 546—Gutenfels Castle and Pfalz Castle, the Classic Rhine View: Burg Gutenfels (see white-painted *Hotel* sign) and the shipshape Pfalz Castle (built in the river in the 1300s) worked very effectively to tax medieval river traffic. The town of Kaub grew rich as Pfalz raised its chains when boats came, and lowered them only when the merchants had paid their duty. Those who didn't pay spent time touring its prison, on a raft at the bottom of its well. In 1504, a pope called for the destruction of Pfalz, but the locals withstood a six-week siege, and the castle still stands.

Notice the overhanging outhouse (tiny white room—with faded medieval stains—between two wooden ones). Pfalz (also known as Pfalzgrafenstein) is tourable but bare and dull (€3 ferry from

Kaub, €3 entry; March–Oct Tue–Sun 10:00–18:00, until 17:00 in March, closed Mon; Nov and Jan–Feb Sat–Sun 10:00–17:00, closed Mon–Fri; closed Dec; last entry one hour before closing, tel. 0172/262-2800).

In Kaub, on the riverfront directly below the castles, a green statue honors the German general Gebhard von Blücher. He was Napoleon's nemesis. In 1813, as Napoleon fought his way back to Paris after his disastrous Russian campaign, he stopped at Mainz—hoping to fend off the Germans and Russians pursuing him by controlling that strategic bridge. Blücher tricked Napoleon. By building the first major pontoon bridge of its kind here at the Pfalz Castle, he crossed the Rhine and outflanked the French. Two years later, Blücher and Wellington teamed up to defeat Napoleon once and for all at Waterloo.

Km 544—"The Raft Busters": Immediately before Bacharach, at the top of the island, buoys mark a gang of rocks notorious for busting up rafts. The Black Forest, upstream from here, was once poor, and wood was its best export. Black Foresters would ride log booms down the Rhine to the Ruhr (where their timber fortified coal-mine shafts) or to Holland (where logs were sold to shipbuilders). If they could navigate the sweeping bend just before Bacharach and then survive these "raft busters," they'd come home reckless and likely horny—the German folkloric equivalent of American cowboys after payday.

Km 543—Bacharach and Stahleck Castle (Burg Stahleck): Cross to the other side of the train. The town of Bacharach is a great stop (see details and accommodations on page 302). Some of the Rhine's best wine is from this town, whose name likely derives from "altar to Bacchus." Local vintners brag that the medieval Pope Pius II ordered Bacharach wine by the cartload. Perched above the town, the 13th-century Burg Stahleck is now a hostel.

Km 540—Lorch: This pathetic stub of a castle is barely visible from the road. Check out the hillside vineyards. These vineyards once blanketed four times as much land as they do today, but modern economics have driven most of them out of business. The vineyards that do survive require government subsidies. Notice the small car ferry (3/hr, 10 min), one of several along the bridgeless stretch between Mainz and Koblenz.

Km 538—Sooneck Castle: Cross back to the other side of the train. Built in the 11th century, this castle was twice destroyed by people sick and tired of robber barons.

Km 534—Reichenstein Castle and **Km 533—Rheinstein Castle:** Stay on the other side of the train to see two of the first castles to be rebuilt in the Romantic era. Both are privately owned, tourable, and connected by a pleasant trail. See my listing for Rheinstein Castle on page 301.

Km 530—Ehrenfels Castle: Opposite Bingerbrück and the Bingen station, you'll see the ghostly Ehrenfels Castle (clobbered by the Swedes in 1636 and by the French in 1689). Since it had no view of the river traffic to the north, the owner built the cute little *Mäuseturm* (mouse tower) on an island (the yellow tower you'll see near the train station today). Rebuilt in the 1800s in Neo-Gothic style, it's now used as a Rhine navigation signal station.

Km 528—Niederwald Monument: Across from the Bingen station on a hilltop is the 120-foot-high Niederwald monument, a memorial built with 32 tons of bronze in 1877 to commemorate "the reestablishment of the German Empire." A lift takes tourists to this statue from the famous and extremely touristy wine town of Rüdesheim.

From here, the Romantic Rhine becomes the industrial Rhine, and our tour is over.

SIGHTS

The following sights—Marksburg Castle, the Loreley Visitors Center, and Rheinstein Castle—are listed in the order you'd see them on the Rhine Blitz Tour, described above.

▲▲Marksburg Castle

Medieval invaders decided to give Marksburg a miss thanks to its formidable defenses. This best-preserved castle on the Rhine

can be toured only with a guide. Tours are in German (4/hr in summer, 1/hr in winter). There are no explanations in English in the castle itself, but your ticket includes an English handout. It's an awesome castle, and between the handout and my self-guided tour (next page), you'll feel fully informed.

Cost, Hours, Location: €5, family card-€13, daily Easter–Oct 10:00–18:00, Nov–Easter 11:00–17:00, last tour departs one hour before closing, tel. 02627/206, www.marksburg.de. Marksburg caps a hill above the Rhine town of Braubach (a short hike or shuttle train from the boat dock).

Getting There: Marksburg Castle is above the village of Braubach, on the east bank of the Rhine. By **train,** it's a 10-minute trip from Koblenz (1–2/hr); from Bacharach or St. Goar, it can take 1–2 hours, depending on the wait in Koblenz (€9.90 one-way). The train is quicker than the **boat** (downstream from Bacharach to Braubech-2.25 hours, upstream return-3.5 hours; €19.70

one-way, €25 round-trip). Consider taking the downstream boat to Braubach, and the train back. If traveling with luggage, store it in the convenient lockers in the underground passage at the Koblenz train station (Braubach has no station—and no lockers).

Once you reach Braubach, **walk** into the old town (follow *Altstadt* signs—coming out of tunnel from train platforms, it's to your right); then follow the *Zur Burg* signs to the path up to the castle. Allow 20–30 minutes for the climb up. Scarce **taxis** charge about €10 from the station to the castle. A green **tourist train** circles up to the castle, but there's no fixed schedule, so don't count on it (Easter–Oct only, €2.50 one-way, €4 round-trip, leaves from Barbarastrasse, tel. 06773/587, www.ruckes-reisen.de). Even if you take the train, you'll still have to climb the last five minutes up to the castle from the parking lot (€2).

➲ **Self-Guided Tour:** The tour starts inside the castle's first gate.

1. Inside the First Gate: While the dramatic castles lining the Rhine are generally Romantic rebuilds, Marksburg is the real McCoy—nearly all original construction. It's littered with bits of its medieval past, like the big stone ball that was swung on a rope to be used as a battering ram. Ahead, notice how the inner gate—originally tall enough for knights on horseback to gallop through—was made smaller, and therefore safer from enemies on horseback. Climb the Knights' Stairway carved out of slate rock and pass under the murder hole—handy for pouring boiling pitch on invaders. (Germans still say someone with bad luck "has pitch on his head.")

2. Coats of Arms: Colorful coats of arms line the wall just inside the gate. These are from the noble families who have owned the castle since 1283. In that year, financial troubles drove the first family to sell to the powerful and wealthy Katzenelnbogen family (who made the castle into what you see today). When Napoleon took this region in 1803, an Austrian family who sided with the French got the keys. When Prussia took the region in 1866, control passed to a friend of the Prussians who had a passion for medieval things—typical of this Romantic period. Then it was sold to the German Castles Association in 1900. Its offices are in the main palace at the top of the stairs.

3. Romanesque Palace: White outlines mark where the larger original windows were located, before they were replaced by easier-to-defend smaller ones. On the far right, a bit of the original plaster survives. Slate, which is soft and vulnerable to the elements, needs to be covered—in this case, by plaster. Because this is a protected historic building, restorers can use only the traditional plaster methods...but no one knows how to make plaster that works as well as the 800-year-old surviving bits.

4. Cannons: The oldest cannon here—from 1500—was back-loaded. This was advantageous because many cartridges could be pre-loaded. But since the seal was leaky, it wasn't very powerful. The bigger, more modern cannons—from 1640—were one piece and therefore airtight, but had to be front-loaded. They could easily hit targets across the river from here. Stone balls were rough, so they let the explosive force leak out. The best cannonballs were stones covered in smooth lead—airtight and therefore more powerful and more accurate.

5. Gothic Garden: Walking along an outer wall, you'll see 160 plants from the Middle Ages—used for cooking, medicine, and witchcraft. *Schierling* (hemlock, in the first corner) is the same poison that killed Socrates.

6. Inland Rampart: This most vulnerable part of the castle had a triangular construction to better deflect attacks. Notice the factory in the valley. In the 14th century, this was a lead, copper, and silver mine. Today's factory—Europe's largest car-battery recycling plant—uses the old mine shafts as vents (see the three modern smokestacks).

7. Wine Cellar: Since Roman times, wine has been the traditional Rhineland drink. Because castle water was impure, wine—less alcoholic than today's beer—was the way knights got their fluids. The pitchers on the wall were their daily allotment. The bellows were part of the barrel's filtering system.

Stairs lead to the...

8. Gothic Hall: This hall is set up as a kitchen, with an oven designed to roast an ox whole. The arms holding the pots have notches to control the heat. To this day, when Germans want someone to hurry up, they say, "give it one tooth more." Medieval windows were made of thin sheets of translucent alabaster or animal skins. A nearby wall is peeled away to show the wattle-and-daub construction (sticks, straw, clay, mud, then plaster) of a castle's inner walls. The iron plate to the left of the next door enabled servants to stoke the heater without being seen by the noble family.

9. Bedroom: This was the only heated room in the castle. The canopy kept in heat and kept out critters. In medieval times, it was impolite for a lady to argue with her lord in public. She would wait for him in bed to give him what Germans still call "a curtain lecture." The deep window seat caught maximum light for needlework and reading. Women would sit here and chat (or "spin a yarn") while working the spinning wheel.

10. Hall of the Knights: This was the dining hall. The long table is an unattached plank. After each course, servants could replace it with another pre-set plank. Even today, when a meal is over and Germans are ready for the action to begin, they say, "Let's lift up the table." The action back then consisted of traveling minstrels who sang and told of news gleaned from their travels.

Notice the outhouse—made of wood—hanging over thin air. When not in use, its door was locked from the outside (the castle side) to prevent any invaders from entering this weak point in the castle's defenses.

11. Chapel: This chapel is still painted in Gothic style with the castle's namesake, St. Mark, and his lion. Even the chapel was designed with defense in mind. The small doorway kept out heavily armed attackers. The staircase spirals clockwise, favoring the sword-wielding defender (assuming he was right-handed).

12. Linen Room: About the year 1800, the castle—with diminished military value—housed disabled soldiers. They'd earn a little extra money working raw flax into linen.

13. Two Thousand Years of Armor: Follow the evolution of armor since Celtic times. Because helmets covered the entire head, soldiers identified themselves as friendly by tipping their visor up with their right hand. This evolved into the military salute that is still used around the world today. Armor and the close-range weapons along the back were made obsolete by the invention of the rifle. Armor was replaced with breastplates—pointed (like the castle itself) to deflect enemy fire. This design was used as late as the start of World War I. A medieval lady's armor hangs over the door. While popular fiction has men locking up their women before heading off to battle, chastity belts were actually used by women as protection against rape when traveling.

14. The Keep: This served as an observation tower, a dungeon (with a 22-square-foot cell in the bottom), and a place of last refuge. When all was nearly lost, the defenders would bundle into the keep and burn the wooden bridge, hoping to outwait their enemies.

15. Horse Stable: The stable shows off bits of medieval crime and punishment. Cheaters were attached to stones or pillories. Shame masks punished gossipmongers. A mask with a heavy ball had its victim crawling around with his nose in the mud. The handcuffs with a neck hole were for the transport of prisoners. The pictures on the wall show various medieval capital punishments. Many times the accused was simply taken into a torture dungeon to see all these tools and, guilty or not, confessions spilled out of him. On that cheery note, your tour is over.

The Loreley Visitors Center (Besucherzentrum Loreley)

Easily reached from St. Goar, this lightweight exhibit reflects a little on Loreley, but focuses mainly on the landscape, culture, and people of the Rhine Valley. Though English explanations accompany most of the geological and cultural displays, the information about the famous mythical *Mädchen* is given in German only—making this place not worth its admission price. The 3-D movie is essentially a tourist brochure for the region, with scenes of the grape harvest over Bacharach that are as beautiful as the sword-fighting is lame (€2.50, daily March 10:00–17:00, April–mid-Nov 10:00–18:00, closed mid-Nov–Feb, tel. 06771/599-093, www.loreley-besucherzentrum.de). Far more exciting than the exhibit is the view from the cliffs themselves. A five-minute walk from the bus stop and visitors center takes you to the impressive viewpoint overlooking the Rhine Valley from atop the famous rock. From there, it's a steep 15-minute hike down to the riverbank.

Getting There: For a good two-hour **hike** from St. Goar up to the Loreley, catch the ferry across to the village of St. Goarshausen (€2.60 round-trip, every 15–20 min, Mon–Sat 6:00–21:00, Sun 8:00–21:00, May–Sept until 23:00). Then follow green *Burg Katz* (Katz Castle) signs up Burgstrasse under the train tracks to find steps on right *(Loreley über Burg Katz)* leading to the Katz Castle (privately owned) and beyond. Traverse the hillside, always bearing right toward the river. You'll pass through a residential area, hike down a 50-yard path through trees, then cross a wheat field until you reach the Loreley Visitors Center (with shops and restaurants) and rock-capping viewpoint. From here, it's a steep 15-minute hike back down to the river, where the riverfront road takes you back to St. Goarshausen and the St. Goar ferry.

If you're not up for a hike, you can catch the hourly **bus** from St. Goarshausen up to the visitors center, and hike or bus back down again. From the St. Goarshausen ferry ramp, walk to your left along the river about 40 yards to get the bus (€2.20 each way; first bus at 10:15, then at :30 past each hour 11:30–16:30; last bus down leaves at 16:42).

▲▲Rheinstein Castle (Schloss Burg Rheinstein)

This castle seems to rule its chunk of the Rhine from a commanding position. While its 13th-century exterior is medieval as can be, the interior is mostly a 19th-century duke's hunting palace. Visitors wander freely (with an English flier) among trophies, armor, and Romantic Age decor.

Cost and Hours: €4, mid-March–mid-Nov daily 9:30–17:30, off-season Sat–Sun only 10:00–16:30, closed mid-Dec–Jan, tel. 06721/6348, www.burg-rheinstein.de.

Getting There: This castle (at river kilometer marker

#533, 2 kilometers upstream from Trechtingshausen on the main highway, B-9) is easy by **car** (small, free parking lot on B-9, steep 5-min hike from there), or **bike** (35 min upstream from Bacharach, stick to the great riverside path, after kilometer marker #534 look for small *Burg Rheinstein* sign and Rösler–Linie dock). It's less convenient by **boat** (no K-D stop nearby) or **train** (nearest stop in Trechtingshausen, 30-min walk away).

Bacharach

Once prosperous from the wine and wood trade, Bacharach (BAHKH-ah-rahkh, with a guttural *kh* sound) is now just a pleasant half-timbered village of a thousand people working hard to keep its tourists happy.

ORIENTATION

Tourist Information

The TI, on the main street in the Posthof courtyard next to the church, will store bags for day-trippers (April–Oct Mon–Fri 9:00–17:00, Sat–Sun 10:00–15:00; Nov–March Mon–Fri 9:00–12:00, closed Sat–Sun; Oberstrasse 45, from train station turn right and walk 5 blocks down main street with castle high on your left, tel. 06743/919-303, www.bacharach.de or www.rhein-nahe-touristik.de, Herr Kuhn and his team).

Helpful Hints

Shopping: The **Jost** German gift store, across the main square from the church, carries most everything a souvenir-shopper could want (from beer steins to cuckoo clocks). The Josts offer a 10 percent discount to readers of this book who pay cash, and can ship things to the US (March–Oct Mon–Fri 8:30–18:00, Sat 8:30–17:00, Sun 10:00–16:00; Nov–Feb shorter hours and closed Sun; Blücherstrasse 4, tel. 06743/1224, www.phil-jost-germany.com, phil.jost@t-online.de).

Internet Access: The Rhine's cheapest Internet café is in the basement of the Lutheran-church-run kindergarten at Koblenzer Strasse 10, a few doors past the Altes Haus (€1/hr, Mon–Tue and Thu–Fri 16:00–21:00, closed Sat–Sun and Wed). The TI has a coin-op terminal (€0.50/15 min).

Post Office: It's inside a shop, at Oberstrasse 37 between the train station and the TI (Mon–Fri 9:00–12:00 & 14:00–18:00, Sat 9:00–12:00, closed Sun).

Grocery Store: Across from the Altes Haus is a **Nahkauf,** a basic grocery store (Mon–Fri 8:00–12:30 & 14:00–18:00, Sat 8:00–15:00, closed Sun, Oberstrasse 46).

Bike Rental: While many hotels loan bikes to guests, the only real bike-rental business in the town center is run by Erich at Hotel Hillen (see listing on page 310). He rents 25 bikes daily from 9:00 until dark (€12/day for non-guests, €7/day for guests, Langstrasse 18, tel. 06743/1287).

Local Guides and Walking Tours: Get acquainted with Bacharach by taking a walking tour. Charming **Herr Rolf Jung,** retired headmaster of the Bacharach school, is a superb English-speaking guide who loves sharing his town's story with Americans (€30, 90 min, call to reserve, tel. 06743/1519). **Manuela Mades** (tel. 06743/2759), **Birgit Wessel** (tel. 06743/937-514), and Aussie **Joanne Augustin,** who works at the youth hostel (tel. 06743/919-300, mobile 0179-231-1389), also give good tours. If none of the above is available, call the TI for advice, or take my self-guided walk (see below). On Saturdays at 11:00 from May to October, the TI offers a 90-minute walking tour (€4.50) in German only.

SELF-GUIDED WALK

Welcome to Bacharach

• *Start at the Köln–Düsseldorfer ferry dock (next to a fine picnic park).*

View the town from the parking lot—a modern landfill. The Rhine used to lap against Bacharach's town wall, just over the present-day highway. Every few years the river floods, covering the highway with several feet of water. The **castle** on the hill is now a youth hostel. Two of the town's original 16 towers are visible from here (up to five if you look really hard). The huge roadside wine keg declares that this town was built on the wine trade.

Reefs farther upstream forced boats to unload upriver and reload here. Consequently, in the Middle Ages, Bacharach became the biggest wine-trading town on the Rhine. A riverfront crane hoisted huge kegs of prestigious "Bacharach" wine (which, in practice, was from anywhere in the region). The tour buses next to the dock and the flags of the biggest spenders along the highway remind you that today's economy is basically founded on tourism.

• *Before entering the town, walk upstream through the riverside park.*

This park was laid out in 1910 in the English style: Notice how the trees were planted to frame fine town views, highlighting

Bacharach

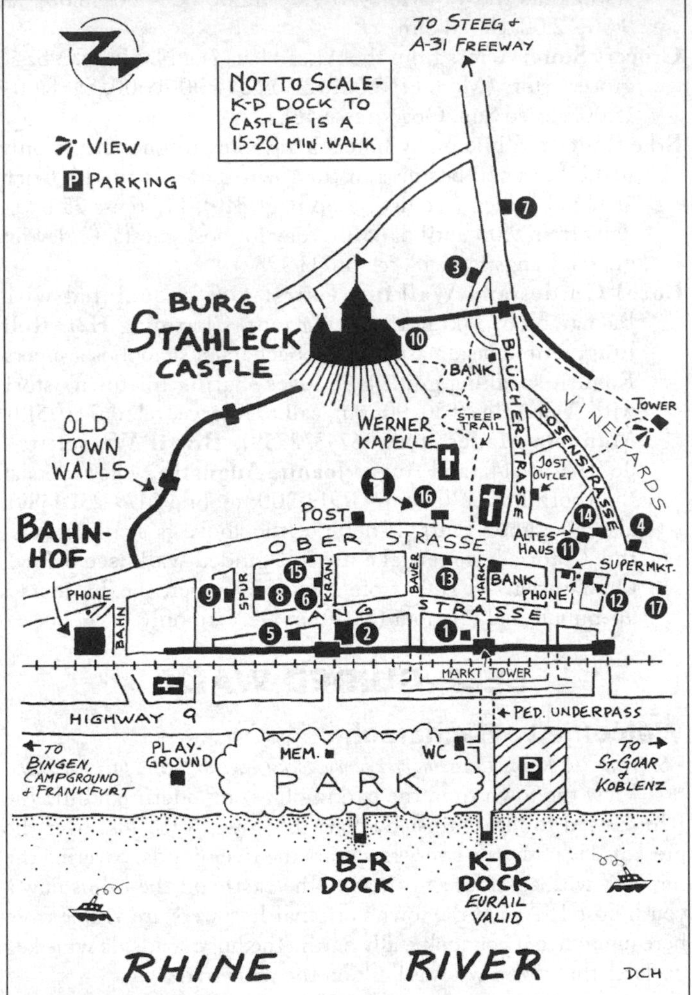

1. Rhein Hotel & Stüber Rest.
2. Hotel/Rest. Kranenturm
3. Pension im Malerwinkel
4. Pension Binz
5. Hotel Hillen & Bike Rental
6. Pension Lettie
7. Pension Winzerhaus
8. Ursula Orth B & B
9. Irmgard Orth B & B
10. Jugendherberge Stahleck Hostel
11. Altes Haus Restaurant
12. Kurpfälzische Münze Restaurant
13. Eis Café Italia
14. Bastian's Weingut zum Grüner Baum
15. Weingut Karl Heidrich
16. Old Posthof
17. Internet Café

the most picturesque bits of architecture. Until recently, stepping on the grass was *verboten*. The dark, sad-looking monument—its "eternal" flame long snuffed out—is a war memorial. The German psyche is permanently scarred by war memories. Today, many Germans would rather avoid monuments like this, which revisit the dark periods before Germany became a nation of pacifists. Take a close look at the monument. Each panel honors sons of Bacharach who died for the Kaiser: in 1864 against Denmark, in 1870 against France, in 1914 during World War I. The military Maltese cross—flanked by classic German helmets—has a *W* at its center, for Kaiser Wilhelm.

• *Continue to where the park meets the playground, and then cross the highway to the fortified riverside wall of the Catholic church—decorated with high-water marks recalling various floods.*

Check out the metal ring on the medieval slate wall. Before the 1910 reclamation project, the river extended out to here, and boats would use the ring to tie up. Upstream from here, there's a trailer park, and beyond that there's a campground. In Germany, trailer vacationers and campers are two distinct subcultures. Folks who travel in trailers, like many retirees in the US, are a nomadic bunch, hauling around the countryside in their mobile homes and paying about €6 a night to park. Campers, on the other hand, tend to set up camp—complete with comfortable lounge chairs and even TVs—and stay put for weeks, even months. They often come back to the same plot year after year, treating it like their own private estate. These camping devotees have made a science out of relaxing.

• *At the church, go under the 1858 train tracks and hook right past the yellow floodwater yardstick and up the stairs onto the town wall. Atop the wall, turn left and walk under the long arcade. After a few steps, notice a well on your left. This is one of 40 such wells that, until 1900, provided water to the townsfolk. You'll pass the Rhein Hotel (see listing on page 308; hotel is before the Markt tower, which marks one of the town's 15 original 14th-century gates), descend, pass another well, and follow Marktstrasse toward the town center, the two-tone church, and the town's main intersection.*

From here, Bacharach's main street (Oberstrasse) goes right to the half-timbered, red-and-white Altes Haus (from 1368, the oldest house in town) and left 400 yards to the train station. To the left (south) of the church, a golden horn hangs over the old **Posthof** (home to the TI, free WC upstairs in courtyard). The post horn symbolizes the postal service throughout Europe. In olden days, when the postman blew this, traffic stopped and the mail sped through. This post station dates from 1724, when stagecoaches ran from Köln to Frankfurt and would change horses here, Pony Express–style.

Step past the old oak doors into the courtyard—once a carriage house and inn that accommodated Bacharach's first VIP visitors. Notice the fascist eagle (from 1936, on the left as you enter; a swastika once filled its center) and the fine view of the church and a ruined chapel above. The Posthof is on a charming square. Spin around to enjoy the higgledy-piggledy building style.

Two hundred years ago, Bacharach's main drag was the only road along the Rhine. Napoleon widened it to fit his cannon wagons. The steps alongside the church lead to the castle. Return to the church, passing the Italian ice-cream café (Eis Café Italia), where friendly Mimo serves his special invention: Riesling wine–flavored gelato (see "Eating," page 312).

Inside the Protestant church (April–Oct daily 9:30–18:00, closed Nov–March, English info on table near door), you'll find Grotesque capitals, brightly painted in medieval style, and a mix of round Romanesque and pointed Gothic arches. To the left of the altar, some medieval frescoes survive where an older Romanesque arch was cut by a pointed Gothic one.

• *Continue down Oberstrasse to the* ***Altes Haus.***

Notice the 14th-century building style—the first floor is made of stone, while upper floors are half-timbered (in the ornate style common in the Rhine Valley). Some of its windows still look medieval, with small flattened circles as panes (small because that's all that glass-blowing technology of the time would allow), pieced together with molten lead. Frau Weber welcomes visitors to enjoy the fascinating ground floor of her Altes Haus, with its evocative old photos and etchings (consider eating here later—see "Eating," page 311).

• *Keep going down Oberstrasse to the* ***old mint*** *(Münze), marked by a crude coin in its sign.*

Across from the mint, the Bastian family's wine garden is the liveliest place in town after dark (see page 312). Above you in the vineyards stands a lonely white-and-red tower—your destination.

At the next street, look right and see the mint tower, painted in the medieval style (illustrating that the Dark Ages weren't really *that* dark), and then turn left. Wander 30 yards up Rosenstrasse to the **well.** Notice the sundial and the wall painting of 1632 Bacharach with its walls intact. (The town is working to reconstruct the wall's missing sections—you may be able to walk the whole length of the wall in 2009.) Climb the tiny-stepped lane behind the well up into the vineyard and to the tall tower. The slate steps lead to a small path through the vineyard that deposits you at a viewpoint atop the stubby remains of the old town wall. If the tower's open, hike to its top floor for the best view.

A grand medieval town spreads before you. For 300 years

(1300–1600), Bacharach was big (population 4,000), rich, and politically powerful.

From this perch you can see the chapel ruins and six surviving **city towers.** Visually trace the wall to the castle. The castle was actually the capital of Germany for a couple of years in the 1200s. When Holy Roman Emperor Frederick Barbarossa went away to fight the Crusades, he left his brother (who lived here) in charge of his vast realm. Bacharach was home of one of seven electors who voted for the Holy Roman Emperor in 1275. To protect their own power, these elector-princes did their best to choose the weakest guy on the ballot. The elector from Bacharach helped select a two-bit prince named Rudolf von Habsburg (from a no-name castle in Switzerland). The underestimated Rudolf brutally silenced the robber barons along the Rhine and established the mightiest dynasty in European history. His family line, the Habsburgs, ruled much of Central and Eastern Europe until 1918.

Plagues, fires, and the Thirty Years' War (1618–1648) finally did in Bacharach. The town, with a population of about a thousand, has slumbered for several centuries. Today, the castle houses commoners—40,000 overnights annually by youth hostelers.

In the mid-19th century, painters such as J. M. W. Turner and writers such as Victor Hugo were charmed by the Rhineland's romantic mix of past glory, present poverty, and rich legend. They put this part of the Rhine on the old Grand Tour map as the "Romantic Rhine." Victor Hugo pondered the ruined 15th-century chapel that you see under the castle. In his 1842 travel book, *Rhein Reise (Rhine Travels),* he wrote, "No doors, no roof or windows, a magnificent skeleton puts its silhouette against the sky. Above it, the ivy-covered castle ruins provide a fitting crown. This is Bacharach, land of fairy tales, covered with legends and sagas." If you're enjoying the Romantic Rhine, thank Victor Hugo and company.

• *To get back into town, take the level path away from the river that leads along the once-mighty wall up the valley past the next tower. Then cross the street into the parking lot. Pass Pension Malerwinkel on your right, being careful not to damage the old arch with your head. Follow the creek past a delightful little series of half-timbered homes and cheery gardens known as "Painters' Corner" (Malerwinkel). Resist looking into some pervert's peep show (on the right) and continue downhill back to the village center. Nice work.*

SLEEPING

(area code: 06743)

Ignore guest houses and restaurants posting *Recommended by Rick Steves* signs. If they're not listed in the current edition of this book, I do not recommend them. Parking in Bacharach is simple along the highway next to the tracks (3-hour daytime limit is generally not enforced) or in the boat parking lot. For locations, see the map on page 304.

$$$ Rhein Hotel, with 14 spacious and comfortable rooms, is classy, well-run, decorated with a modern flair, and overlooks the river. Since it's right on the train tracks, its river- and train-side rooms come with four-paned windows and air-conditioning. This place has been in the Stüber family for six generations (Sb-€55, Db-€90 with this book and direct reservation in 2009, cheaper for longer stays, half-board option, non-smoking, free loaner bikes for guests, Wi-Fi, directly inland from the K-D boat dock at Langstrasse 50, tel. 06743/1243, fax 06743/1413, www.rhein-hotel-bacharach.de, info@rhein-hotel-bacharach.de). For a culinary splurge, consider dining here (see "Eating," page 311).

$$ Hotel Kranenturm, offering castle ambience without the climb, combines hotel comfort with *Zimmer* coziness right downtown. Run by hardworking Kurt Engel and his intense but friendly wife, Fatima, this hotel is part of the medieval fortification. Its former *Kran* (crane) towers are now round rooms. When the riverbank was higher, cranes on this tower loaded barrels of wine onto Rhine boats. While just 15 feet from the train tracks, a combination of medieval sturdiness, triple-paned windows, and included earplugs makes the riverside rooms sleepable (Sb-€39–45, small Db-€56–62, regular Db-€58–65, Db in huge tower rooms with castle and river views-€72–80, Tb-€83–95, Qb great for families with small kids-€100–115, honeymoon special-€85–105, lower price May–Oct with 3-night stay and Nov–April with 2-night stay, family deals, cash preferred, Rhine views come with train noise, back rooms are quiet, non-smoking, showers can be temperamental, kid-friendly, good breakfast, pay Internet access, free Wi-Fi, laundry service-€12.80, Langstrasse 30, tel. 06743/1308, fax 06743/1021, www.kranenturm.com, hotel-kranenturm@t-online.de). Kurt, a good cook, serves €8–14 dinners.

Sleep Code

(€1 = about $1.50, country code: 49)
S = Single, **D** = Double/Twin, **T** = Triple, **Q** = Quad, **b** = bathroom, **s** = shower only. All hotels speak some English. Breakfast is included and credit cards are accepted unless otherwise noted.

To help you sort easily through these listings, I've divided the rooms into three categories, based on the price for a standard double room with bath:

$$$ Higher Priced—Most rooms €80 or more.
$$ Moderately Priced—Most rooms between €60-80.
$ Lower Priced—Most rooms €60 or less.

The Rhine is an easy place for cheap sleeps. B&Bs and *Gasthäuser* with €25 beds abound (and normally discount their prices for longer stays). Rhine-area hostels offer €17 beds to travelers of any age. Each town's TI is eager to set you up, and finding a room should be easy any time of year (except for winefest weekends in Sept and Oct). Bacharach and St. Goar, the best towns for an overnight stop, are 10 miles apart, connected by milk-run trains, riverboats, and a riverside bike path. Bacharach is a much more interesting town, but St. Goar has the famous castle (for St. Goar recommendations, see page 321).

$$ Pension im Malerwinkel sits like a grand gingerbread house that straddles the town wall in a quiet little neighborhood so charming it's called "Painters' Corner" *(Malerwinkel)*. The Vollmer family's 20-room place is super-quiet and comes with a sunny garden on a brook, views of the vineyards, and easy parking (Sb-€38, Db-€62 for 1 night, €56 for 2 nights, €53 for 3 nights or more, cash only, some rooms have balconies, no train noise, non-smoking, bike rental-€6/day; from Oberstrasse, turn left at the church, and stay to the left of the babbling brook until you reach Blücherstrasse 41; tel. 06743/1239, fax 06743/93407, www.im-malerwinkel.de, pension@im-malerwinkel.de, Armin and Daniela).

$$ Pension Binz offers four large, bright, plainly furnished rooms in a good location with no train noise (Sb-€35, Db-€60, third person-€18, slightly cheaper for 3 nights or more, apartment with kitchen but no breakfast and 2-night minimum-€65, Koblenzer Strasse 1, tel. 06743/1604, fax 06743/937-9916, pension .binz@freenet.de, warm Carla speaks a little English).

$ Hotel Hillen, a block south of the Hotel Kranenturm, has a little less charm and similar train noise (with the same ultra-thick windows). It offers spacious rooms, good food, and friendly owners (S-€30, Sb-€35, D-€40, Ds-€45, Db-€50, Tb-€65, Qb-€80, these special prices with a 2-night stay when you reserve directly with this book in 2009, €5 more for 1-night stays, closed mid-Nov–mid-March, family rooms, Langstrasse 18, tel. 06743/1287, fax 06743/1037, hotel-hillen@web.de, kind Iris speaks some English). The Hillen also rents bikes (see page 303).

$ At **Pension Lettie,** effervescent and eager-to-please Lettie offers four bright rooms. Lettie speaks English (she worked for the US Army before they withdrew) and does laundry for €10.50/load (Sb-€38, Db-€53, Tb-€70, Qb-€90, 5b-€105, these prices valid with this book in 2009 if you reserve direct rather than through TI, €3–5 discount for 2-night stays, 10 percent more if paying with credit card, strictly non-smoking, buffet breakfast with waffles and eggs, no train noise, pay Wi-Fi, a few doors inland from Hotel Kranenturm, Kranenstrasse 6, tel. 06743/2115, fax 06743/947564, pension.lettie@t-online.de).

$ Pension Winzerhaus, a 10-room place run by friendly Sybille and Stefan, is outside the town walls, 200 yards up the side-valley road from the town gate, directly under the vineyards. Though you can't hear the train, there is slight noise from passing cars. The rooms are simple, clean, and modern, and parking is easy (Sb-€30, Db-€49, Tb-€65, Qb-€75, 10 percent off in 2009 when you show this book at check-in, cash only, non-smoking, 3 free loaner bikes for guests, Blücherstrasse 60, tel. 06743/1294, winzer haus@gmx.de).

$ Orth *Zimmer*: Delightful sisters-in-law run two fine little B&Bs across the lane from each other (from station, walk down Oberstrasse, turn right on Spurgasse, and look for *Orth* sign). **Ursula Orth** rents five rooms, speaks a smidge of English, and is proud of her homemade jam (Sb-€22, Db-€37, Tb-€45, cash only, rooms 4 and 5 on ground floor, Spurgasse 3, tel. 06743/1557). **Irmgard Orth** rents three fresh rooms, two of which share a bathroom on the hall. She speaks even less English but is exuberantly cheery and serves homemade honey with breakfast (S-€22, D-€34–35, Db-€37, cash only, Spurgasse 2, look for beehive signs, tel. 06743/1553). Their excellent prices assume you're booking direct, instead of through the TI.

$ Jugendherberge Stahleck hostel is a 12th-century castle on the hilltop—500 steps above Bacharach—with a royal Rhine view. Open to travelers of any age, this is a gem with 168 beds and a private modern shower and WC in most rooms. The steep 20-minute climb on the trail from the town church is worth it for the view, even if you're not sleeping there. The hostel serves hearty €6.50 all-you-can-eat buffet dinners, and its pub serves cheap local wine and snacks until midnight. To reach the hostel with luggage from the train station, call an €8 taxi at 06743/1653 or 06743/1418 (€17.40 dorm beds with breakfast and sheets, non-members-€3.10 extra, couples can share one of five €46 Db, no smoking in rooms, pay Internet access, laundry-€5.50, dorm beds normally available but call and leave your name—they'll hold a bed until 18:00, tel. 06743/1266, fax 06743/2684, www.diejugendherbergen.de, bacharach@diejugendherbergen.de). If driving, don't go in the driveway; park on the street and walk 200 yards.

EATING

Restaurants

You can easily find inexpensive (€10–15), atmospheric restaurants offering indoor and outdoor dining. There's also a cozy pizzeria and a *Döner Kebab* joint (daily until 23:00) on the main street.

The Rhein Hotel's **Stüber Restaurant** is Bacharach's best top-end choice. Chef Andreas Stüber is the sixth generation to prepare regional, seasonal plates, served on river- and track-side seating or indoors with a spacious wood-and-white-tablecloth elegance. Consider their €14 William Turner pâté sampler plate, named after the British painter who liked Bacharach (€9–19 entrées, March–mid-Dec Wed–Mon 12:00–14:00 & 17:30–21:00, closed Tue and mid-Dec–Feb, call to reserve on weekends or for an outdoor table, facing the K-D boat dock just below the center of town, Langstrasse 50, tel. 06743/1243).

Altes Haus, the oldest building in town (see page 306), serves reliably good food with Bacharach's most romantic atmosphere. Find the cozy little dining room with photos of the opera singer who sang about Bacharach, adding to its fame (€9–15 entrées, Easter–Nov Thu–Tue 12:00–15:30 & 18:00–23:00, closed Wed and Dec–Easter, dead center by the church, tel. 06743/1209).

Kurpfälzische Münze, while more expensive than Altes Haus, is a popular standby for lunch or a drink on its sunny terrace or in its pubby candlelit interior (main dishes-€7–14 at lunch and €10–20 at dinner, daily 10:00–22:00; in the old mint, a half-block down from Altes Haus; tel. 06743/1375).

Hotel Kranenturm is another good value, with hearty dinners (Kurt prides himself on his *Sauerbraten*—marinated beef with potato dumplings and red cabbage) and good main-course salads. If you're a train-spotter, sit on their track-side terrace and trade travel stories with new friends over dinner, letting screaming trains punctuate your conversation. If you prefer charming old German decor, sit inside (€8–14 main dishes, open 6 days a week 17:00–21:00—closed day varies, see hotel listing on page 308). Kurt and Fatima are your hosts.

Eis Café Italia, on the main street and run by friendly Mimo Calabrese, is known for its refreshing, not-too-sweet Riesling-flavored gelato. Notice the big sundae bowls on the shelves. To enjoy your *Eis* German-style, sit down and order ice cream off the menu, or just stop by for a cone before an evening stroll (€0.70/scoop, no tastes offered, April–mid-Oct daily 10:00–22:00, closed off-season, opposite Posthof at Oberstrasse 48).

Wine-Tasting

Bacharach is proud of its wine. Two places in town—Bastian's rowdy and rustic Grüner Baum, and sophisticated Weingut Karl Heidrich—offer visitors an inexpensive chance to join in on the fun. Each creates carousels of local wines that small groups of travelers (who don't mind sharing a glass) can sample and compare.

At **Bastian's Weingut zum Grüner Baum,** groups of 2–6 people pay €14 for a wine carousel of 15 glasses—14 different white wines and one lonely rosé—and a basket of bread. Your mission: Team up with others who have this book to rendezvous here after dinner. Spin the Lazy Susan, share a common cup, and discuss the taste. Doris Bastian insists: "After each wine, you must talk to each other." They offer soup and cold cuts, and good ambience indoors and out (Mon–Wed and Fri from 13:00, Sat–Sun from 12:00, closed Thu and Feb–mid-March, just past Altes Haus, tel. 06743/1208). To make a meal of a carousel, consider the *Käse Teller* (7 different cheeses, including *Spundekäse,* the local soft cheese).

Weingut Karl Heidrich is a fun, family-run wine shop and *Stube* in the town center (at Oberstrasse 18, near Hotel Kranenturm), where Markus proudly shares his family's wine while passionately explaining its fine points to travelers. They offer a variety of carousels with six wines and bread (€10), which are ideal for the more sophisticated wine-taster (Easter–Oct Thu–Tue 11:00–22:00, closed Wed and Nov–Easter, tel. 06743/93060).

TRANSPORTATION CONNECTIONS

Train Connections from the Rhine

Milk-run trains stop at Rhine towns each hour starting as early as 6:00, connecting at Mainz and Koblenz to trains farther afield. Trains between St. Goar and Bacharach depart at about :20 after the hour in each direction (€3, buy tickets from the machine in the unstaffed stations). The ride times listed below are calculated from Bacharach; for St. Goar, the difference is only 12 minutes. Train info: tel. 11861 (€0.60/min).

From Bacharach by Train to: St. Goar (hourly, 12 min), **Moselkern** near Burg Eltz (hourly, 1.75 hrs, change in Koblenz), **Cochem** (hourly, 1.5 hrs, change in Koblenz), **Trier** (hourly, 2.5 hrs, change in Koblenz), **Köln** (hourly, 1.75 hrs, change in Koblenz), **Frankfurt Airport** (hourly, 1.25–1.5 hrs, most change in Mainz or Bingen, **Frankfurt** (hourly, 1.5–2 hrs, change in Mainz or Bingen), **Rothenburg ob der Tauber** (every 2 hrs, 4–5 hrs, 3–4 changes), **Munich** (hourly, 5 hrs, 2 changes), **Berlin** (hourly, 5.5–6.5 hrs, 1–3 changes), **Amsterdam** (6/day, 5 hrs, 2 changes).

Route Tips for Drivers

This area is a logical first (or last) stop in Germany. If you're using Frankfurt Airport, here are some tips.

Frankfurt Airport to the Rhine: Driving from Frankfurt to the Rhine or Mosel takes 90 minutes (follow blue autobahn signs from airport, major cities are signposted).

The Rhine to Frankfurt: From St. Goar or Bacharach, follow the river to Bingen, then autobahn signs to *Mainz,* then *Frankfurt.* From there, head for the airport *(Flughafen)* or downtown (signs to *Messe,* then *Hauptbahnhof,* to find the parking under Frankfurt's main train station—see "Arrival in Frankfurt—By Car," page 268).

St. Goar

St. Goar is a classic Rhine town. Its hulk of a castle overlooks a half-timbered shopping street and leafy riverside park, busy with sightseeing ships and contented strollers. Rheinfels Castle, once the mightiest on the Rhine, is the single best Rhineland ruin to explore. From the riverboat docks, the main drag—a dull pedestrian mall without history—cuts through town before ending at the road up to the castle.

While the town of St. Goar itself isn't much more than a few hotels and restaurants—and is less interesting than Bacharach—it still makes a good base for hiking or biking the region. A tiny car ferry will shuttle you back and forth across the busy Rhine from here. (One of my favorite pastimes in St. Goar is chatting with friendly Heike at the K-D boat kiosk.) For train connections, see Bacharach's "Transportation Connections."

ORIENTATION

Tourist Information

The helpful St. Goar TI, which books rooms and stores bags for free, is on the pedestrian street, three blocks from the K-D boat dock and train station (May–Sept Mon–Fri 9:00–12:30 & 13:30–18:00, Sat 10:00–12:00, closed Sun; April and Oct Mon–Fri until 17:00, closed Sat–Sun; Nov–March Mon–Thu until 17:00, Fri 9:00–14:00, closed Sat–Sun; from train station, go downhill around church and turn left, Heerstrasse 86, tel. 06741/383, www.st-goar.de).

Helpful Hints

Picnics: St. Goar's waterfront park is hungry for a picnic. You can buy picnic fixings at the tiny **St. Goarer Stadtladen** grocery store on the pedestrian street (Mon–Fri 8:00–18:00, Sat 8:00–13:00, closed Sun, Heerstrasse 106).

Shopping: The helpful Montag family runs two shops (one specializes in steins and the other in cuckoo clocks) and a hotel, all at the base of the castle hill road. The stein shop under the hotel has Rhine guides, fine steins, and copies of this year's *Rick Steves' Germany* guidebook (April–Oct daily 8:30–18:00). Both shops offer 10 percent off any of their souvenirs (including Hummels) for travelers with this book (€5 minimum purchase). On-the-spot VAT refunds cover about half of your shipping costs (if you're not shipping, they'll give you a VAT form to claim your refund at airport). Another good souvenir shop is across from the K-D boat dock.

Internet Access: Hotel Montag offers very expensive coin-op access (€7.50/hr, 6 terminals, Heerstrasse 128, tel. 06741/1629). If you're headed to nearby Bacharach, Internet is cheaper there (see page 302).

Bike Rental: Goarbike, run by Herr Langhans, is five doors from the train station (€6/6 hrs, €11.50/day, April–Oct Mon–Fri 9:00–13:00 & 18:00–20:00, Sat–Sun 9:00–20:00, go right as you exit station, tel. 06741/1735).

Parking: There's a free lot at the downstream end of town.

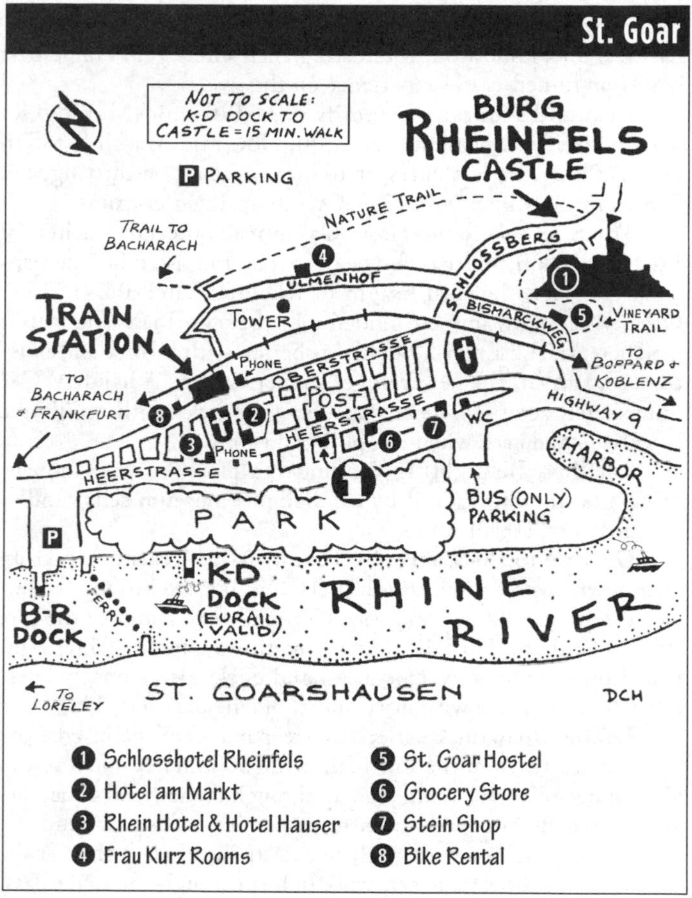

SIGHTS

Rheinfels Castle

Sitting like a dead pit bull above St. Goar, this mightiest of Rhine castles rumbles with ghosts from its hard-fought past. Burg Rheinfels *was* huge—once the biggest castle on the Rhine (built in 1245). It withstood a siege of 28,000 French troops in 1692. But in 1797, the French Revolutionary army destroyed it. For years, the castle was used as a source of building stone, and

today—while still mighty—it's only a small fraction of its original size. This hollow but interesting shell offers your single best hands-on ruined-castle experience on the river.

Cost and Hours: €4, family card-€10; mid-March–Oct daily 9:00–18:00, last entry at 17:00; Nov–mid-March Sat–Sun only 11:00–17:00, last entry at 16:00—weather permitting; tel. 06741/7753, in winter 06741/383, www.burg-rheinfels.com.

Tours and Information: Call in advance or gather 10 English-speaking tourists and beg to get an English tour—perhaps from Günther, the "last knight of Rheinfels" (tel. 06741/7753). Otherwise, follow my self-guided tour (below). The castle map is mediocre; the €2 English booklet is better, with history and illustrations. If it's damp, be careful of slippery stones. A handy WC is immediately across from the ticket booth (check out the guillotine urinals—stand back when you pull to flush).

Let There Be Light: If planning to explore the mine tunnels, bring a flashlight, or do it by candlelight (museum sells candles with matches, €0.50).

Getting to the Castle by Taxi or Mini-Train: A taxi up from town costs €5 (tel. 06741/7011). Or take the kitschy "tschu-tschu" tourist train (€2 one-way, €3 round-trip, 7 min to the top, April–Oct daily 10:00–17:00 but sometimes unpredictable, 2/hr, runs from square between station and dock, also stops by beer-stein shop, complete with lusty music, mobile 0171-496-3762).

Hiking Up to the Castle: Two steep but scenic paths take you up to the castle from the town (allow 15–20 minutes up). You can also simply follow the main road up through the railroad underpass at the top end of the pedestrian street, but it's not as much fun.

To take the **vineyard trail,** start at the beer-stein shop at the end of the pedestrian street, walk uphill through the underpass, make an immediate right on Bismarcksweg along the railroad tracks following the *Fussweg Burg Rheinfels* and yellow *Zur Burg* signs, pass the youth hostel, and then follow the yellow *Zur Burg* signs up the hill through the vineyard. The last couple hundred yards are along the road.

To take the **nature trail,** start at the St. Goar train station. Take the underpass under the tracks at the north end of the station, climb the steep stairs uphill, and turn right (following *Burg Rheinfels* signs) along the path just above the old city wall, which takes you to the castle in 10 minutes.

➲ **Self-Guided Tour:** Rather than wander aimlessly, visit the castle by following this tour: From the ticket gate, walk straight. Pass *Grosser Keller* on the left (where we'll end this tour) and walk through an internal gate past the *zu den gedeckten Wehrgängen* sign on the right (where we'll pass later) uphill to the museum (open 10:00–12:30 & 13:00–17:30, included in castle entry) in the only finished room of the castle. The museum is pleasant, with good English descriptions, but it's not as important as seeing the castle itself—skip the museum if you're short on time.

❶ **Museum and Castle Model:** The seven-foot-tall carved stone immediately inside the door (marked *Keltische Säule von Pfalzfeld*)—a tombstone from a nearby Celtic grave—is from 400 years before Christ. There were people here long before the Romans...and this castle. Find the old wooden library chair near the tombstone. If you smile sweetly, the man behind the desk may demonstrate—pull the chair's back forward and it becomes stairs for accessing the highest shelves.

The sweeping castle history exhibit in the center of the room is well-described in English. The massive fortification was the only Rhineland castle to withstand Louis XIV's assault during the 17th century. At the far end of the room is a model reconstruction of the castle (not the one with the toy soldiers) showing how much bigger it was before French Revolutionary troops destroyed it in the 18th century. Study this. Find where you are. (Hint: Look for the tall tower.) This was the living quarters of the original castle, which was only the smallest ring of buildings around the tiny central courtyard (13th century). The ramparts were added in the 14th century. By 1650, the fortress was largely complete. Ever since its destruction by the French in the late 18th century, it's had no military value. While no WWII bombs were wasted on this ruin, it served St. Goar as a stone quarry for generations. The basement of the museum shows the castle pharmacy and an exhibit of Rhine-region odds and ends, including tools and an 1830 loom. Don't miss the photos of ice-breaking on the Rhine. While once routine, ice-breaking hasn't been necessary here since 1963.

• *Exit the museum and walk 30 yards directly out, slightly uphill into the castle courtyard.*

❷ **Medieval Castle Courtyard:** Five hundred years ago, the entire castle circled this courtyard. The place was self-sufficient and ready for a siege, with a bakery, pharmacy, herb garden, brewery, well (top of yard), and livestock. During peacetime, 300–600 people lived here; during a siege, there would be as many as 4,000. The walls were plastered and painted white. Bits of the original 13th-century plaster survive.

• *Continue through the courtyard and out Erste Schildmauer, turn left into the next courtyard, and walk straight to the two old, wooden, upright posts. Find the pyramid of stone catapult balls on your left.*

St. Goar's Rheinfels Castle

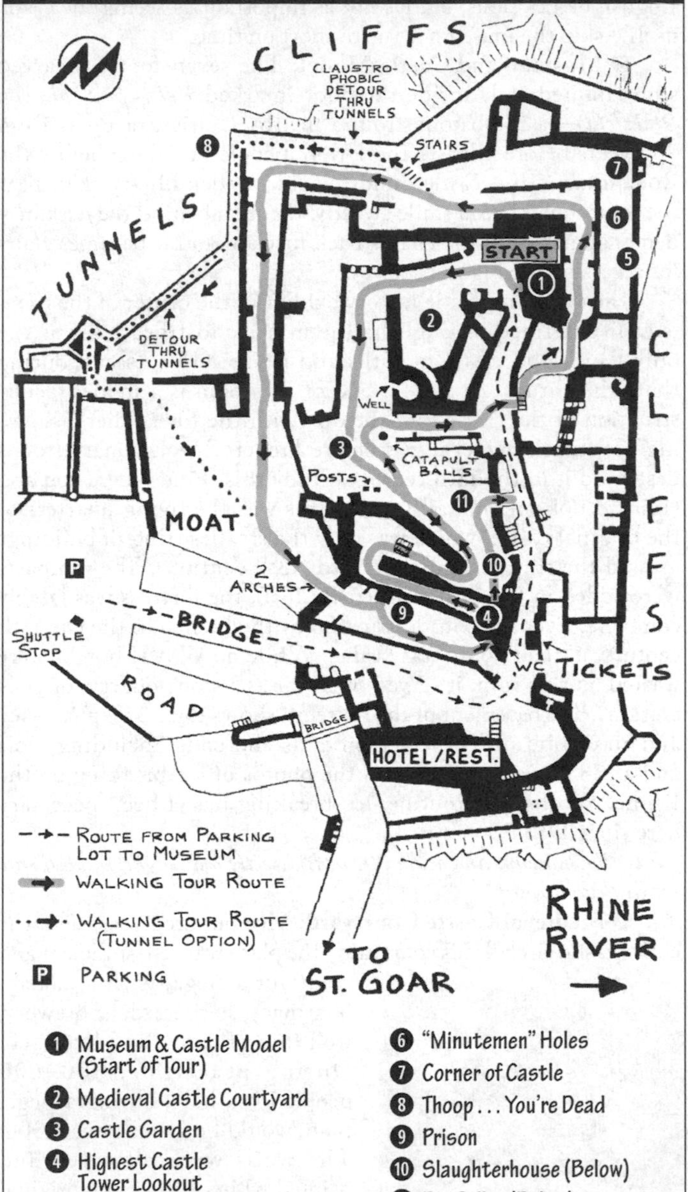

1. Museum & Castle Model (Start of Tour)
2. Medieval Castle Courtyard
3. Castle Garden
4. Highest Castle Tower Lookout
5. Covered Defense Galleries
6. "Minutemen" Holes
7. Corner of Castle
8. Thoop . . . You're Dead
9. Prison
10. Slaughterhouse (Below)
11. Big Cellar (Below)

❸ **Castle Garden:** Catapult balls like these were too expensive not to recycle—they'd be retrieved after any battle. Across from the balls is a well—essential for any castle during the age of sieges. Look in. Spit. The old posts are for the ceremonial baptizing of new members of the local trading league. While this guild goes back centuries, it's now a social club that fills this court with a huge wine party the third weekend of each September.

• *If weary, skip to #5; otherwise, climb the cobbled path up to the castle's best viewpoint—up where the German flag waves.*

❹ **Highest Castle Tower Lookout:** Enjoy a great view of the river, the castle, and the forest. Remember, the fortress once covered five times the land it does today. Notice how the other castles (across the river) don't poke above the top of the Rhine canyon. That would make them easy for invading armies to see.

• *Return to the catapult balls, walk down the road, go through the tunnel, veer left through the arch marked* zu den gedeckten Wehrgängen *("to the covered defense galleries"), go down two flights of stairs, and turn left into the dark, covered passageway. From here, we will begin a rectangular walk taking us completely around (counterclockwise) the perimeter of the castle.*

❺ & ❻ **Covered Defense Galleries with "Minutemen" Holes:** Soldiers—the castle's "minutemen"—had a short commute: defensive positions on the outside, home in the holes below on the left. Even though these living quarters were padded with straw, life was unpleasant. A peasant was lucky to live beyond age 45.

• *Continue straight through the dark gallery and to the corner of the castle, where you'll see a white painted arrow at eye level. Stand with your back to the arrow on the wall.*

❼ **Corner of Castle:** Look up. A three-story, half-timbered building originally rose beyond the highest stone fortification. The two stone tongues near the top just around the corner supported the toilet. (Insert your own joke here.) Turn around and face the wall. The crossbow slits below the white arrow were once steeper. The bigger hole on the riverside was for hot pitch.

• *Follow that white arrow along the outside to the next corner. Midway you'll pass stairs on the right leading down* zu den Minengängen *(sign on upper left). Adventurers with flashlights can detour here (see* *"Optional Detour—Into the Mine Tunnels," page 321**). You may come out around the next corner. Otherwise, stay with me, walking level to the corner. At the corner, turn left.*

❽ **Thoop...You're Dead:** Look ahead at the smartly placed crossbow slit. While you're lying there, notice the stonework. The little round holes were for scaffolds used as they built up. They indicate this stonework is original. Notice also the fine stonework on the chutes. More boiling pitch...now you're toast, too.

• *Continue along the castle wall around the corner. At the gray railing, look up the valley and uphill where the sprawling fort stretched. Below, just outside the wall, is land where attackers would gather. The mine tunnels are under there, waiting to blow up any attackers (see next page).*

Keep going along the perimeter, jog left, go down five steps and into an open field, and walk toward the wooden bridge. You may detour here into the passageway (on right) marked 13 Halsgraben. *The "old" wooden bridge is actually modern. Angle left through two arches (before the bridge) and through the rough entry to the* Verliess *(prison) on the left.*

❾ **Prison:** This is one of six dungeons. You just walked through an entrance prisoners only dreamed of 400 years ago. They came and went through the little square hole in the ceiling. The holes in the walls supported timbers that thoughtfully gave as many as 15 residents something to sit on to keep them out of the filthy slop that gathered on the floor. Twice a day, they were given bread and water. Some prisoners actually survived longer than two years in here. While the town could torture and execute, the castle had permission only to imprison criminals in these dungeons. Consider this: According to town records, the two men who spent the most time down here—2.5 years each—died within three weeks of regaining their freedom. Perhaps after a diet of bread and water, feasting on meat and wine was simply too much.

• *Continue through the next arch, under the white arrow, then turn left and walk 30 yards to the* Schlachthaus.

❿ **Slaughterhouse:** Any proper castle was prepared to survive a six-month siege. With 4,000 people, that's a lot of provisions. The cattle that lived within the walls were slaughtered in this room. The castle's mortar was congealed here (by packing all the organic waste from the kitchen into kegs and sealing it). Notice the drainage gutters. "Running water" came through from drains built into the walls (to keep the mortar dry and therefore strong... and less smelly).

• *Back outside, climb the modern stairs to the left. A skinny, dark passage (yes, that's the one) leads you into the...*

⓫ **Big Cellar:** This *Grosser Keller* was a big pantry. When the castle was smaller, this was the original moat—you can see the rough lower parts of the wall. The original floor was 13 feet deeper. The drawbridge rested upon the stone nubs on the left. When the castle expanded, the moat became this cellar. Halfway up the walls on the entrance side of the room, square holes mark spots where timbers made a storage loft, perhaps filled with grain. In the back, an arch leads to the wine cellar (sometimes blocked off) where finer wine was kept. Part of a soldier's pay was wine... table wine. This wine was kept in a single 180,000-liter stone barrel (that's 47,550 gallons), which generally lasted about 18 months.

The count owned the surrounding farmland. Farmers got to keep 20 percent of their production. Later, in more liberal feudal times, the nobility let them keep 40 percent. Today, the German government leaves the workers with 60 percent...and provides a few more services.

• *You're free. Climb out, turn right, and leave. For coffee on a terrace with a great view, visit Schlosshotel Rheinfels, opposite the entrance (WC at base of steps).*

Optional Detour—Into the Mine Tunnels: In about 1600, to protect their castle, the Rheinfellers cleverly booby-trapped the land just outside their walls by building tunnels topped with thin slate roofs and packed with explosives. By detonating the explosives when under attack, they could kill hundreds of invaders. In 1626, a handful of underground Protestant Germans blew 300 Catholic Spaniards to—they figured—hell. You're welcome to wander through a set of never-blown-up tunnels. But be warned: It's 600 feet long, assuming you make no wrong turns; it's pitch-dark, muddy, and claustrophobic, with confusing dead-ends; and you'll never get higher than a deep crouch. It cannot be done without a light (candles available at entrance). At stop #6 of the above tour, follow the stairs on the right leading down *zu den Minengängen* (sign on upper left).

The *Fuchsloch* sign welcomes you to the foxhole. Walk level (take no stairs) past the first steel railing (where you hope to emerge later) to the second steel railing. Climb down. The "highway" in this foxhole is three feet high. The ceiling may be painted with a white line indicating the correct path. Don't venture into the narrower side aisles. These were once filled with the gunpowder. After a small decline, take the second right. At the T-intersection, go right (uphill). After about 10 feet, go left. Take the next right and look for a light at the end of the tunnel. Head up a rocky incline under the narrowest part of the tunnel and you'll emerge at that first steel railing. The stairs on the right lead to freedom. Cross the field, walk under the bigger archway, and continue uphill toward the old wooden bridge. Angle left through two arches (before the bridge) and through the rough entry to the *Verliess* (prison) on the left. Rejoin the tour here at stop #9.

SLEEPING

(€1 = about $1.50, country code: 49, area code: 06741)
Parking in St. Goar is tight; ask at your hotel.

$$$ Schlosshotel Rheinfels ("Rheinfels Castle Hotel") is the town splurge. Part of the castle, but in a purpose-built new building, this luxurious 60-room place is good for those with money and a car (Db-€165–225 depending on river views and balconies, extra adult bed-€65, extra bed for kids ages 12–18-€45, extra bed for kids ages 7–11-€30, kids under age 7 free, elevator, non-smoking rooms,

Internet access, free Wi-Fi, indoor pool and sauna, dressy restaurant, free parking, Schlossberg 47, tel. 06741/8020, fax 06741/802-802, www.schloss-rheinfels.de, info@schloss-rheinfels.de).

$$ Hotel am Markt, well-run by Herr and Frau Velich, is rustic and a good deal, with all the modern comforts. It features a hint of antler with a pastel flair, 18 bright rooms, and a good restaurant. It's a good value and a stone's throw from the boat dock and train station (S-€40, Sb-€50, standard Db-€65, bigger riverview Db-€80, cheaper March–mid-April and Oct, closed Nov–Feb, Markt 1, tel. 06741/1689, fax 06741/1721, www.hotel-am-markt-sankt-goar.de, hotel.am.markt@gmx.de).

$$ Rhein Hotel, two doors away and run by the Velichs' energetic son Gil (a trained chef), has 10 rooms of similar quality and its own restaurant (Sb-€50, Db-€65–85, higher price is for Rhine-view rooms with balcony, non-smoking, free Wi-Fi at reception, closed mid-Nov–Feb, Heerstrasse 71, tel. 06741/981-240, fax 06741/981-267, www.rheinhotel-st-goar.de, info@rheinhotel-st-goar.de).

$ Hotel Hauser, across the square from Hotel am Markt, is another good deal, warmly run by another Frau Velich. Its 12 simple rooms sit over a fine restaurant (S-€22, D-€46, Db-€54, great Db with Rhine-view balconies-€58, these prices promised with this book and cash through 2009, cash preferred, à la carte half-pension-€14, expensive Wi-Fi in lounge, Heerstrasse 77, tel. 06741/333, fax 06741/1464, www.hotelhauser.de, hotelhauser@t-online.de).

$ Frau Kurz offers St. Goar's best B&B, renting three delightful rooms (sharing 2.5 bathrooms) with refrigerators, bathrobes, a breakfast terrace, garden, fine view, and homemade marmalade (S-€28, D-€48, 2-night minimum, cash only, non-smoking, free and easy parking, honor your reservation or call to cancel, Ulmenhof 11, tel. & fax 06741/459, www.gaestehaus-kurz.de, jeanette.kurz@superkabel.de). It's a memorably steep five-minute hike from the train station: Exit left from the station, take an immediate left at the yellow phone booth, pass under the tracks, go up the stairs, and follow the zigzag path, turning right through an archway onto Ulmenhof; #11 is just past tower.

$ St. Goar Hostel, the big beige building down the hill from the castle, rents 18 doubles and piles of beds in 4- to 10-bed dorms. It has a well-run, strong, institutional atmosphere with a 22:30 curfew (but you can borrow the key) and hearty €6 dinners (dorm beds-€15, D-€36, includes breakfast, non-members-€3.10 extra, non-smoking, expensive Wi-Fi, all ages welcome, open all day, Bismarckweg 17, tel. 06741/388, fax 06741/2869, st-goar@diejugendherbergen.de). It's a fairly level 10-minute walk from the train station: Veer left and go all the way down narrow, red-brick Oberstrasse, then turn left through the underpass and make an immediate right on Bismarcksweg, following the red *Jugendherberge* signs.

EATING

Hotel am Markt serves tasty traditional meals with plenty of game and fish (specialties include marinated roast beef and homemade cheesecake) at fair prices with good atmosphere and service (€9–16 main dishes, March–Oct daily 8:00–21:00, closed Nov–Feb, Markt 1, tel. 06741/1689).

Schlosshotel Rheinfels is your Rhine splurge, with an incredible view terrace in an elegant, dressy setting. As it's at the hilltop castle, you'll have to hike, taxi, or drive up (€18–21 main dishes, €36 three-course fixed-price meals, daily 12:00–14:00 & 18:30–21:00, call to reserve a window table, tel. 06741/8020; see also hotel listing). Their downstairs **Burgschänke** has no view, but is family-friendly and cheaper (€9–12 main dishes, Sun–Thu 11:00–18:00, Fri–Sat 11:00–21:00, tel. 06741/802-806).

Other Options: There are a couple of Italian places in town and plenty of ways to gather a picnic to enjoy on the riverside park. For more options, take the quick train to Bacharach, which leaves and returns hourly (last train at 22:00).

MOSEL VALLEY

Cochem • Burg Eltz • Beilstein • Zell

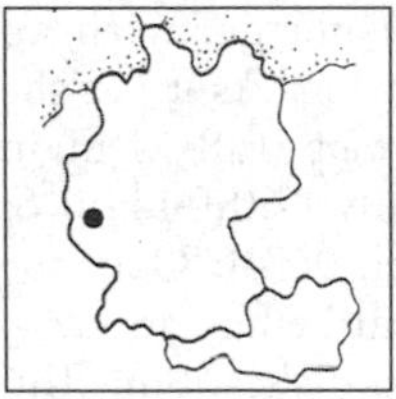

The misty Mosel is what some visitors hope the Rhine will be: peaceful, sleepy, romantic villages slipped between impossibly steep vineyards and the river; fine wine; a sprinkling of castles (Burg Eltz is tops); and lots of friendly small pensions. Boat, train, and car traffic here is a trickle compared to the roaring Rhine. While the swan-speckled Mosel moseys 300 miles from France's Vosges mountain range to Koblenz (where it dumps into the Rhine), the most scenic piece of the valley lies between the towns of Bernkastel-Kues and Cochem. I'd savor only this section. Cochem and Trier (see next chapter) are easy day trips from each other (1 hour by train, 55 miles by car). Cochem is the handiest home base, unless you have a car and want the peace of Beilstein. Zell is yet another home-base alternative (also better with a car).

Throughout the region on summer weekends and during the fall harvest, wine festivals with oompah bands, dancing, and colorful costumes are powered by good food and wine. You'll find a wine festival in some nearby village any weekend, June through September. The tourist season lasts from April through October. Things close down tight through the winter.

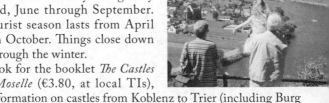

Look for the booklet *The Castles of the Moselle* (€3.80, at local TIs), with information on castles from Koblenz to Trier (including Burg Eltz, Cochem, and Metternich in Beilstein). The booklet not only has historical and structural information, but also some drawings of what the now-ruined castles looked like originally.

Getting Around the Mosel Valley

By Train and Bus: Fast trains zip you between Koblenz, Cochem, Bullay, and Trier in a snap. Other destinations require changing to a slow train or bus. Zell is a 10-minute bus ride from Bullay; Beilstein is a 20-minute ride on bus #716 from Cochem (Mon–Fri about hourly, no buses after 18:30, Sat–Sun 3–4/day, €3). Burg Eltz is a scenic 90-minute hike from the tiny Moselkern train station (see page 334). For bus times, pick up printed schedules at train stations and TIs, or check the regional transit website (http://vrminfo.de) or Germany's train timetable (http://bahn.hafas.de/bin/query.exe/en).

By Boat: The Kolb Line has the most frequent departures and allows you to cruise the most scenic stretch of the Mosel between Cochem, Beilstein, and Zell (tel. 02673/1515, www.moselfahrplan.de). A simple and fun outing is the one-hour cruise between **Cochem** and **Beilstein,** passing through the Fankel lock (4–5/day in each direction May–Oct, no boats off-season, first departure from Cochem about 10:30, last departure from Beilstein about 17:30, €10 one-way, €12 round-trip). You can also sail between **Zell** and **Beilstein** (2 hrs) or **Cochem** (3 hrs), but check the schedules in advance—these boats don't run as often, so you may need to take the bus or train one way if planning a round-trip (1–2/day May–Oct, but none on Fri and Mon May–June; Zell–Beilstein: €12 one-way, €17 round-trip; Zell–Cochem: €15 one-way, €22 round-trip). Another option is the boat in the other direction (downstream) from **Cochem** to **Treis-Karden** (mid-July–Aug 3/day, May–mid-July and Sept–Oct Wed and Sat–Sun only, 45 min, €8 one-way, €10 round-trip). From Treis-Karden, you can get to Burg Eltz via a long hike (2 hours, steep in places), train-and-hike combination, or a taxi ride, but it's much easier to reach Burg Eltz from the Moselkern train station (see page 334). Kolb also runs one-hour **sightseeing cruises** and two-hour **dancing cruises** from Cochem (€9 sightseeing cruises 5/day April–Oct; €15 dancing cruises with live music mid-July–Aug daily at 20:15, May–mid-July and Sept–Oct Tue and Sat only).

The KD (Köln–Düsseldorfer) line sails the lower Mosel, between **Cochem** and **Koblenz,** but only once a day in each direction (€23.90 one-way, mid-June–Sept daily, May–mid-June Fri–Mon only, none in winter, Koblenz to Cochem 9:45–15:00, Cochem to Koblenz 15:40–20:00; free with a German railpass or any Eurailpass that covers Germany, but uses up a day of a flexipass; tel. in Cochem 02671/980-023, www.k-d.com).

In early to mid-June, the Mosel locks close for 10 days of annual maintenance, and none of the boats listed here run. With all the locks, Mosel cruises feel more like a canal-boat ride than the cruises on the mighty Rhine.

Mosel Valley

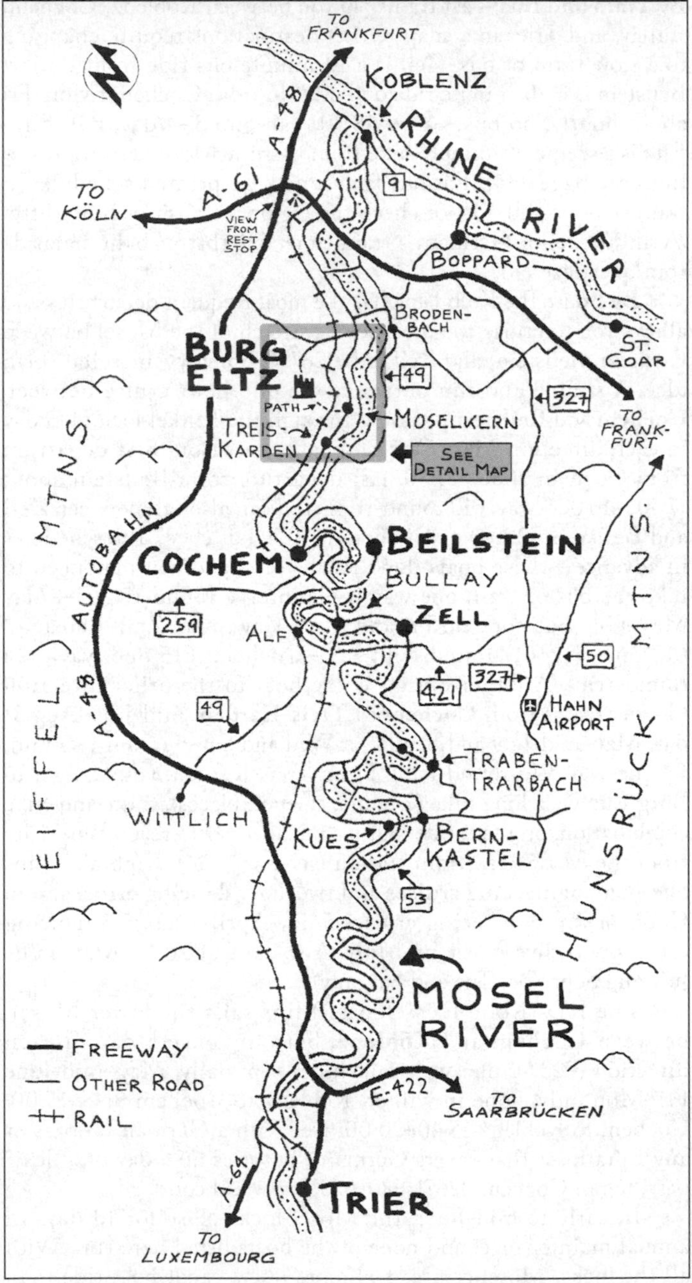

By Car: The easygoing Mosel Wine Route turns anyone into a relaxed Sunday driver. Pick up a local map at a TI or service station. Two-lane roads run along both riverbanks. While riverside roads are a delight, the river valley is very windy. Shortcuts overland can "cut the corners" and save you serious time—especially between Burg Eltz and Beilstein (see "Getting to Burg Eltz," page 334) and if you're driving between the Mosel and the Rhine (note the Brodenbach–Boppard shortcut). Koblenz and Trier have car-rental agencies.

By Bike: Biking along the Mosel is the rage among Germans. You can rent bikes in most Mosel towns (see listings for Cochem, Beilstein, and Zell in this chapter). A fine bike path follows the river (with some bits still sharing the road with cars) from Koblenz to Zell. From Cochem, allow an hour to Beilstein and 2.5 hours for the full trip to Zell, and about 10 minutes from Bullay to Zell. Many pedal one-way and relax on a return cruise or train ride.

By Ferry: About a dozen car-and-passenger ferries *(Fähre)* cross the Mosel between Koblenz and Trier. These are marked *AF* for auto and *PF* for pedestrian on the *Moselle Wine Road/Mosellauf* brochure.

By Air: The confusingly named Frankfurt Hahn Airport, a popular hub for low-fare airlines such as Ryanair, is actually near the Mosel (www.hahn-airport.de). Buses (2–4/day) run from the airport to Zell and Bullay for €6.20, or you can use the subsidized taxi service (Cochem to airport-€9.50/person, arrange 24 hours in advance, www.vuag.de/airporthahn or www.5c5.de, email them at fax@5c5.de).

Cochem

With a majestic castle and picturesque medieval streets, Cochem is the hub of the middle Mosel. With 6,000 inhabitants, it's a larger, more bustling town than Beilstein, Zell, Bacharach, or St.

Goar. Duck into a damp wine cellar to sample the local white wine (*Weinprobe* means "wine-tasting"). Stroll pleasant paths along the idyllic riverbank, play life-size chess, or just grab a bench and watch Germany at play. River-cruise passengers clog the old town during the day, but evenings are peaceful.

ORIENTATION

(area code: 02671)

Tourist Information

The information-packed TI is by the bridge at the main bus stop. Most of the pamphlets (free map with town walk, town history flier) are kept behind the desk—ask. Their thorough 24-hour room listing in the window comes with a free phone connection. The TI also has information on special events, wine-tastings held by local vintners, public transportation to Burg Eltz, area hikes, and the informative €3 *Mosellauf* brochure or the cartoony €1 *Moselle Wine Road* map (May–Oct Mon–Fri 9:00–17:00, Sat 9:00–15:00, closed Sun; July–Oct also Sat until 17:00 and Sun 10:00–12:00; off-season closed weekends and at lunch; tel. 02671/60040, www.cochem.de).

Arrival in Cochem

By Train: Cochem's train station has no lockers, but you can leave your bags at the Taxi-Zentrale storefront (€1.50/day, daily 9:00–18:00, to the right as you exit the station at Bahnhofsvorplatz 3). Make a hard right out of the station and walk about 10 minutes along Ravenéstrasse to the TI and bus station (both on your left, before the bridge). To get to the main square (Markt) and colorful medieval town center, continue under the bridge (€0.30 WC), then angle right and follow Bernstrasse.

By Car: Drivers can park in the multi-story garage just up Endertstrasse from the bridge, or in a lot behind the train station (€1.50/day, reach it by circling around on Ravenéstrasse and Pinnerstrasse).

Helpful Hints

Internet Access: The very pleasant **Espresso I-O** cafe has two terminals (€1/15 min, €3.50/hr, also has Wi-Fi, Mon–Fri 7:00–18:00, Sat 10:00–18:00, Sun 13:00–18:00, between TI and train station at Ravenéstrasse 18–20). After 18:00, head for the **Log-In Netzwerk Café** at Brückenstrasse 4, just before the railroad underpass (€4/hr, daily 10:00–24:00, ages 16 and over only).

Bike Rental: The **K-D boat kiosk** at the dock rents bikes (€8/24 hrs, May–Oct daily 10:00–18:00, closed Nov–April, small selection, tel. 02671/980-023). **Radsport Schrauth,** between the station and TI, is run by serious cyclists, with a good selection and helpful service (€5/half-day, €7/day, €10/day for mountain bikes, Mon–Fri 9:30–18:00, Sat 9:00–13:00, Sun only May–Oct 10:00–12:00, arrange weekend drop-off time, leave driver's license for deposit, Ravenéstrasse 20, tel. 02671/7974). Consider taking a bike on the boat or train and riding back.

Festival: Cochem's biggest wine festival is held the last weekend in August (Aug 27–31 in 2009). High season for wine aficionados lasts from August through October.

SIGHTS AND ACTIVITIES

Cochem Castle (Reichsburg Cochem)—This pretty, pointy castle on a hill above town is the work of overly imaginative 19th-century restorers. It can only be visited on a tour (€4.50; follow one of the frequent 40-min German tours while reading English explanation sheets, or gather 12 English speakers and call a day ahead to schedule an English tour; mid-March–mid-Nov daily from 9:00, last tour at 17:00, closed off-season, tel. 02671/255, www.reichsburg-cochem.de). Below the entrance, the resident falconer frequently shows off his flock; check the notice at the gate to see if the birds are in fine feather (€3.50, 40-min show, Tue–Sun at 11:00, 13:00, 14:30, and 16:00, no shows Mon, look for *Falknerei* sign).

Getting There: From the old town's main square (Markt), the castle is a very scenic 25-minute walk up a mostly gentle slope: Look for the red "A" hanging over Herrenstrasse and head down it until it veers left to meet Burgfrieden Street, marked by the helpful man pointing to the castle; from there, the path is easy to follow. If you've already *probed* a little *Wein* and would rather ride up, consider the shuttle bus that runs from the bus station (next to the TI) to the castle—but you still have to walk the last 10 minutes uphill (€2 one-way, 1–3/hr, May–Oct only, first bus up 10:30, last bus down 17:48, look for *Reichsburg Shuttle-Bus* sign at bus station).

Chairlift and Hikes—For great views, you could ride the *Sesselbahn* chairlift, which ascends the hill on the opposite side of town from the castle (€4.30 one-way, €5.80 round trip, mid-March–mid-Nov 10:00–18:00, closed off-season, tel. 02671/989-065, www.cochemer-sesselbahn.de). You can scramble up the narrow path under the lift for 20 minutes of heart-pounding, aerobic excitement. Or take the trail up to the same point from behind the train station (find trailhead behind station parking lot). For the best of all worlds, ride the lift up, take in the view from the restaurant, then follow the path to the station *(Bahnhof)*, down through the forest and then the vineyards to a wine-tasting at Weingut Rademacher.

Wine-Tasting—At **Weingut Rademacher,** behind the train station, you can taste four local wines for €2.90. There's no charge for tasting if you buy at least three bottles or are staying in their rooms (normally open Mon–Sat 9:00–20:00, Sun 9:00–13:00, different hours during festivals, call ahead to confirm, tel. 02671/4164, www.weingut-rademacher.de; see "Sleeping," for directions). Other wine cellars in town also offer tastings. For a unique treat, look for the Roter-Weinbergs-Pfirsich Likör—a local cordial made from the small, tart "red peaches" that are unique to the Mosel Valley.

Swimming, Tennis, and Golf—Cochem's Moselbad and Freizeit Zentrum offers an array of family-friendly activities: an indoor wave pool, an outdoor pool, a sauna, tennis courts, and mini-golf. The downside: It's 30 minutes on foot from the center of town (indoor pool-€7.70/3 hrs, Tue–Fri 10:00–22:00, Sat–Sun 10:00–19:00, closed Mon; other activities have different hours and prices; 10 min beyond youth hostel at Moritzburger Strasse 1, tel. 02671/97990, www.moselbad.de).

Cruise—The Kolb Line offers one-hour sightseeing cruises and schmaltzy two-hour "Tanz Party" dancing cruises with live music (see "Getting Around the Mosel Valley," page 325).

Sightseeing Train—A little yellow **tourist train** leaves from under the bridge at the TI and does a 25-minute sightseeing loop through town. Since the commentary is only in German (ask for English flier), and Cochem is such a pedestrian-friendly town anyway, this is worth it only if you're bored and lazy (€4.70, includes a glass of wine, 1–2/hr, Easter–Oct daily 10:00–17:00, doesn't run Nov–Easter).

SLEEPING

(area code: 02671)

Cochem is a good base for train travelers. Weingut Rademacher is a five-minute walk from the train station; all the other listings are within a 10- to 15-minute walk. August is very tight, with various festivals and generally inflated prices. Cochem has no launderette.

$$$ Hotel Lohspeicher, an upscale-rustic hotel just off the main square on a street with tiny steps, is for those willing to pay a bit extra for quality lodgings in the thick of things. Its nine high-ceilinged rooms have modern comforts (Sb-€60, Db-€90–114, includes big breakfast in a fine stone-and-timber room, elevator, Wi-Fi, fancy restaurant, parking-€5/day, closed Feb, Obergasse 1, tel. 02671/3976, fax 02671/1772, www.lohspeicher.de, service@lohspeicher.de, Ingo).

$$$ Hotel am Hafen, across the bridge from the TI, offers views over the river to Cochem amidst a mellow atmosphere. Some of the 20 rooms have balconies (Sb-€70–85, Db-€85, slightly nicer

Sleep Code

(€1 = about $1.50, country code: 49)
S = Single, **D** = Double/Twin, **T** = Triple, **Q** = Quad, **b** = bathroom, **s** = shower only. Unless otherwise noted, credit cards are accepted, English is spoken, and breakfast is included.

To help you sort easily through these listings, I've divided the rooms into three categories based on the price for a standard double room with bath:

$$$ Higher Priced—Most rooms €75 or more.
$$ Moderately Priced—Most rooms between €50–75.
$ Lower Priced—Most rooms €50 or less.

Db-€108, deluxe Db-€120, €10 less Nov–June or for 2 nights, free Internet access, Uferstrasse 3, tel. 02671/97720, fax 02671/977-227, www.hotel-am-hafen.de, hotel-am-hafen.cochem@t-online.de).

$$ Weingut Rademacher rents six beautiful ground-floor rooms, which share a TV room with a fridge and microwave. Wedged between vineyards and train tracks, with a pleasant garden, it's a great value. Charming hostess Andrea and her husband Hermann own the vineyards behind the house and will happily show you the wine cellar after breakfast (Sb-€30, Db on train side-€48, Db on vineyard side-€54, cheaper for 3 nights, family deals, non-smoking, free parking; exit station at rear and walk diagonally across the municipal parking lot to Pinnerstrasse 10—see map on website; tel. 02671/4164, fax 02671/91341, www.weingut-rademacher.de, webmaster@weingut-rademacher.de). This place also offers wine-tastings to guests and non-guests alike (described previously in "Sights and Activities").

$ Haus Andreas has 10 clean rooms at fair prices in the old town (Sb-€25–30, Db-€38–42, Tb-€57–63, prices vary by length of stay, cash only, free parking, Schlossstrasse 9, reception is often across the street in shop at #16, tel. 02671/1370 or 02671/5155, fax 02671/1370, best to reserve by fax, kind Frau Pellny speaks a little English). From the main square, take Herrenstrasse (go straight if coming from the station); after a block, angle right up the steep hill on Schlossstrasse.

$ Gasthaus zum Fröhlichen Weinberg, also in the old town, is a relaxed jumble of nine inexpensive rooms, some with low ceilings and tiny bathrooms. Frau Wolf presides and runs a small café on the side (Sb-€23, Db-€45, ask about family rooms, lower prices for longer stays, cash only, lots of stairs, Schlaufstrasse 11, tel. 02671/4193, fax 02671/917-559). From the main square, go up Oberbachstrasse and then go left up tiny Schlaufstrasse.

$ ***Hostel:*** Cochem's hostel is a huge, family-friendly complex just across the river from the train station, with 146 beds, picnic tables, grill pit, playground, game room, bar, restaurant, and a sundeck over the Mosel (dorm bed-€18, Db-€48, €3 more for non-members, includes sheets and breakfast, half- and full-board options available, fills up—reserve in advance, Klottener Strasse 9, tel. 02671/8633, fax 02671/8568, www.diejugendherbergen.de, cochem@diejugendherbergen.de). From the train station, walk straight down to the river, turn left, and use the stairway to cross the modern bridge to the hostel.

EATING

Zum Stüffje, in the old town, is a traditional half-timbered *Weinstube* with €10–24 main dishes and €9 veggie options (Wed–Mon 11:30–14:00 & 17:30–21:00, closed Tue, Oberbachstrasse 14, enter on side street, tel. 02671/7260).

Gaststätte Noss is one of several restaurants along the riverside promenade. It's open later than most and supplies meat from its own butcher shop—a plus in Germany. Don't confuse it with the hotel of the same name (€10–15 entrées; June–Oct daily 10:00–22:00; Nov–May Fri–Wed 10:00–15:00 & 17:30–22:00, closed Thu; Moselpromenade 4, tel. 02671/7067).

Alte Gutschänke, better known as "Arthur's place," is where locals go for a glass of wine in a cozy cellar. Seating is at long, wooden, get-to-know-your-neighbor tables (extensive wine list and basic pub food, Easter–Oct Tue–Fri from 18:00, Sat–Sun from 14:00, closed Mon and in winter, just uphill from the old town's Markt square at Schlossstrasse 6, tel. 02671/8950).

Picnics: The **Diewald supermarket** is at Ravenéstrasse 33, between the train station and TI; enter from the side lane (Mon–Fri 7:00–18:30, Sat 8:00–16:00, closed Sun).

TRANSPORTATION CONNECTIONS

From Cochem by Train to: Bullay (where you catch the bus to Zell; 2/hr, 10 min), **Moselkern** (for hike to Burg Eltz; hourly, 20 min), **Trier** (2/hr, 1 hr), **Frankfurt** and **Frankfurt Airport** (hourly, 2.25–3 hrs, most change in Koblenz), **Köln** (hourly, 1.75 hrs, most with transfer in Koblenz), **Bacharach** (hourly, 1.5 hrs, change in Koblenz), **Rothenburg** (every 2 hrs, 5 hrs, 3 changes), **Berlin** (hourly, 6–7 hrs, 1–3 changes), **Paris** (hourly, 4–5 hrs, 1–2 changes). Train info: tel. 11861 (€0.60/min). Bus info: tel. 02671/8976.

Burg Eltz

My favorite castle in all of Europe—worth ▲▲▲—lurks in a mysterious forest. It's been left intact for 700 years and is furnished throughout as it was 500 years ago. Thanks to smart diplomacy and clever marriages, Burg Eltz was never destroyed. (It survived one five-year siege.) It's been in the Eltz family for 850 years. The scenic, 90-minute walk up the Elz Valley to the castle makes a great half-day outing if you're staying anywhere along the Mosel—and a fun day trip if you're staying on the Rhine.

Elz is the name of a stream that runs past the castle through a deep valley before emptying into the Mosel. The first record of a *Burg* (castle) on the Elz is from 1157. By 1472, the castle looked like it does today, with the homes of three big landlord families gathered around a tiny courtyard within one formidable fortification. Today, the excellent 45-minute tour winds you through two of those homes, while the third remains the fortified quarters of the Eltz family. The elderly countess of Eltz—whose family goes back 33 generations here (you'll see a photo of her family)—enjoys flowers. Each week for 40 years, she's had grand arrangements adorn the public castle rooms.

It was a comfortable castle for its day: 80 rooms made cozy by 40 fireplaces and wall-hanging tapestries. Its 20 toilets were automatically flushed by a rain drain. The delightful chapel is on a lower floor. Even though "no one should live above God," this chapel's placement was acceptable because it fills a bay window, which floods the delicate Gothic space with light. The three families met—working out common problems as if sharing a condo—in the large "conference room." A carved jester and a rose look down on the big table, reminding those who gathered that they were free to discuss anything ("fool's freedom"—jesters could say anything to the king), but nothing discussed could leave the room (the "rose of silence"). In the bedroom, have fun with the suggestive decor: the jousting relief carved into the canopy, and the fertile and phallic figures hiding in the lusty green wall paintings.

Near the exit, the **treasury** fills the four higgledy-piggledy floors of a cellar with the precious, eccentric, and historic mementos of this family that once helped elect the Holy Roman Emperor and, later, owned a sizable chunk of Croatia (Habsburg favors).

Cost, Hours, Information: €8 castle entry (includes guided tour—see below—and treasury, credit cards accepted), April–Oct daily from 9:30, last tour departs at 17:30, closed Nov–March. Pick up the free English descriptions at entry. Tel. 02672/950-500, www.burg-eltz.de, burg@eltz.org.

Tours: The only way to see the castle is with a 45-minute tour (included in entry price). Guides speak English and thoughtfully collect English-speakers into their own tours—well worth waiting for (30-minute wait at most; visit treasury in the meantime). In early spring and late fall, call ahead to see when an English tour is expected. In a pinch, you can also join a German tour (with helpful English fact sheets, €0.60).

Eating: The café serves soups and bratwurst-and-fries cuisine for €4–5 (April–Oct daily 9:30–17:30, cash only, no nearby ATM).

Getting to Burg Eltz

While the castle isn't served by public transportation, it's a pleasant walk from the nearest train station. The 90-minute walk along the footpath to Burg Eltz from the little village of Moselkern is not difficult, and it's the most fun and scenic way to visit the castle. If the weather is poor or you'd prefer not to walk, take a taxi. Cars (and taxis) park in a lot near, but not quite at, Burg Eltz. From the lot, hike 10 minutes downhill to the castle or wait (10 minutes at most) for the red castle shuttle bus (€1.50 each way).

Hiking from Moselkern

The hike between Moselkern train station and Burg Eltz runs through a magical pine forest, where sparrows carry crossbows, and maidens, disguised as falling leaves, whisper "watch out." You can do the hike in 70 minutes at a steady clip, but allow 90 minutes to enjoy the scenery. A few uneven parts are slippery when wet, and a steep flight of stairs leads up to the castle at the end, but the trail is mostly gentle, and the rise from the river to the castle is less than 400 feet.

To start the hike, take the slow milk-run train (hourly) to Moselkern from Cochem (20 min, €3.70) or Koblenz (30 min). The Moselkern train station is unstaffed, and has no lockers, phones, or taxis. The path up to the castle begins at the other end of Moselkern village. To reach this path, turn right from the station along Oberstrasse. Cross the intersection with Weinbergsstrasse and continue straight along narrow Oberstrasse, passing the village church on your right after about five minutes. Keep going straight a few

Burg Eltz Area

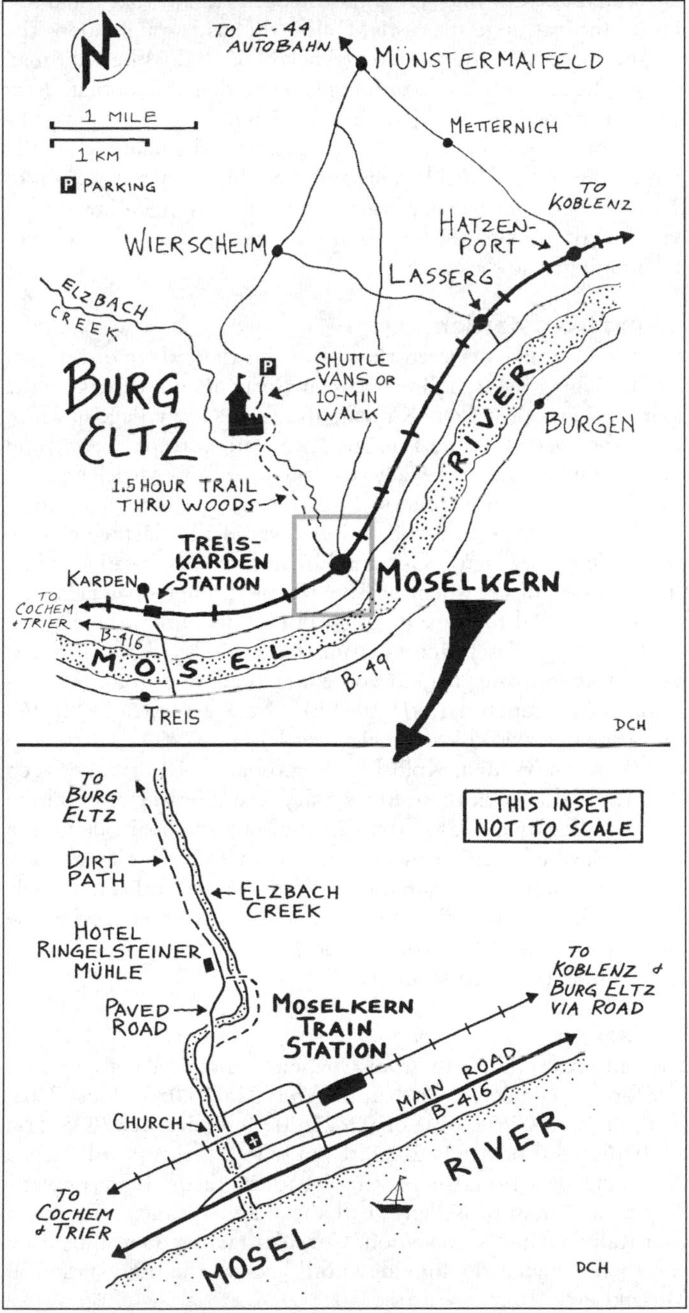
TO E-44 AUTOBAHN
MÜNSTERMAIFELD
1 MILE
1 KM
P PARKING
METTERNICH
TO KOBLENZ
HATZEN-PORT
WIERSCHEIM
LASSERG
ELZBACH CREEK
SHUTTLE VANS OR 10-MIN WALK
BURG ELTZ
RIVER
BURGEN
1.5 HOUR TRAIL THRU WOODS
TREIS-KARDEN STATION
KARDEN
MOSELKERN
TO COCHEM & TRIER
B-416
MOSEL
B-49
TREIS
DCH
TO BURG ELTZ
DIRT PATH
ELZBACH CREEK
THIS INSET NOT TO SCALE
HOTEL RINGELSTEINER MÜHLE
TO KOBLENZ & BURG ELTZ VIA ROAD
PAVED ROAD
MOSELKERN TRAIN STATION
MAIN ROAD
B-416
CHURCH
RIVER
TO COCHEM & TRIER
MOSEL
DCH

houses past the church; then, as the street ends, turn right through the underpass. On your left is the Elzbach stream that you'll follow all the way up to the castle. Follow the road straight along the stream through a mostly residential neighborhood. Where the road crosses the stream on a stone bridge, take either the footpath (stay right) or the bridge—they join up again later.

About 30 minutes from the train station, the road ends at the parking lot of the Hotel Ringelsteiner Mühle. Stay to the right of the hotel and continue upstream along the easy-to-follow trail—which starts out paved but soon changes to dirt—for another 45–60 minutes to the castle.

Hiking from Karden

You can also hike between the castle and the village of Karden, which is along the train line between Cochem and Moselkern (its train station, called Treis-Karden, also serves the village of Treis, across the river). This hike is longer (two hours), steep in places, and harder to follow and less shady than the hike from Moselkern.

The path from Karden to Burg Eltz starts at the far end of Karden village, beyond the white-towered St. Castor's church (follow *Burg Eltz* signs). Get a trail map (available locally) and be prepared for full sun when the hike travels through open fields.

If you need to **store luggage** during the hike, the elegant Schloss-Hotel Petry, across from the Treis-Karden station, is happy to guard your bags if you eat at their restaurant (€10–22 main dishes, lunch daily 11:30–14:15, St. Castorstrasse 80, tel. 02672/9340, www.schloss-hotel-petry.de).

Boats to Karden: Kolb Line riverboat cruises run between Cochem and Karden three times a day (see "Getting Around the Mosel Valley," page 325). You can combine the boat ride with a visit to Burg Eltz, either by hiking directly from Karden to Burg Eltz, continuing on by train (hourly) from Treis-Karden to Moselkern and hiking from there, or taking a taxi from Karden to the castle (see below). If you come by boat, make sure to disembark in Karden (not Treis, across the river).

By Taxi

You can taxi to the castle from **Cochem** (30 min, about €40 one-way for up to 4 people, Cochem taxi tel. 02671/8080), **Moselkern** (€20, taxi tel. 02672/1407 or 02625/2022), or **Karden** (€25, taxi tel. 02672/1407 or 02625/2022). Even with a taxi, you still have a 10-minute walk from the parking lot to the castle. If you're planning to taxi from Moselkern, call ahead and ask the taxi to meet your train at Moselkern station. Consider taxiing up to Burg Eltz and then enjoying the hike downhill back to the train station in Moselkern.

By Car

From Koblenz, leave the river at Hatzenport, following the white *Burg Eltz* signs through the towns of Münstermaifeld and Wierschem. From Cochem, follow the *Münstermaifeld* signs from Moselkern. (Note that the *Eltz* signs at Moselkern lead to Hotel Ringelsteiner Mühle and the trailhead for the hour-long hike to the castle. To drive directly to the castle, ignore the *Eltz* signs until you reach Münstermaifeld.) The castle parking lot (€1.50/day, daily 9:00–18:30) is just over a mile past Wierschem.

Variation: If you're traveling by car but would enjoy the path up to the castle, you can drive to Moselkern, follow the *Burg Eltz* signs up the Elz Valley, park at the Hotel Ringelsteiner Mühle (€2, buy ticket from machine), and enjoy the 45–60-minute hike up to the castle from there (described above).

Shortcut to Beilstein or Zell: If driving from Burg Eltz to Beilstein or Zell, you'll save 30 minutes with this shortcut: Cross the river at Treis-Karden, go through town, and bear right at the swimming pool (direction: Bruttig–Fankel). This overland route deposits you in Bruttig, a scenic three-mile riverside drive from Beilstein (21 miles from Zell).

Beilstein

Just upstream from Cochem is the quaintest of all Mosel towns. Cozy Beilstein (BILE-shtine) is Cinderella-land—touristy but tranquil, except for its territorial swans. Beilstein has no food shop, one bus stop, one mailbox, and 180 residents who run about 30 guest houses and eateries.

Planning Your Time

Car travelers use Beilstein as a base, day-tripping from here to Cochem, Trier, Burg Eltz, and the Rhine. If you're staying in Cochem and using public transportation, you can day-trip to Beilstein: Take the bus to Beilstein, follow my self-guided walk up to the castle, have lunch, and then return by boat (take the boat both ways if you have more time).

Getting to Beilstein

Beilstein has no train station, but it's easy to reach from Cochem—either by **bus** (#716, hourly, no buses after 19:00 and only 3–4/day on weekends, 20 min, €2.90), by **taxi** (€25), or by **river cruise** (4–5/day in each direction May–Oct, no boats off-season, first departure from Cochem at about 10:30, last departure from Beilstein at about 17:30, €10 one-way, €12 round-trip). The best way to get between Zell and Beilstein is by riverboat (1–2/day May–Oct, 2 hrs, €12 one-way, €17 round-trip); by bus or train from Zell, you'll need to change at least twice (in Bullay, Cochem, and/or Ellenz Fähre). If **driving,** you can park for free in any space you find along the riverside road.

ORIENTATION

Beilstein has no TI, but there is an **information board** by the bus stop, and cafés and guest houses can give you town info.

Herr Nahlen rents **bikes** for pleasant riverside rides (€6/day, daily 9:00–12:00, return bikes between 16:00–19:00, reservations smart for groups, Bachstrasse 47, tel. 02673/1840).

SELF-GUIDED WALK

Welcome to Beilstein

Explore the narrow lanes, ancient wine cellar, resident swans, and ruined castle by following this short walk.

• *Stand where the village hits the river.*

Beilstein's Riverfront: In 1963, the big road and the Mosel locks were built, making the river peaceful today. Before then, access to Beilstein was limited to a tiny one-way lane and the small ferry. The cables that tether the ferry once allowed the motorless craft to go back and forth powered only by the current and an angled rudder. Today, it shuttles people (€1.30), bikes, and cars constantly (Easter–Oct daily 9:00–12:00 & 13:00–18:00, no ferries off-season). The campground across the river is typical of German campgrounds—80 percent of its customers set up their trailers and tents at Easter and use them as summer homes until October, when the regular floods chase them away for the winter. If you stood where you are now through the winter, you'd have cold water up to your crotch five times.

Look inland. The Earl of Beilstein—who ruled from his castle above town—built the Altes Zollhaus in 1634 to levy tolls from river traffic. Today, the castle is a ruin, the once-mighty monastery (see the big church high on the left) is down to one monk, and the town's economy is based only on wine and tourists.

Beilstein's tranquility is a result of Germany's WWI loss. This war cost Germany the region of Alsace (now part of France). Before World War I, the Koblenz–Trier train line—which connects

Alsace to Germany—was the busiest in the country. It tunnels through the grape-laden hill across the river in what was the longest train tunnel in Germany. The construction of a supplemental line destined to follow the riverbank (like the lines that crank up the volume on the Rhine) was stopped in 1914 and, since Alsace went to France in 1918, the plans were scuttled.

Follow Bachstrasse into town. You'll notice blue plaques on the left marking the high-water *(Hochwasser)* points of historic floods.

At the first corner, Fürst-Metternich-Strasse leads left to the monastery (to get there, climb stairs marked *Klostertreppe*). While its population is down to one Carmelite, Rome maintains a handsome but oversized-for-this-little-town Catholic church that runs a restaurant with a great view.

Bachstrasse ("Creek Street") continues straight through Beilstein, covering up the brook that once flowed through town providing a handy disposal service 24/7. Today, Bachstrasse is lined by wine cellars. The only way for a small local vintner to make any decent money these days is to sell his wine directly to customers in inviting little places like these.

• *Your first right leads to...*

Market Square (Marktplatz): For centuries, neighboring farmers sold their goods on Marktplatz. The *Zehnthaus* (tithe house) was the village IRS, where locals would pay one-tenth *(Zehnte)* of their produce to their landlord (either the Church or the earl). Pop into the Zehnthauskeller. Stuffed with peasants' offerings 400 years ago, it's now packed with vaulted medieval ambience. It's fun at night for candlelit wine-tasting, soup and cold cuts, and schmaltzy music (often live Fri and Sat). The Bürgerhaus (above the fountain) had nothing to do with medieval fast food. First the village church, then the *Bürger*'s (like a mayor) residence, today it's *the* place for a town party or wedding. Haus Lipmann (on the riverside, now a recommended hotel and restaurant—see "Sleeping") dates from 1727. It was built by the earl's family as a residence after the French destroyed his castle. Haus Lipmann's main dining hall was once the knights' hall.

• *The stepped lane leads uphill (past the Zehnthaus, follow signs for* Burgruine Metternich*) to...*

Beilstein's Castle: Beilstein once rivaled Cochem as the most powerful town on this part of the Mosel. Its castle (officially named Burg Metternich) is a sorry ruin today, but those who make the steep 10-minute climb are rewarded with a postcard Mosel view and a chance to hike even higher to the top of its lone surviving tower (€2.50, Easter–Oct daily 9:00–18:00, closed Nov–Easter, view café/restaurant, tel. 02673/93639, www.burgmetternich.de).

For more exercise and an even better view, exit through the turnstile at the rear of the castle and continue uphill 100 yards, where you'll find the ultimate "castle–river bend–carpets of vineyards" photo op. The derelict roadside vineyard is a sign of recent times—the younger generation is abandoning the family plots, opting out of all that hard winemaking work.

From this viewpoint, a surprising sight—a small but evocative Jewish cemetery *(Jüdische Friedhof)*—is 200 yards farther up the road. During the 700 years leading up to 1942, Beilstein hosted a Jewish community. As in the rest of Europe, wealthy Jews could buy citizenship and enjoy all the protections afforded to residents. These *Schutzjuden,* or "protected Jews," were shielded from the often crude and brutal "justice" of the Middle Ages. In 1840, 25 percent of Beilstein's 300 inhabitants were Jewish. But no payment could shield this community from Hitler—so there are no Jews in Beilstein today. (A small Jewish community in Koblenz maintains this lovely cemetery.)

To reach the viewpoint and the cemetery without going through the castle, continue up the road past the castle entrance, then follow the signs for *Jüdische Friedhof.*

• *From here, you can return to the castle gate, ring the bell* (Klingel), *and show your ticket to get back in and retrace your steps; or continue on the road, which curves and leads downhill (a gravel path at the next bend on the left leads back into town).*

SLEEPING

(€1 = about $1.50, country code: 49, area code: 02673)
Many of Beilstein's hotels shut down from mid-November through March.

$$$ Hotel Haus Lipmann is your chance to live in a medieval mansion with hot showers and TVs. A prizewinner for atmosphere, it's been in the Lipmann family for 200 years. The creaky wooden staircase and the elegant dining hall, with long wooden tables surrounded by antlers, chandeliers, and feudal weapons, will get you in the mood for your castle sightseeing, but the riverside terrace may mace your momentum. There are six guest rooms in the main building and six larger rooms in an equally old building next door (Sb-€75–90, Db-€85–100, Tb-€105–125, Qb-€125–150, price depends on length of stay and day of week, sometimes €20 higher Fri–Sat, cash only, €15 half-board deals, free Internet access and Wi-Fi, closed Nov–April, Marktplatz 3, tel. 02673/1573, fax 02673/1521, www.hotel-haus-lipmann.com, hotel.haus.lipmann@t-online.de). The entire family—Marion (née Lipmann) and her husband Jonas, their hardworking son David, and his wife Anja—hustle for their guests.

$$$ Hotel Lipmann Am Klosterberg, run by Marion's brother Joachim and his wife Malene, is a big, modern place with 17 comfortable rooms at the extremely quiet top of town (Sb-€50, Db-€75–90, closed mid-Nov–Easter, elevator, Auf dem Teich 8, up the main street 200 yards inland, tel. 02673/1850, fax 02673/1287, www.hotel-lipmann.de, lipmann@t-online.de).

$$$ Hotel Lipmann Altes Zollhaus, run by Joachim Lipmann's daughter Julia, packs all the comforts into eight tight, bright riverfront rooms (same prices and contact details as Hotel Lipmann Am Klosterberg; adjoining restaurant Alte Stadtmauer, run by daughter Christina, is open daily 11:00–23:00, closed mid-Nov–Easter).

$$ Hotel Gute Quelle offers half-timbers, a good restaurant (see "Eating"), and 13 inviting rooms, plus seven more in an annex across the street (Sb-€40, D-€60, Db-€64, less for longer stays, closed Dec–March, Wi-Fi, Marktplatz 34, tel. 02673/1437, fax 02673/1399, www.hotel-gute-quelle.de, info@hotel-gute-quelle.de, helpful Susan speaks Irish).

$ The welcoming **Gasthaus Winzerschenke an der Klostertreppe** is a great value, with five rooms right in the tiny heart of town at the bottom of the stairs to the cloister (Db-€50, bigger Db-€60, cash only, discount for 4-night stays, open weekends only Nov–Easter, free Internet access, go up main street and take second left onto Fürst-Metternich-Strasse, reception in restaurant, tel. 02673/1354, fax 02673/962-371, www.winzerschenke-beilstein.de, winzerschenke-beilstein@t-online.de, young and eager Stefanie and Christian Sausen).

EATING

You'll have no problem in Beilstein finding a characteristic dining room or a relaxing riverview terrace.

Restaurant Haus Lipmann serves good, fresh food with daily specials on a glorious, leafy riverside terrace (€8–19 entrées, May–Oct daily 10:00–23:00, closed Nov–April).

The **Zehnthauskeller** on the Marktplatz is *the* place for wine-tasting with soup, cold plates, and lively *Schlager* music (kitschy German folk-pop) while old locals on holiday sit under a dark medieval vault (Easter–Oct Tue–Sun 11:00–23:00, closed Mon and Nov–Easter, run by Joachim Lipmann's daughter Sabine).

The recommended **Hotel Gute Quelle** runs a popular restaurant (€10–20 entrées, daily 11:00–21:00, closed Dec–March, Marktplatz 34).

Zell

With a fine riverside promenade, a pedestrian bridge over the water, and plenty of *Zimmer,* Zell makes a decent overnight stop for car travelers. While the town lacks some of the charm of Cochem or Beilstein, Zell (pop. 4,700) has a long pedestrian zone filled with colorful shops, restaurants, and *Weinstuben* (wine bars). A fun oompah folk band plays on weekend evenings on the main square, making evenings here a delight.

Getting to Zell

Trains go every 30 minutes from Cochem or Trier to Bullay, from where the bus takes you to Zell (€2.25, Mon–Fri hourly, Sat–Sun every 2 hrs—check in advance, usually at :20 past the hour, 10 min; last bus at 20:20 Mon–Fri, at 19:20 Sat–Sun). In Zell, get off at the Lindenplatz stop, at the base of the pedestrian bridge.

ORIENTATION

Tourist Information

The TI is in the Rathaus at #44 on the pedestrianized Balduinstrasse, four blocks upriver from the pedestrian bridge and bus stop (turn inland by the fountain with the black-cat statue). A handy map of town is posted outside the door (Aug–Oct Mon–Fri 9:00–18:00, Sat 10:00–15:00, closed Sun except during festivals; Nov–March Mon–Thu 9:00–12:30 & 13:30–16:30, Fri 9:00–13:00, closed Sat–Sun; April Mon–Fri 9:00–17:00, closed Sat–Sun; May–July Mon–Fri 9:00–17:00, Sat 9:00–13:00, closed Sun; tel. 06542/96220, www.zellmosel.de).

Helpful Hints

Internet Access: Berliner Kaffekännchen/Brotkörbchen, a bakery and café next to the Lindenplatz bus stop at the base of the pedestrian bridge, has two Internet terminals (€1.50/15 min, €5/hr, Mon–Tue and Thu–Fri 8:00–18:30, Sat

8:00–18:00, Sun 14:00–18:00, closed Wed, Balduinstrasse 107, tel. 06542/5450).

Bike Rental: Gästehaus Mesenich rents bikes for €6/day (10–15-min walk from TI along Balduinstrasse in the direction of Bullay—street changes name to Schlossstrasse and then Corray, ring *Fahrradverleih* bell at Corray 33, tel. 06542/5769).

Views: For a village view, walk up to the medieval wall's gatehouse and through the cemetery to the old munitions tower.

SIGHTS

Mosel Museum—The little Wein und Heimatmuseum features Mosel history (open only May–Oct Wed and Sat 14:30–17:00, in same building as TI).

Winery Tour—Locals know Zell for its Schwarze Katze ("Black Cat") wine. Peter Weis, who runs the **F. J. Weis winery,** gives a clever, entertaining, and free tour of his 40,000-bottle-per-year wine cellar—usually daily at 17:00, but it's important to call ahead to reserve (open April–mid-Nov daily 10:30–18:00, usually closed at lunchtime, closed mid-Nov–March except with advance notice, he also rents apartments—see next page, tel. 06542/41398, mobile 0172-780-7153, www.weingut-fjweis.de, f.j.weis@t-online.de). Buy a bottle or two to keep this fine tour going. A blue flag marks his *Weinkeller* south of town, 200 yards past the bridge toward Bernkastel, riverside at Notenau 30.

SLEEPING

(€1 = about $1.50, country code: 49, area code: 06542)

Try sleeping in Zell if Cochem and Beilstein are booked up. Zell's hotels and pensions generally offer discounts to those staying more than one night. Most of these listings (except for Peter Weis' apartments) are near the TI on the main pedestrian drag.

$$$ Hotel zum Grünen Kranz, with 29 rooms, is the place if you're looking for room service, a sauna, a pool, and an elevator (Sb-€60, Db-€90–130, price depends on season and day of week, Balduinstrasse 13, tel. 06542/98610, fax 06542/986-180, www.zumgruenenkranz.de, info@zumgruenenkranz.de). They also have 10 immense rooms in the annex across the street (prices on request).

$$$ Hotel Weinhaus Mayer, run by English-speaking Ruth Mayer, has 26 rooms in two buildings near each other, both with Mosel views. Their shop sells wine from the family vineyards (Db-€88 in newer building at Balduinstrasse 5–7, Db-€72 in older building at Balduinstrasse 15, tel. 06542/61169, fax 06542/61160, www.hotel-weinhaus-mayer.de, info@hotel-weinhaus-mayer.de).

$$ Hotel Ratskeller runs a pizzeria and rents 13 sharp rooms with tile flooring and fair rates (Sb-€45, Db-€72, €10 cheaper Nov–mid-April, Balduinstrasse 36, tel. 06542/98620, fax 06542/986-244, www.hotel-ratskeller-zell.de, info@hotel-ratskeller-zell.de, Perrotta family).

$$ Peter Weis, of the F. J. Weis winery (recommended above), rents two luxurious apartments with kitchen facilities (Db-€60, less for 2 or more nights, extra person-€12, breakfast-€7, important to call in advance, a little outside the center—200 yards beyond bridge on Bernkastel road, riverside at Notenau 30, tel. 06542/41398, fax 06542/961-178, www.weingut-fjweis.de, f.j.weis@t-online.de).

$ Gasthaus Gertrud Thiesen is very comfortable and a great value, with a terrace and TV/living/breakfast room that overlook the Mosel. There are four big, bright rooms (D-€40, Db-€45, cash only, closed Nov–Feb, Balduinstrasse 1, tel. 06542/4453, reserve by phone, Frau Thiesen's husband speaks English).

TRIER

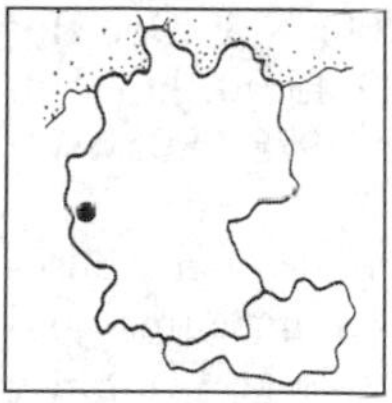

Germany's oldest city lies at the head of the scenic Mosel Valley, near the border with Luxembourg. An ancient Roman capital, Trier brags that it was inhabited by Celts for 1,300 years before Rome even existed. Today, Trier is thriving and feels very young. A short stop here offers you a look at Germany's oldest Christian church, one of its most enjoyable market squares, and its best Roman ruins.

Founded by Augustus in 16 B.C., Trier served as the Roman town Augusta Treverorum for 400 years. When Emperor Diocletian (who ruled A.D. 285–305) divided his overextended Roman Empire into four sectors, he made Trier the capital of the west: roughly modern-day Germany, France, Spain, and England. For most of the fourth century, this city of 80,000—with a four-mile wall, four great gates, and 47 round towers—was the favored residence of Roman emperors. Emperor Constantine used the town as the capital of his fading Western Roman Empire. Many of the Roman buildings were constructed under Constantine before he left for Constantinople. In 480, Trier fell to the Franks.

Today, Trier's Roman sights include the huge city gate (Porta Nigra), basilica, baths, and amphitheater. Trier's main draw is the chance to experience Germany's Roman and early Christian history. If you're more interested in wine-tasting and scenery, stay elsewhere on the Mosel River (see previous chapter).

ORIENTATION

(area code: 0651)

Tourist Information

Trier's cramped and busy TI is just through the Porta Nigra. The TI sells an easily readable map for €1.50, but cheapskates can squint at the free and sufficient small-print map. The TI also sells a useful little guide to the city called *Trier: History and Monuments* (€4) and hands out the *Holiday Region Trier* brochure (free, lists opening hours of Trier's sights, info on city tours, Mosel boat excursions, events, leisure activities, and more). Also consider the booklet *Walking Tours Through Trier* (€3), which has little information on sights but a great map and proposed walking routes (Roman, medieval, Jewish, rainy day). The TI also offers tours (see "Tours," next page) and a free room-booking service (May–Oct Mon–Thu 9:00–18:00, Fri–Sat 9:00–19:00, Sun 10:00–17:00; Nov–Dec and March–April Mon–Sat 9:00–18:00, Sun 10:00–15:00; Jan–Feb Mon–Sat 9:00–17:00, Sun 10:00–13:00; tel. 0651/978-080, www.trier.de).

Discount Deals: The **Trier Card** allows free use of city buses and roughly 25 percent discounts on city tours, museums, and Roman sights (€9, family-€15, valid for 3 days, sold at TI). Since the town is small and walkable, this is only a good deal if you'll be here for two or three days and plan to visit lots of sights. If you're visiting at least three Roman sights (including the Porta Nigra, Imperial Baths, Viehmarkt Baths, and amphitheater, but not the Archaeological Museum), buy the **Roman sights combo-ticket** instead (€6.20, family ticket-€14.80, each sight costs €2.10 individually or €5.10 for families—do the math and decide, available at participating sights).

Arrival in Trier

By Train: The *Reisezentrum* at the train station can answer your train-schedule questions and book tickets for you (Mon–Fri 6:50–19:15, Sat 8:30–17:15, Sun 10:30–18:15). The station also has lockers (€1.50–2.50), a WC (€0.50), and bike rental (see "Helpful Hints," next page). To reach the town center from the train station, walk 10 boring minutes and four blocks up Theodor-Heuss-Allee to the big black Roman gate (Porta Nigra), and turn left under the gate to find the TI. From here, the main pedestrian mall (Simeonstrasse) leads right to the sights: Market Square and the cathedral (a five-minute walk) and the basilica (five more minutes).

By Car: Drivers get off at Trier Verteilerkreis and follow signs to *Zentrum*. There's parking near the gate and TI.

Helpful Hints

Laundry: A well-maintained, self-service launderette is just beyond Karl Marx's House (€7.50/load, daily 8:00–22:00, instructions in English, Brückenstrasse 19).

Internet Access: Arcor/ITS-Trier, across the busy intersection from the Porta Nigra, charges a low hourly rate (€1.50/hr, Mon–Fri 9:00–22:00, Sat–Sun 12:00–22:00, US keyboards, Porta Nigra Platz 4).

Bike Rental: A local citizens' group called **Bürgerservice** rents bikes for reasonable daily rates. Find them just off track 11 at the train station (€9/24 hrs, €2 extra for mountain bikes, leave €30 and ID as deposit; mid-April–Oct daily 9:00–19:00; Nov–mid-April Mon–Fri 10:00–18:00, closed Sat–Sun; tel. 0651/148-856).

TOURS

Walking Tours—The TI offers a €7 two-hour walking tour in English on Saturdays at 13:30 (May–Oct only), and €80 private two-hour tours (tel. 0651/978-0821).

Bus Tours—For a live guide and a big, air-conditioned bus, take the one-hour tour offered by the TI (€7, May–Oct daily at 13:00 in English, at 11:00 and 12:00 in German, no tours Nov–April).

Tourist Train—If you're tired and want a city overview, consider riding the hokey little red-and-yellow tourist train, the Römer-Express, for its 35-minute loop of Trier's major old-town sights (€7, daily April–Oct 2/hr 10:00–18:00, daily March and Nov–Dec hourly 10:00–17:00, Jan–Feb may run Sat–Sun hourly 11:00–16:00—weather permitting, recorded narration in English, departs from TI, buy tickets from driver or at TI, tel. 0651/9935-9525, www.roemer-express.de).

SELF-GUIDED WALK

Welcome to Trier

This fun walk, offering a taste of Trier old, new, and in-between, will take you to the historic city's top sights.

• *Start at the...*

▲Porta Nigra

Roman Trier was built as a capital. Its architecture mirrored the grandeur of the empire. Of the four-mile town wall's four huge gates, only this northern gate survives. This is the most impressive Roman fortification in Germany, and it was built without mortar—only iron pegs hold the sandstone blocks together. While the other three gates were destroyed by medieval metal and stone scavengers, this "black gate" (originally red sandstone, but darkened by time) survived because it became a church. St. Simeon—a pious Greek recluse—lived inside the gate for seven years. After his death in 1035, the St. Simeon monastery was established, and the gate was made into a two-story church—lay church on the bottom, monastery church on top. Napoleon wanted everything non-Roman about the structure destroyed in 1803, but the 12th-century Romanesque apse—the round part at the east end—survived. You can climb around the gate, but there's little to see aside from a fine town view.

The entrance is through the adjacent City Museum (€2.10, €6 for both Porta Nigra and City Museum—described below, daily April–Sept 9:00–18:00, March and Oct 9:00–17:00, Nov–Feb 9:00–16:00, last entry 30 min before closing). As you go in, look for pictures of how the gate looked during various eras, including its church phase.

The arcaded courtyard and buildings of the monastery of St. Simeon remain, next to the Porta Nigra, and are now home to the TI and a slick new **City Museum** (Stadtmuseum Simeonstift). The museum's collection seems to be largely made up of anything old that turned up in townspeople's basements, and most of the items on display are only mildly interesting. However, the third level holds a fascinating model—painstakingly constructed over 19 years—of Trier as it looked in 1800, which might just make this museum worth the admission price (€5, includes audioguide, €6 combo-ticket with Porta Nigra, Tue–Sun 10:00–18:00, closed Mon, tel. 0651/718-1459, www.museum-trier.de).

• *Trier's main pedestrian drag, which leads away from the gate, is named for St. Simeon. As you walk to Market Square, you'll glimpse, about halfway down Simeonstrasse on your left at #19, the...*

House of the Three Magi (Dreikönigshaus)

Now a restaurant, this colorful Venetian-style building was constructed in the 13th century as a keep. Look for the floating door a story above the present-day entrance. A wooden staircase to this door was once the only way in or out. If the town was in danger, the staircase could be burned or torn down, in order to fend off enemies and protect inhabitants. (Look for another medieval keep with a floating door—the Frankenturm—just off Market Square, near the recommended hotel of the same name.)

• *Continue down the pedestrian street until you reach the...*

▲▲Market Square (Hauptmarkt)

Trier's Hauptmarkt is a people-filled swirl of fruit stands, flowers, painted facades, and fountains (with a handy public WC). This is one of Germany's most in-love-with-life market squares.

For an orientation to the sights, go to the square's centerpiece, a market cross, and stand on the side of the cross closest to the big stone **cathedral** a block away. This cathedral was the seat of the archbishop. In medieval times, the cathedral was its own walled city, and the archbishop of Trier was one of the seven German electors who chose the Holy Roman Emperor. This gave the archbishop tremendous political, as well as spiritual, power (for more on the cathedral, see page 351).

The pink-and-white building (now an H&M department store) on the corner of the lane leading to the cathedral was a **palace** for the archbishop. Notice the seal above the door: a crown flanked by a crosier, representing the bishop's ecclesiastical power, and a sword, demonstrating his political might. This did not sit well with the townspeople of Trier. The square you're standing in was the symbolic battlefield of a centuries-long conflict between Trier's citizens and its bishop.

The stone market **cross** (a replica of the A.D. 958 original, now in the City Museum) was the archbishop's way of bragging about the trading rights granted to him by King Otto the Great. This was a slap in the face to Trier's townspeople. They'd wanted Trier to be designated a "free imperial city," with full trading rights and beholden only to the Holy Roman Emperor, not a local prince or bishop.

Look across the square from the lane to the cathedral, to the 15th-century **Town Hall** (Steipe). The people of Trier wanted a Town Hall, but the bishop wouldn't allow it—so they built this "assembly hall" instead, with a knight on each second-story corner. The knight on the left, facing Market Square, has his mask up, watching over his people. The other knight, facing the cathedral

TRIER

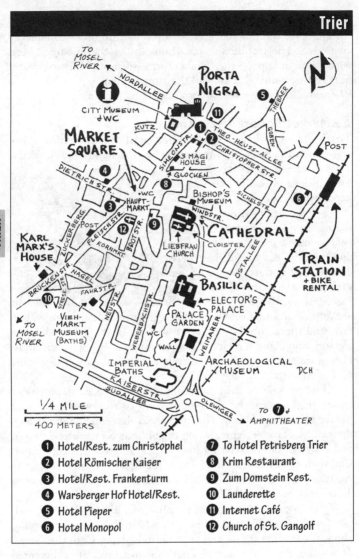

Trier

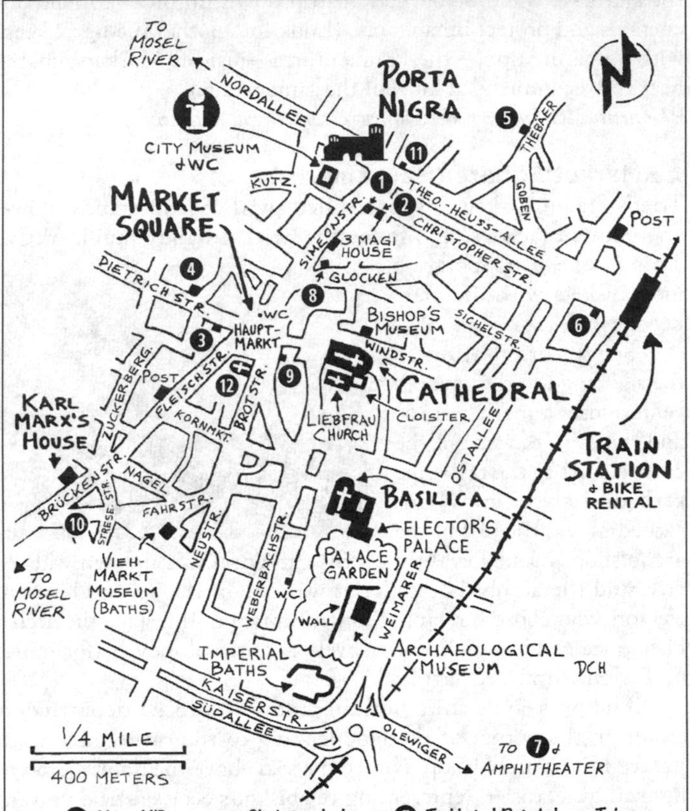

1. Hotel/Rest. zum Christophel
2. Hotel Römischer Kaiser
3. Hotel/Rest. Frankenturm
4. Warsberger Hof Hotel/Rest.
5. Hotel Pieper
6. Hotel Monopol
7. To Hotel Petrisberg Trier
8. Krim Restaurant
9. Zum Domstein Rest.
10. Launderette
11. Internet Café
12. Church of St. Gangolf

and the bishop, has his mask down and his hand on his sword, ready for battle.

Tensions mounted 30 years later. Look to the left, at the tall white steeple with yellow trim. This is the Gothic tower of the **Church of St. Gangolf,** the medieval townspeople's church and fire watchman's post. (From medieval times until the present day, a bell has rung nightly at 22:00, reminding local drunks to go home. When the automatic bell-ringer broke a few years back, concerned locals flooded the mayor with calls.) In 1507, Trier's mayor built

this new Gothic tower to make the people's church higher than the cathedral. A Bible verse in Latin adorns the top in gold letters: "Stay awake and pray." In retaliation, the bishop raised one tower of his cathedral (all he could afford). He topped it with a threatening message of his own, continuing the Town Hall's verse: "For you never know the hour when the Lord will come."

Look farther to the left, to the Renaissance **St. Peter's Fountain** (1595). This fountain symbolizes thoughtful city government, with allegorical statues of justice (sword and scale), fortitude (broken column), temperance (wine and water), and prudence (a snake and, formerly, a mirror—but since the mirror was stolen long ago, she's now empty-handed). The ladies represent idealized cardinal virtues—but notice the rude monkeys hiding on the column behind them, showing the way things are really done. The recommended **Zum Domstein** restaurant is next to the fountain (see page 359).

The rest of the square is a textbook of architectural styles. Notice the half-timbered houses at the north end of the square (toward the Porta Nigra), marking Trier's 14th-century Jewish ghetto. Nearby, look for the Art Deco hotel that now houses a McDonald's (the locals have dubbed its famous arches "the golden horn").

• *When you're finished on the square, head down Sternstrasse to the...*

▲▲Cathedral (Dom)

This is the oldest Christian church in Germany. After Emperor Constantine legalized Christianity in the Roman Empire in A.D. 312, his mother, Helena (now a saint), allowed part of her palace in Trier to be used as the first church on this spot. In A.D. 326, to celebrate the 20th anniversary of his reign, Constantine began the construction of St. Peter's in Rome and this huge cathedral in Trier—also called St. Peter's. The Dom information center is on the courtyard across from the cathedral, on the site of the original church; ask if any excavations from the earliest part of Constantine's cathedral are open for public viewing.

TRIER

Begin your visit in the large front courtyard of the cathedral. As you face the cathedral, look in the corner behind you and to your left (near the pink palace); you'll see a large patch of light-colored bricks in an L shape in the ground. The original Roman cathedral was more than four times its present size; these light-colored bricks mark one corner of this massive "double cathedral." (The opposite corner was at the back of the smaller Liebfrau church, waaay across the courtyard.) The plaque by the corner shows the floor plan of the original Roman cathedral.

Enter the cathedral (free, €0.50 English info brochure, daily April–Oct 6:30–18:00, Nov–March 6:30–17:30, www.trierer-dom.de). You'll see many altars lining the nave, dedicated not to saints, but to bishops. These ornate funeral altars were a fashionable way for the powerful archbishop-electors to memorialize themselves. Even the elaborate black-and-white altar at the back of the church (where you entered) is not a religious shrine, but a memorial for a single rich bishop.

The "pilgrim's walk" (the stairway to the right of the altar) leads to the chapel holding the cathedral's most important relic: the Holy Robe of Christ, found by St. Helena on a pilgrimage to Jerusalem (rarely on view, but you can see its reliquary; look for photos of the robe itself after the first flight of stairs). Also up this stairway is the entrance to the **treasury** *(Schatzkammer)*, displaying huge bishops' rings, the sandal of St. Andrew (in a box topped with a golden foot), and a holy nail supposedly from the Crucifixion (€1.50; April–Oct Mon–Sat 10:00–17:00, Sun 12:30–17:00; Nov–March Mon 13:30–16:00, Tue–Sat 11:00–16:00, Sun 12:30–16:00; last entry 15 min before closing). From the treasury, you can fight the crowds up the last few stairs to the chapel (same hours as treasury). Back down the stairs, the door on your left leads to the peaceful Domkreuzgang **cloister** between the Dom and the Liebfrau church.

A door from inside the cathedral leads to the adjoining **Liebfrau Church,** which claims to be the oldest Gothic church in Germany (it dates from 1235). Unfortunately, the church is closed for renovation until the end of 2009 (but still viewable from outside). This church was built when Gothic was in vogue, so French architects were brought in—and paid with money borrowed from the bishop of Köln when funds ran dry. It's now filled with colorful, modern stained glass.

Leaving the cathedral the way you came in, notice the controversial modern (1972) paintings at the back of the church, representing the Alpha (Paradise/Creation, to the left) and the Omega (the Last Judgment, to the right).

If you want to visit the Bishop's Museum (described next),

go right as you exit the cathedral's main door and turn down the first street on your right (Windstrasse). As you walk with the cathedral on your right, you'll be able to see the different eras of its construction. The big red cube that makes up the back half of the present-day cathedral is all that remains of the enormous, original fourth-century Roman construction (at one time twice as tall as what you see here). Arched bricks in the facade show the original position of Roman windows and doors. Around this Roman nucleus, chunks were grafted on over a millennium and a half of architectural styles: the front half of the cathedral facing the big courtyard, added in the 11th century; the choir on the back, from the 12th century; and the transept and round Baroque shrine on the far back, from the 18th century.

If you look at the original Roman construction squarely, you'll see that it's not perfectly vertical. Locks were built along the Mosel River in the 1960s, depleting groundwater—which was the only thing preserving the church's original wooden foundation. The foundation disintegrated, and the walls began to sag. Architects competed to find a way to prevent the cathedral from collapsing, and the winner—a huge steel bracket above the main nave, holding the walls up with cables—seems to be working.

• *Just past the cathedral on Windstrasse to the left is the...*

▲Bishop's Museum (Bischöfliches Diözesanmuseum)

This museum offers exhibits on the history of the cathedral. Inside and to the right, find the small model of the original Roman church, and the bigger model showing some of the present-day excavations of its various pieces. Don't miss the pieced-together remains of fine ceiling frescoes (dating from A.D. 310–320) from St. Helena's palace. The 50,000 pieces of the frescoes were discovered while cleaning up from WWII bombs. The vivid reds, greens, and blues of the restored works depict frolicking cupids, bejeweled women, and a philosopher clutching his scroll (all described in German). A good €4.60 English book clearly explains the palace ceiling's elaborate structure and the fresco restoration process. Elsewhere in the museum, the stone capitals, gold chalices, vestments, and icons are meaningless to most, unless you can read German (€3.50; April–Oct Mon–Sat 9:00–17:00, Sun 13:00–17:00; Nov–March Tue–Sat 9:00–17:00, Sun 13:00–17:00, closed Mon; Windstrasse 6, tel. 0651/710-5255, www.museum.bistum-trier.de).

• *Return to the front of the cathedral and head two blocks south (away from Market Square), bearing left on An der Meerkatz, to the 200-foot-by-100-foot...*

▲▲Basilica/Imperial Throne Room (Konstantin Basilica)

This building is the largest intact Roman structure outside of Rome. It's best known as a basilica, but it actually started as a throne room. Go inside (free, good €1 English booklet brings the near-empty shell to life; April–Oct Mon–Sat 10:00–18:00, Sun 12:00–18:00; Nov–March Tue–Sat 11:00–12:00 & 15:00–16:00, Sun 12:00–13:00, closed Mon; tel. 0651/72468, www.konstantin-basilika.de).

Standing inside the vast structure, look up: Each of the squares in the ceiling above you is 10 feet by 10 feet—as big as your hotel room. Picture this throne room in ancient times, decorated with golden mosaics, rich marble, colorful stucco, and busts of Constantine and his family filling the seven niches. The emperor sat in majesty under a canopy on his altar-like throne. The windows in the apse around him were smaller than the ones along the side walls, making his throne seem even bigger.

The last emperor moved out in A.D. 395, and petty kings set up camp in the building throughout the Middle Ages. By the 12th century, the bishops had taken it over and converted it to a five-story palace. The building became a Lutheran church in 1856, and it remains the only Protestant church in Trier. It was badly damaged by WWII bombs, and later partially restored.

A Rococo wing, the Elector's Palace, was added to the basilica in the 18th century to house the archbishop-elector; today, it houses local government offices (closed to the public).

• *The Rococo wing faces a fragrant, picnic-riffic garden. Beyond the garden are three more sights: an interesting archaeological museum, the remains of a Roman bath, and a 25,000-seat Roman amphitheater. Cut across the garden toward Weimarer Strasse (the main street in the distance) and veer right to the entrance of the...*

▲Archaeological Museum (Rheinisches Landesmuseum)

This is not only a great museum, but also an active research center. The permanent exhibit focuses on Roman times, as do most of the temporary exhibits. Upstairs, in the back and to the right, is a huge model of Roman Trier (try to pick out the buildings that you're visiting today: cathedral, basilica, baths). Downstairs, explore the huge funerary monuments. Once these were all painted like the replica in the courtyard; today, they tell archaeologists volumes about daily life in Roman times. Find the woman visiting a beauty salon. (Hint: She's on the tallest monument.) The mosaics room is a highlight. On the wall, find the mosaic of four horses surrounding the superstar charioteer Polydus (mosaic floors were the *Sports Illustrated* covers of the Roman world), discovered intact at the Imperial Baths (€3, more for temporary exhibits, Tue–Sun 9:30–17:30, closed Mon, English descriptions, tel. 0651/97740, www.landesmuseum-trier.de).

• *Exit the Archaeological Museum to the right, paralleling the main Weimarer Strasse, then follow the* Tourist Route *signs through the archway in the wall to the modern, red-brick entry arcade of the...*

Imperial Baths (Kaiserthermen)

Built by Constantine, these were the biggest of Trier's three Roman baths, and the most intricate baths of the Roman world.

Trier's cold northern climate, the size of the complex, and the enormity of Constantine's ego meant that these Imperial Baths required a two-story subterranean complex of pipes, furnaces, and slave galleys to keep the water at a perfect 47 degrees Celsius (120 degrees Fahrenheit). Explore the underground tunnels (almost a mile's worth), noticing the chest-high holes in the walls for the beams that used to hold the floor (slaves above, pipes below). It's an impressive complex—too bad the baths never quite worked right, and were left unfinished after Constantine split (€2.10, daily April–Sept 9:00–18:00, March and Oct 9:00–17:00, Nov–Feb 9:00–16:00, €2.50 English booklet, tel. 0651/436-2550, www.burgen-rlp.de).

• *For the unexceptional* ***amphitheater*** *(same price and hours as Imperial Baths, tel. 0651/73010), follow the signs through the pedestrian underpass, then follow Hermesstrasse another half-mile as it curves up the hill and then turn left on Olewigerstrasse.*

Otherwise, consider heading back to town via another (less interesting) Roman bath: Leaving the Imperial Baths, walk left along the red-brick arcade, cross the street to the Fischers Maathes restaurant, then follow Wechselstrasse two blocks. At Neustrasse, jog right to find Viehmarktstrasse, which leads to an open square (Viehmarktplatz). To your right is a modern glass box covering the bath excavations in the...

Viehmarkt Baths Museum

Locals grouse that these ruins sat in the rain for years before their tax money was used to build this expensive new house. The red bricks in the square outside show the intersection of the original Roman roads, laid out as a grid (€2.10, April–Sept Tue–Sun 9:00–18:00, Oct–March Tue–Sun 9:00–17:00, closed Mon, last entry 30 min before closing, €1.50 English brochure, tel. 0651/994-1057, www.burgen-rlp.de). To get here from Market Square, walk down Brotstrasse, and head right on Fahrstrasse—past a cool fountain showing Trier craftsmen at work—to the museum entrance.

• *Our walk is over. From here, you can amble back to Market Square for more food, flowers, fountains, and people-watching; or, if Market Square's capitalism makes you see red, you can walk a few yards toward town on Stresemannstrasse, and make a hard left on Brückenstrasse for...*

Karl Marx's House

Communists can lick their wounds at Karl Marx's birthplace, where early manuscripts, letters, and photographs of the influential economist/philosopher fill several rooms. The free audioguide translates the well-done exhibit into English. Oblivious to their slide out of a shrinking middle class, some people still sneer (€3, includes free brochure; April–Oct daily 10:00–18:00; Nov–March Tue–Sun 10:00–13:00 & 14:00–17:00, Mon 14:00–17:00; tel. 0651/970-680, www.fes.de/Karl-Marx-Haus). From Market Square, it's a 10-minute walk down Fleischstrasse—which becomes Brückenstrasse—to the house at Brückenstrasse 10.

SLEEPING

For locations, see the map on page 350.

Next to the Porta Nigra

$$$ Hotel zum Christophel offers top comfort in its 11 classy rooms, above a fine restaurant and with a kind owner. It's an easy roll from the train station with your luggage (Sb-€65, Db-€90–

Sleep Code

(€1 = about $1.50, country code: 49, area code: 0651)
S = Single, **D** = Double/Twin, **T** = Triple, **Q** = Quad, **b** = bathroom, **s** = shower only. Unless otherwise noted, credit cards are accepted, English is spoken, and breakfast is included.

To help you sort easily through these listings, I've divided the rooms into three categories, based on the price for a standard double room with bath:

$$$ Higher Priced—Most rooms €90 or more.
$$ Moderately Priced—Most rooms between €50-90.
$ Lower Priced—Most rooms €50 or less.

95, elevator, Am Porta Nigra Platz 1, tel. 0651/979-4200, fax 0651/74732, www.zumchristophel.de, info@zumchristophel.de).

$$$ Hotel Römischer Kaiser, next door, is also nice, but a lesser value—charging more for a polished lobby and 43 comparable rooms (Sb-€70–80, Db-€100–120, more during festivals, elevator, free Wi-Fi in lobby, free parking, Am Porta Nigra Platz 6, tel. 0651/977-0100, fax 0651/9770-1999, www.hotels-trier.de, rezeption@hotels-trier.de).

Near Market Square

$$ Hotel Frankenturm, decked out in modern style with track lighting and cheery color schemes, has 12 rooms above a lively saloon and next to a medieval keep of the same name. The six rooms with private baths are on the first floor up; the other six rooms are two floors up, with a shared bath (S-€45, Sb-€65, D-€55, Db-€85, T-€65, Tb-€95, no elevator, Dietrichstrasse 3, tel. 0651/978-240, fax 0651/978-2449, www.hotel-frankenturm.de, frankenturm@t-online.de).

$ Warsberger Hof, run by a local citizens' league, is a clean, simple hostel and budget hotel two blocks from Market Square, with 168 beds and an inexpensive restaurant. This is your best value for cheap sleeps in town (€20.50 per bed in 3- to 6-bed dorms, includes sheets, S-€26–28, D-€45–49, T-€68, Q-€82, showers down the hall, breakfast-€5, pay Internet access, Dietrichstrasse 42, tel. 0651/975-250, fax 0651/975-2540, www.warsberger-hof.de, info@warsberger-hof.de).

Near the Train Station

$$ Hotel Pieper, a good value, is run by the friendly Becker family (he cooks and she keeps the books). They rent 20 comfortable rooms furnished with dark wood over a pleasant neighborhood restaurant (Sb-€48, Db-€78, Tb-€115, pay Wi-Fi, 8-min walk from station, 2 blocks off main drag, Thebäerstrasse 39, tel. 0651/23008, fax 0651/12839, www.hotel-pieper-trier.de, info@hotel-pieper-trier.de). From the station, follow Theodor-Heuss-Allee (toward Porta Nigra) to the second big intersection, angle right onto Göbenstrasse, and continue as the road curves and becomes Thebäerstrasse.

$$ Hotel Monopol, at the train station, has 35 older but clean rooms. It's dark but handy (S-€39, Sb-€47, D-€68, Db-€77, Tb-€105, Qb-€120, elevator, Bahnhofsplatz 7, tel. 0651/714-090, fax 0651/714-0910, www.hotel-monopol-trier.de, bernd.glatzel@hotel-monopol-trier.de).

Outside the Center

$$$ Hotel Petrisberg Trier, up a steep road behind the amphitheater, is top-quality and ideal if you have a car. It's on a hillside overlooking the city, exuding old-school elegance without being stuffy. The Pantenburg family takes great care to spoil all their guests; Helmut whips up tasty egg breakfasts, while his niece Christina—the 2001 Trier Wine Queen—works reception. A pleasant footpath brings you downhill to the cathedral in 20 minutes (35 rooms, Sb-€65, Db-€95, non-smoking, free Internet access, Wi-Fi in breakfast room, Sickingenstrasse 11–13, tel. 0651/4640, fax 0651/46450, www.hotel-petrisberg.de, info@hotel-petrisberg.de).

EATING

Good eateries abound on the side streets leading away from the pedestrian drag (Simeonstrasse) and from Market Square. Most of the recommended hotels have good-value restaurants.

Hotel Frankenturm, a few doors down Dietrichstrasse from Market Square, offers German cuisine with a twist of Asian and Mediterranean in a modern pub-style atmosphere (€9–16 main dishes, €4–8 weekday lunch specials, Mon–Sat 8:00–24:00, Sun 17:00–24:00, Dietrichstrasse 3, tel. 0651/978-240).

Warsberger Hof Eateries: A few doors farther down Dietrichstrasse, in the big yellow pastel building on the right, the recommended **Warsberger Hof hostel** runs three inexpensive eateries: the **Leonardy** pub and cafe (daily 11:30–24:00), the **Rautenstrauch** restaurant (€11–17 main dishes, daily 11:30–14:30 & 18:00–22:00, nice enclosed terrace, kid-friendly), and the **Lothar's** self-service cafeteria, serving cheap lunches (Mon–Fri 11:30–14:15, closed Sat–Sun).

At **Krim,** also just off Market Square, young locals enjoy trendy Mediterranean cuisine (€9–16 main dishes, cheaper lunch specials, Mon–Sat 9:00–24:00, Sun 10:00–24:00, Glockenstrasse 7, tel. 0651/73943).

Zum Domstein, right on Market Square, serves standard German fare and also has a special, pricier menu of entrées based on ancient Roman recipes. The Roman menu was inspired during renovations, when the owner discovered a Roman column in her cellar. (In Trier, you can't put a rec room in your basement without tripping over Roman ruins.) The finished cellar dining room incorporates the column, plus a mini-museum of Roman crockery (€10–20 main dishes, cheaper lunch specials, open daily 11:30–22:00, Roman dishes served in cellar 18:00–21:00, Am Hauptmarkt 5, tel. 0651/74490).

The recommended **Hotel zum Christophel** also has a reasonably priced restaurant with a view of the Porta Nigra (daily 11:00–23:00, Am Porta Nigra Platz).

Picnics: One of several supermarkets in the center is in the basement of the Karstadt department store on Simeonstrasse (open Mon–Sat 9:00–19:00, closed Sun).

TRANSPORTATION CONNECTIONS

From Trier by Train to: Cochem (2/hr, 1 hr), **Bullay** (where you can transfer to a bus to **Zell;** hourly, 40 min), **Koblenz** (1 fast train/hr, 90 min), **Köln** (hourly, 2.5–3 hrs, some change in Koblenz), **St. Goar/Bacharach** (hourly, 2.5 hrs, change in Koblenz), **Frankfurt Airport** (1–2/hr, 3–4 hrs, 1–2 changes). Train info: tel. 11861 (€0.60/min).

KÖLN and the UNROMANTIC RHINE

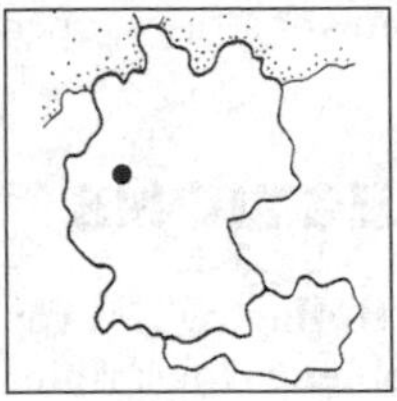

Romance isn't everything. Köln is an urban Jacuzzi that keeps the Rhine churning. It's home to Germany's greatest Gothic cathedral and its best collection of Roman artifacts, a world-class art museum, and a healthy dose of German urban playfulness.

Peaceful Bonn, which offers good people-watching and fun pedestrian streets, used to be the capital of West Germany. The small town of Remagen had a bridge that helped defeat Hitler in World War II, and unassuming Aachen, near the Belgian border, was once the capital of Europe.

Köln

Germany's fourth-largest city, Köln ("Cologne" in English) has a compact, lively center. The Rhine was the northern boundary of the Roman Empire and, 1,700 years ago, Constantine—the first Christian emperor—made Colonia the seat of a bishopric. Five hundred years later, under Charlemagne, Köln became the seat of an archbishopric. With 40,000 people within its walls, it was the largest German city and an important cultural and religious center throughout the Middle Ages.

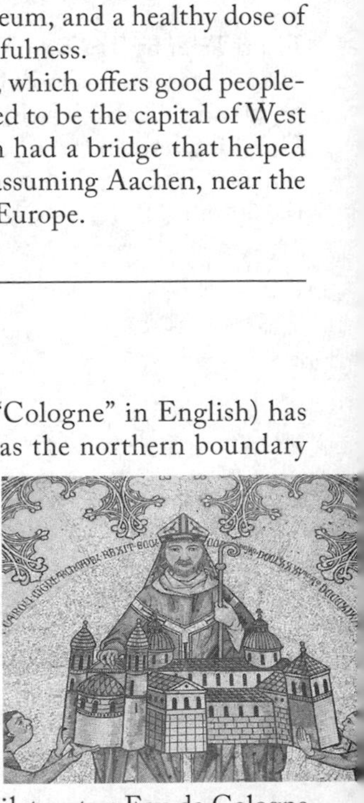

Today, the city is most famous for its toilet water: Eau de Cologne was first made here by an Italian chemist in 1709.

Even though WWII bombs destroyed 95 percent of Köln (population down from 800,000 to 40,000), it has become, after a remarkable recovery, a bustling commercial and cultural center, while keeping its traditions intact.

Planning Your Time

Köln makes an ideal on-the-way stop; it's a major rail junction, and its top sights are clustered near the train station. With an hour or two, you can toss your bag in a locker, zip through the cathedral, and make it back to the station for your train. If you're planning that short of a stop, make sure you'll be here when the whole church is open (see page 364 for times). More time (or an overnight) allows you to delve into a few of the city's fine museums and take in an old-time beer pub.

ORIENTATION

(area code: 0221)

Köln's old-town core was bombed out, then rebuilt in mostly modern styles with a sprinkling of quaint. There are two areas that you need to know. One is the section right around the train station and cathedral. Here you'll find most sights, all my recommended hotels, plus the TI and plenty of eateries and services. Hohe Strasse, Köln's pedestrian shopping street, begins near the cathedral.

The other is the area around Alter Markt and Frankenwerft, a few blocks to the south. This section is known for its pubs, small streets, and waterfront park. From the park, look back at the Hohenzollernbrücke, which crosses the Rhine at the cathedral and is the busiest railway bridge in the world (30 trains per hour all day long). A little farther upstream is Köln's famous chocolate museum.

Tourist Information

Köln's energetic TI, opposite the cathedral entrance, has a basic €0.20 city map and can find you a room (Mon–Sat 9:00–20:00, Sun 10:00–17:00, Kardinal-Höffner-Platz 1, tel. 0221/2213-0400, www.koelntourismus.de). They also offer a range of private guided walking tours, covering such topics as architecture, medieval Köln, and Romanesque churches (call TI to reserve).

Arrival in Köln

Köln couldn't be easier to visit—its three important sights cluster within two blocks of the TI and train station. This super pedestrian zone is a constant carnival of people.

Köln's busy **train station** has everything you need: a drugstore, food court, juice bar, shopping mall with grocery store, pricey "McClean" WC (€1.10), travel center (*Reisezentrum,*

Köln

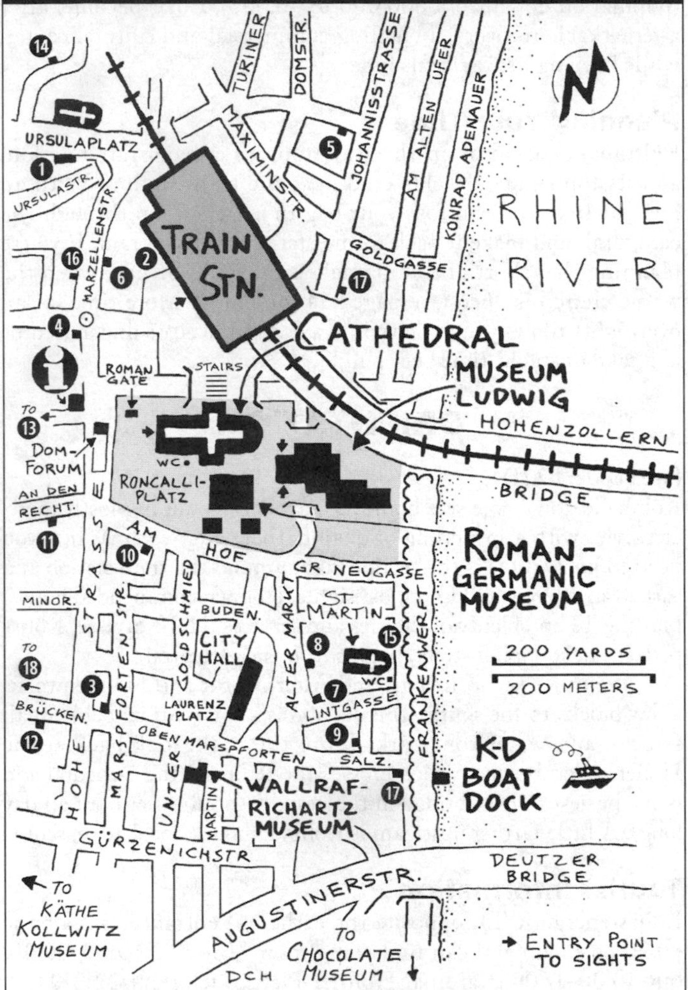

1. Hotel Cristall & Classic Hotel Harmonie
2. Hotel Ibis Koeln am Dom
3. Hotel Engelbertz
4. Central Hotel am Dom
5. Hotel Müller
6. Station Hostel
7. Gaffel Haus Restaurant
8. Papa Joe's Klimperkasten Pub
9. Papa Joe's Jazzlokal
10. Früh am Dom Restaurant
11. To Holtmann's im MAK
12. Café Eigel
13. To Päffgen Restaurant
14. Schreckenskammer Rest.
15. Frankenwerft Bars & Eateries
16. Internet Café
17. Bike Rentals (2)
18. To Kolumba Diocesan Museum

Mon–Fri 6:00–22:00, Sat–Sun 7:00–21:00), and high-tech lockers (€4/24 hrs, accepts coins and €5 and €10 bills, put money in and wait 30 seconds for door to open, your luggage—up to four pieces—is transferred to storage via an underground conveyor belt and retrieved when you re-insert your ticket; next to *Reisezentrum*). Exiting the front of the station (the end near track 1), you'll find yourself smack-dab in the shadow of the cathedral. If your jaw drops, pick it up. Up the steps and to the right is the main entrance to the cathedral (TI across street). For Hotel Müller, leave the station from the back (near track 11).

If you **drive** to Köln, follow signs to *Zentrum,* then continue to the huge Parkhaus am Dom pay lot under the cathedral (€2/hr, €18/day).

If you're arriving on a K-D Line **boat,** exit the boat to the right, then walk along the waterside park until just before the train bridge, when the cathedral comes into view on the left.

Helpful Hints

Closed Day: Note that most museums are closed on Monday. The cathedral remains open Monday, but has limited public hours on Sunday due to frequent services. For information on Köln's museums, visit www.museenkoeln.de.

Sightseeing Discount Cards: Köln has two different cards, one of which is worth considering. The **MuseumCard** is valid for two consecutive days. It covers all local public transportation on the first day (including local trains to Bonn—but not the slick InterCity and ICE trains), and also includes the Roman-Germanic Museum, Museum Ludwig, Wallraf-Richartz Museum, and quite a few lesser museums (but not the cathedral sights). If you're visiting all three of these museums, this card will save you money (€12.20/person, or €20.40 for a family pass—includes 2 adults and 2 kids up to 18, available at participating museums, www.museenkoeln.de). The **WelcomeCard** is a waste of money; though it covers the city's transit system, you can easily reach the top sights on foot. The card gives only a measly 20 percent discount on major museums (Roman-Germanic Museum, Ludwig, and Wallraf-Richartz), and even smaller discounts on other attractions like the Chocolate Museum (€9/24 hrs, €14/48 hrs, €19/72 hrs; family and group cards available, www.koelntourismus.de).

Internet Access: Consider **Via Phone Internet Café,** a block from the station at Marzellenstrasse 3–5 (€2/hr, also sells cheap phone cards, Mon–Sat 9:00–24:00, Sun 10:00–24:00, tel. 0221/1399-6200).

Baggage Storage: The station's baggage service is the most convenient (see previous section, "Arrival in Köln"), but cheapskates can save a few euros by using Museum Ludwig's €0.50 lockers. From the station's underground passage, take the escalator to Platform 1, do a U-turn at the top, and walk past Section A, all the way down to where the platform joins the street—look straight ahead for the museum's large sign.

Bike Rental: Convenient rental is available at friendly **Radstation,** tucked under the train-track arcade (€5/3 hrs, €10/day, Mon–Fri 5:30–22:30, Sat 6:30–20:00, Sun 8:00–20:00, exit station by track 11 to Breslauer Platz, turn right and cross street, tel. 0221/139-7190). You can also rent bikes from the riverside **Kölner Fahrradverleih,** a 10-minute walk from the station (€2/hr, €10/day, April–Oct daily 10:00–18:00, on Markmannsgasse, 100 yards upstream from K-D Line docks, mobile 0171-629-8796). Consider biking the path along the Rhine River up past the convention center *(Messe)* to the Rheinpark for a picnic. Or consider a guided bike tour (described under "Tours," below).

Gadget Supply: You can pick up a new memory card or whatever high-tech gizmo you're lacking for a fair price at **Media Markt,** Germany's version of Best Buy, conveniently located two blocks from the cathedral (Mon–Thu 10:00–20:00, Fri–Sat 10:00–21:00, closed Sun, corner of Hohe Strasse and Minoritenstrasse).

Festival: Köln's Lichter Festival lights up the sky on July 11 in 2009, with fireworks, music, and lots of boats on the river (get details from TI or at www.koelner-lichter.de).

TOURS

Bus Tours—The TI sells tickets for 90-minute bus tours of the city (€10, in both German and English; April–Oct daily at 10:00, 12:00, and 14:00, Fri–Sat also 16:00; Nov–March daily at 11:00 and 14:00; departs from TI).

Bike Tours—Kölner Fahrradverleih (listed under "Bike Rental," above) offers German/English guided bike tours of the city (€15, 3–3.5 hrs, daily April–Oct at 13:30, rain poncho provided just in case, 10-person max, reservations recommended, mobile 0171-629-8796, www.koelnerfahrradverleih.de).

SIGHTS

▲▲▲Köln's Cathedral (Dom)

The Neo-Gothic Dom—Germany's most exciting church—looms immediately up from the train station.

Cost and Hours: Free, open daily 6:00–19:30; no tourist visits during Mass (generally Mon–Sat at 6:30, 7:15, 8:00, 9:00, and

18:30; Sun at 7:00, 8:00, 9:00, 10:00, 12:00, 17:00, and 19:00; get schedule at Domforum office or www.koelner-dom.de).

Tours: The one-hour English-only tours are reliably excellent (€6, Mon–Sat at 10:30 and 14:30, Sun at 14:30, meet inside front door of Dom, tel. 0221/9258-4730). Your tour ticket also gives you free entry to the 20-minute English video in the Domforum directly following the tour (see "Domforum," page 369).

➲ **Self-Guided Tour:** If you don't take the guided tour, follow this seven-stop walk (note that stops 3–7 are closed off during confession Sat 14:00–18:00, and any time services are underway).

❶ **Roman Gate and Cathedral Exterior:** The square in front of the cathedral has been a busy civic meeting place since ancient times. A Roman temple once stood where the cathedral stands today. The north gate of the Roman city, from A.D. 50, marks the start of Köln's 2,000-year-old main street.

Look for the life-size replica tip of a spire. The real thing is 515 feet above you. The cathedral facade, finished according to the original 13th-century plan, is Neo-Gothic from the 19th century.

Postcards show the church after the 1945 bombing. The Roman-Germanic Museum lies beyond the facade to the right, and the modern-art Museum Ludwig sits behind that (both described later in this chapter).

• *Step inside the church. Grab a pew in the center of the nave.*

❷ **Nave:** If you feel small, you're supposed to. The 140-foot-tall ceiling reminds us of our place in the vast scheme of things. Lots of stained glass—enough to cover three football fields—fills the church with light, representing God.

The church was begun in 1248. The choir—the lofty area from the center altar to the far end ahead of you—was finished in 1322. Later, with the discovery of America and routes to the Indies by sea, trade shifted away from inland ports like Köln. Funds dried up and eventually construction stopped. For 300 years, the finished end of the church was walled off and functioned as a church, while the unfinished torso (where you now sit) waited. For centuries, the symbol of Köln's skyline was a huge crane that sat atop the unfinished west spire.

With the rise of German patriotism in the early 1800s, Köln became a symbol of German unity. And the Prussians—the movers and shakers behind German unity—mistakenly considered Gothic a German style. They initiated a national tax that funded

Köln Cathedral

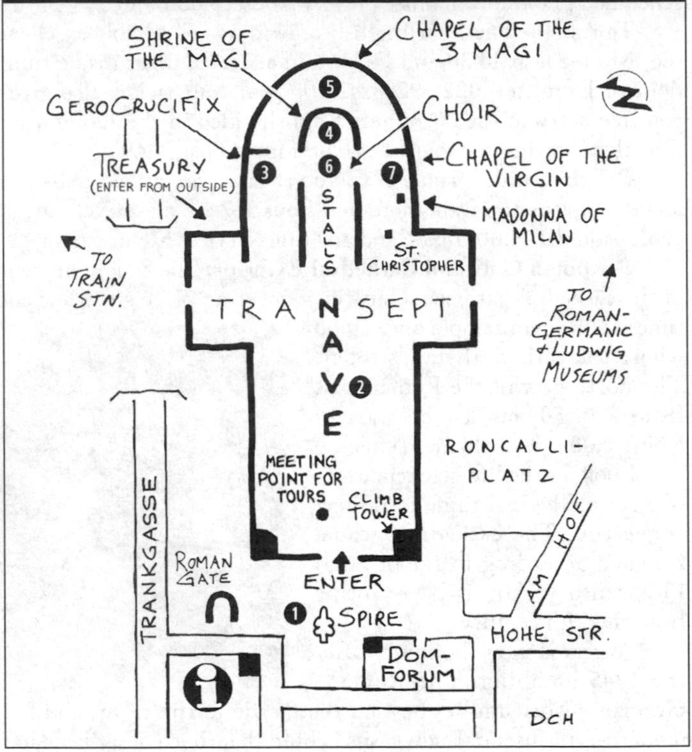

the speedy completion of this gloriously Gothic German church. Nearly 700 workers (compared to 100 in the 14th century) finished the church in just 38 years (1842–1880). The great train station was built in the shadow of the cathedral's towering spire.

The glass windows in the front of the church are medieval. The glass surrounding you in the nave is not as old, but it's precious nevertheless. The glass on the left is Renaissance. Notice the many coats of arms, which depict the lineage of the donors. One of these windows would have cost as much as two large townhouses. The glass on the right—a gift from Ludwig I, grandfather of the "Mad" King Ludwig who built the fairy-tale castles—is 19th-century Bavarian. Compare both the colors and the realism of the faces between the windows to see how techniques advanced over the centuries.

While 95 percent of Köln was destroyed by WWII bombs, the structure of the cathedral survived fairly well. In anticipation of the bombing, the glass and art treasures were taken to shelters and saved. The new "swallow's nest" organ above you was installed to celebrate the cathedral's 750th birthday in 1998. Attaching it to the wall would have compromised the cathedral's architectural integrity, so the organ is actually suspended from precarious-looking steel wires. Relics (mostly skulls) fill cupboards on each side of the nave. The guys in the red robes are cathedral cops, called *Schweizer* (after the Swiss guard at the Vatican); if a service is getting ready to start, they hustle tourists out (but you can stay for the service if you like).

• *Leave the nave by stepping through the gate on the left, into the oldest part of the church. As you enter, look down.*

This ninth-century mosaic shows a saint holding the Carolingian Cathedral, which stood on this spot for several centuries before this one was built.

❸ **Gero-Crucifix:** Ahead of you on the left, the Chapel of the Cross features the oldest surviving monumental crucifix from north of the Alps. Carved in 976 with a sensitivity that was 300 years ahead of its time, it shows Jesus not suffering and not triumphant—but with eyes closed... dead. He paid the price for our sins. It's quite a two-fer: great art and powerful theology in one. The cathedral has three big pilgrim stops: this crucifix, the Shrine of the Magi, and the *Madonna of Milan* (both coming up).

• *Continue to the front end of the church, stopping to look at the big golden reliquary in the glass case behind the high altar.*

❹ **Shrine of the Magi:** Relics were a big deal in the Middle Ages. Köln's acquisition of the bones of the Three Kings in the 12th century put it on the pilgrimage map and brought in enough money to justify the construction of this magnificent place. By some stretch of medieval Christian logic, these relics also justified the secular power of the local king. This reliquary, made in about 1200, is the biggest and most splendid I've seen. It's seven feet of gilded silver, jewels, and enamel. Old Testament prophets line the bottom, and 12 New Testament apostles—with a wingless angel in the center—line the top.

Inside sit the bones of the Magi...three skulls with golden crowns. So what's the big deal about these three kings (of Christmas-carol fame)? They were the first to recognize Jesus as the Savior and the first to come as pilgrims to worship him. They inspired medieval pilgrims and countless pilgrims since. For a thousand years, a theme of this cathedral has been that life is a pilgrimage...a search for God.

❺ **Chapel of the Three Magi:** The center chapel, at the far end, is the oldest. It also features the church's oldest window (center, from 1265). The design is typical: a strip of Old Testament scenes on the left with a theologically and visually parallel strip of New Testament scenes on the right (such as, on bottom panels: to the left, the birth of Eve; to the right, the birth of Mary with her mother Anne on the bed).

Later glass windows (which you saw lining the nave) were made from panes of clear glass that were painted and glazed. This medieval window, however, is actually colored glass, which is assembled like a mosaic. It was very expensive. The size was limited to what pilgrim donations could support. Notice the plain, budget design higher up.

• *Peek into the center zone between the high altar and the carved wooden central stalls. (You can usually get inside only if you take the tour.)*

❻ **Choir:** The choir is surrounded by 13th- and 14th-century art: carved oak stalls, frescoed walls, statues painted as they would have been, and original stained glass high above. Study the fanciful oak carvings. The woman cutting the man's hair is a Samson-and-Delilah warning to the sexist men of the early Church.

• *The nearby chapel holds one of the most precious paintings of the important Gothic School of Köln.*

❼ **Chapel of the Virgin:** *The Patron Saints of Köln* was painted in 1442 by Stefan Lochner. Notice the photographic realism and believable depth. There are literally dozens of identifiable herbs in the grassy foreground. During the 19th century, the city fought to move it to a museum. The Church went to court to keep it. The judge ruled that it could stay in the cathedral only as long as a Mass was said before it every day. For more than a hundred years, that happened at 18:30. Now, 21st-century comfort has trumped 19th-century law—in winter, services take place in the warmer Sacraments Chapel instead. (For more on the School of Köln art style, see "Wallraf-Richartz Museum," page 371.)

Overlooking the same chapel, the *Madonna of Milan* sculpture (1290), associated with miracles, was a focus of pilgrims for centuries. Its colors, scepter, and crown were likely added during a restoration in 1900.

The reclining medieval knight in the cage at the back of the chapel (just before the gate) was a wealthy but childless patron who donated his entire county to the cathedral. Worried that his angry brother and cousin would avenge this snub, his grave was covered to protect his body—an honor usually reserved for priests.

As you head for the exit, look into the transept on your left. The stained-glass windows above you are mostly clear. The local artist Gerhard Richter is designing new windows to create a "harmony of colors." Before leaving, find the statue of St. Christopher (with Jesus on his shoulder and the pilgrim's staff). Since 1470, pilgrims and travelers have looked up at him and taken solace in the hope that their patron saint is looking out for them.

• *Go in peace.*

More Cathedral Sights

Church Spire Climb—For 509 steps and €2, you can enjoy a fine city view from the cathedral's south tower (€5 combo-ticket also includes treasury, daily May–Sept 9:00–18:00, March–April and Oct until 17:00, Nov–Feb until 16:00). From the *Glockenstube* (only 400 steps up), you can see the Dom's nine huge bells, including *Dicke Peter* (24-ton Fat Peter), claimed to be the largest free-swinging church bell in the world.

Treasury—The treasury sits outside the cathedral's left transept (when you exit through the front door, turn right and continue right around the building to the gold pillar marked *Schatzkammer*). The six dim, hushed rooms are housed in the cathedral's 13th-century stone cellar vaults (€4, €5 combo-ticket also includes spire climb, daily 10:00–18:00, last entry 30 min before closing, lockers at entry with €1 coin deposit, tel. 0221/1794-0530).

Spotlights shine on black cases filled with gilded chalices and crosses, medieval reliquaries (bits of chain, bone, cross, and cloth in gold-crusted glass capsules), and plenty of fancy bishop garb: intricately embroidered miters and vestments, rings with fat gemstones, and six-foot gold crosiers. Displays come with brief English descriptions, but the little €4 book sold inside the cathedral shop provides extra information.

Domforum—This helpful visitors center, across from the entrance of the cathedral, is a good place to support the Vatican Bank (notice the Pax Bank ATM just outside the entrance), or just to take a break (Mon–Fri 10:00–18:30, Sat 10:00–17:00, Sun 13:00–17:00, plenty of info, welcoming lounge with €1 coffee and juice, clean WC downstairs—free but donation requested, tel. 0221/9258-4720, www.domforum.de). They offer an English "multi-vision" video on the history of the church (Mon–Sat at 11:30 and 15:30, Sun at 15:30 only, starts slow but gets a little better, 20 min, €2 or included with church tour).

Kolumba Diocesan Museum—This museum contains some of the cathedral's finest art. It's at the corner of Kolumba and Brückenstrasse (a few blocks southwest of the cathedral; walking down Hohe Strasse from the cathedral, turn right on Minoritenstrasse, then left two blocks later). Built around the

Madonna in the Ruins church, the museum is conceived as a place of reflection (€5, Wed–Mon 12:00–17:00, closed Tue, tel. 0221/257-7672, www.kolumba.de).

Near the Cathedral

▲▲Roman-Germanic Museum (Römisch-Germanisches Museum)—Germany's best Roman museum offers minimal English among its elegant and fascinating display of Roman artifacts: glassware, jewelry, and mosaics. All these pieces are evidence of Köln's status as an important site of civilization long before the cathedral was ever imagined. The permanent collection is downstairs and upstairs; temporary exhibits are on the ground floor.

Budget travelers can view the museum's prize piece, a fine mosaic floor, for free from the big window facing the square. Once the dining-room floor of a rich Roman merchant, this is actually its original position (the museum was built around it). It shows scenes from the life of Dionysus...wine and good times, Roman-style. The tall monument over the Dionysus mosaic is the mausoleum of a first-century Roman army officer. Upstairs, you'll see a reassembled, arched original gate to the Roman city with the Roman initials for the town, CCAA, still legible, and incredible glassware that Roman Köln was famous for producing (€6, Tue–Sun 10:00–17:00, closed Mon, Roncalliplatz 4, tel. 0221/2212-4590, www.museenkoeln.de/rgm). The gift shop's €0.50 brochure provides too little information on the collection, and the €20 *Roman-Germanic Cologne* book too much.

▲▲Museum Ludwig—Next door and more enjoyable, this museum—in a slick and modern building—offers a stimulating trip through the art of the last century, including American Pop and post-WWII art. Displays include German and Russian Expressionists, Picasso, and works from the Blaue Reiter (Blue Rider) school (which is better represented at the Lenbachhaus in Munich—see page 57). The floor plan is a mess. Just enjoy the art (€9, often more because of special exhibitions, Tue–Sun 10:00–18:00, closed Mon, €0.50 lockers mandatory for big bags, free WC in entry hall, exhibits are fairly well-described in English; classy but a bit pricey cafeteria—€6–13 salads, pastas, sandwiches, and soups; Heinrich-Böll-Platz, tel. 0221/2212-6165, www.museum-ludwig.de).

Hohe Strasse—The Roman arch in front of the cathedral reminds us that even in Roman times, this was an important trading street and a main road through Köln. In the Middle Ages, when Köln was a major player in the heavyweight Hanseatic League of Northern European merchant towns, two major trading routes crossed here. This high street thrived. Following its complete destruction in World War II, Hohe Strasse emerged once again as an active trading street—the first pedestrian shopping mall in Germany.

Farther from the Cathedral

These museums are several blocks south of the cathedral.

▲▲Wallraf-Richartz Museum—Housed in a cinderblock of a building near the City Hall, this minimalist museum features a world-class collection of old masters, from medieval to northern Baroque and Impressionist. You'll see the best collection anywhere of Gothic School of Köln paintings (1300–1550), offering an intimate peek into those times. Included are German, Dutch, Flemish, and French works by masters such as Albrecht Dürer, Peter Paul Rubens, Rembrandt, Frans Hals, Jan Steen, Vincent van Gogh, Pierre-Auguste Renoir, Claude Monet, Edvard Munch, and Paul Cézanne (€6–9, price depends on special exhibitions, Tue–Fri 10:00–18:00, Thu until 22:00, Sat–Sun 11:00–18:00, closed Mon, English descriptions and good €2.50 audioguide for permanent exhibit, Martin Strasse 39, tel. 0221/2212-1119, www.museenkoeln.de/wrm).

Imhoff Chocolate Museum (Schokoladenmuseum)—Chocoholics love this place, cleverly billed as the "MMMuseum." Three levels of displays—well-described in English—follow the cocoa bean from its origin to the finished product. You can see displays on the history and culture of chocolate and watch the treats trundle down the conveyor belt in the functioning chocolate factory, the museum's highlight. The top-floor exhibit of chocolate advertising is fun. Some find that the museum takes chocolate too seriously, and wish the free samples weren't so meager—you'll have to do your indulging in the fragrant, choc-full gift shop (€6.50, Tue–Fri 10:00–18:00, Sat–Sun 11:00–19:00, closed Mon, last entry one hour before closing, Am Schokoladenmuseum 1a, tel. 0221/931-8880, www.schokoladenmuseum.de).

Getting There: The museum is a pleasant 10-minute walk south on the riverfront, between the Deutzer and Severins bridges. Or take the handy Schoko-Express tourist train from Roncalliplatz (€3 one-way, €5 round-trip, 2/hr—or 1/hr if it's raining, pick-up point changes depending on events on the church square—either by TI or by the ticket office, confirm location at TI).

Käthe Kollwitz Museum—This contains the largest collection of the artist's powerful Expressionist art, welling from her experiences living in Berlin during the tumultuous first half of the last century (€3, Tue–Fri 10:00–18:00, Sat–Sun 11:00–18:00, closed Mon, Neumarkt 18–24, tel. 0221/227-2899, www.kollwitz.de).

Getting There: From Hohe Strasse, go west on Schildergasse for about 10 minutes; go past Neumarkt Gallerie to Neumarkt

Passage, enter Neumarkt Passage, and walk to the glass-domed center courtyard. Take the glass elevator to the fifth floor.

SLEEPING

Köln is *the* convention town in Germany. Consequently, hotels are either jam-packed, with their rooms going for €180–200, or empty and hungry for guests. Unless otherwise noted, prices listed are the non-convention weekday rates. Prices are soft on weekends (always ask) and for slow-time drop-ins. During conventions, rates double or even triple. Outside of convention times, the TI can always get you a discounted room in a business-class hotel (free by phone or Internet, walk-ins pay a €3 booking fee).

An updated list of dates for conventions in 2009 is posted in German at www.koelnmesse.de (click on "Messen und Veranstaltungen," then "Messetermine 2009"). Unlisted smaller conventions can lead to small price increases. Big conventions in nearby Düsseldorf can also fill rooms and raise rates in Köln.

All the options listed here are an easy roll from the train station with your luggage.

Classy Hotels on Ursulaplatz

Two good business-class splurge hotels stand side-by-side a five-minute walk northwest of the station (exit straight out, near track 1, then turn right on Marzellenstrasse, up to Ursulaplatz). These can be pricey but are an excellent value on non-convention weekends.

$$$ Classic Hotel Harmonie is a lesson in elegance, striking a perfect balance between modern and classic. Its 72 rooms include some luxurious "superior" rooms (with hardwoods and swanky bathrooms, including a foot-warming floor). Rates are plenty pricey during conventions, but become affordable on weekends and a downright steal when business is slow (it's important to check—call ahead and ask the helpful staff for prices). So *this* is how the other half lives (Sb-€60–90, Db-€80–110, price depends on room category, non-smoking rooms, most doubles have air-con, elevator, Internet access, pay Wi-Fi, Ursulaplatz 13–19, tel. 0221/16570, fax 0221/165-7200, www.classic-hotel-harmonie.de, harmonie@classic-hotels.com).

$$$ Hotel Cristall is a modern "designer hotel" with 85 cleverly appointed rooms (enjoy the big easel paintings). The deeply hued breakfast room and lounge are so hip that German rock stars have photo shoots here (Sb-€66, Db-€96, prices can drop—especially in summer, request quiet room to escape street and train noise, non-smoking rooms, elevator, pricey pay Wi-Fi, limited parking-€9/day—reserve in advance, Ursulaplatz 9–11, tel. 0221/16300, fax 0221/163-0333, www.hotelcristall.de, info@hotelcristall.de).

Sleep Code

(€1 = about $1.50, country code: 49, area code: 0221)
S = Single, **D** = Double/Twin, **T** = Triple, **Q** = Quad, **b** = bathroom, **s** = shower only. Unless otherwise noted, credit cards are accepted, English is spoken, and breakfast is included.

To help you sort easily through these listings, I've divided the rooms into three categories, based on the price for a standard double room with bath:

$$$ Higher Priced—Most rooms €95 or more.
$$ Moderately Priced—Most rooms between €70-95.
$ Lower Priced—Most rooms €70 or less.

Mid-Range Hotels near the Station

The first three of these moderately priced hotels, centrally located along the pedestrian zone, are more convenient than charming. Hotel Müller is on the other side of the station, in a quieter neighborhood.

$$ Hotel Ibis Koeln am Dom, a 71-room chain hotel, offers predictability, tidiness, and an extremely short walk from the train station—but no personality (Sb-€79, Db-€94; convention rate: Sb-€139, Db-€159; breakfast-€9.50, non-smoking rooms, air-con, elevator, free Internet access, pricey pay Wi-Fi, Hauptbahnhof, entry across from station's *Reisezentrum,* tel. 0221/912-8580, fax 0221/9128-58199, www.ibishotel.com, h0739@accor.com).

$$ Hotel Engelbertz is a fine, family-run, 40-room enterprise. It's an eight-minute walk from the station and cathedral at the end of the pedestrian mall (specials in 2009 for readers with this book who request a discount during non-convention times: Sb-€55 and Db-€79 if you reserve on same day or day before, Sb-€65 and Db-€89 if you reserve in advance; regular rate Sb-€75 and Db-€108, convention rate Db-€195, elevator, pay Internet access and Wi-Fi, just off Hohe Strasse at Obenmarspforten 1–3, coming from station turn left at Hohe Strasse 96, tel. 0221/257-8994, fax 0221/257-8924, www.hotel-engelbertz.de, info@hotel-engelbertz.de).

$$ Central Hotel am Dom's location—just two blocks from the cathedral and one block from the station—and its clean, uncluttered rooms make it a good value (Sb-€59, Db-€80–90, can be cheaper in summer, non-smoking rooms, pay Wi-Fi, An den Dominikanern 3, tel. 0221/135-088, fax 0221/135-080, www.centralamdom.de, info@centralamdom.de).

$$ Hotel Müller, run with great pride by enthusiastic Frau Müller, has 15 recently renovated rooms offering three-star quality at two-star prices (because it doesn't have an elevator). Enjoy the grotto-like basement breakfast room/bar and the courtyard terrace (Sb-€60, Db-€75, non-smoking rooms, pay Wi-Fi; exit station by track 11 to Breslauer Platz, walk 2 blocks up Johannisstrasse, then left on Brandenburger Strasse to #20; tel. 0221/912-8350, fax 0221/9128-3517, www.hotel-mueller-koeln.de, info@hotel-mueller.net). If it's full, there are other affordable, family-run hotels on Brandenburger Strasse and the nearby Domstrasse.

Budget Rooms

$ Station Hostel, with 200 beds, is a five-minute walk from the train station and full of young travelers (dorm bed-€17–22, S-€30, Sb-€37, twin-bed D-€45, Db-€52, Tb-€72, includes sheets, key deposit-€1, kitchen, does not include breakfast—café on premises, no curfew, Internet access and Wi-Fi, laundry-€4, tel. 0221/912-5301, fax 0221/912-5303; exit station on cathedral side, walk straight 1 block, turn right on Marzellenstrasse to #44–56; www.hostel-cologne.de, station@hostel-cologne.de).

EATING

The city's distinct type of beer, called *Kölsch,* is pale, hoppy, and highly fermented. Most of Köln's breweries (such as Gaffel and Päffgen) run their own restaurants, which you'll find in districts like Alter Markt and Friesenplatz.

Near Alter Markt

Gaffel Haus, run by the Gaffel Kölsch brewery, serves good local food. Look for the wall filled with coats of arms of Köln's old guilds *(Gaffeln)*—see how many crafts you can guess by their pictures (€10–17 main dishes, daily 11:00–24:00, near Lintgasse at Alter Markt 20–22, tel. 0221/257-7692).

Papa Joe's Klimperkasten is a dark pub packed with memorabilia and live jazz daily (€5–10 meals, daily 11:00–24:00, live piano jazz Sept–May Sun–Thu from 20:00, Alter Markt 50–52, tel. 0221/258-2132). A couple minutes' walk away is its rowdier sibling, **Papa Joe's Jazzlokal** (live bands nightly from 20:00, Buttermarkt 37, tel. 0221/257-7931, www.papajoes.de for jazz schedule). Both of these win the "atmosphere award."

Near the Train Station and Cathedral

Früh am Dom, close to the cathedral, offers three floors of touristy, traditional German drinking and dining options. Head to the back wall to check out a painting of what the city looked like in 1534 (€9–14 main dishes, daily 8:00–24:00, Am Hof 12–14, tel. 0221/261-3211).

Holtmann's im MAK, a museum café with sophisticated locals enjoying light fare, is a good option for a non-*Bräuhaus* lunch. If you eat here on a Sunday morning, be sure to sit outside and enjoy a free organ concert al fresco—the courtyard abuts a church (€5–10 meals, Tue–Sun 11:00–17:00, closed Mon, on other side of Hohe Strasse from the cathedral in Museum of Applied Arts—Museum für Angewandte Kunst—at An der Rechtschule 1, inside front door and down the stairs, no museum ticket needed, tel. 0221/2779-8860).

Café Eigel, just off Hohe Strasse near the recommended Hotel Engelbertz, is a good option for *Kaffee und Küchen* (afternoon cake and coffee) or for a light lunch of salads or omelets. It's been in the same location for 50 years, but was recently remodeled in a fresh, sleek, modern style. Enjoy delicious pastries in the airy atrium, and be sure to pick up some homemade chocolates (€7–10 main dishes, €3 slices of cake, Mon–Fri 9:00–19:00, Sat 9:00–18:00, Sun 14:00–18:00, Brückenstrasse 1–3, tel. 0221/257-5858).

Schreckenskammer is a down-home joint just behind the St. Ursula church, near the recommended Harmonie and Cristall hotels and the Station Hostel. The sand on the floor, swept out and replaced each morning, buffs the hardwood and also keeps it clean. The *kammer* is small and cozy, so be prepared to share a table and make new friends over a *Kölsch* or two. Most meals (choose from the *Tageskarte,* or daily specials) start with a complimentary cup of *Brühe* (broth). Don't mistake this as an act of hospitality—it only serves to make you thirstier. This eatery is really popular with locals, so arrive early or make a reservation (€7–14 main dishes, €6–10 lunch specials, Mon–Fri 11:00–13:45 & 16:30–22:30, Sat 11:00–14:00, closed Sun, cash only, Ursulagartenstrasse 11–15, tel. 0221/132-581).

Near Friesenplatz

This neighborhood, a 20-minute walk west from the cathedral and train station, is thick with restaurants, clubs, and pubs (some run by breweries). **Päffgen** is one brewery outlet where the *Köbes* (Köln's traditionally grumpy waiters) really live up to their reputation as they dish out traditional *Kölsch* food. Beers are served in delicate glasses (by Bavarian standards) and shuttled around in small, wreath-like trays *(Bierkranz).* This is the place to satisfy your cravings for blood sausage *(Blutwurst)* and kidneys *(Nierchen)*...or, for something a little more mainstream, try the tasty *Rheinischer Sauerbraten* with *Klössen* (dumplings) and applesauce (€7–15 main dishes, daily 10:00–24:00, food served 11:30–23:00, Friesenstrasse 64–66, tel. 0911/135-461).

TRANSPORTATION CONNECTIONS

From Köln by Train to: Bonn (5/hr, 20–30 min), **Remagen** (2–3/hr, 30–50 min), **Aachen** (2/hr, 50–60 min), **Frankfurt** (direct trains hourly, 70 min; also slower, cheaper trains), **Frankfurt Airport** (1–2/hr, 1 hr), **Bacharach** or **St. Goar** (hourly, 1.75 hrs, transfer in Koblenz), **Cochem** (hourly, 1.75 hrs; most with transfer in Koblenz), **Trier** (at least hourly, 2.5–3 hrs, some change in Koblenz), **Würzburg** (almost hourly, 2.5 hrs, usually 1–2 changes), **Munich** (2/hr, 4.5 hrs), **Berlin** (hourly, 4.5 hrs), **Paris** (6/day direct, 4 hrs, Thalys train—requires seat reservation, slower options also available), **Amsterdam** (6/day direct, 2.5 hrs). Train info: tel. 11861 (€0.60/min).

The Unromantic Rhine

Highlights

▲Bonn—Bonn was chosen for its sleepy, cultured, and peaceful nature as a good place to plant West Germany's first post-Hitler government. Since the two Germanys became one again in 1989, Berlin has taken back its position as capital.

Today, Bonn is sleek, modern, and, by big-city standards, remarkably pleasant and easygoing. The pedestrian-only old town stretching out from the station will make you wonder why the US can't trade in its malls for real, people-friendly cities. The market square and Münsterplatz—filled with street musicians—are a joy. People-watching doesn't get much better, though the actual sights are disappointing. There's a sparse exhibit at Beethoven's House (€5; April–Oct Mon–Sat 10:00–18:00, Sun 11:00–18:00; Nov–March Mon–Sat 10:00–17:00, Sun 11:00–17:00; last entry 25 min before closing, free English brochure, tel. 0228/981-7525, www.beethoven-haus-bonn.de). The **TI** is a five-minute walk from the station (Mon–Fri 9:00–18:30, Sat 9:00–16:00, Sun 10:00–14:00, go straight on Windeckstrasse, next to Karstadt department store, tel. 0228/775-000, www.bonn.de).

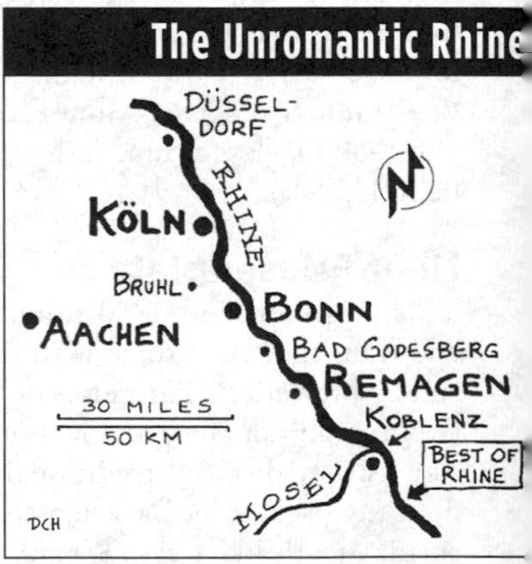

▲**Remagen**—Midway between Koblenz and Köln are the scant remains of the Bridge at Remagen, of WWII (and movie) fame. But the memorial and the bridge stubs are enough to stir the emotions of Americans who remember when it was the only bridge that remained, allowing the Allies to cross the Rhine and race to Berlin in 1945. A small museum tells the bridge's fascinating story in English. It was built during World War I to help supply the German forces on the Western Front. Ironically, one war later, Eisenhower said the bridge was worth its weight in gold for its service *against* Germany. Hitler executed four generals for their failure to blow it up. Ten days after US forces arrived, the bridge did collapse, killing 28 American soldiers. Today you can pay your respects at the bridge and visit its "Peace Museum" (€3.50, early March–mid-Nov daily 10:00–17:00, May–Oct until 18:00, closed mid-Nov–early March; it's on the Rhine's west bank, south side of Remagen town, follow *Brücke von Remagen* signs; www.bruecke-remagen.de). Remagen **TI:** tel. 02642/20187.

▲**Aachen (Charlemagne's Capital)**—This city was the capital of Europe in A.D. 800, when Charles the Great (Charlemagne) called it Aix-la-Chapelle. The remains of his rule include an impressive Byzantine- and Ravenna-inspired church, with his sarcophagus and throne. Enjoy the town's charming historic pedestrian center and festive Christmas market. See the headliner newspaper museum and great fountains, including a clever arrange-'em-yourself version.

Lowlights

Heidelberg—This famous old university town attracts hordes of Americans. Any surviving charm is stained almost beyond recognition by commercialism. It doesn't make it into Germany's top three weeks.

Mainz, Wiesbaden, and Rüdesheim—These towns are all too big or too famous. They're not worth your time. Mainz's Gutenberg Museum is also a disappointment.

NÜRNBERG

Nürnberg (sometimes spelled "Nuremberg" in English), Bavaria's second city, is known for its glorious medieval architecture, its important Germanic history museum, its haunting Nazi past, its famous Christmas market (Germany's biggest), and its little bratwurst (Germany's tiniest). Nürnberg was one of Europe's leading cities in about 1500, and its large imperial castle marks it as a stronghold of the Holy Roman Empire. Today, though Nürnberg has half a million residents, the charming Old Town with its red-sandstone Gothic buildings makes visitors feel like they are in a far smaller city.

Planning Your Time

Nürnberg is a handy stop between other German destinations, and an easy add-on to any itinerary that includes Munich, Würzburg, or Rothenburg (each about an hour away by frequent trains). For the quickest visit to Nürnberg, toss your bag in a locker at the station and head directly to the former Nazi Rally Grounds. If you are staying one night or day-tripping from elsewhere, visit the Nazi sites, stroll through the Old Town from the train station up to the castle (following my self-guided walk), and—on the way back to the station (or your hotel)—dip into the wonderful Germanic National Museum. If you have two days (only worthwhile if you have a serious interest in Nazi history), spend one on Nazi sites and the other in the Old Town.

ORIENTATION

(area code: 0911)

Nürnberg's Old Town (containing all the non-Nazi sights) is surrounded by its three-mile-long wall and moat, and beyond that, a ring road. At the southeast corner of the ring is the train station; across the street, just inside the ring, is the medieval Frauentor gate. From the Frauentor, sights cluster along a straight line (Königstrasse) downhill to the small Pegnitz River, then back uphill through the main market square (Hauptmarkt) to the castle (Kaiserburg). The former Nazi Rally Grounds are southeast of the center (easily accessible by tram or S-Bahn; see page 395).

Tourist Information

Nürnberg's handy and helpful TI is across the ring road from the station, in the modern building just opposite the Frauentor (Mon–Sat 9:00–19:00, closed Sun, Königstrasse 93, tel. 0911/233-6132, www.tourismus.nuernberg.de). Pick up the free city map (with updated sight hours and prices on the back) and get information about bus and walking tours. The TI also offers free Internet access (15-min maximum), books rooms (no fee), and sells transit passes and the Nürnberg Card (see below). The TI has a small branch office at #18 on the Hauptmarkt (Mon–Sat 9:00–18:00, also open Sun May–Oct and during the Christmas market 10:00–16:00).

Discount Deals: Buy a €5 ticket for any of Nürnberg's city-run museums—including the Nazi Documentation Center, Albrecht Dürer House, Toy Museum, and the City Museum—and you can visit all the others as well for no extra charge on the same day (see www.museen.nuernberg.de). Because this is such a great value, I'd skip the two other available deals: the **"Take Five" Ticket** (€19, covers five entrances into your choice of seven different museums, shareable by multiple people, sold at participating sights and at Frauentor TI) and the **Nürnberg Card** (€19/2 days, free for kids 12 and under, sold at the TI and most hotels, covers all of your local transportation and admission to all of Nürnberg's museums, plus small discounts off bus and walking tours, only available to those spending at least one night in Nürnberg). Finally, another €12 combo-ticket offers admission to the National Germanic Museum and Albrecht Dürer House (otherwise €11) and includes a handheld computer guide to the museums and the walking route connecting them (€20 deposit for computer).

Arrival in Nürnberg

By Train: Nürnberg's stately old Hauptbahnhof—with a shiny new interior—is conveniently located just outside the old city walls and ring road. The station has WCs, lockers, ATMs, and lots of shops.

You can get train information and buy tickets at the *Reisezentrum* in the main hall (center of building, Mon–Fri 6:00–21:00, Sat–Sun 8:00–21:00).

To reach the **Frauentor** (the medieval city's southern gate)—which is near most recommended hotels and is also the starting point for exploring the Old Town—follow signs for *Ausgang/City* down the escalator, then signs to *Königstor/Frauentor* and *Altstadt* in the underpass. When you emerge, the TI is on your right and the Frauentor tower is on your left.

To go directly to the **former Nazi Rally Grounds** from the station, follow the pink *Tram* signs in the underpass to the stop in front of the Postbank Center, and catch tram #9 in the direction of Doku-Zentrum (leaves every 10 min).

Getting Around Nürnberg

Most of Nürnberg's sights are in the strollable Old Town, but the Nazi sites are far beyond walking distance. Nürnberg's public transportation network has trams, buses, U-Bahns (subways), and S-Bahns (faster suburban trains). All work on the same tickets, which you can buy at vending machines (marked *VAG Fahrausweise*) on the tram platform or before entering the U- or S-Bahns, or on board (buses only). A single ticket *(Einzelfahrkarte)* costs €1.90 (good for 90 min of travel in one direction, including transfers). A **day ticket** is €3.80 (*TagesTicket Solo,* good for one calendar day or Sat and Sun; the €6.40 *TagesTicket Plus* covers 2 adults and up to 4 children; day tickets also sold at TI). For more information in English, see www.vgn.de. While the day tickets come date-stamped, single tickets must be validated on board (for the bus or tram) or before going down to the platform (for the subway).

Helpful Hints

Internet Access: While there are several Internet cafés in the city center, save some euros and take advantage of free Internet access in the **TI** (15-min time limit).

Laundry: An **SB-Waschsalon** coin launderette with instructions in English is at Pirckheimerstrasse 121, right at the Wurzelbauerstrasse stop of tram #9 (5 stops from train station, direction Thon, same tram as Nazi Rally Grounds but in the other direction; daily 6:00–23:00).

TOURS

Walking Tours—Tours in English of Nürnberg's Old Town leave from the branch TI at Hauptmarkt 18 daily in the tourist season at 13:00 (May–Oct and Dec, €9 plus castle admission, kids under 14 free, 2.5 hrs, no reservation needed, buy ticket from TI or guide, www.nuernberg-tours.de). This is the only way to see the sights in the castle interior with an English-speaking guide (see "Imperial Castle" on page 390).

Bus Tours—These tours, which include some walking, leave daily at 9:30 May through October from the Old Granary at Hallplatz, two blocks up from the Frauentor TI (€13, buy ticket on bus or at TI, 2.5 hrs, in German and English, tel. 0911/202-290, www.neukam.de).

Tourist Train—A goofy little tourist train makes the rounds in the Old Town (€6, 40 min, live narration in German only, written information in English, schedule posted at fountain, leaves Hauptmarkt about hourly 10:30–16:00).

Private Guide—For a good and charming local guide, call **Doris Ritter** (€95/3 hrs, tel. 0911/518-1719, mobile 0176-2421-5863, doris.ritter@nuernberg-tours.de). Guides can also be booked through the TI (tel. 0911/233-6123, fuehrung@ctz-nuernberg.de).

SELF-GUIDED WALK

▲▲Nürnberg's Old Town

Nürnberg's best sights are conveniently clustered along a straight-line thoroughfare connecting the train station (Hauptbahnhof) with the main market square (Hauptmarkt) and the castle (Kaiserburg). For a good orientation, take the following self-guided stroll. Plan on an hour, not including stops.

• *Begin at the Frauentor (where you emerge from the Hauptbahnhof underpass). Review the lay of the land on the 10-foot-tall city map posted in front of the tunnel (find the four towers). This tour will take you from the red dot at the bottom to the* Burg *(castle) at the top.*

NÜRNBERG

Frauentor

This tower guards one of the four medieval entrances to Nürnberg's Old Town. Of the three miles of wall that once surrounded the city, 90 percent survives. Many Central European cities (such as Vienna) tore down their walls to make way for expansion in the 1800s, and Nürnberg nearly did the same. Now they're glad they didn't—it's better for tourism.

• *Between the walls just next to the gate, you'll see the entrance to the...*

Craftsmen's Courtyard (Handwerkerhof)

This hokey collection of half-timbered houses was built in 1971 to celebrate craftsmanship and to honor the 500th birthday of Nürnberg's famous resident Albrecht Dürer. Nürnberg did not have abundant natural resources or a navigable waterway, so its citizens made their living through trade and crafts (such as making scientific instruments, weapons, and armor). Dürer, arguably

Central Nürnberg

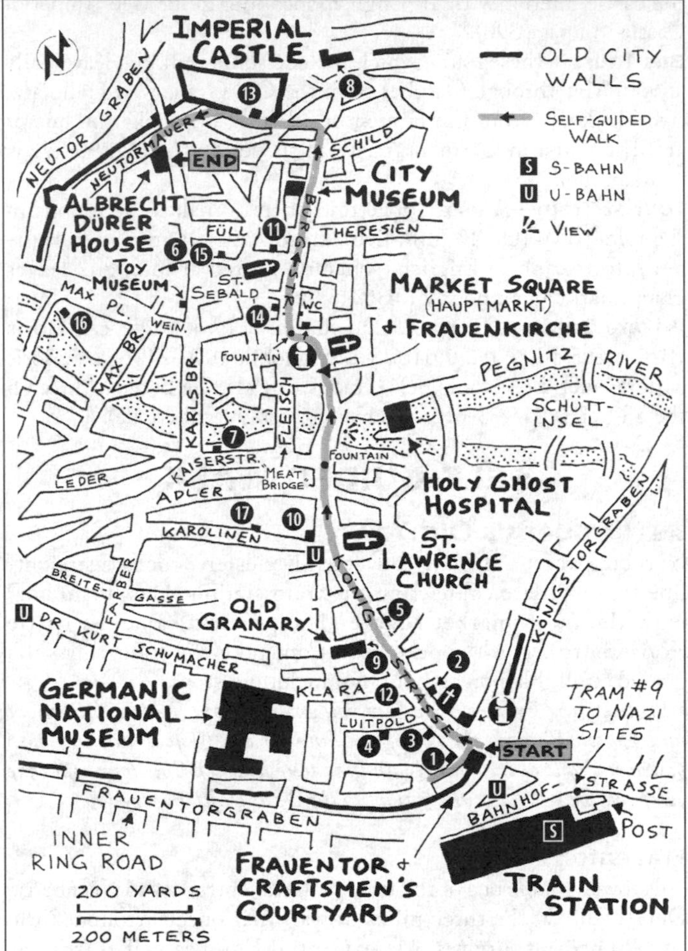

1. Hotel Victoria
2. Hotel Drei Raben & Aldi Supermarket
3. Ibis Altstadt Hotel
4. Hotels Probst & Keiml
5. City Hotel
6. Hotel Elch
7. Hotel Lucas
8. Nürnberg Youth Hostel
9. Barfüsser Beer Cellar
10. Nassauer Keller Restaurant
11. Goldenes Posthorn Rest.
12. Literaturhaus Nürnberg Rest.
13. Burgwächter Restaurant
14. Bratwursthäusle Rest.
15. Restaurant Sebald
16. Kettensteg Biergarten
17. Karstadt Supermarket

Germany's best painter, was considered the ultimate craftsman. The proud medieval tradition of craftsmanship continues today, as the city is home to some of Germany's top goldsmiths and glassblowers.

While a bit kitschy, this courtyard is good for picking up a medieval vibe as you enter the Old Town. It's packed with replicas of medieval shops, where artisans actually make—and, of course, sell—leather, pottery, and brass goods. In the Middle Ages, this area between the walls was not a medieval mall but *Passkontrolle*—a customs and security checkpoint zone where all visitors had to register before they could enter the town.

At the back of the courtyard, step through the old gate and out onto a bridge over what was the moat. The bridge marks one of four entries into the medieval town. Look up at the mighty round Frauentor tower. It was originally square, but was made round after the development of better cannons (so balls would glance off rather than hit it head-on). Imagine cannons lined up under the eaves of the tower, set to defend the city. When local kids look at the mighty train station (across the street), they remember that the first train in Germany choo-chooed from here in 1835.

• *When you're finished poking around the courtyard, head into town (with the train station at your back) on...*

Königstrasse

Though it had always been one of the four primary entrances to Nürnberg, this street became the city's main drag only after the train station was built in the early 20th century. It's lined with key sights, several recommended hotels and restaurants, and some wonderful Gothic and Neo-Gothic architecture.

Nürnberg hit its peak in the 14th century, and a 1356 conference held here issued a decree called the Golden Bull, which regularized the election of the Holy Roman Emperor. From then throughout the Middle Ages, German emperors were elected in Frankfurt, crowned in Aachen, and were supposed to hold their first Imperial Diet (a gathering of German nobles and VIPs) right here in Nürnberg...though not all bothered to follow through on such democratic notions.

Nürnberg's low point came during World War II. By the end of the war, 90 percent of the Old Town was destroyed—the only German city hit worse was Dresden. If a building was only damaged, it was repaired in the original Gothic style—check out the building with the Peschke Optik shop at Königstrasse 81. But some buildings were completely destroyed. Instead of rebuilding these exactly as they were, or replacing them with modern-style buildings, postwar German architects compromised, creating styles that were at once modern and traditional. In Nürnberg, they often rebuilt in local sandstone. Look 50 yards down the street at #71. The design is modern, but it replicates some of the Gothic lines and uses the same distinctive red stone as older buildings.

Ahead, on the left, is the small **Clara Church** (Klarakirche). In the Middle Ages, Nürnberg had nine monasteries like this one. When the Reformation hit, Nürnberg turned Lutheran, and most of the monasteries were torn down. As they fell, so did Nürnberg's importance; the city was now Lutheran, but the emperors were still Catholic. They moved the increasingly frequent Imperial Diet—once Nürnberg's claim to fame—to more Catholic-friendly Regensburg. (Today, this church is an "ecumenical free church"—meaning it's neither Lutheran nor Catholic and welcomes all stripes.)

Across the street from Clara Church, look for Mary on the second-story corner. Statues like this bless houses all over Nürnberg.

• *Continue down Königstrasse to Hallplatz and the Old Granary (where the pedestrian stretch begins). The minimalist metal arch (left) remembers the German refugees of World War II, and the hospitality of the Bavarians who took them in. If you want to visit the excellent Germanic National Museum (described on page* 392*) now, detour left at Hallplatz and walk 200 yards. Otherwise, check out the...*

Old Granary (Mauthalle)

Medieval Nürnberg had 11 of these huge granaries to ensure that they'd have enough food in case of famine or siege. The grain was stored up above in the attic (behind all those little dormer windows). Today, the cellar is home to a lively beer hall, Barfüsser (see "Eating," page 401).

Go around the right side of the building and find the fun little **Vom Fass shop,** which sells liquor, wine, vinegar, and oils "from the tap" (as the name indicates). You bring or buy a container of any size, fill it with what you like (tastes allowed), and they'll even write a gifty message right on the bottle (An der Mauthalle 2, Mon–Fri 10:00–19:00, Sat 10:00–18:00, closed Sun, Herr Eduard Stöber).

Continue down pedestrians-only Königstrasse. This drag used to have more cars and trams than any other street in town. But when the U-Bahn came in the 1970s, this part of the street became traffic-free.

• *After another two blocks, you'll see...*

▲▲St. Lawrence Church (Lorenzkirche)

The church is a massive house of worship, but it's not a cathedral—because Nürnberg never had a bishop (a fact locals were very proud of...a bishop would have threatened their prized independence). The name of Königstrasse ("King's Street")—where you've been walking—is misleading. When most royals came to town, they actually preferred to come through the west gate, so they could approach this masterful facade head-on. Stand in front of the church's main door. Flip around and imagine the Holy Roman Emperor parading—right past Starbucks—toward this magnificent Oz-like church.

Study the 260-foot-tall **facade** (completed c. 1360). Adam and Eve flank the doors (looking for a sweater). In the first row above the left door, you'll see two scenes: an intimate take on Jesus' birth on top, and the visit from the Magi on the bottom (with the starfish of Bethlehem shining from above). Over the right door, you'll see the slaughter of the innocents (with a baby skewered by a Roman sword—classic medieval subtlety), and below that, the presentation of Jesus in the temple and the flight to Egypt. Above those scenes is the Passion story (from lowest to highest: trial, scourging, carrying the cross, Crucifixion, deposition, entombment, Resurrection, and people coming out of their graves for Judgment Day). The saved (Peter—with his huge key—and company) are on the left, and the sorry chain gang of the damned (including kings and bishops) is shuttled off literally into the jaws of hell on the right. Above it all stands the triumphant resurrected Christ, with the sun and moon at his feet, flanked by angels tooting alphorns.

Step inside (enter around right side, €1 donation requested, €5 for a pass to take photos, Mon–Sat 9:00–17:00, Sun 12:00–16:00).

The **interior** wasn't completely furnished until more than a century after the church was built—just in time for the Reformation (so the Catholic decor adorned a now-Lutheran church). Most of the decorations inside were donated by wealthy Nürnbergers trying to cut down on their time in purgatory. Through the centuries, this art survived three separate threats: the iconoclasm of the Reformation, the whitewashing of the Baroque age, and the bombing of World War II. While Nürnberg was the first "Free Imperial City" to break with the Catholic Church and become Lutheran, locals didn't go wild (like Swiss Protestants did) in tearing down the rich, Mary-oriented decor of their fine churches.

Luther told the iconoclasts, "Tear the idols out of your heart, and you'll understand that these statues are only pieces of wood."

Suspended over the altar, the woodcarving called ***The Annunciation*** is by a Nürnberg citizen who was one of Central Europe's best woodcarvers, Veit Stoss. Carved in 1517, it shows the angel Gabriel telling Mary that she'll be giving birth to the Messiah. Startled, she drops her prayer book. This is quite Catholic (notice the rosary frame with beads, and a circle of roses—one for each Hail Mary, and with a medallion depicting the "Joys of Mary"). The dove sits on Mary's head, and God the Father—looking as powerful as a Holy Roman Emperor—looks down. The figures are carved from linden trees. This survived the Reformation covered in a sack, revealed only on special occasions. Around back, enjoy more details—Mary's cascading hair, and the sun and the moon. Nearby, the altar painting at the very front of the church (behind the altar) shows the city of Nürnberg in 1483 (before the city's square towers were made round).

To the left of the altar, the frilly **tabernacle** tower is the "house of sacraments" that stored the consecrated Communion wafer. After the Mass, leftovers needed a worthy—even heavenly—home...and this was it. The cupboard behind the gold grate was the appropriate receptacle for "the body of Christ." The theme of the carving is the Passion. The scenes ascend in chronological order: Last Supper, Judas' kiss, arrest, Crucifixion, and so on. Everything is carved of stone except for the risen Christ (way up high). He was living, and so was this...it's made of wood. The man holding the tabernacle on his shoulders is the artist who created it, Adam Kraft. In the Middle Ages, artists were faceless artisans, no more important than a blacksmith or a stonemason. But in the 1490s, when this was made, the Renaissance was in the air, and artists like Kraft began putting themselves into their works. Kraft's contemporary, the painter Albrecht Dürer, actually signed his works—an incredible act in Germany at that time (see "Albrecht Dürer House," page 391). In anticipation of the Allied bombs of World War II, this precious work was encased in protective concrete except for the top 22 feet—which was the only part destroyed when the church was hit.

Adam Kraft is looking up at a **plaque** honoring the American philanthropist who donated nearly a million Deutschmarks in 1950 to help rebuild the church. Though the church was devastated by WWII bombs, everything movable had been hidden away in bunkers, including the stained glass you see today. The plaque is in English, but it's hard to read, as it's written in the Gothic Fraktur font. In the back of the church, a silent **video** (with dates in the upper corner) shows the preparations in anticipation of WWII bombs, the destruction, and the reconstruction.

As you leave, notice that the church has many **side chapels**—employing an innovative trick of expanding the nave out so the buttresses are actually inside the church.

From St. Lawrence Church to the River: Back outside, find the castle-like building on the corner across from the church facade. This is the only remaining **tower house** in Nürnberg. It was built in 1200, when there was no city wall, and the locals had to defend their own homes. It's basically a one-family castle. (In the basement, you'll find an appropriately medieval restaurant—complete with suits of armor—called the Nassauer Keller; see "Eating," page 401.)

Continue downhill to the river. American moralists might shield their eyes from the kinky **Fountain of the Seven Virtues.** Otherwise, play a game: Circle the sprightly fountain and try to identify the classic virtues by the symbolism: justice (on top), faith, love, hope (anchor), courage (lion), temperance (moderation), patience. Are any birds sipping?

• *Continue down the street. Caution: You'll pass Kaiserstrasse on your left—the most expensive shopping street in town (with a little shop filled with insanely expensive Steiff teddy bears). When you get to the bridge, look to the right.*

Holy Ghost Hospital (Heilig-Geist-Spital)

This river-spanning hospital was donated to Nürnberg in the 14th century by the city's richest resident, eager to do his part to help the poor...and hopefully skip purgatory altogether. (A statue of him hangs out on the second-story corner of the Spital Apotheke, the first building after the bridge.) He funded this very scenic hospital to care for ill, disabled, and elderly Nürnbergers. The wing over the river dates from the 16th century. The dove beneath the middle window under the turret represents the Holy Ghost, the hospital's namesake.

If you look in the distance to the right—beyond the hospital and the next two bridges—you'll see a half-timbered fragment of the town wall. The big white building to the right of that is Germany's biggest multiplex cinema, with 21 screens (most underground).

Cross to the other side of the bridge, and look at the next bridge over (the **"Meat Bridge"**). This is the narrowest point of the river, and flooding was a big concern. Since this bridge doesn't have any piers, there's less chance of a collapse. When this was built in 1596, it was considered an engineering feat—the most high-tech bridge in Central Europe, inspired by Venice's single-span Rialto Bridge. The river once powered the town's medieval water mills.

Continue across the bridge and study the monument depicting characters from a 15th-century satire called ***The Ship of Fools*** *(Das Narrenschiff)*. It's adapted to follies that plague modern society: violence, technology, and apathy. Hey, how about the quiet, people-friendly ambience created by making this big city traffic-free in the center? Do a slow 360-degree spin and imagine this back home.

• *Now enter the...*

▲▲Market Square (Hauptmarkt)

When Nürnberg boomed in the 13th century, it consisted of two distinct walled towns separated by the river. As the towns grew and it became obvious that the two should merge, the middle wall came down. This square, built by the Holy Roman Emperor Charles IV, became the center of the newly united city. Though Charles is more often associated with Prague (he's the namesake for the Charles Bridge and Charles University), he also loved Nürnberg—and visited 60 times during his reign.

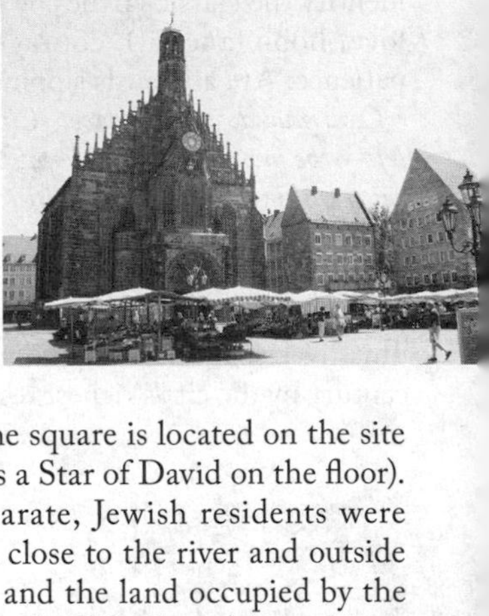

The **Frauenkirche** church on the square is located on the site of a former synagogue (inside, there's a Star of David on the floor). When Nürnberg's towns were separate, Jewish residents were required to live in this swampy area close to the river and outside the walls. When the towns merged and the land occupied by the Jewish quarter became valuable, Charles IV allowed his subjects to force out the Jews—and 600 were killed in the process...a somber reminder that anti-Semitism predated the Nazis. Charles IV, the most powerful man in Europe in his time, oversees the square from a perch high on the church facade. He's waiting for noon, when the electors dance around him.

Year-round, the Hauptmarkt is lively with fruit, flower, and souvenir stands. For a few weeks before Christmas, it hosts Germany's largest **Christmas market** (*Christkindlmarkt,* more than 2 million visitors annually, starts the Friday before the first Sunday in Advent).

Walk across the square to the pointy, gold **Beautiful Fountain** (Schöner Brunnen). Medieval tanneries, slaughterhouses, and the

hospital you just saw dumped their byproducts into the river. So this fountain brought clean drinking water into the square. Of course, it's packed with allegorical meaning. Step up to the iron railing. The outermost figures ringing the bottom represent the arts (such as philosophy, music, and astronomy). On the pillars just above them are the four church fathers and the four Evangelists, showing that religion is higher than the arts. On the column itself, the lowest figures are the seven electors of the Holy Roman Emperor and nine heroes: three Christian (including King Arthur and Charlemagne); three Jewish (such as King David); and three heathen (such as Julius Caesar). At the very top are eight prophets, hovering above—but granting legitimacy to—worldly power. On the side of the fountain facing the McDonald's, you'll probably see tourists fussing over a gold ring. If you believe in such silly tour-guide tales, spinning this ring three times brings good luck...okay, go ahead and spin it. The black ring opposite (nearest the stork bearing a baby—look for the rice on the ground) brings fertility. Civic marriage ceremonies that take place at the adjacent City Hall often end up here for photos.

• *Leave the square straight uphill from the fountain, heading for the castle. Along the way, you'll pass St. Sebald (Sebaldkirche), Nürnberg's second great Gothic church. About 100 yards farther up the hill, you'll see the...*

City Museum (Stadtmuseum Fembohaus)

This museum is packed with fine artifacts, but you'll need the English audioguide to give them meaning (included in admission, €20 deposit). Check out the top-floor model of Nürnberg. The museum's Noricama Nürnberg Film is a fascinating 50-minute video shown on the hour (in English with headphones) that gives a fun and thoughtful overview of the city, its history, and its great sights in a comfortable little theater (museum-€5, film-€4, €7 combo-ticket includes both, Tue–Fri 10:00–17:00, Sat–Sun 10:00–18:00, closed Mon, Burgstrasse 15, tel. 0911/231-2595, www.museen.nuernberg.de).

• *Now huff the rest of the way up to the Imperial Castle. The cobbled path forks at the castle's base. The right fork leads to the Castle Garden and youth hostel. The left fork leads to the castle courtyard (see big, round tower high above) and over the Burgwächter restaurant (see page 402). For now, take the left fork and visit the...*

▲Imperial Castle (Kaiserburg)

In the Middle Ages, Holy Roman Emperors stayed here when they were in town. The huge complex has 45 buildings. The part on the right, which housed the stables and stored grain, is now a youth hostel (see page 401).

The castle interior and museum are standard fare. The most interesting bits are the so-called Deep Well (which, at 165 feet, is...well, deep) and the Romanesque double-decker chapel (higher nobility in the upper chapel, lower nobility down below, plus a special balcony for the emperor). The tower climb offers only a higher city view and lots of exercise.

The castle grounds are free, but unfortunately, you can only see the interior sights with a German-language tour (€6 for 1-hour tour of museum, palace, chapel, well, and then the chance to visit the museum and climb the tower on your own; €3 to visit just the well and then climb tower on your own; tickets sold in office at top end of courtyard; daily April–Sept 9:00–18:00, Oct–March 10:00–16:00, tel. 0911/244-6590, www.schloesser.bayern.de). There is one alternative: Go with the TI's English tour of the entire Old Town, which includes the castle (departs at 13:00, see "Tours," earlier in this chapter).

Deep Well visits (about 4/hr), even with the German guide, are simple, quick, and fun: You'll see water poured way, waaay down—into an incredible hole dug in the 14th century. Then a small candle is lowered until it almost disappears into the water table.

• *Now you get to walk downhill again. The quick way down is to retrace your steps to the Burgwächter restaurant; then turn right and walk beneath the castle along Am Ölberg and Obere Schmiedgasse to Tiergärtnertorplatz (see next page). The scenic route, which takes an extra 15 minutes, leads you around the back of the castle through the...*

Castle Garden (Burggarten)

Find the entrance to the castle garden. It's at the back of the hill, between the main complex and the youth hostel, and signposted *Burggarten,* but a bit hidden (you may have to ask). The garden, wrapped around the back of the castle, offers great views of the

town's 16th-century fortifications and former moat.

• *Follow the path around the castle. Either make a quick return through the first archway on your left, or continue another five minutes through landscaped gardens along the old city walls. Eventually you'll be spit out in between two archways in front of a round tower (Neutor). Go through the archway on your left, then turn left, and walk two slightly uphill blocks along Neutormauer to the square with the giant rabbit statue. This is...*

Tiergärtnertorplatz

Near the top of the square, inspect the giant rabbit. While it looks like roadkill with mice gnawing at it, it's actually a modern interpretation of one of the best-known paintings by medieval Nürnberg artist Albrecht Dürer, *The Hare.* (The original painting is in Vienna.)

• *The rabbit faces a half-timbered building at the bottom of the square. That's the...*

▲Albrecht Dürer House (Albrecht-Dürer-Haus)

Nürnberg's most famous local lived in this house for the last 20 years of his life. Albrecht Dürer (1471–1528), a contemporary of Michelangelo, studied in Venice and brought the Renaissance to stodgy medieval Germany. He did things that were unthinkable to other northern European artists of his time—such as signing his works, or painting things like hares simply for study (not on commission).

Nothing in the museum is original (all of the paintings are replicas—the only Dürer originals in Nürnberg are in the Germanic National Museum, described later in this chapter). But the museum does a fine job of capturing the way that Dürer actually lived, and includes a replica of the workshop where he printed his woodcuts with a working printing press. In one room, a 17-minute movie plays continuously (in English on your headphones). The top floor is a gallery with copies of Dürer's most famous paintings and woodcuts. On Saturdays at 14:00, you can meet Dürer's wife, Agnes, who speaks English and takes you through their house (€5, includes Agnes-led audioguide, live Agnes tour-€2.50 extra, €1.50 English brochure also available, €12 combo-ticket with Germanic National Museum—described on next page, Tue–Sun 10:00–17:00, Thu until 20:00, closed Mon except July–Sept and Dec 10:00–17:00, Albrecht-Dürer-Strasse 39, tel. 0911/231-2568, www.albrecht-duerer-haus.de).

• You've walked from the southern gate of Nürnberg to the northern gate, and your tour is over. If heading from here to the Nazi sites, bus #36 from Hauptmarkt or a taxi are your best bets. Or, for more sightseeing on your way back to the Frauentor, two more Old Town museums are listed in the next section.

SIGHTS

In the Old Town

Toy Museum (Spielzeugmuseum)—Nürnberg is famous for woodworking. You can see some examples of this local craft—and lots more—at this entertaining, interactive collection of toys from across the ages. The chronological display starts on the ground floor and heads up through four more floors. Highlights are: for history buffs—the militarization of the 1930s and the rubble years through the 1950s section; for Nebraskans—the Omaha train station in miniature; and for kids—the top-floor play zone. The English coverage of this fine exhibit is mediocre. Ask about an audioguide, or consider the good little €3 booklet (€5/adult, €10.50/family, Tue–Fri 10:00–17:00, Sat–Sun 10:00–18:00, closed Mon, Karlstrasse 13–15, near Albrecht Dürer House, tel. 0911/231-3164, www.museen.nuernberg.de).

▲▲Germanic National Museum (Germanisches Nationalmuseum)—This sprawling, sweeping museum is dedicated to the cultural history of the German-speaking world. It occupies an interconnected maze of buildings, old and new, in the southern part of the Old Town, near the station and recommended hotels.

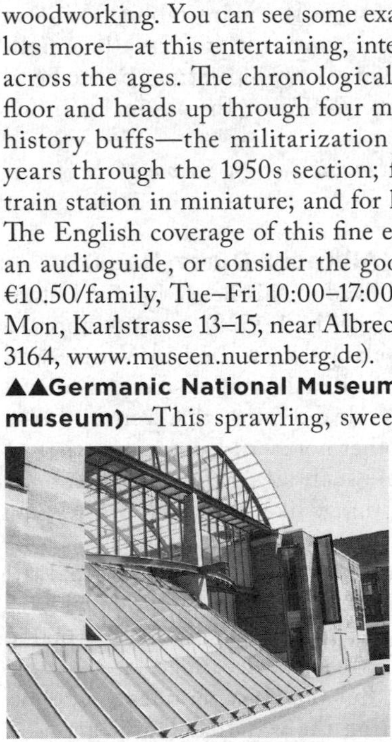

The museum is huge, and covers a vast spectrum of German culture from fine arts to prehistory to science to musical instruments. There are also regular temporary exhibits. You could spend days here, but the best approach is to get the bilingual "Floor Plan" brochure *(Orientierungsplan),* which lists the different collections. Pick out a few things you are really interested in. Note the room numbers and the color codes of the wings you're headed for. Few labels or signposts are in English, but free English brochures on some of the exhibitions are available in a rack by the entrance.

Highlights of the museum's medieval art collection are works by Dürer (the only originals in town), Rembrandt, and Tilman Riemenschneider, often arranged into temporary exhibitions.

Other "must-sees" generally on display include an early globe (since it dates from 1492, the Americas are conspicuously missing) and the delicate wooden *Nürnberg Madonna* (1515). This intimate, anonymous carving of the favorite hometown girl was the symbol of the city during the Romantic Age (19th century).

Coming in the entrance, you'll stand before a wall of street signs from East Germany dating from the time when the Soviets had renamed the main drag in many towns *Strasse der Befreiung* ("Street of the Liberation"—from the Nazis and capitalism). Also check out room 219 in the 20th-century collection (wing E, blue signs), which shows "approved Nazi art" that promoted the ideals of Nazism.

Entering the museum along Kartäusergasse, you walk along the "Way of Human Rights." Designed by an Israeli artist, its pillars trumpet each of the provisions of the United Nations' Universal Declaration of Human Rights.

Cost and Hours: €6, free Wed 18:00–21:00, worthwhile €1.50 audioguide, €12 combo-ticket includes entrance to Albrecht Dürer House as well as a handheld computer tour of both museums and the route between them (€20 deposit for computer); Tue–Sun 10:00–18:00 (upper floor closes at 17:00), Wed all floors until 21:00, closed Mon; free English tours every other Sun at 14:00, mandatory bag check (lockers with €1 refundable deposit), Kartäusergasse 1, 2 blocks west of Königstrasse (enter on far side of building), tel. 0911/13310, www.gnm.de.

Nazi Sites

Though the city tries to recast itself as the "City of Human Rights," its reputation as Hitler's favorite place for a really big party is hard to shake. To understand Nürnberg's role in the Nazi movement, visit Hitler's vast Nazi Party Rally Grounds (Reichsparteitagsgelände), and the excellent museum—the Nazi Documentation Center—set amid the mute remains of the Third Reich.

Planning Your Time: World War II buffs might want to make this an all-day visit (a café in the museum serves lunch). With half a day, spend two hours in the museum and then another hour following the path around the lake. On a lightning visit, see the museum, peek into the courtyard of the Congress Hall, and if time allows, walk to Zeppelin Field and back. Only part of the outdoor circuit is shaded, so bring a hat and sunscreen on a hot day. Make sure to pick up the free map and the €1 English guidebook from the museum counter before doing the walk around the lake.

Getting to the Nazi Documentation Center and Rally Grounds: The sprawling complex is wrapped around a pond called Dutzendteich, southeast of the Old Town. Take handy tram #9, which leaves from the front of the Postbank Center at the train station (Hauptbahnhof) every 10 minutes (direction: Doku-Zentrum, 15-min trip). Get off at the Doku-Zentrum stop, and check return times before going to the sites. From the Hauptmarkt or City Hall, you can also hop on the made-for-tourists bus #36, which takes you to the same place. Both options cost the same (€1.90 one-way, it's better to purchase the €3.80 day ticket—see page 380). As you get off the tram or bus, you'll see the...

▲▲▲Nazi Documentation Center (Dokumentationszentrum)

Visitors to Europe's Nazi and Holocaust sites inevitably ask the same haunting question: How could this happen? This superb museum does its best to provide an answer. It meticulously traces the evolution of the National Socialist (Nazi) movement, focusing on how it both energized and terrified the German people (the exhibit's title is "Fascination and Terror"). Special attention is paid to Nürnberg's role in the Nazi movement, including the construction and use of the Rally Grounds, where Hitler's largest demonstrations took place. This is not a World War II or Holocaust museum; those events are almost an afterthought. Instead, the center frankly analyzes the Nazi phenomenon, to understand how it happened—and to prevent it from happening again.

The museum is housed in one small wing of Hitler's cavernous, unfinished Congress Hall—the largest surviving example of Nazi architecture. The building was planned to host the mammoth annual Nazi Party gatherings. Today, it's symbolically sliced open by its modern entryway to show the guts and brains of the Nazi movement.

The exhibit is a one-way walk. Allow two hours just for the fine videos you can see along the way. WWII history buffs should allow an extra hour for the two movies that play continuously in the *Kino* at the start of the exhibit, offering excellent insights into the mass hypnosis of the German nation (interviews and old footage with English subtitles). Once you're in the exhibit, the included audioguide gives each display additional meaning (turns on automatically at video presentations, you dial room numbers for overviews and specific numbers for details of displays—if rushed, listen to the overviews only). You'll see parts of Leni Riefenstahl's 1934 propaganda classic *Triumph of the Will*, and just before the end, footage of the Nürnberg Trials. The last stop (before the long ramp back to the start) is a catwalk giving

Nazi Documentation Center and Rally Grounds

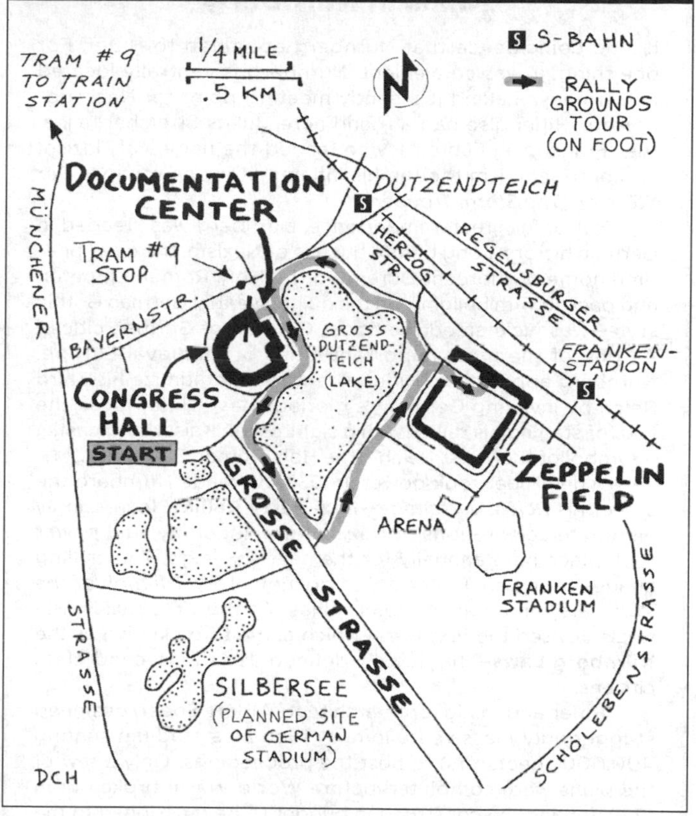

you a look into the core of what would have been a Congress Hall filled with 50,000 cheering Nazis (an artist's sketch is on a nearby wall).

Cost, Hours, Location: €5, includes audioguide, Mon–Fri 9:00–18:00, Sat–Sun 10:00–18:00, Bayernstrasse 110, tel. 0911/231-5666, www.museen.nuernberg.de.

▲Rally Grounds (Reichsparteitagsgelände)

The Rally Grounds occupy four square miles behind the museum. Albert Speer, Hitler's favorite architect, designed this immense complex of buildings for the Nazi rallies. Not many of Hitler's ambitious plans were completed, but you can visit the courtyard of the Congress Hall, Zeppelin Field (where Hitler addressed his followers), and a few other remains. The easiest way to see them is to follow the circular route around the lake that's shown in the map above and on the museum's free, bilingual area plan *(Geländeplan)*.

Nazis in Nürnberg

It's no coincidence that Nürnberg appealed to Hitler. For one thing, it was convenient: Nürnberg is centrally located in Germany, making it a handy meeting point for Nazi supporters. Hitler also had a friend here, Julius Streicher (a.k.a. the "Franconian Führer"), who fanned the flames of Nazism and anti-Semitism though his inflammatory newspaper *Der Stürmer (The Storm Trooper).*

But of far greater importance, Nürnberg was steeped in German history. Long before the rise of Nazism, the city—onetime home of Albrecht Dürer and the Holy Roman Emperor, and packed with buildings in the quintessential German Gothic style—was nicknamed the "most German of German cities." As one of the most important cities of medieval Europe, Nürnberg appealed to Hitler as a way to legitimize his Third Reich by invoking Germany's glorious past. Hitler loved the idea of staging his rallies within sight of the Kaiserburg castle, a symbol of the "First Reich" (the Holy Roman Empire).

When Hitler took power in 1933, he made Nürnberg the site of his *Reichsparteitage*—**Nazi Party Rallies.** Increasingly elaborate celebrations of Nazi culture, ideology, and power took place here annually for the next six years. The chilling images from Leni Riefenstahl's documentary *Triumph of the Will* were filmed at the 1934 rallies. At the 1935 rallies, the Nazis devised the first laws—which came to be known as the **Nürnberg Laws**—that legally defined Jews as second-class citizens.

Hitler and his favorite architect, Albert Speer, designed staggeringly massive buildings (such as a stadium seating 400,000 spectators) to host the proceedings. Only a few of the plans were completed before World War II broke out in 1939, forcing the construction budget to be reassigned to the war effort. Today, it's possible to walk around the still-unfinished remains of Hitler's megalomaniacal super-structures (see "Rally Grounds" on previous page). The Rally Grounds were the ultimate example of Hitler's preferred architecture style: stark, huge, and Neoclassical.

As the war drew to a close, the world puzzled over what to do with the Nazi officers who had overseen some of the most gruesome atrocities in the history of humankind. It was finally decided that they should be tried as war criminals by an international tribunal (spearheaded by the US and based on the Anglo-American code of law). These trials took place right here, in the **Nürnberg Trials Courtroom** (see page 398). The Nürnberg Trials—the first ever international war-crimes tribunal—brought about a new concept of international law, which continues today in The Hague, Netherlands.

The numbers on the plan correspond to the information pillars that you'll find on-site (this information also appears at www.reichsparteitagsgelaende.de).

Figure an hour round-trip from the Documentation Center to do the full circuit. If you have less time, you can visit the courtyard of the Congress Hall, or walk to Zeppelin Field and back, without doing the full loop. If you're really short on time, remember that you'll get the best sense of the Rally Grounds simply from the exhibits inside the Documentation Center.

I've listed the main sites here in the order you reach them while circling the lake.

Congress Hall (Kongresshalle): This huge building—big enough for an audience of 50,000—was originally intended to be topped with a roof and skylight. The Nazi Documentation Center occupies part of the hall. To see the vast, Colosseum-like courtyard, turn right as you leave the Documentation Center, and walk along the side of the building. Dip through the archway into the courtyard to appreciate its dimensions. Part of the hall is now used by the Nürnberg Symphony Orchestra. Turn around and return to the main path. When you get to the end, turn right again and continue walking with the Congress Hall on your right. Continue past the end of the building, and then turn left (under the *Kommen Sie gut nach Hause* sign) onto the...

Great Road (Grosse Strasse): At 200 feet wide, the Great Road was big enough to be used as a runway by the Allies after the war. Now it's a parking lot for trucks serving the nearby conference center. The road points toward Nürnberg's imperial palace, Kaiserburg—Hitler's symbolic connection to the Holy Roman Empire (the "First Reich"). The lights you see in the distance hover above the Franken Stadium (a soccer field before Hitler, then used for Nazi rallies, and most recently, during the 2006 World Cup soccer tournament).

Ahead and to the right was to be the site of the **German Stadium (Deutsches Stadion)**—the biggest in the world (with 400,000 seats). They got as far as digging a foundation before funding was redirected to the war effort. Today, the site of the stadium is a park surrounding the big lake, Silbersee—which was the hole for the never-built stadium's foundation. If you like, you can detour across the road to an information sign about the stadium. Otherwise, follow the Dutzenteich lakeshore to the left for about 15 minutes until you hit a parking lot. To your right is the huge...

Zeppelin Field (Zeppelinwiese): This was the site of the Nazis' biggest rallies, including those famously filmed by Leni Riefenstahl. You can climb up on the grandstand and stand on the platform in front of the Zeppelin Tribune, where Hitler stood to survey the masses (up to 250,000 people at a time). The Tribune is based on the design of the ancient Greek Pergamon Altar (now in Berlin's Pergamon Museum); it was originally topped by a towering swastika, which was blown up by the Allies soon after the end of the war. Warning: Clowning around on the speaking platform with any Nazi gestures is illegal and taken seriously by the police.

From Zeppelin Field, continue the rest of the way around the lake back to the Documentation Center.

Nürnberg Trials Courtroom (Nürnberger Prozesse)

In 1945, in courtroom *(Saal)* #600 of Nürnberg's Palace of Justice (Justizgebäude), 21 Nazi war criminals stood trial before an international tribunal of judges appointed by the four victorious countries. After a year of trials and deliberations, 12 Nazis were sentenced to death by hanging, three were acquitted, and the rest were sent to prison. One of the death sentences was for Hitler's right-hand man, Hermann Göring. He wanted to be shot by firing squad—a proper military execution—but his request was denied. Instead, two hours before his scheduled hanging, Göring committed suicide with poison he had smuggled into his cell, infuriating many who thought that this death was too easy for him.

This historic courtroom is closed until sometime in 2010, as the city builds a new exhibit about the trials. For the latest on the opening date, try the website www.museen.nuernberg.de (west of Old Town at Fürther Strasse 110, enter on Bärenschanzstrasse, take U-1 to Bärenschanze, it's just behind *Pit Stop* sign, tel. 0911/231-5666).

SLEEPING

Prices spike up during major conventions in the spring and fall, and in December—when the Christmas market brings visitors from around the world. July and August are generally low season and come with the lowest prices.

Sleep Code

(€1 = about $1.50, country code: 49, area code: 0911)
S = Single, **D** = Double/Twin, **T** = Triple, **Q** = Quad, **b** = bathroom, **s** = shower only. Unless otherwise noted, credit cards are accepted, English is spoken, and breakfast is included.

To help you sort easily through these listings, I've divided the rooms into three categories, based on the price for a standard double room with bath:

$$$ Higher Priced—Most rooms €100 or more.
$$ Moderately Priced—Most rooms between €70-100.
$ Lower Priced—Most rooms €70 or less.

Near the Frauentor, on Königstrasse

These hotels cluster along Königstrasse, just inside the Frauentor and the city walls, and are convenient to both the train station and city sightseeing. From the station, you can roll your luggage here in five minutes without a single stair.

$$$ Hotel Victoria offers friendly staff and 64 fresh, new-feeling rooms behind its historic 1896 facade just inside the Frauentor. The standard rooms are a better value than the slightly bigger business rooms (standard rooms: S-€50–60, Sb-€80–90, Db-€100–110; business rooms €10 extra, discounts on slow summer weekends, 3 of 4 floors non-smoking, elevator, Wi-Fi in common areas, cable Internet in business rooms, parking garage-€11/day, Königstrasse 80, tel. 0911/24050, fax 0911/227-432, www.hotelvictoria.de, book@hotelvictoria.de).

$$$ Hotel Drei Raben is an artsy and fun splurge, with a super-stylish lobby, 25 comfortable rooms, a huge breakfast buffet (ask for eggs or a cappuccino), and lots of elegant touches. In this "theme hotel," you might get the Dürer room, the soccer room, the toys room, or even the graffiti room (Sb/Db-€100, €120, or €150 depending on size; spacious suites with freestanding bathtubs: Db-€185; ask for special summer discounts—especially on weekends; non-smoking, air-con, elevator, Wi-Fi, parking garage-€15/day, Königstrasse 63, tel. 0911/274-380, fax 0911/232-611, www.hoteldreiraben.de, info@hoteldreiraben.de).

$ Ibis Altstadt Hotel, sandwiched between a bunch of fast-food joints, offers 53 good-value, cookie-cutter rooms in a convenient location (Sb-€69 Mon–Thu, €59 Fri–Sun; Db-€69 Mon–Sat, €59 Sun; Sb/Db-€75 during Christmas market, €109 during conventions; breakfast-€10, elevator, free Internet access, expensive Wi-Fi, Königstrasse 74, tel. 0911/232-000, fax 0911/209-684, www.ibishotel.com, h1069@accor.com).

$ City Hotel, with 20 old, very basic rooms, has decent prices for the location and amenities (Sb-€40, Db-€55, elevator, reception on third floor, Königstrasse 25–27, tel. 0911/232-645, fax 0911/203-999, Widtmann family).

Near the Frauentor, on Luitpoldstrasse

These two affordable hotels are next door to each other, just around the corner from the ones above, set amidst a harmless sprinkling of strip clubs and sex shops. Either will do if you're watching your budget, but some guests complain about noise, so ask for a room on the back side (especially if staying on Friday or Saturday night).

$$ Hotel Probst is run by the hardworking Probst family. They rent 37 clean, cheap rooms on floors 2–4 of an older apartment building (Ss-€40, Sb-€56, Db-€67–75, Tb-€87–93, prices soft, non-smoking rooms, elevator to 3rd floor, Luitpoldstrasse 9, tel. 0911/203-433, fax 0911/205-9336, www.hotel-garni-probst.de, info@hotel-garni-probst.de).

$ Hotel Keiml is run by gracious Frau Keiml, who has been welcoming guests here since 1975. She rents 22 spacious, bright, and homey rooms up several flights of stairs (no elevator) in another former apartment building (Sb-€45, Db-€65–70, these prices with this book and cash in 2009, non-smoking rooms, Wi-Fi, Luitpoldstrasse 7, tel. 0911/226-240, fax 0911/241-760, reservations by fax preferred).

Closer to the Castle

These accommodations are closer to the castle at the far side of Old Town. Getting here is a €8 taxi ride or a long hike from the station. You can get partway by taking the U-Bahn (line #1) to Lorenzkirche and exiting toward Kaiserstrasse.

$$ Hotel Elch, the oldest hotel in town (with 500-year-old exposed beams adding to its classic, elk-friendly woodiness), is buried deep in the Old Town near the castle. It rents 12 charming and well-equipped rooms and has a small restaurant (Sb-€70, Db-€95, a bit cheaper Fri–Sun; extra bed free for kids under age 14, non-smoking, Wi-Fi, nearby parking garage-€10/day, behind St. Sebald Church at Irrerstrasse 9, tel. 0911/249-2980, fax 0911/2492-9844, www.hotel-elch.com, info@hotel-elch.com).

$$ Hotel Lucas, recently renovated, is in the heart of the Old Town just a short walk from the Hauptmarkt (market square). With only 13 rooms, you can expect personalized care from Herr Singer and his team. Rooms are modern and cheerful, making this a great, non-smoking home base (Sb-€50–65, Db-€75–90, lower prices are for weekends; breakfast is simple, but ask for extras like eggs at no extra charge; attached restaurant, Kaiserstrasse 22, tel. 0911/227-845, fax 0911/244-9158, www.hotel-lucas.de, info@hotel-lucas.de).

$ *Hostel:* The **Nürnberg Youth Hostel** is romantically situated at the top of the Old Town inside the castle complex (at the far right as you face it). It's scenic, but can be crowded with school-age groups in the summer. Those over age 26 pay €4 extra, unless traveling as a family (bed in 3- to 6-bed dorm-€21.40; limited singles and doubles: S-€39, D-€48; dorm dwellers pay less for longer stays, €3.10 more for non-members; includes breakfast and sheets, curfew at 1:00 in the morning, tel. 0911/230-9360, fax 0911/2309-3611, www.nuernberg.jugendherberge.de, jhnuernberg@djh-bayern.de).

EATING

Nürnberg is famous for its pinkie-sized bratwurst (called, like local residents, *Nürnberger*). Nürnbergers—the people—insist that size doesn't matter; they maintain that *in der Kürze liegt die Würze* (in the shortness lies the tastiness). All over town, signs read *3 im Weckle,* meaning "three *Nürnberger* bratwurst in a little bun" (a good snack for about €2). Old-timers go for mustard, while children like ketchup. Restaurant menus often offer them in 6-, 8-, or 10-weenie servings with *Beilagen* (side dishes, generally potato salad and/or kraut). Nürnberg's butchers churn out 1.3 billion of the little buggers every year.

For convenience, I've listed restaurants that are on (or near) Königstrasse, the main drag connecting the station to the castle. Only the last two places are away from this tourist zone—buried in the west end of the Old Town, and known only to locals.

Barfüsser Beer Cellar serves its own popular microbrew and fills the basement of the old grain storehouse *(Mauthalle)* with jovial Germans munching meat-on-the-bone (from pork knuckle to duck) and swilling beer. This is good, German fun. On hot nights, the cellar's empty and tables spill out onto Königstrasse. Locals love the *Schäufele,* oven-roasted pork shoulder in home-brewed dark beer sauce, and the *Frankenschmaus,* a "greatest hits" platter of sausages, pork shoulder, kraut, and dumplings (€6–11 meals, daily 11:00–24:00, Hallplatz 2, tel. 0911/204-242).

Nassauer Keller is a snug and classy 13th-century vaulted cellar filled with suits of armor and diners enjoying the romantic atmosphere and traditional food. A small door leads down steep steps (watch your head) into a dressy dining room—popular for roast shoulder of pork and venison dishes. It's a little pricey and worth the extra euros in wintertime—but avoid this place on hot days (€10–15 meals, Mon–Sat 12:00–15:00 & 18:00–24:00, kitchen closes at 14:00 and at 22:00, closed Sun, reservations smart, across from Lorenzkirche at Karolinenstrasse 2–4, tel. 0911/225-967).

Goldenes Posthorn is a venerable institution and—while no longer in its original historic location—was once Albrecht Dürer's favorite hangout. Come here to enjoy everything from Franconian specialties and bratwurst to daily fish and vegetarian plates, either in the light-wood, chalet-chic interior or on the patio in the shadow of St. Sebald Church (€6–12 meals, daily 11:00–23:00, daily specials, cash only, Glöckleingasse 2, tel. 0911/225-153).

Literaturhaus Nürnberg is a Parisian-style café run by the local book club and popular for readings. It serves theme breakfasts (daily until 15:00) and creative international dishes for €8–14. Locals like to order several varied plates tapas-style, or just enjoy its bookish café ambience for drinks and desserts (Mon–Sat 9:00–24:00, Sun 9:00–22:00, 2 blocks from Frauentor just off Königstrasse at Luitpoldstrasse 6, tel. 0911/234-2658).

Burgwächter is just under the castle, and therefore both touristy and practical. It serves up German cuisine—in its cozy restaurant and on a covered patio with big, rustic picnic tables (€5–15 main dishes, good salads, daily 12:00–23:00, Am Ölberg 10, tel. 0911/222-126).

Bratwursthäusle is a high-energy, woody-yet-mod place with a leafy terrace (and enjoyable people-watching). Its cozy interior feels like a big farmhouse with tables gathered around an open grill. The menu is very limited, with little more than bratwurst and some nasty pickled animal parts. You come here for the best bratwurst in town—all made in-house by the *Häusle*'s own butcher, and dished up with efficient service. Chat up the owner, friendly Herr Behringer, and he'll be happy to tell you about Bratwurst Saints (Mon–Sat 10:00–22:00, closed Sun, midway between Hauptmarkt and the castle on the main drag, Rathausplatz 1, tel. 0911/227-695). For bratwurst to go, pay €2 at the little door, take your receipt to the grill...and in seconds, you'll be on your way with Nürnberg's "Little Mac" (three *Nürnberger* in a fresh roll).

Sebald is an upscale, bratwurst-free bistro serving well-presented, Italian-inspired cuisine in a white-tablecloth, indoor/outdoor setting. It's friendly, stylish, and into smooth jazz. The local clientele appreciates their €8–17 daily blackboard specials (€19–29 main dishes, Mon–Sat 11:30–24:00, Sun 11:30–22:00, 2 blocks west of St. Sebald Church toward the wall at Weinmarkt 14, tel. 0911/381-303).

Kettensteg Biergarten, the usual Bavarian jumble of picnic tables under trees, enjoys an above-average setting overlooking the city's river and medieval wall. It's named after, and is next to, Germany's first iron suspension bridge (built in 1824). Its youthful energy and big flames give it a tribal vibe after dark. This is ideal on a balmy evening for leafy outdoor dining surrounded by happy locals and in-the-know foreign students. After 17:00, the lower-level self-service section opens, with cheaper prices and a limited menu (€8–13 meals, modern German cuisine and decent salads, daily in summer 11:00–23:00, west of Hauptmarkt where the river hits the wall, Maxplatz 35, tel. 0911/221-081).

Picnic: There's an Aldi discount **supermarket** near recommended hotels at Königstrasse 83 (limited selection, Mon–Sat 8:00–20:00, closed Sun), and a more upscale supermarket in the sub-basement of the Karstadt department store (enter across from Karolinenstrasse 15 and take the escalators down two flights, Mon–Sat 9:30–20:00, closed Sun).

TRANSPORTATION CONNECTIONS

From Nürnberg by Train to: Rothenburg (hourly, 1–1.5 hrs, change in Ansbach and then Steinach), **Würzburg** (2–3/hr, 1–1.25 hrs), **Munich** (2–3/hr, 1–1.25 hrs), **Frankfurt** (1–2/hr, 2 hrs), **Frankfurt Airport** (1–2/hr, 2.5 hrs), **Berlin** (hourly, 4.5 hrs), **Salzburg** (hourly with change in Munich, 3 hrs). Train info: tel. 11861 (€0.60/min).

DRESDEN

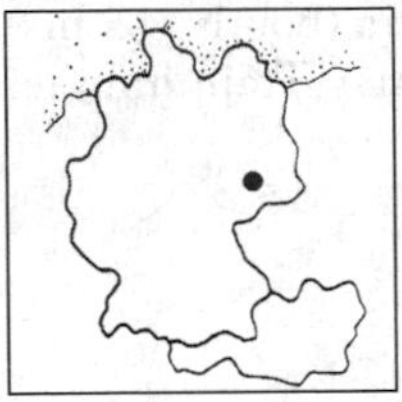

Dresden, the capital of Saxony, surprises visitors with fanciful Baroque architecture and excellent museums. It's historic, intriguing, and fun. While the city is packed with tourists, 90 percent of them are German or Russian. Until Americans rediscover Dresden's Baroque glory, you'll feel like you're in on a secret.

At the peak of its power in the 18th century, this capital of Saxony ruled most of present-day Poland and eastern Germany from the banks of the Elbe River. Dresden's "Louis XIV" was Augustus the Strong. As both prince elector of Saxony and king of Poland, he imported artists from all over Europe, peppering his city with stunning Baroque buildings and filling his treasury with lavish jewels and artwork. Dresden's grand architecture and dedication to the arts—along with the gently rolling hills surrounding the city—earned it the nickname "Florence on the Elbe."

Sadly, these days Dresden is better known for its destruction in World War II. American and British pilots firebombed the city on the night of February 13, 1945. More than 25,000 people were killed, and 75 percent of the historical center was destroyed. American Kurt Vonnegut, who was a POW in Dresden during the firebombing, later memorialized the event in his novel *Slaughterhouse-Five.*

When Germany was divvied up at the end of World War II, Dresden wound up in the Soviet sector. Forty years of communist rule left the city in an economic hole, from which it is just emerging. Some older Dresdeners feel nostalgia for the Red old days, when "everyone had a job." During the Cold War, Dresden was known as the "Valley of the Clueless," since it was one of the only spots in East Germany where you couldn't get Western television.

But in the two decades since the Berlin Wall fell, Dresden has made real progress in getting back on its feet—and most locals are enjoying capitalism with gusto. Today's Dresden is a young and vibrant city, crawling with happy-go-lucky students who barely remember communism.

Under the communists, Dresden patched up some of its damaged buildings, left many others in ruins, and replaced even more with huge, modern, ugly sprawl. But today, Dresden seems all about rebuilding. Circa-1946 photos are displayed everywhere, and the city's most important and beautiful historic buildings in the Old Town have been restored. Across the river, the New Town was missed by the bombs. While well-worn, it retains its prewar character and has emerged as the city's fun and lively people zone. Most tourists never cross the bridge away from the famous Old Town museums...but a visit to Dresden isn't complete without a wander through the New Town.

Planning Your Time

Dresden, conveniently located about halfway between Prague and Berlin, is well worth even a quick stop. If you're short on time, Dresden's top sights can be seen in a midday break from your Berlin–Prague train ride (each one is less than a 2.5-hour ride away). Catch the early train, throw your bag in a locker at the station (€2.50), follow my self-guided walk (page 408), and visit some museums before taking an evening train out. If possible, reserve far ahead to visit one of Dresden's top sights, the Historic Green Vault (for reservations details, see page 418).

If you have more time, Dresden merits an overnight stay. The city is a handy home base for getting back to nature at Saxon Switzerland National Park (see page 423), or side-tripping to the town of Görlitz for its intriguing mix of rich architecture and culture (see next chapter).

ORIENTATION

(area code: 0351)

Dresden is big, with half a million residents. Its city center hugs a curve on the Elbe River. Despite the city's size, most of its sights are within easy strolling distance along the south bank of the Elbe in the Old Town (Altstadt). South of the Old Town (a 5-min tram ride or 15-min walk away) is the main train station (Hauptbahnhof). North of the Old Town, across the river, you'll find the residential-feeling New Town (Neustadt). While the New Town boasts virtually no sights, it's lively, colorful, and fun to explore—especially at night—and has some recommended hotels and restaurants.

Dresden

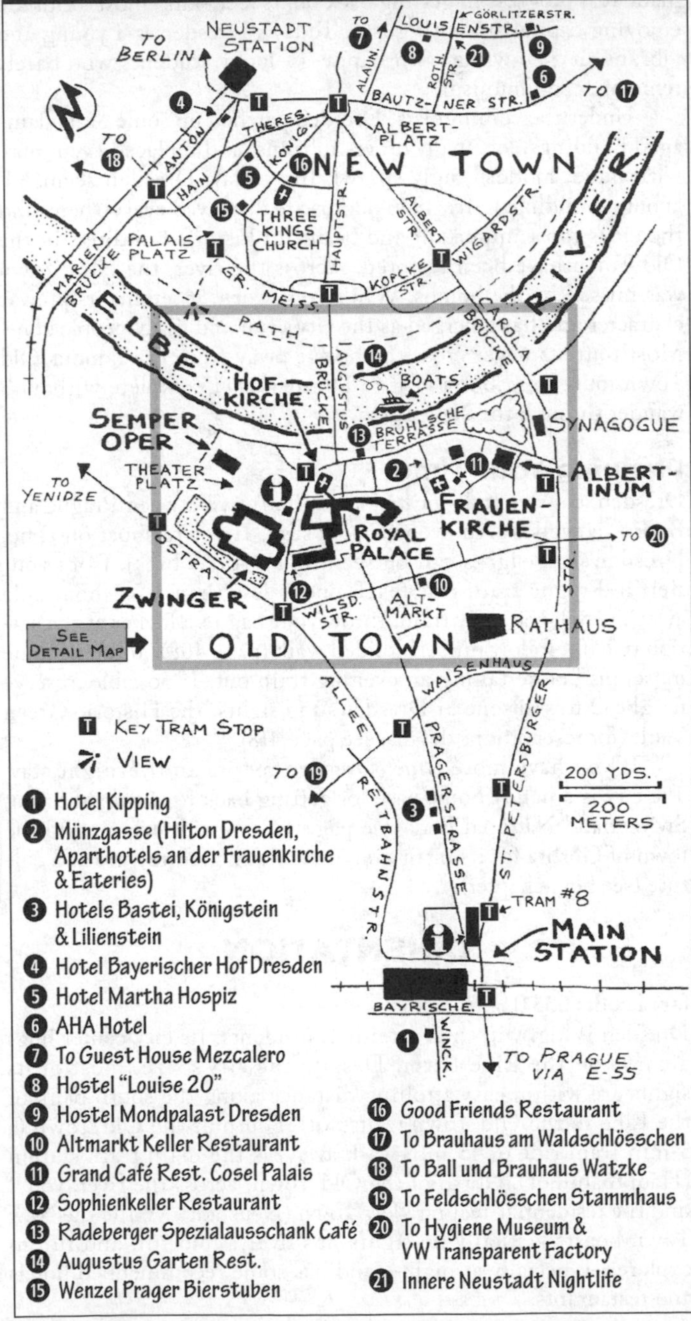

TO BERLIN
NEUSTADT STATION
TO 7
LOUISENSTR.
GÖRLITZERSTR.
ALAUN.
ROTH. STR.
BAUTZNER STR.
TO 17
ALBERT-PLATZ
THERES.
KÖNIG.
ANTON.
HAIN
TO 18
NEW TOWN
THREE KINGS CHURCH
HAUPTSTR.
ALBERT STR.
WIGARDSTR.
RIVER
PALAIS PLATZ
MARIEN-BRÜCKE
GR. MEISS.
KOPCKE STR.
CAROLA BRÜCKE
PATH
ELBE
AUGUSTUS BRÜCKE
BOATS
HOF-KIRCHE
SEMPER OPER
BRÜHLSCHE TERRASSE
SYNAGOGUE
THEATER PLATZ
ALBERT-INUM
TO YENIDZE
FRAUEN-KIRCHE
ROYAL PALACE
TO 20
OSTRA.
ZWINGER
WILSD. STR.
ALT-MARKT
RATHAUS
SEE DETAIL MAP
OLD TOWN
WAISENHAUS
ST. PETERSBURGER STR.
ALLEE
KEY TRAM STOP
VIEW
TO 19
REITBAHN STR.
PRAGERSTRASSE
200 YDS.
200 METERS
TRAM #8
MAIN STATION
BAYRISCHE.
WINCK.
TO PRAGUE VIA E-55
1 Hotel Kipping
2 Münzgasse (Hilton Dresden, Aparthotels an der Frauenkirche & Eateries)
3 Hotels Bastei, Königstein & Lilienstein
4 Hotel Bayerischer Hof Dresden
5 Hotel Martha Hospiz
6 AHA Hotel
7 To Guest House Mezcalero
8 Hostel "Louise 20"
9 Hostel Mondpalast Dresden
10 Altmarkt Keller Restaurant
11 Grand Café Rest. Cosel Palais
12 Sophienkeller Restaurant
13 Radeberger Spezialausschank Café
14 Augustus Garten Rest.
15 Wenzel Prager Bierstuben
16 Good Friends Restaurant
17 To Brauhaus am Waldschlösschen
18 To Ball und Brauhaus Watzke
19 To Feldschlösschen Stammhaus
20 To Hygiene Museum & VW Transparent Factory
21 Innere Neustadt Nightlife

Tourist Information

Dresden has two TIs: one in the **Old Town** at Theaterplatz (in the Schinkelwache building, next to the Zwinger); and another one 100 yards from the **main train station,** in the Prager Spitze shopping center at Prager Strasse 2a (both open Mon–Sat 10:00–19:00, Old Town also Sun 10:00–16:00, Prager Strasse closed Sun; tel. 0351/491-920, www.dresden-tourist.de). Both TIs book rooms (€3/person), offer the Dresden City Card museum pass (see below), sell concert and theater tickets, and operate travel agencies. Get the handy, free, one-page city map with a listing of key sights, hours, and prices on the back. For live entertainment and cultural events, skim the monthly *Theater Konzert Kunst* (free, in German only).

Discount Deals: The **Dresden City Card** offers you entry into all of Dresden's top museums (except the Historic Green Vault), discounts on some lesser museums, and unlimited use of the city's transit system (€21/48 hours, €32/72-hour regional pass that includes outlying areas, €42/48-hour Family City Card covers two adults and up to four children, all sold at TI). If you're only here for the day, skip it and buy a one-day ***Tageskarte*** museum pass instead (€12, covers all state museums except the Historic Green Vault, no transit, sold at participating museums but not the TI). The website for all Dresden state museums is www.skd-dresden.de.

Arrival in Dresden

Dresden has two major train stations: Hauptbahnhof and Neustadt. (Note that express trains from Berlin stop first at Neustadt, then at Hauptbahnhof.)

If you're coming for the day and want the easiest access to the sights, use the **Hauptbahnhof** (main train station), which owes its chic new look to Sir Norman Foster of Reichstag Dome fame. Exit the station following signs for the city, taxis, and trams. To take a **tram** into the center, cross the tram tracks at Wiener Platz. Veer right (through the five-story rounded glass building) to find tram #8 or #11 (departing to your left), which zips you to the historical center (Theaterplatz or Postplatz). The 15-minute **walk** to the Old Town offers an insightful glimpse of the communist era as you stroll down Prager Strasse (described on page 422; from the station, continue straight through Wiener Platz, under and past the towering Mercure Hotel).

The **Neustadt** station serves the New Town north of the river, near some recommended hotels. From this station, tram #11 runs to Am Zwingerteich, a park in the center of the Old Town right next to the sights.

Trains run between the Hauptbahnhof and Neustadt stations every 10 minutes (€1.80, 10-min ride, most trains stop at each station—ask; the stations are also connected by slower tram #3).

Helpful Hints

Sightseeing Strategies: Note that many of Dresden's top museums are closed either Monday or Tuesday. The incredible treasury—the Historic Green Vault—requires a reservation well in advance; if you don't get one, try to line up early to buy a same-day ticket, sold at 10:00 (for all the details, see page 418). Once you have your appointed Historic Green Vault visit time, plan the rest of your day around it (it's conveniently located right in the center of the Old Town). The Hofkirche hosts free pipe-organ concerts twice a week (Wed and Sat at 11:30).

Internet Access: To check your email in the main train station, find the Sidewalk Express computers in the **Point Shop To Go** (€2/hr, one-hour minimum, open long hours daily).

Local Guides: Genteel **Maren Koban** (tel. 0351/311-1315, mobile 0176-2922-6374) and **Liane Lowe** (lianeloewe@gmx.de) each enjoy sharing the story of their hometown with visitors (€100/half-day).

Getting Around Dresden

Dresden's efficient **trams** and **buses** work well for the visitor. The tram network is so slick, you might just spend the hour your €1.80 ticket gets you joyriding—marveling at the huge investment this city is making as it rebuilds. Buy tickets at the machines on the platforms or in the trams (€1.80 for a single ticket, or *Einzelfahrkarte;* €4.50 for a 4-pack of *Kurzstrecke*—short-ride tickets; machines accept coins only). A day ticket (*Tageskarte,* €4.50 for one calendar day) works for sightseeing within the city. Validate your ticket by date-stamping it in the little boxes on train platforms and on board buses and trams (for the day ticket, stamp it only the first time you ride). Free use of public transit is included with the Dresden City Card (see previous page).

Taxis are reasonable, plentiful, and generally honest (€2.50 to start, then €1.20/kilometer).

SELF-GUIDED WALK

▲▲▲Do-It-Yourself Dresden Baroque Blitz Tour

Dresden's major sights are conveniently clustered along a delightfully strollable promenade next to the Elbe River. Get to know this sightseeing zone by taking this walk. Though the city has a long and colorful history, we'll focus on the four eras that have shaped it the most: Dresden's Golden Age in the mid-18th century under Augustus the Strong; the city's destruction by firebombs in World War II; the communist regime (1945–1989); and the current "reconstruction after reunification" era.

Central Dresden

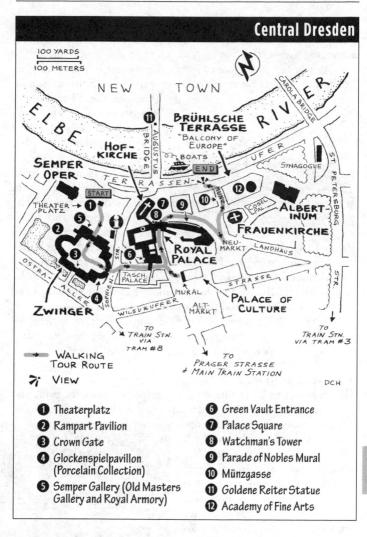

1. Theaterplatz
2. Rampart Pavilion
3. Crown Gate
4. Glockenspielpavillon (Porcelain Collection)
5. Semper Gallery (Old Masters Gallery and Royal Armory)
6. Green Vault Entrance
7. Palace Square
8. Watchman's Tower
9. Parade of Nobles Mural
10. Münzgasse
11. Goldene Reiter Statue
12. Academy of Fine Arts

The following walk laces together Dresden's top sights in about an hour, not counting museum stops. It includes the three major sights (Zwinger, Royal Palace with Historic Green Vault treasuries, and Frauenkirche), each of which is described later in the chapter. Incorporating these visits into the walk will fill your day.

• *Begin at Theaterplatz (a convenient drop-off point for tram #8 from the Hauptbahnhof).*

Theaterplatz

Face the equestrian statue (King John, an unimportant mid-19th-century ruler) in the middle of the square. In front of you, behind the statue, is the Saxon State Opera House—nicknamed the **Semperoper** after its architect, Gottfried Semper (visits only with a tour, see page 421).

As you face the Opera House, the nearest building on your left is the Neoclassical guardhouse called the Schinkelwache (housing the TI and opera box office). The big building behind it is the vast Zwinger palace complex (your next stop). Across the square from the Opera House is the Hofkirche, with its distinctive green-copper steeple, and to its right is the sprawling Royal Palace (with shiny new clock; both described later). All the buildings you see here—Dresden's Baroque treasures—are thoroughly reconstructed. The originals were destroyed in a single night by American and British bombs. For more than 60 years, Dresden has been rebuilding—and there's more work to do.

• *Walk through the passageway into the Zwinger courtyard, noticing the Crown Gate on the opposite side lowering majestically into view. Stop in the middle of the courtyard, where we'll survey all four wings.*

▲▲The Zwinger

This palace complex is a Baroque masterpiece—once the pride and joy of the Wettin dynasty, and today filled with fine museums. The Wettins ruled Saxony for more than 800 years, right up until the end of the First World War (like so many of Europe's royal families). Saxony wasn't ruled by a king, but by a prince elector—one of a handful of nobles who elected the Holy Roman Emperor. The prince elector of Saxony was one of Germany's most powerful people. In the 18th century, the larger-than-life Augustus the Strong—who was both prince elector of Saxony and king of Poland—kicked off Saxony's Golden Age (see sidebar on opposite page).

"Zwinger" means the no-man's-land running along the city wall. This empty space gradually evolved into the complex of buildings you see today. By Augustus' time, the Zwinger was used for celebrations of Saxon royalty. Imagine an over-the-top royal wedding in this complex. The courtyard served as an open-air palace, complete with orange trees in huge Chinese porcelain pots.

DRESDEN

Augustus the Strong
(1670–1733)

Friedrich Augustus I of the Wettin family exemplified royal excess, and made Dresden one of Europe's most important cities of culture. Legends paint Augustus as a macho, womanizing, powerful, ambitious, properly Baroque man—a real Saxon superstar. A hundred years after his death, historians dubbed Augustus "the Strong." Today, tour guides love to impart silly legends about Augustus, who supposedly fathered 365 children and could break a horseshoe in half with his bare hands.

As prince elector of Saxony, Augustus wheeled and dealed—and converted from his Saxon Protestantism to a more Polish-friendly Catholicism—to become King Augustus II of Poland. Like most Wettins, Augustus the Strong was unlucky at war, but a clever diplomat and a lover of the arts.

The Polish people blame Augustus and his successors—who were far more concerned with wealth and opulence than with sensible governance—for Poland's precipitous decline after its own medieval Golden Age. According to Poles, the Saxon kings did nothing but "eat, drink, and loosen their belts" (it rhymes in Polish).

Whether you consider them the heroes of history, or the villains, Augustus and the rest of the Wettins—and the nobles who paid them taxes—are to thank for Dresden's rich architectural and artistic heritage.

Let's get oriented. Face the north wing (with the Crown Gate on your left). You're looking at the **Rampart Pavilion** (Wallpavillon), the first wing of the palace—an orangerie capped with a sun pavilion built for Augustus' fruit trees and parties. Up top is Atlas (who happens to have Augustus' features) with the Earth on his back—a fitting symbol for Augustus the Strong. Stairs lead to a fine view from the terrace above. This wing of the Zwinger houses the fun **Mathematics-Physics Salon** (closed until 2010).

Turn to the left, facing the **Crown Gate** (Kronentor). The gate's golden crown is topped by four golden eagles supporting a smaller crown—symbolizing Polish royalty (since Augustus was also king of Poland).

Turn again to the left to see

the **Glockenspielpavillon.** The glockenspiel near the top of the gate has 40 bells made of Meissen porcelain (bells chime every 15 minutes, and play a sweet three-minute melody at 10:15, 14:15, and 17:15). This wing of the Zwinger also houses Augustus the Strong's **Porcelain Collection** (see page 418).

Turn once more to the left (with the Crown Gate behind you) to see the **Semper Gallery.** This Zwinger wing was added to the original courtyard a hundred years later by Gottfried Semper (of Opera House fame). It houses Dresden's best painting collection, the **Old Masters Gallery,** as well as the **Royal Armory** (see page 417).

Throughout the city, you'll see the local sandstone looking really sooty. Locals claim that it's not pollution, but natural oxidation that turns the stone black in about 30 years. Once restored, the statues are given a silicon treatment that lets the stone breathe but keeps it from going black.

Take time to enjoy some of the Zwinger's excellent museums. Anticipating WWII bombs, Dresdeners preserved their town's art treasures by storing them in underground mines and cellars in the countryside. This saved these great works from Allied bombs... but not from the Russians. Nearly all of the city's artwork ended up in Moscow until after Stalin's death in 1953, when the art was returned by the communist regime to win over their East German subjects. Today, Russians invade only as tourists.

When you're finished with the museums, exit the Zwinger through the Glockenspielpavillon (south gate). Halfway through the corridor, look for the **timelines** telling the history of the Zwinger in German: to the right, its construction, and to the left, its destruction and reconstruction. Notice the Soviet spin: On February 13, 1945, gangs of Anglo-American bombers obliterated *(vernichtet)* the city. On May 8, 1945, the Soviet army liberated *(befreite)* Dresden from "fascist tyranny" *(faschistischen Tyrannei),* and from 1945 to 1964, the Zwinger was rebuilt with the "power of the workers and peasants" *(Arbeiter- und Bauern-Macht).*

• *As you exit the corridor, cross the street and the tram tracks and jog left, walking down the perpendicular Taschenberg Strasse with the yellow Taschenberg Palace on your right (ruined until 1990, today the city's finest five-star hotel). The yellow-windowed sky bridge ahead connects the Taschenberg, which was the crown prince's palace, with the prince electors'* ***Royal Palace.*** *This is where you can enter the spectacular* ***Green Vault*** *treasuries (described on pages 418 and 419; entrance is before crossing under the sky bridge, through fancy gate on left). But if your Historic Green Vault reservation is for later today, you can continue this walk for now.*

Exiting the Royal Palace, go under the sky bridge. Ahead of you and to the right, the blocky modern building is the...

Palace of Culture (Kulturpalast)

Built by the communist government in 1969, this hall is still used for concerts today. Notice the mural depicting communist themes: workers; strong women; care for the elderly; teachers and students; and, of course, the red star and the seal of former East Germany. The bronze doors on the street side give a Marxist interpretation of the history of Dresden. Little of this propaganda, which once inundated the lives of locals, survives in post-communist Germany.

• *Now turn left (with the Palace of Culture behind you). Walk along the palace wall toward the two copper spires, through a tunnel with (mostly Russian) musicians, until you emerge into the* ***Palace Square.*** *Ahead of you and to the left is the...*

Hofkirche (Cathedral)

Why does Dresden, a stronghold of local-boy Martin Luther's Protestant Reformation, boast such a beautiful Catholic cathedral? When Augustus the Strong died, his son wanted to continue as king of Poland, like his father. The pope would allow it only if Augustus Junior built a Catholic church in Dresden. Now, thanks to Junior's historical kissing-up, the mere 5 percent of locals who are Catholic get to enjoy this fine church. The elevated passageway connecting the church with the palace allowed the royal family to avoid walking in the street with commoners.

Step inside the cathedral (free, enter through side door facing palace, Mon–Thu 9:00–17:00, Fri 13:00–17:00, Sat 10:00–18:00, Sun 12:00–16:00, tel. 0351/484-4712, www.kathedrale-dresden.de). The fine Baroque pulpit—hidden in the countryside during World War II—is carved out of linden wood. The glorious 3,000-pipe organ filling the back of the nave is played for the public on Wednesdays and Saturdays at 11:30 (free).

The **Memorial Chapel** (facing the rear of the church, on the left) is dedicated to those who died in the WWII firebombing and to all victims of violence. Its evocative *pietà* altarpiece was made in 1973 of Meissen porcelain. Mary offers the faithful the crown of thorns made from Dresden's rubble, as if to remind us that Jesus—on her lap, head hanging lifeless on the left—died to save humankind. Jesus' open heart shows us his love, offers us atonement for our sins, and proves that reconciliation is more powerful than hatred. The altar (freestanding, in front) shows five flaming heads. It seems to symbolize how Dresdeners suffered...in the presence of their suffering savior. The dates on the high altar (30-1-33 and 13-2-45) mark the dark period between Hitler's rise to power and the night Dresden was destroyed.

The basement houses the **royal crypt,** including the heart of the still-virile Augustus the Strong—which, according to legend, still beats when a pretty woman comes near (crypt open only for one 45-min German tour each day).

• *As you leave the Hofkirche, you're facing the palace complex entry (with the* ***Watchman's Tower*** *above on the right—**see page 419**). To the left, next to the palace's main entrance, you'll see a long, yellow mural called the...*

▲▲Parade of Nobles (Fürstenzug)

This mural is painted on 24,000 tiles of Meissen porcelain. Longer than a football field, it illustrates 700 years of Saxon royalty. It was built to commemorate Saxon history and heritage after Saxony became a part of Germany in 1871. The artist carefully studied armor and clothing through the ages, allowing you to accurately trace the evolution of weaponry and fashions for seven centuries. (This is great for couples—try this for a switch: As you stroll, men watch the fashions, women the weaponry.)

The very last figure (or the first one you see, coming from this direction) is the artist himself, Wilhelm Walther. Then come commoners (miners, farmers, carpenters, teachers, students, artists), and then the royals, with 35 names and dates marking more than 700 years of Wettin rule. Stop at 1694. That's August II (Augustus the Strong), the most important of the Saxon kings. His horse stomps on the rose (symbol of Martin Luther, the Protestant movement, and the Lutheran church today) to gain the Polish crown. The first Saxon royal is Konrad der Grosse ("the Great"). And waaay up at the very front of the parade, an announcer with a band and 12th-century cheerleaders excitedly herald the arrival of this wondrous procession. The porcelain tiles, originals from 1907, survived the bombing. When created, they were fired three times at 2,400 degrees Fahrenheit...and then fired again during the 1945 firestorm, at only 1,800 degrees.

• *When you're finished looking at the mural, dogleg right and walk into the big square. Find a statue of Martin Luther.*

Neumarkt Square

This "New Market Square," once a town center ringed by rich merchants' homes, is being rebuilt and will soon be a lively people-and-café center. The statue of Martin Luther holds not just any Bible, but the Word of God he translated into German so that regular people could get their minds on it without Church control—basically what the Reformation was all about. Toppled in 1945, he's cleaned up and back on his feet again.

• *The big church looming over the square is the...*

▲▲▲Frauenkirche (Church of Our Lady)

This church is the heart and soul of Dresden. The people of Dresden, jealous of the mighty Catholic domes of Venice and London, mobilized their Protestant pride to raise the money, and built this impressive Lutheran church. When completed in 1743, this was Germany's biggest Protestant church (310 feet high). Its unique central-stone-cupola design gave it the nickname "the stone bell." While it's a great church, this building garners the world's attention primarily because of its tragic history and phoenix-like resurrection: On the night of February 13, 1945, the firebombs came. When the smoke cleared the next morning, the Frauenkirche was smoldering but still standing. It burned for two days before finally collapsing. After the war, the Frauenkirche was kept in rubble as a peace monument. It was the site of many memorial vigils. In 2005, completely rebuilt, it reopened to the public. (For touring details and more information, see page 419.)

A big hunk of the bombed **rubble** stands in the square (near door E, river side of church) as a memorial. Notice the small relief of the dome that shows where this piece came from.

• *From here, stroll downhill through a busy little restaurant-lined street, Münzgasse, and up the stairs to Dresden's grand river-view balcony. Find a bulge in the promenade 30 yards to the right. Belly up to that banister.*

▲▲Brühlsche Terrasse

This so-called "Balcony of Europe," a delightful promenade, was once Dresden's defensive rampart. Look along the side of the terrace facing the Elbe River to see openings for cannons. By Baroque times, fortresses were no longer necessary, and this became one of Europe's most charming promenades, with a leafy canopy of linden trees.

Dresden claims to have the world's largest and oldest fleet of historic paddleboat steamers: nine riverboats from the 19th century. The hills in the distance (to the left) are home to Saxon vineyards, producing some of Germany's northernmost wine. Because only a small amount of the land is suitable for vineyards, Saxony's respected, expensive wine (mostly white) is consumed almost entirely by Saxons.

Below you to the left is the **Augustus Bridge** (Augustusbrücke), connecting Dresden's old and new towns. During the massive floods of August 2002, the water reached two-thirds of the way up the arches. At the far end of the Augustus Bridge, look for the golden equestrian statue, a symbol of Dresden. It's Augustus the Strong, the **Goldene Reiter** (Golden Rider), facing east to his kingdom of Poland.

The area across the bridge is the **New Town** (Neustadt). While three-quarters of Dresden's Old Town was decimated by Allied firebombs, much of the New Town survived. The 18th-century apartment buildings here were restored—giving the area a Baroque look instead of the blocky Soviet style predominant on the Old Town side of the river. Today, the New Town is a trendy district, and well worth exploring (see page 422). The **Three Kings Church** (Dreikönigskirche, steeple visible above the Goldene Reiter) marks a neighborhood with some recommended restaurants (see page 429).

The interesting **mosque-shaped building** in the distance to the far left (marked *Yenidze*), originally a tobacco factory designed to advertise Turkish cigarettes, is now an office building with restaurants and nightclubs. A few steps to your left is the recommended **Radeberger Spezialausschank Café**—the best place for a drink or meal with a river view (see page 429).

Behind you on the right, you'll see the glass domes of the **Academy of Fine Arts,** capped by a trumpeting gold angel. (Locals call the big dome on the right "the lemon juicer.")

• *Your tour is over. Stairs at the end of the promenade lead back to the Palace Square; just beyond the Hofkirche is Theaterplatz, where you began.*

DRESDEN

SIGHTS

The Zwinger Museums

The museums around the Zwinger courtyard all have the same hours (Tue–Sun 10:00–18:00, closed Mon, tel. 0351/4914-2000, www.skd-dresden.de). Entrance to all of the museums (except the Porcelain Collection) costs €7, and are all covered by the €12

Tageskarte museum pass (buy at any sight) or the Dresden City Card (which also includes transit).

▲▲▲Old Masters Gallery (Gemäldegalerie Alte Meister)—Dresden's best museum features works by Raphael, Titian, Rembrandt, Peter Paul Rubens, Jan Vermeer, and more. While it hangs 750 paintings at a time, it feels particularly enjoyable for its "quality, not quantity" approach to showing off great art. Locals remember the Old Masters Gallery as the first big public building reopened after the war, in 1956 (€7, includes Royal Armory entry, €3 audioguide, consider the good €13 English guidebook, in Zwinger's Semper Gallery).

Entering, you'll pass a small room with portraits of the Wettin kings who patronized the arts and founded this collection. The next room shows five cityscapes of Dresden, painted by Canaletto during the city's Golden Age. These paintings of mid-18th-century Dresden—showing the Hofkirche (still under construction) and the newly completed Frauenkirche—offer a great study of the city. Next, you enter a world of Rubens and Belgian Baroque. This high-powered Catholic art is followed by the humbler, quieter Protestant art of the Dutch Masters, including a fine collection of Rembrandts (don't miss his jaunty self-portrait—with Saskia on his lap and a glass of ale held aloft) and a pristine Vermeer *(Girl at a Window Reading a Letter)*. The German late-Gothic/early-Renaissance rooms include exquisite canvases by Lucas Cranach and Albrecht Dürer. Farther on, the Venetian masters include a sumptuous *Sleeping Venus* by Giorgione (1510). He died while still working on this, so Titian stepped in to finish it. Giorgione's idealized Venus sleeps soundly, at peace with the plush nature.

The collection's highlight: Raphael's masterful *Sistine Madonna*. The portrait features the Madonna and Child, two early Christian martyrs (Saints Sixtus and Barbara), and wispy angel faces in the clouds. Mary is in motion, offering the Savior to a needy world. But today, the stars of this painting are the pair of whimsical angels in the foreground—which Raphael added after the painting was completed, just to fill the empty space. These lovable tykes—of T-shirt and poster fame—are bored...just hanging out, oblivious to the exciting arrival of the Messiah just behind them. They connect the heavenly world of the painting with you and me.

Royal Armory (Rüstkammer)—One big room packed with swords and suits of armor, the armory is especially interesting for its tiny children's armor and the jousting exhibit in the back (included with €7 ticket to Old Masters Gallery, across the entry passage from gallery).

Sculpture Collection (Skulpture im Zwinger)—With the Albertinium closed until 2010, some pieces from its sculpture collection are on loan to the Zwinger. Look for Degas' *Fourteen-Year-Old Dancer* (included in the €7 ticket to the Old Masters Gallery and in the €6 ticket to the Porcelain Collection, entrance on the courtyard).

Mathematics-Physics Salon (Mathematisch-Physikalischer Salon)—This fun collection features globes, lenses, and clocks from the 16th to the 19th centuries (north end of Zwinger courtyard, closed until 2010).

▲▲Porcelain Collection (Porzellansammlung)—Every self-respecting European king had a porcelain works, and the Wettins had the most famous: Meissen. The Saxon prince electors were pioneers in European porcelain production. They inspired other royal courts to get into the art form. They also collected other types—from France to Japan and China. Augustus the Strong was obsessed with the precious stuff...he liked to say he had "porcelain sickness." Here you can enjoy some of his symptoms, under chandeliers in elegant galleries (€6, good English descriptions, south end of Zwinger courtyard).

Royal Palace (Residenzschloss)

This Renaissance palace was once the residence of the Saxon prince elector. Formerly one of the finest Renaissance buildings in Germany, it's been rebuilt since its destruction in World War II. The grand state rooms of Augustus the Strong are scheduled to open in 2009. For now, the prince's treasures are the big draw here: The New Green Vault is remarkable enough, but the Historic Green Vault (reservation required) is arguably the most impressive treasury in Europe. The entire complex has the same hours (Wed–Mon 10:00–18:00, closed Tue, Historic Green Vault until 19:00), but each attraction has its own entrance fee (Historic Green Vault-€10, not covered by €12 *Tageskarte;* New Green Vault-€9, Watchman's Tower-€3, both covered by *Tageskarte*).

▲▲▲Historic Green Vault (Historisches Grünes Gewölbe)—The famed, glittering Baroque treasury collection was begun by Augustus the Strong in the early 1700s. It evolved as the royal family's extravagant treasure trove of ivory, silver, and gold knickknacks. Your visit is thrilling in the Baroque style of wowing visitors—starting easy and crescendoing to a climax, taking a quick break, and finishing again with a flurry. Following the included (and essential) audioguide, you'll spend one hour progressing: the amber room, the ivory room, the silver room, the sumptuous crown jewels room, the soothing bronze room, and another jewels room.

The incredible pieces in the crown jewels room (especially the Obeliscus Augustalis) are fine examples of *Gesamtkunstwerk*—a symphony of artistic creations. Your audioguide also describes treasures in the "pre-vault" (where you pick up and drop off the audioguide). In this room, don't miss photos of vaults before the war and Luther's signature ring.

Reservations: To protect this priceless collection and the extravagant rooms in which it's displayed, the number of visitors each day is carefully controlled. This means you have to reserve in advance (you'll be given a 15-minute entry window for your visit—once inside, you can stay as long as you like). You'll pass through a "dust sluice" as you enter to be sure you're free of irritants—a good feeling. To be assured entry, make a reservation far in advance (reserve at www.skd-dresden.de, email museum@dresden-tourist.de, or call 0351/4919-2285). If the Internet booking system shows your dates as sold out, keep checking back, since tour groups often cancel at short notice. While advance entry times can be booked six months in advance, 270 tickets are saved for each day (the number of spots still available and entry times—*Freie Plätze*—are indicated at the ticket desk). These are sold starting at 10:00—line up early. If all else fails, you can try walking up to the ticket office to see if a tour group canceled. Once I got in within 20 minutes this way, even after being told that the vault was sold out for months. When planning your visit, remember that the Historic Green Vault is closed Tuesday.

▲▲New Green Vault (Neues Grünes Gewölbe)—This collection shows off more of the treasure in a modern setting. Don't miss the 6.2-carat, one-of-a-kind, green diamond that "mysteriously" appeared here from India. Invest in the €3 audioguide, which beautifully describes the best 65 objects in 90 minutes.

Watchman's Tower (Hausmannsturm)—This palace tower is completely rebuilt (and feels entirely modern). For €3 (included in the €12 *Tageskarte*), you can climb past an underwhelming coin collection, see the rebuilt medieval clock mechanism from behind, peruse an extensive series of dome-damage photos, and earn a good city view after a long climb. In bad weather, the view terrace is closed, and you'll peer through small windows—a big disappointment. If climbing the Frauenkirche tower (which affords the best view in town but costs €8), skip this.

▲▲▲Frauenkirche (Church of Our Lady)

This landmark church was originally built by local donations—Protestant people-pride. Destroyed by the Allied firebombing in World War II, the church sat in ruins for decades. Finally, in 1992, the reconstruction of the church began. The restorers used these guidelines: rebuild true to the original design; use as much of the

original material as possible; maximize modern technology in the procedure; use no concrete or rebar; and make it a lively venue for 21st-century-style worship. The church was fitted together like a giant jigsaw puzzle, with about a third made of original stones (notice the dark ones, placed in their original spots). The reconstruction cost more than €100 million, 90 percent of which came from donors around the world.

Now open, the church is as worthwhile for its glorious **interior** as for its tragic, then uplifting recent history. Stepping inside, you're struck by the shape—not so wide (150 feet) but very tall (inner dome 120 feet, under a 225-foot main dome). The color scheme is pastel, in an effort to underline the joy of faith and enhance the festive ambience of the services and ceremonies held here. The curves create a community feeling. The seven entrances are perfectly equal (as people are, in the eyes of God). When the congregation exits, the seven exits point to all quarters—a reminder of "go ye," the Great Commission to spread the Word everywhere.

The Baroque sandstone **altar** shows Jesus praying in the Garden of Gethsemane the night before his crucifixion. Soldiers, led by Judas, are on their way, but Christ is firmly in the presence of God and his angels. Eighty percent of today's altar is from original material—in the form of 2,000 individual fragments that were salvaged and pieced back together by restorers.

The **Cross of Nails** at the high altar is from Coventry, England—Dresden's sister city. Two fire-blackened nails found in the smoldering ruble of Coventry's bombed church are used as a symbol of peace and reconciliation. Coventry was bombed as thoroughly as Dresden (so thoroughly, it gave the giddy Luftwaffe a new word for "to bomb to smithereens"—to "coventrate"). From the destroyed town of Coventry was born the Community of the Cross of Nails, a worldwide network promoting peace and reconciliation through international understanding.

Near the exit stands the church's **twisted old cross,** which fell 300 feet and burned in the rubble. Lost until 1993, it was

found relatively intact and stands exactly on the place in the rubble where it was found. A copy—a gift from British people in 2000 on the 55th anniversary of the bombing—crowns the new church. It was crafted by an English coppersmith whose father dropped bombs on the church on that fateful night. As they leave, visitors are invited to light a candle before this cross and enter a wish for peace in the guest book.

Cost, Hours, Location: Free but donation requested, enter through door D, Mon–Fri 10:00–12:00 & 13:00–18:00, open between services and concerts on Sat–Sun, €2.50 for 45-min audioguide, www.frauenkirche-dresden.de.

Climbing the Dome: Those feeling energetic can get a great view over the city by climbing the stairs to the top of the dome. After an elevator takes you a third of the way, you still have a long climb (€8—consider it a donation to the church, enter through door G, follow signs to *Kuppelaufstieg,* Mon–Sat 10:00–18:00, Sun 12:00–19:00).

More Sights in Dresden

▲Semperoper—This elegant opera house watches over Theaterplatz in the heart of town. Three opera houses have stood in this spot: The first was destroyed by a fire in 1869, the second by firebombs in 1945. The rebuilt Semperoper continues to be a world-class venue, and tickets for the Saxon State Orchestra (the world's oldest) are hard to come by (on sale a year in advance, box office in Schinkelwache TI across the square sells day-of tickets only, Mon–Fri 10:00–18:00, Sat 10:00–13:00, closed Sun, tel. 0351/491-1705, fax 0351/491-1700, www.semperoper.de).

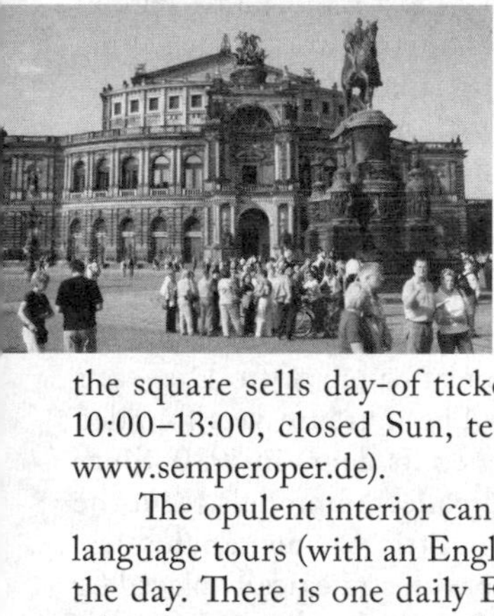

The opulent interior can only be visited with a tour. German-language tours (with an English handout) go regularly throughout the day. There is one daily English tour at 14:00 (€7, €2 extra to take photos, 1 hour, tour schedule depends on rehearsal schedule, enter on right side, tel. 0351/491-1496).

Albertinum—This historic building, at the end of the Brühlsche Terrasse, is closed for renovation until 2010. When it reopens, it may once again house two good museums: the Sculpture Collection (Skulpturensammlung) and the New Masters Gallery (Gemäldegalerie Neue Meister). In the meantime, its collections have been lent to other museums (in other cities) or put in storage. Art-lovers can ask at the TI if any works from the New Masters Gallery are on display in Dresden. This collection includes paintings and sculptures by 19th- and 20th-century greats such as Pierre-Auguste Renoir, Auguste Rodin, Vincent van Gogh, Edgar Degas, and Gustav Klimt. I especially enjoy Otto Dix's moving triptych *War* (painted between the world wars), Klimt's *Buchenwald,* and one of Rodin's *Thinkers*.

Prager Strasse—This communist-built pedestrian mall, connecting the train station and the historic center, was in ruins until the 1960s. Even today, "Prague Street" reflects Soviet ideals: big, blocky, functional buildings without extraneous ornamentation. As you stroll down Prager Strasse, imagine these buildings without much color or advertising (which were unnecessary back in the no-choices days of communism). Today, the street is filled with corporate logos, shoppers with lots of choices, and a fun summertime food circus. When all the construction is finished, this will be an impressive people zone.

▲New Town (Neustadt)—A big sign across the river from the old center declares, "Dresden continues here." This seems directed at tourists who visit the city and stay exclusively in the Old Town. Don't be one of them—make a point to explore Dresden's New Town, too. While there are no famous sights in the New Town, it's the only part of Dresden that predates World War II. Today, it's thriving with cafés, shops, clubs, and—most important—regular people. I've listed several hotels and restaurants worth considering in the neighborhood (see "Sleeping" and "Eating").

Hygiene Museum (Deutsches Hygiene Museum)—Many Germans are fanatical about hygiene and public health. This museum is a highly conceptual compilation of vaguely health-related exhibits. The building has the dubious honor of once being the headquarters of the Nazi eugenics (genetic engineering through "proper" breeding) and racial studies administration. The exterior fresco—by German Expressionist painter Otto Dix—sets the tone for the unsettling interior. The museum was founded in 1911, and the current location opened its doors in 1930. Since then, the museum has produced and collected models from the 16th century to the present, including little wooden anatomical figures with removable parts (complete with strategically placed fig leaves), X-ray machines from the 1930s, and graphic wax models of venereal diseases. The exhibit is divided into weirdly themed sections (Life and Death, Disease, Physiology, Reproduction, and Grooming). There are some English explanations, or you can rent the €2 audioguide, but most of the exhibits speak (or shriek) for themselves. Perhaps a reflection of the typically German pragmatism toward sexuality, this place is usually filled with school groups or families with young kids. People who enjoyed the Dieter sketches on *Saturday Night Live* will get a kick out of this highly interactive museum, but those easily disturbed should stay away (€6, Tue–Sun 10:00–18:00, closed Mon; Lingnerplatz 1, take tram #1, #2, or #4 from Postplatz to the Deutsches Hygiene Museum stop; tel. 0351/484-6670, www.dhmd.de).

Volkswagen Transparent Factory (Gläserne Manufaktur)—Car buffs will want to make a pilgrimage to this new VW factory on the southeastern edge of town. Two floors of this fascinating, transparent building are open to visitors interested in the assembly of one of VW's high-end cars. You don't have to custom-order a luxury-model Phaeton to see how they're manufactured. (But if you do buy a car, you can bring a folding chair, park yourself on the platform, and follow it through every moment of the 36-hour "birth" process.) The parts are delivered to the logistics plant just on the edge of town, then transported to this manufacturing plant by "cargo trams" (which are used to avoid adding to traffic congestion in town). While you're basically paying to experience a VW ad, it is interesting to see the wild building, peek at the assembly line, and play with the informative, high-tech, English touchscreen displays (€4, daily 8:00–20:00, Lennestrasse 1, toll tel. 01805-896-268—costs €0.14/min, www.glaesernemanufaktur.de). Take tram #1, #2, or #4 from Theaterplatz or Prager Strasse, or tram #10 from the Hauptbahnhof (main train station), to Strassburgerplatz, from which it's a 100-yard walk.

Near Dresden: Saxon Switzerland National Park

Consider a break from big-city sightseeing to spend a half-day taking a *wunderbar* hike through this scenic national park.

Twenty miles southeast of Dresden (an easy 45-min S-Bahn ride away), the Elbe River cuts a scenic swath through the beech forests and steep cliffs of Saxon Switzerland (Sächsische Schweiz) National Park. You'll share the trails with serious rock climbers and equally serious Saxon grandmothers. Allow five hours (including lunch) to enjoy this day trip.

Take the S-Bahn line 1 from either the Hauptbahnhof or the Neustadt station (direction Bad Schandau, departs hourly; round-trip-€5.10, family day ticket-€14, day ticket for a group of up to five adults-€22). Get off at the Kurort Rathen stop, follow the road downhill five minutes through town to the dock, and take the ferry across the Elbe (€1.70 round-trip, pay on board, crossing takes 2 min, runs continuously). When the ferry docks on the far (north) side of the river, turn your back on the river and walk 100 yards through town, with the little creek on your right. Turn left after the Sonniges Eck Restaurant (tasty lunch option, check out the 2002 flood photos in their front dining room) and walk up the lane. The trail begins with stairs on your left just past Hotel Amselgrundschlösschen (follow *Bastei* signs).

A 45-minute walk uphill through the woods leads you to the Bastei Bridge and stunning views of gray sandstone sentries rising several hundred feet above forest ridges. Elbe Valley sandstone was used to build Dresden's finest buildings (including the Frauenkirche and Zwinger), as well as Berlin's famous Brandenburg Gate. The multiple-arch bridge looks straight out of Oz—built in 1851 specifically for Romantic Age tourists, and scenic enough to be the subject of the first landscape photos ever taken in Germany. Take the time to explore the short, 50-yard spur trails that reward you with classic views down on the Elbe 900 feet below. Watch the slow-motion paddleboat steamers leave V-shaped wakes as they chug upstream toward the Czech Republic, just around the next river bend. If you're not afraid of heights, explore the maze of catwalks through the scant remains of the Felsenberg Neurathen, a 13th-century Saxon fort perched precariously on the bald stony spires (€1.50, entrance 50 yards before Bastei Bridge).

Just a five-minute uphill hike beyond the bridge is the Berg Hotel Panorama Bastei, with a fine restaurant, a snack bar, and memorable views. Return back down to the Elbe ferry via the same trail.

NIGHTLIFE

To really connect with Dresden as it unfolds, you need to go to the **Innere Neustadt** ("Inner New Town," a 10-min walk from Neustadt train station). This area was not bombed in World War II, and after 1989 it sprouted the first entrepreneurial cafés and bistros. While eateries are open long hours, the action picks up after 22:00. The clientele is young, hip, pierced, and tattooed.

Rather than seek out particular places in this continuously evolving scene, I'd just get to the epicenter (corner of Görlitzer Strasse and Louisenstrasse) and wander. Pop through the Kunsthofpassage, a Hundertwasser-type apartment block with some fun spots (Görlitzer Strasse 23). At Böhmischestrasse 34 (a half-block off Lutherplatz), the Russian-flavored Kneipe Raskolnikoff has an imported beach, giving it a Moscow/Maui ambience. The Carte Blanche Transvestite Bar is a hoot for some (€25, most nights from 20:00, Priessnitzstrasse 10, tel. 0351/204-720).

For more sedate entertainment, stroll along the New Town's riverbank after dark for fine floodlit views of the Old Town.

SLEEPING

Dresden is packed with big, conference-style hotels. Characteristic, family-run places are harder to come by. (The communists didn't do "quaint" very well.) Peak season for the big business-class hotels is May, June, September, and October. Peak season for hostels is July and August (especially weekends). For locations, see the map on page 406.

In or near the Old Town

$$$ Hilton Dresden has 330 luxurious rooms (some with views of the Frauenkirche) in the heart of the Old Town, one block from the river. Complete with porters, fitness club, pool, and several restaurants, it's everything you'd expect from a soulless, four-star chain hotel (Sb/Db-€125–239, breakfast-€22, parking-€19/day, An der Frauenkirche 5, tel. 0351/86420, fax 0351/864-2725, www.hilton.de, info.dresden@hilton.com).

$$ Hotel Kipping, with 20 tidy rooms 100 yards behind the Hauptbahnhof, is professionally run by the friendly and proper Kipping brothers (Rainer and Peter). The building was one of few in this area to survive the firebombing—in fact, people took shelter here during the attack (Sb-€70–110, Db-€95–130, 1-person suite-€115–130, 2-person suite-€130–145, child's bed-€25; higher prices are for weekends, May–June, and Sept–Oct; elevator, free parking, exit the station following signs to *Bayerische Strasse* near track 6, it's at Winckelmannstrasse 6, tram #8 whisks you to the Old Town, tel. 0351/478-500, fax 0351/478-5090, www.hotel-kipping.de, reception@hotel-kipping.de). Their restaurant serves international cuisine and Saxon specialties (€9–12 main dishes, Mon–Sat 18:00–22:30, closed Sun).

$$ Aparthotels an der Frauenkirche rents 50 new units just above all the restaurant action on Münzgasse. Designed for longer stays but also welcoming two-nighters (minimum), these modern, comfortable apartments come with kitchens and the lived-in works. The Drescher family also owns two other apartment-hotels in the immediate area (Db-€65–150, extra bed-€15, breakfast-€10, cheaper for longer stays and off-season, parking at nearby garage-€10/day, Münzgasse 10, tel. 0351/438-1111, www.aparthotels-frauenkirche.de, info@aparthotels-frauenkirche.de).

Sleep Code

(€1 = about $1.50, country code: 49, area code: 0351)
S = Single, **D** = Double/Twin, **T** = Triple, **Q** = Quad, **b** = bathroom, **s** = shower only. All of these places speak English and accept credit cards. Unless otherwise noted, breakfast is included.

To help you sort easily through these listings, I've divided the rooms into three categories, based on the price for a standard double room with bath:

$$$ Higher Priced—Most rooms €120 or more.
$$ Moderately Priced—Most rooms between €80–120.
$ Lower Priced—Most rooms €80 or less.

$$ Hotels Bastei, Königstein, and **Lilienstein** are cookie-cutter members of the Ibis chain, goose-stepping single-file up Prager Strasse (listed in order from the station to the center). Each is practically identical, with 360 rooms. Though utterly lacking in charm, they are a good value in a convenient location between the Hauptbahnhof and the Old Town (Sb-€70, Db-€85, apartment-€128 for a family of 4, breakfast-€9.50, parking-€6.50/day, reservations for all: tel. 0351/4856-2000; individual receptions: tel. 0351/4856-5445, tel. 0351/4856-6445, and tel. 0351/4856-7445, respectively; www.ibis-dresden.de).

In the New Town

The first two hotels are fancy splurges in a tidy residential neighborhood surrounding the Neustadt train station. The rest are cheap and funky, buried in the trendy, newly happening café-and-club zone called the Innere Neustadt ("Inner New Town," about a 10-min walk from Neustadt station—see page 424).

$$$ Hotel Bayerischer Hof Dresden, 100 yards toward the river from the Neustadt train station, offers 50 rooms and elegant, inviting public spaces in a grand old building (Sb-€99, Db-€138, pricier suites, non-smoking rooms, elevator, free parking, Antonstrasse 33–35, yellow building across from station, tel. 0351/829-370, fax 0351/801-4860, www.bayerischer-hof-dresden.de, info@bayerischer-hof-dresden.de).

$$$ Hotel Martha Hospiz, with 50 rooms near the recommended restaurants on Königstrasse, is bright and cheery. The two old buildings that make up the hotel have been smartly renovated and connected in back with a glassed-in winter garden and an outdoor breakfast terrace. It's a 10-minute walk to the historical center, and a five-minute walk to the Neustadt station (S-€55, Sb-€79–86, Db-€113–121, extra bed-€27, elevator; leaving Neustadt station, turn right on Hainstrasse, left on Theresenstrasse, and then right on Nieritzstrasse to #11; tel. 0351/81760, fax 0351/8176-222, www.vch.de/marthahospiz.dresden, marthahospiz.dresden@t-online.de).

$$ AHA Hotel may have an unassuming facade on a big, noisy street, but inside you'll find a homey and welcoming ambience. The 30 simple-but-neat apartments all come with kitchens; most (except the top floor) have balconies. It's a bit farther from the center—10 minutes by foot east of Albertplatz, a 20-minute walk or a quick ride on tram #11 from the Old Town—but its friendliness, coziness, and good value make it a winner (Sb-€67, Db-€101–108, small Db about €10 cheaper, breakfast-€9, request quieter back side, non-smoking rooms, elevator, Bautzner Strasse 53, tel. 0351/800-850, fax 0351/8008-5114, www.ahahotel-dresden.de, kontakt@ahahotel-dresden.de).

$ Guest House Mezcalero, decorated Mexican from top to bottom, is a 22-room enterprise that's a 10-minute walk from the Neustadt station at the edge of the lively Innere Neustadt zone. It feels smart yet comfy, with an adobe ambience (S-€35, D-€55, Db-€65, dorm bed-€17 plus a one-time €2.50 fee for sheets and towels, breakfast-€6, from either station catch tram #7 to Bischofsweg, Königsbrücker Strasse 64, tel. 0351/810-770, fax 0351/810-7711, www.mezcalero.de, info@mezcalero.de).

$ Hostel "Louise 20" rents 83 beds in the heart of the Innere Neustadt. Though located in the wild-and-edgy nightlife district, it feels safe, solid, clean, and comfy. The newly furnished rooms, guests' kitchen, cozy common room, and friendly staff make it the best place in town for cheap beds (S-€32, D-€43, small dorm-€17/bed—€2.50 less if you have sheets; breakfast extra, no lockers, generally booked on summer weekends, Louisenstrasse 20, tel. 0351/8894-894, www.louise20.de, info@louise20.de).

$ Hostel Mondpalast Dresden is young and hip, in the heart of the Innere Neustadt above a cool bar. It's good for backpackers with little money and an appetite for late-night fun (S-€34, Sb-€44, D-€44, Db-€52, dorm bed-€15, one-time €2 fee for sheets, breakfast-€5, lockers, kitchen, lots of facilities, tram #7 from Hauptbahnhof or #11 from Neustadt station, near Kamenzer Strasse at Louisenstrasse 77, tel. 0351/563-4050, fax 0351/563-4055, www.mondpalast.de, info@mondpalast.de).

EATING

As the city comes back to life, nearly every restaurant seems bright, shiny, and modern. While Old Town restaurants are touristy, the prices are reasonable, and it's easy to eat for €10–15 just about anywhere. For cheaper prices and authentic local character, leave the famous center, cross the river, and wander through the New Town.

The special local dessert sold all over town is *Dresdner Eierschecke,* an eggy cheesecake with vanilla pudding, raisins, and almond shavings.

In the Old Town

Münzgasse, the busy and touristy lane that connects the Brühlsche Terrasse promenade and the Frauenkirche, is the liveliest street in the Old Town, with a fun selection of eateries. Choose from tapas, Aussie, goulash, crêpes, and even antiques (Kunst Café Antik scatters its tables among a royal estate sale of fancy furniture and objets d'art—around the corner, riverside). Service is a necessary evil, the clientele is international, and the action spills out onto the cobbled pedestrian lane on balmy evenings.

Altmarkt Keller, a few blocks farther from the river on Altmarkt square, is a festive beer cellar that serves nicely presented Saxon and Bohemian food (from separate menus) and has good Czech beer on tap. The lively crowd, cheesy music (live Sat only), and jolly murals add to the fun. While the on-square seating is fine, the vast-but-stout air-conditioned cellar offers your best memories. The giant mural inside the entryway—representing the friendship between Dresden and Prague—reads, "The sunshine of life is drinking and being happy" (€8–13 main dishes, daily 11:00–24:00, Altmarkt 4, to the right of McDonald's, tel. 0351/481-8130).

Grand Café Restaurant Cosel Palais serves Saxon and French cuisine in the shadow of the newly rebuilt Frauenkirche. This is a Baroque, chandeliered dining experience with fine, if touristy, courtyard seating—great for an elegant meal or tea and pastries (€10–19 meals, daily specials, daily 10:00–24:00, An der Frauenkirche 12, tel. 0351/496-2444).

Erlebnisgastronomie ***("Experience Gastronomy"):*** All the rage among Dresdeners (and German tourists in Dresden) is *Erlebnisgastronomie.* Elaborately decorated theme restaurants have sprouted next to the biggest-name sights around town, with over-the-top, theme-park decor and historically costumed waitstaff. These can offer a fun change of pace and aren't the bad value you might suspect. The best is **Sophienkeller,** which does its best to take you to the 18th century and the world of Augustus the Strong. The king himself, along with his countess, musicians, and magicians, stroll and entertain, while court maidens serve traditional

Saxon food from a "ye olde" menu. Read their colorful brochure to better understand the place. It's big (470 seats), and it even has a rotating carousel table with suspended swing-chairs that you sit in while you eat. Before choosing a seat, survey the two big and distinct zones—one bright and wide open, the other more intimate and cellar-like (€10–15 main dishes, daily 11:00–24:00, under the five-star Taschenberg Palace Hotel, Taschenberg 3, tel. 0351/497-260).

With a River View: **Radeberger Spezialausschank Café** is dramatically situated on the Brühlsche Terrasse promenade, with a rampart-hanging view terrace and three levels taking you down to the river. For river views from the "Balcony of Europe," this is your spot. The inviting-yet-simple menu includes daily Saxon specials and cheap wurst and kraut. This is the only place in town that serves Radeberger's unfiltered beer. The cool river-level bar comes with big copper brewery vats (daily 11:00–24:00, reservations smart for view terrace, Terrassenufer 1, tel. 0351/484-8660).

In the Main Train Station: For a quick bite at the Hauptbahnhof, the healthy market-style **Marché Cafeteria** is fast and reasonable (daily 5:30–21:00).

In the New Town

Venture to these eateries—across Augustus Bridge from the Old Town—for lower prices and a more local scene. I've listed them nearest to farthest from the Old Town.

Just Across Augustus Bridge

Augustus Garten is a lazy, crude-yet-inviting beer garden with super-cheap self-service food (pork knuckle, kraut, cheap beer, and lots of mustard). You'll eat among big bellies—and no tourists—with a fun city-skyline-over-the-river view. While enjoyable in balmy weather, this place is dead when it's cool (€3–8.50 main dishes, €2–5 beers, €2 refundable deposit on beer glasses, daily 11:00–24:00, closed in bad weather, Wiesentorstrasse 2, tel. 0351/404-5854). As you walk across the bridge from the Old Town, it's on your immediate right.

On Königstrasse

For trendy elegance without tourists, have dinner on Königstrasse. After crossing the Augustus Bridge, hike five minutes up the communist-built main drag of the New Town, then turn left to find this charming Baroque street. As this is a fast-changing area, you might survey the other options on and near Königstrasse (be sure to tuck in to a few courtyards) before settling down.

Wenzel Prager Bierstuben serves country Bohemian cuisine in a woodsy bar that spills out into an airy, glassed-in gallery—made doubly big by its vast mirror. Stepping inside, you immediately feel this is a winner. They offer a fun Bohemian menu with great Czech beer on tap (€7 dinner-with-beer specials on Tue–Thu, €8–13 main dishes, open daily 11:00–24:00, Königstrasse 1, tel. 0315/804-2010).

Good Friends is a favorite for Thai and Vietnamese food, and a welcome relief from pork and potatoes (€6–12 main dishes, Mon–Fri 11:30–15:00 & 17:30–23:00, Sat–Sun 12:00–23:00, An der Dreifaltigkeitskirche 9, tel. 0351/646-5814). Walk down Königstrasse to the towering Three Kings Church. It's under the steeple.

Beer Halls

All of Dresden's famous beer halls were destroyed in the war, and the communists refused to rebuild them. But after unification, ambitious Dresdeners began recreating this tradition. Beer halls usually serve their own brew and hearty Saxon cuisine. Saxons love to eat and talk, so a beer hall is a great place to meet locals and get a taste of life outside of tourist areas. All of these places are far from the city center, but are easily reached by public transportation.

Brauhaus am Waldschlösschen is fun and lively, with nightly music that really gets going after 21:00. The restaurant serves traditional Saxon cuisine with some fine salads (main dishes under €15). The view of Dresden's Old Town from the self-service beer garden (with snacks under €6.50) can't be beat (daily 11:00–24:00, Am Brauhaus 8b, tram #11 to Waldschlösschen, tel. 0351/652-3900). They offer brewery tours daily at 16:00—in German only, but still enjoyable.

Ball und Brauhaus Watzke, the oldest of the beer halls, started life as a ballroom (it still holds public balls once a month). It sits pleasantly on the banks of the Elbe, with nice views of the Old Town. Watzke serves traditional beer-hall food in huge portions, and features €8 dinner-with-beer specials nightly except Sunday (€9 main dishes, open daily 11:00–24:00, Kötzschenbroderstrasse 1, tram #4 or #9 to Altpieschen, tel. 0351/852-920). The brewery also operates the **Brauereiausschank am Goldenen Reiter** pub in New Town. It has the same beer and menu, with a good view of the Frauenkirche, but with little of the original's ambience (daily 11:00–24:00, Hauptstrasse 1—in front of the Golden Rider statue, tel. 0351/810-6820).

Feldschlösschen Stammhaus was the original brewery and hop warehouse for Feldschlösschen beer, but the company moved to another part of Dresden in the 1970s. Although significantly farther afield than the other beer halls, the Stammhaus is a cozy, energy-filled spot in a sea of East German prefab apartments. Traditional fare dominates the menu, but Stammhaus sneaks in large portions of fresh vegetables and fresh homemade bread (€11 main dishes, €9 dinner specials with a beer, daily 11:00–24:00,

Budapester Strasse 32, bus #82 from the Prager Strasse Transit Center to the Arbeitsamt stop, tel. 0351/471-8855).

TRANSPORTATION CONNECTIONS

From Dresden by Train to: Görlitz (hourly, 1.5 hrs), **Bautzen** (about hourly, 30–45 min; Bautzen-bound trains continue on to Görlitz), **Zittau** (better from Neustadt, hourly, 1.5–2 hrs), **Berlin** (every 2 hrs, more with a transfer in Leipzig, 2.25 hrs), **Prague** (every 2 hrs, 2.25–2.5 hrs), **Frankfurt** (hourly, 4.75 hrs), **Nürnberg** (hourly, 4.5 hrs, transfer in Leipzig), **Munich** (about hourly, 5.75–6.25 hrs, transfer in Leipzig or Nürnberg), **Vienna** (2/day, 7 hrs; plus 1 night train/day, 9 hrs), **Budapest** (1/day, 9 hrs). There are overnight trains from Dresden to Zürich, the Rhineland, and Munich. Train info: tel. 11861 (€0.60/min).

GÖRLITZ

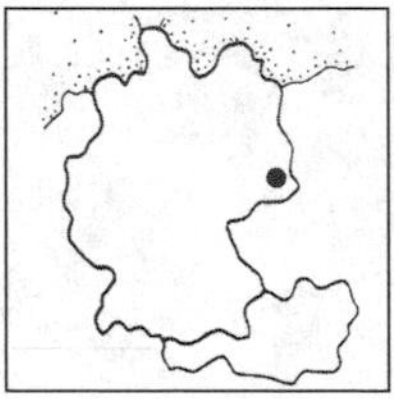

Tucked away in Germany's easternmost corner, the surprisingly beautiful town of Görlitz is a treasure trove of architecture and one of this country's best-kept secrets.

During the Middle Ages, Görlitz was a major European crossroads, at the intersection of trade routes from Moscow to Barcelona and from the Baltic Sea to Venice. Trade in cloth and beer made the city flourish. Görlitz's rich cultural tapestry was gradually enhanced as the centuries passed, leaving it a delightful collage of architectural styles. The town escaped most of World War II's bombs, but soon after was split down the middle along its river—with half of the town in Germany, the other half in Poland. Görlitz's historic buildings were preserved by the East German government, saving it from the unsightly communist-era blemishes that mark most former East German towns.

Since the Wall fell, Görlitz has sprung back to life and is busily polishing its gorgeous facades. The town offers a unique opportunity to venture to the eastern fringes of Germany, sample Silesian culture and cuisine, and appreciate some breathtaking architecture and stay-a-while squares. Best of all, although German tourists fill Görlitz on weekends during the summer, it's virtually undiscovered by foreign tourists—making it a real Back Door experience.

Planning Your Time

Although Görlitz is an ideal day trip from Dresden (hourly trains, 1.5 hrs), the city's subtle charm warrants an overnight stay. Görlitz opens up on long summer nights, as pubs and cafés spill out into the cobbles. Get lost and wander the back streets and alleys.

ORIENTATION

(area code: 03581)
With a population of about 56,000, Görlitz is the largest city in what's left of German Silesia. While Görlitz lost a third of its population to Poland in 1945, the historic center and most sights of interest to travelers remain in Germany. The compact Old Town (Altstadt), containing almost everything to see and do, is an easy stroll, roughly between Marienplatz and the western bank of the Neisse River. The focal point of the Old Town is its twin market squares, Upper (Obermarkt) and Lower (Untermarkt).

Tourist Information

The TI, called Görlitzinformation, sells €1 maps and can book you a room for free. Information in English is sparse, but there are a few English guidebooks available, and people seem genuinely helpful and welcoming (Mon–Fri 9:00–19:00, Sat–Sun 9:00–18:00, between Obermarkt and Untermarkt at Obermarkt 32, tel. 03581/475-723, www.europastadt-goerlitz.de). Pick up the €6.90 *Görlitz Town Guide,* a small but informative do-it-yourself walking tour, but skip the €3 map. The *Architectural Guide Through the Old Town of Görlitz* (€7) is overkill for most visitors but indispensable for architecture buffs, describing almost every building in the Old Town in a convenient flip-out format.

To arrange for a guided **tour** in English, call 03581/475-713.

Arrival in Görlitz

By Train: Görlitz's train station, about a half-mile southwest of the city center, is a sight in itself. Built in 1901, the main hall is a pearl of Prussian *Jugendstil,* while the building itself is Neoclassical. Its opening hours are shorter than those at larger stations, and it's virtually deserted after 21:00. Lockers are in the passage between the tracks and the main hall (€1–2). You'll also find handy WCs (€0.50, deposit coin, then wait for buzzer) and a *Reisezentrum* for train information and tickets (Mon and Thu–Fri 6:30–18:30, Tue–Wed 7:30–13:00 & 13:45–17:00, Sat 7:30–13:00, Sun 12:30–18:00).

To get into town (a 15-min walk), exit straight out the front entrance and follow Berliner Strasse. At the first large square *(Postplatz),* the road veers left, and you'll see the Hertie department store (marking Marienplatz and the start of my self-guided walking tour). You can also take tram #2 or #3 to Demianiplatz (departs from the platform on your right as you exit the station; €1.20, 5 min).

Görlitz: A Silesian Brew

Görlitz is a city with an identity crisis, much like the entire region of Silesia. Silesia, which has never been a "nation" of its own, encompasses parts of Germany (where it's called "Schlesien"), Poland ("Śląsk"), and the Czech Republic ("Slezsko"). Silesians are proud of this diversity, and of their pragmatic ability to work and live peacefully with each other despite the borders that separate them. Just like the Silesians themselves, their cuisine, folk art, and customs are a mish-mash of German, Polish, and Czech.

After Slavic Sorbs founded Gorelec in 1071, the village—renamed Görlitz—came under the German sphere of cultural influence in the 12th century, and has been predominantly German ever since. For most of its early existence, the city technically belonged to Bohemia, but was ceded to Saxony after the Peace of Prague in 1635. In 1815, Görlitz fell into Prussian hands at the Congress of Vienna and became the largest city in the province of Lower Silesia.

The city's unusual experience in World War II made it the unique place it is today: While Görlitz almost miraculously escaped destruction (only its Old Town Bridge was bombed), it was split in two by the Potsdam Agreement in 1945. This treaty determined the Neisse River—which runs through the center of Görlitz—to be the border between Germany and Poland. The following year, Poland expelled all Germans from its country, which included booting them out of Silesia and, therefore, out of the Polish side of Görlitz.

This expulsion created two ethnically distinct halves: the German town of Görlitz on the west side of the river, and the Polish town of Zgorzelec, which is still part of Poland on the east. Although most German Silesians have long since abandoned any hope of re-establishing their lost homeland, they have gone to great efforts to stress the unity between Silesians of all ethnic backgrounds—Germans, Poles, and Czechs—by re-establishing cultural connections across the rivers and mountains. Czechs and Poles are strong participants at all city festivals. After German, Polish and Czech are the most common languages you'll hear spoken in the streets and see on signs in Görlitz.

In 2004, German Görlitz and Polish Zgorzelec completed the reconstruction of a new, pedestrians-only Old Town Bridge (Altstadtbrücke) across the Neisse. Locals like to think this largely symbolic gesture makes Görlitz the most European city in Europe. And now that Poland has joined the open-borders Schengen Agreement, anyone can freely cross the bridge without even having to flash a passport.

Getting Around Görlitz

The communists left little Görlitz with a highly developed and efficient public-transportation system (€1.20/ride, *Einzelfahrt Normal;* €3 day pass, *Tageskarte Normal;* €6.50 pass for up to 5 people, *Kleingruppenkarte*). Tickets are valid on both trams and buses. Buy tickets from bus drivers or the machines on the platforms and trams (coins only), and validate tickets in the little blue box on board. All buses and trams converge at Demianiplatz. The Old Town is compact, so unless you're planning to visit the Holy Sepulcher or go out to the Landeskrone mountain, you'll probably only use public transit to get from the train station into the city center.

SELF-GUIDED WALK

Welcome to Görlitz

The joy of Görlitz is simply wandering the Old Town and appreciating the architecture. Begin this orientation walk at Marienplatz, the small square right outside the former city walls.

Marienplatz

The unique *Jugendstil* **Hertie department store** (completed in 1911) has a richly decorated facade concealing an ornate glass-domed interior with intricate staircases and galleries (Mon–Sat 9:00–19:00, closed Sun).

Behind Hertie is the **Church of our Lady** (Frauenkirche), a 15th-century, late-Gothic church built near the hospital and poorhouse outside the city walls. Although this church seems unremarkable, take a moment to step inside (free, Mon–Sat 10:00–18:00, Sun 11:00–18:00; Mon–Fri try to catch the *Mittagsrast* prayer and organ music at 12:00). Imagine being here in the fall of 1989, shortly before the Berlin Wall came down. This church served as a forum for discussions and peace prayers *(Friedensgebete)*. A poster announcing the first prayer meeting was placed in the glass cabinet on the front of the church. Soon, like-minded shopkeepers began to follow suit, and 580 people attended the first meeting. Just two weeks later, 1,300 people showed up, and subsequent meetings swelled to 5,000—so large that they spilled over into other churches. The meetings became a forum for discussing impending political changes, civil rights, and environmental issues. As each participant came forward and voiced their concerns, a candle was blown out until the church was dark. Then, as those who had a hopeful or positive experience came forward, a candle was lit until the church was illuminated once again. The East German secret police, the *Stasi,* stationed plainclothes police in the buildings across the street to document who was participating in these "acts of civil disobedience." Many people lost their jobs or were

Görlitz

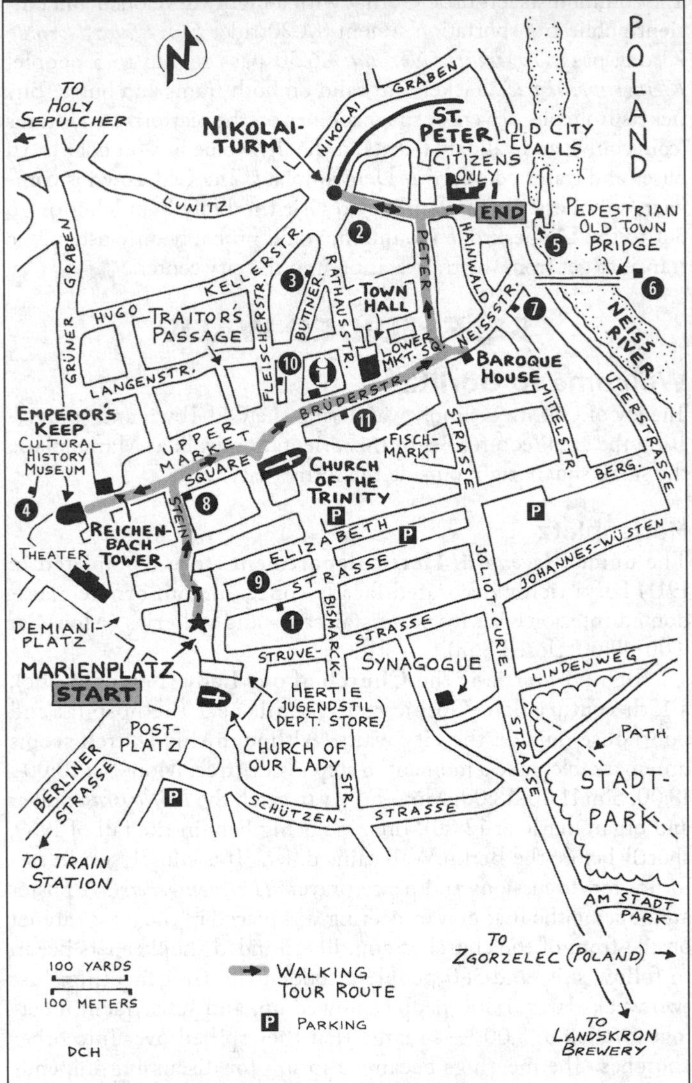

1. Hotel Bon Apart
2. Die Destille Pension/Rest.
3. Hotel und Gasthof Dreibeiniger-Hund
4. Zur Goldenen Sonne Rest.
5. Vierradenmühle Rest.
6. Piwnica Staromiejska Pub
7. Bürgerstübl Rest.
8. Lebensmittel Weiss Grocery
9. Farmers' Market
10. Görlitzer Weinachts Haus (Christmas Shop)
11. Schlesische Schatztruhe Shop

punished. But the hope for democracy and self-determination had already caught on, and today, this church stands as a symbol of peace and solidarity.

To the north, the **Fat Tower** (Dicker Turm) is the second-oldest tower in the city's defensive network. Although the tower itself is Gothic (from 1270), it's topped by a copper Renaissance cupola. The tower was attached to the so-called Women's Gate (Frauen Tor) in 1477. It's decorated with a sandstone relief of the Görlitz city coat of arms, featuring a Bohemian lion and a Silesian black eagle—representing Görlitz as an independent and free city.

• *Walk down the street to the left of the tower (Steinstrasse) and onto the...*

Upper Market Square (Obermarkt)

This square dates from the 13th century, and is lined with mainly Baroque houses. The **Reichenbach Tower** dominates the western end of the square. The tower formed the western city wall and dates from the 13th century, although the cylindrical portion was added in 1485 and is topped with a Baroque cupola from 1782. The tower housed city guards and watchmen—who among other things kept a lookout for fires—until the last "tower family" moved out in 1904. Inside is an impressive collection of armaments, early 20th-century photographs, and an interesting exhibit on the daily lives of the tower's occupants (€1.50, May–Oct Tue–Sun 10:00–17:00, closed Mon and Nov–April, Platz des 17 Juni, tel. 03581/671-355). The view from the top is worth the 165 steps.

In 1490, Görlitz strengthened its city fortifications by building a circular bastion outside Reichenbach Tower. The structure came to be known as the **Emperor's Keep** (Kaisertruz) when the Swedish troops made their last stand against the Imperial Saxon army during the Thirty Years' War. Since then, the Emperor's Keep has been used as an archive, and today houses the Cultural History Museum (closed for renovation until 2011).

• *The tall tower on Obermarkt belongs to the...*

Church of the Trinity (Dreifaltigkeitskirche)

In 1245, Franciscan monks consecrated this church, at the southeast side of Obermarkt. Although originally a Romanesque structure, renovations in 1380 gave the church its current late-Gothic appearance. When the Reformation took hold in Silesia in 1563, the monks surrendered the keys to the church and monastery—with

Görlitz Architecture

Although no bombs fell on Görlitz itself during World War II (only on its bridge), the city didn't escape partial destruction during the Thirty Years' War or the ravages of three great city fires. Each wave of devastation allowed Görlitz to rebuild in the architectural style of the time. The results are an astonishing collection of exemplary buildings from every architectural era: Gothic, Renaissance, Baroque, *Gründerzeit* (late 19th century), and *Jugendstil*. The East German government placed the entire city under a protection order, rescuing it from the bleak communist aesthetic of the late 20th century. More than 3,700 buildings are registered historical monuments. This, combined with energetic reconstruction, makes Görlitz the gem that it is today.

the condition that the monastery be used as a school. A school operates in the former monastery to this day.

Go inside the church (free, daily 9:00–18:00, tel. 03581/311-311). The interior seems austere, but upon careful inspection, reveals delightful little details. As you enter, go immediately to your left. This is the oldest part of the church. Pillars from the original 13th-century Romanesque chapel are integrated into the walls. The fancy balcony is where the nobility sat. If you've been to Dresden, the high altar will look familiar, as it was built by artists brought from Dresden, and resembles the crown gate of the Zwinger. The swirly clouds identify this as Rococo. The missing crucifix on the left wall (now in Warsaw) is a reminder of the artifacts that were pillaged from this church during various wars, but the choir stalls, carved in the 1430s, are original. As you follow signs to the *Marienaltar,* look up at the vaulted ceiling, and notice how complex it gets as you walk into newer parts of the church.

The church's trophy is the beautiful 15th-century carved triptych, the *Marienaltar.* The simple side was used on regular worship days, while the gilded side—containing an almost life-size carving of the Virgin Mary—was reserved for high feast days. Today, you can usually see it open, and can admire the closed panels via the display on the bench to the right of the altar. (If the altar is closed, ask one of the guides to open it for you.) It's an eyeful—rich with action and symbolism. The symmetry and order of the checked tablecloth is replaced in the other panels by lots of action and purposefully conflicting lines that create energy and tension. Notice the symbolism—there's a turban-wearing Ottoman (archenemy of the time) and Jesus wearing a Franciscan frock (a nod to the church's Franciscan heritage). Behind you, an exhausted Jesus, reminiscent of Auguste Rodin's *The Thinker,* ponders the fate of man. This statue, from 1910, used to sit on the grass outside of the Holy Sepulcher (see page 443)—notice the rotting wood at the base.

This is an active church, still very much alive; during a recent celebration based on the theme, "Christ carries you—have no fear," parish kids rappelled down from the balconies.

The church's **tower** is unusually thin—the locals call it the *Mönch* ("Monk"). The clock doesn't keep very good time, thanks to one in a series of Cloth-Maker Rebellions. In the Middle Ages, Görlitz was run by the powerful guilds of the cloth trade and the brewers, who neglected the rights of their workers and forbade non-members from practicing their trades. Finally, in the early 16th century, the workers rose up against the corrupt city council, which allowed the guilds to continue their unfair practices. The rebels ended their meetings punctually at midnight to avoid the night watchmen, who would be on the other side of town at that hour. But the city council was one step ahead: They ordered the church bell to chime seven minutes before midnight to fool the conspirators out onto the street and into the waiting arms of the guard. Fourteen of the conspirators were executed, and 25 more banished from the city. To this day, the bell chimes seven minutes early.

Across the square is the **Traitor's Passage** (Verrätergasse), a dark, sinister passageway used by the instigators of the rebellion to sneak in and out of the main marketplace.

• *To leave Obermarkt, walk down...*

Brüderstrasse

This street, connecting Obermarkt and Untermarkt, is home to a fine collection of Renaissance houses. The orange-and-gray house at the end of Brüderstrasse (#8) claims to be Germany's oldest Renaissance civic building (from 1526) and now houses the **Silesian Museum of Görlitz** (Schlesisches Museum zu Görlitz), a state museum featuring Silesian culture (€4, Tue–Sun 10:00–17:00, closed Mon, Brüderstrasse 8, tel. 03581/87910, www.schlesisches-museum.de).

As you pass Schwarzestrasse, look left. The street's flying buttresses are typical of Görlitz's Old Town—these two are remnants of a series of brick barriers used to keep insurgents out of the inner city during the Cloth-Maker Rebellions.

• *At the end of Brüderstrasse, you'll reach...*

Lower Market Square (Untermarkt)

The remarkably well-preserved Untermarkt is typical of Central European squares: It's built up in the middle to make maximum use of this prime real estate. The square shows just how prosperous the cloth trade made Görlitz.

Ignoring the tall tower (we'll get to it later), take a look around the square. The building at #14 (east end of the square) housed the city **scales** and was one of the most important commercial buildings since, at its peak, more than 1,000 wagons per day entered Görlitz. Everything had to be weighed and duties paid here. The late-Gothic ground floor, which housed the scales, is topped off with three Renaissance levels. The column-topping busts are a virtual Who's Who of the town's masons and scale-masters.

Around the corner from the scales, on the northern edge of the square, the city established a **commodity exchange** at the beginning of the 18th century. The building was also a kind of department store used to drive simple street vendors away from the financial center. With the rabble banished, the Baroque building with its adorning portal was a favored place for merchants to meet and deal.

• *Untermarkt is dominated by the tall Gothic tower of the...*

Town Hall

Görlitz had no town hall until 1350, when the city purchased this building from a prominent citizen. The tower was extended to 195 feet in 1368. A lightning strike blew the top off the tower on July 9, 1742, prompting the addition of the current Baroque turret. The tower houses two clocks: The upper clock measures day, month, and phase of the moon, while the lower clock tells the time. The warrior's head used to stick out his tongue every hour, but now just seems to open his mouth. The date inscribed on the clock, 1584, commemorates the year when Bartholomäus Sculteus, an astronomer and mathematician, first divided the clock into 12 points. Sculteus also helped develop the Gregorian calendar. The city honored Sculteus, a Görlitz native, by being the first city in Germany to adopt both the new calendar and the clock. The Town Hall stairs represent the height of Görlitz Renaissance sculpture, and lead from the street level to the building's then-main entrance. Local officials used the balcony to make public announcements and decrees. If you look closely at the statue of Justice (1591), she's not blindfolded—in other words, the city is the highest authority.

• *For evidence that Görlitz is definitely a Protestant town, head down Neissstrasse to #29. There you'll find the...*

Biblical House

Since the Church banned religious depictions on secular buildings, the carvings on the Biblical House made it clear that the Reformation had come to stay. The houses in the Neissstrasse had all burned to the ground in 1526. Hanz Heinz, a cloth trader, purchased this house and rebuilt it completely in the Renaissance style. The house is named after the sandstone reliefs decorating the facade between the first and second floor parapets. The top level represents the New Testament, with (from left to right) the Annunciation, birth of Jesus, Jesus' baptism, the Last Supper, and the Crucifixion. The bottom row depicts the creation of Eve, the Fall of Man, Isaac's sacrifice, Moses receiving the Ten Commandments, and Moses banishing serpents.

• *Next door, step into the...*

Baroque House (Barockhaus)

This museum offers a peek at life in the 17th and 18th centuries. There's also an exhibit honoring Görlitz's favorite son (the philosopher Jacob Böhme, who lived here from 1575–1624), and a fascinating library, which is accessible only with an escort (request a viewing when you buy your ticket). This amazing library is still functioning today—for a €2.50 annual fee, you can have access to any of the books three days a week...anyone interested in tax records from 1475? The rest of the exhibit includes elaborately painted farm furniture, formal 18th-century apartments, a glass exhibit, and a unique lab of electrophysical instruments that belonged to a local contemporary of scientist (and "volt" namesake) Alessandro Volta. The natural sciences library holds geological samples, topographic models, and a first edition of a book by Benjamin Franklin—it's in the last room of books, on the shelf to your right by the window, fifth shelf from the bottom (€3.50, Tue–Sun 10:00–17:00, closed Mon, little English information but ask for the free explanatory fliers, tel. 03581/671-355, www.museum-goerlitz.de).

• *Backtrack to Untermarkt and hang a right onto...*

Peterstrasse

On the corner of Peterstrasse is the **City Apothecary** (Ratsapotheke). The owner attempted to transform a Gothic building into a Renaissance masterpiece, but ended up only combining the two styles. The two sundials on the southern facade were added in 1550. The left dial (Solarium) displays the time using the Arabic, local, Roman, and Babylonian clocks. The dial on the right (*Arachne*, "spider" in Greek) displays the position of the planets and the signs of the zodiac. The City Apothecary houses one of the city's best cafés, Kretschmer Ratscafé.

Peterstrasse is yet another impressive street. Look inside #14—the staircase seems to hang in mid-air. The house at #6 is a perfect example of renovations gone wrong: The building is Renaissance, with Gothic doors and windows, Ionic columns, and Baroque decorations—the combination doesn't really work, does it?

At the end of Peterstrasse, you can turn either right or left. Left leads to the **Nikolaiturm** (open to the public only on rare occasions), the oldest of Görlitz's towers, which marks the site of the original village of Gorelec. The Nikolaiturm, like all of the city-wall towers, got a facelift in the 18th century that replaced its pointy top with its current round dome. The city walls and gates were destroyed in 1848—the stones were used to build the Jägerkaserne, a barracks off in the distance to the left of the Nikolaiturm. The only remaining section of the city wall is now a pleasant park that curves around from the base of the Nikolaiturm to the back of the Church of St. Peter. Alternatively, to the right of the park entrance, a small alleyway (Karpfengurnd) snakes its way back to the Peterstrasse.

• *If you turn right at the end of Peterstrasse, you'll reach the...*

Church of St. Peter (Peterskirche)

The church was completed—after many setbacks, landslides, and Hussite invasions—in 1457, and renovated after fire destroyed the interior in 1691. The spires were added in 1890. The facade looks like a thousand other Gothic churches, but it's what's inside that counts: The Silesian-Italian Eugenio Casparini's **Sun Organ** (Sonnenorgel) is a spectacular, one-of-a-kind musical instrument and the center of Görlitz's musical life since 1701. The organ gets its name not from the golden sun at the center (which spins when air is pushed through the pipe), but for the circularly arranged pipes that shoot out like the sun's rays. Take in a free concert Thursday or Sunday at noon (Nov–March Sun only). The colorful baptistery, from 1617, is also worth a look.

• *Your walk is finished. Consider visiting some of Görlitz's other sights (described next), or relax with a local Landskron beer.*

SIGHTS

In Görlitz

▲Holy Sepulcher (Heiliges Grab)—One of Görlitz's most unusual and interesting sights, this is the only complete and relatively accurate replica of the garden of Gethsemane and the

holy places in Jerusalem, as they appeared in the 15th century. It takes a bit longer to visit than other sights in Görlitz, but pilgrims find it well worth ▲▲▲.

After making a pilgrimage to Jerusalem, Georg Emmerich commissioned this site as an offering to those who could not make such a journey themselves (built 1480–1503). The first building is the two-story Chapel of the Holy Cross. Reflecting the traditional belief that Christ was crucified on the site of Adam's grave, the crypt represents the tomb of Adam with the Golgotha Chapel above. Next door is the Salbhaus, a tiny chapel with a statue of Mary anointing Jesus' dead body. Finally, the Church of the Holy Sepulcher is a much smaller version of the original, but nonetheless is an interesting fusion of Middle Eastern and European architecture. This version actually predates the restored Jerusalem site, which was damaged by fire in the 16th century. Medieval pilgrims to this site purchased a *Görlitzer Scheckel*—gold, silver, or pewter, according to their means—as payment to the church and a symbol of their pilgrimage (€1.50, daily April–Sept 10:00–18:00, Oct–March 10:00–16:00, English handout, Heilige-Grab-Strasse 79, tram #1, #2, or #3 to Heilige Grab, www.heiligesgrab-goerlitz.de).

▲▲Landskron Brewery—Beer has been brewed in Görlitz since the 12th century. The last remaining (and best) brewery is Landskron, which brews 11 different beers, including the best *Hefeweizen* (wheat-beer) in Germany. It's also one of the last breweries to use open fermentation. The brewery offers tours in German, but the staff tries to be accommodating to English-speakers. In the end, it's all about the taste samples anyway. There are two tour versions: the ".331 Tour" (€5, 1.5 hours) or the ".51 Tour" (€8, 2.5 hours). Contact the brewery in advance to check the tour schedule and reserve—although it's usually possible to sneak into an already scheduled tour, if you ask nicely (An der Landskronbrauerei 116, tel. 03581/465-121, www.landskron.de, besichtigung@landskron.de). In the summer, the brewery hosts concerts and other events.

▲Landeskrone—On the outskirts of the city is a dormant volcano that stretches 1,376 feet above sea level. The city of Görlitz purchased the Landeskrone from the aristocracy and incorporated it into the city in 1440. The mountainside provided wood for building (especially for rebuilding the town after fire) and basalt for cobblestones, and gave the city a commanding view into three countries at once—helping to defend the city against marauding robber-barons. The observation tower on top, built on the ruins of a Bohemian fort, came in the 18th century, and was followed by a small restaurant and hotel in 1844 (the current version was rebuilt in 1951). The entire area is a park, ideal for short hikes. To get here, take tram #2 to the stop Biesnitz/Landeskrone. It's about a 40-minute hike from the tram stop to the top.

Near Görlitz

Three Silesian towns near Görlitz offer an interesting and diverse glimpse into this unique cultural crossroads.

▲Zgorzelec—When everything east of the Neisse River (and, farther north, the Oder River) became a part of Poland, Görlitz lost its eastern suburb. By 1946, Poles transplanted from Belarus and Ukraine eliminated all traces of the German past and created the city of Zgorzelec. On both sides of the river, government and citizenry are making great strides to glue the city back together (at least culturally) in a united Europe. And now, since Germany and Poland opened their borders in late 2007, you can stroll freely between the two countries. A walk into Poland is an interesting experience and offers a stark contrast to wonderfully restored Görlitz. Zgorzelec is obviously the less wealthy part of the city, but offers a fine collection of patrician and burgher houses (along ulica Warszawska). Some have been lovingly renovated, but others are in desperate need of repair.

GÖRLITZ

The main part of Zgorzelec is across the Pope John Paul II Bridge (Neissebrücke), south of the Old Town. Once across the bridge, turn to the right and go up the hill to reach the Upper Lusatian Memorial Hall (nowadays the Dom Kultury, or Civic House of Culture), a memorial to Kaiser Wilhelm I. Wander north through Poland, then cross back into Germany at the pedestrian Old Town Bridge, behind the Church of St. Peter.

Zittau and Oybin Castle (Burg Oybin)—Although Zittau is a splendid city in its own right, with pretty squares and a town hall by Karl Friedrich Schinkel, the real reason to come here is to take the narrow-gauge steam railroad to the castle ruins at Oybin. Bohemian Emperor Charles IV built the fortress and monastery Burg Oybin in the 14th century. The structure fell into disuse by the 16th century, and was repeatedly struck by lightning in the 18th and 19th centuries. The ruins are huge and fun to poke around, and the views of the unique geological formations of the Zittau Mountains are grand (castle entry-€4, daily April–Oct 9:00–18:00, Nov–March 10:00–16:00, www.burgundkloster-oybin.de).

Bautzen/Budyšin—This town, about halfway between Dresden and Görlitz, is the cultural capital of the Sorbs (or Wends, as they are known in the US). The Sorbs—not to be confused with the Serbs of the former Yugoslavia, much farther south—are of Slavic descent, and still speak a distinct language that's a hybrid of Polish and Czech. About 20,000 Sorbs live in Germany, making up the country's only indigenous ethnic minority.

Bautzen's dual-language signs and slightly Mediterranean feel of spacious squares and public fountains, combined with intact city walls and a tower that's more off-center than Pisa's, make this town a perfect stopover between Dresden and Görlitz. Bautzen is also home to Germany's only Simultaneous Church, a house of worship shared by Catholics on one side and Protestants on the other. Germany's best spicy mustard comes from Bautzen. For lunch, try **Restaurant Wjelbik,** which serves wonderful Sorbian food (Kornstrasse 1). For more information on the town, see www.bautzen.de.

SHOPPING

Görlitzer Weinachts Haus celebrates Christmas all year long. Stop here for good deals on traditional crafts such as nutcrackers, incense burners shaped like smoking men, and Nativity scenes. Big draws are traditional paper stars from Herrnhut, handblown Sorbian glass eggs, and Thuringian glass (Mon–Fri 10:00–18:00, Sat 10:00–17:00, Sun 11:00–16:00 in summer only, otherwise closed Sun, Fleischerstrasse 19, just off Obermarkt—look for the huge nutcracker out front, tel. 03581/649-205).

Schlesische Schatztruhe is one-stop shopping for all your Silesian souvenir needs: books, posters, maps, cookbooks, and more. This is the first place to stop for Silesian ceramics and "Polish pottery" from Bolesławiec (Bunzlau in German). Unfortunately, they don't ship pottery to the US—you'll have to ship or carry it yourself. Their *Streuselkuchen* pastry seems to stay fresh forever (Mon–Fri 9:00–18:00, Sat–Sun 10:00–18:00, Brüderstrasse 13, tel. 03581/410-956, www.schlesien-heute.de).

Sleep Code

(€1 = about $1.50, country code: 49, area code: 03581)
S = Single, **D** = Double/Twin, **T** = Triple, **Q** = Quad, **b** = bathroom, **s** = shower only. Unless otherwise noted, credit cards are accepted, English is spoken, and breakfast is included.

To help you sort easily through these listings, I've divided the rooms into two categories, based on the price for a standard double room with bath:

$$ Higher Priced—Most rooms €75 or more.
$ Lower Priced—Most rooms less than €75.

SLEEPING

$$ Hotel Bon Apart is a comfortable hotel with an eclectic interior design that can only be described as "Gothic meets Baroque." It's a great value, with the best breakfast buffet in town. The rooms and suites have kitchens, and they brew their own beer (Sb-€80–95, Db-€95–130, 1-person suite-€130, 2-person suite-€150, family suites-€170–225, Elisabethstrasse 41, tel. & fax 03581/48080, www.bon-apart.de, hotel@bon-apart.de). Owner François recently opened the new, slightly cheaper **Am Stadtpark,** a pension with renovated rooms in a gorgeous old building on the edge of the city park, a little farther from the center.

$ Die Destille ("The Distillery") is a clean, friendly, family-run pension with well-apportioned rooms near the Nikolaiturm. A good breakfast is left in the refrigerator near your room, so you can have breakfast whenever you want. During renovation of the building in the 1990s, workers discovered a *mikveh* (ritual Jewish bath) in the basement (Sb-€50, Db-€68, cash only, Nikolaistrasse 6, tel. & fax 03581/405-302, www.destille-goerlitz.de).

$ Hotel und Gasthof Dreibeiniger-Hund ("Three-Legged Dog"), down the street from Die Destille, is a small, meticulously restored pension offering 13 cozy and romantic rooms in a 14th-century shell (Sb-€55, Db-€75, cash only, book ahead in summer, Büttnerstrasse 13, tel. 03581/423-980, www.dreibeinigerhund.de).

EATING

Silesians are a hearty people, and their cooking combines German, Polish, and Czech elements into one of Germany's most interesting regional cuisines. *The* Silesian specialty is *Schlesisches Himmelreich* ("Silesian Heaven"), a mix of pork roast and ham with stewed fruit in a white sauce served with dumplings. For dessert, try Silesian

Streuselkuchen, a yummy crumb cake available everywhere. Landskron is Görlitz's ubiquitous brew, and one of the best pilsners in Germany.

Die Destille (see "Sleeping"), literally in the shadow of the Nikolaiturm, is a delightful restaurant oozing comfortable country elegance, with a friendly staff to boot. They excel at extremely traditional Silesian dishes, including the best *Schlesisches Himmelreich* in Görlitz. It's small, so come early or be prepared to share a table (€7–12 plates, daily 11:30–15:00 & 17:00–22:00, Nikolaistrasse 6, tel. 03581/405-302).

The **Dreibeiniger-Hund** (see "Sleeping") has a personal and homey restaurant. Regional cuisine with fresh seasonal specialties makes the "Dog" a must. In summer, sit outside under the sprawling oak tree (€6–12 plates, daily 11:00–23:00, Büttnerstrasse 13, tel. 03581/423-980).

Zur Goldenen Sonne, a favorite among the artsy clientele from the neighboring theater, serves traditional Silesian cuisine as well as exotic meats such as ostrich, bison, and crocodile. Don't worry—you can get a steak or a schnitzel here, too. Or try one of the excellent *Pfannen* dishes, served in a cast-iron skillet. Housed in a former stable, the Sonne has a cozy ambience and reasonable prices, and offers a sunny Mediterranean break from dumplings (€6–18 plates, daily 12:00–14:30 & 17:00–23:00, closed Mon for lunch, Demianiplatz 54, tel. 03581/311-609).

Vierradenmühle, Germany's easternmost restaurant, is the perfect place to ponder the division and reunification of Europe. The restaurant sits on top of a water-filtration station and former power plant (with museum) in the Neisse River, so the eastern foundation wall is actually the German–Polish border. The two sides of the border are marked by wooden poles on either side in the colors of the respective country: white and red for Poland, and black, red, and yellow for Germany. The food is mediocre and overpriced, but the location is great—making it the ideal spot to enjoy a cold beer (Mon–Sat 11:00–24:00, Sun 10:00–22:00, at the end of Neissstrasse at Hotherstrasse 20, tel. 03581/406-661).

In Poland: **Piwnica Staromiejska** ("Old Town Pub"), in a former grain mill on the Polish side of the Old Town Bridge, serves traditional eastern Polish specialties. The lively, largely Polish crowd welcomes visitors from both sides of the city, and the friendly and helpful staff will explain the menu. Don't worry about paying with Polish *złoty*—the restaurant accepts euros, and won't cheat you on the exchange (€3–12 plates, *pelmeni* dumplings and a Żywiec beer-€5, lavish salads, daily 12:00–22:00, ulica Wrocławska 1, Zgorzelec, from Germany dial 00-48-75-775-2692).

Near the Lower Market Square: Good eateries abound near the Untermarkt. The best are on Peterstrasse, between the market and the Church of St. Peter; and on Neissstrasse, stretching from

Untermarkt to the river. Almost every building on Neissstrasse was once a brewery. The pick of the litter is the **Bürgerstübl,** which was recently renovated with the help of the Landskron brewery and has a secret *Biergarten* in the back (€7–10 plates, open daily from 18:00, Sat–Sun also 12:00–14:00, Neissstrasse 27, tel. 03581/879-579).

Picnic Supplies: The only grocery store in the city center is the **Lebensmittel Weiss,** at the corner of Steinstrasse and Obermarkt (Mon–Fri 8:00–18:30, Sat 8:00–16:00, closed Sun). For fresh fruit and produce, try the **Farmer's Market,** on Elisabethstrasse across from Hotel Bon-Apart (Mon–Fri 6:00–18:00, Sat 6:00–12:00, closed Sun).

TRANSPORTATION CONNECTIONS

From Görlitz by Train to: Zittau (hourly, 45 min, not covered by railpass—see below), **Bautzen** (about hourly, 30–45 min; Bautzen-bound trains continue on to Dresden), **Dresden** (hourly, 1.5 hrs), **Berlin** (hourly, 2.5 hrs, transfer in Cottbus, not fully covered by railpass—see below). Train info: tel. 11861 (€0.60/min).

Important Note: If you have a railpass (such as a German Railpass, or a Eurailpass that includes Germany), it covers the trip from Görlitz to Bauten and on to Dresden. However, your railpass is *not* valid between Görlitz and Cottbus (where you transfer to Berlin), or between Görlitz and Zittau, as these blue-and-yellow trains are not part of the Deutsche Bahn system (you can buy tickets at the Deutsche Bahn ticket window, but it's easier just to get them on the train). If you are day-tripping from Görlitz to Zittau, your best bet is the **Tageskarte Lausitz** day pass—at the ticket machine, choose *Tageskarte Lausitz,* then *1* (€10); or *Kleingruppenkarte Lausitz*, then *1* (€20 for up to 5 adults).

BERLIN

No tour of Germany is complete without a look at its historic and reunited capital. Over the last decade, Berlin has been a construction zone. Standing over ripped-up tracks and under a canopy of cranes, visitors witnessed the rebirth of a great European capital. Today, as we enjoy the thrill of walking over what was the Wall and through the well-patched Brandenburg Gate, it's clear that history is not contained in some book, but is an exciting story that we are a part of. Historians find Berlin exhilarating.

Berlin had a tumultuous 20th century. After the city was devastated in World War II, it was divided by the Allied powers: The American, British, and French sectors became West Berlin, and the Soviet sector, East Berlin. In 1948 and 1949, the Soviet Union tried to starve the Western half into submission, but the siege was foiled by the United States' Berlin Airlift, which flew in supplies from Frankfurt (2008–2009 marks its 60th anniversary). The East–West division was set in stone in 1961, when the East German government boxed in West Berlin by building the Berlin Wall. The Wall stood for 28 years. In 1990, less than a year after the Wall fell, the two Germanys—and the two Berlins—officially became one. When the dust settled, Berliners from both sides of the once-divided city faced the monumental challenge of reunification.

While the work is far from over, a new Berlin has emerged. Berliners joke that they don't need to go anywhere because their city's always changing. Spin a postcard rack to see what's new. A five-year-old guidebook on Berlin covers a different city.

Reunification has had its negative side, and locals are fond of saying, "The Wall survives in the minds of some people." Some "Ossies" (impolite slang for Easterners) miss their security.

Some "Wessies" miss their easy ride (military deferrals, subsidized rent, and tax breaks). For free spirits, walled-in West Berlin was a citadel of freedom within the East.

The city government has been eager to charge forward, with little nostalgia for anything that was Eastern. Big corporations and the national government have moved in, and the dreary swath of land that was the Wall and its notorious "death strip" has been transformed. City planners have boldly made Berlin's reunification and the return of the national government a good opportunity to make Berlin a great capital once again.

Today, Berlin feels like the nuclear fuel rod of a great nation. It's so vibrant with youth, energy, and an anything-goes-and-anything's-possible buzz that Munich feels spent in comparison. Berlin is both extremely popular and surprisingly affordable. As a booming tourist attraction, Berlin welcomed more visitors than Rome in 2008. But the city is so spread out, you'll often feel like you have the place to yourself.

Planning Your Time

Because of Berlin's inconvenient location, try to enter and/or leave by either night train or plane. On a three-week trip through Germany, I'd give Berlin at least two days and spend them this way:

Day 1: Begin your day getting oriented to this huge city: Either take the 10:00 "Discover Berlin" guided walking tour offered by Original Berlin Walks (see page 459) or follow my "Do-It-Yourself Orientation Tour" by bus to the Reichstag (page 464), then continue by foot down Unter den Linden (page 474). Focus on sights along Unter den Linden, including the Reichstag dome (most crowded 10:00–16:00; best to visit 8:00–9:00 or 21:00–22:00), the German History Museum, and Museum Island (with the Pergamon and Egyptian museums).

Day 2: Concentrate on the sights in central Berlin, and in eastern Berlin south of Unter den Linden. Here's a plan to do just that: Spend the morning with the paintings at the Gemäldegalerie. After lunch, hike via Potsdamer Platz to the Topography of Terror exhibit and along the surviving Zimmerstrasse stretch of the Wall to the Museum of the Wall at Checkpoint Charlie. If you're not museum-ed out yet, swing by the magnificent Jewish Museum. Finish your day in the lively East—ideally in the once glum, then edgy, now fun-loving and trendy Prenzlauer Berg district.

If you're maximizing your sightseeing, you could squeeze a hop-off, hop-on bus tour into Day 1. The Reichstag dome and the Museum of the Wall are open late.

Berlin merits additional time if you have it. There's much more in the city. And the concentration camp memorial at Sachsenhausen and the palace at Potsdam are both worthwhile side-trips.

Berlin Sightseeing Modules

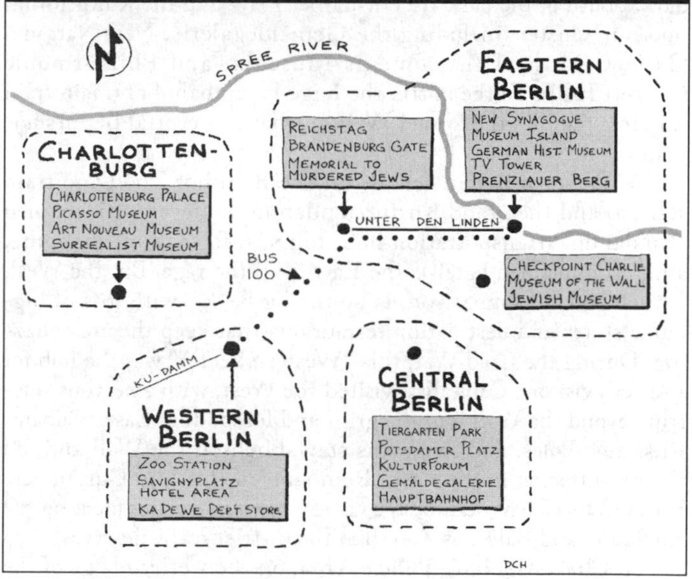

ORIENTATION

(area code: 030)

Berlin is huge, with 3.4 million people. But the tourist's Berlin can be broken into four digestible chunks:

1. Eastern Berlin has the highest concentration of notable sights and colorful neighborhoods. Near the famous Brandenburg Gate, you'll find the Reichstag building, Pariser Platz, and the new Holocaust Memorial. From the Brandenburg Gate, the famous Unter den Linden boulevard runs eastward through the former East Berlin, passing the marvelous German History Museum and Museum Island (Pergamon Museum, Egyptian Museum, and Berlin Cathedral) on the way to Alexanderplatz (TV Tower). The intersection of Unter den Linden and Friedrichstrasse is emerging as the new center of the city. South of Unter den Linden, you'll find the delightful Gendarmenmarkt square, most Nazi sites (including the Topography of Terror exhibit), the Jewish Museum, the best Wall-related sights (Museum of the Wall at Checkpoint Charlie, and East Side Gallery), and the colorful Turkish neighborhood of Kreuzberg. North of Unter den Linden are these worth-a-wander neighborhoods: around Oranienburger Strasse (Jewish Quarter and New Synagogue), Hackescher Markt, and Prenzlauer Berg (several recommended hotels and a very lively restaurant/nightlife zone).

2. Central Berlin is dominated by the giant Tiergarten park. South of the park are Potsdamer Platz and the Kulturforum museum cluster (including the Gemäldegalerie, New National Gallery, Musical Instruments Museum, and Philharmonic Concert Hall). To the north, the huge Hauptbahnhof (main train station) straddles the former Wall in what was central Berlin's no-man's-land.

3. Western Berlin centers on the Bahnhof Zoo (Zoo train station) and the grand Kurfürstendamm boulevard, nicknamed "Ku'damm" (transportation hub, tours, information, shopping, and recommended hotels). The East is all the rage. But the West, while staid in comparison, is bouncing back—with lots of big-name stores and destination restaurants that keep the area buzzing. During the Cold War, this "Western Sector" was the hub for Western visitors. Capitalists visited the West, with a nervous side-trip beyond the Wall into the grim and foreboding East. (Cubans, Russians, Poles, and Angolans stayed behind the Wall and did their sightseeing in the East.) Remnants of this Iron Curtain–era Western focus have left today's visitors with a stronger focus on the Ku'damm and Bahnhof Zoo than the district really deserves.

4. Charlottenburg Palace Area, on the western edge of the city center, is home to a palace and nearby museums (Picasso, Art Nouveau, and Surrealist). This area is of least interest to a visitor on a tight schedule.

Tourist Information

With any luck, you won't have to use Berlin's TIs—they're for-profit agencies working for the city's big hotels, which colors the information they provide. TI branches, appropriately called "infostores," are unlikely to have the information you need (tel. 030/250-025, www.berlin-tourist-information.com). You'll find them at the **Hauptbahnhof** train station (daily 8:00–22:00, by main entrance on Europaplatz), **Ku'damm** (Kurfürstendamm 21, in the glass-and-steel Neues Kranzler Eck building, Mon–Sat 10:00–20:00, Sun 10:00–18:00, shorter hours in winter), the **Reichstag** (on Scheidemannstrasse, daily April–Oct 8:00–20:00, Nov–March 10:00–18:00), and the **Brandenburg Gate** (daily April–Oct 9:30–19:00, Nov–March 10:00–19:00).

Skip the TI's €1 map, and instead pick up any of the walking tour companies' brochures—they include better maps for free (most hotels also provide free city maps). While the TI does sell the three-day Museumspass (described next), it's also available at major museums. If you take a walking tour, your guide is likely a better source of nightlife or shopping tips than the TI. The TI offers a €3 room-finding service (but only to hotels that give them kickbacks—many don't).

Museum Passes: The three-day **Museumspass** (Schaulust MuseenBerlin) gets you into 70 museums (including the national museums and most of the recommended biggies) on three consecutive days for €19. As you'll routinely pay €5–8 per admission, this pays for itself in a hurry. And you'll enjoy the ease of popping in and out of museums that you might not otherwise want to pay for. Buy it at the TI or any participating museum. Note that if a museum is closed on one of the days of your Museumspass, you have access to that museum on a fourth day to make up for lost time. The pass won't, however, enable you to skip lines: Many museums want passholders to stand in line to get a free ticket that lets you through the turnstile. The €12 **Museum Island Pass** (Standortkarte Museumsinsel) covers all the museums on the island (otherwise €8 each) and is a fine value—but for €7 more, the three-day Museumspass gives you triple the days and many more entries. TIs also sell the **Welcome Card,** a transportation pass that also gives some museum discounts (see page 457).

Local Publications: Various magazines can help make your time in Berlin more productive (all available at the TI and most at newsstands). ***Berlin Programm*** is a comprehensive German-language monthly, especially strong in high culture, that lists upcoming events and museum hours (€2, www.berlin-programm.de). ***Berlin To Go*** is a sketchier German/English, TI-produced bimonthly magazine offering timely features on Berlin and a partial calendar of events (€1). ***Exberliner Magazine*** is the only real English monthly (published mostly for expat Americans, but very helpful for curious travelers). It has an edgy, youthful focus and gives a fascinating insider's look at this fast-changing city (€2, www.exberliner.com). The free, informative magazines that promote the tour companies **New Berlin Tours** and **Insider Tours** (both described on page 462) are also useful.

Arrival in Berlin

By Train

Berlin's newest and grandest train station is **Berlin Hauptbahnhof** (main train station, a.k.a. simply "der Bahnhof"). All long-distance trains now arrive at Europe's biggest, mostly underground train station. Tracks 1–8 are underground, while tracks 11–16 are a floor above ground level (along with the S-Bahn).

It's a "transfer station"—unique for its major lines coming in at right angles—where the national train system meets the city's train system (S-Bahn).

BERLIN

It's also the home of 80 shops with long hours—some locals call the station a "shopping mall with trains" (daily 8:00–22:00, even Sunday). The Kaisers supermarket (above track 2) is handy for assembling a picnic for the ride.

Services: While the station has no lockers, the Gepäck Center is an efficient and secure deposit service (€4/day per bag, always open, on the upper level—signed as *UG* or *+1,* directly under track 14). The WC Center (public toilets) is next to the Virgin Megastore.

Train Information: The station has two DeutscheBahn ***Reisezentrum*** information counters (one upper level, one lower—just follow signs; both open daily 6:00–22:00). If you're staying in the West, keep in mind that the info center at the Bahnhof Zoo station is just as good and much less crowded.

EurAide is an English-speaking information desk with answers to your questions about train travel around Europe. It operates from a single counter in the lower-level *Reisezentrum* (labeled *-1,* not *+1;* follow signs to tracks 5–6). It's American-run, so communication is simple. This is an especially good place to make fast-train and *couchette* reservations for later in your trip. EurAide also gives out a helpful, free city map (April–Sept daily 10:00–20:00; Oct–March Mon–Fri 11:00–19:00, closed Sat–Sun; www.euraide.com).

Getting into Town: While taxis and buses await outside the station, the S-Bahn is probably your best means of connecting to your destination within Berlin. The crosstown express S-Bahn line connects the station with my recommended hotels in a few minutes. It's simple: All S-Bahn trains are on tracks 15 and 16 at the top of the station. All trains on track 15 go east (toward the Ostbahnhof and Hackescher Markt), and trains on track 16 go west (toward Bahnhof Zoo and Savignyplatz). Your train ticket or railpass into the station covers you on your connecting S-Bahn ride into town (and your ticket out includes the transfer via S-Bahn to the Hauptbahnhof). U-Bahn rides are not covered by tickets or railpasses.

If you're sleeping in the West, catch any train on track 16 to Savignyplatz, and you're a five-minute walk from your hotel (see map on page 510). Savignyplatz is one stop after **Bahnhof Zoo** (rhymes with "toe," a.k.a. Bahnhof Zoologischer Garten), the once-grand train hub now eclipsed by the Hauptbahnhof. Nowadays it's useful mainly for its shops, uncrowded train-information desk, and BVG transit office (outside the entrance, amid the traffic).

If you're sleeping in eastern Berlin, take any train on track 15 two stops to Hackescher Markt, then catch tram #M1 north (see map on page 512).

By Plane

For information on reaching the city center from Berlin's airports, see "Transportation Connections" at the end of this chapter.

Helpful Hints

Medical Help: "Call a Doc" is a non-profit referral service designed for tourists (tel. 01804-2255-2362, phone answered 24 hours a day, www.calladoc.com). Payment is arranged between you and the doctor, and is likely far more affordable than similar care in the US. The US Embassy also has a list of local English-speaking doctors (www.usembassy.de).

Museum Hours: Many major Berlin museums are closed on Monday. All national museums, including the Pergamon and Gemäldegalerie (plus others as noted in "Sights," page 466), are free for the last four hours on Thursdays (for example, if it closes at 18:00, it's free from 14:00 on; www.museen-berlin.de).

Monday Activities: Since many museums close on Monday, save the day for Berlin Wall sights, the Reichstag dome, my "Do-It-Yourself Orientation Tour" and strolling Unter den Linden, walking/bus tours, the Jewish Museum, churches, the zoo, or shopping (the Kaufhaus des Westens—KaDeWe—department store is a sight in itself). Be aware that when Monday is a holiday—as it is several times a year—museums are open then and closed Tuesday.

Addresses: Many Berlin streets are numbered with odd and even numbers on the same side of the street, often with no connection to the other side (for example, Ku'damm #212 can be across the street from #14). To save steps, check the white street signs on curb corners; many list the street numbers covered on that side of the block.

Internet Access: You'll find Internet access in most hotels and hostels, as well as at small Internet cafés all over the city. The **easyInternetcafé** outlets—generally paired with Dunkin' Donuts (daily 6:00–23:00)—have handy locations, including Hardenbergplatz 2 (across from Bahnhof Zoo, next to McDonald's), Ku'damm 224 (10-min walk from Bahnhof Zoo, near several recommended hotels), and Rathaus-Passagen (on Alexanderplatz). Buy a ticket at the self-service machines and follow the English instructions. Unused time can be used at any branch in Berlin for up to a week.

Bookstore: Berlin Story, a big, fun bookshop, has the best selection anywhere in town of English-language books on Berlin. They also have a fascinating, free little museum in the back with a model of Unter den Linden from 1930 and a room showing a good 25-minute Berlin history video (in English). The shop has a knowledgeable staff and stocks an amusing mix of knick-knacks and East Berlin nostalgia souvenirs (daily 10:00–20:00, Unter den Linden 26, tel. 030/2045-3842, www.berlinstory.de).

Laundry: Schnell und Sauber Waschcenter is a chain of handy launderettes, with a location in western Berlin's Charlottenburg at Kaiserdamm 100 (while waiting, grab a beer at Alt-Berlin, a locals-only pub next door), and another in eastern Berlin at Torstrasse 115, around the corner from the Circus Hostel (€5–9/load wash and dry, daily 6:00–23:00). Also near my recommended hotels in Prenzlauer Berg, try **Eco-Express Waschsalon** (€4–9/load wash and dry, daily 6:00–22:00, self- or full-serve, attached café, Danziger Strasse 7).

Travel Agency: Last Minute Flugbörse can help you find a flight in a hurry (discount flights, no train tickets, in Europa Center near Bahnhof Zoo, Mon–Sat 10:00–20:00, closed Sun, tel. 030/2655-1050, www.lastminuteflugboerse.de). **American Express** is a few blocks off Unter den Linden at Friedrichstrasse 172 (sells train tickets for €4 service fee, Mon–Fri 9:00–19:00, Sat 10:00–14:00, closed Sun, tel. 030/201-7400).

Getting Around Berlin

Berlin's sights spread far and wide. Right from the start, commit yourself to the city's fine public-transit system.

By Subway and Bus: Berlin's many modes of transportation are consolidated into one system that uses the same tickets: U-Bahn (*Untergrund-Bahn,* Berlin's subway), S-Bahn (*Schnell-Bahn*, or "fast train," mostly above ground and with fewer stops), *Strassenbahn* (streetcars, called "trams" by locals), and buses. Here are your options:

• A basic ticket *(Einzelfahrschein)* for two hours of travel in one direction on buses or subways—€2.10. It's easy to make this ticket stretch to cover several rides...as long as they're all in the same direction.

• A cheap, short-ride ticket *(Kurzstrecke)* for a single short ride of six bus stops or three subway stations (one transfer allowed)—€1.20.

• A four-trip ticket *(4-Fahrten-Karte),* four basic tickets at a small discount—€8.

• A day pass *(Tageskarte)* covering zones A and B, the city proper—€6.10 (good until 3:00 the morning after). To get out to Potsdam, you need a ticket covering zone C—€6.30. (For longer stays, a 7-day pass—*Sieben-Tage-Karte*—is also available for €26.20, or €32.30 including zone C; or buy 2 WelcomeCards, described next.) The *Kleingruppenkarte* lets groups of up to five travel all day for €16.

• The **WelcomeCard** covers transportation, and gives you a 25 percent discount on lots of minor and a few major museums (including Checkpoint Charlie), sightseeing tours (including 25 percent off the recommended Original Berlin Walks), and music and theater events. Choose between two versions: Berlin only (covers transit zones A and B, €16.50/48 hrs, €21.50/72 hrs) and Berlin with Potsdam (covers zones A, B, and C, €18/48 hrs, €24.50/72 hrs). Both versions of the card are valid for an adult and up to three kids younger than 14. If you plan to cover a lot of ground using public transportation during a two- or three-day visit, this is usually the best transit deal.

Buy your U- and S-Bahn tickets from machines at stations. (They are also sold at BVG pavilions at train stations, airports, and the TI, and aboard trams and buses—drivers give change.) *Erwachsener* means "adult"—anyone 14 or older. Don't be afraid of the automated machines: First select the type of ticket you want, then load in the coins or paper bills. As you board the bus or tram, or enter the subway system, punch your ticket in a red or yellow clock machine to validate it (or risk a €40 fine; for an all-day or multi-day pass, validate it only the first time you ride). Within Berlin, Eurailpasses are good only on S-Bahn connections from the train station when you're arriving, and to the station when you're departing.

The S-Bahn crosstown express is a river of public transit through the heart of the city, in which many lines converge on one basic highway. Get used to this and you'll leap within a few minutes between: Savignyplatz (hotels), Bahnhof Zoo (Ku'damm, bus #100, walking tour meeting spot), the Hauptbahnhof (all major trains in and out of Berlin), Friedrichstrasse (heart of Unter den Linden), Hackescher Markt (Museum Island, hotels, restaurants, nightlife), and Alexanderplatz (eastern end of Unter den Linden).

Sections of the U- or S-Bahn sometimes close temporarily for repairs. In this situation, a bus route often replaces the train (*Ersatzverkehr*, or "replacement transportation").

Berlin's public transit is operated by BVG (except the S-Bahn, run by Deutsche Bahn). Bus schedules are available on the helpful BVG website, www.bvg.de.

By Taxi: Taxis are easy to flag down, and taxi stands are common. A typical ride within town costs €8–10, and a crosstown trip (for example, Bahnhof Zoo to Alexanderplatz) will run you about €15. ***Money-Saving Taxi Tip:*** For any ride of less than two kilometers (about a mile), you can save several euros if you take advantage of the ***Kurzstrecke*** (short-stretch) rate. To get this rate, it's important that you flag the cab down on the street—not at or even near a taxi stand. Also, you must ask for the *Kurzstrecke* rate as soon as you hop in: Confidently say *"Kurzstrecke, bitte"* (KOORTS-shtreh-keh BIT-teh), and your driver will flip the meter to a fixed €3.50 rate.

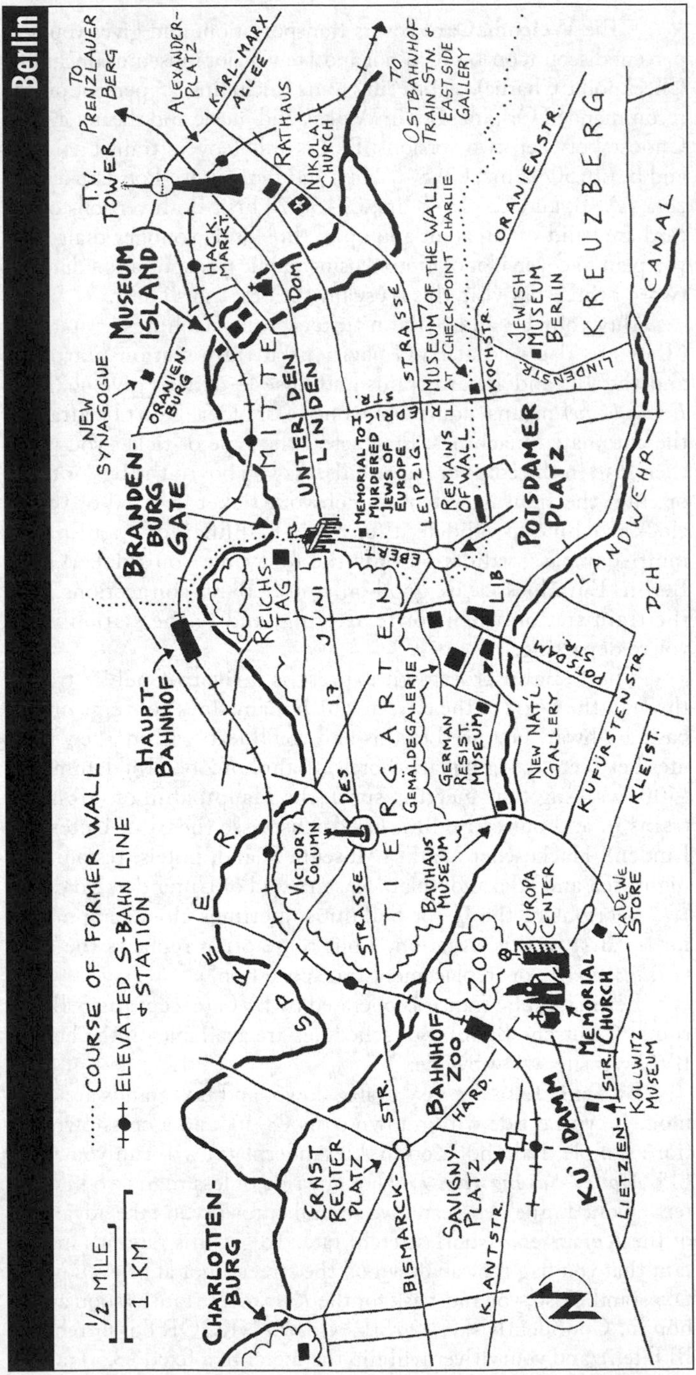

Berlin
1/2 MILE
1 KM
COURSE OF FORMER WALL
ELEVATED S-BAHN LINE + STATION
CHARLOTTEN-BURG
ERNST REUTER PLATZ
BISMARCK-STR.
SAVIGNY-PLATZ
KANT STR.
HARD.
BAHNHOF ZOO
KU'DAMM
LIETZEN-STR.
KOLLWITZ MUSEUM
MEMORIAL CHURCH
ZOO
EUROPA CENTER
KADEWE STORE
SPREE R.
STRASSE DES 17 JUNI
TIERGARTEN
VICTORY COLUMN
BAUHAUS MUSEUM
GERMAN RESIST. MUSEUM
GEMÄLDEGALERIE
NEW NAT'L GALLERY
POTSDAM STR.
KUFÜRSTEN STR.
KLEIST.
HAUPT-BAHNHOF
REICHS-TAG
BRANDEN-BURG GATE
EBERT STR.
MEMORIAL TO MURDERED JEWS OF EUROPE
LEIPZIG STRASSE
REMAINS OF WALL
POTSDAMER PLATZ
LIB
LANDWEHR CANAL
DCH
UNTER DEN LINDEN
MITTE
FRIEDR. STR.
NEW SYNAGOGUE
ORANIEN-BURG STR.
MUSEUM ISLAND
DOM
HACK. MARKT
T.V. TOWER
TO PRENZLAUER BERG
ALEXANDER-PLATZ
KARL-MARX ALLEE
RATHAUS
NIKOLAI CHURCH
TO OSTBAHNHOF TRAIN STN. & EAST SIDE GALLERY
MUSEUM OF THE WALL AT CHECKPOINT CHARLIE
KOCHSTR.
LINDENSTR.
JEWISH MUSEUM BERLIN
ORANIENSTR.
KREUZBERG

By Bike: Flat Berlin is a very bike-friendly city, but be careful—Berlin's motorists don't brake for bicyclists (and bicyclists don't brake for pedestrians). Fortunately, some roads and sidewalks have special red-painted bike lanes. Just don't ride on the regular sidewalk—it's *verboten.*

In western Berlin, you can rent good bikes at the **Bahnhof Zoo** left-luggage counter, next to the lockers at the back of the station (€10/day, €23/3 days, €35/7 days; bikes come with lock, air pump, and mounted basket; daily 7:00–21:00, there's a limited supply of bikes and they've been known to run out). In the East, **Fahrradstation** near the Friedrichstrasse S-Bahn station has a huge number of bikes (€15/day, April–Oct daily 8:00–20:00; Nov–March Mon–Fri 10:00–19:00, Sat 10:00–16:00, closed Sun; leave the S-Bahn station via Friedrichstrasse exit, turn left on Dorotheenstrasse and walk 500 yards, and you'll find it at the entrance to the parking garage at Dorotheenstrasse 30; tel. 030/2045-4500).

TOURS

▲▲▲Walking Tours

Berlin is an ideal city to get to know with a walking tour. The city is a battle zone of extremely competitive and creative walking-tour companies, all offering employment to American and British expats and students and cheap, informative tours to visiting travelers. Unlike many other European countries, Germany has no regulations controlling who can give city tours. Berlin is home to a large number of expatriates and academics, and it seems that every year some of them get together and form a new tour company. Some of these upstarts run great tours, but you'll generally get the best quality with one of the more established companies. All give variations on the same themes: general introductory walk, Hitler and Nazi sites walk, communism walk, and day trips to Potsdam and the Sachsenhausen Concentration Camp Memorial. The youth-oriented outfits also do nightly pub crawls. For details, see the various websites. Here's my take on the current situation:

Original Berlin Walks—This is the most established operation, with tours aiming at a clientele that's curious about the city's history. They don't offer "free tours" or pub crawls, and their guides are professionals. I've enjoyed the help of O.B.W.'s high-quality, high-energy guides for many years, and routinely hire them when my tour groups are in town. I'm always impressed with founder Nick Gay's ability to assemble guides of such high caliber. Tours generally cost €12 (€9 with WelcomeCard, or €10 if you're under 26). Readers of this book get a €1 discount (off the adult or youth price) per tour in 2009.

Berlin at a Glance

▲▲▲**Reichstag** Germany's historic Parliament building, topped with a striking dome you can climb. **Hours:** Daily 8:00–24:00, last entry at 22:00. To avoid long lines, go very early (8:00) or late (after 21:00). See page 466.

▲▲▲**German History Museum** The ultimate swing through the tumultuous history of this country. **Hours:** Daily 10:00–18:00. See page 479.

▲▲▲**Museum of the Wall at Checkpoint Charlie** Moving museum near the former site of the famous border checkpoint between the American and Soviet sectors, with stories of brave escapes during the Cold War and the gleeful days when the Wall fell. **Hours:** Daily 9:00–22:00. See page 486.

▲▲▲**Jewish Museum Berlin** User-friendly museum celebrating Jewish culture, in a highly conceptual building. **Hours:** Daily 10:00–20:00, Mon until 22:00. See page 488.

▲▲▲**Gemäldegalerie** Germany's top collection of 13th- through 18th-century European paintings, featuring Dürer, Van Eyck, Rubens, Titian, Raphael, Caravaggio, and more. **Hours:** Tue–Sun 10:00–18:00, Thu until 22:00, closed Mon. See page 497.

▲▲**Berlin Wall** Mostly gone, but parts of the Wall are still visible—including the East Side Gallery, the Documentation Center on Bernauer Strasse, and a chunk near the Topography of Terror (former SS and Gestapo headquarters). **Hours:** Always open. See page 470.

▲▲**Brandenburg Gate** One of Berlin's most famous landmarks, a massive columned gateway, at the former border of East and West. **Hours:** Always open. See page 471.

▲▲**Memorial to the Murdered Jews of Europe** New Holocaust memorial with almost 3,000 symbolic pillars, plus an exhibition about Hitler's Jewish victims. **Hours:** Memorial always open; exhibition open Tue–Sun 10:00–20:00, closed Mon. See page 473.

▲▲**Unter den Linden** Leafy boulevard through the heart of former East Berlin, lined with some of the city's top sights. **Hours:** Always open. See page 474.

▲▲**Pergamon Museum** World-class museum of classical antiquities on Museum Island (just off Unter den Linden), featuring the fantastic second-century B.C. Greek Pergamon Altar. **Hours:** Daily 10:00–18:00, Thu until 22:00. See page 480.

▲▲**Egyptian Museum/Altes Museum** Proud home (on Museum Island) of the exquisite 3,000-year-old bust of Queen Nefertiti. **Hours:** Daily 10:00–18:00, Thu until 22:00. See page 480.

▲▲**Gendarmenmarkt** Inviting square bounded by twin churches (one with a fine German history exhibit), a chocolate shop, and a concert hall. **Hours:** Always open. See page 484.

▲**Deutsche Kinemathek Film and TV Museum** An entertaining look at German film and TV from *Metropolis* to Dietrich, from Hitler through the Communist days. **Hours:** Tue–Sun 10:00–18:00, Thu until 20:00, closed Mon. See page 496.

▲**New Synagogue** Largest prewar synagogue in Berlin, damaged in WWII, with a facade that has since been rebuilt. **Hours:** Generally Sun–Fri 10:00–17:00 or later, closed Sat. See page 490.

▲**Prenzlauer Berg** One of Berlin's most colorful and lively neighborhoods, worth exploring. **Hours:** Always bustling. See page 491.

▲**Potsdamer Platz** The "Times Square" of old Berlin, long a postwar wasteland, now rebuilt with huge glass skyscrapers, an underground train station, and—covered with a huge canopy—the Sony Center mall with eateries. **Hours:** Always open. See page 495.

▲**Kaiser Wilhelm Memorial Church** Evocative destroyed church in the heart of the former West Berlin, with a modern annex. **Hours:** Church open Mon–Sat 10:00–16:00, closed Sun, annex open daily 9:00–19:00. See page 499.

▲**Käthe Kollwitz Museum** The black-and-white art of the Berlin artist who conveyed the suffering of her city's stormiest century. **Hours:** Daily 11:00–18:00. See page 500.

▲**Potsdam's Palaces** Frederick the Great's escapist, *über*-frilly palaces, nestled in a vast, leafy park. **Hours:** Sanssouci interior open April–Oct Tue–Sun 9:00–17:00, Nov–March Tue–Sun 9:00–16:00, closed Mon year-round. See page 503.

There's no need to reserve ahead—just show up. All tours meet at the taxi stand in front of the Bahnhof Zoo, and start at 10:00 unless otherwise noted. The Discover Berlin and Jewish Life tours have a second departure point 30 minutes later opposite eastern Berlin's Hackescher Markt S-Bahn station, outside the Weihenstephaner Restaurant; if you're staying in the East, save time by showing up here.

Discover Berlin, their flagship introductory walk, covers the birthplace of the city, Museum Island, then heads up Unter den Linden, stops at the Reichstag, and then goes on to Checkpoint Charlie (no interior visits, 4 hrs, English only, daily year-round, meet at 10:00 at Bahnhof Zoo, April–Oct also daily at 14:30). Other tours include: **Infamous Third Reich Sites** (April–Oct Tue and Thu at 10:00, Sat at 14:30, Sun at 10:00; less frequently off-season—check their website or pick up a flier for the schedule); **Jewish Life in Berlin** (April–Oct Mon at 10:00 at Bahnhof Zoo); **Potsdam** (€15, see page 503); and the newest itinerary, **Nest of Spies** (April–Oct only, Sat at 12:30). Many of the Third Reich and Jewish history sights are difficult to pin down without these excellent walks.

Their six-hour trip to the **Sachsenhausen Concentration Camp Memorial** intends to "provide a challenging history lesson with universal applications" (€15, April–Oct Tue, Thu, Fri, and Sun at 10:15 from Bahnhof Zoo meeting point, also from Hackescher Markt meeting point at 10:15, runs less off-season—check website or flier for details).

You can confirm these starting times at EurAide or by phone with Nick or his wife and business partner, Serena (tel. 030/301-9194, www.berlinwalks.de, info@berlinwalks.de). They can also arrange private guides (€150/3 hrs).

Insider Tour—This group offers essentially the same itineraries as Original Berlin Walks, as well as hugely successful **pub crawls** (€12, nightly, with profit supplemented by featured bars—for details see "Nightlife"). The basic introductory city walks leave daily at 10:30 and 15:00 from Coffeemamas at Hackescher Markt S-Bahn station--just show up (€12, 4 hours, no afternoon tours Nov–March, will also pick you up from McDonald's opposite Bahnhof Zoo 30 min before tour starts, www.insidertour.com).

New Berlin Tours—This company targets a young crowd and offers free introductory tours—hoping you'll then sign up for one of their other walks (€10–12 each, roughly the same list of itineraries as O.B.W. and Insider Tour, including a nightly pub crawl, listed under "Nightlife"). The basic city walks leave daily at 11:00 and 13:00 (free but tip expected, 3.5 hours, meet at Starbucks at Brandenburg Gate/Pariser Platz, or 30 min earlier from Dunkin' Donuts opposite Bahnhof Zoo, just show up). For all the details, see their free magazine—which includes a practical map—or visit www.newberlintours.com.

Brewer's Berlin Tours—For a more exhaustive (or, for some, exhausting) walking tour of Berlin, consider Brewer's Berlin Tours. These are run by Terry (retired from the British diplomatic service—he worked at the embassy in East Berlin) and his well-trained and engaging staff (all native English speakers). Their All-Day Berlin tours are legendary for their length, and best for those with a long attention span and a serious interest in Berlin (€12, tour lasts 8 hours or more and covers the entire old center, departs daily at 10:30 year-round from Bandy Brooks ice cream shop at Friedrichstrasse U- and S-Bahn station, tel. 030/2248-7435, mobile 0177-388-1537, www.brewersberlintours.com). Just show up. They also do all-day Potsdam tours (May–Oct Wed and Sun; for details, see "Near Berlin: Potsdam's Palaces" on page 503).

Berlin Underground Association (Berliner Unterwelten Verein)—Much of Berlin's history lies beneath the surface, and this group has an exclusive agreement with the city to explore and research what is hidden underground. Their one-of-a-kind tour of a WWII air-raid bunker features a chilling explanation of the air war over Berlin (April–Oct Mon–Thu at 11:00, Nov–March Mon and Thu at 11:00). They also have access to the inside of the Humboldthain air defense tower (April–Oct Thu at 13:00) and to a completely stocked and fully functional nuclear emergency bunker (Sat–Mon at 13:00). The English tours are usually led by Nick Jackson, one of the best tour guides in the city (all tours cost €9, meet in the hall of the Gesundbrunnen U-Bahn/S-Bahn station, follow signs to *Humboldthain/Brunnenstrasse* exit and walk up the stairs to their office, www.berlinerunterwelten.de, tel. 030/4991-0517). Nick also gives private tours by arrangement (mobile 0179-973-0397).

Bus Tours

Full-Blown Bus Tours—Severin & Kühn offers a long list of bus tours in and around Berlin; their three-hour "Big Berlin Tour" is a good introduction (€22, daily at 10:00 and 14:00, two stops: Checkpoint Charlie and Brandenburg Gate, live guides in two languages, departs from Ku'damm 216, buy ticket at bus, tel. 030/880-4190, www.severin-kuehn-berlin.de).

Hop-on, Hop-off City Circle Tours—Several companies cooperate so that you can make a circuit of the city with unlimited hop-on, hop-off privileges (about 14 stops) on buses with boring recorded commentary (€20, 4/hr, daily 10:00–18:00, last bus leaves all stops at 16:00, 2-hr loop). Just hop on where you like and pay the driver. On a sunny day, when some convertible double-decker buses go topless, these are a photographer's delight, cruising slowly by just about every major sight in town. In the winter (Nov–March), the buses come only twice an hour and the last departure is at 15:00.

Bike Tours

Fat Tire Bike Tours—Choose among three different four-hour, six-mile tours (€20 each): City Tour (daily March–Nov at 11:00, June–Aug also at 16:00), Berlin Wall Tour (mid-May–Sept Mon, Thu, and Sat at 10:30), and Third Reich Tour (mid-May–Sept Wed, Fri, and Sun at 10:30). For any tour, meet at the TV Tower at Alexanderplatz (no need to reserve for the Wall or Third Reich tours, tel. 030/2404-7991, fax 030/2404-8837, www.fattirebiketoursberlin.com, info@fattirebiketoursberlin.com).

New Berlin Tours—The young guides who offer New Berlin's free walking tours also give quite good four-hour bike tours (free but tip expected, daily at 11:30 and 15:00, meet on the corner of Oranienburger Strasse and Tucholskystrasse, S-Bahn: Oranienburger Strasse, no need to reserve, for contact info see page 462).

SELF-GUIDED TOUR

Do-It-Yourself Orientation Tour: Bus #100 from Bahnhof Zoo to the Reichstag

This tour narrates the route of convenient bus #100, which connects my recommended hotel neighborhood in western Berlin with the sights in eastern Berlin. If you have the €20 and two hours for a hop-on, hop-off bus tour (described earlier), take that instead. But this short €2.10 bus ride provides a fine city introduction. Bus #100 is a sightseer's dream, stopping at Bahnhof Zoo, the Berlin Zoo, Victory Column (Siegessäule), Reichstag, Brandenburg Gate, Unter den Linden, Pergamon Museum, and Alexanderplatz. While you could ride it to the end, it's more fun to get out at the Reichstag and walk down Unter den Linden at your own pace (using my commentary on page 474). When combined with the self-guided walk down Unter den Linden, this tour merits ▲▲▲. Before you take this bus into eastern Berlin, consider checking out the sights in western Berlin (see page 498).

The Tour Begins: Buses start from Hardenbergplatz in front of Bahnhof Zoo. Buses come every 10 minutes, and single tickets are good for two hours—so take advantage of hop-on-and-off privileges. Climb aboard, stamp your ticket (giving it a starting time), and grab a seat on top. This is about a 15-minute ride. The upcoming stop will light up on the reader board inside the bus.

➲ On your left and then straight ahead you'll see the bombed-out hulk of the **Kaiser Wilhelm Memorial Church,** with its post-war sister church (described on page 499) and the **Europa Center.** This shopping district, once the center of West Berlin, is still a bustling people zone with big department stores nearby. When the Wall came down, East Berliners flocked to this area's department stores (especially KaDeWe, described on page 500). Soon after, the biggest, swankiest new stores were built in the East. Now the West is trying to win those shoppers back by building even bigger and better shopping centers around the Europa Center.

➲ At the stop in front of Hotel Palace: On the left, the elephant gates mark the entrance to the **Berlin Zoo** and its aquarium (described on page 500).

➲ Cruising down Kurfürstenstrasse, you'll pass several Asian restaurants—a reminder that, for most, the best food in Berlin is not German. Turning left, with the huge Tiergarten park in the distance ahead, you'll cross a canal and see the famous **Bauhaus Archive** behind the trees on the right (hard to see—it's the off-white, blocky building with scoopy roof ducts). The Bauhaus movement ushered in a new age of modern architecture that emphasized function over beauty, giving rise to blocky steel-and-glass skyscrapers in big cities around the world. On the left is Berlin's new embassy row. The big turquoise wall marks the communal home of all five Nordic embassies. This building is "green," run entirely on solar power.

➲ The bus enters a 400-acre park called the **Tiergarten,** packed with cycling paths, joggers, and—on hot days—nude sunbathers. Straight ahead, the **Victory Column** (Siegessäule, with the gilded angel, described on page 493) towers above this vast city park that was once a royal hunting grounds, now nicknamed the "green lungs of Berlin."

➲ A block after leaving the Victory Column (on the left) is the 18th-century, late-Rococo **Bellevue Palace.** Formerly the official residence of the Prussian (and later German) crown prince, and at one time a Nazi VIP guest house, it's now the residence of the federal president (whose power is mostly ceremonial—the chancellor wields the real power). If the flag's out, he's in.

➲ Driving along the Spree River, look left for the next sights: This park area was a residential district before World War II. Now it's filled with the buildings of the **national government.** The huge brick "brown snake" complex was built to house government workers—but it didn't sell, so now its apartments are available to anyone. A metal Henry Moore sculpture entitled *Butterfly* floats in front of the slope-roofed House of World Cultures (Berliners have nicknamed this building "the pregnant oyster"). The modern tower (next on left) is a carillon with 68 bells (from 1987).

➲ Leap out at the Platz der Republik stop. (While you could continue on bus #100, it's better on foot from here.) Through the trees on the left you'll see Germany's new and sprawling **Chancellery.** Started during the more imperial rule of Helmut Kohl, it's now considered overly grand. The big open space is the **Platz der Republik,** where the Victory Column stood until

Hitler moved it. The Hauptbahnhof (Berlin's vast main train station, marked by its tall tower with the *DB* sign) is across the field between the Chancellery and the Reichstag. Watch your step—excavators found a 250-pound, undetonated American bomb here.

➲ Just down the street stands an old building with a new dome...the **Reichstag.**

SIGHTS

Eastern Berlin

I've arranged the following sights in the order of a convenient self-guided orientation walk, picking up where my "Do-It-Yourself Orientation Tour" (previous section) leaves off. Allow a comfortable hour for this walk from the Reichstag to Alexanderplatz, including time for lingering (but not museum stops).

Near the Brandenburg Gate

▲▲▲Reichstag Building—The parliament building—the heart of German democracy—has a short but complicated and emotional history. When it was inaugurated in the 1890s, the last emperor, Kaiser Wilhelm II, disdainfully called it the "house for chatting." It was from here that the German Republic was proclaimed in 1918. In 1933, this symbol of democracy nearly burned down. While the Nazis blamed a communist plot, some believe that Hitler himself (who needed what we'd call today a "new Pearl Harbor") planned the fire, using it as a handy excuse to frame the communists and grab power. As World War II drew to a close, Stalin ordered his troops to take the Reichstag from the Nazis by May 1 (the workers' holiday). More than 1,500 Nazis (mostly French SS troops) made their last stand here—extending World War II by two days. On April 30, 1945, it fell to the Red Army. It was hardly used from 1933 to 1999. For the building's 101st birthday in 1995, the Bulgarian-American artist Christo wrapped it in silvery-gold cloth. It was then wrapped again—in scaffolding—and rebuilt by British architect Lord Norman Foster into the new parliamentary home of the Bundestag (Germany's lower house, similar to the US House of Representatives). To many Germans, the proud resurrection of the Reichstag symbolizes the end of a terrible chapter in German history.

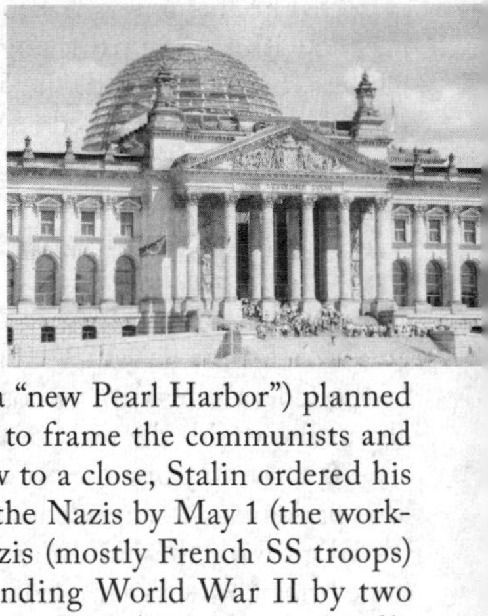

The **glass cupola** rises 155 feet above the ground. Its two sloped ramps spiral 755 feet to the top for a grand view. Inside the

Eastern Berlin

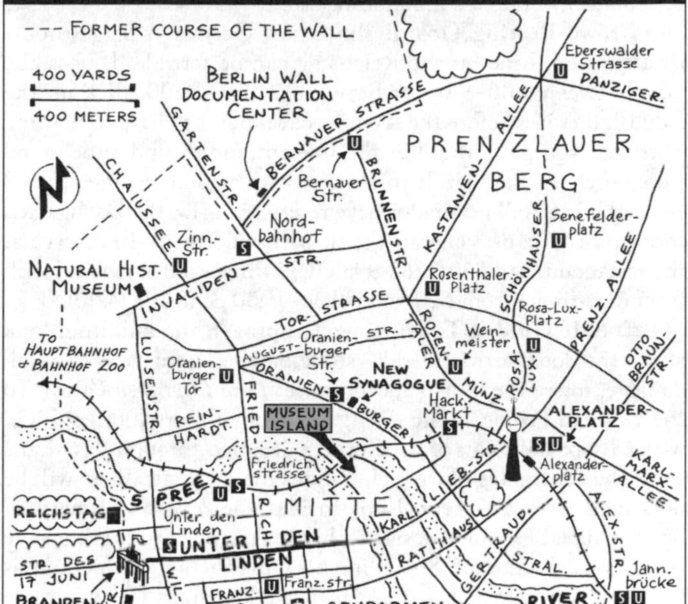

dome, a cone of 360 mirrors reflects natural light into the legislative chamber below. Lit from inside at night, this gives Berlin a memorable nightlight. The environmentally friendly cone also helps with air circulation, drawing hot air out of the legislative chamber (no joke) and pulling in cool air from below.

Cost, Hours, Location: Free, daily 8:00–24:00, last entry at 22:00, most crowded 10:00–16:00 (wait in line to go up—good street musicians, metal detectors, no big luggage allowed, some hour-long English tours when parliament is not sitting), Platz der

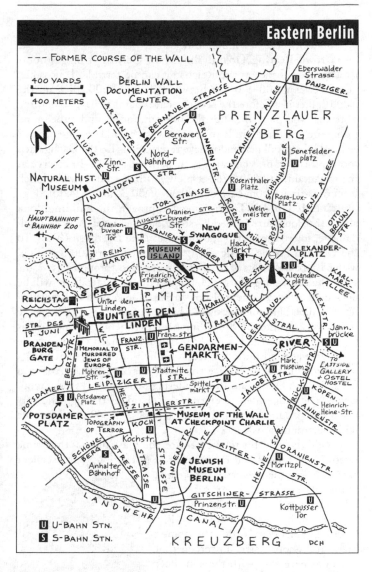

Republik 1, S- or U-Bahn: Friedrichstrasse or Unter den Linden, tel. 030/2273-2152, www.bundestag.de.

Crowd-Beating Tips: Berlin is now Germany's biggest tourist attraction. Lines at the Reichstag can be terrible. If possible, visit between 8:00–9:00 or between 21:00–22:00. Pick up the English flier just before the security checkpoint to have something to read as you wait. The skip-the-line entrance is under the grand front porch on the right. If you're here with a child (younger than 8 years old) or a frail person, or have reservations for the Dachgarten rooftop restaurant, you can get in without a wait. To reserve at the restaurant, call 030/2262-9933 (€58 three-course meals, lunch from €15, dinner from €20, daily 9:30–16:30 & 18:30–24:00).

➲ **Self-Guided Tour:** As you approach the building, look above the door, surrounded by stone patches from WWII bomb damage, to see the motto and promise: *Dem Deutschen Volke* ("To the German People"). The open, airy lobby towers 100 feet high, with 65-foot-tall colors of the German flag. See-through glass doors show the **central legislative chamber.** The message: There will be no secrets in government. Look inside. The seats are "Reichstag blue," a lilac-blue color designed by the architect to brighten the otherwise gray interior. Spreading his wings behind the podium is the *Bundestagsadler* (a.k.a. "the fat hen"), a stylized German eagle representing the Bundestag (each branch of government has its own symbolic eagle). Notice the doors marked "Yes," "No," and "Abstain"...an homage to the Bundestag's traditional "sheep jump" way of counting votes by exiting the chamber through the corresponding door (although for critical issues, all 669 members vote with electronic cards).

Ride the elevator to the base of the glass **dome.** Take time to study the photos and read the circle of captions—an excellent exhibit telling the Reichstag story. Then study the surrounding architecture: a broken collage of new on old, torn between antiquity and modernity, like Germany's history. Notice the dome's giant and unobtrusive sunscreen that moves as necessary with the sun. Peer down through the skylight to look over the shoulders of the elected representatives at work. For Germans, the best view from here is down—keeping a close eye on their government.

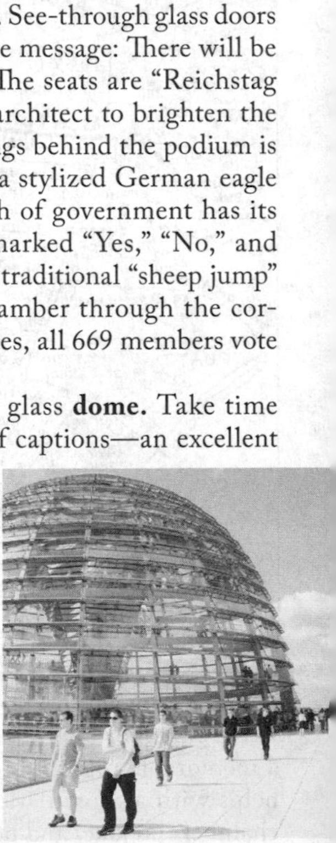

Start at the ramp nearest the elevator and wind up to the top of the **double ramp.** Take a 360-degree survey of the city as you hike: First, the big park is the **Tiergarten,** the "green lungs of Berlin." Beyond that is the **Teufelsberg,** or "Devil's Hill" (built of rubble from the destroyed city in the late 1940s, and famous during the Cold War as a powerful ear of the West—notice the telecommunications tower on top). Knowing the bombed-out and bulldozed story of their city, locals say, "You have to be suspicious when you see the nice, green park." Find the **Victory Column** (Siegessäule, moved by Hitler in the 1930s from in front of the Reichstag to its present position in the Tiergarten). Next, scenes of the new Berlin spiral into your view—**Potsdamer Platz,** marked by the conical glass tower that houses Sony's European headquarters. The yellow building to the right is the Berlin Philharmonic Concert Hall, marking the museums at the Kulturforum. Continue circling left, and find the green chariot atop the **Brandenburg Gate.** The new **Memorial to the Murdered Jews of Europe** stretches south of the Brandenburg Gate. Next, you'll see **former East Berlin** and the city's next huge construction zone, with a forest of 300-foot-tall skyscrapers in the works. Notice the TV Tower (featuring the Pope's Revenge—explained on page 483), the Berlin Cathedral's massive dome, the red tower of the City Hall, the golden dome of the New Synagogue, and the Reichstag's **Dachgarten Restaurant** (see "Crowd-Beating Tips," previous page).

Follow the train tracks in the distance to the left toward Berlin's huge main train station, the **Hauptbahnhof.** Just in front of it, alone in a field, is the Swiss Embassy. It used to be surrounded by buildings, but now it's the only one left. Complete your spin-tour with the blocky **Chancellery,** nicknamed by Berliners "the washing machine." It may look like a pharaoh's tomb, but it's the office and home of Germany's most powerful person, the chancellor (currently Angela Merkel).

Memorial to Politicians Who Opposed Hitler—As you leave the Reichstag, look for the row of slate slabs imbedded in the ground by the park across from the main entry (looks like a fancy slate bicycle rack). This is a memorial to the 96 politicians (the equivalent of our members of Congress) who were murdered and persecuted because their politics didn't agree with Chancellor Hitler's. They were part of the Weimar Republic, the weak and ill-fated attempt at post-WWI democracy in Germany. These were the people who could have stopped Hitler...so they became his first victims. Each slate slab remembers one man—his name, party (mostly KPD—Communists, and SPD—Social Democrats), and date and location of death—generally in concentration camps. (*KZ*

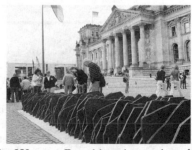

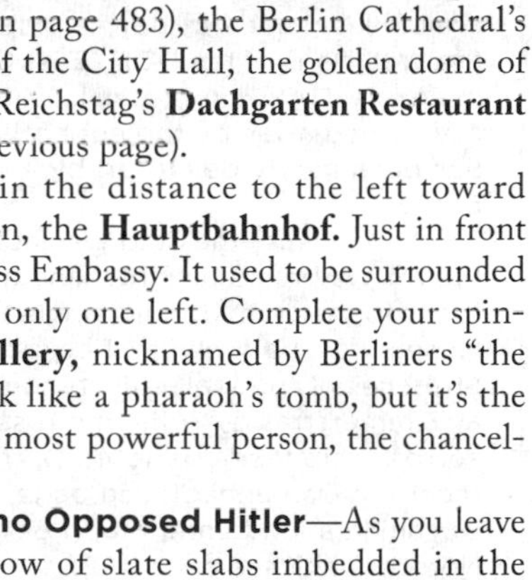

BERLIN

The Berlin Wall

The 100-mile "Anti-Fascist Protective Rampart," as it was called by the East German government, was erected almost overnight in 1961 to stop the outward flow of people (three million leaked out between 1949 and 1961). The 13-foot-high Wall *(Mauer)* had a 16-foot tank ditch, a no-man's-land (or "death strip") that was 30–160 feet wide, and 300 sentry towers. During the Wall's 28 years, border guards fired 1,693 times and made 3,221 arrests, and there were 5,043 documented successful escapes (565 of these were East German guards).

The carnival atmosphere of those first years after the Wall fell is gone, but hawkers still sell "authentic" pieces of the Wall, flags of the DDR (East Germany), and military paraphernalia to gawking tourists. When it fell, the Wall was literally carried away by the euphoria. What managed to survive has been nearly devoured by a decade of persistent "Wall-peckers."

Americans—the Cold War victors—have the biggest appetite for Wall-related sights, and a few bits and pieces remain for us to seek out. Berlin's single best Wall-related sight is the Museum of the Wall at Checkpoint Charlie (see page 486). Stretches of the Wall still standing include the short section at Zimmerstrasse/Wilhelmstrasse (near the Topography of Terror exhibit; see page 487), the longer East Side Gallery (near the Ostbahnhof; see page 489), and at the Berlin Wall Documentation Center along Bernauer Strasse (near S-Bahn: Nordbahnhof; see page 492).

stands for "concentration camp.") They are honored here, in front of the building in which they worked.

To the Brandenburg Gate: Let's continue our walk and cross what was the Berlin Wall. Leaving the Reichstag, return to the busy road and walk around the building. At the rear of the building (across the street, at the edge of the park) is a small memorial to some of the East Berliners who died trying to cross the Wall. Look at the faces of these exceptionally free spirits. The Wall was built on August 13, 1961. Of these people—many of whom died within months of the wall's construction—most died trying to swim the river to freedom. In the park just behind this memorial, another memorial is planned. It will remember the Roma (Gypsy) victims of the Holocaust. (The Roma, as disdained by the Nazis as the Jews were, lost the same percentage of their population to Hitler.)

The Brandenburg Gate is ahead. Stay on the park side of the street for a better view of the gate. As you cross at the light, notice the double row of **cobblestones**—it goes around the city, marking where the Wall used to stand. (You could go directly to the Jewish memorial from here, but we'll go through the Brandenburg Gate first, then reach the memorial through Pariser Platz.)

▲▲Brandenburg Gate (Brandenburger Tor)—The historic Brandenburg Gate (1791) was the grandest, and is the last survivor, of 14 gates in Berlin's old city wall (this one led to the neighboring region of Brandenburg). The gate was the symbol of Prussian Berlin...and later the symbol of a divided Berlin. It's crowned by a majestic four-horse chariot with the Goddess of Peace at the reins. Napoleon took this statue to the Louvre in Paris in 1806. After the Prussians defeated Napoleon and got it back (1813), she was renamed the Goddess of Victory.

The gate sat unused, part of a sad circle dance called the Wall, for more than 25 years. Now postcards all over town show the ecstatic day—November 9, 1989—when the world enjoyed the sight of happy Berliners jamming the gate like flowers on a parade float. Pause a minute and think about struggles for freedom—past and present. (There's actually a special room built into the gate for this purpose—see the sidebar on the next page.) Around the gate, look at the information boards with pictures of how much this area changed throughout the 20th century. The latest chapter: The shiny white gate was completely restored in 2002 (but you can still see faint patches marking war damage). The TI within the gate is open daily (April–Oct 9:30–19:00, Nov–March 10:00–19:00, S-Bahn: Unter den Linden).

The Brandenburg Gate, the center of old Berlin, sits on a major boulevard running east to west through Berlin. The western segment, called Strasse des 17 Juni (named for a workers' uprising against the DDR government in 1953), stretches for four miles from the Brandenburg Gate and Victory Column to the Olympic Stadium. But we'll follow this city axis in the opposite direction, east, walking along what is known as Unter den Linden—into the core of old imperial Berlin and past what was once the palace of the Hohenzollern family who ruled Prussia and then Germany. The palace—the reason for just about all you'll see—is a phantom sight, long gone (though the facade—which we'll see later on

The Brandenburg Gate, Arch of Peace

Two hundred years ago, the Brandenburg Gate was designed as an arch of peace, crowned by the Goddess of Peace and showing Mars sheathing his sword. The Nazis misused it as a gate of triumph and aggression. Today a Room of Silence, built into the gate, is dedicated to the peaceful message of the original Brandenburg Gate (daily 11:00–18:00). As you consider the history of Berlin in this room—which is carefully not dedicated to any particular religion—you may be inspired to read the prayer of the United Nations:

"Oh Lord, our planet Earth is only a small star in space. It is our duty to transform it into a planet whose creatures are no longer tormented by war, hunger, and fear, no longer senselessly divided by race, color, and ideology. Give us courage and strength to begin this task today so that our children and our children's children shall one day carry the name of man with pride."

this walk—is now being partially rebuilt). Alexanderplatz, which marks the end of this walk, is near the base of the giant TV Tower hovering in the distance.

Ponder the fact that you're standing in what was the so-called "death strip." Now cross through the gate, into...

▲Pariser Platz—"Parisian Square," so named after the Prussians defeated Napoleon in 1813, was once filled with important government buildings—all bombed to smithereens in World War II. For decades, it was an unrecognizable, deserted no-man's-land. But now, sparkling new banks, embassies (the French Embassy rebuilt where it was before WWII), a palace of coffee (Starbucks), the small Kennedys Museum (described later), and a swanky rebuilt hotel have filled in the void. The winners of World War II got prime real estate: The American, French, British, and Soviet (now Russian) embassies are all on or near this square.

Face the gate and look to your left. The **US Embassy** moved back here in 2008. This new embassy has been controversial: For safety's sake, Uncle Sam wanted it away from other buildings, but the Germans preferred it in its original location. A compromise was reached, building the embassy by the gate—but routing roads farther from it (at the expense of American taxpayers) to reduce the security risk. Throughout the world, American embassies are the most fortified buildings in town.

Just to the left, the **DZ Bank building** is by Frank Gehry, the unconventional American architect famous for Bilbao's organic Guggenheim Museum, Prague's Dancing House, Seattle's Experience Music Project, Chicago's Millennium Park, and Los

Angeles' Walt Disney Concert Hall. Gehry fans might be surprised at the DZ Bank building's low profile. Structures on Pariser Platz are designed to be bland so as not to draw attention away from the Brandenburg Gate. (The glassy facade of the Academy of Arts, next to Gehry's building, is controversial for drawing attention to itself.) For your fix of the good old Gehry, step into the lobby and check out its undulating interior. It's a fish—and you feel like you're both inside and outside of it. Gehry's vision is explained on a nearby plaque.

The **Academy of Arts** (Akademie der Kunst), with its notorious glass facade, is next door. Its doors lead to a mall (daily 10:00–22:00), which leads directly to the vast...

▲▲Memorial to the Murdered Jews of Europe (Denkmal für die Ermordeten Juden Europas)—The new Holocaust memorial, consisting of 2,711 gravestone-like pillars and completed in 2005, is an essential stop for any visit to Berlin. This is the first formal German government–sponsored Holocaust memorial. Jewish American architect Peter Eisenman won the competition for the commission (and built it on time and on budget—€27 million). It's controversial for the focus—just Jews. The government promises to make memorials to the other groups targeted by the Nazis.

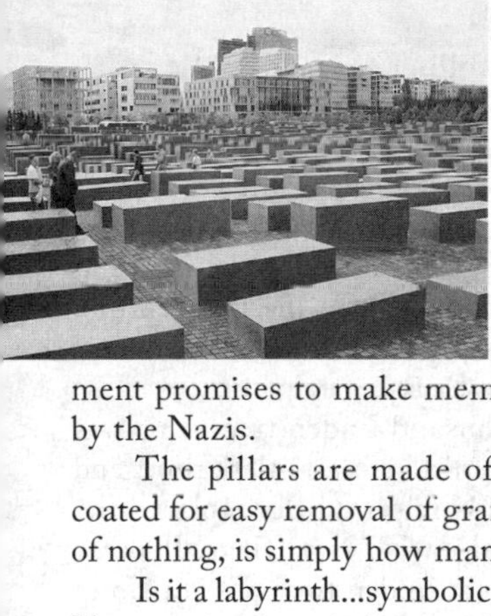

The pillars are made of hollow concrete, each chemically coated for easy removal of graffiti. The number of pillars, symbolic of nothing, is simply how many fit on the provided land.

Is it a labyrinth...symbolic cemetery...intentionally disorienting? The meaning is entirely up to the visitor to derive. The idea is for you to spend time pondering this horrible chapter in human history.

The pondering takes place under the sky. For the learning, go under the field of concrete pillars to the state-of-the-art information center (there may be a short line because visitors must go through a security check). This studies the Nazi system of extermination, humanizes the victims, traces stories of individual families and collects vivid personal accounts, and lists 200 different places of genocide (all well-explained in English, free, Tue–Sun 10:00–20:00, closed Mon, last entry 45 min before closing, S-Bahn: Unter den Linden or Potsdamer Platz, tel. 030/2639-4336, www.stiftung-denkmal.de). The €3 audioguide augments the experience.

The location—where the Wall once stood—is coincidental. It's just a place where lots of people will experience it. Nazi propagandist Joseph Goebbels' bunker was discovered during the work and left buried under the northeast corner of the memorial. Hitler's bunker is just 200 yards away, under a nondescript parking lot. Such Nazi sites are intentionally left hidden to discourage neo-Nazi elements from creating shrines.

Now backtrack to Pariser Platz (through the yellow building). Across the square, consider dropping into the...

Kennedys Museum—This crisp new private enterprise facing the Brandenburg Gate recalls Kennedy's Germany trip in 1963, with great photos and video clips as well as a photographic shrine to the Kennedy clan in America. It's a small, overpriced, yet delightful experience with interesting mementos—such as JFK's notes with the phonetic "ish bin ein Bear lee ner." Jacqueline Kennedy commented on how strange it was that this was her husband's most quotable quote (€7, €3.50 to a broad array of visitors—dream up a discount and ask for it, daily 10:00–18:00, Pariser Platz 4a, tel. 030/2065-3570).

Leave Pariser Platz and begin strolling...

▲▲Along Unter den Linden

Unter den Linden is the heart of former East Berlin. In Berlin's good old days, Unter den Linden was one of Europe's grand boulevards. In the 15th century, this carriageway led from the palace to the hunting grounds (today's big Tiergarten). In the 17th century, Hohenzollern princes and princesses moved in and built their palaces here so they could be near the Prussian emperor.

Named centuries ago for its thousand linden trees, this was the most elegant street of Prussian Berlin before Hitler's time, and the main drag of East Berlin after his reign. Hitler replaced the venerable trees—many 250 years old—with Nazi flags. Popular discontent actually drove him to replant linden trees. Today, Unter den Linden is no longer a depressing Cold War cul-de-sac, and its pre-Hitler strolling café ambience is returning. Notice how it is divided, roughly at Friedrichstrasse, into a business section that stretches toward the Brandenburg Gate, and a culture section that spreads out toward Alexanderplatz. Frederick the Great wanted culture, mainly the opera and the university, closer to his palace, and to keep business (read: banks) farther away, near the city walls.

As you walk toward the giant TV Tower, the big building you see jutting out into the street on your right is the **Hotel Adlon.** It hosted such notables as Charlie Chaplin, Albert Einstein, and Greta Garbo. This was where Garbo said, "I want to be alone" during the filming of *Grand Hotel.* And, perhaps fresher in your memory, this is where Michael Jackson shocked millions by dangling his little baby over the railing (second balcony up, center of facade). Destroyed by Russians just after World War II, the grand

Unter den Linden

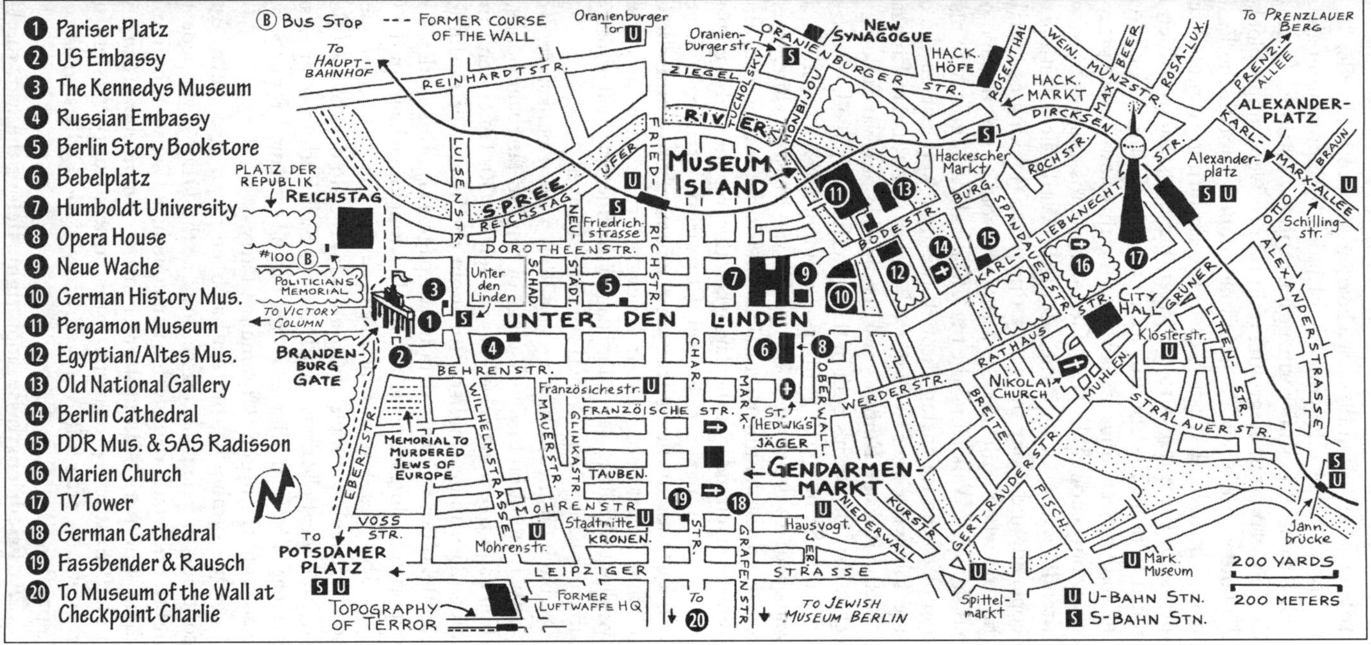

Adlon was rebuilt in 1996. See how far you can get inside.

Descend into the Unter den Linden S-Bahn station ahead of you. It's one of Berlin's former **ghost subway stations.** During the Cold War, most underground train tunnels were simply blocked at the border. But a few Western lines looped through the East. To make a little hard Western cash, the Eastern government rented the use of these tracks to the West, but the stations (which happened to be in East Berlin) were strictly off-limits. For 28 years, the stations were unused, as Western trains slowly passed through, seeing only eerie DDR (East German) guards and lots of cobwebs. Literally within days of the fall of the Wall, these stations were reopened, and today they are a time warp (looking essentially as they did when built in 1931, with dreary old green tiles and original signage). Walk along the track (the walls are lined with historic photos of the Reichstag through the ages) and exit on the other side, following signs to *Russische Botschaft* (the Russian Embassy).

The **Russian Embassy** was the first big postwar building project in East Berlin. It's built in the powerful, simplified, Neoclassical style that Stalin liked. While not as important now as it was a few years ago, it's immense as ever. It flies the Russian white, blue, and red. Find the hammer-and-sickle motif decorating the window frames—a reminder of the days when this was the USSR embassy.

Continuing past the Aeroflot airline offices, look across Glinkastrasse to the right to see the back of the **Komische Oper** (Comic Opera; program and view of ornate interior posted in window). While the exterior is ugly, the fine old theater interior—amazingly missed by WWII bombs—survives.

Back on the main drag, at #26, is a great bookstore, **Berlin Story.** In addition to a wide range of English-language books, this shop has a free museum (with a model of 1930s Unter den Linden) and a 25-minute English film about the history of Berlin (daily 10:00–20:00; for more details, see page 455). This is also a good opportunity to pick up some nostalgic knickknacks from the Cold War. The West lost no time in consuming the East; consequently, some are feeling a wave of *Ost*-algia for the old days of East Berlin. In 2006 local elections, nearly half of East Berlin's voters—and 6 percent of West Berliners—voted for the extreme left party, which has ties to the bygone Communist Party.

One symbol of that era has been given a reprieve. As you continue to Friedrichstrasse, look at the DDR-style pedestrian lights, and you'll realize that someone had a sense of humor back then. The perky red and green men—***Ampelmännchen***—were under threat of replacement by the far less jaunty Western signs. Fortunately, after a 10-year court battle, the DDR signals will be kept after all.

At **Friedrichstrasse,** look right. Before the war, the Unter den Linden/Friedrichstrasse intersection was the heart of Berlin. In the 1920s, Berlin was famous for its anything-goes love of life. This was the cabaret drag, a springboard to stardom for young and vampy entertainers like Marlene Dietrich. (Born in 1901, Dietrich starred in the first German "talkie" and then headed straight to Hollywood.) Over the last few years, this boulevard—lined with super department stores (such as Galeries Lafayette) and big-time hotels (such as the Hilton and Regent)—has slowly begun to replace Ku'damm as the grand commerce and café boulevard of Berlin. (More recently, the West is retaliating with some new stores of its own.) Across from Galeries Lafayette is American Express (handy for any train-ticket needs—see page 456). Consider detouring to Galeries Lafayette, with its cool marble and glass waste-of-space interior (Mon–Sat 9:30–20:00, closed Sun; belly up to its amazing ground-floor viewpoint, or have lunch in its basement cafeteria—see page 518).

If you continued down Friedrichstrasse, you'd wind up at the sights listed in "South of Unter den Linden," on page 484—including the Museum of the Wall at Checkpoint Charlie (a 10-min walk from here). But for now, continue along Unter den Linden. You'll notice big, colorful **water pipes** around here, and throughout Berlin. As long as the city remains a gigantic construction zone, it will be laced with these drainage pipes—key to any building project. Berlin's high water table means any new basement comes with lots of pumping out.

The **VW Automobil Forum** shows off the latest models from the many car companies owned by VW (free, corner of Friedrichstrasse and Unter den Linden, VW art gallery in the basement).

Continue down Unter den Linden a few more blocks, past the large equestrian statue of Frederick II ("the Great"), and turn right into the square called **Bebelplatz.** Stand on the glass window in the center.

Frederick the Great—who ruled from 1740 to 1786—established Prussia not just as a military power, but as a cultural and intellectual heavyweight, as well. This square was the center of the "new Rome" that Frederick envisioned. His grand palace was just down the street (see page 482).

Look down through the glass you're standing on (center of Bebelplatz): The room of empty bookshelves is a memorial to the notorious Nazi **book burning.** It was on this square in 1933 that staff and students from the university threw 20,000 newly forbidden books (like Einstein's) into a huge bonfire on the orders of the Nazi propaganda minister Joseph Goebbels. A memorial plaque nearby reminds us of the prophetic quote by the German Jewish poet Heinrich Heine. In 1820, he said, "When you start by burning books, you'll end by burning people." A century later, his books were among those that went up in flames on this spot.

Great buildings front Bebelplatz. Survey the square counter-clockwise:

Humboldt University, across Unter den Linden, is one of Europe's greatest. Marx and Lenin (not the brothers or the sisters) studied here, as did the Grimms (both brothers) and more than two-dozen Nobel Prize winners. Einstein, who was Jewish, taught here until taking a spot at Princeton in 1932 (smart guy).

The former **state library** is where Vladimir Lenin studied during much of his exile from Russia. If you climb to the second floor of the library and go through the door opposite the stairs, you'll see a 1968 vintage stained-glass window depicting Lenin's life's work with almost biblical reverence. On the ground floor is Tim's Canadian Deli, a great little café with light food, student prices, and garden seating (€2 plates, Mon–Sat 7:00–20:00, closed Sun, easy WC).

The **German State Opera** was bombed in 1941, rebuilt to bolster morale and to celebrate its centennial in 1943, and bombed again in 1945.

The round, Catholic **St. Hedwig's Church**—nicknamed the "upside-down teacup"—was built by the pragmatic Frederick the Great to encourage the integration of Catholic Silesians after his empire annexed their region in 1815. (St. Hedwig is the patron saint of Silesia, a region now shared by Germany, Poland, and the Czech Republic—see page 434.) When asked what the church should look like, Frederick literally took a Silesian teacup and slammed it upside-down on a table. Like all Catholic churches in Berlin, St. Hedwig's is not on the street, but stuck in a kind of back lot—indicating inferiority to Protestant churches. You can step inside the church to see the cheesy DDR government renovation.

Continue down Unter den Linden. The next square on your right holds the **Opera House.** The Opernpalais, preening with fancy prewar elegance, hosts the pricey Operncafé. With the best desserts and the longest dessert bar in Europe, it's popular with Berliners for *Kaffee und Kuchen* (see page 517).

Cross Unter den Linden to the university side. The Greek-temple-like building set in the small, chestnut-tree-filled park is the **Neue Wache** (the emperor's "New Guardhouse," from 1816). When the Wall fell, this memorial to the victims of fascism was transformed into a new national memorial. Look inside, where a

BERLIN

replica of the Käthe Kollwitz statue, *Mother with Her Dead Son,* is surrounded by thought-provoking silence. This marks the tombs of Germany's unknown soldier and the unknown concentration camp victim. The inscription in front reads, "To the victims of war and tyranny." Read the entire statement in English (on wall, left of entrance). The memorial, open to the sky, incorporates the elements—sunshine, rain, snow—falling on this modern-day *pietà*.

After the Neue Wache, the next building you'll see is Berlin's pink-yet-formidable Zeughaus, or arsenal. Dating from 1695, it's considered the oldest building on the boulevard and now houses the...

▲▲▲German History Museum (Deutsches Historisches Museum)—This fantastic museum is a two-part affair: the pink former Prussian arsenal building, and the I. M. Pei–designed annex. The main building (fronting Unter den Linden) houses the permanent collection. Two huge rectangular floors are packed with more than 8,000 artifacts telling the story of Germany—making this the top history museum in town. Historical objects, photographs, and models are intermingled with multimedia stations to help put everything in context. The first floor traces German history from 1 B.C. to 1918, with exhibits on early cultures, the Middle Ages, Reformation, Thirty Years' War, German Empire, and World War I. Exhibits on the ground floor continue with the Weimar Republic, Nazism, World War II, Allied occupation, and a divided Germany, wrapping up with reunification and a quick look at Germany today (€5, daily 10:00–18:00, excellent €3 audioguide has six hours of info for you to choose from, tel. 030/2030-4751, www.dhm.de).

For architecture buffs, the big attraction is the Pei annex behind the history museum, which complements the museum with often-fascinating temporary history exhibits. From the old building (with the Pei glass canopy over its courtyard), take a tunnel to the new wing, emerging under a striking glass spiral staircase that unites four floors with surprising views and lots of light. It's here that you'll experience why Pei—famous for his glass pyramid at Paris' Louvre—is called the "perfector of classical modernism," "master of light," and a magician of uniting historical buildings with new ones. (If the museum is closed, or you don't have a ticket, venture down the street—Hinter dem Giesshaus—to the left of the museum to see the Pei annex from the outside.)

Back on Unter den Linden, head toward the **Spree River.** Just before the bridge, wander left along the canal through a tiny but colorful arts-and-crafts market (weekends only; a larger flea market is just outside the Pergamon Museum). Canal tour boats leave from here (€7, 1 hour, departures on the half-hour, tour in German only but so dull it hardly matters). Continue up the riverbank two blocks and cross the Spree at the footbridge, which takes you to...

Museum Island (Museumsinsel)

This island, home of Berlin's first museum, is undergoing a formidable renovation. The grand vision is to integrate the city's major museums with a grand entry and tunnels that will lace the complex together (intended completion date: 2015). The complex was originally built in about 1871, when Germany was newly unified as one nation—and when Berlin was calling itself the "Athens on the Spree River." Today, its imposing Neoclassical buildings host four grand museums: the Pergamon (classical antiquities), the Altes Museum (housing the Egyptian Museum, with the bust of Queen Nefertiti), the Old National Gallery (19th-century German Romantic painting), and the Bode Museum (European statuary through the ages, coins, and Byzantine art). The museums function as one with the same prices, phone number, and a €12 comboticket that's far better than buying individual €8 entries (all are also included in the city's €19 Museumspass; Pergamon, Altes, and Bode museums open daily 10:00–18:00, Thu until 22:00, free on Thu after 18:00; Old National Gallery open same hours except closed Mon; tel. 030/2090-5577, www.museumsinsel-berlin.de). The nearest S-Bahn station is Hackescher Markt.

Consider visiting any of these museums, and other Museum Island attractions (mentioned later), before continuing our walk. Once you're finished, skip over to "Museum Island to Alexanderplatz," page 482, to resume the self-guided tour.

▲▲Pergamon Museum—This world-class museum, part of Berlin's Collection of Classical Antiquities (Antikensammlung), stars the fantastic Pergamon Altar. From a second-century B.C. Greek temple, the altar shows the Greeks under Zeus and Athena beating the giants in a dramatic pig pile of mythological mayhem. Check out the action spilling onto the stairs. The Babylonian Ishtar Gate (glazed blue tiles from the sixth century B.C.) and many ancient Greek and Mesopotamian treasures are also impressive. The superb "Pergamon in 30 Minutes" audioguide (free with admission, but €4 during free Thu extended hours) covers the museum's highlights and broadens your experience by introducing you to wonders you might not otherwise notice.

▲▲Egyptian Museum (Ägyptisches Museum)/Altes Museum—Showing off one of the world's top collections of Egyptian art, this wonderfully presented museum fills the second floor of Berlin's Altes Museum (Old Museum). If you're not interested in the Altes Museum, you can go directly up to the second floor to the Egyptian collection.

The curator welcomes you on the included audioguide and

encourages a broader approach to the museum than just seeing its claim to fame, the bust of Queen Nefertiti (described next). The fine audioguide celebrates new knowledge about ancient Egyptian civilization and offers fascinating insights into workaday Egyptian life as it describes the vivid papyrus collection, slice-of-life artifacts, and dreamy wax portraits decorating mummy cases.

But let's face it: The main reason to visit is to enjoy one of the great thrills in art appreciation—gazing into the still-young-and-beautiful face of 3,000-year-old **Queen Nefertiti,** the wife of King Akhenaton. This bust of Queen Nefertiti (c. 1340 B.C.) is the most famous piece of Egyptian art in Europe. Discovered in 1912, Nefertiti—with all the right beauty marks: long neck, symmetrical face, and just the right makeup—is called "Berlin's most beautiful woman." The bust never left its studio, but served as a master model for all other portraits of the queen. (That's probably why the left eye was never inlaid.) Buried for more than 3,000 years, she was found in the early 1900s by a German team who, by agreement with the Egyptian government, got to take home any workshop models they found. Although this bust is not particularly representative of Egyptian art in general, it has become a symbol for Egyptian art by popular acclaim. (Note that the Egyptian collection is destined to move in a few years to the island's fifth museum, the New Museum.)

Old National Gallery (Alte Nationalgalerie)—This gallery, behind the Egyptian Museum/Altes Museum, is designed to look like a Greek temple. It shows mostly paintings: three floors with French and German Impressionists on the second, and Romantic German paintings (which I find most interesting) on the top (audioguide is free).

Lustgarten—For 300 years, the island's big central square has flip-flopped between being a military parade ground and a people-friendly park, depending upon the political tenor of the time. In 1999, it was made into a park again (read the history posted in corner opposite church). On a sunny day, it's packed with relaxing locals and is one of Berlin's most enjoyable public spaces.

Berlin Cathedral (Berliner Dom)—This century-old church towers over Museum Island (€5 includes access to dome gallery, not covered by Museum Island ticket, Mon–Sat 9:00–20:00, Sun 12:00–20:00, until 19:00 in winter, www.berliner-dom.de; many organ concerts—generally Sat at 20:00, tickets about €10 always available at the door, tel. 030/2026-9136). Inside, the great reformers (Luther, Calvin, and company) stand around the brilliantly restored dome like stern saints guarding their theology. Frederick I rests in an ornate tomb (right transept, near entrance to dome). The 270-step climb to the outdoor dome gallery is tough, but offers pleasant, breezy views of the city at the finish line (last entry 45 min before closing). The crypt downstairs is not worth a look.

Site of the Palace of the Republic—Across Unter den Linden from Berlin Cathedral is a construction site that once held the decrepit Palace of the Republic—formerly East Berlin's parliament building/futuristic entertainment complex, and a symbol of the communist days. Much of Frederick the Great's earlier palace actually survived World War II, but was replaced by the communists with this blocky Soviet-style building. The landmark building fell into disrepair after reunification, and was eventually dismantled in 2007. After long debate, the German Parliament decided to construct a building that will include the rebuilt facade of the old palace. Investing a huge sum, they will create a huge new public venue to be filled with museums, shops, galleries, and concert halls.

Museum Island to Alexanderplatz

Continue walking down Unter den Linden. Before crossing the bridge (and leaving Museum Island), look right. The pointy twin spires of the 13th-century Nikolai Church mark the center of medieval Berlin. This Nikolaiviertel (*Viertel* means "quarter") was restored by the DDR and was trendy in the last years of socialism. Today, it's a lively-at-night riverside restaurant district.

As you cross the bridge, look left in the distance to see the gilded **New Synagogue dome,** rebuilt after WWII bombing (see page 490).

Across the river to the left of the bridge is the giant **SAS Radisson Hotel** and shopping center, with a huge aquarium in the center. The elevator goes right through the middle of a deep-sea world. (You can see it from the unforgettable Radisson hotel lobby—tuck in your shirt and walk past the guards with the confidence of a guest who's sleeping there.) Here in the center of the old communist capital, it seems that capitalism has settled in with a spirited vengeance.

At the river side of the SAS Radisson Hotel, the little **DDR Museum** offers an interesting peek at a humbler life before capitalism took hold. You'll crawl through a Trabant car, see a DDR kitchen, and be surrounded by former DDR residents reminiscing about the bad old days (steep €5.50 admission, daily 10:00–22:00, Karl-Liebknecht Strasse 1, tel. 030/847-123-731).

In the park immediately across the street (a big jaywalk from the Radisson) are grandfatherly statues of **Marx and Engels** (nicknamed by locals "the old pensioners"). Surrounding them are stainless-steel monoliths with evocative photos that show the struggles of the workers of the world.

Walk toward **Marien Church** (from 1270, an artist's rendering helps you follow the interesting but very faded old "Dance of Death" mural which wraps around the narthex inside the door), just left of the base of the TV Tower. The big, redbrick building past the trees on the right is the **City Hall,** built after the revolution of 1848 and arguably the first democratic building in the city.

The 1,200-foot-tall **TV Tower** (Fernsehturm) offers a fine view from halfway up (€9.50, daily March–Oct 9:00–24:00, Nov–Feb 10:00–24:00). The tower offers a handy city orientation and an interesting view of the flat, red-roofed sprawl of Berlin—including a peek inside the city's many courtyards *(Höfe).* Consider a kitschy trip to the observation deck for the view and lunch in its revolving restaurant (mediocre food, €12 plates, horrible lounge music, reservations smart for dinner, tel. 030/242-3333). It's very retro and somewhat trendy these days, so expect a line for the elevator. Built (with Swedish know-how) in 1969, the tower was meant to show the power of the atheistic state at a time when DDR leaders were having the crosses removed from church domes and spires. But when the sun shined on their tower—the greatest spire in East Berlin—a huge cross was reflected on the mirrored ball. Cynics called it "The Pope's Revenge." East Berliners dubbed the tower the "Tele-Asparagus." They joked that if it fell over, they'd have an elevator to the West.

Farther east, pass under the train tracks into **Alexanderplatz.** This area—especially the Kaufhof department store—was the commercial pride and joy of East Berlin. Today, it's still a landmark, with a major U- and S-Bahn station.

Our orientation stroll is finished. For a ride through workaday eastern Berlin, with its Lego-hell apartments (dreary even with their new facelifts), hop back on bus #100 from here. It loops five minutes to the end of the line and then, after a couple minutes' break, heads on back. (This bus retraces your route, finishing at Bahnhof Zoo.) Or consider extending this foray into eastern Berlin to...

Karl-Marx-Allee

The buildings along Karl-Marx-Allee in East Berlin (just beyond Alexanderplatz) were completely leveled by the Red Army in 1945. As an expression of their adoration to the "great Socialist Father" (the "cult of Stalin" was in full gear), the DDR government decided to rebuild the street better than ever (the USSR provided generous subsidies) and made it intentionally one meter wider than the Champs-Elysées. They named it Stalinallee. Today, this street, done in the bold "Stalin Gothic" style so common in Moscow in the 1950s, has been restored, renamed after Karl Marx, and lined with "workers' palaces"—providing a rare look at Berlin's communist days. Distances are a bit long for convenient walking, but you can cruise Karl-Marx-Allee by taxi, or ride the U-Bahn to Strausberger Platz (which was built to resemble an Italian promenade) and walk to Frankfurter Tor, reading the good information posts along the way. Notice the Social Realist reliefs on the buildings and the lampposts, which incorporate the wings of a phoenix (rising from the ashes) in their design.

The **Café Sibylle,** just beyond the Strausberger Platz U-Bahn station, is a fun spot for a coffee, traditional DDR ice-cream treats, and a look at its free, informal museum that tells the story of the most destroyed street in Berlin. While the humble exhibit is nearly all in German, it's fun to see the ear and half a moustache from what was the largest statue of Stalin in Germany (the centerpiece of the street until 1961) and a few intimate insights into apartment life in a DDR flat. The café is known for its good coffee and *Schwedeneisbecher mit Eierlikor*—an ice-cream sundae with a shot of liqueur, popular among those nostalgic for communism (daily 10:00–20:00, Karl-Marx-Allee 72, at intersection with Koppenstrasse, a block from U-Bahn: Strausberger Platz, tel. 030/2935-2203).

Heading out to Karl-Marx-Allee (just beyond the TV Tower), you're likely to notice a giant colorful **mural** decorating a blocky communist-era skyscraper. This was the Ministry of Education, and the mural is a tile mosaic trumpeting the accomplishments of the DDR's version of "No Child Left Behind."

South of Unter den Linden

The following sights—heavy on Nazi and Wall history—are listed roughly north to south (as you reach them from Unter den Linden).

▲▲Gendarmenmarkt—This delightful and historic square is bounded by twin churches, a tasty chocolate shop, and the Berlin Symphony's concert hall (designed by Karl Friedrich Schinkel, the man who put the Neoclassical stamp on Berlin). In summer, it hosts a few outdoor cafés, *Biergartens*, and sometimes concerts. Wonderfully symmetrical, the square is considered by Berliners to be the finest in town. The name of the square—part

French and part German (after the *Gens d'Armes,* Frederick the Great's royal guard who were headquartered here)—reminds us that in the 17th century, a fifth of all Berliners were French émigrés, Protestant Huguenots fleeing Catholic France. Back then, tolerant Prussia was a magnet for the persecuted. These émigrés vitalized Berlin with new ideas and know-how.

The German Cathedral (described below) on the square has an exhibit worthwhile for history buffs. The French Cathedral (Französischer Dom) offers a humble museum on the Huguenots (€2, Tue–Sun 12:00–17:00, closed Mon, U-Bahn: Französische Strasse or Stadtmitte). Fun fact: Neither of these churches are true cathedrals, as they never contained a bishop's throne; their German title of *Dom* (cathedral) is actually a mistranslation from the French word *dôme* (cupola).

Fassbender & Rausch, on the corner near the German Cathedral, claims to be Europe's biggest chocolate store. After 150 years of chocolate-making, this family-owned business proudly displays its sweet delights—250 different kinds—on a 55-foot-long buffet. Truffles are sold for about €0.60 each—it's fun to compose a fancy little eight-piece box of your own for about €5 (daily 10:00–20:00, corner of Mohrenstrasse at Charlottenstrasse 60, tel. 030/2045-8440). Upstairs is an elegant hot chocolate café with fine views.

Gendarmenmarkt is buried in what has recently emerged as Berlin's new "Fifth Avenue" shopping district. For the ultimate in top-end shops, find the corner of Jägerstrasse and Französische Strasse and wander through the Quartier 206 (Mon–Fri 10:30–19:30, Sat 10:00–18:00, closed Sun, www.quartier206.com).

▲German Cathedral (Deutscher Dom)—This cathedral, bombed flat in the war and rebuilt only in the 1980s, houses the thought-provoking *Milestones, Setbacks, Sidetracks (Wege, Irrwege, Umwege)* exhibit, which traces the history of the German parliamentary system. The parliament-funded exhibit—while light on actual historical artifacts—is well done and more interesting than it sounds. It takes you quickly from the revolutionary days of 1848 to the 1920s, and then more deeply through the tumultuous 20th century. There are no English descriptions, but you can follow the essential, excellent, and free 90-minute English audioguide or buy the wonderfully detailed €10 guidebook. If you think this museum is an attempt by the German government to develop a more sophisticated and educated electorate in the interest of stronger democracy, you're exactly right. Germany knows (from its own troubled history) that a dumbed-down electorate, manipulated by clever spin-meisters and sound-bite media blitzes, is a dangerous thing (free, May–Sept Tue–Sun 10:00–19:00, Oct–April Tue–Sun 10:00–18:00, closed Mon year-round, on Gendarmenmarkt just off Friedrichstrasse, tel. 030/2273-0431).

▲▲▲Museum of the Wall at Checkpoint Charlie (Mauermuseum Haus am Checkpoint Charlie)—While the famous border checkpoint between the American and Soviet sectors is long gone, its memory is preserved by one of Europe's most interesting, though cluttered, museums. During the Cold War, the House at Checkpoint Charlie stood defiantly—spitting distance from the border guards—showing off all the clever escapes over, under, and through the Wall. Today, while the drama is over and hunks of the Wall stand like victory scalps at its door, the museum still tells a gripping history of the Wall, recounts the many ingenious escape attempts (early years—with a cruder wall—saw more escapes), and includes plenty of video coverage of those heady days when people-power tore down the Wall (€12.50, assemble 20 tourists and get in for €7.50 each, €3 audioguide, discount with WelcomeCard but not covered by Museumspass, cash only, daily 9:00–22:00, U-6 to Kochstrasse or—better from Zoo—U-2 to Stadtmitte, Friedrichstrasse 43–45, tel. 030/253-7250, www.mauermuseum.de). If you're pressed for time, this is a good after-dinner sight. With extra time, consider the "Hear We Go" audioguide about the Wall that takes you outside the museum (€7, 90 min, leave ID as deposit).

▲▲Checkpoint Charlie Street Scene—Where Checkpoint Charlie once stood, notice the thought-provoking post with larger-than-life posters of a young American soldier facing east and a young Soviet soldier facing west. The area has become a Cold War freak show. The rebuilt guard station now hosts two actors playing American guards who pose for photos. Across the street is Snack Point Charlie. The old checkpoint was not named for a person, but because it was checkpoint number three—as in Alpha (at the East–West German border, a hundred miles west of here), Bravo (as you enter Berlin proper), and Charlie (the most famous because it was where most foreigners would pass). A fine photo exhibit stretches down the street with great English descriptions telling the story of the Wall. While you could get this information from a book, it's poignant to stand here in person and ponder the gripping history of this place. A few yards away (on Zimmerstrasse), a glass panel describes the former checkpoint. From there, a double row of cobbles in Zimmerstrasse traces the former path of the Wall. These innocuous cobbles run throughout the city, even through some modern buildings.

Follow the cobbles one very long block to Wilhelmstrasse, a surviving stretch of Wall, and the...

Hitler and Third Reich Sites

While many come to Berlin to see Hitler sites, these are essentially invisible. The German Resistance Memorial is in German only and difficult for the tourist to appreciate (see page 493). The Topography of Terror (SS and Gestapo headquarters) is a fascinating exhibit but all that remains of the building is its foundation. (Both museums have helpful audioguides in English.) Hitler's bunker is completely gone (near Potsdamer Platz). Your best bet for "Hitler sites" is to take the Infamous Third Reich Sites walking tour offered by Original Berlin Walks (see "Tours," page 459).

Topography of Terror (Topographie des Terrors)—The park behind the Zimmerstrasse/Wilhelmstrasse bit of Wall marks the site of the command center of Hitler's Gestapo and SS. Because of the horrible things planned here, the rubble of these buildings will always be left as rubble. The SS, Hitler's personal bodyguards, grew to become a state-within-a-state, with its talons in every corner of German society. Along an excavated foundation of the building, an exhibit tells the story of National Socialism and its victims in Berlin (free, info booth open daily May–Sept 10:00–20:00, Oct–April 10:00–18:00 or until dark, tel. 030/2548-6703, www.topographie.de). Posted information is in both German and English, but the free English audioguide is helpful (available only until 18:45 in summer).

Across the street (facing the Wall) is the **German Finance Ministry** (Bundesministerium der Finanzen). Formerly the headquarters of the Nazi Luftwaffe (Air Force), this is the only major Hitler-era government building that survived the war's bombs. The communists used it to house their—no joke—Ministry of Ministries. Walk up Wilhelmstrasse (to the north) to see an entry gate (on your left) that looks much like it did when Germany occupied nearly all of Europe. On the north side of the building (farther up Wilhelmstrasse, at corner with Leipziger Strasse) is a wonderful example of communist art. The mural, Max Lingner's *Aufbau der Republik* (*Building the Republic,* 1953), is classic Socialist Realism, showing the entire society—industrial laborers, farm workers, women, and children—all happily singing the same patriotic song.

This was the communist ideal. For the reality, look at the ground in the courtyard in front of the mural to see an enlarged photograph from a 1953 uprising here against the communists...quite a contrast.

▲▲▲Jewish Museum Berlin (Jüdisches Museum Berlin)—This museum is one of Europe's best Jewish sights. The highly conceptual building is a sight in itself, and the museum inside—an overview of the rich culture and history of Europe's Jewish community—is excellent. The Holocaust is appropriately remembered, but it doesn't overwhelm this celebration of Jewish life. Even though the museum is in a nondescript residential neighborhood (a 10-min walk from the Hallesches Tor U-Bahn station or the Checkpoint Charlie museum), it's well worth the trip.

Designed by American architect Daniel Libeskind (who is redeveloping New York City's World Trade Center site), the zinc-walled building's zigzag shape is pierced by voids symbolic of the irreplaceable cultural loss caused by the Holocaust. Enter through the 18th-century Baroque building next door, then go through an underground tunnel to reach the museum interior.

Before you reach the exhibit, your visit starts with three memorial spaces. Underground, follow the Axis of Exile to a disorienting slanted garden with 49 pillars. Then the Axis of Holocaust leads to an eerily empty tower shut off from the outside world. A detour near the bottom of the long stairway leads to the "Memory Void," a thought-provoking space of "fallen leaves": heavy metal faces that you walk on, making un-human noises with each step.

Finally, climb the stairs to the top of the museum, from where you stroll chronologically through the 2,000-year story of Judaism in Germany. The exhibit, on two floors, is engaging. Interactive bits (for example, spell your name in Hebrew) make it lively for kids. English explanations interpret both the exhibits and the design of the very symbolic building.

Cost and Hours: €5, covered by Museumspass, discount with WelcomeCard, daily 10:00–20:00, Mon until 22:00, last entry one hour before closing, closed on Jewish holidays. Tight security includes bag check and metal detectors. If you're here in

December, be sure to check out their "Hannumas" holiday market. Tel. 030/2599-3300, www.jmberlin.de.

Getting There: Ride U-Bahn line 1, 6, or 15 to Hallesches Tor, take the exit marked *Jüdisches Museum,* exit straight ahead, then turn right on Franz-Klühs-Strasse. The museum is a five-minute walk ahead on your left, at Lindenstrasse 9.

Eating: The museum has a good, but not kosher, café/restaurant (€9 daily specials, lunch served 12:00–16:00, snacks at other times, tel. 030/2593-9760).

East Side Gallery—The biggest remaining stretch of the Wall is now "the world's longest outdoor art gallery." It stretches for nearly a mile and is covered with murals painted by artists from around the world. The murals are routinely whitewashed so new ones can be painted. This segment of the Wall makes another poignant walk. For a quick look, take the S-Bahn to the Ostbahnhof station (follow signs to Stralauerplatz exit; once outside, TV Tower will be to your right; go left and at next corner look to your right—the Wall is across the busy street). The gallery is slowly being consumed by developers. If you walk the entire length of the East Side Gallery, you'll find a small Wall souvenir shop at the end and a bridge crossing the river to a subway station at Schlesisches Tor (in Kreuzberg). The bridge, a fine example of Brandenburg Neo-Gothic brickwork, has a fun neon "rock, paper, scissors" installment poking fun at the futility of the Cold War.

Kreuzberg—This district—once abutting the dreary Wall and inhabited mostly by poor Turkish guest laborers and their families—is still run-down, with graffiti-riddled buildings and plenty of student and Turkish street life. It offers a gritty look at melting-pot Berlin, in a city where original Berliners are as rare as old buildings. Berlin is the fourth-largest Turkish city in the world, and Kreuzberg is its "downtown." But to call it a "little Istanbul" insults the big one. You'll see *Döner Kebab* stands, shops decorated with spray paint, and mothers wrapped in colorful scarves looking like they just got off a donkey in Anatolia. But lately, an influx of immigrants from many other countries has diluted the Turkishness of Kreuzberg. Berliners come here for fun ethnic eateries. For a dose of Kreuzberg without getting your fingers dirty, joyride on bus #129 (catch it near Jewish Museum). For a colorful stroll, take the U-Bahn to Kottbusser Tor and wander—ideally on Tuesday and Friday between 12:00 and 18:00, when the Turkish Market sprawls along the Maybachufer riverbank.

North of Unter den Linden

While there are few major sights to the north of Unter den Linden, this area has some of Berlin's trendiest, most interesting neighborhoods.

▲New Synagogue (Neue Synagogue)—A shiny gilded dome marks the New Synagogue, now a museum and cultural center on Oranienburger Strasse. Only the dome and facade have been restored—a window overlooks the vacant field marking what used to be the synagogue. The largest and finest synagogue in Berlin before World War II, it was desecrated by Nazis on "Crystal Night" (Kristallnacht) in 1938, bombed in 1943, and partially rebuilt in 1990. Inside, past tight security, there's a small but moving exhibit on the Berlin Jewish community through the centuries with some good English descriptions (ground floor and first floor). On its facade, the *Vergesst es nie* message—added by East Berlin Jews in 1966—means "Never forget." East Berlin had only a few hundred Jews, but now that the city is reunited, the Jewish community numbers about 12,000 (€3; March–Oct Sun–Mon 10:00–20:00, Tue–Thu 10:00–18:00, Fri 10:00–17:00, closed Sat; Nov–Feb Sun–Thu 10:00–18:00, Fri 10:00–14:00, closed Sat; Oranienburger Strasse 28/30, U-Bahn: Oranienburger Tor, tel. 030/8802-8300 and press 1, www.cjudaicum.de).

Cheer things up 50 yards away with every local kid's favorite traditional candy shop—**Bonbonmacherei**—where you can see candy being made the old-fashioned way (at Oranienburger Strasse 32, in another example of a classic Berlin courtyard).

A block from the synagogue, walk 50 yards down Grosse Hamburger Strasse to a little park. This street was known for 200 years as the "street of tolerance" because the Jewish community donated land to Protestants so that they could build a church. Hitler turned it into the "street of death" *(Todes Strasse)*, bulldozing 12,000 graves of the city's oldest Jewish cemetery and turning a Jewish nursing home into a deportation center. Because of the small but growing radical Muslim element in Berlin, and a smattering of persistent neo-Nazis, several police officers and an Israeli secret agent keep watch over this park and the Jewish high school nearby.

▲Oranienburger Strasse—Berlin is developing so fast, it's impossible to predict what will be "in" from year to year. The area around Oranienburger Strasse is definitely trendy (but is being challenged by hip Friedrichshain, farther east, and Prenzlauer Berg, described later). While the area immediately around the synagogue is dull, 100 yards away things get colorful. The streets behind Grosse Hamburger Strasse flicker with atmospheric cafés, *Kneipen* (pubs), and art galleries. At night (from about 20:00), techno-prostitutes line Oranienburger Strasse. Prostitution is decriminalized here, but there's a big debate about taxation. Since they don't get unemployment insurance, why should they pay taxes?

Hackescher Markt—This area, in front of the S-Bahn station by the same name, is a great people scene day and night. The brick

Stolpersteine (Stumbling Stones)

As you wander through the Hackesche Höfe and Oranienburger Strasse neighborhoods—and throughout Germany—you might stumble over small brass plaques in the sidewalk called *Stolpersteine*. *Stolpern* means "to stumble," which is what you are meant to do. These plaques are placed in front of former homes of residents who were killed during World War II. The *Stolpersteine* serve not only to honor the victims, but also to stimulate thought and discussion on a daily basis (rather than only during visits to memorial sites) and to put an individual's name on the mass horror.

More than 7,500 of these plaques have been installed across Germany. They're made of brass so they stay polished as you walk over them, instead of fading into the sidewalk. On each plaque is the name of the person who lived in that spot, and how and where they died. While some Holocaust memorials formerly used neutral terminology like "perished," now they use words like "murdered"—part of the very honest way in which today's Germans are dealing with their country's past. Installation of a *Stolperstein* can be sponsored for €95 and has become popular in schools, where the students research the memorialized person's life as a class project.

trestle supporting the train track is another classic example of the city's Brandenburg Neo-Gothic brickwork. Most of the brick archways are now filled with hip shops, which have official—and newly trendy—addresses such as "S-Bahn Arch #9, Hackescher Markt." Within 100 yards of the S-Bahn station, you'll find Hackesche Höfe (see below), recommended Turkish and Bavarian restaurants, walking-tour and pub-crawl departure points, and tram #M1 to Prenzlauer Berg.

Hackesche Höfe (a block in front of the Hackescher Markt S-Bahn station) is a series of eight courtyards bunny-hopping through a wonderfully restored 1907 *Jugendstil* building. Berlin's apartments are organized like this—courtyard after courtyard leading off the main roads. This complex is full of trendy restaurants (including a good Turkish place, Hasir—see page 518), theaters, and cinema (playing movies in their original languages). This is a wonderful example of how to make huge city blocks livable. Two decades after the Cold War, this area has reached the final evolution of East Berlin's urban restoration—this is where Prenzlauer Berg is heading. (These courtyards also serve a useful lesson for visitors: Much of Berlin's charm hides off the street front.)

▲**Prenzlauer Berg**—Young, in-the-know locals agree that "Prenzl'berg" is one of Berlin's most colorful neighborhoods (roughly between Helmholtzplatz and Kollwitzplatz and along Kastanienallee, U-Bahn: Senefelderplatz and Eberswalder Strasse; or take the S-Bahn to Hackescher Markt and catch tram #M1 north). This part of the city was largely untouched during World War II, but its buildings slowly rotted away under the communists. Since the Wall fell, it's been overrun with laid-back hipsters, energetic young families, and clever entrepreneurs who are breathing life back into its classic old apartment blocks, deserted factories, and long-forgotten breweries. While it's no longer "up-and-coming," but on the road to gentrification, Prenzlauer Berg is a celebration of life and a joy to stroll through. The area feels strangely wholesome and family-friendly, as former ruffians with tattoos, piercings, and an appetite for the cutting-edge life are now responsible young parents. Though it's a few blocks farther out than the neighborhoods described earlier, it's a fun area to explore and have a meal (see page 519) or spend the night (see page 511).

Natural History Museum (Museum für Naturkunde)—This museum is worth a visit just to see the largest dinosaur skeleton ever assembled. While you're there, meet "Bobby" the stuffed ape (€4, Tue–Fri 9:30–17:00, Sat–Sun 10:00–18:00, closed Mon, last entry 30 min before closing, U-Bahn line 6 to Zinnowitzer Strasse, Invalidenstrasse 43, tel. 030/2093-8591, www.museum.hu-berlin.de).

Berlin Wall Documentation Center (Dokumentationszentrum Berliner Mauer)—The last surviving complete "Wall system" (with both sides of its Wall and its no-man's-land, or "death strip," all still intact) is now part of a sober little memorial and "Doku-Center." Though it's directed at German-speakers and far from other sights, it's handy enough to the S-Bahn that any Wall aficionado will find it worth a quick visit. The Documentation Center has a photo gallery and rooftop viewpoint (accessible by elevator), from which you can view the "Wall system." It's poignantly located where a church was destroyed to make way for the Wall; today, a memorial chapel has been built where the church once stood (free, April–Oct Tue–Sun 10:00–18:00, Nov–March until 17:00, closed Mon year-round, Bernauer Strasse 111, tel. 030/464-1030, www.berliner-mauer-dokumentationszentrum.de). Take the S-Bahn to Nordbahnhof and walk 200 yards along Bernauer Strasse, which is still lined with a long chunk of Wall.

Central Berlin

Tiergarten Park and Nearby

Berlin's "Central Park" stretches two miles from Bahnhof Zoo to the Brandenburg Gate.

Victory Column (Siegessäule)—The Tiergarten's centerpiece, the Victory Column, was built to commemorate the Prussian defeat of Denmark in 1864...then reinterpreted after the defeat of France in 1870. The pointy-helmeted Germans rubbed it in, decorating the tower with French cannons and paying for it all with francs received as war reparations. The three lower rings commemorate Bismarck's victories. I imagine the statues of Moltke and other German military greats—which lurk in the trees nearby—goose-stepping around the floodlit angel at night. Originally standing at the Reichstag, in 1938 the tower was moved to this position and given a 25-foot lengthening by Hitler's architect Albert Speer, in anticipation of the planned re-envisioning of Berlin as "Germania"—the capital of a world-wide Nazi empire. Streets leading to the circle are flanked by surviving Nazi guardhouses—built in the bold style that fascists loved. At the memorial's first level, notice how WWII bullets chipped the fine marble columns. More recently, the column has been the epicenter of the Love Parade (Berlin's city-wide techno-hedonist street party) and the backdrop for Barack Obama's summer 2008 visit to Germany as a presidential candidate. Climbing its 285 steps earns you a breathtaking Berlin-wide view and a close-up look at the gilded bronze statue of the goddess Victoria (go ahead, call her "the chick on a stick"—everybody here does). You might recognize Victoria from Wim Wenders' 1987 art-house classic *Wings of Desire,* or the *Stay (Faraway, So Close!)* video he directed for U2 (€2.20; April–Sept Mon–Thu 9:30–18:30, Fri–Sun 9:30–19:00; Oct–March daily 9:30–17:30; closes in the rain, WCs for paying guests only, no elevator, bus #100, tel. 030/8639-8560). From the tower, the grand Strasse des 17 Juni leads east to the Brandenburg Gate.

Flea Market—A colorful flea market with great antiques, more than 200 stalls, collector-savvy merchants, and fun German fast-food stands thrives weekends on Strasse des 17 Juni (Sat–Sun 6:00–16:00, right next to S-Bahn: Tiergarten).

German Resistance Memorial (Gedenkstätte Deutscher Widerstand)—This memorial and museum, just south of the Tiergarten, tells the story of several organized German resistance movements against Hitler. The Bendlerblock was a military headquarters where an ill-fated attempt to assassinate Hitler was plotted (the actual attempt occurred in Rastenburg, eastern Prussia; the event is dramatized in the 2009 Tom Cruise film *Valkyrie*). Claus Schenk Graf von Stauffenberg and several of his co-conspirators were shot here in the courtyard. While posted explanations are in German only and there are no real artifacts, the spirit that haunts the place is multilingual (free, Mon–Fri 9:00–18:00, Thu until 20:00, Sat–Sun 10:00–18:00, free and good English audioguide with passport, €3 printed English translation, no crowds, near

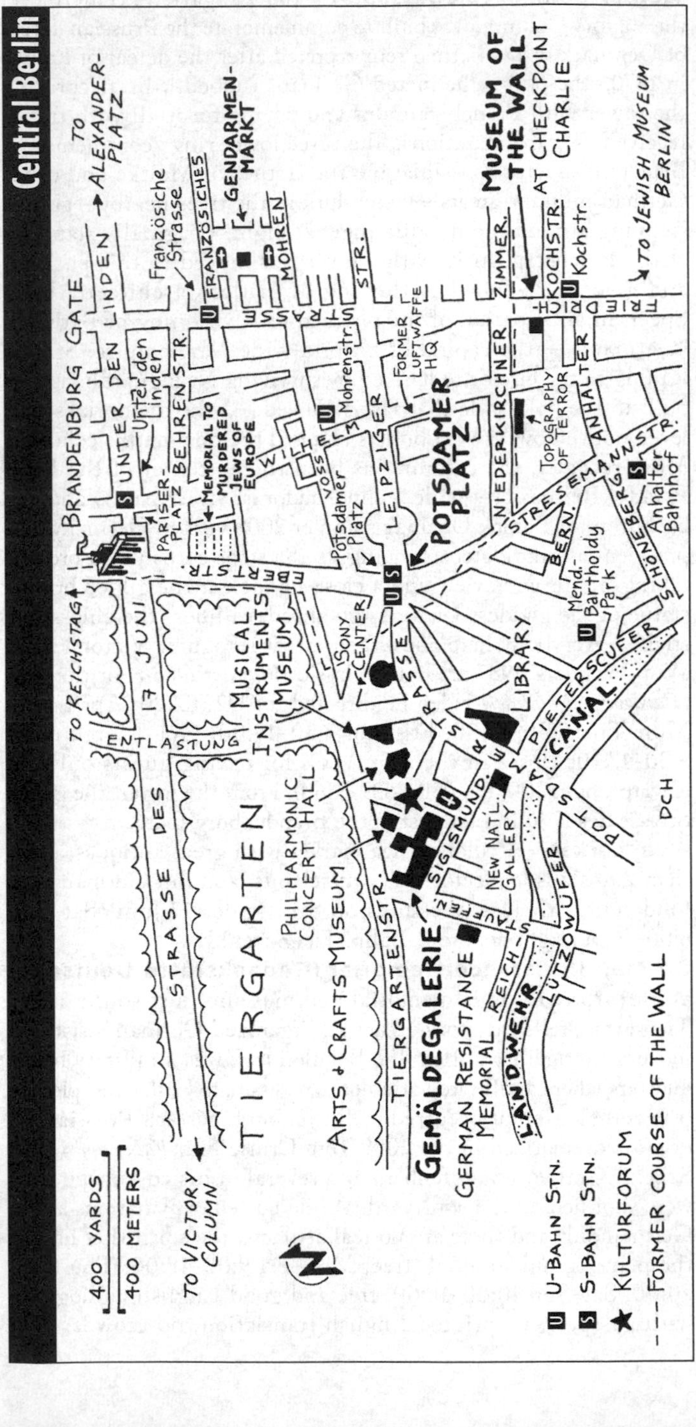
Central Berlin
TO REICHSTAG
BRANDENBURG GATE
TO ALEXANDER-PLATZ
UNTER DEN LINDEN
Unter den Linden
PARISER-PLATZ
BEHRENSTR.
EBERTSTR.
MEMORIAL TO MURDERED JEWS OF EUROPE
Französiche Strasse
FRANZÖSICHES
GENDARMEN-MARKT
MOHREN
STRASSE
Mohrenstr.
WILHELM
VOSS
Potsdamer Platz
LEIPZIGER
STR.
FORMER LUFTWAFFE HQ
POTSDAMER PLATZ
MUSEUM OF THE WALL AT CHECKPOINT CHARLIE
ZIMMER.
KOCHSTR.
Kochstr.
FRIEDRICH
TO JEWISH MUSEUM BERLIN
NIEDERKIRCHNER
TOPOGRAPHY OF TERROR
ANHALTER
STRESEMANNSTR.
SCHÖNEBERG.
Anhalter Bahnhof
BERN.
Mend.-Bartholdy Park
17 JUNI
ENTLASTUNG
STRASSE DES
TIERGARTEN
MUSICAL INSTRUMENTS MUSEUM
SONY CENTER
POTSDAMER STRASSE
LIBRARY
PIETERSCUFER
CANAL
PHILHARMONIC CONCERT HALL
ARTS & CRAFTS MUSEUM
TIERGARTENSTR.
SIGISMUND.
NEW NAT'L GALLERY
STAUFFEN.
REICHPIETSCHUFER
LÜTZOWUFER
LANDWEHR
GEMÄLDEGALERIE
GERMAN RESISTANCE MEMORIAL
POTSDAMER
DCH
400 YARDS
400 METERS
TO VICTORY COLUMN
N
U U-BAHN STN.
S S-BAHN STN.
★ KULTURFORUM
- - - FORMER COURSE OF THE WALL

Kulturforum at Stauffenbergstrasse 13, enter in courtyard, door on left, main exhibit is on third floor, bus #M29, tel. 030/2699-5000).

▲Potsdamer Platz

The "Times Square of Berlin," and possibly the busiest square in Europe before World War II, Potsdamer Platz was cut in two by the Wall and left a deserted no-man's-land for 40 years. Today, this immense commercial/residential/entertainment center, sitting on a futuristic transportation hub, is home to the European corporate headquarters of several big-league companies.

The new Potsdamer Platz was a vision begun in 1991, when it was announced that Berlin would resume its position as capital of Germany. Sony, Daimler-Chrysler, and other major corporations have turned the square once again into a center of Berlin. Like great Christian churches were built upon pagan holy grounds, Potsdamer Platz—with its corporate logos flying high and shiny above what was the Wall—trumpets the triumph of capitalism.

While Potsdamer Platz tries to give Berlin a common center, the city has always been—and remains—a collection of towns. Locals recognize 28 distinct neighborhoods that may have grown together but still maintain their historic orientation. While Munich has the single dominant Marienplatz, Berlin will always have Charlottenburg, Savignyplatz, Kreuzberg, Prenzlauer Berg, and so on. In general, Berliners prefer these characteristic neighborhoods to an official city center. They're unimpressed by the grandeur of Potsdamer Platz, and consider it simply a good place for movies, with overpriced, touristy restaurants.

While most of the complex just feels big (the arcade is like any huge, modern, American mall), the entrance to the complex and Sony Center are worth a visit, and German-film buffs will enjoy the Deutsche Kinemathek museum (described later).

For an overview of the new construction, and a scenic route to the Sony Center, start at the Bahnhof Potsdamer Platz (east end of Potsdamer Strasse, S- and U-Bahn: Potsdamer Platz, exit following *Leipziger Platz* signs to see the best view of skyscrapers as you emerge). Find the green hexagonal clock tower with the traffic lights on top. This is a replica of the first automatic traffic light in Europe, which once stood at the six-street intersection of Potsdamer Platz. On either side of Potsdamer Strasse, you'll see enormous cubical entrances to the new underground Potsdamer Platz train station. Near these entrances, notice the slanted glass cylinders sticking out of the ground. The mirrors on the tops of the tubes move with the sun to collect light and send it underground (saving piles of euros in energy costs). A line in the pavement indicates where the Berlin Wall once stood. Notice also the slabs of the Wall re-erected where the Wall once stood. Imagine when the first piece was cut out (see photo and history on nearby panel). These hang at the gate of Fort Capitalism...look up at the towering corporate headquarters: Market forces have won a clear victory. Now descend into one of the train station entrances and follow signs to *Sony Center.*

You'll come up the escalator into the **Sony Center** under a grand canopy (designed to evoke Mount Fuji). At night, multicolored floodlights play on the underside of this tent. Office workers and tourists eat here by the fountain, enjoying the parade of people. The modern Bavarian Lindenbräu beer hall—the Sony boss wanted a *Bräuhaus*—serves traditional food (€5–16, daily 11:00–24:00, big salads, three-foot-long taster boards of eight different beers, tel. 030/2575-1280). The adjacent Josty Bar is built around a surviving bit of a venerable hotel that was a meeting place for Berlin's rich and famous before the bombs (expensive, daily 10:00–24:00, tel. 030/2575-9702). CineStar is a rare cinema that plays mainstream movies in their original language (www.cinestar.de).

▲Deutsche Kinemathek Film and TV Museum—This exhibit is the most interesting place to visit in the Sony Center. Your admission ticket gets you into several floors of exhibits (third floor is permanent exhibits, first and fourth floor are temporary exhibits) made meaningful by the included (and essential) English audioguide. The film section takes you from the German film industry's beginnings, with emphasis on the Weimar Republic period in the 1920s, when Berlin rivaled Hollywood (*Metropolis* was a 1927 German production). Three rooms are dedicated to Marlene Dietrich, and another section features Nazi use of film as propaganda. The TV section tells the story of *das Booben Tube* from its infancy (when it was primarily used as a Nazi propaganda tool) to today. The 30-minute kaleidoscopic review—kind of a frantic fast-forward montage of greatest hits in German TV history—is great fun even if you don't understand a word of it (it plays all day long, with 10-minute breaks). Upstairs is a TV archive where you can dial through a wide range of new and classic German TV standards (€6, includes 90-min audioguide, Tue–Sun 10:00–18:00, Thu until 20:00, closed Mon, tel. 030/2474-9888). The Kino

Arsenal theater downstairs shows offbeat artistic films in their original language.

Across Potsdamer Strasse, you can ride what's billed as "the fastest elevator in Europe" to skyscraping rooftop views at the **Panaromapunkt.** You'll travel at nearly 30 feet per second to the top of the 300-foot-tall Kollhoff Tower. Its sheltered but open-air view deck provides a fun opportunity to survey Berlin's ongoing construction from above (€3.50, daily 11:00–20:00, last lift at 19:30, closed Mon in winter, in red-brick building at Potsdamer Platz 1, tel. 030/2529-4372, www.panoramapunkt.de).

Kulturforum

Just west of Potsdamer Platz, with several top museums and Berlin's concert hall—home of the world-famous Berlin Philharmonic orchestra—is the city's cultural heart (admission to all Kulturforum sights covered by a single €8 "Standortkarte Kulturforum" combo-ticket or the Museumspass; phone number for all museums: tel. 030/266-2951). Of its sprawling museums, only the Gemäldegalerie is a must (S- or U-Bahn to Potsdamer Platz, then walk along Potsdamer Platz; or from Bahnhof Zoo, take bus #200 to Philharmonie).

▲▲▲Gemäldegalerie—Germany's top collection of 13th-through 18th-century European paintings (more than 1,400 canvases) is beautifully displayed in a building that's a work of art in itself. Follow the excellent free audioguide. The North Wing starts with German paintings of the 13th to 16th centuries, including eight by Albrecht Dürer. Then come the Dutch and Flemish—Jan van Eyck, Pieter Brueghel, Peter Paul Rubens, Anthony van Dyck, Frans Hals, and Jan Vermeer. The wing finishes with German, English, and French 18th-century art, such as Thomas Gainsborough and Antoine Watteau. An octagonal hall at the end features an impressive stash of Rembrandts. The South Wing is saved for the Italians—Giotto, Botticelli, Titian, Raphael, and Caravaggio (free Thu after 18:00, open Tue–Sun 10:00–18:00, Thu until 22:00, closed Mon, clever little loaner stools, great salad bar in cafeteria upstairs, Matthäikirchplatz 4).

New National Gallery (Neue Nationalgalerie)—This features 20th-century art, with ever-changing special exhibits (Tue–Fri 10:00–18:00, Thu until 22:00, Sat–Sun 11:00–18:00, closed Mon, café downstairs, Potsdamer Strasse 50).

Museum of Arts and Crafts (Kunstgewerbemuseum)—Wander through a thousand years of applied arts—porcelain, fine

Jugendstil furniture, Art Deco, and reliquaries. There are no English descriptions and no crowds (Herbert-von-Karajan-Strasse 10).

▲Musical Instruments Museum (Musikinstrumenten Museum)—This impressive hall is filled with 600 exhibits from the 16th century to modern times. Wander among old keyboard instruments and funny-looking tubas. There's no English, aside from a €0.10 info sheet, but it's fascinating if you're into pianos (Tue–Fri 9:00–17:00, Thu until 22:00, Sat–Sun 10:00–17:00, closed Mon, low-profile white building east of the big, yellow Philharmonic Concert Hall, tel. 030/254-810).

Philharmonic Concert Hall—Poke into the lobby of Berlin's yellow Philharmonic building and see if there are tickets available during your stay (ticket office open Mon–Fri 15:00–18:00, Sat–Sun 11:00–14:00, must purchase tickets in person, box office tel. 030/2548-8132). You can often get inexpensive and legitimate tickets sold on the street before the performance. The interior is famous for its extraordinary acoustics. Even from the outside, this is a remarkable building, designed by a nautical engineer to look like a ship—notice how different it looks from each angle.

Western Berlin

Throughout the Cold War, Western travelers—and most West Berliners—got used to thinking of western Berlin's Kurfürstendamm boulevard as the heart of the city. But those days have gone the way of the Wall. With the huge changes the city has undergone since 1989, the real "city center" is now, once again, Berlin's historic center (the Mitte district, around Unter den Linden and Friedrichstrasse). While western Berlin has long had the best infrastructure to support your visit, and still works well as a home base, it's no longer the obvious base from which to explore Berlin. And after the new Hauptbahnhof essentially put the Bahnhof Zoo out of business in 2006, the area was left with an identity crisis. Now, almost 20 years after reunification, the west side is back and has fully embraced its historical role as a chic, classy suburb. There are a few interesting sights here, all within walking distance of Bahnhof Zoo and the Savignyplatz hotels.

For a detailed map of this area, see page 510.

▲Kurfürstendamm—Western Berlin's main drag, Kurfürstendamm boulevard (nicknamed "Ku'damm"), starts at Kaiser Wilhelm Memorial Church and does a commercial cancan for two miles. In the 1850s, when Berlin became a wealthy and important capital, her new rich chose Kurfürstendamm as their street. Bismarck made it Berlin's Champs-Elysées. In the 1920s, it became a chic and fashionable drag of cafés and boutiques. During the Third Reich, as home to an international community of diplomats and journalists, it enjoyed more freedom than the rest of

Berlin. Throughout the Cold War, economic subsidies from the West made sure that capitalism thrived on Ku'damm. And today, while much of the old charm has been hamburgerized, Ku'damm is still a fine place to enjoy elegant shops (around Fasanenstrasse), department stores, and people-watching.

▲Kaiser Wilhelm Memorial Church (Gedächtniskirche)—This church was originally dedicated to the first emperor of Germany. Reliefs and mosaics show great events in the life of Germany's favorite *Kaiser,* from his coronation in 1871 to his death in 1888. The church's bombed-out ruins have been left standing as a memorial to the destruction of Berlin in World War II (free, Mon–Sat 10:00–16:00, closed Sun, Breitscheidplatz, S-Bahn: Zoologischer Garten or U-Bahn: Wittenbergplatz, www.gedaechtniskirche.com).

Under a Neo-Romanesque mosaic ceiling, a small exhibit features interesting photos about the bombing and before-and-after models of the church. As you enter the church, turn immediately right to find a simple charcoal sketch of the Virgin Mary wrapped in a shawl. During the Battle of Stalingrad, German combat surgeon Kurt Reuber rendered the Virgin on the back of a stolen Soviet map to comfort the men in his care. On the right are the words "Light, Life, Love" from the gospel of John; on the left, "Christmas in the cauldron 1942"; and at the bottom, "Fortress Stalingrad." Though Reuber died in captivity a year later, his sketch had been flown out of Stalingrad on the last medical evacuation flight, and post-war Germany embraced it as a symbol of the wish for peace. Copies of the drawing, now known as the *Stalingrad Madonna,* hang in the Berlin Cathedral, in England's Coventry, and in Russia's Volgograd (formerly Stalingrad), as a sign of reconciliation between the nations.

After the war, some Berliners wanted to tear down the church and build it anew. Instead, it was decided to keep the ruin as a memorial, and stage a competition to design a modern add-on section. The winning selection—the short, modern building (1961) next to the church—offers a world of 11,000 little blue windows (free, daily 9:00–19:00). The blue glass was given to the church by the French as a reconciliation gift. For more information on both churches, pick up the English booklet (€2.60).

The lively square between the churches and the Europa Center (a once-impressive, shiny high-rise shopping center built as a showcase of Western capitalism during the Cold War) usually attracts street musicians.

The Story of Berlin—Filling most of what seems like a department store right on Ku'damm (at #207), this sprawling history exhibit is a business venture making money by telling the stormy 800-year story of Berlin in a creative way. While there are almost no real historic artifacts, the exhibit does a good job of cobbling together many dimensions of the life and tumultuous times of this great city. However, for similar information, the German History Museum on Unter den Linden is a far better use of your time and money (see page 479).

▲Käthe Kollwitz Museum—This local artist (1867–1945), who experienced much of Berlin's stormiest century, conveys some powerful and mostly sad feelings about motherhood, war, and suffering through the stark faces of her art. This small yet fine collection (the only one in town of Kollwitz's work) consists of three floors of charcoal drawings, topped by an attic with a handful of sculptures (€5, €1 pamphlet has necessary English explanations of a few major works, daily 11:00–18:00, a block off Ku'damm at Fasanenstrasse 24, U-Bahn: Uhlandstrasse, tel. 030/882-5210, www.kaethe-kollwitz.de).

▲Kaufhaus des Westens (KaDeWe)—The "Department Store of the West" celebrated its 100th birthday in 2007. With a staff of 2,100 to help you sort through its vast selection of 380,000 items, KaDeWe claims to be the biggest department store on the Continent. You can get everything from a haircut and train ticket (basement) to souvenirs (third floor). The theater and concert box office on the sixth floor charges an 18 percent booking fee, but they know all your options (cash only). The sixth floor is a world of gourmet taste treats. The biggest selection of deli and exotic food in Germany offers plenty of classy opportunities to sit down and eat. Ride the glass elevator to the seventh floor's glass-domed Winter Garden self-service cafeteria—fun but pricey (Mon–Fri 10:00–20:00, Sat 9:30–20:00, closed Sun, S-Bahn: Zoologischer Garten or U-Bahn: Wittenbergplatz, tel. 030/21210, www.kadewe.de). The Wittenbergplatz U-Bahn station (in front of KaDeWe) is a unique opportunity to see an old-time station. Enjoy its interior.

Berlin Zoo (Zoologischer Garten Berlin)—More than 1,400 different kinds of animals call Berlin's famous zoo home...or so the zookeepers like to think. The recent big hit here is Knut, a young polar bear who first made headlines for being born in captivity, but quickly became an international star after he was abandoned by his mother and raised by zookeepers. Germans also enjoy seeing the pandas at play (straight in from the entrance). I enjoy seeing the Germans at play (€11 for zoo, €12 for world-class aquarium, €18 for both, children half-price, daily mid-March–mid-Oct generally 9:00–19:00, mid-Oct–mid-March generally

9:00–17:00, aquarium closes 30 min earlier; feeding times—*Fütterungszeiten*—posted on map just inside entrance, the best feeding show is the sea lions—generally at 15:30; enter near Europa Center in front of Hotel Palace or opposite Bahnhof Zoo on Hardenbergplatz, Budapester Strasse 34, tel. 030/254-010, www.zoo-berlin.de).

Erotic Art Museum—This offers two floors of graphic art (especially East Asian), old-time sex-toy knickknacks, and a special exhibit on the queen of German pornography, the late Beate Uhse. This amazing woman, a former test pilot for the Third Reich and groundbreaking purveyor of condoms and sex ed in the 1950s, was the female Hugh Hefner of Germany and CEO of a huge chain of porn shops. She is famously credited with bringing sex out of the bedroom, and onto the kitchen table (€6, Mon–Sat 9:00–24:00, Sun 13:00–24:00, last entry at 23:00, hard-to-beat gift shop, at corner of Kantstrasse and Joachimstalerstrasse, a block from Bahnhof Zoo, tel. 030/8862-6613). If you just want to see sex, you'll see much more for half the price in a private video booth next door.

Charlottenburg Palace Area

The Charlottenburg district—with a cluster of museums across the street from a grand palace—is an easy side-trip from downtown. The palace isn't much to see, but if the surrounding museums appeal to you, consider making the trip. To get here, ride U-2 to Sophie-Charlotte Platz and walk 10 minutes up the tree-lined boulevard Schlossstrasse (following signs to *Schloss*), or—much faster—catch bus #M45 (direction Spandau) direct from Bahnhof Zoo.

Eating near Charlottenburg Palace: For a Charlottenburg lunch, the **Bräuhaus Lemke** is a comfortable brewpub restaurant with a copper and woody atmosphere, good local microbeers (*dunkles* means "dark," *helles* is "light"), and traditional German grub (€8–15 meals, daily 9:00–24:00, fun for groups, across from palace at Luisenplatz 1, tel. 030/3087-8979). Or consider lunching like the Russians, who have been part of Charlottenburg ever since Frederick the Great invited them in the 18th century. Small **Samovar** serves traditional Russian specialties in a comfortable, intimate setting (€6–12 meals, Russian tea-€3.40, daily 11:00–22:00, just past Bräuhaus Lemke at Luisenplatz 3, tel. 030/341-4154).

▲Charlottenburg Palace (Schloss Charlottenburg)—If you've seen the great palaces of Europe, this Baroque palace, also known as the Altes Schloss, comes in at about number 10 (behind Potsdam, too). It's the largest former residence of the royal Hohenzollern family in Berlin, and contains the largest collection of 17th-century French fresco painting outside of France (€10,

Charlottenburg Palace Area

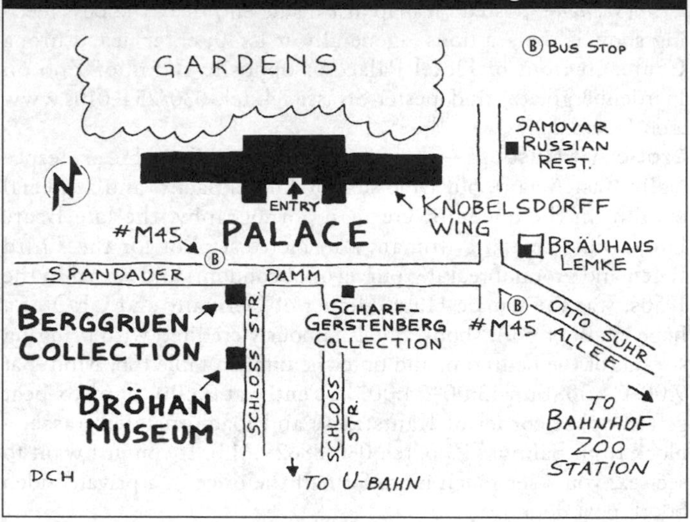

includes audioguide, Tue–Sun 10:00–18:00, closed Mon, last entry at 17:30, tel. 030/320-911, www.spsg.de).

The Neue Flügel (a.k.a. the Knobelsdorff Wing) features a few royal apartments. Go upstairs and take a substantial hike through restored-since-the-war, gold-crusted white rooms (€6, more during special exhibitions, free English audioguide, Wed–Mon 10:00–17:00, closed Tue, last entry at 16:30, when facing the palace walk toward the right wing, tel. 030/3209-1442).

▲Berggruen Collection: Picasso and His Time—This tidy little museum is a pleasant surprise. Climb three floors through a fun and substantial collection of Picassos. Along the way, you'll see plenty of notable works by Henri Matisse. Enjoy a great chance to meet Paul Klee (€6, covered by Museumspass, free Thu after 14:00, open Tue–Sun 10:00–18:00, closed Mon, Schlossstrasse 1, tel. 030/326-9580).

▲Bröhan Museum—Wander through a dozen beautifully furnished *Jugendstil* and Art Deco living rooms, a curvy organic world of lamps, glass, silver, and posters. English descriptions are posted on the wall of each room on the main floor. While you're there, look for the fine collection of Impressionist paintings by Karl Hagemeister (€5–6 depending on special exhibits, covered by Museumspass excluding special exhibits, Tue–Sun 10:00–18:00, closed Mon, Schlossstrasse 1A, tel. 030/3269-0600, www.broehan-museum.de).

▲Scharf-Gersternberg Collection—Opened in 2008, this small museum houses a collection of more than 250 works of Surrealist and pre-Surrealist art. The *Surreal Worlds* exhibit shows just how freaky and weird the world looked to artists like Salvador Dalí, Paul Klee, and Francisco de Goya. Be sure to check out Dalí's film of his birth from an egg on the beach (€8, covered by Museumspass, free Thu after 14:00, open Tue–Sun 10:00–18:00, closed Mon, Schlossstrasse 70, tel. 030/3435-7315).

▲Near Berlin: Potsdam's Palaces

Featuring a lush park strewn with the escapist whimsies of Frederick the Great, the sleepy town of Potsdam has long been Berlin's holiday retreat. Frederick's super-Rococo Sanssouci Palace is one of Germany's most dazzling. His equally extravagant New Palace, built to disprove rumors that Prussia was running out of money after the costly Seven Years' War, is on the other side of the park (it's a 30-minute walk between palaces). Potsdam's much-promoted Wannsee boat rides are exceedingly dull.

Getting to Potsdam: Potsdam is easy to reach from Berlin (17 min on direct Regional Express/RE trains from Hauptbahnhof, Bahnhof Zoo, or Friedrichstrasse every 30 min; round-trip covered by €6.30 transit day pass with zones A, B, and C; any train to Brandenburg or Magdeburg stops in Potsdam). Once in Potsdam, bus #695 runs from the Potsdam train station to the palaces, and is invariably packed (3/hr, 20 min, leaves from lane 4; April–Oct bus #X15 runs the same route on weekends). A less-crowded option is to take tram #91 to Luisenplatz (3/hr, 11 min, leaves from lane 1), then walk 20 minutes through the park and enjoy a classic view of Sanssouci Palace. The tram is also the better option if you're taking the Potsdam TI's tour (see "Tours at Potsdam," below). Use the same bus #695 to shuttle between the sights in the park.

Orientation and Information: Unless you're planning on spending time exploring the town of Potsdam itself, skip the Potsdam **TI** (April–Oct Mon–Fri 9:30–18:00, Sat–Sun 9:30–16:00; Nov–March Mon–Fri 10:00–18:00, Sat–Sun 9:30–14:00; tel. 0331/275-580, Brandenburger Strasse 3, www.potsdamtourismus.de) and head straight to the **palace information office** (across the street from windmill near Sanssouci entrance, helpful English-speaking staff, daily April–Oct 8:30–17:00, Nov–March 9:00–16:00, tel. 0331/969-4202, www.spsg.de; clean WC in same building, €0.30). To supplement the English tour handouts, consider picking up the gray "official guide" booklets (available for all of the sights, €3 each at palace information office and gift shop).

Combo-Ticket: If you plan on seeing several of the buildings, save money by getting a **Premium Day Ticket** (€15, available only at the Sanssouci ticket office—the regular day ticket does not include Sanssouci).

Tours at Potsdam: The Potsdam TI offers a bus tour of Potsdam sights, plus the interior of Sanssouci Palace. This normally

Greater Berlin

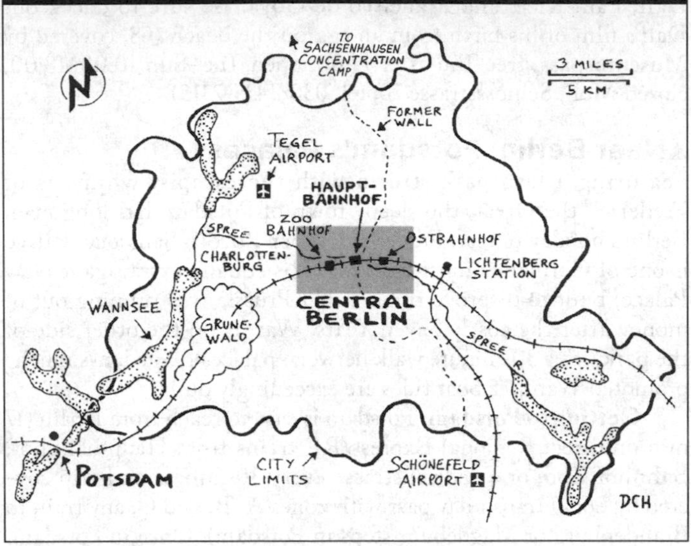

wouldn't be worth the time...except that it's the only way to get into Sanssouci with a live, English-speaking guide (often with some German, too; €26 covers tour, palace, and park; Sun–Tue at 11:00, no tours Mon, 3.5 hrs, departs from TI at Luisenplatz, reserve by phone, in summer reserve at least 2 days in advance, tel. 0331/275-5850).

Tours from Berlin: Original Berlin Walks, Brewer's Tours, and New Berlin Tours all offer inexpensive all-day tours from Berlin through Potsdam (small groups, English-language only, no reservations necessary, admissions and public transportation not included, doesn't actually go into Sanssouci Palace). These tours are the best way to get the most out of Potsdam, and can help you avoid a lot of stress. **Original Berlin Walks'** tour leaves from the taxi stand outside Berlin's Bahnhof Zoo at 9:50 every Sunday, April through October (also on Thu July–Aug; €15, meet at taxi stand at Bahnhof Zoo, tel. 030/301-9194). The guide takes you to Cecilienhof Palace (site of postwar Potsdam conference attended by Churchill, Stalin, and Truman), through pleasant green landscapes to the historic heart of Potsdam for lunch, and finishes outside Sanssouci Palace. The **Brewer's** tour is similar (€12, Wed and Sun, May–Oct only, leaves at 9:20 from Bandy Brooks ice cream shop at Friedrichstrasse U- and S-Bahn station, call to confirm and hold a spot, tel. 030/2248-7435, mobile 0177-388-1537, www.brewersberlintours.com). **New Berlin**'s entertaining tour leaves daily at 11:00 from their starting point in front of Starbucks on Pariser Platz (€14, tel. 030/5105-0030, www.newberlintours.com).

Sanssouci Palace—Visits to this palace include an interesting audioguide. *Sans souci* means "without a care," but for the most stress-free visit, arrive early: In the summer, if you arrive by 9:00, you'll get right in; if you arrive after 10:00, plan on a wait (€6 with audioguide, €12 with live guide, April–Oct Tue–Sun 9:00–17:00, Nov–March Tue–Sun 9:00–16:00, closed Mon year-round).

New Palace (Neues Palais)—This palace's apartments are underwhelming and frustrating for non-German speakers (€6, includes audioguide, April–Oct Sat–Thu 9:00–17:00, Nov–March Sat–Thu 9:00–16:00, closed Fri year-round). If you also want to see the king's apartments, you must take a required 45-minute tour in German (included in entrance fee, offered May–Oct daily at 10:00, 11:00, 14:00, and 16:00). Off-season (Nov–April), the king's apartments are closed, and you can visit the rest of the New Palace only on a German tour (€5); it can take up to an hour for enough people to gather.

Bornstedt Royal Estate (Krongut Bornstedt)—Designed to look like an Italian village, this warehouse-like complex once provided the royal palaces with food and other supplies. Today the estate houses the Bornstedt Buffalo brewery and distillery, which delivers fine brews and schnapps, as it has since 1689. The restaurant is a good place for lunch, serving local specialties (€6–12 plates). The grounds also house a wood-fired bakery with fresh bread and pastries. You can watch hat-makers, candle-makers, coopers, potters, and glassmakers produce (and sell) their wares using traditional techniques (free except during special events, daily 10:00–19:00, restaurant serves until 21:30, from Sanssouci walk toward the windmill and follow the street An der Orangerie about 500 yards to Ribbeckstrasse 6, tel. 0180-5766-488, www.krongut-bornstedt.de).

Cecilienhof—The former residence of Crown Prince William and the site of the 1945 Potsdam Conference is a short bus ride away (€5, April–Oct Tue–Sun 9:00–17:00, Nov–March Tue–Sun 9:00–16:00, closed Mon year-round; take bus #695 from Sanssouci Palace to Reiterweg, then transfer to bus #692; tel. 0331/969-4224). If you're hungry at Cecilienhof, try the brewery called **Meierei** ("Creamery"). Its nice beer garden offers spectacular views of the lake, solid German food, and great homemade beer. When you walk down the hill into the restaurant, note the big open field to the right—it used to be the Berlin Wall (€6-15 meals, daily 11:00–22:00, follow *Meierei* signs to Im Neuen Garten 10, tel. 0331/704-3211).

NIGHTLIFE

Berlin is a happening place for nightlife—whether it's nightclubs, pubs, jazz music, cabaret, hokey-but-fun German variety shows, theater, or concerts.

Sources of Entertainment Info: *Berlin Programm* lists a non-stop parade of concerts, plays, exhibits, and cultural events (€2, in German, www.berlin-programm.de); *Exberliner Magazine* (€2, www.exberliner.com) and the TI-produced *Berlin To Go* (€1) have less information, but are in English (all sold at kiosks and TIs). For the young and determined sophisticate, *Zitty* and *Tip* are the top guides to alternative culture (in German, sold at kiosks). Also pick up the free schedules *Flyer* and *030* in bars and clubs. The free magazines by walking-tour companies such as New Berlin Tours (www.newberlintours.com) and Insider Tour (www.insidertour.com) are also good, providing the English-language inside scoop on nightlife, cheap eats, and pub crawls (available all over town).

Visit KaDeWe's ticket office for your music and theater options (sixth floor, 18 percent fee but access to all tickets; see page 500). Ask about "competitive improvisation" and variety shows.

Western Berlin Jazz—To enjoy live music near my recommended Savignyplatz hotels in western Berlin, consider **A Trane Jazz Club** (all jazz, great stage and intimate seating, €7–18 cover depending on act, opens at 21:00, live music nightly 22:00–2:00 in the morning, Bleibtreustrasse 1, tel. 030/313-2550) and **Quasimodo Live** (mix of jazz, rock, and blues, €5–12 cover, Tue–Sat from 22:00, closed Sun–Mon, Kantstrasse 12A, under Delphi Cinema, tel. 030/312-8086, www.quasimodo.de).

Berliner Rock and Roll—Berlin has a vibrant rock and pop scene, with popular venues at the Spandau Citadel and at the outdoor Waldbühne ("Woods Stage"). Check out what's playing on posters in the U-Bahn, in *Zitty*, or at any ticket agency. Great Berlin bands include Wir Sind Helden, The Beatsteaks, Jennifer Rostock, and the funky ska band Seeed.

Cabaret—Bar Jeder Vernunft offers modern-day cabaret a short walk from the recommended hotels in western Berlin. This variety show—under a classic old tent perched atop a modern parking lot—is a hit with German speakers, but can still be worthwhile for those who don't speak the language (as some of the music shows are in a sort of "Denglish"). Even some Americans perform here periodically. Tickets are generally about €20, and shows change regularly (performances start Mon–Sat at 20:30, Sun at 20:00, Wed is non-smoking, seating can be a bit cramped, south of Ku'damm at Schaperstrasse 24, tel. 030/883-1582, www.bar-jeder-vernunft.de).

German Variety Show—To spend an evening enjoying Europe's largest revue theater, consider Revue Berlin at the Friedrichstadt Palast. This super-kitschy German Moulin Rouge–type show basically depicts the history of Berlin, and is choreographed in a funny and musical way that's popular with the Lawrence Welk–type German crowd (€17–61, Tue–Sat 20:00, Sat–Sun also at 16:00, no shows Mon, U-Bahn: Oranienburger Tor, tel. 030/2326-2326, www.friedrichstadtpalast.de).

Nightclubs and Pubs—Oranienburger Strasse's trendy scene (page 490) is being eclipsed by the action at Friedrichshain (farther east). To the north, you'll find the hip Prenzlauer Berg neighborhood, packed with everything from smoky pubs to small art bars and dance clubs (best scene is around Helmholtsplatz, U-Bahn: Eberswalder Strasse; see page 491).

Dancing—Cut a rug at **Clärchens Ballhaus,** an old ballroom that's been a Berlin institution since 1913. At some point everyone in Berlin comes through here, as the dance hall attracts an eclectic Berlin-in-a-nutshell crowd of grannies, elegant women in evening dresses, yuppies, scenesters, and hippies. The music (swing, waltz, tango, or cha-cha) changes every day, with live music on Friday and Saturday (daily from 10:00 until the last person goes home, in the heart of the Auguststrasse gallery district at Auguststrasse 24, S-Bahn: Oranienburger Strasse, tel. 030/282-9295, www.ballhaus.de). Dancing lessons are also available (€8, Mon–Tue and Thu at 19:00, 90 min). The restaurant serves decent food and good pizzas.

Art Galleries—Berlin, a magnet for new artists, is a great city for gallery visits. Galleries—many of which stay open late—welcome visitors who are "just looking." The most famous gallery district is in eastern Berlin's Mitte neighborhood, along **Auguststrasse** (branches off from Oranienburger Strasse at the Tacheles building). Check out the Berlin outpost of the edgy-yet-accessible art of the New Leipzig movement at **Galerie Eigen+Art** (Tue–Sat 11:00–18:00, closed Sun–Mon, Auguststrasse 26, tel. 030/280-6605, www.eigen-art.com). The other gallery area is in western Berlin, along **Fasanenstrasse**.

Pub Crawls—Insider Tours and New Berlin Tours each offer €12 pub crawls (or, some would say, "pub brawls"). Insider Tours leaves at 20:30 from Hackescher Markt; New Berlin Tours leaves at 21:00 from the Oranienburger Strasse S-Bahn station. Those who show up early are treated to a warm-up keg. After the recent (unrelated) binge-drinking death of a German teenager, the tours enforce an 18-year-old minimum. A new marketing slogan for one organization: "Our mission: To show you Berlin's great nightlife...not to hospitalize you." Both tours generally visit four bars and two clubs, and provide a great way to get drunk with new

English-speaking friends from around the world while getting a peek at Berlin's bar scene...or at least how its bars look when invaded by 50 loud tourists.

SLEEPING

When in Berlin, I sleep in the former West, on or near Savignyplatz. While Bahnhof Zoo and Ku'damm are no longer the center of Berlin, the trains, TI, and walking tours are all still handy to the Zoo. And the streets around the tree-lined Savignyplatz (a 10-min walk behind the station) have a neighborhood charm. While towering new hotels are being built in the new center, simple, small, friendly, good-value places abound here. My listings are generally located a couple of flights up in big, run-down buildings. Inside, they're clean, quiet, and spacious enough so that their well-worn character is actually charming. Rooms in back are on quiet courtyards.

For those interested in staying in a livelier, more colorful district, I've also listed some suggestions in eastern Berlin's youthful and increasingly popular Prenzlauer Berg neighborhood.

Berlin is packed and hotel prices go up on holidays, including Green Week in mid-January, Easter weekend, the first weekend in May, Ascension weekend in May, German Unity Day (Oct 3), Christmas, and New Year's. Keep in mind that many hotels have limited staff after 20:00, so if you're planning to arrive after that, let the hotel know in advance.

In Western Berlin: Near Savignyplatz and Bahnhof Zoo

These hotels and pensions are a 5- to 15-minute walk from Bahnhof Zoo and Savignyplatz (with S- and U-Bahn stations). Asking for a quieter room in back gets you away from any street noise. The area has an artsy charm going back to the cabaret days in the 1920s, when it was the center of Berlin's gay scene. Of the accommodations listed in this area, Pension Peters offers the best value for budget travelers.

$$$ Hotel Askanischerhof is the oldest B&B in Berlin, posh as can be with 16 sprawling, antique-furnished living rooms you can call home. Photos on the walls brag of famous movie-star guests. Frau Glinicke offers Old World service and classic Berlin atmosphere (Sb-€105, Db-€125, extra bed-€25, elevator, free parking, Ku'damm 53, tel. 030/881-8033, fax 030/881-7206, www.askanischer-hof.de, info@askanischer-hof.de).

$$$ Hecker's Hotel is an ultra-modern, four-star business hotel with 69 rooms and all the sterile Euro-comforts (Sb-€125, Db-€150, all rooms €200 during conferences but generally only

Sleep Code

(€1 = about $1.50, country code: 49, area code: 030)
S = Single, **D** = Double/Twin, **T** = Triple, **Q** = Quad, **b** = bathroom, **s** = shower only. Unless otherwise noted, credit cards are accepted, English is spoken, and breakfast is included.

To help you sort easily through these listings, I've divided the rooms into three categories, based on the price for a standard double room with bath:

$$$ Higher Priced—Most rooms €125 or more.
$$ Moderately Priced—Most rooms between €85-125.
$ Lower Priced—Most rooms €85 or less.

€100 July–Aug, breakfast-€15, non-smoking rooms, elevator, parking-€9–12/day, between Savignyplatz and Ku'damm at Grolmanstrasse 35, tel. 030/88900, fax 030/889-0260, www.heckers-hotel.com, info@heckers-hotel.com).

$$$ Hotel Astoria is a friendly, three star, business-class hotel with 32 comfortably furnished rooms and affordable summer and weekend rates (high-season Db-€108–160; prices drop to Db-€70–94 during low season of July–Aug and Nov–Feb—check their website for deals; breakfast-€10 extra, non-smoking floors, elevator, Internet access, parking-€5/day, around corner from Bahnhof Zoo at Fasanenstrasse 2, tel. 030/312-4067, fax 030/312-5027, www.hotelastoria.de, info@hotelastoria.de).

$$ Hotel Carmer 16, with 30 bright and airy (if a bit dated) rooms, is both business-like and homey, and has an inviting lounge and charming balconies (Db-€93–160, ask for Rick Steves discount, extra person-€20, some rooms have balconies, elevator and a few stairs, Carmerstrasse 16, tel. 030/3110-0500, fax 030/3110-0510, www.hotel-carmer16.de, info@hotel-carmer16.de).

$$ Hotel-Pension Funk, the former home of a 1920s silent-movie star, is delightfully quirky. Kind manager Herr Michael Pfundt offers 14 elegant old rooms with rich Art Nouveau furnishings (S-€34–57, Ss-€41–75, Sb-€52–82, D-€62–82, Ds-€93, Db-€98–105, extra person-€23, cash preferred, a long block south of Ku'damm at Fasanenstrasse 69, tel. 030/882-7193, fax 030/883-3329, www.hotel-pensionfunk.de, berlin@hotel-pensionfunk.de).

$$ Hotel Bogota is a once-elegant old slumbermill renting 115 rooms in a sprawling old maze of a building that used to house the Nazi Chamber of Culture. Today, pieces of the owner's modern-art collection lurk around every corner (S-€44, Ss-€57, Sb-€72, D-€69, Ds-€77, Db-€98, extra bed-€22, children under 12 free, elevator, 10-min walk from Savignyplatz at Schlüterstrasse

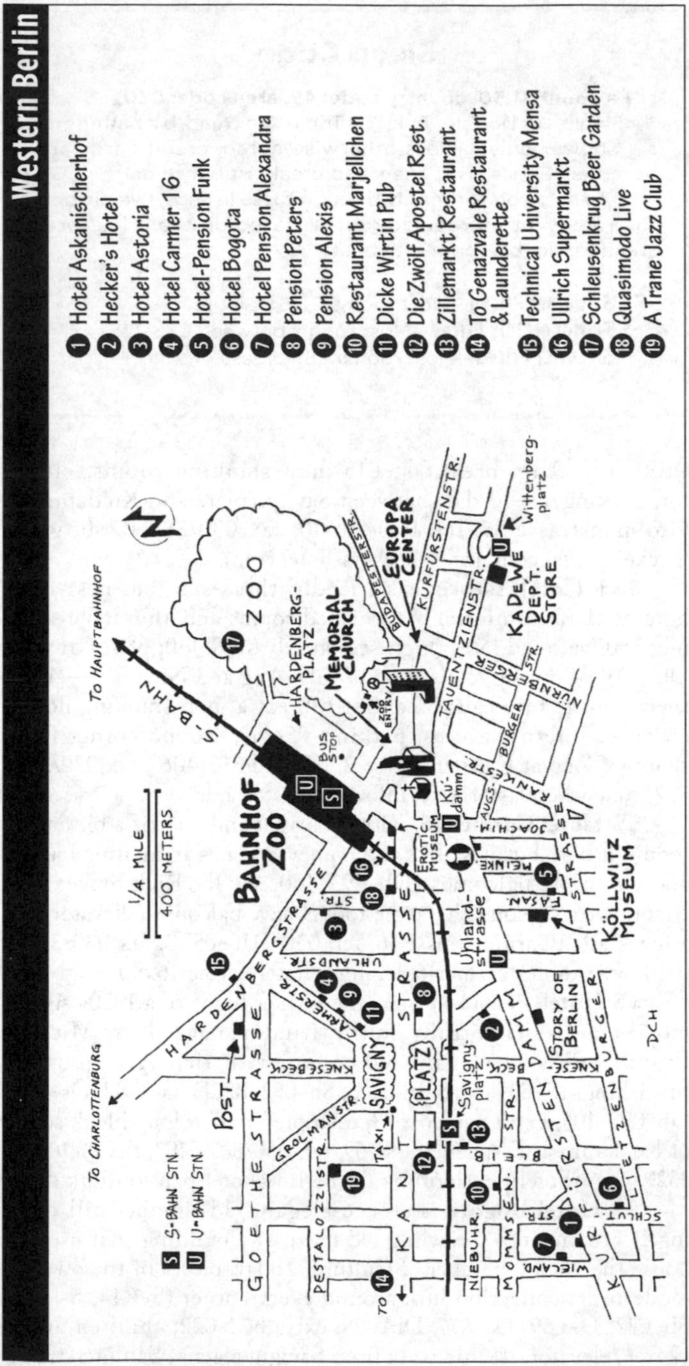
Western Berlin
1 Hotel Askanischerhof
2 Hecker's Hotel
3 Hotel Astoria
4 Hotel Carmer 16
5 Hotel-Pension Funk
6 Hotel Bogota
7 Hotel Pension Alexandra
8 Pension Peters
9 Pension Alexis
10 Restaurant Marjellchen
11 Dicke Wirtin Pub
12 Die Zwölf Apostel Rest.
13 Zillemarkt Restaurant
14 To Genazvale Restaurant & Launderette
15 Technical University Mensa
16 Ullrich Supermarkt
17 Schleusenkrug Beer Garden
18 Quasimodo Live
19 A Trane Jazz Club
S S-BAHN STN.
U U-BAHN STN.
1/4 MILE
400 METERS
TO CHARLOTTENBURG
TO HAUPTBAHNHOF
S-BAHN
ZOO
BAHNHOF ZOO
HARDENBERGSTRASSE
HARDENBERG-PLATZ
MEMORIAL CHURCH
EUROPA CENTER
BUDAPESTERSTR.
KURFÜRSTENSTR.
TAUENTZIENSTR.
KADEWE DEPT. STORE
Wittenberg-platz
NÜRNBERGER STR.
BURGER
RANKESTR.
AUGS.
JOACHIM
MEINEKE
FASAN.
STRASSE
KÖLLWITZ MUSEUM
EROTIC MUSEUM
Ku'damm
ZOO ENTRY
BUS STOP
Uhlandstrasse
UHLANDSTR.
CARMERSTR.
KNESEBECK
SAVIGNY PLATZ
Savignyplatz
GROLMANSTR.
POST
GOETHESTRASSE
PESTALOZZISTR.
KANTSTRASSE
TAXI
TO 14
NIEBUHR.
MOMMSEN STR.
BLEIBTREU STR.
KURFÜRSTENDAMM
STORY OF BERLIN
KNESEBECK
WIELAND.
SCHLÜT.
LIETZENBURGER
DCH

BERLIN

45, tel. 030/881-5001, fax 030/883-5887, www.hotelbogota.de, hotel-bogota@t-online.de).

$$ Hotel Pension Alexandra has 11 pleasant rooms on a tree-lined street between Savignyplatz and Ku'damm. Expect the usual high ceilings and marble entryway found in these turn-of-the-century buildings, but with added touches—most rooms and the elegant breakfast room are decorated with original antique furniture (Ss-€69, Sb-€89, Ds-€95, Db-€105–120, lower prices off-season, extra bed-€35, Wielandstrasse 32, tel. 030/881-2107, fax 030/885-77818, www.hotelalexandra.de, info@hotelalexandra.de, Frau Kuhn and Mariane).

$ Pension Peters, run by a German–Swedish couple, is sunny and central, with a cheery breakfast room. Decorated sleek Scandinavian, with each of its 37 rooms renovated, it's a winner (S-€36, Ss-€47, Sb-€55, D-€51, Ds-€68, Db-€75–78, extra bed-€10, these special prices offered only with this book in 2009—mention when you reserve, up to 2 kids under 13 free with 2 paying adults, family room, cash preferred, Internet access, 10 yards off Savignyplatz at Kantstrasse 146, tel. 030/3150-3944, fax 030/312-3519, www.pension-peters-berlin.de, info@pension-peters-berlin.de, Annika and Christoph). The same family also rents apartments in Prenzlauer Berg (ideal for small groups and longer stays; see "Steiner Apartments," page 514).

$ Pension Alexis is a classic Old World four-room pension in a stately 19th-century apartment run by Frau and Herr Schwarzer (who speak just enough English). The shower and toilet facilities are old and cramped, but this, more than any other Berlin listing, has you feeling at home with a faraway grandmother (S-€43, D-€67, T-€97, Q-€128, 2-night minimum, cash only, big rooms, Carmerstrasse 15, tel. 030/312-5144).

In Eastern Berlin: Prenzlauer Berg

If you want to sleep in the former East Berlin, set your sights on the youthful, colorful, and fun Prenzlauer Berg district (or "Prenzl'berg" for short). After decades of neglect, this corner of the East has quickly come back to life. Gentrification has brought Prenzlauer Berg great hotels, tasty ethnic and German eateries (see page 519), and a happening nightlife scene. Think of all the graffiti as just some people's way of saying they care. The huge and impersonal concrete buildings are now enlivened with a street fair of fun little shops and eateries. Prenzlauer Berg is about a mile and a half north of Alexanderplatz, roughly between Kollwitzplatz and Helmholtzplatz, and to the west, along Kastanienallee (known affectionately as "Casting Alley" for its extra share of beautiful people). The closest U-Bahn stops are Senefelderplatz at the south end of the neighborhood and Eberswalder Strasse at the north end.

Prenzlauer Berg Neighborhood

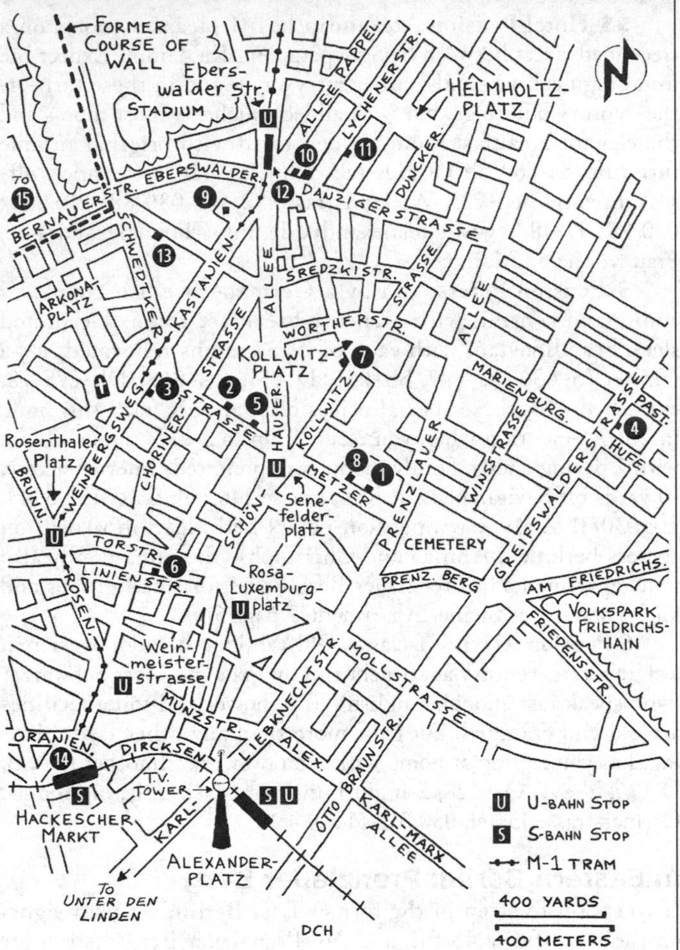

1. Myer's Hotel
2. Hotel Jurine
3. Hotel Kastanienhof
4. Hotel Transit Loft
5. EastSeven Hostel
6. Steiner Apartments
7. Gugelhof Restaurant
8. Metzer Eck
9. Prater Biergarten
10. Zum Schusterjungen Speisegaststätte & Launderette
11. La Bodeguita del Medio Cuban Bar Restaurant
12. Knoppke's Imbiss
13. Kauf Dich Glücklich
14. Walking Tour & Pub Crawl Departure Point
15. To Berlin Wall Documentation Center, Nordbahnhof S-Bahn & Natural History Museum

Or, for less walking, take the S-Bahn to Hackescher Markt, then catch tram #M1 north.

$$$ Myer's Hotel is a boutique-hotel splurge renting 52 simple, small, but elegant rooms. The gorgeous public spaces include a patio and garden. Details done right and impeccable service set this place apart. This peaceful hub—off a quiet courtyard and tree-lined street, just a five-minute walk from Kollwitzplatz or the nearest U-Bahn stop (Senefelderplatz)—makes it hard to believe you're in a capital city (Sb-€79–139, Db-€99–189, price depends on size of room, Metzer Strasse 26, tel. 030/440-140, fax 030/4401-4104, www.myershotel.de, info@myershotel.de).

$$ Hotel Jurine (yoo-REEN) is a pleasant 53-room business-style hotel whose friendly staff aims to please. Enjoy the breakfast buffet surrounded by modern art, or relax in the lush backyard (Sb-€75, Db-€105, Tb-€135, extra bed-€37, prices can zoom up during conventions, check website for discounts in July–Aug, breakfast-€14, parking garage-€13/day, Schwedter Strasse 15, 10-min walk to U-Bahn: Senefelderplatz, tel. 030/443-2990, fax 030/4432-9999, www.hotel-jurine.de, mail@hotel-jurine.de).

$$ Hotel Kastanienhof is a basic, less-classy hotel offering 35 sleepable but slightly overpriced rooms (Sb-€79, Db-€105, reception closed 22:00–6:30, 40 yards from the M1 tram stop at Kastanienallee 65, tel. 030/443-050, fax 030/4430-5111, www.kastanienhof.biz, info@kastanienhof.biz).

$ Hotel Transit Loft is technically a hostel, but feels more like an upscale budget hotel. Located in a refurbished factory, it offers clean, bright, modern, new-feeling, mostly blue rooms with an industrial touch. The reception—staffed by friendly, hip Berliners—is open 24 hours, with a bar serving drinks all night long (4- to 6-bed dorms-€21/bed, Sb-€62, Db-€72, Tb-€96, includes sheets and breakfast, no age limit, cheap Internet access, fully wheelchair-accessible, Emmanuelkirchstrasse 14A, U-Bahn: Alexanderplatz then tram M4 to Hufelandstrasse and walk 50 yards, tel. 030/4849-3773, fax 030/4405-1074, www.transit-loft.de, loft@hotel-transit.de).

$ EastSeven Hostel rents the best cheap beds in Prenzlauer Berg. It's sleek and modern, with all the hostel services and more: 24-hour reception, inviting lounge, fully equipped guests' kitchen, lockers, garden, and bike rental. Children are welcome. While most hostels—especially in Prenzlauer Berg—are annoyingly youthful to people over 30, easygoing people of any age are comfortable here (S-€37, D-€50, T-€63, €17 for a bed in a 4-, 5-, or 6-bed dorm, bathrooms always down the hall, one-time €3 fee for sheets, free Internet access and Wi-Fi, laundry-€5, 100 yards from U-Bahn: Senefelderplatz at Schwedter Strasse 7, tel. 030/9362-2240, www.eastseven.de, info@eastseven.de).

$ Steiner Apartments, run by Pension Peters, are nine well-located, modern, and comfortable apartments near Hackescher Markt (Sb-€55, Db-€70, Tb-€80, Qb-€90, cash only, up to 2 children under 13 sleep free with 2 paying adults, fully equipped as if you live there, Linienstrasse 60—enter on Gormannstrasse, 350 yards from S-Bahn: Hackescher Markt, even closer to U-Bahn: Rosenthaler Platz, www.pension-peters-berlin.de, info@pension-peters-berlin.de; to book, contact Pension Peters, described on page 511).

Hostels

Berlin is known among budget travelers for its fun, hip hostels. Here are some good bets. The first one is south of Bahnhof Zoo, the next two are in Prenzlauer Berg, and the last is in Friedrichshain.

$ Studentenhotel Meininger 10 (€14/bed in 8-bed dorms, D-€46, includes sheets, no curfew, elevator, free parking, near City Hall on JFK Platz, Meininger Strasse 10, a 200-yard walk from U-Bahn: Rathaus Schöneberg, tel. 030/7871-7414, www.meininger-hostels.de).

$ Circus is a brightly colored, well-run place with 230 beds, a Dylanesque ambience, and a bar downstairs (€18/bed in 4- to 8-bed dorms, S-€33, Sb-€46, D-€50, Db-€62, T-€63, Q-€76, 2-person apartment with kitchen-€77, 4-person apartment-€134, sheets-€2, breakfast-€5, no curfew, Internet access; U-Bahn: Rosenthaler Platz, Weinbergsweg 1a; tel. 030/2839-1433, www.circus-berlin.de, info@circus-berlin.de).

$ Mitte's Backpacker Hostel (€15/bed in 32-bed dorms, S-€30–35, D-€48–56, T-€63, Q-€80, sheets-€2.50, no breakfast, could be cleaner, no curfew, Internet access, English newspapers, laundry, bike rental, U-Bahn: Zinnowitzer Strasse, Chauseestrasse 102, tel. 030/2839-0965, fax 030/2839-0935, www.backpacker.de, reservation@backpacker.de).

$ Ostel is a fun, retro-1970s-DDR apartment building that recreates the lifestyle and interior design of a country relegated to the dustbin of history. All the furniture and room decorations have been meticulously collected and restored to their former socialist glory—only the psychedelic wallpaper is a replica. Guests buy ration vouchers (€3.50 per person) for breakfast in the attached restaurant. Kitschy and tacky, sure—but also clean and memorable (€9 for a bed in a 4- or 6-bed "Pioneer Camp" room, S-€33, Sb-€40, D-€54, Db-€61, 4-person apartments-€120, Wi-Fi, free bike rental, free parking, free collective use of the people's own barbeque, right behind Ostbahnhof station on the corner of Strasse der Pariser Kommune at Wriezener Karree 5, tel. 030/2576-8660, www.ostel.eu, contact@ostel.eu).

EATING

Don't be too determined to eat "Berlin-style." The city is known only for its mildly spicy sausage. Still, there is a world of restaurants in this ever-changing city to choose from. Your best approach may be to select a neighborhood, rather than a particular restaurant.

Colorful pubs—called *Kneipen*—offer light, quick, and easy meals and the fizzy local beer, *Berliner Weiss.* Ask for it *mit Schuss* for a shot of fruity syrup in your suds. Germans—especially Berliners—consider their food old-school; when they go out to eat, they're not usually looking for the "traditional local" fare many travelers are after. Nouveau German is California cuisine with scant memories of wurst, kraut, and pumpernickel. In 2008, Berlin banned smoking in restaurants.

If the kraut is getting the wurst of you, try one of the many Turkish, Italian, and Balkan restaurants. Eat cheap at *Imbiss* snack stands, bakeries (sandwiches), and falafel/kebab counters. Train stations have grocery stores, as well as bright and modern fruit-and-sandwich bars.

In Western Berlin

Near Savignyplatz

Many good restaurants are on or within 100 yards of Savignyplatz, near my recommended western Berlin hotels. Take a walk and survey these; continue your stroll along Bleibtreustrasse to discover many trendier, more creative little eateries.

Restaurant Marjellchen is a trip to East Prussia. Dine in a soft, jazzy elegance in one of two six-table rooms. While it doesn't have to be expensive (€25 for two courses), plan to go the whole nine yards here, as this can be a great Prussian experience with a great and caring service. The menu is inviting, and the Königsberg meatballs are the specialty. Reservations are smart (daily 17:00–23:30, family-run, Mommsenstrasse 9, tel. 030/883-2676).

Dicke Wirtin is a pub with traditional old-Berlin *Kneipe* atmosphere, six good beers on tap, and good, solid home cooking at reasonable prices—such as their famously cheap *Gulaschsuppe* (€3.40). Their interior is fun and pubby; their streetside tables are also inviting (€5 daily specials, open daily from 12:00 with dinner served from 18:00, just off Savignyplatz at Carmerstrasse 9, tel. 030/312-4952).

Die Zwölf Apostel ("The Twelve Apostles") is trendy for good Italian food. Choose between indoors with candlelit ambience, outdoors on a sun-dappled patio, or overlooking the people-parade on its pedestrian street. A dressy local crowd packs this restaurant for excellent €10 pizzas and €15–30 meals (open 24 hours daily, cash only, immediately across from Savignyplatz S-Bahn entrance, Bleibtreustrasse 49, tel. 030/312-1433).

Zillemarkt Restaurant, which feels like an old-time Berlin *Biergarten,* serves traditional Berlin specialties in the garden or in the rustic candlelit interior. Their *Berliner Allerlei* is a fun way to sample a bit of nearly everything (for a minimum of two people...but it can feed up to five). They have their own microbrew (€10 meals, daily 12:00–24:00, near the S-Bahn tracks at Bleibtreustrasse 48A, tel. 030/881-7040).

Genazvale ("Best Friends") serves traditional fare from the Republic of Georgia, and is popular with Charlottenburg's immigrant Russian community. Sample some Georgian wines—virtually impossible to find in North America—and try their warm *catchapuri* (cheese bread) or a delicious plate of *chinkali* (cheese dumplings). The best way to enjoy Georgian food is to order several appetizers and split a main dish, which is usually grilled meat or stew (€8–15 main dishes, daily 17:00–23:00, live music and dancing on Georgian holidays, on the corner of Kantstrasse at Windscheidstrasse 14, tel. 030/4508-6026).

Technical University Mensa, a student cafeteria with impossibly cheap prices, puts you in a modern university scene with fine food and good indoor or streetside seating (€5 meals, Mon–Fri 11:00–15:30, closed Sat–Sun, general public entirely welcome, cheap coffee bar downstairs with Internet access, just north of Uhlandstrasse at Hardenbergstrasse 34).

Ullrich Supermarkt is the neighborhood grocery store (Mon–Sat 9:00–22:00, Sun 11:00–22:00, Kantstrasse 7, under the tracks near Bahnhof Zoo). There's plenty of fast food near Bahnhof Zoo and on Ku'damm.

Near Bahnhof Zoo

Schleusenkrug beer garden is hidden in the park between the Bahnhof Zoo and Tiergarten stations. Choose from an ever-changing self-service menu of huge salads, pasta, and some German dishes. English breakfast is served until 15:00 (€7–12 plates, €3–5 grill snacks, daily 10:00–24:00, Müller-Breslau-Strasse; standing in front of Bahnhof Zoo, turn left and follow the path into the park between the zoo and train tracks; tel. 030/313-9909).

Self-Service Cafeterias: The top floor of the famous department store, **KaDeWe,** holds the Winter Garden Buffet view cafeteria, and its sixth-floor deli/food department is a picnicker's nirvana. Its arterials are clogged with more than 1,000 kinds of sausage and 1,500 types of cheese (Mon–Fri 10:00–20:00, Sat 9:30–20:00, closed Sun, U-Bahn: Wittenbergplatz). **Wertheim** department store, a half-block from Kaiser Wilhelm Memorial Church, has cheap food counters in the basement and a city view from its self-service cafeteria, Le Buffet, located up six banks of escalators (Mon–Sat 9:30–20:00, closed Sun, U-Bahn: Ku'damm). **Marche,** a chain that's popped up in big cities all over Germany, is another inexpensive, self-service cafeteria within a half-block of Kaiser Wilhelm Memorial Church (Mon–Thu 8:00–22:00, Fri–Sat 8:00–24:00, Sun 10:00–22:00, plenty of salads, fruit, made-to-order omelets, Ku'damm 14, tel. 030/882-7578).

In Eastern Berlin

Along Unter den Linden

These eateries are listed as you'll reach them as you walk along Unter den Linden from west to east.

At the Opera House (Opernpalais): The **Operncafé** is perhaps the classiest coffee stop in Berlin, with a selection of 50—count 'em: 50—different decadent desserts (daily 8:00–24:00, across from university and war memorial at Unter den Linden 5, tel. 030/202-683). The **Schinkel Klause Biergarten** serves good €9–14 meals on its shady terrace with a view of the Unter den Linden scene when sunny, or in its cellar otherwise (daily 11:30–24:00).

Near the Pergamon Museum: Georgenstrasse, a block behind the Pergamon Museum and under the S-Bahn tracks, is lined with fun eateries filling the arcade of the train trestle—close to the sightseeing action but in business mainly for students from nearby Humboldt University. **Deponie3** is a trendy Berlin *Kneipe* usually filled with students. Garden seating in the back is nice if you don't mind the noise of the S-Bahn passing directly above you. The interior is a cozy, wooden wonderland of a bar with several inviting spaces. They serve basic sandwiches, salads, traditional Berlin dishes, and hearty daily specials (€3–7 breakfasts, €5–11 lunches and dinners, open daily from 9:00, sometimes live music, Georgenstrasse 5, tel. 030/2016-5740). A branch of **Die Zwölf Apostel** is nearby (daily until 24:00, described earlier under "Near Savignyplatz").

In the Heart of Old Berlin's Nikolai Quarter: The *Nikolaiviertel* marks the original medieval settlement of Cölln, which would eventually become Berlin. The area was destroyed during the war, but rebuilt for Berlin's 750th birthday in 1987. The whole area has a cute, cobbled, and characteristic old town...Middle Ages meets Socialist Realism. Today, the district is pretty soulless by day, but is a popular restaurant zone at night. **Bräuhaus Georgbrau** is a thriving beer hall serving homemade suds on a picturesque courtyard overlooking the Spree River. Eat in the lively and woody but mod-feeling interior, or outdoors with fun riverside seating—thriving with German tourists. It's a good place to try one of the few typical Berlin dishes: *Eisbein* (boiled ham hock) with sauerkraut and mashed peas with bacon (€9.99 with a beer and schnapps). The statue of St. George once stood in the courtyard of Berlin's old castle—until the Nazis deemed it too decadent and not "German" enough, and removed it (cheap plates, three-foot-long sampler board with a dozen small glasses of beer, daily 10:00–24:00, 2 blocks south of Berlin Cathedral and across the river at Spreeufer 4, tel. 030/242-4244).

South of Unter den Linden, near Gendarmenmarkt

The twin churches of Gendarmenmarkt seem to be surrounded by people in love with food. The lunch and dinner scene is thriving with upscale restaurants serving good cuisine at highly competitive prices to local professionals. If in need of a quick-yet-classy lunch, stroll around the square and along Charlottenstrasse.

Lutter & Wegner Restaurant is well-known for its Austrian cuisine (*Schnitzel* and *Sauerbraten*) and popular with businesspeople. It's dressy, with fun sidewalk seating or a dark and elegant interior (two-course lunch with wine-€15 Mon–Fri, €20 Sat–Sun; fixed-price gourmet dinner-€34, daily 11:00–24:00, Charlottenstrasse 56, tel. 030/202-9540).

Maredo Argentine Steak Restaurant, a family-friendly chain restaurant, is generally a good value with a fine €6.20 salad bar that can make a healthy and cheap meal (behind French Cathedral at Gendarmenmarkt, at Charlottenstrasse 57, tel. 030/2094-5230).

Galeries Lafayette Food Circus is a festival of fun eateries in the basement of the landmark department store (Mon–Sat 10:00–20:00, closed Sun, U-Bahn: Französische Strasse).

Turkish and Bavarian Cuisine at Hackescher Markt

Hasir Turkish Restaurant is your chance to dine with candles, hardwood floors, and happy Berliners as snappy Turkish waiters bring plates piled high with meaty Anatolian specialties. As Berlin is one of the world's largest Turkish cities, it's no wonder you can find some good Turkish restaurants here. But while most locals think of Turkish food as fast and cheap, this is a dining experience. The restaurant, in a courtyard next to the Hackesche Höfe shopping complex (see page 491), offers indoor and outdoor tables filled with an enthusiastic local crowd (€14 plates, huge and splittable portions, daily from 11:30 until late, a block from the Hackescher Markt S-Bahn station at Oranienburger Strasse 4, tel. 030/2804-1616).

Weihenstephaner Bavarian Restaurant serves upmarket Bavarian traditional food for around €15 a plate, offers an atmospheric cellar and a busy people-watching street-side terrace, and, of course, has excellent beer (daily 11:00–24:00, Neue Promenade 5 at Hackescher Markt, tel. 030/2576-2871).

In Prenzlauer Berg

Prenzlauer Berg is packed with fine restaurants—German, ethnic, and everything in between. (For more on this district, see page 491.) Before making a choice, I'd spend half an hour strolling and browsing through this bohemian wonderland of creative eateries. **Kollwitzplatz** is an especially good area to prowl for dinner—this square, home of the DDR student resistance in 1980s, is now trendy and upscale. With its leafy playground park in the center, it's a good place for up-market restaurants. Walk the square and choose. Just about every option offers sidewalk seats in the summer—these are great on a balmy evening. Nearby **Helmholtzplatz** (especially Lychener Strasse) is a somewhat younger, hipper, and edgier place to eat and drink.

Gugelhof, right on Kollwitzplatz, is the Prenzlauer Berg stop for visiting dignitaries. It's an institution famous for its Alsatian German cuisine. You'll enjoy French quality with German proportions. It's highly regarded with a boisterous and enthusiastic local crowd filling its minimalist yet classy interior (3-course-meal-€25, daily from 16:00, reservations required during peak times, where Knaackstrasse meets Kollwitzplatz, tel. 030/442-9229).

Metzer Eck is a time-warp *Kneipe* with a family tradition dating to 1913 and a cozy charm. It serves cheap basic typical Berlin food with Czech Budvar beer on tap (€5–7 meals, daily from 18:00, Metzer Strasse 33, on the corner of Metzer Strasse and Strassburger Strasse, tel. 030/442-7656).

Prater Biergarten offers two great eating opportunities: a rustic restaurant indoors and a mellow, shady, super-cheap, and family-friendly beer garden outdoors—each proudly pouring its own microbrew. In the beer garden—Berlin's oldest—you step up to the counter and order (simple €3–5 plates and an intriguing selection of beer munchies). The restaurant serves serious traditional *Biergarten* cuisine and good salads (€8–14 plates, Mon–Sat 18:00–24:00, Sun 12:00–24:00, cash only, Kastanienallee 7, tel. 030/448-5688).

Zum Schusterjungen Speisegaststätte ("The Cobbler's Apprentice") is a classic old-school, German-with-attitude eatery that retains its circa-1986 DDR decor. Famous for its schnitzel and filling €7–8 meals, it's a no-frills place with quality ingredients and a strong local following. It serves the eating needs of those Berliners lamenting the disappearance of solid traditional German cooking amid the flood of ethnic eateries (small 40-seat dining hall, daily 11:00–24:00, corner of Lychener Strasse and Danziger Strasse 9, tel. 030/442-7654).

La Bodeguita del Medio Cuban Bar Restaurant is purely fun-loving Cuba—Christmas lights, graffiti-caked walls, Che Guevara posters, animated staff, and an ambience that makes you want to dance. Come early to eat or late to drink. It seems the waiters know the regulars' drinks. This restaurant has been here for more than a decade—and in fast-changing Prenzlauer Berg, that's an eternity. Cuban ribs and salad for €7 is a hit (€4–10 tapas, struggle with a menu in German and Spanish, puff a Cuban cigar, daily 17:00–24:00, 1 block from U-Bahn: Eberswalder Strasse at Lychener Strasse 6, tel. 030/4171-4276).

Knoppke's Imbiss, a super-cheap German-style hot-dog stand, has been a Berlin institution for over 70 years—it was family-owned even during DDR times. Berliners say Knoppke's cooks up the city's best *Currywurst* (grilled hot dog with curry-infused ketchup, €2). There are a few tables under a nearby tent for sit-down wurst-munching (Mon–Sat 6:00–20:00, closed Sun; Kastanienallee dead-ends at the elevated train tracks, and under them you'll find Knoppke's at Schönhauser Allee 44A). Don't be fooled by the Currystation at the foot of the stairs coming out of the station; Knoppke's is actually across the street, under the tracks.

For Dessert: **Kauf Dich Glücklich** makes a great capper to a Prenzlauer Berg dinner. It serves an enticing array of sweet Belgian waffles and ice cream in a candy-sprinkled, bohemian, retro setting under WWII bullet holes on a great Prenzlauer Berg street (daily until late, indoor and outdoor seating, Oderberger Strasse 44—it's the only un-renovated building on the street, tel. 030/4435-2182).

TRANSPORTATION CONNECTIONS

Berlin used to have several major train stations. But now that the Hauptbahnhof has emerged as the single, massive central station, all the others have wilted into glorified subway stations. Virtually every long-distance train passes through the Hauptbahnhof—ignore the other stations.

EurAide is an agent of the German Railroad that sells high-speed- and overnight-train reservations, with staff that can answer your travel questions in English (located in the Hauptbahnhof; see "Arrival in Berlin," on page 453).

From Berlin by Train to: Dresden (every 2 hrs, more with a transfer in Leipzig, 2.25 hrs), **Frankfurt** (hourly, 4 hrs), **Bacharach** (hourly, 5.5–6.5 hrs, 1–3 changes), **Würzburg** (hourly, 4 hrs, 1 change in Fulda or Hannover), **Nürnberg** (hourly, 4.5 hrs), **Munich** (hourly, 5.75–6.25 hrs), **Köln** (hourly, 4.5 hrs), **Amsterdam** (3/day direct, 3 more with change in Duisberg, 6.5 hrs), **Budapest** (3/day, 13 hrs; these go via Czech Republic and Slovakia, where Eurailpass is not valid, for an overnight you need to go to Vienna and then change), **Copenhagen** (5/day, 6.5 hrs, reservation required, change in Hamburg; also consider the direct overnight train-plus-ferry route to Malmö, Sweden, which is just 20 min from Copenhagen—

covered by a railpass that includes Germany or Sweden), **London** (5/day, 10–11.5 hrs, 2 changes—but you're better off flying cheap on easyJet or Air Berlin, even if you have a railpass—see next page), **Paris** (9/day, 8–9 hrs, 1–2 changes, 1 direct 12-hr night train, many connections go via Belgium), **Zürich** (hourly, 8.5 hrs, 1 direct 12-hr night train), **Prague** (6/day, 4.5–5 hrs, no overnight trains), **Warsaw** (3/day, 6 hrs, 1 night train; reservations required on all Warsaw-bound trains), **Kraków** (1/day direct, 2 more with transfer in Warsaw, 10 hrs, 1 night train), **Vienna** (8/day, most with 1 change, 9.5 hrs, some via Czech Republic—for second-class ticket, Eurailers pay an extra €40; the Berlin–Vienna via Passau train avoids Czech Republic—nightly at 20:55—as do connections with a change in Nürnberg or Munich). It's wise but not required to reserve in advance for trains to or from Amsterdam or Prague. Train info: tel. 11861 (€0.60/min). Before buying a ticket for any long train ride from Berlin (over 7 hours), consider taking a cheap flight instead (buy it well in advance to get a super fare).

Eurailpasses don't cover the Czech Republic, so if you're headed to Prague you need to buy a ticket for the Czech portion of the trip. You can either buy that in the station before leaving Berlin (€14), or save about €5 by buying it directly from the Czech conductor. (German stations charge twice what Czechs do for Czech tickets; note that you can only buy tickets on board on long-distance trains—if you go to Prague indirectly via a milk-run train, you can be fined heavily for boarding without a ticket.)

There are **night trains** from Berlin to these cities: Munich, Frankfurt, Köln, Brussels, Paris, Vienna, Kraków, Warsaw, Malmö, Basel, and Zürich. There are no night trains from Berlin to anywhere in Italy or Spain. A *Liegeplatz*, or *couchette* berth (€13–36), is a great deal; inquire at EurAide at the Hauptbahnhof for details. Beds generally cost the same whether you have a first- or second-class ticket or railpass. Trains are often full, so reserve your *couchette* a few days in advance from any travel agency or major train station in Europe.

The **Berlin–Paris night train** goes through Belgium. If you're using a railpass, either the pass must include Benelux, or you'll have to pay extra for the Belgian segment of the trip (roughly €50 in second class).

Berlin's Two Airports

Tegel Airport handles most flights from the United States and Western Europe (4 miles from center, no subway trains, catch the faster bus #X9 to Bahnhof Zoo, or bus #109 to Ku'damm and Bahnhof Zoo for €2.10; bus #TXL goes between Tegel Airport, the Hauptbahnhof, and Alexanderplatz in eastern Berlin; taxi from Tegel Airport costs €15 to Bahnhof Zoo, €25 to

Alexanderplatz). Flights from the east and discount airlines usually arrive at **Schönefeld Airport** (12.5 miles from center, 3-min walk to S-Bahn station where you catch the regional express train into the city—going direct to Savignyplatz, Hauptbahnhof, and Hackescher Markt, railpass valid, taxi €35 to city center). The central telephone number for both airports is 01805-000-186. For British Air, tel. 01805-266-522; Delta, tel. 01803-337-880; SAS, tel. 01805-117-002; Lufthansa, tel. 01803-803-803.

Berlin, the New Discount Airline Hub: Berlin's Schönefeld Airport is now the Continental European hub for discount airlines such as easyJet (with lots of flights to Spain, Italy, Eastern Europe, the Baltics, and more—book long in advance to get the incredible €30-and-less fares, www.easyjet.com). Ryanair (www.ryanair.com) and Air Berlin (www.airberlin.com) are also making the London–Berlin trip (and other routes) dirt-cheap, so consider this option before booking an overnight train. Consequently, British visitors to the city are now outnumbered only by Americans. For more on cheap flights, see page 557.

GERMAN HISTORY

There was no Germany before 1871, but the cultural heritage of the German-speaking people (of modern-day Germany and Austria) stretches back 2,000 years.

Romans (A.D. 1–500)

German history begins in A.D. 9, when Roman troops were ambushed and driven back by the German chief Arminius. For the next 250 years, the Rhine and Danube rivers marked the border between civilized Roman Europe (to the southwest) and "barbarian" German lands (northeast). While the rest of Europe's future would be Roman, Christian, and Latin, Germany would follow its own pagan, *Deutsch*-speaking path.

Rome finally fell to the Germanic chief Theodoric the Great (a.k.a. Dietrich of Bern, A.D. 476). After that, Germanic Franks controlled northern Europe, ruling a mixed population of Romanized Christians and tree-worshipping pagans.

Charlemagne and the Franks (A.D. 500–1000)

For Christmas in A.D. 800, the pope gave Charlemagne the title of Holy Roman Emperor. Charlemagne, the king of the Franks, was the first of many German kings to be called *Kaiser* ("emperor," from "Caesar") over the next thousand years. Allied with the pope, Charlemagne ruled an empire that included Germany, Austria, France, the Low Countries, and northern Italy.

Charlemagne (Karl der Grosse, or Charles the Great, r. 768–814) stood a head taller than his subjects, and his foot became a standard measurement. The stuff of legend, Charles the Great had five wives and four concubines, producing descendants with names like Charles the Bald, Louis the Pious, and Henry the Quarrelsome. After Charlemagne died of pneumonia (814),

Why We Call Deutschland "Germany"

Our English name "Germany" comes from the Latin *Germania,* the name of one of the "barbarian" tribes. The French and Spanish call it *Allemagne* and *Alemania,* respectively, after the Alemanni tribe. Italians call the country *Germania,* but in Italy the German language is known as *tedesco,* after another Germanic tribe. Completely confused by all this, the Slavic peoples of Eastern Europe simply throw up their hands and call Germany *Německo* (Czech), *Niemcy* (Polish), *Németország* (Hungarian), or other variations of a word that means "mute."

To Germans, their country is *Deutschland,* a name used for at least 1,200 years. It probably derives from *Deutsch*—which is what eighth-century folks called the common language that developed in the eastern half of the Frankish empire. *Alles klar?*

his united empire did not pass directly to his oldest son but was divided into (what would become) Germany, France, and the lands in between (Treaty of Verdun, 843).

The Holy Roman Empire (1000-1500)

Chaotic medieval Germany was made of more than 300 small, quarreling dukedoms ruled by the Holy Roman Emperor. The title was pretty bogus, implying that the German king ruled the same huge European empire as the ancient Romans. In fact, he was "Holy" because he was blessed by the Church, "Roman" to recall ancient grandeur, and the figurehead "Emperor" of only a scattered kingdom.

Germany's emperors had less hands-on power than other kings around Europe. Because of the custom of electing emperors by nobles and archbishops, rather than bestowing the title through inheritance, they couldn't pass the crown father to son. This system gave nobles great power, and the peasants huddled close to their local noble's castle for protection from attack by the noble next door. There were no empire-wide taxes and no national capital.

When Emperor Henry IV (r. 1056–1106) tried to assert his power by appointing bishops, he was slapped down by the nobles, and forced to repent to the pope by standing barefoot in the alpine snow for three days at Canossa (in northern Italy, 1077).

Emperor Frederick I Barbarossa (1152–1190), blue-eyed and red-bearded (hence *barba rossa*), gained an international reputation as a valiant knight, gentleman, bon vivant, and lover of poetry and women. Still, his great victories were away in Italy and Asia (on the Third Crusade, where he drowned in a river), while back home nobles wielded real power.

This was the era of Germany's troubadours *(Meistersingers)*, who traveled from castle to castle singing love songs *(Minnesang)* and telling the epic tales of chivalrous knights (Tristan and Isolde, Parzival, and the Nibelungen) that would later inspire German nationalism and Wagnerian operas.

While France, England, and Spain were centralizing power around a single ruling family to create modern nation-states, Germany remained a decentralized, backward, feudal battleground.

Medieval Growth

Nevertheless, Germany was located at the center of Europe, and trading towns prospered. Several northern towns (especially Hamburg and Lübeck) banded together into the Hanseatic League, promoting open trade around the Baltic Sea. To curry favor at election time, emperors granted powers and privileges to certain towns, designated Free Imperial Cities. Some towns, such as Köln, Mainz, Dresden, and Trier, held higher status than many nobles, as hosts of one of the seven Electors of the emperor.

Textiles, mining, and the colonizing of eastern lands made Germany an economic powerhouse with a thriving middle class. In towns, middle-class folks (burghers), not the local aristocrats, began running things. In about 1450, Johann Gutenberg of Mainz invented moveable type for printing, an invention that would allow the export of a new commodity: ideas.

Religious Struggles and the Thirty Years' War (1500–1700)

Martin Luther—German monk, fiery orator, and religious whistle-blower—sparked a century of European wars by speaking out against the Catholic Church (see sidebar, next page).

Luther's protests ("Protestantism") threw Germany into a century of turmoil, as each local prince took sides between Catholics and Protestants. In the 1525 Peasant Revolt, peasants attacked their feudal masters with hoes and pitchforks, fighting for more food, political say-so, and respect. The revolt was brutally put down.

The Holy Roman Emperor, Charles V (r. 1519–1556), sided with the pope. Charles was the most powerful man in Europe, having inherited an empire that included Germany and Austria, plus the Low Countries, much of Italy, Spain, and Spain's New World possessions. But many local German nobles took the opportunity to go Protestant—some for religious reasons, but also to seize Church assets and powers.

The 1555 Peace of Augsburg allowed each local noble to decide the religion of his realm. In general, the northern lands became Protestant, while the south (today's Bavaria, along with Austria) remained Catholic.

Martin Luther
(1483-1546)

One of the most influential Germans of all time was Martin Luther, who defied the Catholic Church and forever divided its congregation. Luther was born on November 10, 1483, in Eisleben, south of Berlin. His dad owned a copper smelter, affording Luther a middle-class upbringing—a rarity in the medieval hierarchy of nobles, clergy, and peasants. At the University of Erfurt, Luther earned a liberal-arts degree, entered law school, and earned himself two nicknames—"the philosopher" for his wide-ranging mind, and "the king of hops" for his lifelong love affair with beer.

In 1505, while riding back to school after a trip home, a bolt of lightning knocked him to the ground. Terrified, he vowed to become a monk. By age 23, he was ordained a priest in Erfurt Cathedral, and was on the fast track to become a professor of theology.

Luther soon got a teaching job at a brand-new university in Wittenberg—the progressive city that would be his home for the rest of his life. Luther taught theology and mingled with the town's brightest thinkers and artists; he also spent hours alone in his cell (living quarters) in the Augustinian monastery. Consumed with the notion that he was a sinner, he devoured the Bible, looking for an answer and finding it in Paul's letter to the Romans. Luther realized that God makes sinners righteous through their faith in Jesus Christ, not by earning it through good deeds. As this concept of grace took hold, Luther said, "I felt myself to have been born again."

Energized, he began a series of Bible lectures at Wittenberg's twin-towered St. Mary's City Church. The pews were packed as Luther quoted passages directly from the Bible. Speaker and audience alike began to see discrepancies between what the Bible said and what the Church was doing.

Coincidentally, a representative of the pope arrived in Wittenberg to raise money by selling letters of indulgence promising "full forgiveness for all sins." Luther was outraged at the idea that God's grace could be bought, and thought the subject should be debated openly. On October 31, 1517, Luther approached Wittenberg's Castle Church and nailed 95 "theses"—or topics for discussion—to the door, which was then used as a public bulletin board. The theses questioned indulgences and other Church practices and beliefs. Luther's propositions were printed and circulated from Wittenberg's newfangled presses (some of Europe's first). It was the talk of Germany, and Luther became famous—or infamous—almost overnight.

The pope ordered Luther's writings to be burned and sent a letter excommunicating the rebellious monk. Luther was branded a heretic and ordered to Rome to face charges, but he refused to go. Finally, the most powerful man in Europe, Emperor Charles V, stepped in to arbitrate, calling an Imperial Diet (congress) at Worms (1521). Luther made a triumphal entry into Worms, greeted by cheering crowds.

The Diet convened, and Luther took his place in the center of the large hall, standing next to a stack of his books. Inquisitors grilled him while the ultra-Catholic Charles looked on from his throne. Luther refused to disavow his beliefs or books. "Here I stand," he told the assembly, "I can do no other. So help me God. Amen."

Given a few days to reconsider, Luther disappeared. Rumor was he was kidnapped, but in fact he'd escaped to safety in Wartburg Castle, overlooking his teenage home of Eisenach. Protected by a German prince opposed to Rome, he spent a year fighting depression and translating the New Testament from Greek into German. This "German King James Version" was revolutionary, bringing the Bible to the masses and shaping the modern German language. Finally, wearing a fake beard and disguised as a knight, Luther returned home to Wittenberg.

In 1525, 41-year-old Martin met 25-year-old Katherine von Bora, and within months, the ex-monk married the ex-nun in St. Mary's City Church. He and "Katie" moved from the monastery to their own house. Martin and Katherine had six children and raised four orphans.

Though living in Wittenberg under the protection of German princes, Luther traveled, spreading the Protestant message. In 1529, at Marburg Castle just north of Frankfurt, he attended a summit of leading Protestants to try and forge an alliance against Catholicism (1529). They agreed on everything except a single theological point: whether Christ was present in the wine and bread of Communion in a physical sense (according to Luther) or symbolic sense (per Ulrich Zwingli). The disagreement doomed the Protestant movement to splinter into dozens of sects.

In his 50s, Luther's health declined and he grew bitter, a fact made clear in such writings as "Against the Papacy at Rome Founded by the Devil" and "Of the Jews and Their Lies." He died on February 18, 1546, and was buried in Wittenberg. To this day, pilgrims bring flowers.

Unresolved religious and political differences eventually expanded into the Thirty Years' War (1618–1648). This Europe-wide war, fought mainly on German soil, involved Denmark, Sweden, France, and Bohemia (in today's Czech Republic), among others. It was one of history's bloodiest wars, fueled by religious extremism and political opportunism, and fought by armies of brutal mercenaries who worked on commission, and were paid in loot and pillage.

By the war's end (Treaty of Westphalia, 1648), a third of all Germans had died, France was the rising European power, and the Holy Roman Empire was a medieval mess of scattered, feudal states. In 1689, France's Louis XIV swept down the Rhine, gutting and leveling its once-great castles, and Germany ceased to be a major player in European politics until the modern era.

Austria and Prussia (1700s)

The German-speaking lands now consisted of three "Germanys": Austria in the south, Prussia in the north, and the rest in between.

Prussia—originally colonized by celibate ex-Crusaders called Teutonic Knights—was forged into a unified state by two strong kings. Frederick I (the "King Sergeant," r. 1701–1713) built a modern state around a highly disciplined army, a centralized government, and national pride. His grandson, Frederick II "The Great" (r. 1740–1786), added French culture and worldliness, preparing militaristic Prussia to enter the world stage. A well-read, flute-playing lover of the arts and liberal ideals, Frederick also ruled with an iron fist—the very model of the "enlightened despot."

Meanwhile, Austria thrived under the laid-back rule of the Habsburg family. Habsburgs gained power in Europe by marrying it. They acquired the Netherlands, Spain, Bohemia, and Hungary that way—a strategy that didn't work so well for Marie-Antoinette, who wed the king of France.

In the 1700s, the Germanic lands became a cultural powerhouse, producing musicians (Bach, Haydn, Mozart, Beethoven), writers (Goethe, Schiller), and thinkers (Kant, Leibniz). But politically, feudal Germany was no match for the modern powers.

After the French Revolution (1789), Napoleon swept through Germany with his armies, deposing feudal lords, confiscating church lands, and forcing the emperor to hand over his crown (1806). After a thousand years, the Holy Roman Empire (or *Reich*) was dead.

German Unification (1800s)

Napoleon's invasion helped unify the German-speaking peoples by rallying them against a common foreign enemy. After Napoleon's defeat, the Congress of Vienna (1815), presided over by the

Germany Before Unification

Austrian Prince Metternich, realigned Europe's borders. The idea of unifying the three Germanic nations—Prussia, Austria, and the German Confederation, a loose collection of small states in between—began to grow. By mid-century most German-speaking people favored forming a modern nation-state. The only question was whether the confederation would be under Prussian or Austrian dominance.

Economically, Germany was becoming increasingly modern, with a unified trade organization (1834), railroads (1835), mechanical-engineering prowess, and factories booming on a surplus of labor.

Energetic Prussia took the lead in unifying the country. Otto von Bismarck (served 1862–1890), the strong minister of Prussia's weak king, used cunning politics to engineer a unified Germany under Prussian dominance. First, he started a war with Austria, ensuring that any united Germany would be under Prussian control. (The Austrian Empire would remain a separate country.) Next, Bismarck provoked a war with France (Franco-Prussian War, 1870–1871). This action united Prussia and the German Confederation against their common enemy, France.

Fueled by hysterical patriotism, German armies swept through France and, in the Hall of Mirrors at Versailles, crowned Prussia's Wilhelm I as Emperor *(Kaiser)* of a new German Empire uniting Prussia and the German Confederation (but excluding Austria). This Second Reich (1871–1918) featured elements of democracy (an elected *Reichstag*, or parliament), offset by a strong military and an emperor with veto powers.

A united and resurgent Germany was suddenly flexing its muscles in European politics. With strong industry, war spoils, overseas colonies, and a large and disciplined military, it sought its rightful place in the sun. *Volk* art flourished (Wagner's operas, Nietzsche's essays), fueled by nationalist fervor, reviving medieval German myths and Nordic gods. The rest of Europe saw Germany's rapid rise and began arming themselves to the teeth.

World War I and Hitler's Rise (1914–1939)

When Archduke Franz Ferdinand, the heir to the Austro-Hungarian Empire, was assassinated in 1914, all of Europe took sides as the political squabble quickly escalated into World War I. Germany and Austria-Hungary attacked British and French troops in France, but were stalled at the Battle of the Marne. Both sides dug defensive trenches, then settled in for four years of bloodshed, boredom, mud, machine-gun fire, disease, and mustard gas.

Finally, at 11:00 in the morning of November 11, 1918, the fighting ceased. Germany surrendered, signing the Treaty of Versailles in the Hall of Mirrors at Versailles. The war cost the defeated German nation 1.7 million men, precious territory, colonies, their military rights, reparations money, and national pride.

A new democratic government called the Weimar Republic (1919) dutifully abided by the Treaty of Versailles, and tried to maintain order among Germany's many divided political parties. But the country was in ruins, its economy a shambles, and the war's victors demanded heavy reparations. Communists rioted in the streets, fascists plotted coups, and a loaf of bread cost a billion inflated Marks. War vets grumbled in their beer about how their leaders had sold them out. All Germans, regardless of their political affiliations, were fervently united in their apathy toward the new democracy. When the worldwide depression of 1929 hit Germany with brutal force, the nation was desperate for a strong leader with answers.

Adolf Hitler (1889–1945) was a disgruntled vet who had spent the post–World War I years homeless, wandering the streets of Vienna with sketchpad in hand, hoping to become an artist. In Munich, he joined other disaffected Germans to form the National Socialist (Nazi) party. In stirring speeches, Hitler promised to restore Germany to its rightful glory, blaming the country's current problems on communists, foreigners, and Jews. After an unsuccessful coup attempt (the Beer Hall Putsch in Munich, 1923), Hitler was sent to jail, where he wrote an influential book of his political ideas, called *Mein Kampf (My Struggle).*

By 1930, the Nazis—now wearing power suits and working within the system—had become a formidable political party in Germany's democracy. They won 38 percent of the seats in the *Reichstag* in 1932, and Hitler was appointed chancellor (1933). Two months later, the *Reichstag* building was mysteriously set on fire—an apparent act of terrorism with a September 11–size impact—and a terrified Germany gave Chancellor Hitler sweeping powers to preserve national security.

Hitler wasted no time in using this Enabling Act to jail opponents, terrorize the citizenry, and organize every aspect of German life under the watchful eye of the Nazi party. Plumbers' unions, choral societies, school teachers, church pastors, filmmakers, and artists all had to account to a Nazi Party official about how their work furthered the Third Reich.

For the next decade, an all-powerful Hitler proceeded to revive Germany's economy, building the autobahns and rebuilding the military. Defying the Treaty of Versailles and world opinion, Hitler occupied the Saar region (1935) and the Rhineland (1936), annexed Austria and the Sudetenland (1938), and invaded Czechoslovakia (March 1939). The rest of Europe finally reached its appeasement limit, and World War II began (see sidebar, next page).

Two Germanys (1945–1990)

After World War II, the Allies divided occupied Germany into two halves, split down the middle by an 855-mile border that Winston Churchill called an "Iron Curtain." By 1949, Germany was officially two separate countries. West Germany (the Federal Republic of Germany) was democratic and capitalist, allied with the powerful United States. East Germany (the German Democratic Republic, or DDR) was a socialist state under Soviet control. The former capital, Berlin, sitting in East German territory, was itself split into two parts, allowing a tiny pocket of Western life in the Soviet-controlled East. Armed guards prevented Germans from crossing the border to see their cousins on the other side.

In 1948, Soviet troops blockaded West Berlin. The Allies responded by airlifting food and supplies into the stranded city, forcing the Soviets to back off. In 1961, the East Germans erected a 12-foot-high concrete wall through the heart of Berlin. The Berlin Wall—built at the height of the Cold War between the United States and the USSR—was designed to prevent the westward flow of East German citizens. It came to symbolize divided Germany.

Germany During World War II
(1939–1945)

1939 Soldiers singing *"Muss ich denn, Muss ich denn"* ("I must leave, I must leave my happy home") march off to war. On September 1, Germany invades Poland, sparking World War II. Germany, Italy, and Japan (the Axis) would eventually square off against the Allies—Britain, France, the United States, and the Soviet Union.

1940 The Nazi *Blitzkrieg* (lightning war) quickly sweeps through Denmark, Norway, the Low Countries, France, Yugoslavia, and Greece. With fellow fascists ruling Italy (Mussolini), Spain (Franco), and Portugal (Salazar), all of the Continent is now dominated by fascists, creating a "fortress Europe."

1941 Hitler invades his former ally, the USSR. Bombastic victory parades in Berlin celebrate the triumph of the Aryan race over the lesser peoples of the world.

1942 Allied bombs begin falling on German cities. That autumn and winter, German families receive death notices from the horrific Battle of Stalingrad. On the worst days, 50,000 men died (by comparison, America lost 58,000 total in Vietnam). Back home, Nazi officials begin their plan for the "final solution to the Jewish problem"—systematic execution of Europe's Jews in specially built death camps.

In West Germany, Chancellor Konrad Adenauer (who had suffered imprisonment under the Nazis) tried to restore Germany's good name, paying war reparations and joining international organizations of nations. Thanks to US aid from the Marshall Plan, West Germany was rebuilt, democracy was established, and its "economic miracle" quickly exceeded pre-WWII levels. Adenauer was succeeded in 1969 by the US-friendly Willy Brandt.

East Germany was ruled with an iron fist by Walter Ulbricht (who had been exiled by the Nazis). In 1953, demonstrations and protests against the government were brutally put down by Soviet—not German—troops. Erich Honecker (having endured a decade of Nazi imprisonment) succeeded Ulbricht as ruler of the East in 1971. Honecker was a kinder, gentler tyrant.

Throughout the 1970s and 1980s, both the US and the Soviet Union used divided Germany as a military base. West Germans debated whether US missiles aimed at the Soviets should be placed in their country. Economically, West Germany just got stronger while East Germany stagnated.

On November 9, 1989, East Germany unexpectedly opened

1943 Germany has to fight a two-front war: against tenacious Soviets on the chilly Eastern Front, and against Brits and Yanks advancing north through Italy on the Western Front. Germany's industrial output tries desperately to keep up with the Allies'. The average German suffers through shortages, rationing, and frequent trips to the bomb shelter.

1944 Hitler's no-surrender policy is increasingly unpopular, and he narrowly survives being assassinated by a bomb planted in an office. After the Allies reach France on D-Day, Germany counterattacks with a last-gasp offensive (the Battle of the Bulge) that slows but does not stop the Allies.

1945 Soviet soldiers approach Berlin from the east, and Americans and Brits advance from the west. Adolf Hitler commits suicide, and families lock up their daughters to protect them from rapacious Soviet soldiers. When Germany finally surrenders on May 8, the country is in ruins, occupied by several foreign powers, divided into occupation zones, and viewed by the world as an immoral monster.

In the war's aftermath, many German citizens learn for the first time of the mass killings and atrocities committed by their leaders.

the Berlin Wall (see "The Berlin Wall" sidebar, page 470). Astonished Germans from both sides climbed the Wall, hugged each other, shared bottles of beer, sang songs, and chiseled off souvenirs. At first, most Germans—West and East—looked forward to free travel and better relations between two distinct nations. But before the month was out, negotiations and elections to reunite the two Germanys had already begun. October 3, 1990, was proclaimed German Unification Day, and Berlin re-assumed its status as German capital in 1991.

Germany Today (1990–present)

Differences between "Ossies" (rude slang for former East Germans) and "Wessies" remain, but they're diminishing as the two economies find equilibrium. Germany remains a major economic and political force in Europe. After a decade of a center-right government (under Chancellor Helmut Kohl), and a decade under the center-left Chancellor Gerhard Schroeder, Germany is at a crossroads. Elections in 2005 left no dominant political party, and the government is currently led by a

Benedict XVI, the German Pope

When Josef Ratzinger became the 265th pope in 2005, he introduced himself as "a simple, humble worker in the vineyard of the Lord." But the man has a complex history, a reputation for intellectual brilliance, a flair for the piano, a penchant for controversy for his unbending devotion to traditional Catholic doctrine...and a Bavarian accent.

Born in 1927 in the small Bavarian town of Marktl am Inn (southeast of Munich), young Josef went to school in nearby Traunstein, studying in the seminary. When Hitler took power, he lived life under Nazi rule as many Germans did—outwardly obeying leaders while inwardly conflicted. Like many Germans, he joined the Hitler Youth, was drafted into the Army, sprayed flak from anti-aircraft guns (guarding a BMW plant), and saw Jews transported to death camps. Near the war's end, he deserted, and subsequently spent a brief time in an American POW camp near Ulm.

After the war, Ratzinger became a priest and a professor of theology, first at Munster, then at the University of Tübingen. Originally a voice of liberal Catholicism, he became increasingly convinced that Church tradition was needed to offset the growing chaos of the world.

In 1977, he was made Archbishop of Munich. Ratzinger became Pope John Paul II's closest advisor and good friend. Every Friday afternoon for two decades, they met for lunch, intellectual sparring, and friendly conversation.

Under John Paul II, Ratzinger served as the Church's "enforcer" of doctrine, earning the nickname "God's Rottweiler." He spoke out against ordaining women, chastised Latin American priests for fomenting class warfare, reassigned bishops who were soft on homosexuality, reaffirmed opposition to birth control, and wrote thoughtful papers challenging the secular world's moral relativism.

The name of "Benedict" recalls both Pope Benedict XV (who healed World War I's divisions) and Europe's patron St. Benedict (c. 480–543), who symbolizes Europe's Christian roots.

loose coalition headed by a conservative Christian Democrat, Chancellor Angela Merkel. German-American relations suffered when the US invaded Iraq (Germany opposed the invasion), but the relationship remains fundamentally strong. Germany is fully integrated into the international community as a member of the European Union—an organization whose chief aim was to avoid future wars with an aggressive Germany by embracing it in the economic web of Europe.

APPENDIX

CONTENTS

RESOURCES

Tourist Offices

In the US

Germany's national tourist information office in the US is a wealth of information. They have maps, Rhine schedules, and information on festivals, castles, biking, genealogy, cities, and regions. Most materials can be downloaded from their website; if you want tourist materials sent to you, a small donation is requested.

Contact: tel. 800-651-7010, www.cometogermany.com.

In Germany

The local tourist information office (abbreviated **TI** in this book) is your best first stop in any new town or city. Try to arrive, or at least telephone, before it closes. Throughout Germany, you'll find TIs are usually well-organized and have English-speaking staff.

As national budgets tighten, many TIs have been privatized. This means they have become sales agents for big tours and hotels, and their "information" is unavoidably colored. While TIs are eager to book you a room, you should use their room-finding service only as a last resort. TIs can as easily book you a bad room as a good one—they are not allowed to promote one place over another. It's better to book direct, using the listings in this book.

Resources from Rick Steves

Guidebooks and Online Updates

This book is updated every year in person. The telephone numbers and hours of sights listed in this book are accurate as of mid-2008—but even with annual updates, things change. For the very latest, visit www.ricksteves.com/update. Also at my website, you'll find a valuable list of reports and experiences—good and bad—from fellow travelers (www.ricksteves.com/feedback).

This book is one of more than 30 titles in my series on European travel, which includes country guidebooks, city and regional guidebooks, and my budget-travel skills handbook, *Rick Steves' Europe Through the Back Door.* My phrase books—for German, French, Italian, Spanish, and Portuguese—are practical and budget-oriented. My other books are *Europe 101* (a crash course on art and history, newly expanded and in full color), *European Christmas* (on traditional and modern-day celebrations, including Germany's and Austria's), and *Postcards from Europe* (a fun memoir of my travels over 25 years). For a complete list of my books, see the inside of the last page of this book.

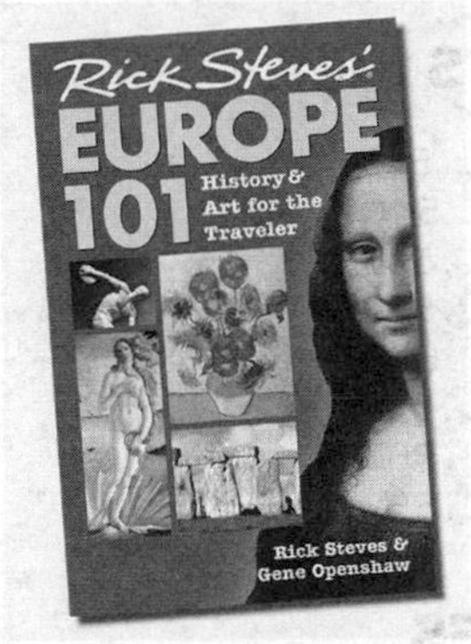

Public Television and Radio Shows

My TV series, *Rick Steves' Europe,* covers European destinations in 70 shows, with four episodes on Germany. My weekly public radio show, *Travel with Rick Steves,* features interviews with travel experts from around the world, including several hours on Germanic culture. All the TV scripts and radio shows (which are easy and free to download to an iPod or other MP3 player) are at www.ricksteves.com.

Free Audiotours

If your travels take you beyond Germany to France or Italy, you could take advantage of free, self-guided audiotours we offer of the major sights in Paris, Florence, Rome, and Venice. The audiotours, produced by Rick

Begin Your Trip at www.ricksteves.com

At our travel website, you'll find a wealth of free information on European destinations, including fresh monthly news and helpful tips from thousands of fellow travelers.

Our **online Travel Store** offers travel bags and accessories specially designed by Rick Steves to help you travel smarter and lighter. These include Rick's popular carry-on bags (wheeled and rucksack versions), money belts, totes, toiletries kits, adapters, other accessories, and a wide selection of guidebooks, planning maps, and DVDs.

Choosing the right **railpass** for your trip—amidst hundreds of options—can drive you nutty. We'll help you choose the best pass for your needs, plus give you a bunch of free extras.

Rick Steves' Europe Through the Back Door travel company offers **tours** with more than two-dozen itineraries and 450 departures reaching the best destinations in this book... and beyond. We offer a 14-day tour of Germany, Austria, and Switzerland. You'll enjoy great guides, a fun bunch of travel partners (with small groups of generally about 26), and plenty of room to spread out in a big, comfy bus. You'll find European adventures to fit every vacation length. For all the details, and to get our Tour Catalog and a free Rick Steves Tour Experience DVD (filmed on location during an actual tour), visit www.ricksteves.com or call the Tour Department at 425/608-4217.

Steves and Gene Openshaw (the co-author of seven books in the Rick Steves series) are available through iTunes and at www.rick steves.com. Simply download them onto your computer and transfer them to your iPod or other MP3 player. (Remember to bring a Y-jack and extra set of ear buds for your travel partner.)

Maps

The black-and-white maps in this book, drawn by Dave Hoerlein, are concise and simple. Dave, who is well-traveled in Germany and Austria, has designed the maps to help you locate recommended places and get to the tourist offices, where you can pick up a more in-depth map (usually free) of the city or region. Better maps are sold at newsstands—take a look before you buy to be sure the map has the level of detail you want.

European bookstores, especially in touristy areas, have good selections of maps. For drivers, I'd recommend a 1:200,000- or 1:300,000-scale map. Train travelers usually manage fine with the freebies they get with the train pass and from the local tourist offices.

Other Guidebooks

If you're like most travelers, this book is all you need. But if you're heading beyond my recommended destinations, you might want some supplemental information. Considering the improvements they'll make in your $4,000 vacation, $40 for extra maps and books is money well spent. Note that none of the following guidebooks are updated annually; check the publication date before you buy.

Lonely Planet's guide to Germany is thorough, well-researched, and packed with good maps and hotel recommendations for low- to moderate-budget travelers. The similar Rough Guide is written by insightful British researchers.

Students and vagabonds like the highly opinionated Let's Go series, which is updated by Harvard students. Let's Go is best for backpackers who have railpasses, stay in hostels, and are interested in the youth and nightlife scene.

The popular, skinny, green Michelin Guides are excellent, especially if you're driving. Michelin Guides are known for their city and sightseeing maps, dry but concise and helpful information on all major sights, and good cultural and historical background. English editions are sold in Europe at gas stations and tourist shops.

Recommended Books and Movies

To get a feel for Germany past and present, consider these books and films:

Non-Fiction

Germany: A New History (Schulze) is a one-volume compendium covering 2,000 years. Albert Speer's *Inside the Third Reich,* based on 1,200 manuscript pages, is an authoritative account of 1933 through 1945. *Stasiland: True Stories from Behind the Berlin Wall* (Funder) relays the secrets of the Stasi, the East German Ministry for State Security.

Germany and the Germans (Ardagh) is interesting if you'd like to know more about the 1990s reunification. For more on modern Germany, including cultural insights, pick up *Culture Shock! Germany* (Lord), *When in Germany, Do as the Germans Do* (Flippo), and *Of German Ways* (Rippley). Gourmets may want to grab *The Marling Menu-Master for Germany.*

Memoirs: Günter Grass stirred up controversy with his 2007 memoir, *Peeling the Onion,* which revealed he was a soldier in the dreaded Waffen-SS. *A Time of Gifts* (Fermor) tells of the author's walking tour of Europe—and Germany—in the 1930s. In *A Tramp Abroad,* Mark Twain recounts his amusing European adventures, including some in Germany.

Fiction

Classics of German fiction include the works of Thomas Mann (*Buddenbrooks* and *The Magic Mountain*) and Hermann Hesse (*Narcissus and Goldmund* and *Siddhartha*).

Some of the best modern German literature has wrestled with the country's warmongering past. *All Quiet on the Western Front,* a classroom classic by Erich Maria Remarque, speaks with eloquence about World War I. First published before World War II, *Address Unknown* (Kathrine Kressman Taylor) is a novella with a cautionary tone about what would follow. In *The Tin Drum,* Günter Grass broke the post-WWII silence, creating a landmark work of literature in the process. *The Silent Angel* is a complex love story set after the war (by Nobel Prize winner Heinrich Böll).

A book of science fiction and time travel, *1632* (Flint) sends West Virginians back to 17th-century Germany. *The Good German* (Kanon), set during the postwar years, is part thriller, part historical fiction. *Berlin Noir* (Kerr) is filled with stories of secrets and crime.

For a recently written read, consider the following books, published since the mid-1990s. Esther Freud, the daughter of artist Lucien Freud, set *Summer at Gaglow* during the Great War. *Stones from the River,* the story of a dwarf in Nazi Germany, and *Floating in My Mother's Palm,* which takes place in a small town on the Rhine, have brought Ursula Hegi accolades. Told by a sympathetic narrator, *The Reader* (Schlink) challenges readers to think, "What if my loved ones had been Nazis?" *Saints and Villains* (Giardina) is the fictionalized account of Dietrich Bonhoeffer, a Protestant theologian who protested against Hitler's rise. *Marrying Mozart* (Cowell) reveals a more intimate side of the famous composer.

Films

Leni Riefenstahl's *Triumph of the Will* (1935) is infamous Nazi propaganda turned film classic. Orson Welles infuses *The Third Man* (1949, actually shot in a bombed-out and Soviet-occupied Vienna) with noir foreboding. *The Tin Drum* (1979) is based on Günter Grass' seminal novel (see previous page).

Other meditations on the war years—films filled with allegory and metaphor about the Nazis' rise to power—include *Mephisto* (1981) and Rainer Werner Fassbinder's *The Marriage of Maria Braun* (1979). *Downfall* (2004) tells of the Führer's final days. *Schindler's List* (1993)—about a factory owner's inspirational efforts to save his Jewish employees from deportation to concentration camps—won Steven Spielberg the Best Picture and Best Director Oscars.

Shoah (1985) is a 9.5-hour Holocaust documentary that includes no wartime footage, only interviews with those who lived through it. The well-respected *Das Boot* (1981) has a strong pacifist message, as do the films about the students who defied Hitler—and were ultimately sentenced to die: *The White Rose* (1982) and the beautiful, devastating *Sophie Scholl: The Final Days* (2005).

But German film is not comprised of only dramatic, war-themed movies. *Cabaret* (1972, about the crazy Berlin scene in the late 1920s) made Liza Minnelli a star. Set in Berlin, *Wings of Desire* (1987) is Wim Wenders' best film, showing an angel who falls in love and falls to earth. *Amadeus* (1984) made Mozart into a flesh-and-blood man (who giggles), as did *Immortal Beloved* (1994) for Beethoven. *Run Lola Run* (1998) was an art-house phenomenon, combining action, love, and mobsters. Jewish refugees settle in 1930s Kenya in *Nowhere in Africa* (2001). *Good Bye, Lenin!* (2003) is a funny, poignant look at a son's struggle to re-create long-gone Eastern Europe for his mother, while the former GDR's harsh secrets are exposed in *The Lives of Others* (2006).

TELEPHONES, EMAIL, AND MAIL

Telephones

Smart travelers learn the phone system and use it daily to book or reconfirm rooms, get tourist information, reserve restaurants, confirm tour times, or phone home.

Types of Phones

You'll encounter various kinds of phones in Germany:

Hurdling the Language Barrier

German—like English, Dutch, Swedish, and Norwegian—is a Germanic language, making it easier on most American ears than Romance languages (such as Italian and French). These tips will help you pronounce German words: The letter *w* is always pronounced as "v" (e.g., the word for "wonderful" is *wunderbar*, pronounced VOON-der-bar). In the vowel combinations *ie* and *ei*, you pronounce only the second letter, so *ie* sounds like the letter *e* (as in *hier* and *Bier*, the German words for "here" and "beer"), while *ei* sounds like the letter *i* (as in *nein* and *Stein*, the German words for "no" and "stone"). The vowel combination *au* is pronounced "ow" (as in *Frau*). The vowel combinations *eu* and *äu* are pronounced "oy" (as in *neu*, *Deutsch*, and *Bräu*, the German words for "new," "German," and "brew"). To pronounce *ö* and *ü*, purse your lips when you say the vowel; the other vowel with an umlaut, *ä*, is pronounced the same as *e* in "men." (In written German, these can be depicted as the vowel followed by an *e*—*oe*, *ue*, and *ae*, respectively.) The letter *Eszett (ß)* represents *ss*. Written German always capitalizes all nouns.

Use the German Survival Phrases on page 565. Give it your best shot. The locals will appreciate your efforts.

Card-operated phones—in which you insert a locally bought phone card into a public pay phone—are fairly common.

Coin-operated phones are becoming scarce in Germany, though you might see them at gas stations and in the lobbies of big hotels.

Hotel room phones are sometimes cheap for local calls (confirm at the front desk first), but can be a rip-off for long-distance calls ($1–2/minute unless you use an international phone card—described on the next page). But incoming calls are free, making this a cheap way for friends and family to stay in touch, provided they have a good long-distance plan for calls to Europe.

American mobile phones work in Europe if they're GSM-enabled, tri-band or quad-band, and on a calling plan that includes international calls. They're convenient, but pricey. For example, with a T-Mobile phone, you'll pay $1 per minute for calls and about $0.35 for text messages.

German mobile phones are affordable to buy and come without contracts. These phones are loaded with prepaid calling time that you can recharge as you use up the minutes. As long as you're not "roaming" outside the phone's home country, incoming calls are free. If you're traveling to multiple countries within Europe, make sure the phone is electronically "unlocked," so that you can swap out its SIM card (a fingernail-sized chip that holds the phone's information) for a new one in other countries.

For example, T-Mobile sells a cheapo phone in Germany for €15, including a SIM card and €5 of credit. You'll need to provide an address (either your hotel or your home will work) and show your passport. Calls are generally no more than €0.50 per minute and often less, and the SIM card can be used in other European countries (ask about rates). Receiving calls within Germany is free (but you will pay extra to reach other mobile phones). Refill cards (to add extra calling time) come in €15, €30, and €50 denominations.

If you already own an unlocked multi-band GSM phone, all you'll need is a German SIM card (T-Mobile sells one for €10, including €10 worth of calling credit).

For more information on mobile phones, see www.ricksteves.com/phones.

Using Phone Cards

Get a phone card for your calls. Prepaid phone cards come in two types: international and insertable.

International Phone Cards: These offer the cheapest way to make international calls from Germany (they also work for local calls). Some even work in multiple countries—if traveling to both Germany and Austria, try to buy a card that will work in both places.

The cards are sold at small newsstand kiosks and hole-in-the-wall long-distance shops. There are many different brands of cards, so ask the clerk which one has the best rates for calls to America. Some cards are rechargeable; you can call the number on the card, give your credit-card number, and buy more time. Because cards are occasionally duds, avoid the high denominations.

You can use international phone cards from any type of phone, even your hotel-room phone (check to make sure that your phone is set on tone instead of pulse, and ask at the desk about hidden fees for toll-free calls).

Avoid using international phone cards at pay phones, because the German phone company slaps on hefty surcharges. From a pay phone, you'll get far fewer minutes for your money (for example, 10 min instead of 100 on a €5 card) than if you call from your hotel room.

To use a card, scratch off the back to reveal your PIN (Personal Identification Number). Dial the number listed on the card, reaching an automated operator. When prompted, dial in the PIN code. Then dial your number (if you need help, see "How to Dial," next page.

Remember that you don't need the actual card to use a card account, so it's sharable. You can write down the access number and PIN code in your notebook and share it with friends. Give the number of a still lively card to another traveler if you're leaving the country.

Insertable Phone Cards: These cards can be used only at pay phones, and are sold in denominations starting at about €5 at TIs, tobacco shops, post offices, and train stations. To use the card, you physically insert it into a slot in the pay phone. The price of the call is automatically deducted while you talk. Calling the US with an insertable phone card is reasonable (about 2–3 min per euro), but more expensive than using an international phone card. Note that insertable phone cards don't work outside of Germany.

Given the prevalence of mobile phones, public phones (especially the type that accepts phone cards) are getting harder to find.

Using Hotel Room Phones, VoIP, or US Calling Cards

The best way to call home is using an international phone card, but there are other alternatives:

Calling from the phone in your **hotel room** is convenient...but expensive (unless you use an international phone card, described on previous page). While incoming calls (made by folks back home) can be the cheapest way for you to keep in touch, charges for *outgoing* calls can be a very unpleasant surprise. Before you dial, get a clear explanation from the hotel staff of the charges, even for local (and supposedly) toll-free calls.

If your family has an inexpensive way to call Europe, either through a long-distance plan or prepaid calling card, have them call you in your hotel room. Give them a list of your hotels' phone numbers before you go. Then, as you travel, send them an email to set up a time for them to give you a ring.

If you're traveling with a laptop, consider trying **VoIP (Voice over Internet Protocol).** With VoIP, two computers act as the phones, allowing for a free Internet-based call. The major providers are Skype (www.skype.com) and Google Talk (www.google.com/talk).

US Calling Cards (such as the ones offered by AT&T, MCI, or Sprint) are the worst option. You'll nearly always save a lot of money by paying with a phone card (see previous page).

How to Dial

Calling from the US to Europe, or vice versa, is simple—once you break the code. The European calling chart on the next page will walk you through it.

Dialing Domestic Calls

Germany, like much of the US, uses an area-code dialing system. If you're dialing within an area code, you just dial the local number

APPENDIX

European Calling Chart

Just smile and dial, using this key:
AC = Area Code, LN = Local Number.

European Country	Calling long distance within...	Calling from the US or Canada to...	Calling from a European country to...
Austria	AC + LN	011 + 43 + AC (without the initial zero) + LN	00 + 43 + AC (without the initial zero) + LN
Belgium	LN	011 + 32 + LN (without initial zero)	00 + 32 + LN (without initial zero)
Bosnia-Herzegovina	AC + LN	011 + 387 + AC (without initial zero) + LN	00 + 387 + AC (without initial zero) + LN
Britain	AC + LN	011 + 44 + AC (without initial zero) + LN	00 + 44 + AC (without initial zero) + LN
Croatia	AC + LN	011 + 385 + AC (without initial zero) + LN	00 + 385 + AC (without initial zero) + LN
Czech Republic	LN	011 + 420 + LN	00 + 420 + LN
Denmark	LN	011 + 45 + LN	00 + 45 + LN
Estonia	LN	011 + 372 + LN	00 + 372 + LN
Finland	AC + LN	011 + 358 + AC (without initial zero) + LN	999 + 358 + AC (without initial zero) + LN
France	LN	011 + 33 + LN (without initial zero)	00 + 33 + LN (without initial zero)
Germany	AC + LN	011 + 49 + AC (without initial zero) + LN	00 + 49 + AC (without initial zero) + LN
Greece	LN	011 + 30 + LN	00 + 30 + LN
Hungary	06 + AC + LN	011 + 36 + AC + LN	00 + 36 + AC + LN
Ireland	AC + LN	011 + 353 + AC (without initial zero) + LN	00 + 353 + AC (without initial zero) + LN

European Country	Calling long distance within...	Calling from the US or Canada to...	Calling from a European country to...
Italy	LN	011 + 39 + LN	00 + 39 + LN
Montenegro	AC + LN	011 + 382 + AC (without initial zero) + LN	00 + 382 + AC (without initial zero) + LN
Netherlands	AC + LN	011 + 31 + AC (without initial zero) + LN	00 + 31 + AC (without initial zero) + LN
Norway	LN	011 + 47 + LN	00 + 47 + LN
Poland	LN	011 + 48 + LN (without initial zero)	00 + 48 + LN (without initial zero)
Portugal	LN	011 + 351 + LN	00 + 351 + LN
Slovakia	AC + LN	011 + 421 + AC (without initial zero) + LN	00 + 421 + AC (without initial zero) + LN
Slovenia	AC + LN	011 + 386 + AC (without initial zero) + LN	00 + 386 + AC (without initial zero) + LN
Spain	LN	011 + 34 + LN	00 + 34 + LN
Sweden	AC + LN	011 + 46 + AC (without initial zero) + LN	00 + 46 + AC (without initial zero) + LN
Switzerland	LN	011 + 41 + LN (without initial zero)	00 + 41 + LN (without initial zero)
Turkey	AC (if no initial zero is included, add one) + LN	011 + 90 + AC (without initial zero) + LN	00 + 90 + AC (without initial zero) + LN

- The instructions above apply whether you're calling a land line or mobile phone.
- The international access codes (the first numbers you dial when making an international call) are 011 if you're calling from the US or Canada, or 00 if you're calling from virtually anywhere in Europe (except Finland, where it's 999).
- To call the US or Canada from Europe, dial 00, then 1 (the country code for the US and Canada), then the area code and number. In short, 00 + 1 + AC + LN = Hi, Mom!

to be connected; but if you're calling outside your area code, you have to dial both the area code (which starts with a 0) and the local number. You'll find area codes listed throughout this book, or you can get them from directory assistance (tel. 11833).

For example, Munich's area code is 089 and the number of one of my recommended Munich hotels is 515-530. To call the hotel within Munich, you'd dial 515-530. To call it from Frankfurt, you'd dial 089/515-530.

Don't be surprised if local phone numbers in Germany have different numbers of digits within the same city or even the same hotel (for example, a hotel can have a 6-digit phone number and an 8-digit fax number).

Be aware that some numbers, typically those that start with 018 (including some train and airline information numbers) are actually premium toll calls, costing more than a regular land-line call. The per-minute charge should be listed in small print next to the phone number.

Dialing Internationally

If you want to make an international call, follow these three steps:

1. Dial the international access code (00 if you're calling from Europe, 011 from the US or Canada).

2. Dial the country code of the country you're calling (49 for Germany, or 1 for the US or Canada).

3. Dial the area code (without its initial 0) and the local number.

For example, to call the recommended Munich hotel from the US, dial 011 (the US international access code), 49 (Germany's country code), 89 (Munich's area code without the initial 0), and 515-530.

To call my office in Edmonds, Washington, from Germany, I dial 00 (Europe's international access code), 1 (the US country code), 425 (Edmonds' area code), and 771-8303.

Useful Phone Numbers

Directory Assistance

National—tel. 11833, International—tel. 11834.
Train info—tel. 11861 (€0.60/min); ask for an English speaker.
German Tourist Offices: Dial the local code, then 19433.

US Embassy

In Berlin: Neustädtische Kirchstrasse 4–5, tel. 030/83050; consular services at Clayallee 170, Mon–Fri 8:30–12:00, closed Sat–Sun, tel. 030/832-9233—Mon–Fri 14:00–16:00 only, www.usembassy.de, consberlin@state.gov.

Email and Mail

Email: Many travelers set up a free email account with Yahoo, Microsoft (Hotmail), or Google (Gmail). Internet cafés are easy to find in big cities. Most of the small towns I cover in this book also have Internet cafés. Many libraries offer free access, but they also tend to have limited opening hours, restrict your online time to 30 minutes, and may require reservations. Look for the places listed in this book, or ask the local TI, computer store, or your hotelier.

Most hotels have a dedicated desktop computer for guests' email needs. Small places with no guest computer or Wi-Fi sometimes let clients (who've asked politely) sit at their desk for a few minutes just to check their email. But don't abuse their courtesy by camping out on their computer.

Internet access for laptop users is becoming commonplace at most hotels and even smaller *Gasthof*s. Many hotels that offer this do so for free, but some charge (about €8/hr, up to €18–25/day at fancier places). You'll either access the hotel's wireless Internet (Wi-Fi, also called "WLAN" in Europe), sometimes using a password provided by the hotelier; or plug your computer directly into an Internet wall socket (they can usually loan you a cable). These days, I can get online at most hotels in this book, and I've noted this in each listing. If I say "Internet access," there's a public terminal in the lobby for guests to use. If I say "Wi-Fi," you can generally access it in your room, but only if you have your own laptop.

Mail: Get stamps at the neighborhood post office, newsstands within fancy hotels, and some mini-marts and card shops. Avoid standing in line at the post office by using the handy yellow stamp *(Briefmarke)* machines found just outside the building. Warning: These machines give change only in stamps, not in coins. Postcard stamps to the US or Canada cost €1.

To arrange for mail delivery, reserve a few hotels along your route in advance and give their addresses to friends. Allow 10 days for a letter to arrive. Phoning and emailing are so easy that I've dispensed with mail stops altogether.

TRANSPORTATION

By Car or Train?

Cars are best for three or more traveling together (especially families with small kids), those packing heavy, and those scouring the countryside. Trains and buses are best for solo travelers, blitz tourists, and city-to-city travelers. While a car gives you the ultimate in mobility and freedom, enables you to search for hotels more easily, and carries your bags for you, the train zips you effortlessly from city to city, usually dropping you in the center and near the tourist office. A car is a worthless headache in cities such as Munich, Berlin, and Frankfurt.

Trains

Trains are generally slick, speedy, and punctual, with synchronized connections. They cover cities well, but some frustrating schedules make a few out-of-the-way recommendations (such as Bavaria's Wieskirche) not worth the time and trouble for the less determined. It's illegal to smoke on Germany's trains, buses, and taxis.

Types of Trains

There are big differences in price, speed, and comfort between Germany's three levels of trains. ICE trains (white with red trim and streamlined noses) are the fastest, zipping from city to city in air-conditioned comfort, and costing proportionately more. Red regional trains (labeled RB, RE, and IRE on schedules) are the slowest—the milk-run RB trains stop at every small station—but cost much less. Mid-level IC and EC trains are white with red trim but look older than the ICEs. If you have a railpass, take the fastest train available—railpass holders don't pay a supplement for the fast ICE trains (with one exception, the "ICE Sprinter"). If you're buying point-to-point tickets, taking a slower train can save a lot of money.

Schedules

Schedules change by season, weekday, and weekend. Verify train times shown in this book—on the Web, check http://bahn.hafas.de/bin/query.exe/en. At staffed train stations, attendants will print out a step-by-step itinerary for you, free of charge. You can also produce an itinerary yourself by using the computerized red-and-blue trackside machines marked *Fahrkarten*. The touch-screen display gives you an English option; choose "Timetable Information," indicate your point of departure and destination, and then hit "Print" for a personalized schedule, including transfers and track numbers. You can also buy tickets from these machines—cash only, since they don't accept non-European bankcards (for more information, see "Type of Tickets," page 552).

You can call Germany's train information number from anywhere in the country: tel. 11861 (€0.60/min). Ask for an English speaker.

Railpasses

The German Pass is a great value for rail travel within Germany. Any pass that covers Germany covers travel all the way to Salzburg, Austria, which counts as the official border point on the train line

Public Transportation

from Munich. If you're traveling in a neighboring country, two-country Eurailpasses allow you to pair Germany with Austria, Switzerland, France, the BeNeLux region, Denmark, Poland, or the Czech Republic. The Eurail Selectpass gives you more travel in three, four, or five adjacent countries (but some Eastern European countries—like the Czech Republic or Poland—are not eligible). If you're planning a whirlwind tour of Europe, another possibility is the 20-country Eurailpass. These passes are available in a Saverpass version, which gives a 15 percent discount on railpasses for two or more companions traveling together. For specifics, check the rail-pass chart on the next page and visit www.ricksteves.com/rail.

APPENDIX

Railpasses

Prices listed are for 2009 and are subject to change. For the latest prices, details, train schedules, and easy online ordering, see my comprehensive Guide to Eurail Passes at www.ricksteves.com/rail. See Web site for more passes, including France-Germany, Germany-Poland, and Germany-Czech passes.

"Saver" prices are per person for two or more people traveling together. "Youth" means under age 26. All passes for Germany cover KD Line boats on the Rhine and Mosel, 20% off Romantic Road bus ride.

GERMAN PASS

	Indiv. 1st Cl.	Indiv. 2nd Cl.	Twin 1st Cl.	Twin 2nd Cl.	Youth 2nd Cl.
4 days in 1 month	$340	$260	$267	$195	$216
Extra rail days (max. 6)	43-47	29-32	30-32	21-24	14-17

Twin prices are per person for two traveling together. The fare for children 6–11 is half the individual fare. Kids under age 6 travel free. Five and ten-day versions available at some stations in Germany.

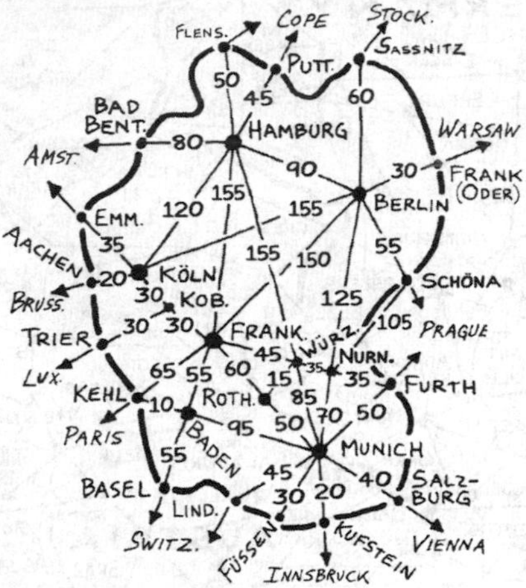

Map key:
Approximate point-to-point one-way second-class rail fares in US dollars. First class costs 50 percent more. Add up the approximate ticket costs for your trip to see if a railpass will save you money.

SELECTPASS

This pass covers travel in three adjacent countries. For four- and five-country options, please visit **www.ricksteves.com/rail**.

	Individual 1st Class	Saver 1st Class	Youth 2nd Class
5 days in 2 months	$435	$370	$284
6 days in 2 months	481	410	315
8 days in 2 months	570	487	370
10 days in 2 months	660	559	427

Selectpass diagram key:
A **Selectpass** can be designed to connect a "chain" of any three, four, or five countries in this diagram linked by direct lines. (Examples that qualify: Norway-Sweden-Germany or Germany-Austria-Switzerland.) "Benelux" is considered one country.

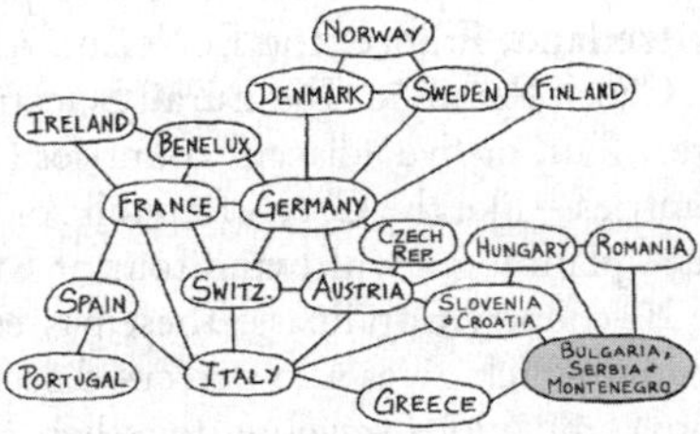

GERMANY–AUSTRIA PASS

	Indiv. 1st Cl.	Indiv. 2nd Cl.	Saver 1st Cl.	Saver 2nd Cl.	Youth 2nd Cl.
5 days in 2 months	$390	$332	$332	$285	$285
6 days in 2 months	429	365	365	315	315
8 days in 2 months	510	434	434	373	373
10 days in 2 months	593	504	504	434	434

The fare for children 4–11 is half the adult individual fare or Saver fare. Kids under age 4 travel free.

GERMANY–SWITZERLAND PASS

	Individual 1st Class	Saver 1st Class	Youth 2nd Class
5 days in 2 months	$412	$351	$290
6 days in 2 months	454	387	320
8 days in 2 months	537	459	377
10 days in 2 months	621	531	437

The fare for children 4–11 is half the adult individual or Saver fare. Kids under age 4 travel free.

BENELUX–GERMANY PASS

	Indiv. 1st Cl.	Indiv. 2nd Cl.	Saver 1st Cl.	Saver 2nd Cl.	Youth 2nd Cl.
5 days in 2 months	$406	$305	$305	$248	$248
6 days in 2 months	449	338	338	271	271
8 days in 2 months	531	399	399	320	320
10 days in 2 months	617	463	463	371	371

The fare for children 4–11 is half the adult individual fare or Saver fare. Kids under age 4 travel free.

DENMARK–GERMANY PASS

	Indiv. 1st Cl.	Indiv. 2nd Cl.	Saver 1st Cl.	Saver 2nd Cl.	Youth 2nd Cl.
4 days in 2 months	$330	$271	$271	$209	$209
5 days in 2 months	371	305	305	235	235
6 days in 2 months	412	338	338	257	257
8 days in 2 months	496	407	407	296	296
10 days in 2 months	596	454	454	335	335

The fare for children 4–11 is half the adult individual fare or Saver fare. Kids under age 4 travel free.

GERMANY RAIL & DRIVE PASS

Any 2 rail days and 2 car days in 1 month.

Car Category	1st Class	2nd Class	Extra Car Day
Economy	$228	$185	$53
Compact	237	194	62
Intermediate	245	202	70
Small automatic	263	220	88

Prices are per person, two traveling together. Extra rail day $65 in 1st Class, $48 in 2nd Class (max. 2).

SELECTPASS RAIL & DRIVE

Any 3 rail days and 2 car days in 2 months within 3 adjoining countries.

Car Category	1st Class	Extra Car Day
Economy	$372	$53
Compact	389	72
Intermediate	398	81
Small Automatic	418	98

Prices are per person, two traveling together. Extra rail days (max. 2) about $40 each. 2-rail-day version also available. Third and fourth persons sharing car get a 3-day out of 2-month railpass for approx. $326 (kids 4-11: $163). A fourth or fifth country each adds about $45 to these prices. Longer durations available for five countries.

To order a Rail & Drive pass, call your travel agent or Rail Europe at 800-438-7245. *These passes are not sold by Europe Through the Back Door.*

Railpass travelers should know what extras are covered by their pass: for example, travel on any German buses marked "DeutscheBahn" or "DB" (run by the train company); travel on city S-Bahn systems (except in Berlin, where only S-Bahn lines between major train stations are covered); covered or discounted boats on the Rhine, Mosel, and Danube rivers; and a 20 percent discount on the Romantic Road bus. Flexipass-holders should note that discounted trips don't use up a flexi-day, but fully covered ("free") trips do. The "used" flexipass day can also cover your train travel on that day (but if you're not planning to travel more that day, it makes sense to pay for, say, a short boat ride rather than use up a day of your pass for it).

Type of Tickets

People of any age buying individual tickets should remember that traveling in second class instead of first class provides the same transportation for 33 percent less. Ticket fares are shown on the map on page 550 and at http://bahn.hafas.de/bin/query.exe/en.

You can buy *Normalpreis* point-to-point tickets at any time; no reservation is needed, so you can easily change your plans and take any train.

Deals: Look into specials available in Germany. For instance, kids under 14 travel free when named on a parent's or grandparent's point-to-point ticket. Off-peak specials in Germany include a wild *Schönes Wochenende* ticket for €32; it gives groups of up to five people unlimited second-class travel on slower regional trains all day Saturday or Sunday. *Länder-Tickets* are a similar deal (€27 for up to 5 people after 9:00 on weekdays on local trains within a single region, such as Bavaria). Round-trip, longer-distance tickets—called *Sparpreis 25* and *50*—are 25–50 percent cheaper when you commit to taking particular trains and buy your ticket at least three days in advance (changing your itinerary costs about €15). Those staying longer in Germany can get additional discounts for a full year by purchasing one of several BahnCards (starting at €55; see www.bahn.de).

Buying Tickets

At the Station: Major German stations have a handy *Reisezentrum* (travel center) where you can ask questions and buy tickets. Many smaller stations, though, are unstaffed, with tickets sold only from machines (marked *Fahrkarten,* which means "tickets").

The new red-and-blue, multilingual, touch-screen machines at larger stations sell short- and long-distance train tickets, and print schedules for free (see "Schedules," page 548). You can pay with bills, coins, or credit cards that have a PIN code.

There are also older ticket machines, still around at major stations and sometimes the only option at smaller stations. These machines sell same-day-only tickets to nearby destinations. In cities, they also sell local public transport tickets. To buy a ticket, press the flag button until it gives you a screen in English. Then look for your destination on the long list of towns on the left side of the machine. If your destination isn't on the list (because it's too far away), you can buy the ticket on board (let the conductor know where you boarded and you won't even have to pay the small markup for buying a ticket on the train). If your destination *is* on the list, note the four-digit code for your destination and enter it in the number pad. The machine will automatically issue you a ticket for a one-way *(Einfache)* second-class fare, but you can alter that with the buttons below the keypad (press *Hin- und Rückfahrt* if you want a round-trip ticket, *1./2. Klasse* for first class, and note the column of buttons for children's tickets). Feed the machine cash (small bills are okay, but it won't take your non-European credit card), then collect your ticket and change. *Gut gemacht!* (Well done!)

On the Train: You can buy a ticket on board from the conductor for a long-distance journey (by paying a small markup), but if you're riding a local (short distance) train, you're expected to board with a valid ticket...or you can get fined.

Online: You can buy German train tickets online and print them out yourself or have them delivered by mail; you'll need to visit http://bahn.hafas.de/bin/query.exe/en and create a login and password.

Train plus Bike

Hundreds of local train stations rent bikes for about $10 a day, and sometimes have easy "pick up here and drop off there" plans. For more on mixing train and bike travel, ask at stations for information booklets.

Renting a Car

Car rental is cheapest if arranged from home. Call several companies, look online, or arrange a rental through your hometown travel agent, who can help you out if anything goes wrong during your trip. Two reputable companies among many are Auto Europe (www.autoeurope.com) and Europe by Car (www.europebycar.com). For the best deal, rent by the week with unlimited mileage (but for long trips, consider leasing).

Expect to pay about $800 per person (based on 2 people sharing the car) for a small economy car for three weeks with unlimited mileage, including gas, parking, and insurance. I normally rent a small, inexpensive model like a Ford Fiesta. For a bigger, roomier, more powerful but inexpensive car, move up to a Ford Focus or VW Polo. Minibuses are a great budget way to go for 5–9 people.

Car-rental companies have age restrictions (confirm age requirements when you book). Most companies will not rent to someone under 21, and restrictions and "underage fees" can apply if you're 21–24. There's generally not a maximum age limit, but if you are 70 or older, it's smart to ask. If you're considered too young or old, look into leasing, which has less-stringent age restrictions (see "Leasing," next page).

If you want an automatic, reserve the car at least a month in advance and specifically request an automatic. You'll pay about 40 percent more to rent a car with an automatic instead of a manual transmission.

When you pick up the car, check it thoroughly and make sure any damage is noted on your rental agreement. Find out how your car's headlights, turn signals, wipers, and gas cap function.

Returning a car at a big-city train station can be tricky; get precise details on the car drop-off location and hours. When you return the car, make sure the agent verifies its condition with you.

If you drop your car off early or keep it longer, you'll be credited or charged at a fair, prorated price. But keep your receipts in case any questions arise about your billing.

Car Insurance Options

When you rent a car, you are liable for a very high deductible, sometimes equal to the entire value of the car. You can limit your financial risk in case of an accident by choosing one of these three options: buy Collision Damage Waiver (CDW) coverage from the car-rental company, get coverage through your credit card (free, if your card automatically includes zero-deductible coverage), or buy coverage through Travel Guard.

CDW includes a very high deductible (typically $1,000–1,500). When you pick up the car, you'll be offered the chance to "buy down" the deductible to zero (for $10–30/day; this is often called "super CDW").

If you opt instead for credit-card coverage, there's a catch. You'll technically have to decline all coverage offered by the car-rental company, which means they can place a hold on your card for the full deductible amount. In case of damage, it can be time-consuming to resolve the charges with your credit-card company. Before you decide on this option, quiz your credit-card company about how it works and ask them to explain the worst-case scenario.

Buying CDW insurance (plus "super CDW") is the easier but pricier option. Using the coverage that comes with your credit card saves money, but can involve more hassle.

Finally, you can buy CDW insurance from Travel Guard ($9/day plus a one-time $3 service fee covers you up to $35,000, $250 deductible, tel. 800-826-4919, www.travelguard.com). It's valid throughout Europe, but some car-rental companies refuse to honor it (especially in the Republic of Ireland and in Italy). Oddly, residents of Washington State aren't allowed to buy this coverage.

For more fine print about car-rental insurance, see www.ricksteves.com/cdw.

Leasing

For trips of two and a half weeks or more, leasing (which automatically includes CDW-type insurance with no deductible) is the best way to go. By technically buying and then selling back the car, you save lots of money on tax and insurance. Leasing provides you a new car with unlimited mileage and a 24-hour emergency assistance program. You can lease for as little as 17 days to as long as six months. Car leases must be arranged from the US. A reliable company offering 17-day lease packages for about $1,100 is Europe by Car (US tel. 800-223-1516, www.europebycar.com).

Driving

Your US driver's license is all you need to drive in Germany, but it's recommended that you also get an International Driving Permit (IDP) at your local AAA office before you go ($15 plus the cost of two passport-type photos, www.aaa.com).

Learn the universal road signs (explained in charts in most road atlases and at service stations). Seat belts are required, and two beers under those belts are enough to land you in jail. You're required to use low-beam headlights if it's overcast, raining, or snowing.

Use good local maps and study them before each drive. Learn

which exits you need to look out for, which major cities you'll travel toward, where the ruined castles lurk, and so on.

To get to the center of a city, follow signs for *Zentrum* or *Stadtmitte.* Ring roads go around a city. For parking, you can pick up a cardboard clock (*Parkscheibe,* available free at gas stations, police stations, and *Tabak* shops). Display your arrival time on the clock and put it on the dashboard, so parking attendants can see you've been there less than the posted maximum stay.

Every long drive between my recommended destinations is via the autobahn (super-freeway), and nearly every scenic backcountry drive is paved and comfortable.

The shortest distance between any two points is the autobahn. Blue signs direct you to the autobahn. To understand the complex but super-efficient autobahn (no speed limit, toll-free), look for the *Autobahn Service* booklet at any autobahn rest stop (free, lists all stops, services, road symbols, and more). Learn the signs: *Dreieck* ("three corners") means a Y in the road; *Autobahnkreuz* is an intersection. Exits are spaced about every 20 miles and often have a gas station (*bleifrei* means "unleaded"), a restaurant, a mini-market, and sometimes a tourist information desk. Exits and intersections refer to the next major city or the nearest small town. Peruse the map and anticipate which town names to look out for. Know what you're looking for—miss it, and you're long autobahn-gone. When navigating, you'll see *nord, süd, ost,* and *west.*

Autobahns in Germany generally have no speed limit, but you will commonly see a recommended speed posted. While no one gets a ticket for ignoring this recommendation, exceeding this speed means your car insurance no longer covers you in the event of an accident. Don't cruise in the passing lane; stay right. Obstructing traffic on the autobahn is against the law—so running out of gas is not only dangerous, it can earn you a big ticket. In fast-driving Germany, the backed-up line caused by an insensitive slow driver is called an *Autoschlange,* or "car snake." What's the difference between a car snake and a real snake? According to locals, "On a real snake, the ass is in the back."

Driving: Distance and Time

Driving in Austria: If you side-trip by car into Austria, bring your US driver's license and get an International Driving Permit (see the beginning of this section). Austria charges drivers who use their major roads. You'll need to have a *Vignette* sticker stuck to the inside of your rental car's windshield (buy at the border crossing, big gas stations near borders, or a rental-car agency). The cost is €8 for 10 days, or €22 for two months. Dipping into the country on regular roads—such as around Reutte in Tirol—requires no special payment. In Austria, green signs direct you to the autobahn, and autobahn speed limits are enforced.

Cheap Flights

If you're visiting one or more cities on a longer European trip, consider intra-European airlines. While trains are usually the best way to connect places that are close together, a flight can save both time and money on longer journeys.

One of the best websites for comparing inexpensive flights is www.skyscanner.net. Other comparison search engines include www.kayak.com, www.mobissimo.com, www.sidestep.com, and www.wegolo.com.

Well-known cheapo airlines in Europe include easyJet (www.easyjet.com) and Ryanair (www.ryanair.com). Those based in Germany are Air Berlin (www.airberlin.com), Germanwings (www.germanwings.com), and TUIfly (www.tuifly.com).

Be aware of the potential drawbacks of flying on the cheap: nonrefundable and nonchangeable tickets, rigid baggage restrictions (and fees if you have more than what's officially allowed), use of airports far outside town, tight schedules that can mean more delays, little in the way of customer assistance if problems arise, and, of course, no frills. Read the small print—especially baggage policies—before you book.

HOLIDAYS AND FESTIVALS

This is a partial list of holidays and festivals. For more information, contact the tourist information office listed at the beginning of this chapter (www.cometogermany.com). Salzburg has music festivals nearly every month.

Jan	Perchtenlaufen (winter festival, parades), Tirol and Salzburg, Austria
Jan–Feb	Fasching (carnival season, balls, parades), throughout Germany
April 10	Good Friday
Easter	April 12 in 2009; Easter Festival, Salzburg
May 1	May Day with maypole dances, throughout Austria and Germany
May 16–24	Spring Horse Races (www.baden-galopp.de), Baden-Baden
May 25–June 1	Meistertrunk Show (medieval costumes, parties in the *Biergartens,* www.meistertrunk.de), Rothenburg
June 1	Pentecost Monday (Pfingstmontag), southern Germany
June 11	Corpus Christi (Fronleichnam), southern Germany
Late June	City Festival (www.elbhangfest.de), Dresden
June	Frankfurt Summertime Festival (arts)
Late June	Midsummer Eve Celebrations, Austria
July 11	Lichter Festival (fireworks and music, www.koelner-lichter.de), Köln

2009

JANUARY

S	M	T	W	T	F	S
				1	2	3
4	5	6	7	8	9	10
11	12	13	14	15	16	17
18	19	20	21	22	23	24
25	26	27	28	29	30	31

FEBRUARY

S	M	T	W	T	F	S
1	2	3	4	5	6	7
8	9	10	11	12	13	14
15	16	17	18	19	20	21
22	23	24	25	26	27	28

MARCH

S	M	T	W	T	F	S
1	2	3	4	5	6	7
8	9	10	11	12	13	14
15	16	17	18	19	20	21
22	23	24	25	26	27	28
29	30	31				

APRIL

S	M	T	W	T	F	S
			1	2	3	4
5	6	7	8	9	10	11
12	13	14	15	16	17	18
19	20	21	22	23	24	25
26	27	28	29	30		

MAY

S	M	T	W	T	F	S
					1	2
3	4	5	6	7	8	9
10	11	12	13	14	15	16
17	18	19	20	21	22	23
24/31	25	26	27	28	29	30

JUNE

S	M	T	W	T	F	S
	1	2	3	4	5	6
7	8	9	10	11	12	13
14	15	16	17	18	19	20
21	22	23	24	25	26	27
28	29	30				

JULY

S	M	T	W	T	F	S
			1	2	3	4
5	6	7	8	9	10	11
12	13	14	15	16	17	18
19	20	21	22	23	24	25
26	27	28	29	30	31	

AUGUST

S	M	T	W	T	F	S
						1
2	3	4	5	6	7	8
9	10	11	12	13	14	15
16	17	18	19	20	21	22
23/30	24/31	25	26	27	28	29

SEPTEMBER

S	M	T	W	T	F	S
		1	2	3	4	5
6	7	8	9	10	11	12
13	14	15	16	17	18	19
20	21	22	23	24	25	26
27	28	29	30			

OCTOBER

S	M	T	W	T	F	S
				1	2	3
4	5	6	7	8	9	10
11	12	13	14	15	16	17
18	19	20	21	22	23	24
25	26	27	28	29	30	31

NOVEMBER

S	M	T	W	T	F	S
1	2	3	4	5	6	7
8	9	10	11	12	13	14
15	16	17	18	19	20	21
22	23	24	25	26	27	28
29	30					

DECEMBER

S	M	T	W	T	F	S
		1	2	3	4	5
6	7	8	9	10	11	12
13	14	15	16	17	18	19
20	21	22	23	24	25	26
27	28	29	30	31		

Late July Kinderzeche Festival, Dinkelsbühl (www.kinderzeche.de)

Late July–Aug Salzburg Festival (music)

Aug 15 Assumption (Mariä Himmelfahrt), Munich

Aug 29–Sept 6 Summer Horse Races (www.baden-galopp.de), Baden-Baden

Sept Berlin Festwochen (arts festival)

Sept 4–6 Reichsstadt Festival (fireworks), Rothenburg

Sept 19–Oct 4 Oktoberfest (www.oktoberfest.de), Munich

Oct 3 German Unity Day (Tag der Deutschen Einheit), Germany

Oct 16–18 Fall Horse Races (www.baden-galopp.de), Baden-Baden

Nov 1	All Saints' Day (Allerheiligen), southern Germany
Nov	Berlin Jazz Festival; St. Martin's Day Celebrations (feasts), Bavaria
Dec	Christmas Fairs

CONVERSIONS AND CLIMATE

Numbers and Stumblers

- Europeans write a few of their numbers differently than we do. 1 = 1, 4 = 4, 7 = 7.
- In Europe, dates appear as day/month/year, so Christmas is 25/12/09.
- Commas are decimal points and decimals commas. A dollar and a half is 1,50, and there are 5.280 feet in a mile.
- When counting with fingers, start with your thumb. If you hold up your first finger to request one item, you'll probably get two.
- What Americans call the second floor of a building is the first floor in Europe.
- On escalators and moving sidewalks, Europeans keep the left "lane" open for passing. Keep to the right.

Metric Conversions (approximate)

1 foot = 0.3 meter	1 square yard = 0.8 square meter
1 yard = 0.9 meter	1 square mile = 2.6 square kilometers
1 mile = 1.6 kilometers	1 ounce = 28 grams
1 centimeter = 0.4 inch	1 quart = 0.95 liter
1 meter = 39.4 inches	1 kilogram = 2.2 pounds
1 kilometer = 0.62 mile	32°F = 0°C

Climate

The first line is the average daily high; the second line, the average daily low. The third line shows the average number of days without rain. For more detailed weather statistics for destinations throughout Germany (as well as the rest of the world), check www.worldclimate.com.

	J	F	M	A	M	J	J	A	S	O	N	D
GERMANY • Berlin												
	35°	37°	46°	56°	66°	72°	75°	74°	68°	56°	45°	38°
	26°	26°	31°	39°	47°	53°	57°	56°	50°	42°	36°	29°
	14	13	19	17	19	17	17	17	18	17	14	16
GERMANY • Munich												
	35°	38°	48°	56°	64°	70°	74°	73°	67°	56°	44°	36°
	23°	23°	30°	38°	45°	51°	55°	54°	48°	40°	33°	26°
	15	12	18	15	16	13	15	15	17	18	15	16

Temperature Conversion: Fahrenheit and Celsius

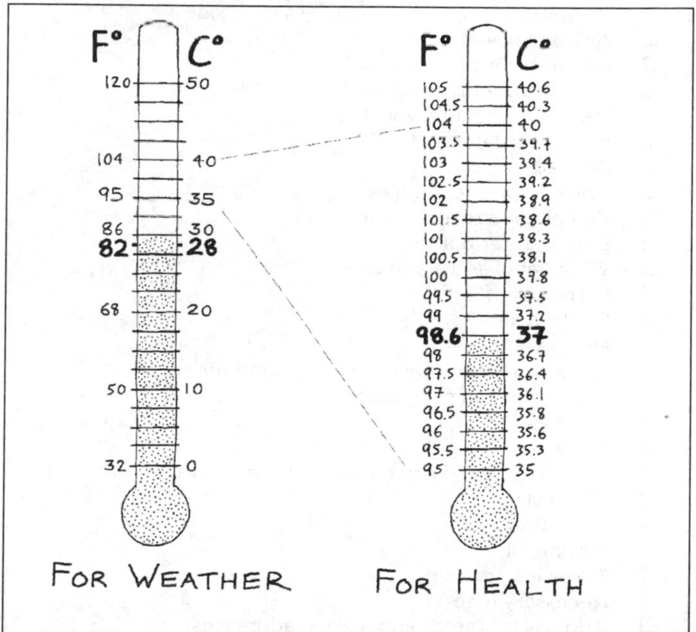

Europe takes its temperature using the Celsius scale, while we opt for Fahrenheit. For a rough conversion from Celsius to Fahrenheit, double the number and add 30. For weather, remember that 28°C is 82°F—perfect. For health, 37°C is just right.

Essential Packing Checklist

Whether you're traveling for five days or five weeks, here's what you'll need to bring. Remember to pack light to enjoy the sweet freedom of true mobility. Happy travels!

- ❑ 5 shirts
- ❑ 1 sweater or lightweight fleece jacket
- ❑ 2 pairs pants
- ❑ 1 pair shorts
- ❑ 1 swimsuit (women only—men can use shorts)
- ❑ 5 pairs underwear and socks
- ❑ 1 pair shoes
- ❑ 1 rain-proof jacket
- ❑ Tie or scarf
- ❑ Money belt
- ❑ Money—your mix of:
  - ❑ Debit card for ATM withdrawals
  - ❑ Credit card
  - ❑ Hard cash in US dollars
- ❑ Documents (and back-up photocopies)
- ❑ Passport
- ❑ Airplane ticket
- ❑ Driver's license
- ❑ Student ID and hostel card
- ❑ Railpass/car rental voucher
- ❑ Insurance details
- ❑ Daypack
- ❑ Sealable plastic baggies
- ❑ Camera and related gear
- ❑ Empty water bottle
- ❑ Wristwatch and alarm clock
- ❑ Earplugs
- ❑ First-aid kit
- ❑ Medicine (labeled)
- ❑ Extra glasses/contacts and prescriptions
- ❑ Sunscreen and sunglasses
- ❑ Toiletries kit
- ❑ Soap
- ❑ Laundry soap (if liquid and carry-on, limit to 3 oz.)
- ❑ Clothesline
- ❑ Small towel
- ❑ Sewing kit
- ❑ Travel information
- ❑ Necessary map(s)
- ❑ Address list (email and mailing addresses)
- ❑ Postcards and photos from home
- ❑ Notepad and pen
- ❑ Journal

Hotel Reservation

To: ______________________ ______________________
hotel *email or fax*

From: ______________________ ______________________
name *email or fax*

Today's date: _____ /______ /_____
day *month* *year*

Dear Hotel ______________________________,
Please make this reservation for me:

Name: ______________________________

Total # of people: _______ # of rooms: _______ # of nights: _______

Arriving: _____ /_____ /_____ My time of arrival (24-hr clock): _______
day *month* *year* (I will telephone if I will be late)

Departing: ____ /____ /_____
day *month* *year*

Room(s): Single___ Double ___ Twin___ Triple___ Quad___

With: Toilet ___ Shower___ Bath___ Sink only___

Special needs: View___ Quiet___ Cheapest ___ Ground Floor___

Please email or fax confirmation of my reservation, along with the type of room reserved and the price. Please also inform me of your cancellation policy. After I hear from you, I will quickly send my credit-card information as a deposit to hold the room. Thank you.

____
Name

____
Address

____
City ***State*** ***Zip Code*** ***Country***

Before hoteliers can make your reservation, they want to know the information listed above. You can use this form as the basis for your email, or you can photocopy this page, fill in the information, and send it as a fax (also available online at www.ricksteves.com/reservation).

German Survival Phrases

When using the phonetics, pronounce ī as the long I sound in "light."

Good day.	**Guten Tag.**	**goo**-tehn tahg
Do you speak English?	**Sprechen Sie Englisch?**	**shprehkh**-ehn zee **ehng**-lish
Yes. / No.	**Ja. / Nein.**	yah / nīn
I (don't) understand.	**Ich verstehe (nicht).**	ikh fehr-**shtay**-heh (nikht)
Please.	**Bitte.**	**bit**-teh
Thank you.	**Danke.**	**dahng**-keh
I'm sorry.	**Es tut mir leid.**	ehs toot meer līt
Excuse me.	**Entschuldigung.**	ehnt-**shool**-dig-oong
(No) problem.	**(Kein) Problem.**	(kīn) proh-**blaym**
(Very) good.	**(Sehr) gut.**	(zehr) goot
Goodbye.	**Auf Wiedersehen.**	owf **vee**-der-zayn
one / two	**eins / zwei**	īns / tsvī
three / four	**drei / vier**	drī / feer
five / six	**fünf / sechs**	fewnf / zehkhs
seven / eight	**sieben / acht**	**zee**-behn / ahkht
nine / ten	**neun / zehn**	noyn / tsayn
How much is it?	**Wieviel kostet das?**	**vee**-feel **kohs**-teht dahs
Write it?	**Schreiben?**	**shrī**-behn
Is it free?	**Ist es umsonst?**	ist ehs oom-**zohnst**
Included?	**Inklusive?**	in-kloo **zoo** veh
Where can I buy / find...?	**Wo kann ich kaufen / finden...?**	voh kahn ikh **kow**-fehn / **fin**-dehn
I'd like / We'd like...	**Ich hätte gern / Wir hätten gern...**	ikh **heh**-teh gehrn / veer **heh**-tehn gehrn
...a room.	**...ein Zimmer.**	īn **tsim**-mer
...a ticket to ___.	**...eine Fahrkarte nach ___.**	ī-neh **far**-kar-teh nahkh
Is it possible?	**Ist es möglich?**	ist ehs **mur**-glikh
Where is...?	**Wo ist...?**	voh ist
...the train station	**...der Bahnhof**	dehr **bahn**-hohf
...the bus station	**...der Busbahnhof**	dehr **boos**-bahn-hohf
...tourist information	**...das Touristen-informationsbüro**	dahs too-**ris**-tehn-in-for-maht-see-**ohns-bew**-roh
...toilet	**...die Toilette**	dee toh-**leh**-teh
men	**Herren**	**hehr**-rehn
women	**Damen**	**dah**-mehn
left / right	**links / rechts**	links / rehkhts
straight	**geradeaus**	geh-**rah**-deh-**ows**
When is this open / closed?	**Um wieviel Uhr ist hier geöffnet / geschlossen?**	oom **vee**-feel oor ist heer geh-**urf**-neht / geh-**shloh**-sehn
At what time?	**Um wieviel Uhr?**	oom **vee**-feel oor
Just a moment.	**Moment.**	moh-**mehnt**
now / soon / later	**jetzt / bald / später**	yehtst / bahld / **shpay**-ter
today / tomorrow	**heute / morgen**	**hoy**-teh / **mor**-gehn

In the Restaurant

I'd like / We'd like...	**Ich hätte gern / Wir hätten gern...**	ikh **heh**-teh gehrn / veer **heh**-tehn gehrn
...a reservation for...	**...eine Reservierung für...**	ī-neh reh-zer-**feer**-oong fewr
...a table for one / two.	**...einen Tisch für ein / zwei.**	ī-nehn tish fewr īn / tsvī
Non-smoking.	**Nichtraucher.**	**nikht**-rowkh-er
Is this seat free?	**Ist hier frei?**	ist heer frī
Menu (in English), please.	**Speisekarte (in Englisch), bitte.**	**shpī**-zeh-kar-teh (in **ehng**-lish) **bit**-teh
service (not) included	**Trinkgeld (nicht) inklusive**	**trink**-gehlt (nikht) in-kloo-**zee**-veh
cover charge	**Eintritt**	**īn**-trit
to go	**zum Mitnehmen**	tsoom **mit**-nay-mehn
with / without	**mit / ohne**	mit / **oh**-neh
and / or	**und / oder**	oont / **oh**-der
menu (of the day)	**(Tages-) Karte**	**(tah**-gehs-) **kar**-teh
set meal for tourists	**Touristenmenü**	too-**ris**-tehn-meh-**new**
specialty of the house	**Spezialität des Hauses**	**shpayt**-see-ah-lee-**tayt** dehs **how**-zehs
appetizers	**Vorspeise**	**for**-shpī-zeh
bread	**Brot**	broht
cheese	**Käse**	**kay**-zeh
sandwich	**Sandwich**	**zahnd**-vich
soup	**Suppe**	**zup**-peh
salad	**Salat**	zah-**laht**
meat	**Fleisch**	flīsh
poultry	**Geflügel**	geh-**flew**-gehl
fish	**Fisch**	fish
seafood	**Meeresfrüchte**	**meh**-rehs-**frewkh**-teh
fruit	**Obst**	ohpst
vegetables	**Gemüse**	geh-**mew**-zeh
dessert	**Nachspeise**	**nahkh**-shpī-zeh
mineral water	**Mineralwasser**	min-eh-**rahl**-vah-ser
tap water	**Leitungswasser**	**lī**-toongs-vah-ser
milk	**Milch**	milkh
(orange) juice	**(Orangen-) Saft**	(oh-**rahn**-zhehn-) zahft
coffee	**Kaffee**	kah-**fay**
tea	**Tee**	tay
wine	**Wein**	vīn
red / white	**rot / weiß**	roht / vīs
glass / bottle	**Glas / Flasche**	glahs / **flah**-sheh
beer	**Bier**	beer
Cheers!	**Prost!**	prohst
More. / Another.	**Mehr. / Noch ein.**	mehr / nohkh īn
The same.	**Das gleiche.**	dahs **glīkh**-eh
Bill, please.	**Rechnung, bitte.**	**rehkh**-noong **bit**-teh
tip	**Trinkgeld**	**trink**-gehlt
Delicious!	**Lecker!**	**lehk**-er

For more user-friendly German phrases, check out *Rick Steves' German Phrase Bo and Dictionary* or *Rick Steves' French, Italian & German Phrase Book.*

INDEX

N

T

Rick Steves®
EUROPEAN TOURS
Experience Europe the Rick Steves way, with great guides, small groups...and no grumps!
See 30 itineraries at ricksteves.com

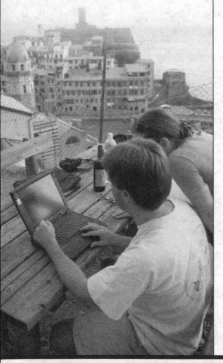

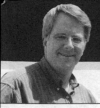

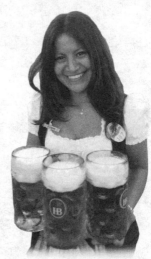

ricksteves.com

turn your travel dreams into affordable reality

▸ Free Audio Tours & Travel Newsletter

Get your nose out of this guidebook and focus on what you'll be seeing with Rick's free audio tours of the greatest sights in Paris, Rome, Florence and Venice.

Subscribe to our free *Travel News* e-newsletter, and get monthly articles from Rick on what's happening in Europe.

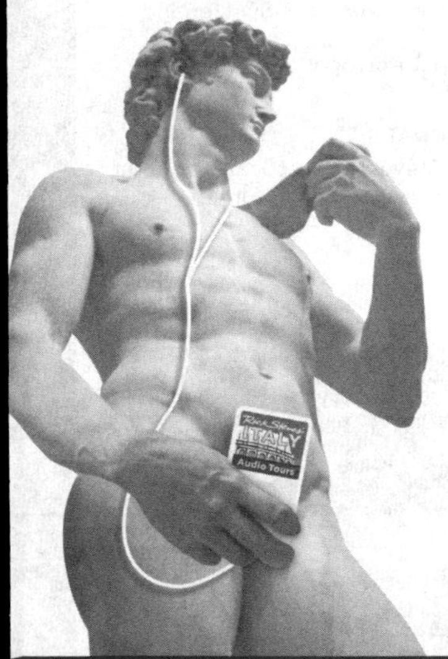

▸ Great Gear from Rick's Travel Store

Pack light and right—on a budget—with Rick's custom-designed carry-on bags, roll-aboards, day packs, travel accessories, guidebooks, journals, maps and DVDs of his TV shows.

130 Fourth Avenue North, PO Box 2009 • Edmonds, WA 98020 USA
Phone: (425) 771-8303 • Fax: (425) 771-0833 • www.ricksteves.com

CREDITS

Researcher

To help update this book, Rick relied on...

Ian Watson

Ian has worked with Rick's guidebooks since 1993, after starting out with Let's Go and Frommer's guides. Originally from upstate New York, Ian speaks several European languages, including German, and makes his home in Reykjavík, Iceland.

Contributor

Gene Openshaw

Gene is the co-author of seven Rick Steves books. For this book, he wrote material on art, history, and contemporary culture. When he's not traveling, Gene enjoys composing music, recovering from his 1973 trip to Europe with Rick, and living everyday life with his daughter.

IMAGES

Location	Photographer
Munich: Marienplatz	Rick Steves
Bavaria and Tirol: Neuschwanstein Castle	Dominic Bonuccelli
Salzburg and Berchtesgaden: Salzburg Overview	Dominic Bonucelli
Baden-Baden and the Black Forest: Baden-Baden	Cameron Hewitt
Rothenburg and the Romantic Road: Rothenburg	David C. Hoerlein
Würzburg: Residenzplatz	Ian Watson
Frankfurt: Frankfurt Scene from Bridge	Rick Steves
Rhine Valley: Bacharach and the Rhine	Dominic Bonucelli
Mosel Valley: Beilstein	Cameron Hewitt
Trier: Market Square	Cameron Hewitt
Köln and the Unromantic Rhine: Köln's Cathedral	Cameron Hewitt
Nürnberg: Market Square	Rick Steves
Dresden: Zwinger	Cameron Hewitt
Görlitz: Church of St. Peter	Lee Evans
Berlin: Gendarmenmarkt	Cameron Hewitt

Rick Steves' Guidebook Series

Country Guides

Rick Steves' Best of Europe
Rick Steves' Croatia & Slovenia
Rick Steves' Eastern Europe
Rick Steves' England
Rick Steves' France
Rick Steves' Germany
Rick Steves' Great Britain
Rick Steves' Ireland
Rick Steves' Italy
Rick Steves' Portugal
Rick Steves' Scandinavia
Rick Steves' Spain
Rick Steves' Switzerland

City and Regional Guides

Rick Steves' Amsterdam, Bruges & Brussels
Rick Steves' Athens & the Peloponnese (new in 2009)
Rick Steves' Budapest (new in 2009)
Rick Steves' Florence & Tuscany
Rick Steves' Istanbul
Rick Steves' London
Rick Steves' Paris
Rick Steves' Prague & the Czech Republic
Rick Steves' Provence & the French Riviera
Rick Steves' Rome
Rick Steves' Venice
Rick Steves' Vienna, Salzburg & Tirol (new in 2009)

Rick Steves' Phrase Books

French
French/Italian/German
German
Italian
Portuguese
Spanish

Other Books

Rick Steves' Europe 101: History and Art for the Traveler
Rick Steves' Europe Through the Back Door
Rick Steves' European Christmas
Rick Steves' Postcards from Europe

(Avalon Travel)

Avalon Travel
a member of the Perseus Books Group
1700 Fourth Street
Berkeley, CA 94710

Printed in the USA by Worzalla. Second printing May 2009.

ISBN (10) 1-59880-112-0
ISBN (13) 978-1-59880-112-5
ISSN 1553-6866

For the latest on Rick's lectures, guidebooks, tours, public radio show, and public television series, contact Europe Through the Back Door, Box 2009, Edmonds, WA 98020, tel. 425/771-8303, fax 425/771-0833, www.ricksteves.com, rick@ricksteves.com.

Thanks to my wife, Anne, for her support. Thanks to Gene Openshaw for writing the tour of Munich's Alte Pinakothek; to Cameron Hewitt for writing the original versions of the Dresden and Nürnberg chapters; and to Lee Evans for writing the original version of the Görlitz chapter.

Europe Through the Back Door Lead Editor: Cameron Hewitt
ETBD Editors: Jennifer Madison Davis, Tom Griffin, Cathy McDonald, Gretchen Strauch, Sarah McCormic, Cathy Lu
ETBD Managing Editor: Risa Laib
Avalon Travel Senior Editor and Series Manager: Madhu Prasher
Avalon Travel Project Editor: Kelly Lydick
Avalon Travel Editorial Assistant: Jamie Andrade
Research Assistance: Ian Watson, Lee Evans, Gretchen Strauch
Copy Editor: Ellie Behrstock
Proofreader: Kay Elliott
Indexer: Carl Wikander
Production & Typesetting: McGuire Barber Design
Cover Design: Kimberly Glyder Design
Maps & Graphics: David C. Hoerlein, Laura VanDeventer, Lauren Mills, Barb Geisler, Mike Morgenfeld
Photography: Cameron Hewitt, Rick Steves, Karoline Vass, Ian Watson, David C. Hoerlein, Pat O'Connor, Gretchen Strauch, Dominic Bonuccelli, Debi Jo Michael, Lee Evans
Front Matter Color Photos: p. i, Bavarian beer maid © Rick Steves; Burg Eltz © Dominic Bonucelli
Cover Photo: © Cephas Picture Library/Alamy